*Welwyn Garden City
to
Cole Green*

GREAT NORTHERN RAILWAY BRANCHES
HATFIELD TO HERTFORD

McMullen & Sons, brewers of Hertford since 1827, operated a fleet of open wagons, of which 5-plank open No. 91 was a typical example.
D. Dent collection

Hertford GNR station, 27 miles 22 chains from London King's Cross and 9 miles 47 chains from Hatfield, showing the 210 feet long curved platform. An ornate canopy fronting the station building provides protection for waiting passengers. Note the bookstall and, at the end of the platform, the signal box provided in 1890 and containing a 26-lever, later 30-lever, frame. The Up starting signal stands sentinel beyond the signal box and beyond that cattle wagons are stabled in the cattle dock road. 'G2' Class No. 249 is waiting to depart with an Up goods train from the run round road. *Author's collection*

GREAT NORTHERN RAILWAY BRANCHES
HATFIELD TO HERTFORD

PETER PAYE

Lightmoor Press

© Peter Paye and Lightmoor Press 2021
Designed by Nigel Nicholson
British Library Cataloguing-in-Publication Data. A catalogue record for this book is available from the British Library
ISBN 9781 911038 89 4
All rights reserved. No part of this publication may be reproduced, stored in a retrieval system or transmitted in any form or by any means, electronic, mechanical, photocopying, recording or otherwise, without the written permission of the publisher

LIGHTMOOR PRESS

Unit 144B, Lydney Trading Estate, Harbour Road, Lydney, Gloucestershire GL15 4EJ

www.lightmoor.co.uk

Lightmoor Press is an imprint of Black Dwarf Lightmoor Publications Ltd
Printed in Poland; www.lfbookservices.co.uk

Hertingfordbury station from the west in 1955 showing that the station nameboard has been removed and foliage is beginning to encroach on the platform.
Author's collection

Contents

Introduction		7
1	A Second Railway to Hertford	9
2	Construction and Expansion	17
3	Opening to Traffic	25
4	Great Northern Takeover	35
5	Consolidation	45
6	L&NER Operation	71
7	Nationalisation and Closure	85
8	The Route Described	97
9	Permanent Way, Signalling and Staff	165
10	Timetables and Traffic	187
11	Locomotives and Rolling Stock	223
Appendices		
	1 Level Crossings	273
	2 Bridges and Culverts	274
Bibliography		278
Acknowledgements		278
Index		279

The approach to Hertford GNR station from the appropriately named Station Road with McMullen's brewery dating from 1827 on the right. The family brewery provided much traffic to and from the railway in the halcyon years of the branch. *D. Dent collection*

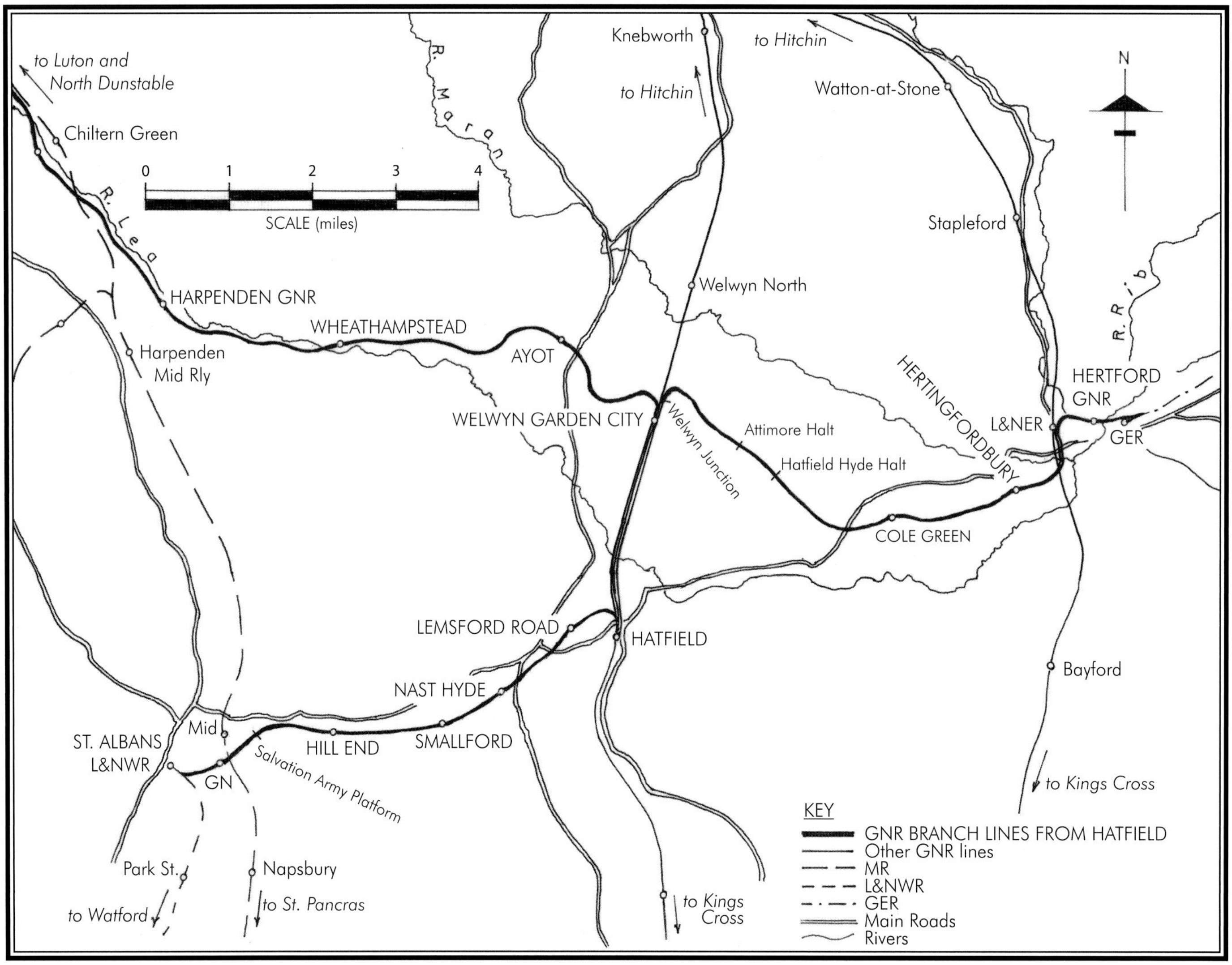

Hertford Cowbridge or Old station on 20th September 1958 with a Class '08' diesel electric shunting locomotive preparing to depart for Hatfield with a goods brake van. In the last years of freight traffic between Hatfield and Hertford a Class '08' locomotive was diagrammed to work out and back from Hatfield each weekday.
Author's collection

Introduction

The East Coast main line from King's Cross on its trajectory to the north encounters the rolling terrain of Hertfordshire where multiple tracks were provided for approximately three miles on the southern approach to the double formation and bottleneck across Welwyn Viaduct. From the 1890s until the late 1930s, along this section main-line expresses hauled by Great Northern Ivatt 'Atlantic' locomotives with their mix of 6-wheel and bogie coaches – and later L&NER Gresley Class 'A3' and 'A4' 'Pacific' engines hauling sleek modern stock – were getting into their stride en route to their various destinations. Passengers had settled into their carriage compartments for the comfortable journey with the occasional glance out of the window to admire the scenery. However, unbeknown to most travellers their train would often be participating in an unofficial race* on this multi-track section; for the shrieking of an engine whistle found businessmen lowering their copy of *The Times*, ladies removing their pince-nez and children placing their noses close to the windows. Running parallel to the sleek modern train on the easternmost line could be found a Great Northern 'Back Tank' or 'Atlantic' tank engine hauling some elderly 6-wheel coaches and later an L&NER Class 'N7' 0-6-2 tank locomotive pulling a 2- or 3-coach train, apparently attempting to overtake the lengthy express. The pounding and vibrating of the tank engine, its coupling rods revolving in a blur, added to the occasion as if the driver and fireman were challenging the crew of the larger steam locomotive to a duel; several passengers on the swaying carriages of the local train would wave to their main-line counterparts and lads would even make rude gestures. What cheek! Who on earth wants to travel on that? This parvenu attempting to outrun the elite service on the main line! All too soon the unofficial race was over, the excitement quelled as the little train braked sharply and disappeared round a sharp curve whilst the express resumed its dignified progress. Where did this upstart come from? And where did it go? Many people, however, wanted to travel on this train from Hatfield to Hertford, a service which served the local community for nearly a century and is now but a distant memory.

Unlike many medium sized communities in the mid-nineteenth century, Hertford, the county town of the shire, benefited as a result of a railway connection as early as 1843 when the Northern & Eastern Railway opened their branch from Broxbourne on the Stratford to Bishop's Stortford main line. The N&ER was taken over by the Eastern Counties Railway in 1844 before extending to Cambridge and Ely with connections to Norwich the following year. The ECR thereafter was concerned to protect their territory from other embryonic companies and proposed an extension from Ware to Huntingdon, but the proposal fell by the wayside. By now, however, local gentry, industrialists and townsfolk of Hertford were keen to encourage the new mode of transport to the west of the town so that malt and barley could be readily conveyed to the flour mills, maltings and breweries in the district. Little positive progress was made but some urgency prevailed after the Great Northern Railway opened their main line from Peterborough to Maiden Lane in 1850 and ultimately to King's Cross two years later. The new line with its northern connections passed six miles west of the town serving nearby Hatfield, the ancestral home of the Marquis of Salisbury.

Meanwhile various proposals had been made, notably by the GNR which, eager to expand their network, obtained an Act of Parliament to construct a railway from St. Albans via Hatfield to Hertford in 1847. When this failed the townsfolk realised the only way forward was to promote their own railway west of the town to connect at the nearest point on the GNR main line, thus avoiding the Hatfield House estate. With the backing and blessing of Earl Cowper of Panshanger, who owned much of the required land, and after much wrangling, the Act authorising the Hertford & Welwyn Junction Railway was obtained in 1854. Provision was made for a junction with the ECR at Hertford and, as well as the GNR, the ECR took close interest in the proposed new line. Almost immediately the H&WJR directors realised their scheme was too parochial and further expansion was desirable. Plans were prepared to build an extension, possibly by bridging the main line at Welwyn Junction and continuing to the industrial centres of Luton and Dunstable, there to make a junction with the London & North Western Railway. The Act was passed in July 1855 but the GNR vehemently objected to the direct line bypassing their system and for a time the development of both Luton and Hertford routes proceeded independently, but amalgamation was thought essential for progress. Advancement was made on the line from Hertford to Welwyn Junction which opened to traffic on 1st March 1858 with traffic worked jointly by the ECR and GNR.

The Hertford, Luton and Dunstable Railway Act authorised amalgamation on 22nd June 1858 but all was not well with the Hertford section, which was *'not working for a profit'*. Several accidents brought into question the safety of the railway. Despite promises to work goods traffic from the north to ECR destinations via the new line, the arrangements left much to be desired and the two main-line companies were constantly in disagreement so that in August 1860 the ECR ceased working across to Welwyn Junction. To provide better connections with the GNR, two months later both Luton and Hertford services were extended to Hatfield, adding more traffic to the already congested two-track main line. On 12th June 1861 the GNR absorbed the HL&DR and immediately instituted improvements including a new station to replace the ramshackle structure at Hertford. Increasing congestion on the main line out of King's Cross found the GNR seeking alternative arrangements, and in June 1865 a proposal was made to construct a new line from Hornsey to Hertford, there to join the Hertford branch with a west facing connection and a north facing curve at Welwyn Junction to allow through running, but in the event the branch – although constructed – terminated at Enfield.

---

* Frowned on by top management; but local supervisors invariably turned a blind eye to the proceedings.

Having lost some promised importance as part of a diversionary route, the branch then continued in relative obscurity as a GNR secondary route, one of three radiating from Hatfield. Proposals were made to combine the GER (which had absorbed the ECR in 1862) and GNR stations at Hertford but all were aborted. In 1876 the Hertford single line was extended from the site of Welwyn Junction through to Hatfield to release the Up main line for the ever expanding GNR traffic, the Luton section had been completed seven years earlier using in part a contractor's ballast line. Traffic to Hertford was increasing and to assist the regulation of trains the block telegraph was installed in 1883. In October of the same year meetings were held to encourage the extension of the Enfield branch through to the Hertford branch, but the resultant 1890 scheme for a Central Hertfordshire Railway failed to raise the necessary finances. Such was the growth in branch traffic with the opening of various sidings that regulation was difficult and congestion ensued over the single line from Hatfield to Hertford, so a crossing loop was installed at the intermediate station at Cole Green in 1891. Further widening on the main line between Digswell, north of Welwyn Junction, to Hatfield was authorised at the same time.

Around the turn of the century many new sidings were opened alongside the Hertford branch, chiefly as a result of Josiah Smart having close associations with the GNR and local landowners including Earl Cowper, and revenue from sand and ballast workings mushroomed. However, passenger receipts were far from encouraging and in late 1904 and early 1905 experiments were conducted with a lightweight 4-wheel petrol railcar; two new halts were opened beside existing level crossings and sidings on 1st January 1905. The experiment was unsuccessful, with the vehicle frequently failing in traffic and unable to haul additional coaches or wagons, and the halts closed on 1st July of the same year.

In 1898 the Enfield to Stevenage extension was authorised but with only minor connections to the Hatfield to Hertford branch. Construction was prolonged and it was 1915 before a temporary connection for construction traffic was made at Hertford. Because of the constraints of World War One the loop line was not opened until March 1918 and even then only as a single line from Cuffley to Langley Junction. During the hostilities the Hatfield to Hertford branch dealt with increased freight and agricultural traffic, and various troop exercises in the area required additional passenger services. The end of the war saw the development of a new town at Welwyn Garden City and in 1921 the first inroads into the monopoly of the branch passenger traffic came with the introduction of bus services serving the local towns and villages, providing an almost door-to-door service. Rapid development was made at the new town and a passenger halt was opened on the Luton/Dunstable single line, but only a contractors halt on the Hertford branch near the site of the former Welwyn Junction station.

In 1922 the GNR in their last action before railway grouping prepared a scheme for a new station at Welwyn Garden City and work continued after grouping to improve the Cuffley to Langwith Junction route, where a new Hertford station was planned. Thus with the creation of the London & North Eastern Railway in 1923 the role of the Hatfield to Hertford branch was to dramatically change. On 2nd June 1924 the route from Cuffley was opened for passenger traffic when the new Hertford North station opened. Thereafter the branch services from Hatfield were diverted to the new station via new connections and the former Hertford station was reduced to the status of a goods depot. With no necessity to travel to London via Hatfield, passengers enjoyed a shorter and more frequent journey to the capital, and branch revenue from the existing intermediate stations at Hertingfordbury and Cole Green slumped. After the opening of Welwyn Garden City station from 20th September 1926, main-line outer suburban services called and few passengers travelled on the branch train from Welwyn Garden City to Hatfield. As a result of the new innovations, passenger services over the single line were drastically reduced to operate during morning and evening peak periods offering a connection to and from main-line services. Proposals were made to withdraw the passenger trains altogether but as freight services required the opening of signal boxes, the skeletal timetable was allowed to continue. This was a fortunate decision: the outbreak of World War Two and petrol rationing removed many buses and motor vehicles from the road and the branch came into its own, conveying munition workers to Hatfield and Hertford for connections via Hertford East to Waltham Cross and Enfield Lock armaments factories. On several occasions during this period the line was used as a diversionary route for essential military traffic.

To cater for increased train movements improvements had been made to the branch signalling in 1941, whilst to release further space on the main-line Hertford branch passenger services were terminated at Welwyn Garden City in 1944 – the former branch single line being converted to an additional Up goods line to Hatfield. After nationalisation, from 1948 British Railways Eastern Region management were seeking economies and the single-track branch conveying few trains and even fewer passengers was ripe for rationalisation. Thus with the easing of petrol rationing and the increase in bus services the passenger services was withdrawn in June 1951, well before the famed Beeching era. Thereafter freight services operated for another decade, but as more industries turned to the internal combustion engine for conveyance of freight so revenue reduced. The loss of much ballast trade, replaced in part by the conveyance of London and Luton household rubbish to fill the resultant blots on the landscape, only served to prolong the inevitable death knell of the branch. By 1963 Hertford North to Hertford Cowbridge was abandoned, with remaining freight handled from Hertford East for a short period. The lifting of the permanent way on the remainder of the branch commenced in 1967 and for a year was forestalled at Holwell Hyde rubbish tip; thereafter track removal continued to the outskirts of Welwyn Garden City until the private sidings near the junction were closed and removed in 1981.

I have attempted to provide the full fascinating story of the branch, which was designed to offer important cross-country connections, but because of successive railway developments played only a secondary role as bridesmaid but was never the bride. Details have been checked with available documents, but apologies are offered for any errors which may have occurred.

Peter Paye
Bishop's Stortford

1

A Second Railway to Hertford

THE COMING OF THE RAILWAYS in the Eastern Counties began with a scheme backed by the Earl of Hardwicke in 1821 for William James to survey an engine railroad from the head of the Stort Navigation at Bishop's Stortford to the River Cam at Cambridge as an alternative to a canal. Extensions were also planned to Norwich, King's Lynn and Lincoln, but the scheme was too ambitious and costly for the period, and, like the canal, fell into oblivion. The idea to link London with the northern coal and industrial centres via Cambridge was revived in 1825 by the Northern Railroad Company surveyed by John and George Rennie. Their route to Cambridge was via the Lea Valley and Barkway and included an extension to the proposed High Peak Railway in Derbyshire. The national depression of the period curtailed further surveys until in 1833 and 1834 Nicholas Cundy surveyed a route for the Great Northern & Eastern Railway via Bishop's Stortford. The following year Joseph Gibbs surveyed a route further to the east via Epping, Dunmow, and Saffron Walden as part of the Great Northern Railway route from London to York. Both of these schemes proposed branches to Norwich. Cundy's scheme was losing favour to the Great Northern Railway route when Handley, a Lincolnshire Member of Parliament, saved it from oblivion. With Cundy's concurrence he financed the resurveying of the route via Bishop's Stortford by James Walker, the engineer of the recently completed Leeds and Selby line, and the new route emerged as the Northern & Eastern Railway Company. The Great Northern promoters objected bitterly to the new scheme and the failure to placate local prejudices and the disturbance of a large number of country estates led to the defeat of the GNR bill at the second reading in the House of Commons by 99 votes to 85. When the GNR was again mooted a decade later it followed a course to the west through Hatfield, Hitchin and Huntingdon.

The Northern & Eastern was subsequently incorporated on 4th July 1836 (6 and 7 William IV cap ciii) but depression delayed the raising of capital with construction commencing in 1839. The railway opened in sections from the south at a cost of over £25,000 per mile as far as Broxbourne on 15th September 1840 and was extended to Harlow on 9th August 1841, then to a temporary terminus at Spelbrook, a mile south of Bishop's Stortford on 22nd November 1841. Because of difficulty with earthworks and lack of finance the railway was not completed to Bishop's Stortford until 16th May 1842.

On the same day as the incorporation of the N&ER the Eastern Counties Railway was enacted with a share capital of £1,600,000 to build a 126-mile line from Shoreditch in east London to Norwich and Yarmouth via Colchester, Ipswich and Eye. The company quickly ran into financial difficulties and by March 1843 had only succeeded in reaching the 51 miles to Colchester at a cost of £1,631,000, which exceeded the original estimate. After a period of soul searching and reorganisation, however, the company resurrected itself and as we shall see became a leading force in the later development of railways in East Anglia and the Home Counties.

In the meantime the N&ER directors and proprietors, concerned that a rival concern would open a line to Cambridge via Ware, took steps to counteract such proposals by submitting a scheme for a branch railway from Broxbourne to Ware and Hertford following closely the course of the River Lea. The bill received the Royal Assent on 21st June 1841 (4 and 5 Vic cap xlii) authorising the company to make and maintain a railway leaving the proposed main line to Cambridge at Valley Marsh in the parish of Broxbourne and terminating in a certain field on the north side of Mead Lane in the Parish of St. John, Hertford. Certain clauses dictated that no part of the said branch line, nor any station, terminus or other works connected therewith, should be constructed within 150 yards of the boundary of any part of the property belonging to Christ's Hospital at Hertford or within 200 yards from the centre door of the County Gaol at Hertford. Three years were allowed for the compulsory purchase of land and five years for the completion of works.

Unfortunately, lack of finance delayed commencement of works and at a special general meeting held on 15th June 1842 at the London Tavern the gathering discussed the execution of the railway to Ware with no mention of Hertford. James Gilbertson of Hertford had, however, attended the meeting with the sole purpose of learning about the extension of the line to Hertford and drew the attention of the gathering to the fact that Hertford had between 6,000 and 7,000 inhabitants, and the Bluecoats School (Christ's Hospital) had many visitors who would use the railway. A correspondent to the *Herts & Bedford Reformer* of 2nd July 1842 urged Hertford residents to become shareholders in the company and by subscribing would encourage the extension of the line beyond Ware to the county town. A public meeting was suggested but there is no evidence it was held. At a shareholders meeting held on 8th October 1842 the chairman advised the extension of the line beyond Ware to Hertford was in abeyance as the company had insufficient funds.

Despite continuing monetary problems and difficulties regarding the turnpike road at Ware, construction eventually commenced and in August 1843 it was optimistically forecast the line would open for traffic in October. The great railway engineer Robert Stephenson was overseeing construction, which was being undertaken by Grissel and Peto. The following month the *Herts & Bedford Reformer* of 16th September was informing its readers that:

> works on the Hertford and Ware branch are progressing rapidly. The line between Ware and Hertford is completed within a short distance of the former town, and the line between Broxbourne and Ware is nearly in the same forward state. The viaduct at Ware is in the course of erection, and stations are building on various parts of the line. Hertford station is completed and a covered way is in the course of erection. We understand the there is little doubt the branch will be opened by the latter end of the ensuing month.

Further altercations with Cheshunt Turnpike Trust regarding the level crossing at Ware failed to stop advancement and following the successful official Board of Trade inspection by Major General Charles William Pasley on 26th October, the line was officially opened to traffic on Tuesday 31st October 1843, laid to a gauge of 5 feet 0 ins. The *Herts & Bedford Reformer* of 4th November reporting the event mentioned:

> A communication will be opened with Bedford through Hertford via the railway to London. The frequency of the communication with Hitchin and other towns on that line of road is also to be increased and Hertford will become the centre to which the locomotive population of a large part of the county and also Bedfordshire will flock.

On and from 1st January 1844 the Northern & Eastern Railway was taken over by the Eastern Counties Railway on a 999 years lease at an annual rent of 5 per cent of the construction costs and a division of the profits and this was confirmed by the Act of 23rd May 1844 (7 Vic cap xx). The ECR line was subsequently extended from Bishop's Stortford through Newport and Cambridge to Brandon to join up with the Norfolk Railway from Norwich on 30th July 1845. The ECR board members were increasingly concerned that the 5 feet 0 inches gauge of both lines would result in isolation from the rest of the embryonic railway empire and following advice from Robert Stephenson decided to convert the lines to standard gauge of 4 feet 8½ inches. The conversion of the main lines was achieved with as little disruption as possible but the Broxbourne Junction to Hertford branch was closed on Wednesday 25th September 1845 and reopened to traffic on Monday 30th September. In the intervening period a horse drawn omnibus maintained a connection from the Salisbury Arms at Hertford to Broxbourne station.

After the opening of the N&ER branch from Broxbourne to Hertford, the land west of the county town became increasingly attractive to railway developers. One such scheme was the Bedfordshire, Hertfordshire & Essex Junction Railway, surveyed by Andrew Trimen and promoted in 1845 to connect Luton with the Essex coastal port of Maldon, which hoped to encourage manufacturers of Luton to send their produce to the Eastern Counties, and in return receive timber and fish from the coast. The bill and associated plans signed by the engineer Hamilton H. Fulton was deposited on 29th November, the route passing by way of Kimpton and Welwyn to Bramfield and Hertford, then on to Ware and across to Harlow and Chelmsford before terminating at Maldon. It came of no surprise that the scheme failed to attract the necessary capital.

A rival and more ambitious scheme deposited on the same day and promoted as the Metropolitan Junction Railway envisaged a 114 miles 5 furlong route circling London and connecting Reigate in the south with Tilbury in the east and running via Dorking, Weybridge, Staines, Uxbridge, Rickmansworth and Watford to St. Albans and Hatfield. The railway would then pass by way of Hertford and Ware to Harlow before swinging south-east to Billericay and Horndon to the Thames. This route, had it been built, would have greatly benefited cross-country travel, relieving London of passenger and goods congestion. The engineers for the scheme costing £2,500,000 were Captain W.S. Moorsom and Robert Stephenson. Through Hertfordshire the line ran from St. Albans to Bishop's Hatfield and thence via Essendon to Bayford, where a 330-yards-long tunnel was envisaged, before swinging south to Hertford and thence parallelling the N&ER route for the next 3½ miles. By January 1846 proposals were made to amalgamate with the Northern & Southern Connecting Railway surveyed by Joseph Gibbs, which had deposited plans on 30th November 1845 for a line from Bishop's Hatfield to St. Albans, Watford, Rickmansworth and on via Weybridge on the London & Southampton Railway, to terminate at Reigate. As one almost duplicated the other, success was envisaged but, as with many other proposals of the time, both schemes fell into oblivion. Yet another unsuccessful proposal, deposited on 30th September 1845 and surveyed by M.A. Borthwick, was the St. Albans, Hatfield & Hertford Junction Railway. Measuring 11 miles 6 furlongs from Hertford, the railway was the brainchild of George Hudson who had joined the ECR board earlier in 1845. He set about promoting schemes to enlarge the ECR empire and whilst some of the plans were genuine, others were put forward to prevent the advance of the embryonic Great Northern Railway. The proposed St. Albans route from a junction with the ECR at Hertford ran by way of Bengeo up a 1 in 224 gradient to Hertingfordbury and then on a direct path to Hatfield, a distance of 3 miles. Beyond Hatfield the line climbed again at 1 in 252 and then descended at 1 in 285 towards Hatfield Paper Mills. The railway terminated at Holywell Bridge in the Parish of St. Michael, St. Albans.

The ECR trying desperately to thwart the southern thrust of the Great Northern Railway also proposed unsuccessfully in 1846 to

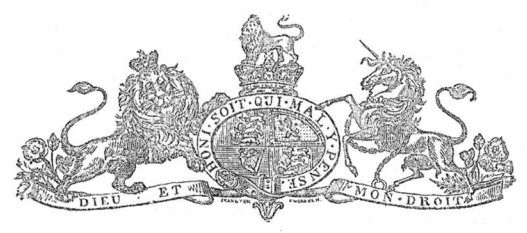

Front page of GNR Act for a railway from St. Albans to Hatfield and Hertford dated 22nd July 1847.

extend their Hertford branch to Huntingdon and then to Hitchin in the following year, where it proposed to join forces with the Midland Railway then pushing south from Bedford. The GNR was an amalgam of two separate schemes – the Direct Northern who employed Rennie and Gravatt to survey their route and the London & York whose engineer was the noted Joseph Locke – which were both pathed through Hatfield, Welwyn, Knebworth, Stevenage and Hitchin. The London & York subsequently chose a route running a mile west of their rivals but when Locke resigned to seek railway construction in France, Samuel Hughes was appointed to the vacancy. Subsequently the rivals merged on 5th May 1846 and the Great Northern Railway Act received the Royal Assent on 26th June 1846. Before construction of the main line was completed, the company, in order to thwart rivals entering their territory, objected to both ECR proposals and in defence obtained sanction to build their own branch line from Hertford via Hatfield to St. Albans.

The Bill received the Royal Assent on 22nd July 1847 as the Great Northern Railway (Hertford, Hatfield and St. Albans Branch) Act 1847 (10 and 11 Vic cap cclxxii). The statute authorised the company to make a railway from St. Albans to the GNR at Hatfield, continuing thence to the town of Hertford. Under the provisions of the Act the railway was to commence in the Parish of St. Albans at the Turnpike Road leading from Watford, before passing through the several parishes of St. Peter St. Albans, St. Stephen St. Albans, St. Peter Hatfield (otherwise Bishop's Hatfield), Hertingfordbury, Brickendon, All Saints Hertford and St. Andrew Hertford, to terminate at or near the Hertford station of the Hertford & Ware branch of the Northern & Eastern Railway in the Parish of St. John's Hertford. In the course of the route the company was not to interfere with part of the possessions of the late Monastery of Sopwell, located partially in the Parish of St. Stephen and partially in the Parish of St. Peter St. Albans. The company was also empowered to construct two short diverging lines as junctions with the GNR at Hatfield. Level crossings were authorised across the following public roads:

Road Numbers	Parish
9 and 28	St. Stephen, St. Albans
83 and 90	St. Peter, St. Albans
60	Hatfield
7, 17 and 51	Hertingfordbury
53, 63 and 65	St. John, Hertford

Whilst bridges were to be provided at:

Road	Parish	Span	Height
16, 28 and 45	St. Peter, St. Albans	25 feet	14 feet
25, 47, 92, 127, 133, 199	Hatfield	25 feet	14 feet
51	Hertingfordbury	25 feet	14 feet

The statute further stipulated the railway was not to be laid on the north east side of the waterworks in the Parish of St. Andrew, Hertford without due permission, neither was it to interfere with the works of the N&ER station at Hertford without due negotiation and at the direction of the N&ER engineer. The Act also specified clauses regarding the crossing of the River Lea and the requirements to deepen the navigation under the bridges and the repair of the towpaths. The company was also required to construct a dock beside the River Lea at Hertford as a penalty for obstructing the navigation of the river. Finally, if the GNR required land attached to Cowbridge House, Hertford for any purpose, prior permission was to be obtained from Thomas Robert, Baron Dimsdale.

For the purposes of building the railway and associated works, the company was authorised to raise shares to the value of £300,000 with borrowing powers of £100,000 when half of the original capital was fully paid up. Three years were allowed for the purchase of the necessary land and five years for the completion of the works. Unfortunately the GNR was suffering a financial crisis, having overspent on their main-line construction, and in 1848 the Hertford to St. Albans scheme was abandoned.

From the opening of the GNR main line together with Hatfield station on 7th August 1850 the town of Hertford was connected to the new railway by Scarborough's horse buses, which ran twice daily from the Dimsdale Arms and the Bull Inn to Hatfield station to connect with the expresses. The horse bus service, however, left much to be desired for the roads were poor, especially in adverse weather, and the connections were often missed. Local townsfolk and travellers agitated for an alternative and in September 1850 an approach was made to the GNR authorities for a branch railway to be built from Hatfield direct to Hertford. The route of the intended line bisected the Hatfield estate of Lord Salisbury and permission for the release of land was abruptly refused. The GNR subsequently withdrew their interest in the scheme and it was thus left to local people to campaign for a railway linking the county town with the nearest point on the GNR main line. The idea received favourable support from certain local gentry, landowners, businessmen and traders of Hertford and in the autumn of 1853 plans were duly prepared, but carefully bypassing Lord Salisbury's land. Because of this factor the route chosen ran in a westerly direction from the town to a point on the main line just south of the small community of Welwyn and south of Welwyn Viaduct, some three miles north of Hatfield station.

The prospectus for the Hertford, Ware & Welwyn Junction Railway published in the *Hertfordshire Mercury* for 19th November 1853 advised the incorporation of the company; construction of Railway and Works and powers to use the GNR with their stations at Welwyn and Hatfield. The official document envisaged a series of lines and junctions, which ultimately attracted objections and proved over ambitious for such a small concern.

Notice is hereby given that application is intended to be made to Parliament in the ensuing session, for leave to bring in a Bill for an Act for making and maintaining the railway and works hereinafter mentioned, with all proper communications, approaches, and conveniences connected therewith (that is to say), a railway commencing by a junction with the Great Northern Railway in the parish of Digswell, in the County of Hertford, at a point four furlongs or thereabout southward from the Welwyn station thereof and thence passing from, in, through or into several parishes, townships, townlands, and extra parochial or other places following or some of them, that is to say, Digswell, Hatfield, otherwise Bishop's Hatfield, Welwyn, Datchworth, Bramfield, Stapleford, Tewin, Hertingfordbury, Bayford, Brickendon, Bengeo, St John Hertford, St Andrew Hertford and All Saints Hertford, all in the county of Hertford, and terminating by a junction with the Hertford branch of the Northern and Eastern Railway, at or near the Hertford station thereof, in the parish of St John Hertford.

Also a branch railway from, and out of the main line of the said intended railway, commencing by a junction therewith, about three furlongs from the junction last mentioned with the Great Northern Railway, and terminating in the said parish of Digswell, by a junction with the Great Northern Railway, at a point near the boundaries of the parishes of Hatfield, otherwise Bishop's Hatfield and Digswell aforesaid.

Also a branch railway from and out of the said intended railway, commencing by a junction therewith at or near a certain field in the parish of St John Hertford, in the county of Hertford belonging to Captain John Townshend R N, and in the occupation of Samuel Hale and Daniel Hale and number 64 in the said parish of St John Hertford on the plans intended to be deposited, with the Clerk of the Peace for the said county of Hertford as hereafter mentioned, and passing thence from, in, through, or into the several parishes, townships, townlands, and extra parochial or other places following, or some of them, that is to say, St John Hertford, All Saints Hertford, Little Amwell, Great Amwell and Ware, all in the county of Hertford, and terminating in a field numbered 10 on the said plans, in the parish of Ware, belonging to Martin Hadsley Gosselin Esq, adjoining or near the road leading from the town of Ware to Ware Park.

And it is proposed by the said intended Act to take powers to construct stations, communications, conveniences and other works in the several parishes, townships, townlands and extra parochial places before mentioned, or in some of them, for the working and using the said railway and branch railways, and also to authorize junctions with any railway or railways at the commencement or termination or in the line or course of the said railway and branch railways and works as before described, in the several parishes, townships, townlands, extra parochial and other places aforesaid, and for deviating from the line laid down on the plans hereinafter mentioned to the extent therein defined; and to cross, divert, alter or stop up, either temporarily or permanently, all such turnpike or other roads, highways, rivers, aqueducts, streams, canals, navigations and sewers.

The *Hertfordshire Mercury* enthused for the new proposed railway, which *'seeks to supply Hertford and Ware in communication with the corn and coal districts through which the Great Northern and Midland lines run and with the leading markets of this and adjoining counties'*. It remonstrated that Ware and Hertford suffered considerable damage by their lack of communication with the western and northern parts of the county and that the advantage of having an (ECR) terminus at Hertford *'affords no compensation for the disadvantages arising from the absence of railway communication in those directions'*. It stressed the formation of the GNR line had *'the practical effect of bringing important districts in the county into nearer connection with London than with some of the chief local towns and markets'* and that *'the only remedy offered to the public'* is the projected Hertford, Ware & Welwyn Junction Railway *'which has already received the support of gentlemen who are well known to have the interests of the town and neighbourhood deeply at heart'*. It concluded: *'we recommend the project – which promises to prove beneficial to the trade of Hertford and Ware'*.

By 14th January 1854 it was announced that a requisite number of shares proposed to finance the future Hertford, Ware & Welwyn Railway had been tentatively subscribed for and the conditions imposed by the Standing Order had been complied with, so that it was envisaged there would be no opposition to the bill being presented to Parliament. On Monday 13th February the proposition of the HW&WR was placed before the examiners, after which the bill and petition was presented to the House of Commons by Thomas Chambers MP. The second reading was heard on the last day of February 1854 and presented for the third hearing on 27th March. Unfortunately for the promoters certain clauses were contested by the Eastern Counties Railway and were debated by the Commons Select Committee the following day. As a result of the opposition the promoters were forced to abandon the part of the bill seeking authority to build a line between Hertford and Ware running almost parallel with the Northern & Eastern Railway Hertford branch operated by the ECR. The ECR directors, however, agreed to revise clauses granting the HW&WR (by now re-titled the Hertford & Welwyn Junction Railway) facilities for continuation of their traffic over the N&ER branch between Hertford and Ware at the same conveyance rates and without transfer of carriage. The Committee considered the agreement granting running powers over the ECR *'most satisfactory'* and the following alterations were included in the amendment bill presented to Parliament on Friday 7th April 1854.

The Eastern Counties Railway shall and are hereby required to afford at all times such reasonable and proper facilities and accommodation upon their line of railway between Hertford and Ware and at the present or at any future station at Ware. The Eastern Counties shall make such arrangements for booking at their station all passengers, animals, goods, parcels and other traffic for the town of Ware to any part of the Hertford and Welwyn Junction Railway.

The Bill was read for the first time in the House of Lords on the same day when it was rumoured the ECR might take advantage of the Bill to close their terminal passenger station and remove the site to a more central position in the town where through running was possible. Unfortunately the passage of the Bill through the upper house was far from smooth for objections against the

The seal of the Hertford & Welwyn Junction Railway incorporated in 1854. *Barry Gray collection*

railway were received from the Marquis of Salisbury and W. Parker, complaining that the conditions of the Standing Orders had not been complied with.

The petitions were presented to the Select Committee on Standing Orders on 28th May 1854 with Lord Redesdale in the chair. In evidence Mr Nicholson, representing Parker, stated the substantive contract for the railway was incorrect and not complied with, as the line originally advised as running from Welwyn to Ware was now terminating at Hertford. Lord Salisbury's only objection to the proposed line was that he had not received notice of the compulsory purchase of two small pockets of land where the route of the railway ran across his estate. Mr Marchant, representing the railway company, advised the chairman that the land known as Nellie Rose Spring was in good faith believed to form part of a public highway 12 to 13 feet in width. After deliberating Lord Redesdale found the railway company to be at default for not advising Lord Salisbury of land requirements. However, all other Standing Orders had been complied with and on receiving the assurance of Mr Marchant that Lord Salisbury would be officially advised of future land requirements the bill was allowed to proceed. The paper was read for the second time in the House of Lords on the following Friday, 2nd June, but once again progress was halted when it was announced forty people had petitioned against the railway.

The bill was placed before the Select Committee of the House of Lords on 20th June 1854 together with the petition against the proposed line signed and presented by many of the merchant traders of Hertford. The committee with Lord Panmure as chairman included the Earl of Ilchester, the Bishop of Carlisle, Lord Wynford and Lord Hamilton. Mr Rodwell appeared on behalf of the Hertford & Welwyn Junction Railway promoters with Mr Marchant as agent. Although forty persons had petitioned only the arguments of three, William Robert Baker, the Marquis of Salisbury and William Parker were presented to counsel. At the conclusion of the presentation Mr Rodwell objected to the argument presented by the Marquis of Salisbury on the grounds that *'he as a landowner was not affected by the bill'*. Amidst uproar the counsel and parties withdrew whilst the committee discussed the legal points. When they were recalled the chairman advised the Marquis of Salisbury that he had no grounds for objecting and therefore no case could be advanced. Having easily overcome the minor complaints of Baker, Rodwell attacked the objections raised by Parker and advised the chairman that the complainant had no valid case to present for he was a shareholder and had in fact signed a contract with the railway company before the case had reached the Select Committee stage. Once again the committee retired before confirming that Parker had no case to argue.

Rodwell then advanced the case for the proposed railway and called upon Thomas Chambers, Member of Parliament for Hertford to give evidence. Chambers advised he was well acquainted with the towns of Hertford, Ware and Hitchin as well as the intermediate district and was a director of the proposed H&WJR. He reminded the committee that great quantities of malt were handled at Ware, *'probably more than any other town in England'*, whilst within four miles of Hertford *'there were more flour mills than elsewhere in the country'*. Although as MP he was an ex officio trustee of the River Lea and was *'well aware of the great necessity for the improved transportation of commodities by other means than water, especially west of Hertford where no navigable river existed and where a great quantity of barley was grown'*. Being well acquainted with the land between Hertford and the GNR he was conscious of the considerable difficulty experienced transporting barley to Ware, especially over the poor roads. The majority of the barley grown in the Hitchin and Royston area was loaded by the GNR and circuitously routed via Cambridge and the ECR to Broxbourne before completing the journey along the branch line to Ware. The aim of the H&WJR was to bring the barley growing districts west of Ware onto a railway system to ease transportation. It was therefore of the utmost importance that the line was built.

On being cross-examined, Chambers advised that he was fully aware of the railways proposed by the ECR and GNR in 1847 which had been abandoned after the change of purpose by the main-line companies. It was because of the failure of the 1847 scheme that the proposed railway had been mooted and was so important, especially to the town of Ware. Most of the promoters and subscribers to the H&WJ scheme lived locally and although it was not being proposed as originally intended, the Hertford and Ware section had been abandoned at the suggestion of the Select Committee of the House of Commons as it duplicated the ECR line between those two places. The MP concluded by advising the committee of the very strong support for the line, so much so that the inhabitants of both Hertford and Ware had signed a petition in favour of the scheme. He had faith that every arrangement made

Front page of Hertford and Welwyn Junction Railway Act 3rd July 1854.

with the ECR and GNR would increase the facilities available for passenger and goods traffic.

John Cass Birkinshaw, the H&WJR Engineer, was then asked by Rodwell to advise on the route and construction of the proposed line. Birkinshaw explained to the gathering that the railway commenced by a junction with the GNR at Welwyn station and followed the nearest direct course as possible to Hertford, avoiding ornamental property on each side of the line. The 7½ miles of route was of easy construction with no residential damage, whilst 6½ miles was over land owned by Lord Cowper and Mr Baker. The purchase price of land had been reasonable. On the engineering aspects Birkinshaw quoted the steepest gradient at 1 in 80 for a quarter of a mile whilst the sharpest curve except at the junction with the GNR was of 20 chains radius. The arrangements made for running powers over the ECR from Hertford to Ware was better and cheaper than providing an independent line. Arrangements with both the GNR and ECR were on a friendly basis. No turnpike roads were crossed and all roads in Hertford were crossed by under or overbridges. Concluding his report the engineer estimated the outlay for the entire line at £65,000 with £12,700 of that absorbed by land purchase. The cost was therefore in the region of £8,000 per mile for the single-track railway, with land available for doubling if future traffic warranted the additional outlay.

After deliberating, the chairman reported in favour of the bill with certain amendments and offered it forward for the third and final reading in the House of Lords. Royal Assent for the Hertford and Welwyn Junction Railway Act 1854 (17 and 18 Vic cap cxxvii) was given on 3rd July 1854. The statute authorised the building of a railway from the Northern & Eastern Railway station at Hertford to a triangular junction at Digswell on the Great Northern Railway with running powers thence to Digswell station.

The first portion of the railway commenced at a junction with the Great Northern Railway in the Parish of Digswell in the County of Hertford at a point where the railway abutted on to fields No's 3 and 4 as prescribed by the GNR and terminated by a junction with the Hertford branch of the Northern & Eastern Railway at or near the Hertford station in the Parish of St. John, Hertford. The second railway was to be a branch out of the main line of the intended railway commencing in the Parish of Digswell and terminating in the same parish by a junction with the GNR at a point near to the boundary of the Parishes of Hatfield, otherwise Bishop's Hatfield, and Digswell. The new line was to pass through the Parishes of Digswell, Bishop's Hatfield, Tewin, Hertingfordbury, St. Andrew Hertford, Bengeo and St. John Hertford, all in the County of Hertford. Clause xix of the statute stated it was not lawful for the railway company to take any portion of wood or spring situated in the Parish of Bishop's Hatfield or Parish of Tewin and owned by the Marquis of Salisbury without the owner's consent.

The Act authorised the railway to cross the following roads by level crossing: No's 8 and 14 in the Parish of Bishop's Hatfield, No. 38 in the Parish of Hertingfordbury, No. 14 in the Parish of Bengeo and No's 55, 63 and 65 in the Parish of St. John's Hertford. The company was also authorised to stop up roads No's 35 and 44 in the Parish of Bengeo and settle all accounts with the Honourable Thomas Robert, Baron Dimsdale before taking possession of any portion of the Cowbridge House Estate at Hertford.

Clause xxvi of the Act stipulated the requirements for bridging the River Lea at Hertford. The company was empowered to build a bridge with a clear span between abutments of not less than 35 feet, measured at right angles from the said abutment together with a 'proper and sufficient' wall 100 yards in length constructed of Kentish Ragstone to protect the towpath at the side of the navigation. The towpath was itself to be not less than 8 feet in width. The soffit of the underside of the bridge was to be not less than 9 feet above the top water level of the navigation as indicated by the groove mark on the iron post fixed by the River Lea Trustees near the stream leading to Dicker Mill. During the course of construction the railway company was to leave a clear navigation of not less than 30 feet with additional room on the bank for the passage of horses. All work was to be constructed and maintained to the satisfaction of the Navigation Trustees.

A further clause required the H&WJR to purchase sufficient land to make and maintain at their own expense, a dock or lay-by at the side of the navigation at or near the railway bridge to accommodate at least two barges and maintain a siding to the dock for the interchange of traffic. The railway company was not to charge tolls for the use of the dock or siding which were to be available at all times for public use, the dock being legally considered a goods station. The plans for the bridge and dock were to be agreed between John Cass Birkinshaw, Engineer of the H&WJR, and Nathaniel Beardmore on behalf of the Navigation Trustees.

Clause xxix enforced the railway not to cross the stream called Paper Mill Ditch at a greater distance than 80 yards from the lower side of the brick arch near the tail water channel of the waterworks belonging to the Borough of Hertford. In a subsequent clause the Mayor, Aldermen and Burgesses of Hertford were authorised to exchange land in the field called Hartham adjoining the route of the proposed line.

All land required for the proposed line was to be purchased within two years and works completed within four years of the passing of the Act. Works at the Welwyn end of the railway were to be agreed with the GNR where the main-line company was to maintain the junction and control the movement of traffic to and from the Hertford line. For this purpose the GNR was to install pointwork and erect the necessary signals. Similarly at the Hertford end of the line the works and junction was to be agreed and worked by the ECR. In accordance with the working agreements the ECR was required to grant H&WJR traffic through running powers to Ware and provide the necessary accommodation and facilities for the interchange of traffic. At the western end of the line by clause lii the GNR was empowered to grant the H&WJR running powers in a northerly direction on the main line to Welwyn station and the use of facilities for the interchange of traffic. The following clause permitted the H&WJR Company to enter into a working agreement with the GNR or the ECR, or both.

The Act authorised the raising of £65,000 in £20 shares with borrowing powers of £21,600 when the whole of the original share issue was subscribed and half actually paid up. The promoters of the railway and initial first directors were the Honourable William Francis Cowper, Thomas Chambers, John Townshend, Harry Inskip and Franklin Haggar. Other interested parties were John Villiers Stuart Townshend, Thomas Jackson, Alfred William Bean, James Gow and Joseph Chuck.

The new management was eager to begin construction and by 12th August 1854 a great portion of the railway was staked out and preparations made to commence work as soon as the crops had been harvested. Evidence of progress prompted many people to apply for the outstanding unsold shares. Heartened by such progress the Honourable W. Cowper, Chairman of the H&WJR, with others was already investigating the possible expansion of the system. The chosen area without a railway lay to the west of the GNR from the proposed Welwyn Junction towards the manufacturing town of Luton and thence to Dunstable where the London & Birmingham Railway had opened a branch line from Leighton Buzzard for goods traffic on 29th May 1848 and for passenger traffic on 1st June. Boosted by the success of the undertaking the H&WJR appeared eager for expansion and on 19th August 1854 a public meeting was held at Luton to engender support for such a venture.

The first ordinary meeting of the H&WJR shareholders held on 30th September 1854 was rather overshadowed by the announcement of plans for the projected line from Welwyn Junction to Luton and Dunstable, which would effectively provide an important cross country railway linking three great railways, the London & North Western at Dunstable, the GNR at Welwyn and the ECR at Hertford. The shareholders were then advised of the progress made on their own line and negotiations with the ECR over the Hertford to Ware section of line. The majority of land had been purchased for the railway and stations. Birkinshaw then announced that Jackson, Bean & Gow had been awarded the contract for building the railway after tendering at £47,078 and had in fact commenced staking out the formation. The contract price excluded the cost of several stations but as the exact siting of these had yet to be decided, additional costs would be entailed.

The Secretary urged shareholders to purchase a greater number of shares so that the company could take advantage of the borrowing powers. The authorised £65,000 had been divided into 3,250 £20 shares but of these only 2,658 had been taken. It was therefore necessary for the remaining 382 £20 shares to be sold before the £21,600 could be borrowed. The financial standing of the company was:

Credit	Shares, deposits	£5,206	16s	0d
Debit	Parliamentary expenses	£2,753	1s	1d
	Interest	£8	12s	2d
Balance		£2,444	2s	5d

By mid November 1854 the engineer and contractor were so confident of rapid progress that arrangements were made for the ceremonial cutting of the first sod. The ceremony was duly performed at 11.30am on Tuesday 28th November 1854 by the Honourable William Francis Cowper MP for Hertford and the company chairman in an upland field known as the Cottager's Gardens on the Hertingfordbury Road near the Sele Mill, Hertford. Despite prior announcements many people missed the ceremony because of a misunderstanding over the exact location of the event. The chairman duly turned the first spit of earth into a barrow and then wheeled the vehicle across planks before offloading the contents. Among those present among the cheering throng were Major J. Gripper and the contractors Jackson & Bean. After speeches advocating the success of the railway, the directors, contractors and friends took lunch at the Dimsdale Arms Hotel. The contractors' supervisors, foremen and agents were entertained to dinner at The Bull, whilst Mr Willmott financed a meal at the Railway Tavern for the men working on the railway. While this great revelry was taking place, labourers and navvies employed by the contractors shared a barrel of ale on the site.

The course of the branch was beset by sharp curves, as shown on the approach to Port Hill, Hertford, in 1966 before the track was lifted.

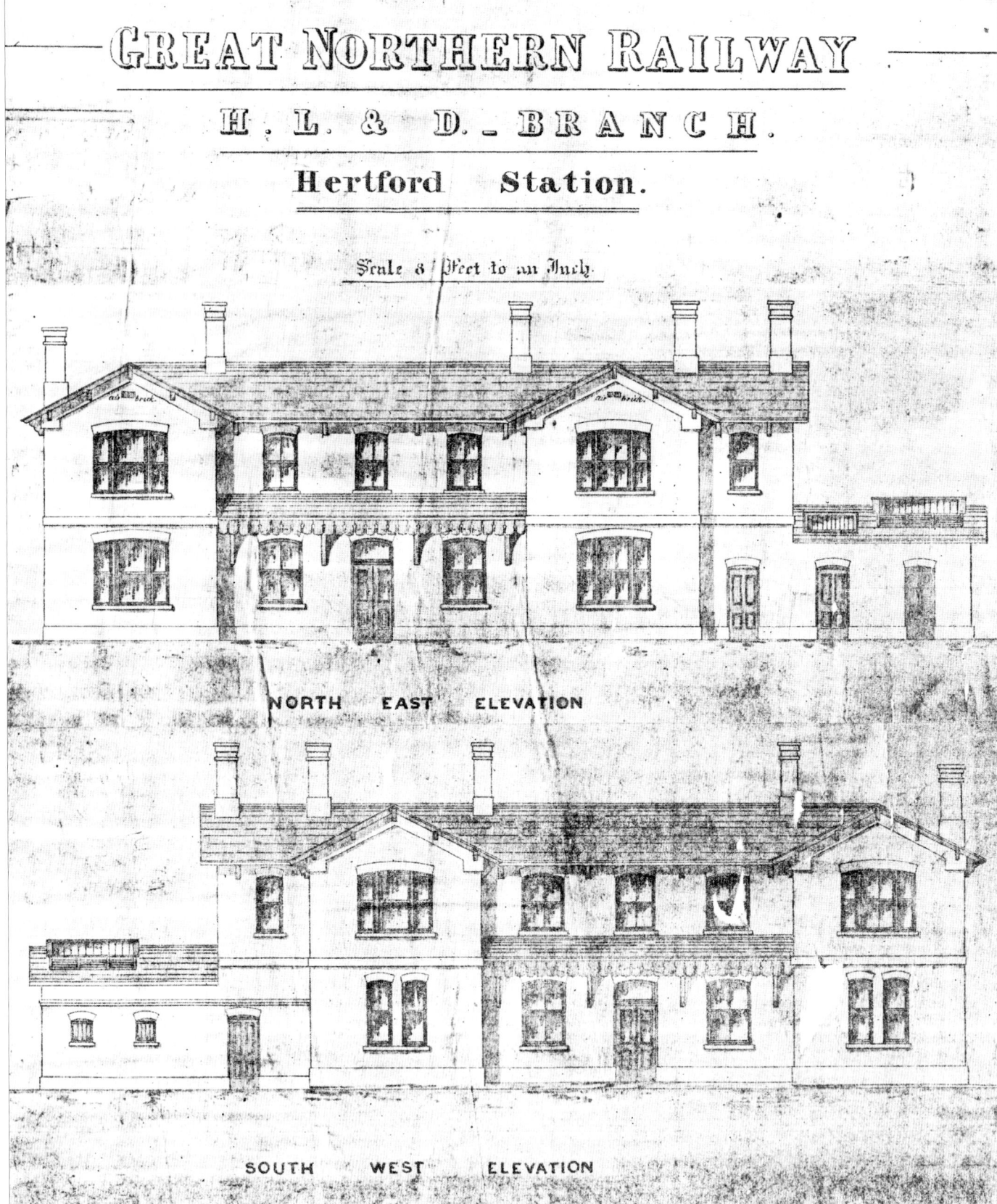

GNR Hertford Cowbridge station building north-east (platform) and south-west (external) elevations.

2
Construction and Expansion

Very little work was carried out on the new railway during the subsequent winter months, but by mid April 1855 the contractor's men were working at several places along the route with the majority of the workforce employed at Digswell and Hertford.

At the half-yearly meeting of the shareholders held at the end of June 1855 J.C. Birkinshaw submitted a report as to progress and state of the works:

> I beg to say that the contractors are now at work at various places between the junction with the Great Northern Railway and Hertford, having broken ground at eleven of the cuttings, and executed upwards of 30,000 cubic yards of earthworks. About three miles of fencing have been fixed, and materials for three or four miles more have been provided. Considerable progress has been made with the bridges and approaches for three public roads and with two river bridges. In consequence of the unexpected difficulties and delay in settling the compensation to be paid to the occupiers of portions of the land required for the railway, the works have been suspended for some time in the neighbourhood of Hertford, and it is only within the last ten days that the contractors have been able to enter upon the land most urgently required. The contractors are now, however, in possession of all the land between Hertford and the Great Northern Railway, a distance of about 6½ miles, excepting one property about half a mile in length, which is not immediately required. It is not proposed to proceed immediately with the works on the remaining portions of the line but preparations are being made to obtaining timely possession of the property so that the contractors may not be delayed when they are ready to proceed. I have only to add, what I have before mentioned, that the period of completion depends mainly on the financial considerations, as there is nothing in the character of the works themselves to prevent the opening of the railway in the present year.

The Act incorporating the Luton, Dunstable & Welwyn Junction Railway received the Royal Assent on 16th July 1855 (18 and 19 Vic cap cxlvi). The initial directors included the Honourable William Francis Cowper and Thomas Chambers who held similar positions on the H&WJR Company, together with John Bennet Lawes, Lionel Ames, James Waller and Henry Tomson. The statute authorised the building of a railway commencing by a junction with the Leighton Buzzard and Dunstable branch of the London & North Western Railway at or near the eastern end of Dunstable L&NWR station, in the Parish of Houghton Regis in the County of Bedford and terminating by a junction with the GNR about one furlong to the south of the road leading from Upper Hanside to Attimore Hall where the road crossed the GNR in the Parish of Bishop's Hatfield, in the County of Hertford. A second railway from and out of the first line in the Parish of Bishop's Hatfield, three furlongs or thereabouts northward from the junction of railway No. 1 and the GNR crossed the main line to terminate at a junction with the authorised Hertford and Welwyn Junction line, three furlongs or thereabouts eastwards from a bridge over the GNR main line near Digswell Lodge Farm in the Parish of Digswell. A north-facing junction was also authorised towards Welwyn, also terminating near Digswell Lodge Farm. Thus the statute authorised a triangular junction with the GNR at Welwyn Junction together with a bridge allowing a direct connecting line over the GNR to join up with the H&WJR to permit through running between the minor lines.

Two years were allowed for the compulsory purchase of land and four years for the completion of works. To finance the scheme the

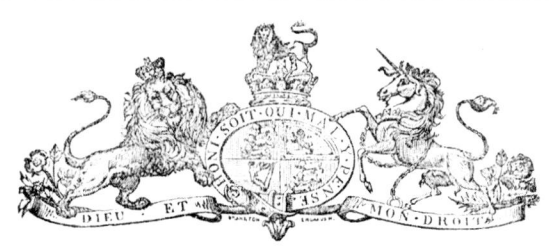

Front page of Luton Dunstable and Welwyn Junction Railway Act 16th July 1855.

new company was authorised to raise a share capital of £120,000 in £20 shares with borrowing powers of £40,000 when all the capital had been subscribed and half paid up.

As construction continued on the Hertford line some macabre human remains were discovered during the excavation of a cutting near East End Green, Hertingfordbury in September 1855. Initially various portions of a man were found, two feet below the surface, embedded in the clay. Nearby lay the stone head of an arrow, the single bone of a girl and four larger bones of a horse.

By the end of June 1855 the H&WJR company was in possession of nearly all the land, whilst the cuttings and embankments were in the course of construction in eleven places. The general balance sheet for the period ending 30th June 1855 showed:

Receipts	£	s	d
Calls on shares	9,142	16	0
Expenditure			
Preliminary expenses	3,287	6	6
Interest	8	6	3
Sundries		18	9
Engineering expenses	950	0	0
Land compensation	958	9	4
Purchase of property	2,414	0	0
Legal expenses	61	8	9
Management expenses	108	12	0
Balance in hand	1,353	14	5
Total	9,142	16	0

The officers of the company at this time were the Right Honourable W.F. Cowper MP, Chairman, with fellow directors T. Chambers, Captain J. Townshend RN MP, H. Inskip and F. Haggar. The Secretary was J. Marchant, Engineer J.C. Birkinshaw of 22 Abingdon Street, Westminster, Auditors William Wilds and Young Crawley of Hertford and the Joint Solicitors E.E. Spence and J.L. Foster, both of Hertford.

Work on the railway from Hertford continued apace and the half yearly meeting of the H&WJR shareholders was held on Wednesday 23rd January 1856 in the Shire Hall, Hertford. The Chairman addressing the gathering announced that nearly all the land required for the Hertford line was in the hands of the company; the land agent and solicitor were concluding negotiations with the remaining landowners regarding the early transfer of property. Cowper also announced that the Luton, Dunstable and Welwyn Junction Railway Company Act had received the Royal Assent and as many were dual holders of both Hertford and Luton railway shares he was certain that all present looked forward to the extension of the Dunstable line to Welwyn, where it would join up with the Hertford line to allow through running between the two sections. It was also hoped traffic from the L&NWR to the Eastern Counties would be routed via the joint lines and vice versa.

The balance sheet for the Hertford section for the half year ending 31st December 1855 was:

Receipts	£	s	d
Calls on shares	13,574	0	0
Interest on calls	9	7	4
	13,583	7	4
Balance brought forward	1,353	14	5
	14,937	1	9
Expenditure			
Engineer's expenses to date	730	0	0
Interest to bankers		18	6
Compensation for land	230	0	0
Purchase of property	804	0	0
Legal expenses	31	4	10
Management expenses	109	19	0
Construction	11,079	0	0
	13,655	2	4
Balance carried forward	1,271	19	5
	14,937	1	9

GNR stable block (built in 1863) to the north of the running lines at Hertford Cowbridge in 1962. Shunting horses as well as goods cartage animals were housed in this block. *P. Whitaker*

The general balance to 31st December 1855 was:

Parliamentary expenses	3,287	6	6
Engineers expenses	1,700	0	0
Sundries		18	9
Compensation for land	1,188	9	4
Purchase of property	3,218	0	0
Legal expenses	92	13	7
Management expenses	278	11	0
Works	11,079	0	0
	21,444	18	2
Balance in hand	1,271	17	5
Total	22,716	18	7

Birkinshaw, the engineer, then reported on the progress of construction announcing the contractor had made considerable advancement with more than three-quarters of the earthworks completed and two-thirds of the boundary fencing erected. Work had commenced between the junction with the ECR and Port Vale Road, Hertford, a distance of about a mile, and most of the material for the outstanding sections of line had been delivered. Of the sixteen bridges on the railway, six were completed and seven in a forward state of construction. Some track had been laid and a considerable part of the ballasting completed.

At the conclusion of the engineer's report the question of the siting of Hertford station was raised. In reply the Secretary advised J.J. Gripper that consultation was still in hand with the ECR and it was probable that the station would be located at Cowbridge. Mr Gardner thought many of the shareholders preferred the station to be at Fore Street, beside the river, and that the company was mistaken in locating the structure at Cowbridge. Gardner voiced the thoughts of many people when he stated that Cowbridge was considered too far from the town centre where trade was concentrated. The only approach in the area was over Mill Bridge where the road was too narrow for pedestrians to cross without endangering themselves to road traffic.

In the ensuing discussion Cowper the Chairman emphasised the directors were anxious to resolve the position of the station in the town as well as the facilities to be provided. The company had purchased a large area of land at Cowbridge and if the station was located elsewhere, other property would have to be purchased at considerable cost and inconvenience. Birkinshaw reminded those present that although other sites were negotiable the ECR would only run their trains as far as Cowbridge. Responding, J.J. Gripper thought it impossible and improbable for the ECR or GNR to work trains to two stations within half a mile distance of each other. Concluding the debate Mr Chambers stated that he had only heard of one other site mentioned, the Priory, but there were greater engineering difficulties in siting the station at that place.

The construction of the railway continued without serious incident until Saturday 14th June 1856 when an earth slip occurred near Port Vale, Hertford. At this point the road from the extreme end of Port Vale to Bengeo Common was being diverted and a new road constructed. In accordance with the Act of Parliament the railway ran through a cutting as the new road crossed the line by an overbridge. On that fateful Saturday morning navvies were excavating earth for the foundation of the new structure. The cutting, some four feet wide, was enclosed on one side by a perpendicular wall of earth twelve feet high, whilst the other side varied from depths of four to five feet. Despite minor slippages the previous day, caused by the loamy soil, Alcock, the contractor in charge of the excavation work, gave direction to the navvies to cut away at the top of the cutting to loosen the pressure on the lower strata. Unfortunately when work commenced at 8.15am the base

HERTFORD AND WELWYN JUNCTION RAILWAY COMPANY.

The Half-Yearly General Meeting of the Proprietors will be held at the Shire Hall, Hertford, on Saturday, the 9th day of August instant, at a quarter-past Eleven o'clock precisely.

REPORT OF THE DIRECTORS.
AUGUST, 1856.

Your Directors beg to present the Half-yearly Report and Statement of Accounts.

Since the date of the last meeting, the Works of the Line have progressed at various points, and between Welwyn and Hertford a considerable portion of the rails and permanent way has been laid; possession of nearly all the Land has been obtained, and the Railway rapidly approaches completion.

Your Directors take the present opportunity of expressing most strongly their conviction, that they will be serving the best interests of the Company by urging on the finishing of the Line, so that it may be opened for Traffic in time for the conveyance of the produce of the approaching Harvest; and, although but a few months intervene between the present time and the next Malting Season, the Line could, as your Directors are informed, be then opened for Public Traffic; provided that, by the prompt co-operation of the Shareholders, the necessary means are immediately placed at their disposal.

The importance of this object can scarcely be too highly estimated, as there is a prospect of an abundant harvest in the counties through and into which the Line will run; and the Traffic in Corn alone during the latter months of the year will probably be very considerable.

The Special Act empowers the Company to borrow on Mortgage or Bond the sum of £21,000, and the Directors have determined to ask the sanction of the Shareholders at this Meeting, to their raising the same at once, to enable them to carry on and complete the Works without delay.

A further Call of £2 per Share has been made since the last Meeting, payable this day; which, together with the Deposit, gives a total of £13 2s. per Share called up to the present time.

The negotiation (alluded to at the last Meeting) which took place with the Directors of the Eastern Counties Railway as to the construction and use of a Joint Station on your own land at Cowbridge, has for the present been abandoned; not, however, from any doubt as to the advantages of the proposed arrangement to both Companies, but because the Eastern Counties Board is uncertain as to whether the adoption of such a scheme is within the authority conferred on them by their several Acts of Parliament. Under these circumstances, and to avoid all difficulty and delay in opening the Line, your Directors have decided on erecting a temporary Station, postponing their final decision as to the locality of the Station and all permanent arrangements for the accommodation of the traffic, until they shall have learnt, by some experience of its character and amount, what is the nature and extent of accommodation which may ultimately be required.

Communications have been addressed by your Board both to the Eastern Counties and Great Northern Railway Companies, stating that the time has now arrived when some plans should be agreed upon for conducting the traffic over your Railway, and for receiving and forwarding it at Welwyn and Hertford; and

H&WJR report of directors 1856.

of the twelve feet high bank gave way burying two men up to their thighs and one other man completely. All hands were quickly at the scene to free the men. The two men partially buried were released without injury whilst the third luckily suffered only bruising. He was taken to Hertford Infirmary for a medical check before being discharged later the same day. The rescue work was watched by a large gathering of local people.

With works at an advanced state Marchant, the H&WJR Secretary, wrote on 15th July 1856 to the GNR advising that his company wished to form the junction in the Parish of Digswell and either purchase or utilise land belonging to the main-line company. The matter was raised at a board meeting at King's Cross the same day when the directors heard that Brydone, the engineer and the General Manager were satisfied with the siting of the junction but their report concluded the exact mode and arrangements for installation were still to be finalised. As a result of the report the H&WJR was advised that only one rod of GNR land would be made available to the company and that the GNR General Manager and Engineer were to liaise with Birkinshaw regarding the installation work at the junction.

On 21st July 1856 the H&WJR Secretary again wrote to King's Cross optimistically intimating that the works of the railway were nearing completion. He advised that his directors were prepared to entertain a proposal from the GNR to work the Hertford line and duly requested a meeting between the two companies as well as the ECR. These tentative arrangements for jointly working the H&WJR were placed before the GNR board six days later.

By August 1856 many of the shareholders were becoming disenchanted with the slow progress being made on the new railway and few bothered to attend the half yearly meeting at the Shire Hall, Hertford on 9th August. The engineer reported nine-tenths of the earthworks were completed and the bridges nearly all finished. The only incomplete bridge was that spanning the River Lea and work on that was to commence later in the month when arrangements had been made to stop up the navigation to allow the foundations of the structure to be laid; rails and sleepers for the remaining section of line were delivered. Birkinshaw concluded his report expecting no difficulty in arranging for the completion of the line ready for opening in October. The Chairman summing up told the meagre gathering that the plans for the joint H&WJR/ECR station at Cowbridge had been postponed when the main-line company solicitor had advised the provision of the station was outside the jurisdiction of the Act. Because of these difficulties the H&WJR directors decided to provide a temporary station at Cowbridge funded entirely by the company. To resolve the monetary problems, J. Marchant, the Company Secretary, advised on 29th August 1856 that the H&WJR directors were prepared to receive tenders for loans on debentures for periods of three or five years, being empowered under the provision of the Act of incorporation to borrow the sum of £21,600, and tenders for the whole amount, or any sum not less than £100, were invited, being addressed to the company office St. Andrew's Street Hertford.

Attempts to finalise a working agreement for the Hertford to Welwyn Junction line soon ran into difficulties. Seymour Clarke, the GNR General Manager, reported the problems to his board on 27th October 1856. Because of the treaty being negotiated for the H&WJR Company traffic to use the ECR station at Hertford, the ECR concluded that under clauses 47 and 67 of their agreement with the GNR the latter ought not to carry Hertford to London traffic. The ECR had, however, no desire to object to the movement of traffic and it had been suggested a committee be set up under clause 3 of the same agreement to arrange the working of the H&WJR traffic to the mutual satisfaction of all parties. After discussion at the board meeting the following day the directors requested Mr Pym to represent the interests of the GNR at the meetings. Almost two months elapsed, however, before any meetings were arranged and it was not until 18th December that the ECR Chairman met Pym for serious discussion.

The New Year found the H&WJR affairs in the doldrums. At the half yearly meeting held on 14th February 1857 at the Shire Hall Hertford, the most important topic on the agenda was the inability of the company to take advantage of the borrowing powers because of the poor state of the money market. All land required for the railway had been purchased and permanent way laid for three-quarters of the distance between Welwyn Junction and Hertford. The engineer reported to the few shareholders present that there was little to complete except for the section from Cowbridge to the junction with the ECR where earthworks near the river bridge were still incomplete. The Secretary reiterated the lack of borrowing powers was delaying such completion and concluded by advising the gathering that negotiations for working the line were pending. At the end of February the ECR directors also notified their shareholders that the company was negotiating the joint working of the H&WJR with the GNR and their actions received the necessary approval.

The lack of progress towards completion of the short section from Cowbridge to the ECR junction was a constant worry to the H&WJR directors, for as one problem was solved another emerged. The bridge over the River Lea was completed by April 1857 at the same time as the Commoners of Hartham Common voiced their dissatisfaction with the railway company over the compulsory purchase of a portion of their land. Matters came to a head on 28th April when the H&WJR directors met members of Hertford Town Council to finalise terms for the acquisition of the land.

At the invitation of Seymour Clark, General Manager of the GNR, Horatio Love, his ECR counterpart, met on 29th July 1857 to discuss the future working of the Hertford to Welwyn Junction line. Neither at the time appeared overly interested in being involved in the minor cross-country railway for both initially agreed the local company should be left to find and fund its own operating resources.

In the meantime improvements in the money market enabled construction to recommence and on 1st August 1857 the *Hertford Mercury* reported:

> *The works at the Hertford end of the railway are in active progress and it is confidently believed the railway will open in October. The site of the station is fixed near Cowbridge House and cottages at the corner of and in Hartham Lane are to be pulled down to make way for the new road to the station.*

Other new works included the construction of a new road connecting Hartham Lane and Port Hill on a bridge over the railway and the placing of a coal depot for local fuel merchants. To the satisfaction of local residents Hartham Lodge was *'untouched by the progress of the railway'*.

The shareholders who attended the half yearly meeting on Saturday 8th August 1857 were gratified to hear the railway directors had overcome most of the legal problems and succeeded in raising the required additional capital. As a result the works were sufficiently completed to enable the commencement of a train service in September. The physical junction with the GNR had yet to be installed but the permanent way was completed from there as far as the Hartham Road level crossing. The contractor was waiting for the annual stop up of the River Lea to complete bridge works and in the meantime was building a dock and lay-by adjacent to the structure to enable the interchange of rail and river traffic. Concluding his report the engineer advised the station at Hartham (sic) was sufficiently completed to enable the line to open, as forecast, in September.

However, when the H&WJR Secretary wrote in early August to the ECR seeking agreement for the connection with that company at Hertford station, the matter was referred to the board on 13th August. In the meantime, Seymour Clarke had reported to his directors at King's Cross who immediately concurred that joint operation of the new railway, however minor, was essential for the territorial protection of the GNR. From thereon correspondence passed almost daily between King's Cross and Bishopsgate. Initially Seymour Clarke again raised the question of the joint working of the line but the ECR response was vague, and within house the GNR Chairman was asking for a reply in the affirmative. Having met the H&WJR committee, Horatio Love, the ECR Chairman incorrectly advised Clarke on 20th August that the Hertford Company was purchasing locomotives and rolling stock to work the line.

By 25th August 1857 the H&WJR committee was again requesting an early decision on the junction at Hertford. The ECR answer was non-committal and as work on the local line was nearing completion the Hertford directors asked for the ECR to receive a deputation. Almost three weeks elapsed before Horatio Love, Lightly Simpson and Robert Sinclair met with Lord Cowper and other members of the H&WJR board on 17th September to discuss the arguments for and against a fork junction or straight junction with the ECR.

By 9th September the new wharf at Hertford, measuring 48 feet in width with a 200-foot frontage to the River Lea, was almost completed. At the same time the new dock adjacent to the structure also in the course of construction was sold to W. Parker for £285. At the other end of the line arrangements for the physical junction at Welwyn Junction with the GNR were concluded in early September and the engineers duly arranged installation. On 19th September the H&WJR Secretary wrote to the GNR requesting the main-line company to execute the work and install the necessary protecting signals with all costs for the work being borne by the local company.

The *Herts Guardian* reported on 19th September 1857 that a temporary station platform measuring 30 feet by 9 feet was being erected in Hartham, together with a small goods shed, and the line was expected to open for traffic in early October. The works were progressing between the Priory and the junction with the ECR although it was still undecided whether the new line would run into the ECR terminal or by the *'burnt engine house'*. Six houses at the north-west corner of Hartham had been demolished: *'Cowbridge House is now seen to better advantage'*. The newspaper was aggrieved that it had not received an invite to the recent shareholders meeting and finally reported there was no truth in the rumour that E.B. Denison was about to relinquish chairmanship of the GNR in order to become chairman and sole manager of the Hertford and Welwyn line.

The junction at Welwyn was installed in early October and arrangements subsequently made for the GNR to arrange a trial run over the new line. On Saturday 10th October 1857 local people gathered at the lineside to watch the passage of the GNR locomotive from Welwyn Junction to Hertford. Having concluded a satisfactory first run to test the permanent way, Jackson and Bean, the contactors, rode on the engine for the return run to the junction. The *Hertford Mercury* reporting the event noted the locomotive was *'a new one belonging to the company'*. Not to be outdone a reciprocal run was made across the line the following day by an ECR ballast engine, which gained access over a temporary junction east of Hertford ECR station.

At a meeting of the GNR committee at King's Cross on 20th October 1857, Clarke reported that traffic arrangements for the new railway had once again been deferred as the H&WJR had advised they intended to hire Manchester, Sheffield & Lincolnshire Railway rolling stock to work the services. How precisely the company intended to transfer such stock when locomotives and carriages would have had to be worked over the GNR or ECR to Welwyn Junction or Hertford is unclear. It would appear to have been a sudden impulse to secure independence without much thought being given that hired stock had still to be maintained and repaired far from the parent system. On hearing of such grandiose plans Horatio Love objected to any such proposals and it would appear Clarke followed suit, for no further mention was made of the MS&LR stock or independent operation by the H&WJR directors.

Despite the optimistic forecast for the opening of the railway in the latter months of 1857, progress at the eastern end of the line was slow, although by now a permanent junction was installed. The negotiations between the GNR locomotive superintendent and his ECR counterpart had raised false hopes for as yet no formal working agreement had been concluded, nor timetables arranged. The New Year arrived and still the railway lay dormant. Matters were hardly better on the Luton and Dunstable line, which had been progressing in tandem with the Hertford line. At a shareholders meeting held at Luton on 9th January 1858, whilst acknowledging the success of the Luton to Dunstable section where opening was imminent, the company was unable to build the line on to Welwyn Junction because of the almost total lack of support by local people. They had therefore taken the only steps available and formally arranged the amalgamation of the LD&WJR with the H&WJR. The scheme was mutually acceptable as several directors served on the board of both companies. To ensure shareholders received due remuneration for their holdings it was agreed that all profits received from the Luton section of the line would be kept for the benefit of that section and similarly all profits from the Hertford section, after the line opened for traffic, would be retained for the Hertford line.

The amalgamation was bitterly opposed by William Willis and several other Luton shareholders who expressed concern that the company was seeking to abandon all connections with the GNR by bridging the main line and joining forces with the H&WJR, which would force passengers to travel via the ECR to London instead of the GNR line to King's Cross. A special meeting was held at Luton on 26th January 1858 when the matter was put to the vote. Many of the objecting shareholders abstained and other shareholders, with the assistance of the contractors Jackson & Bean, who held 4,000 shares in the Luton company as well as shares in the Hertford line, forced the issue and amalgamation was duly agreed.

The question of the junction at Welwyn was raised at the GNR board meeting on Tuesday 26th January 1858 when the General Manager reported that in anticipation of the opening of the Welwyn to Hertford line and to meet the increase in the number of trains, including Midland Railway services south of Hitchin, it had been decided to place two signalmen to operate the signal box at Welwyn Junction. The directors approved of the decision on condition the H&WJR company paid the wages of the staff employed at the junction.

On 8th February 1858 Seymour Clarke, the GNR General Manager and Mr Pym a H&WJR director submitted the two agreements made with the H&WJR and the ECR for the joint working of the Hertford line by the GNR and ECR. The agreement, dated 18th January, signed by Horatio Love on behalf of the ECR, Seymour Clarke for the GNR and the Right Honourable Francis Cowper MP for the H&WJR, stipulated.

1. The Welwyn and Hertford line to be worked jointly by the Eastern Counties Railway and the Great Northern Railway between Hertford and Welwyn Junction.
2. The Welwyn and Hertford Company to find clerks, signalmen and all servants on their own line and stations and pay government duty on their own traffic. The company would pay all rates and taxes and be responsible for all accidents and damages to life and property.
3. The traffic to be worked efficiently and according to the timetable to be agreed with the Welwyn and Hertford Company and the working companies.
4. Payment to be made for engine power including drivers, coke and stores at 1s 3d per train mile.
5. Rolling stock, other than engines, used for traffic to be paid for according to Railway Clearing House mileage arrangements.
6. The Welwyn and Hertford Company to find stations at Hertford for passengers, goods and coals or use those of the Eastern Counties Railway on such terms as may be agreed.
7. The Welwyn and Hertford Company to find their own collection and delivery service for goods, parcels and minerals at Hertford.
8. Trains to be run as far as practicable to fit certain trains on the lines of the Great Northern Railway Company and Eastern Counties Railway Company at times to be agreed between the Welwyn and Hertford Company and the working companies.
9. The Great Northern Railway to call at Welwyn Junction for passengers, goods and mineral traffic passing to or from the Welwyn and Hertford line.
10. The Eastern Counties Railway to make through rates with all places the Great Northern Railway can reach north of the Welwyn Junction and Hertford Railway to and from Victoria Docks, Blackwall, Pepper Warehouse, Barking Road, Stratford, Tottenham, Water Lane, Enfield, Ponders End, Waltham, Broxbourne, St. Margarets and Ware for passenger and goods traffic but not for coals, the rates to be same by both routes whether by way of Cambridge or Welwyn.
11. Through rates via Welwyn between Hertford and all stations north of Welwyn Junction which may be reached by the Great Northern Railway line in connection therewith for all descriptions of traffic, the rates to and from Peterborough and stations north of Peterborough to be not less than by the Eastern Counties Railway via Cambridge.
12. Through rates via Welwyn Junction between Hertford and London for all descriptions of traffic at the rates which may vary from time to time to be the same as that charged by the Eastern Counties Railway via Broxbourne. The Great Northern Railway to hand over to the Eastern Counties Railway 66⅔ per cent of the amount earned from Hertford and London traffic between Welwyn Junction and London and Holloway after deducting the Railway Clearing House terminals and goods and mineral traffic and parcels and government duty on passengers. The goods to be at station-to-station rates and not to be carried at cartage rates either by the Eastern Counties or Great Northern Companies. The charge for collection and delivery in London and Hertford, to be the same by both companies.
13. In consequence of the foregoing concession on the part of the Eastern Counties Railway, the Great Northern Railway agreed to abandon the restriction imposed on the Eastern Counties Railway under the agreement made on 16th July 1852 to permit the carriage and booking through of goods traffic to and from Victoria Docks over the Eastern Counties Railway through Hertford with Manchester, Liverpool and for places in the Counties of Northumberland, Durham, York, Lancaster and in Scotland and such other places as may from time to time be mutually agreed upon. The Great Northern Railway to enable the Eastern Counties Railway to obtain through rates to and from all places and beyond on the Great Northern Railway system such as Manchester, Liverpool, Edinburgh and Glasgow, they themselves may from time to time negotiate with other companies.
14. This agreement to come into operation on the opening if the Welwyn Junction and Hertford line for public traffic and continue until the expiry of the agreement of 16th July 1852 between the Eastern Counties and Great Northern Companies.
15. The Hertford and Welwyn Junction Company to accept the mileage proposed after the deduction of temporary allowances of the rates of through traffic passing over the Hertford and Welwyn line between the Great Northern Railway and the Eastern Counties Railway.
16. The arbitration clause to meet all occurrences of dispute.

The agreement was passed to the H&WJR directors and following a board meeting William Marchant, Secretary of the local company, wrote to King's Cross on 18th February 1858 advising acceptance of the working arrangements.

At the H&WJR Company shareholders meeting held in the Shire Hall, Hertford on 13th February 1858 the Right Honourable W.F. Cowper MP as Chairman reported that works were finally completed. The junctions with the GNR and ECR were installed in compliance of the terms of the Act of Parliament and the line was now awaiting Board of Trade inspection. The negotiations for the working of the line had been protracted and he advised those present that the two companies would jointly work the railway at such times as agreeable to themselves. Through rates and fares were to be quoted between all places north of Welwyn Junction on the GNR, and over the Hertford and Welwyn line to and from Victoria Dock, Blackwall, Barking Road and stations Tottenham to Ware on the ECR, and also between Hertford and London by both routes.

The Chairman then thanked the Marquis Townshend and Earl Cowper for desisting from pressing pecuniary claims against the railway company and for giving full possession of land required for construction from their estates. He explained that a bill to effect the amalgamation of the Luton, Dunstable & Welwyn Junction

Railway with the Hertford & Welwyn Junction Railway was being submitted for Parliamentary approval. The amalgamation, although not welcomed by all, was expected to afford many advantages with economy of staff and working expenses. Despite these reassurances Mr Palmer voiced the thoughts of many when he objected to the merger. He and several others were of the opinion the H&WJR had incurred enough trouble completing their own line. Now they were being forced to amalgamate with a company that was too weak to construct their extension from Luton to Welwyn Junction.

In reply, W.F. Cowper explained that when the railway from Hertford was first mooted there was great interest in the undertaking by the local populace and the shareholders expected the directors to engineer a speedy and successful completion to the scheme. Unfortunately, financial problems had precluded the undertaking remaining commercially independent. It was then thought more economical for a main-line company to work the line but problems arose because the railway formed a junction with two companies, the ECR and GNR. Negotiations were further complicated because the one company would not negotiate without the other for fear of losing territorial advantage. With working arrangements now negotiated, Cowper rather optimistically concluded the H&WJR had only to provide the station accommodation and officers and would eventually become part of an important trunk route from the Midland Railway and the GNR to and from Victoria Docks. He was therefore pleased to announce that subject to satisfactory inspection the line would open to traffic on 1st March 1858, the BOT having been informed an inspection was required.

The balance sheet for the half year ending 31st December 1857 was then presented:

Receipts		£	s	d
	Calls on shares	5,955	3	1
	Interest on arrears	51	7	2
	Loans from bankers	3,000	0	0
	Loans on debentures	58,900	0	0
	Sundry small rents	7	10	0
	Income tax on debenture interest	24	5	8
	Transfer fees		2	6
	Dividend received from Adams & Co.	23	0	0
	Total	68,011	8	5
Expenditure				
	Preliminary expenses	2,312	10	6
	Engineers expenses	2,800	0	0
	Land compensation	1,504	6	4
	Purchase of property	17,124	4	2
	Legal expenses	1,099	12	5
	Management expenses	968	16	0½
	Works	39,328	18	0
	Surveying	263	18	9
	Interest on bankers loans	512	19	3
	Rates and taxes	5	4	0
	Land tax		8	11
	Tithe rent charges	18	3	10½
	Broker's commission	49	0	0
	Amount with Adams & Co.	114	9	7
	Total	67,798	1	6
	Balance in hand	213	6	11
	Total	68,011	8	5

On the same day as the railway meeting, the Town Clerk of Hertford reported that the Hertford & Welwyn Railway Company had taken 17 poles of ground more than they had been given, and *'in accordance with the agreement entered into with the company, as to payment to be made for the excess of land taken, the Corporation would have to receive the sum of £21'*. It was agreed that *'the committee appointed some time since to see that the agreement with the Company was properly carried out, be requested to make a report on the subject'*. It was also pointed out that the Council *'ought to have a proper record of the terms of the agreement having been complied with'*.

Lieutenant Colonel William Yolland carried out the official BOT inspection of the new line on 15th February 1858. The inspector noted that the H&WJ Railway was 7 miles 30 chains in length, commencing at a junction with the GNR at Welwyn and terminating at a junction with the ECR at Hertford. Land had been purchased and overbridges constructed for double line if required, although the railway was single track. The width of land at formations of cuttings and embankments was 18 feet. After inspecting the permanent way Yolland examined the six overbridges and nine underbridges. In addition he found two footpath overbridges. Of the overbridges, two were built entirely of brick, three had brick abutments and cast iron girders whilst the sixth consisted of five arches, one which was spanned by a cast iron girder. Inspection of the underbridges revealed six were built entirely of brick, two with brick abutments and wrought iron girders, whilst one had brick abutments and cast iron girders. The girders of the bridge over a cattle creep were formed of three rails bolted together. The greatest span of the overbridges was 28 feet on the square whilst one of the underbridges had a 42 feet skew span wrought iron girder. Yolland considered all were well constructed and sufficiently strong with the exception of the bridge over the cattle creep with 10 feet span, which exhibited a ⅜ inch deflection under load. The inspector then examined the four wooden viaducts which were considered sufficiently strong but noted that having been erected for some consideration time it was necessary for them to be carefully looked over and wedged up with the nuts and bolts tightened.

Yolland found no unauthorised level crossings and although seven had been authorised by the Act only four had been constructed. There were slight deviations beyond the authorised limits of the railway but these had been made with the sanction of the proprietors of the adjacent land. Only one station was provided on the line at Hertford but a platform was also provided at Welwyn Junction.

In his summary the Lieutenant Colonel thought the line to be in *'fair order'* but urged that it would require looking after once traffic worked over it. He noted the gates of three level crossings, and the goods warehouse at Hertford, were too close to the line. Similarly, the end of the coal drops on the ECR at Hertford abutted the line and at present there was nothing to prevent wagons projecting over the H&WJ Railway. Yolland noted that no turntables were provided at either end of the railway, although the ECR had a turntable at their Hertford engine shed. Noting that both the GNR and ECR were to provide rolling stock for the railway he stipulated *'it will be necessary that provision be made to prevent the necessity for running tender first when the line opens'*. Yolland subsequently refused to sanction the opening of the line because of incompleteness of the works.

Just over a week later the H&WJR Secretary advised the Board of Trade the intended method of operating the line and notified that all remedial work was completed. The BOT advised that Colonel Yolland would re-inspect the line on 27th February and the GNR was asked to provide a special train for the inspection.

At the half yearly meeting of ECR shareholders, Horatio Love formally spoke to the gathering of the conviction with which the H&WJR had been developed to provide through traffic for its livelihood neither being *'cribbed or confined'*, and dependent upon limited traffic from the area through which the line passed. *'Local apathy and apprehension together with foreign indifference had been overcome after a lengthy struggle by the local directors who were to be congratulated on their achievement.'* He concluded that the new railway was to be worked by the GNR and ECR one month at a time.

The H&WJR directors and their ECR and GNR counterparts evidently anticipated no problems regarding the opening of the line, for at 12 noon on 27th February 1858 a special train from Bishopsgate hauled by *'one of the prettiest of locomotives'* arrived at Cowbridge station with a deputation of ECR directors and friends led by the Chairman of the company Horatio Love. Also present were James Goodson, Vice Chairman, Messrs Anderson, Smyth and Walters, Directors and James Robertson, Superintendent of the Line. Cowper and his fellow directors met the train on arrival at the station.

Unlike the ECR train, the GNR train was over an hour late arriving as it conveyed Lieutenant Colonel Yolland making his second inspection of the line. Numerous stoppages were made along the route adding to the delay and on reaching Cowbridge the train continued through the station so that the inspector could examine the bridge over the River Lea and the physical junction with the ECR. The short notice of the inspection and formal opening precluded the GNR directors attending but Mr Mowatt, the Company Secretary, and several minor officers represented the GNR. Mowatt tendered apologies on behalf of his directors who were attending an important board meeting at King's Cross.

At the conclusion of the inspection Yolland noted that all deficiencies previously reported had been rectified except for the provision of an engine turntable at Welwyn Junction. In his report of the same day the Lieutenant Colonel remarked that the H&WJR had already informed the BOT that the passenger traffic would be worked entirely by tank engines until a turntable was installed at the junction with the GNR. At the same juncture the Honourable William Cowper, Chairman of the Company promised in a letter to provide within six months either a turntable or a triangular section of line at the junction with the GNR to enable the engine to be turned. It was also confirmed to the inspector that the ECR turntable at Hertford was available for the use of the engine working the H&WJR line. On learning from the Chairman and Secretary of the local company that the line was to be worked on the One Engine in Steam principle with no more than one engine being used at the same time on either of the two sections of line, Welwyn Junction to Hertford and Hertford to the ECR junction, Yolland recommended the opening of the railway to passenger traffic, adding the rider that because of the sharp curves on the line the speed limit be restricted to 20 mph.

After the inspection and a number of speeches, the directors, officials and ladies were invited to join the GNR train for a return journey to Welwyn Junction. At 1.32pm the train departed from Cowbridge station to the cheers of those remaining on the platform. Passing under Port Vale road bridge the train skirted the fir-covered slopes of Port Hill and then through the cutting to the rear of Port Vale. Beyond George Street and Russell Street the train crossed the substantially-built brick bridge spanning Molewood Mill Road with Molewood marshes in the distance. Continuing at a sedate speed, passengers then enjoyed a view of the River Beane near Haggar's Mill, owned by a director of the railway company. The train then crossed the bridge spanning North Road before leaving the outskirts of Hertford and descending through Camps Hill cutting where a footbridge spanned the line. Skirting the village of Hertingfordbury the train then crossed the Hertingfordbury Road on another bridge. So the journey continued until the train negotiated the sharp curve to the platform at Welwyn Junction, located a mile and a half south of the GNR Digswell station. The reporter from the *Hertford Mercury* reported Welwyn Junction as *'an out of the world place between Welwyn and Hatfield, far from the high road with only at present a signal station and a cottage to remind us that humanity lives and breathes in the neighbourhood'.*

For the intrepid travellers there were more delays, no doubt to the smug satisfaction of the ECR contingent present, for when the locomotive ran round the train ready to re-couple for the return journey the leading wheels derailed at the points, effectively blocking the line. The representative from the *Hertford Mercury* reported *'the engine sent from King's Cross, being of somewhat unusual construction in that the space is longer between the driving wheels and the hind wheels than is usual so that there is no inherent elasticity, the points being adapted for an engine of different construction'.* Embarrassed GNR officials sent an urgent telegraph message for a replacement engine but unfortunately after some two hours' delay, when the locomotive arrived it was entirely unsuitable for the line *'being one of the largest on the GNR'.* To the relief of the frustrated passengers the original engine was re-railed using screw jacks from the larger locomotive. After these frustrations the train made an uneventful return run to Hertford where the guests retired to the Town Hall for a celebratory dinner arranged by S. Halestrop of the Dimsdale Arms. The Mayor of Hertford, J. Woodhouse, presided and introduced the after-dinner speeches advocating success to the new line. Other attendees included the Right Honourable W.F. Cowper, Chairman, other directors of the H&WJR, and Horatio Love, the ECR Chairman.

3

Opening to Traffic

On the same day as the inspection and official first run, the following notice was posted at Hertford station and also appeared in the *Hertford Mercury*.

> **HERTFORD AND WELWYN JUNCTION RAILWAY**
>
> **OPENING OF LINE FOR GOODS TRAFFIC**
>
> The public are respectfully informed that the Hertford and Welwyn Line will be opened for Goods Traffic on the First of March. Rates and any further information can be had on application to the undersigned.
>
> COWBRIDGE STATION   JOHN MAXEY
> HERTFORD   Traffic Manager
> 28 February 1858.

This announcement was made rather prematurely, for on learning of the inspector's agreement to the opening of the line the directors immediately declared the railway officially open on the same day, with the public opening for general traffic on and from Monday 1st March 1858. The timetable showed a total of five trains running in each direction on weekdays only. Later in the month, after an initial disagreement, the ECR Company was permitted to work their goods trains to Cowbridge and to shunt malt traffic routed via the GNR for Mr Palmer at Hertford. When, however, the H&WJR Company demanded a toll of 4d per ton for the use of Cowbridge station the ECR Superintendent was sent post haste to settle the matter. At the same time the GNR was forwarding traffic from Leeds to Southend via Peterborough, prompting the ECR General Manager to advise his King's Cross counterpart that by the terms of the working agreement such traffic was to be routed via Welwyn Junction. In accordance with the working arrangements the GNR operated the line for the remaining days of March whilst the ECR announced at the end of the month they would work the services for the month of April. With this in mind, ECR footplate crews rode with the GNR engine crews to and from Welwyn Junction to familiarise the route.

On 6th May 1858 the H&WJR directors sought tenders for the erection of station houses at Hertingfordbury and Cole Green stations, together with seven cottages at Digswell Junction (*sic*) and gatekeeper's cottages at Attimore Farm level crossing and the level crossing at the road leading to Hatfield Gate. These were to be constructed according to drawings and specifications exhibited on or after Wednesday 12th May at the Traffic Manager's office, Hartham Lane Hertford. Tenders were to be submitted by 22nd May.

In the meantime, and despite objections raised by the L&NWR, the Luton, Dunstable and Welwyn Junction and Hertford and Welwyn Junction Amalgamation Bill was read for the third time and passed the lower house on Thursday 20th May 1858. The GNR authorities were also highly suspicious of the amalgamation bill and equally worried of the territorial gain made by the ECR reaching Welwyn Junction. Although no objections had initially been raised, certain officers were having second thoughts and the company solicitor was requested to prepare a petition against the bill to safeguard GNR interests. These objectives were accomplished by the insertion of a special clause providing that where the LD&WJR and H&WJR or any part of them formed the shortest or part of the shortest and most convenient route to London or any other place then the amalgamated company would offer every facility for the use of such railway to the GNR. Whatever arrangements or agreements were made or thereafter made with the ECR as to the conveyance of traffic or the use of the amalgamated undertaking, the amalgamated company would make equally favourable arrangements with the GNR. The contents of the amendment were made known to the GNR board in a letter from the solicitor on 29th May 1858.

It was not long before problems arose on the new railway, for during shunting operations at Hertford Cowbridge in late May an ECR wagon loaded with malt was damaged when it ran off the rails. At the subsequent investigation the H&WJR Company was ordered to pay for repairs and compensation as no buffer stops had been provided at the end of the siding!

Once the new line was opened for traffic the lethargic attitude of the local populace returned and very few shareholders bothered to attend a special meeting of the H&WJR held at Hertford Town Hall on 7th June 1858 to discuss the amalgamation bill. With the Honourable W.F. Cowper presiding and fellow directors G.F. Thornton and F. Haggar in attendance the only questions raised concerned the issue of preference stock. Later in the month, Marchant, the H&WJR Secretary, wrote to King's Cross requesting free passes for the five directors of the local company for travel between Hertford and King's Cross in exchange for free passes issued to GNR directors for travel between Welwyn Junction and Hertford. The GNR board was terse and the reply of 29th June refused the application outright and considered the request '*objectionable*'.

The Hertford, Luton and Dunstable Railway Act 1858 (21 and 22 Vic cap lxxiv) duly received the Royal Assent on 28th June 1858. The statute authorised the amalgamation of the Hertford & Welwyn Junction Railway and the Luton, Dunstable & Welwyn Junction Railway, as well as the raising of additional capital to complete work on both sections of line. Clause vii included the provision of a new station building and other works at Hertford. The initial directors of the new company were the Right Honourable William Francis Cowper, former Chairman of both the Hertford and Luton companies, Thomas Chambers, a director of both companies, and George Smith Thornton, Henry Inskip and Franklin Haggar, formerly directors of the H&WJR, together with Lionel Ames, Thomas Sworder and John Everitt, formerly LD&WJR directors. One other director could be appointed. The capital of the new Hertford Luton and Dunstable Railway Company was set at £185,000, formed of £65,000 Hertford stock and £120,000 of

Luton stock. The share issue of £54,400 of the Hertford section was to be increased by an authorised new issue of £10,540 by the statute, whilst the £70,000 existing Luton stock was increased by £50,000 new issue. The whole of the original shares were to be converted and the new shares to be issued as £10 shares. The Act also permitted the company to borrow on the Hertford section a sum not exceeding £21,600 and on the Luton section a sum not exceeding £40,000 once the whole of the capital was subscribed and half paid up. The transfer of money from one section account to the other was not permissible and the Hertford and Luton accounts were to be kept separate. If for any reason the company decided to borrow from one section to assist on the other then interest at 5 per cent per annum was to be charged. (The Dunstable route will form a later volume in the branch lines from Hatfield.)

As a result of a new agreement from 1st July 1858 the Hertford traffic was to be worked for a period of three months by the GNR and then for three months by the ECR. Because of ailing finances, the H&WJR board decided to reduce the working expenses and advised both the GNR and ECR companies that no goods trains were to run on the line after 26th July 1858. All goods traffic was to be attached to passenger trains, which were to be down-rated to run as mixed trains. The decision was unacceptable to the ECR when it was found goods traffic was taking an additional day in transit. As a compromise the ECR offered to waive the 20 per cent levy for traffic starting north of Peterborough routed to the ECR at Peterborough and instead demanded only that traffic from the GNR south of Peterborough should be worked via Welwyn Junction. On 4th August the ECR authorities were still awaiting a reply from the GNR and H&WJR.

Evidence of cheap labour employed by the H&WJR management came to light at the Hertford County Magistrates Court on Saturday 24th July 1858 when two lads – Joseph Ballard and Richard Basil, employed as gatekeepers on the line – appeared to answer a charge of neglect of duty. Mr Foster appeared for the company and Mr Armstrong for the defendants. With Thomas Mills MP in the chair, Foster advised from the evidence of engine driver James Head that at about 9.50pm on 17th July he was in charge of a luggage (*sic*) train and approaching the gates in the charge of Joseph Ballard, he noted the barriers had been left open to the road and across the railway. He had no time to apply the brakes and his engine smashed the level crossing gates, some pieces of which flew into the air and would have injured him if he had not been protected by the engine. He stopped the train as quickly as he could and returning to the crossing found Ballard asleep. On being questioned the gatekeeper said he had *'left the gate right, and someone must have meddled with it'*. On cross examination Ballard reported he was engaged to go on duty at 4.00pm in the afternoon and remain on duty until 4.00am the next morning; that he had been engaged by the company in April and had never been relieved, that his duties included Sundays and that his wages were 10s 0d per week. The charge against Basil was that at 4.30am on 18th July he had been found asleep in the crossing keeper's hut next his level crossing; that he was locked in and that three others persons, two men and a woman were with him in the building. Armstrong, for the defendants contended the duties expected from the youths were excessive and *'more than human nature could bear; they were mere lads and it was not to be wondered they should give way to sleep by sheer exhaustion'*. During the times they were asleep there were no passenger trains on the line and only *'two miserable luggage [sic] trains during the whole night – nothing in fact to keep them awake'*. It was contended their wages were utterly insufficient and Ballard had been obliged to take on a second job to get *'sufficient maintenance'*. Armstrong trusted the bench would deal leniently with both as it was their first offence and he hoped they might get fined and not be imprisoned which *'would be their disgrace and entirely ruin the rest of their lives'*. The Bench, after consideration, inflicted a fine of 10s 0d on Ballard and £1 0s 0d on Basil, and the chairman summed up stating *'we think the duties excessive and the pay very inadequate'*. The fines were duly paid.

The first half yearly meeting of the proprietors of the H&WJR was held at Hertford Town Hall on Monday 9th August 1858 under the auspices of the Herttford, Luton, Dunstable & Welwyn Junction Railway syndicate. It was reported that receipts from the Luton and Dunstable section were excellent but traffic on the Hertford section since the opening for traffic on 1st March had been light and receipts disappointing. In order to bring the Hertford section shares in line with the Luton section for accountancy purposes all Hertford section holdings were to be converted to £10 shares. Receipts and expenditure for the Hertford section for the six months ending 30th June 1858 were:

Front page of Hertford and Welwyn Junction Railway and Luton, Dunstable and Welwyn Junction Railway Amalgamation Act 28th June 1858

Receipts		£	s	d
Calls on shares		4,884	2	10
Interest on calls in arrears		10	17	4
Loans from bankers		5,500	0	0
Loans on mortgage		2,000	0	0
Sundry receipts		10	0	0
Income tax on debenture issues		15	11	11
Sale of surplus property		1,634	11	10
Dividend of 1s 0d in the £ for assignees of Adams & Co.		5	13	0
Traffic receipts				
passenger		429	13	5
Goods		249	5	0
Season tickets		16	11	9
Commission on goods balance		10	11	
Deposit of season tickets		1	0	0
	Total	14,747	6	0
Balance from last account		213	6	11
	Total	14,960	0	11
Expenditure				
Engineer's expenses		836	10	6
Land compensation		35	17	7
Purchase of property		5,574	8	3
Legal expenses		63	12	3
Management expenses		183	18	11½
Expenses of Amalgamation Act		100	0	0
Sale of surplus property		146	15	9
Surveyor		70	9	0
Maintenance		127	0	0
Loan repaid to banker		6,000	0	0
Interest and discount on loan		120	18	3
Rates and taxes			4	5
Tithe rent charge		8	0	9
Interest on debenture loan		562	0	0
Land tax		1	0	0
Land tax redemption		89	12	6
Traffic expenses				
Salaries		50	0	0
Wages		232	17	6
Incidentals		57	8	0
Clothing		44	0	9
Stores		8	5	7
Mileage and demurrage		60	11	0
Passenger duty		8	12	7
	Total	14,503	5	7½
Balance in hand		472	1	5
Due in office		14	1	1½
	Total	14,960	6	11

An auction for the sale of surplus railway plant and valuable materials was held at Hertford on Thursday 7th October 1858 when Allcock, the local agent for Jackson & Bean, advised that having completed the contract, disposal would commence at 11.00am at the works near Cowbridge station. Items disposed of included five cart horses, a roan horse and a *'mare of great strength, a powerful brown mare and a hay horse'*. Other items included eight carts, two timber gigs, a stone truck, 611 temporary sleepers, 54 permanent sleepers, three tons of cut nails measuring from 1½ inches to 6 inches, 10 tons of cast iron wheels and 3 tons of metals and wagon axles plus seasoned oak, elm and ash planking.

On 30th September 1858 the GNR ceased their three months' operation of the branch and in accordance with the agreement the ECR assumed responsibility for the next three months ending 31st December. By early November the ECR authorities were reporting that no goods traffic had been conveyed across the branch for several weeks but now that it had resumed the HL&DR were willing to run the trains provided the ECR supplied the locomotives. The ECR agreed to operate the freight services as a temporary measure until a meeting could be arranged with the GNR to discuss the full implications of the workings and charges to be raised for the freight on the branch. The meeting was subsequently held at King's Cross on 1st January 1859 when the parties agreed to a charge of 1s 0d per mile each way for a locomotive with a total mileage of two round trips of 28 miles each night. It was agreed each company would pay a third of the costs for the three-month trial terminating on 31st March 1859, but the agreement was subsequently extended into April. By 2nd February the ECR officers were optimistic that the new arrangements were satisfactory and reported the conveyance of 1,927 tons of coal via the HL&DR route to London together with 10,000 barrels of beer from Burton en route to Blackwall, much to the dismay of McMullen's, the local Hertford brewers. Even Mr Stephens of Ware asked to use the HL&DR lay-by at Hertford for the transfer of corn and flour from his mill.

In the meantime Hertingfordbury and Cole Green stations first appeared in the public timetable in December 1858 but, curiously, not in the working timetable until two years later. At this period the stations were little more than halts and trains only called by request.

At the HL&DR shareholders meeting held at the Town Hall, Luton on Monday 28th February 1859, the Chairman reported the Hertford section had yet to be worked at a profit. The gathering was informed the line would not achieve its full potential until the Dunstable connection was made at Welwyn Junction, when traffic from the North-West and Midlands could traverse the line to Victoria Docks and other destinations. Cowper then advised of a reduction in train services. When the line first opened to Hertford five and very soon six trains ran in each direction but as traffic had not come up to expectations it had been found necessary to reduce the service to cut the cost of locomotive power. Despite the reduction traffic had actually increased with the following comparable results.

	Traffic Receipts £	Locomotive Power £
First four months of operation	766	692
Last four months of operation	980	318

Initially goods tonnages conveyed were minimal but these were increasing as the figures for 1858 showed July 595 tons, October 888 tons, November 1,736 tons and December 1,030 tons.

Unfortunately it was not possible to achieve more favourable charges for locomotive power because of the terms of the working agreement between the ECR and GNR. The Chairman, in summing up, thought the prospect for the railway would have been better if the connection had been ready with the L&NWR. He voiced the thoughts of many when he admitted the prospects for the viability of the Hertford section of line were not as favourable as on the Luton section regarding the future growth of traffic. In answer to allegations made by certain shareholders as to the poor workmanship of the contractors Jackson & Bean, George Leeman, a director of the North Eastern Railway spoke in support of the partnership advising they had constructed a large portion of that railway.

In late December 1858 the HL&DR Chairman had written to the GNR requesting permission to erect a refreshment room adjacent to the booking office and waiting room at Welwyn Junction, on land belonging to the main-line company. Having received no reply Cowper again wrote on 3rd March 1859 stating that B. Young of Hertford was willing to construct the refreshment room at his own expense provided he could remove the building at any time should trade not come up to expectations. The GNR board discussed the matter on 22nd March and ultimately sanctioned the building of the room but on terms *'protective to the interests of the GNR'*.

An accident, which occurred on the afternoon of Saturday 9th April 1859, brought severe criticism of the working arrangements. The 4.05pm mixed train from Hertford to Welwyn Junction was formed of two passenger coaches, five wagons and a brake van, hauled by an ECR locomotive in the charge of Driver John Chapman. The coaches were more crowded than usual as it was a fair day in the town, whilst the wagons were so heavily loaded that three wagons containing bricks, corn and oil had been left behind adjacent to the goods shed as it was thought the combined load of two coaches, eight wagons and brake van would have been too heavy for the engine.

On receiving the 'right away' from the guard, Driver Chapman started the train away from Cowbridge station but soon after being set in motion he realised the engine was struggling with the load and this was confirmed when the locomotive had difficulty climbing the gradient to Molewood Lane bridge and stalled on the incline. With no hope of restarting his engine on the rise the driver decided to reverse the train back to Hertford station and reattempt the climb. Unfortunately Chapman completely miscalculated the weight of his heavy train against his lightweight locomotive and minimal braking power. Having started on the perilous reversal movement the engine could not hold the vehicles or retard the reversing action with the result the train, now with the engine at the rear of the formation, passed two signals at danger before running through Hertford station and colliding with the three stationary wagons standing on the main single line opposite the goods shed, at an estimated speed of 20 mph. So great was the impact that the unbraked heavily laden wagons were driven 241 yards back towards the junction with the ECR before running into a siding and colliding with buffer stops, where they splintered to matchwood leaving three tons of oil, sacks of corn and hundreds of bricks spread across the permanent way. Six passengers received injuries and were treated on site by Doctor Woodhouse, including Mr Reed of Hatfield sustaining a cut nose, a young lady from Woolmer Green who received cuts to face and head, whilst according to the *Herts Guardian 'a lady who was admiring the teeth of a gentleman who sat opposite her, had the pleasure of having a violent collision and indentation of the said teeth in her forehead'*. Other travellers injured were John Taylor of West Moulsley, Surrey with a deep wound in the cheek bone and William Chalkley, a corn dealer of Stevenage with a wound on the nose. The majority of passengers were shaken but unhurt. The Reverend Spencer, the Minister of Cowbridge Independent Chapel, travelling by train to Potters Bar, was one of the relatively uninjured passengers and, although damaging his kneecap, he provided spiritual comfort.

Later in the day J. Marchant, the HL&DR Secretary, visited the injured with Mr Maxey.

The *Herts Guardian* was quick to apportion blame; bad construction of the line with the station at the low point of the gradient, the starting of an overloaded train and, thirdly, the stabling of trucks on the main line instead of a within a siding. It considered the ECR was not to blame as they were working the railway at the behest of the Hertford & Welwyn Company and concluded the accident would *'still incur the local shareholders in greater loss'*.

A local inquiry into the accident revealed that, for economy, the ECR was working the Hertford to Welwyn Junction line with underpowered locomotives. A further admission was made that the ECR entered into such a contract with their drivers to economise on fuel that the locomotive had barely enough fire or steam to work the train. In evidence, Driver Chapman admitted he had disobeyed the signals, neither blowing the engine whistle nor stopping at the signal near Molewood Bridge. A question that was pertinent to the incident was why the train, on reversing down the gradient back towards Hertford, had not become derailed at the points near Port Hill bridge and collided with some cattle wagons standing in the adjacent siding.

The evidence from the local enquiry was forwarded to the BOT who delegated Captain Ross to arrange the full enquiry. The inspector immediately requested the ECR and GNR to arrange for trial trips to run using the same locomotive involved in the incident. Two trial runs were made on Thursday 14th April 1859, the first with the locomotive hauling two passenger coaches, a brake van and five loaded wagons and the second run with an additional wagon added to the tail load. Despite heavy rain causing slippery rails and each wagon being loaded with 4½ tons of merchandise or thirty quarters of barley, the locomotive easily climbed the gradient to Molewood bridge from a standing start at Cowbridge station to arrive at Hertingfordbury station in 7 minutes running time from Hertford.

With attention focused on the accident, on 27th April 1859 the working terms agreed by the ECR and GNR with the Hertford Company were renewed for an unspecified short term.

Although the HL&DR Act of 1858 had authorised the raising of an additional £10,540 for the Hertford section, the preference shares bearing a dividend of 5 per cent remained unissued. Finding that additional time was required to complete the line from Luton to Welwyn Junction the directors decided to incorporate the clause for the additional capital in the application to Parliament. The draft of the bill was duly prepared and presented at a special meeting of shareholders held at the Fendells Hotel, New Palace Yard, Westminster, on 30th April where approval was agreed.

Meanwhile traffic on the Hertford line still fell far short of expectations. Under the existing working arrangements the GNR estimated the railway was making an annual loss of £500 on receipts of £3,350. As losses of this magnitude could not be maintained, representatives of both the ECR and GNR had an urgent meeting with the HL&DR Chairman and directors and advised the distinct possibility of closure of the line. Before such drastic action was taken the authorities at King's Cross proposed an alternative working agreement whereby the railway would continue to be worked by both the ECR and GNR with each company sharing the profits. On 5th May 1859 the ECR board requested R. Moseley, their General Manager, and J. Robertson, the Superintendent of the Line, to investigate the proposed revised arrangements. A week later they recommended acceptance of the GNR plan, especially as it benefited traffic travelling between the Midlands and Victoria Docks.

Early attempts to formulate a permanent working agreement met with failure. Under the initial arrangements the Welwyn Junction signalling costs of £318 per annum were to be shared half by the HL&DR Company and a quarter each by the ECR and GNR. The goods train services were to be worked entirely by the ECR at a rate of 10d per mile whilst the GNR worked the passenger services at 9d per mile. The ECR Committee, however, could not agree to such proposals and thought the passenger workings should alternate between the GNR and ECR. The ECR also directed that the HL&DR Company should pay half the costs of signalling and control of the junction at Hertford. Hardly had the two companies agreed the new arrangements before petty bickering again broke out in June 1859. Grain loaded by the GNR at Newark en route for Romford was routed via Welwyn Junction and Hertford as per the agreement between the parties, but on reflection the GNR goods agent objected to the routing claiming there was a shorter possible route between the two points via Peterborough.

At the end of June Captain George Ross concluded his inquiry into the working of the Hertford section of the Hertford, Luton & Dunstable Railway. In his summary the inspector found the local company directors far from blameless despite their repudiation of all responsibility in respect of locomotive working on their railway. By the arbitration clause in their agreement with the ECR, Ross concluded the directors should have checked whether the company had regular staff employed such as secretary, traffic management and guards besides other railway servants previously referred to by Mr Marchant. *'It was obvious the means existed and should have been exercised by the HL&DR directors to maintain a check.'* From his investigation the directors admitted the line had not been worked efficiently and *'under their false theory of irresponsibility the directors had taken no pains to get proper information how the work was being done'*.

No records had been kept of the failure of engines to get their loads to ascend the incline, no enquiry was called as to the causes of failure and the line was opened without any proper undertaking on the part of the directors as to the control of the driver. In the case of the turntable they thought it proper to follow out their own principles. As they had nothing to do with the locomotive arrangements the provision of the turntable might wait their convenience; in the absence of a direct complaint from the ECR Company they need have no scruple neglecting their engagement for the completion of this necessary adjunct to their line, leaving the locomotive arrangements to take care of themselves.

Ross also reported that from his enquiries he had discovered Driver Chapman had run his train past signals on previous occasions when working the line. Unfortunately the local directors had failed to ask the ECR to enquire into his misdemeanours to discover the true facts of the matter. On taking the subject up with the ECR Locomotive Superintendent, Ross was concerned to learn that the company provided a tank locomotive suitable only for light passenger work with 12 inch cylinders and 6 feet 6 inch diameter driving wheels to work the line. The engines were obviously not suited for the 1 in 63 gradient and were in the habit of slipping to a standstill, but as there were only six of the class the company was at a loss to find another suitable class of engine to work the Hertford to Welwyn services. Ross observed he did not recollect speaking about the turntable to the Locomotive Superintendent but *'the mere facts suggest the necessity of one'*. The inspector concluded by absolving the GNR Company from any blame. Unlike the ECR, the GNR Locomotive Superintendent required daily reports from their drivers when employed working trains on the Hertford, Luton and Dunstable line.

When the findings of the enquiry into the incident at Hertford were published, the GNR authorities were considerably concerned that the BOT inspector had initially admonished the company for the slack working arrangements on the line. The GNR Secretary was immediately ordered to write pointing out that the incident was due entirely to the failings of the ECR and that the GNR was not involved. As a result of the correspondence the directors were informed on 5th July 1859 that a letter had been received from Captain Galton of the BOT apologising for the inspecting officer inadvertently including the GNR in his condemnation of the ECR's method of working the Hertford to Welwyn Junction line.

The Hertford Luton and Dunstable Railway Act 1859 (22 and 23 Vic cap xxxiii) received the Royal Assent on 21st July 1859 and amongst other things authorised the company to create a new issue of shares to the value of £10,000 for the Hertford section as

Front page of Hertford, Luton and Dunstable Railway Further Capital Act 21st July 1859.

additional capital over and above the original allocation of £65,000. If shares were unissued they could be offered to Luton section shareholders in the same amounts as held in Luton section shares. The Act also extended the period for completion of the Luton to Welwyn Junction section for a further two years with an expiry date of 16th July 1861.

By September 1859, relationships between the HL&DR and the GNR were far from cordial. On 5th of the month the General Manager wrote to Cowper seeking payment of £1,000 due from the minor company. Cowper replied, asking time to consult with his fellow directors but after a month of silence the GNR board requested the HL&DR directors to furnish some means of security to ensure the main-line company continued to work the line. Alarmed by this final demand and unable to produce the required £1,000, Cowper sought a meeting with the General Manager to make the payment spread over a period.

The continuing threat of traffic bypassing the GNR by using the proposed bridge connecting the Luton section with the Hertford section at Welwyn Junction caused great concern and indeed alarm at King's Cross. The main-line company finally nullified the scheme by imposing almost impossible conditions on the HL&DR whereby the structure was to be limited to a single span with no abutments on GNR property and built without interference to trains on the main line. Approach embankments were, however, built from earth extracted from Digswell cutting on the Luton line, but never completed.

The proposed joint working of the HL&DR line was still being considered early in the new year by the ECR directors. Certainly the company had little sway in the operation of the branch for in November 1859 the daily ECR locomotive mileage for goods trains amounted to only 28 miles, with a similar figure for passenger trains, equal to four round trips between Hertford and Welwyn Junction. By early March 1860, Seymour Clarke, the GNR General Manager, approached Moseley, his ECR counterpart, and proposed the following working conditions in order to protect GNR interests:

1   The ECR to forego the 60 per cent for Welwyn to London goods and passenger traffic receipts from the Welwyn and Hertford line.
2   The GNR to concede the traffic from Dunstable to Welwyn Junction to the ECR and London Bishopsgate.
3   The GNR to work the Welwyn & Hertford Railway for a sum equal to 50 per cent of the revenue.
4   The GNR to work all traffic between Dunstable and Hertford, with joint working with the ECR for that distance of Welwyn to Hertford only.

Clarke also proposed the resolution that:

1   For past working the HL&DR offered some security bearing interest at 5 per cent to the ECR and GNR and for the future a plan be formulated whereby the GNR may work the traffic and take the proceeds of the Hertford section, paying the balance monthly to the HL&DR Company who would in turn be responsible to the GNR for making good any deficiency in profits.

At the fourth half yearly meeting of the HL&DR, held in the Town Hall at Luton on Saturday 25th February 1860, the directors expressed their regret at the accident at Hertford. Although the Hertford section had shown an increase in earnings the tonnage of goods passing over the line was still unsatisfactory with little sign of improvement. The directors expressed they were fully aware that most of the traffic on the Hertford section was through working of wagons with little generated by or received from local stations and consequently of little benefit to the revenue of the HL&DR.

The Hertford section accounts for the half year ending 31st December 1859 were then presented.

Debits		£	s	d
	Maintenance of the way	262	10	0
	Locomotive power	586	14	8
	Salaries and office expenses	161	8	10
	Traffic wages	217	17	8
	Welwyn Junction expenses	113	16	11
	Goods collection and delivery	60	2	3
	Mileage and demurrage	92	7	5
	Advertising, printing etc	40	10	6
	Stores, oils and greases	32	19	7
	Gas	39	19	0
	Railway Clearing House expenses	16	18	7
	Compensation and losses	14	11	11
	Travelling and other expenses	34	1	1
		1,623	18	5
	Rates and taxes	31	6	6
	Passenger duty	21	12	7
	Interest	1	2	6
	Interest on loans, less received on			
	Calls in arrears	47	12	10
	Debentures	530	18	4
		632	12	9
		2,256	11	2
Credits				
	Passenger and parcels traffic	607	10	5
	Goods and livestock	1,029	10	11
	Coal traffic	429	4	6
	Rents	65	0	0
	Transfer fees	1	5	6
		2,132	10	10
	Balance carried to balance sheet loss	124	0	4
		2,256	11	2

Although a loss had been recorded the Hertford section had earned enough to pay back a £300 loan and it was hoped no further loans would be required. As a result of the retirement of the Right Honourable W. Cowper MP from the board, John Jasper Gripper was selected to become Chairman of the company. After taking his place the directors received a memorandum from the shareholders urging negotiations with the GNR for the working of the line and urging an increase in the train services with at least two through trains to London with the proviso that Hatfield be made the junction station in preference to the rather remote Welwyn Junction. The Chairman intimated the matter would be considered.

After considerable discussion at the ECR board meeting on 14th March 1860 the directors requested Moseley and Robertson to report on the proposals made by the HL&DR. Needless to say the two officers were entirely against such concessionary proposals and the GNR was advised accordingly. Evidently not all work requested in the application for the erection of buildings published on 6th May 1858 was fulfilled, for on 28th March 1860 P.C. Cleasby, the Secretary, Manager and Accountant of the HL&DR, invited tenders from builders and others for the erection of gate houses at Attimore Hall level crossing and Hatfield Hyde Road crossing as well as waiting rooms at Cole Green station. Plans and specifications were to be obtained on application to the station master at Cowbridge station Hertford, with replies required by 14th April 1860. A footnote added that *'the directors do not bind themselves to accept the lowest of any tender'*. No buildings were, however, erected.

The question of the working agreement was again discussed at a local meeting on 10th April 1860, after which their new Secretary, Mr Cleasby, wrote to the GNR of the intention of the HL&DR to determine six months from that date whether the agreement made between the HL&DR, GNR and ECR on 18th January 1859 should continue. The GNR board duly debated the issue on 24th April and requested the General Manager to look into the matter in conjunction with the possible working of the Welwyn Junction to Luton line. The ECR directors met on 19th April.

With a view to protecting their territorial rights the GNR General Manager quickly negotiated with the HL&DR directors and on 9th May submitted a draft agreement proposing the GNR would continue to work both the Hertford and Luton sections of line for a period of five years. Because of the additional traffic the GNR authorities requested an overbridge replace the existing level crossing at Welwyn Junction by the same date of the agreement. Reporting to the directors, the GNR General Manager requested full powers to negotiate better working arrangements for the Luton to Welwyn Junction section and also similar arrangements for negotiating with the ECR for working the Hertford section where the existing arrangements were considered totally unsatisfactory. The directors, whilst agreeing to this course of action, also empowered the General Manager to request adjustments with the existing working and operating receipts due to the GNR. As early as June 1860 the ECR was in dispute with the staffing of the new line at Hertford. It appeared the Railway Clearing House wagon numbertaker was also employed by the HL&DR Company; whether this was an official or unofficial arrangement is not known, but the ECR management objected and demanded an RCH man solely for ECR work.

Within the next few days the GNR General Manager held further talks with the HL&DR directors concerning the future operating policy and traffic working arrangements. It was during these discussions that the talk of a possible takeover of both lines was mooted. In his report of 7th June 1860 the General Manager stressed the special bearing the line had on the GNR stability with the EC, L&NW and Midland railways in the area. On 12th June the GNR board also heard of the proposals made by the ECR directors for extending their working of services to the Luton and Dunstable line. To the GNR this was a blatant attempt by their Bishopsgate rivals to gain territorial advantage connecting with the L&NWR at Dunstable. Evidently with a little scheming the ECR could then takeover both sections of the HL&DR and remove all GNR interests. To obviate such action the GNR General Manager was asked to investigate the prospect of concentrating services from both the Hertford and Dunstable branches at Hatfield, where there were better interchange facilities than at Welwyn Junction, and also the total takeover of both lines by the GNR.

The suggestion was duly placed before the HL&DR directors but during subsequent discussions the company solicitors Mr Leech and Mr Larman were both of the opinion such action would require Parliamentary approval. The General Manager, reporting to the GNR board on 9th July, pointed out that if the company applied for a requisite Act the ECR and L&NWR would almost certainly seek running powers, which would lessen the value of both routes to the GNR. After somewhat lengthy discussion on the value of the HL&DR routes, the GNR directors resolved that the Act authorising takeover of the small company be sought, but if the ECR or L&NWR instituted a clause for running powers the GNR would arbitrarily withdraw the bill and allow the working agreement to lapse.

Meanwhile, on 16th June 1860 the ECR had disputed a charge of £70 13s 3d raised for a 30-wagon coal train destined for Messrs Wood at Waltham Cross. After investigation it was found the wagons had been labelled in error for routing via Welwyn Junction instead of the agreed route via Peterborough and Ely. It was assumed the local agent for the GNR had not questioned the routing and the charge was therefore withdrawn. At the same time there was a dispute on freight charges for earthenware dispatched from stations on the North Eastern Railway destined for Devonshire Street. Although the charges were the same via Welwyn Junction or King's Cross, the former journey was 12 miles longer. The ECR was prepared to accept charges for the additional distance of 4 miles but the GNR insisted on 8 miles and the matter was passed to the Railway Clearing House for arbitration.

By July 1860 the GNR and ECR had reached an amicable agreement on the working of the Welwyn Junction to Hertford line. Although the Luton section was not yet completed the GNR agreed to work all Dunstable to Hertford traffic with the existing traffic routing arrangements preserved. In addition the GNR would pay the ECR 60 per cent of the earnings of the Welwyn Junction to King's Cross traffic. However, on 1st August the ECR Superintendent was reporting a drastic decrease in goods traffic on the Hertford line and complained the majority of traffic was now routed via Camden, King's Cross and Hackney Wick.

Despite the rather harsh possibility of abandoning the HL&DR, the GNR authorities pressed ahead with arrangements for working the Welwyn Junction to Luton line and these were presented to the Executive and Traffic committees for examination on 31st July. After due discussion the GNR directors advised the HL&DR board that the Welwyn Junction to Luton section of line was not to be opened for traffic until their General Manager was satisfied that the railway

Advertisement inviting tenders for the erection of gate houses and waiting rooms, March 1860.

was sufficiently completed, and only then if all construction was to the satisfaction of the GNR Engineer. The railway would only be opened on the understanding that additional works required would be totally financed by the HL&DR Company.

On completion of the line from Dunstable, Colonel William Yolland conducted the official BOT inspection of the Welwyn Junction to Luton line on 11th August 1860 when it was announced that if his report was favourable the line was to formally open for traffic the following Wednesday. Local arrangements were made for the directors, shareholders and friends of the HL&DR, together with GNR officers, to depart by special train from Luton in good time to reach Hertford by 1.00pm. At Hertford station the special train was to be met by the Mayor and Corporation of the town before attending a celebration dinner.

At the half yearly meeting of HL&DR shareholders held at the Shire Hall, Hertford on 17th August 1860 the gathering was informed of the proposed takeover of the line by the GNR. The Chairman, speaking on behalf of the directors, advised the permanent interests of the HL&D Company would be greatly enhanced by the incorporation of their railway into the GNR and he recommended the proprietors to sanction the agreement. The gathering was then advised the terms of the transfer. On the Dunstable to Welwyn section the GNR would pay a fixed dividend on the original capital of £70,000 commencing at 3 per cent during the first year, 4 per cent on the second and third years and 4½ per cent for the fourth and succeeding years. On the Welwyn to Hertford section, 1 per cent would be payable on the original capital of £55,000 until April 1866 and 3½ per cent thereafter. The GNR also undertook the liability of paying interest on the mortgage and preference capital amounting to £152,500, making the total expended on both lines to £277,500. The majority of shareholders present agreed to the necessary course of action whilst noting that Parliamentary sanction had to be obtained before the completion of the transaction.

The balance sheet for the Hertford section was then presented:

Debits		£	s	d
Maintenance of the way		274	18	10
Locomotive power		525	18	0
Wages for pumping water		20	16	0
Shunting at stations		49	14	6
Salaries		79	15	0
Wages of clerks		150	4	10
Welwyn Junction expenses		124	6	11
Collection and delivery of goods		15	12	5
Stores		10	5	1
Fuel and gas		29	13	6
Tickets, printing etc		50	7	3
Compensation and losses		3	2	4
Gatekeepers wages		46	16	0
Mileage and demurrage		32	14	2
		1,414	4	10
Directors		100	4	1
Railway Clearing House expenses		26	3	11
Auditors expenses		15	15	0
Travelling and other expenses		51	16	2
Clerk guarantee			17	6
Insurance from the Junction		3	2	0
Stamps		7	11	4
Rates and taxes		33	0	0
Government duty		17	17	0
Interest	RCH balance	22	19	2
	Cash balance	16	4	7
	Temporary loans	18	16	0
	Debentures	643	0	0
		957	7	7
		2,371	12	5

Hatfield station looking south showing the Up platform fronted by the all-over canopy spanning the Up slow line. In the foreground are the Up and Down fast lines, whilst in the far distance is the Hertford branch bay platform. Covered footbridge No. 60 provided a passenger connection from the Up side to the Down fast and Down bay platforms.
Author's collection

Credits			
Passenger receipts	560	5	3
Parcels	29	12	0
Horses and carriages	6	1	0
Merchandise	1,215	5	3
Livestock	95	14	1
Coal and coke	250	0	0
	2,096	17	7
Commission on goods	2	4	8
Rent on land and buildings	34	0	3
Rent from advanced advertising	25	0	0
	61	4	11
	2,158	2	6

The foregoing showed a working loss of £213 9s 11d for the period.

The gathering was also advised that two-thirds of all traffic on the Hertford line was through traffic and, by agreement dated April 1856 with the ECR and GNR the joint working companies, the receipts were totally absorbed by working and other expenses. Because of the parlous financial standing the Hertford line owed debentures amounting to a total of £21,000 to which could be added interest varying between 5 and 6 per cent. Added to this was the outstanding liability of £26,000 making a total of £47,500, which unless urgent payment was made, would steadily increase.

On 29th August 1860 the ECR directors were advised the GNR Company was to lease the Hertford to Welwyn line from 1st September. From that date the ECR locomotive workings to Welwyn Junction were to cease. Through rates were to be offered from Hertford to stations on the L&NWR via Dunstable and Leighton Buzzard, whilst the company was also seeking through rates from stations east of Hertford. To the satisfaction of the ECR board it was announced the agreement of 16th January 1852 would continue. The gathering was also informed the GNR had advised that traffic exchange at Welwyn Junction to and from Hertford would cease from 1st October 1860, after which traffic would be routed for interchange at Hatfield.

Coinciding with the delayed opening of the Luton and Dunstable line, rationalisation of operating arrangements were made from 1st September 1860, when all services from both the Hertford and Dunstable branches were extended beyond Welwyn Junction along the main line to Hatfield. As a result, the station at Welwyn Junction was closed and passenger facilities withdrawn, although interchange sidings remained for goods traffic. However, with new traffic from the west of the main line and steadily increasing traffic from the Hertford branch, the long section from Welwyn Junction to Hatfield shared on the double track by main-line traffic soon proved an operating inconvenience. On 12th August 1860 the General Manager had requested sanction to provide an intermediate block signalling hut between the two places and this was agreed by the GNR Traffic Committee on 4th September, when the added cost of employing additional signalmen was also authorised. The signal box was subsequently sited at the 19th milepost from King's Cross and bore that title.

Despite the differences of opinion between the ECR and GNR regarding freight charges, it was reported in September 1860 that 570 tons of coal traffic had been routed via the Welwyn Junction and Hertford line during August 1860, primarily for destinations in the City of London.

Continuing wet weather during the late summer brought a spate of flooding as the rivers rose well above their normal level. This caused problems at Hartham where the altered flow caused by the building of the railway resulted in damage to the bridge spanning a stream linking the Old River Lea to Paper Mill Ditch. On 1st October 1860, Mr Longman, the Town Clerk of Hertford, wrote to the GNR requesting compensation but the railway authorities curtly turned down the claim, denying liability.

Preparation for the takeover of the HL&D Railway progressed rapidly during the autumn of 1860 and by 6th November the GNR accountants Johnson, Farquahar & Leek of 65 Moorgate Street London were finalising the wording for the bill incorporating the purchase with additional time for new works at King's Cross, the application being required at the Private Bill Office before 23rd November. In the same month the local railway board was involved in the Chancery Court over false allegations. The action was the subject at the somewhat lengthy and heated extraordinary meeting of the HL&DR at the Town Hall Luton on 22nd November, but after taking legal advice the agitators Whitbread and Parker withdrew their action against the company on 19th December 1860.

THE GREAT NORTHERN RAILWAY COMPANY.

AGREEMENTS.

THE GREAT NORTHERN RAILWAY COMPANY

AND THE

HERTFORD LUTON AND DUNSTABLE RAILWAY COMPANY.

AGREEMENT for the working, by the Great Northern Railway Company, of the Hertford Luton and Dunstable Railway.

Dated 20th November, 1860.

SECRETARY'S OFFICE—KING'S CROSS STATION, LONDON.

1861.

Front page of GNR and HL&DR Agreement dated 20th November 1860.

The ever increasing traffic on the Hertford to Hatfield line and the subsequent need to introduce larger and more powerful tender locomotives to haul the greater loads brought about the need for the provision of a turntable at Hertford, independent of the ECR turntable, to obviate tender-first running. On 3rd December 1860 authority was given to transfer a turntable from Hatfield to Hertford, at the same time sanctioning the provision of a cart road to be laid adjacent to a siding to ease the loading and unloading of station to station goods transferring from railway wagon to cart. The total cost of the scheme was £84, but in the event a turntable was never provided.

On 15th December 1860 the solicitor enclosed to the GNR directors a copy of the HL&DR bill and petition for approval. At the board meeting on the same day the directors advised the Secretary to write to Johnson, Farquahar & Leech asking for the agreement of 30th October 1860 between the HL&DR and the GNR to be superseded by the revised agreement of 20th November.

A fatal accident occurred at Cole Green station on Wednesday 30th January 1861. Anne Strickland, aged 70 years, travelling on the 7.25pm Hertford to Hatfield train alighted at Cole Green but for unknown reasons had not left the railway premises for she was hit by the engine of the following goods train, in charge of Driver William Andrews. At the inquest held at the Cowper Arms, Cole Green the following day the coroner was advised that the guard noticed Strickland alight from the passenger train, the only stopping point en route, but could not account for her movements thereafter. Recording a verdict of accidental death the coroner was critical of the fact that Cole Green station was unmanned at the time of the incident.

The subject of the working agreement between the HL&DR and the GNR was raised in correspondence between the solicitor of the local company and the Board of Trade. Replying in early February 1861 the BOT Secretary advised the new arrangements could be authorised subject to the approval of the shareholders of both companies.

Luton was the venue for the eighth half yearly meeting of the shareholders on 27th February 1861. The main topic of discussion was the impending takeover by the GNR, after which the small gathering heard that receipts from the Hertford line for the six months ending 31st December 1860 were merchandise £222 7s 6d and parcels £10 1s 7d. The Chairman advised that the company was delivering parcels in Hertford at reduced cost.

Early in February 1861 Mr Leeman of the HL&DR twice wrote to the GNR General Manager requesting an advance loan of £4,000 to enable certain liabilities for works to be settled. Before agreeing, the General Manager enquired as to what securities would be offered. In reply the Secretary advised the advance would be repaid out of additional capital included in the Parliamentary bill. The GNR authorities agreed to this measure and granted the loan on 5th March 1861.

The passage of the GNR bill through Parliament was far from smooth, the L&NWR board insisting on additional clauses and safeguards for running powers, much to the distress of the officers at King's Cross. On 19th April the matter was brought before the House of Commons Select Committee when the Chairman eased the tense situation by intimating that in the committee's opinion the running powers would only extend between Dunstable and Luton. By 5th May the bill was read for the second time with the only objection being raised by the ECR.

On Whit Monday 23rd May 1861 eight companies of the Hertfordshire Volunteer Rifle Corps assembled for the first time in Hertford on Hartham Common under the command of the Right Honourable Earl Cowper. Under sunny skies soon after 9.00am a special train arrived on the Hertford & Welwyn line conveying the St. Albans, Royston, and Hitchin corps whilst the ECR provided a special train conveying men from Cheshunt and Ware. Alighting at the Cowbridge station, each corps marched independently into Hartham. As well as the gentry and their ladies in their carriages attending the gathering, hundreds of people arrived on foot to witness the event. The *Herts Guardian* bemoaned the fact that all were *'braving the difficulties of getting into Hartham for the sake of the sight and it is no easy matter getting into the place now'.* It continued: *'there was a time when after opening the lane gates we went into Hartham direct on the greensward but the railway has altered all that; there are large flints to walk over, the line to cross, and the rails to tumble over'.* Despite the grim warning there were no reports of accidents or injuries caused crossing the railway. On another occasion the public could not gain access to Hartham as the railway gates were locked and the station staff had left the keys in the station premises. With several clambering over the barriers a member of staff duly arrived after half an hour to open the gates. This was a recurring theme, however, of how construction of the railway affected access to Hartham, which caused some discontent amongst the townsfolk of Hertford. It was probably the reason that Earl Cowper staged subsequent volunteer days at Panshanger.

The problems associated with the takeover were partially forgotten as a result of an incident at Hertford on Monday 3rd June 1861. After the arrival of the first Down passenger train from Hatfield, the empty coaching stock was shunted into the siding leading to the engine shed located between Port Hill bridge and the station shortly after 9.00am. The movement was made to allow a goods train to occupy the main single line so that parcels could be unloaded from vans onto the platform. After unloading was completed the foreman porter in charge of train movements failed to notice the points still lay towards the engine shed sidings. The unfortunate individual then gave the signal to the driver to shunt the wagons but on discovering his error he reversed the points to stop the vehicles colliding with the empty coaching stock. In saving the collision he succeeded in derailing three wagons containing sacks of manure, which were badly damaged as they toppled sideways tearing the coping stones from the edge of the station platform. As a result of the incident the train service was curtailed for the rest of the morning.

Two days after the incident, on Wednesday 5th June South Herts Yeomanry held their annual races at Hatfield Park and despite the poor weather with heavy rain in the morning thousands were expected to attend the event. At 11.55am there were more passengers at Hertford station than could be accommodated on the train so that additional carriages had to be provided. The extra load proved almost too much for the locomotive, for after starting out for Hatfield soon after 12.10pm the engine was struggling on the incline after crossing the River Beane bridge. The *Herts Guardian* stated: *'the engine had its work to do to get up the ascent to Cole Green, the pace was slow and tedious, the train all but coming to a dead stop'.* Beyond Cole Green the driver appeared to try to make up lost time and arrival at Hatfield was at 12.40pm, 25 minutes late. With improving conditions it was reported that by three o'clock far more vehicles were in the grounds *'than we had ever seen before, even before the Hertford and Welwyn Junction Railway was made'.*

4

Great Northern Takeover

The Act authorising the takeover of the HL&D Railway by the GNR received the Royal Assent on 12th June 1861 (24 Vic cap lxx). The statute stipulated the GNR would on taking possession of both the Hertford and Luton sections of line repair and maintain the railway in good order. Clause 27 empowered the GNR to afford the L&NWR running powers between Dunstable and Luton, the L&NWR affording the GNR reciprocal powers into their station at Dunstable. In return for the takeover of the line the GNR was to pay a dividend at the rate of 4 per cent per annum on the £28,400 preference shares of the Hertford section and 5 per cent per annum on the Luton stock valued at £50,000. In addition, 1 per cent per annum was payable on the Hertford line ordinary shares totalling £55,000 until 1st April 1866 and 3½ per cent thereafter. On the £70,000 ordinary shareholding on the Luton section the GNR was required to pay 3 per cent per annum until 1st September 1861, then 4 per cent per annum until 1st September 1863 and thereafter at a rate of 4½ per cent per annum. Finally, 4 per cent per annum was payable on the £15,000 authorised share issue.

During a detailed inspection of the Hertford line prior to the passing of the Act the GNR engineer had found the fencing along the entire route in poor condition. Reporting to the board meeting on 24th June 1861 the Secretary questioned the liability, bearing in mind the main-line company had recently absorbed the minor railway. Fabor, one of the GNR directors, was requested to negotiate with Parker of the former HL&DR and arrange settlement of the repair costs for the fencing and other items requiring remedial action.

It soon became clear to the GNR operating authorities that staffing of their newly acquired branches would be an early problem. Within a fortnight of takeover, and following complaints from crossing keepers of lack of proper amenities, the General Manager recommended the provision of gate lodges at Attimore Hall and Hatfield Hyde level crossings for the accommodation of staff at an estimated cost of £150 each. Similarly, at Cole Green station no house was available for the resident clerk-in-charge and to rectify the deficiency the General Manager recommended the provision of accommodation attached to the station at an estimated cost of £250. The application, although approved by the Traffic Committee on 26th June 1861, was only passed to the directors for sanctioning on 9th July. At this period Earl Cowper through his land agent requested the provision of a siding at Attimore crossing and on 29th June 1861 Seymour Clarke the GN General Manager had written:

I am now in a position to agree to your putting in the siding at Attimore Hall subject to the approval of the engineer of the GN Railway, who will of course put the points in the main line, charging you for the work done. We must stipulate for two 25 feet wrought iron distant signals, but we will forgo the station signal on the understanding that the siding is only worked during daylight. The GN Company will keep the key of the points, which will be worked by a Great Northern Capstan and therefore easily locked. Of course it is compliant to you to give such instructions with respect to the gate of the lane leading to the siding, as they may seem proper to you. The estimate for the work which will be required to be done is £186 15s 0d for the siding and £102 for the two distant signals.

Evidently Cowper's staff were willing to carry out some of the work, possibly to reduce costs, for on 3rd July 1861 Clarke again wrote to Cowper's Land Agent:

I have no objection to you finding the points and putting them in at Attimore siding if done to the entire satisfaction of the

Front page of GNR and HL&DR Amalgamation Act 12th June 1861.

engineer of the GN Company, both as to materials, construction and platelayers' work. With respect to the iron signals, you will recollect that you appealed to us to go for them with respect to the [Lord Cowper's] siding near the junction, because you had already provided wooden ones, but I cannot take this view with respect to Attimore siding. With regard to the height, I will ask the engineer to arrange to meet you on the ground to determine the point and also the distance at which they must be placed.

Although their railway had been absorbed, the former HL&DR directors continued to clear outstanding items including debts. On 10th July 1861 they approached the GNR for a £2,000 loan to clear the balance owing to the Railway Clearing House. The application was declined on 23rd July leaving the directors no alternative but to seek other sources. A month later an irate landowner wrote to King's Cross stating the HL&D Company had purchased a portion of his property without paying. After investigation the GNR amicably settled by offering shares in full settlement of the transaction.

Over the next few months the GNR authorities began the process of bringing both the Luton and Hertford sections up to the standard of the main-line company. The increase in goods traffic was most noticeable, especially at Hertingfordbury where local farmers were keen to forward their produce by rail. Delays were often incurred through lack of accommodation and on 9th January 1862 the General Manager requested additional siding accommodation at the station at a cost of £74. Authority was duly given five days later and the siding was installed by the early summer. During these investigations the lack of adequate facilities at stations also became apparent, especially at Hertford where only a temporary structure had been erected. It was of the utmost importance to provide a permanent station in the town with full accommodation for both passenger and parcels traffic. On 3rd February the General Manager reported to his directors that the estimated cost for completion of the station at Hertford was £3,500. After the directors visited the line during a tour of inspection, sanction was given for the necessary expenditure and the contract for the construction of the building was awarded to Kirk & Parry.

The intermediate station at Cole Green was next to receive attention. The station was essentially a private structure, having been provided by a Mr Young of Hertford at a cost of £138, by arrangement with the HL&DR on the understanding that he received 6 per cent annually on the outlay and for which he permitted the general public to use the station. Arrangements had been made whereby the GNR had the option to purchase by repaying Young the amount expended, less 1 per cent per annum from the date of completion and full occupancy of the station. The directors readily agreed on 29th April 1862 to the early completion of the transfer.

Financial problems pertaining to the takeover were still being raised in early May when Mr Leeman wrote urging the GNR to retain out of the 4 per cent preference stock exchanged for similar HL&DR stock an amount equal to the smaller company's debt to the main-line company in order to clear the liability of the local shareholders.

The Volunteer Field Day on 9th June 1862 was held at Panshanger, with the 2nd Herts Battalion of Volunteer Rifles mustering at 10.30am at Cole Green to be joined by London companies at 1.00pm. The day was declared a public holiday in Hertford with most tradesmen closing their shops. Although the general public were allowed to view the proceedings the intention of the gathering was for volunteers to practice military movements. The GNR entered into the spirit of the occasion with a special train departing Cowbridge at 9.40am for Cole Green where a spacious temporary platform was erected at the station to handle the crowds. The special trains conveying the volunteers at a special return fare of 1s 0d departed King's Cross for Cole Green at 11.30am, 11.35am and 11.40am. So great were the numbers traveling, estimated at 2,500, that the volunteers were accommodated in open *'seated wagons'* as the railway company had committed all their carriages to other services.

The derailment of a coal train at Wood Green on Tuesday 22nd July 1862 brought repercussions on the Hertford branch services. Passengers unaware of the incident and catching the 8.15am train from Hertford to Hatfield found on arrival at the junction there were no through trains to King's Cross. In an attempt to catch the 9.30am ECR empty coaching stock train from Hertford to Bishopsgate, the passengers returned on the first Down GNR train from Hatfield but a temporary blockage of the line at Cowbridge resulted in a late arrival. Because of the number of passengers travelling the GNR arranged to strengthen the 10.40am departure from Hertford to Hatfield when it was known the main line had subsequently been cleared.

THE GREAT NORTHERN RAILWAY COMPANY.

AGREEMENTS.

THE HERTFORD, LUTON AND DUNSTABLE RAILWAY COMPANY

TO

THE GREAT NORTHERN RAILWAY COMPANY.

CONVEYANCE of the undertaking of the former to the latter Company.

Dated 5th June, 1862.

SECRETARY'S OFFICE, KING'S CROSS STATION, LONDON.

1862.

Front page of HL&DR and GNR Agreement dated 5th June 1862.

The road frontage to Hertford GNR station with the ornate canopy over the entrance to the booking hall. The station master's accommodation was located on the first floor. The structure built by Kirk & Parry was completed in 1863. Note the proliferation of signs, placards and billboards adorning the station. Although much altered in the latter years before demolition in 1990, the structure has a clone at St. Albans where the building on the former branch from Hatfield has been preserved and is in daily use as offices. *Author's collection*

Having leased or taken over the working of all major railways in East Anglia the ECR was the principal party to a scheme being prepared for the amalgamation of the Eastern Counties, Eastern Union, East Anglian, Newmarket and Norfolk railways into a new undertaking to be known as the Great Eastern Railway. The Act sanctioning the amalgamation, the Great Eastern Railway Act 1862 (25 and 26 Vic cap ccxxiii) received the Royal Assent on 7th August 1862 but took effect retrospectively from July of that year. Fortunately most of the chief officers of the new company were former ECR personnel and thus, for GNR management, continuity was maintained in matters concerning the Hertford to Hatfield branch.

During the summer of 1862 work commenced on the new station at Hertford. On 13th September the *Hertford Mercury* reported *'the GNR are building a new and commodious station at Cowbridge with waiting rooms, a residence for a station master, a goods shed and other amenities'*. The *Herts Guardian* not to be outsmarted by its press rival added:

the new station is being erected in Hartham, north of the temporary building. It will be both an elegant and commodious structure and we hope the directors of the Great Eastern Railway will follow the example and erect a new station near Kings Mead Lane.

Unfortunately the operation of the branch remained rather primitive for when a goods train from Hatfield became derailed just before 8am on 8th October near the bridge over the River Beane at Hertford, the line remained blocked for some hours as dislodged timber derailed a wagon effectively marooning the engine. London passengers were directed to use the GER services. The absence of telegraphic communication with Hatfield meant the Hertford station master had to hire the services of a post cart to get to Hatfield and summon another engine and coaches. The station master then returned with the empty stock train, which formed the 9.30am Hertford to Hatfield service.

Kirk & Parry completed the construction of the new station at Hertford in 1863, and would continue their good work by building the stations at Harpenden, New Mill End and Luton on the Dunstable line the following year. During the final weeks of work, on 12th February 1863 there was an altercation between James Hutchinson, the foreman carpenter and Charles Stanley, a booking clerk employed at the station. At the subsequent court case in early March, Mr Shepherd appeared for the prosecution while Hutchinson, who showed signs of irritability, conducted his own defence. In opening the case Shepherd advised the court that it was not the first time that Hutchinson had been before the court on a similar charge and it appeared that the penalty of a fine had not resulted in the desired effect of calming the man down. He was of the opinion the bench should commit the defendant without the option of a fine. The evidence showed that Stanley, conveying a letter for M. De Wind, the company's engineer, was going through the station building when Hutchinson seized him by the collar and arm and threw him violently off the platform, forcing him to go onto the Up line before recovering his footing. De Wind's office was nearly in direct line from the existing booking office through the new buildings and as a company servant Stanley thought he had a right to go that way. Several witnesses said that Hutchinson threw the booking clerk over the Down line so that he first touched the ground in the 'six foot' between the Up and Down lines. The defendant denied touching Stanley, who, he affirmed, jumped off the platform of his own accord. The Bench convicted Hutchinson and ordered him to pay a fine of £1 including costs. Certain threats having been used during the hearing, the Chairman warned Hutchinson to *'take care they were not carried out, or he would find himself in a much worse position'*.

The continuing growth of goods traffic at Hertford led the GNR to introduce horse power for shunting wagons in the yard as well as delivery work in the town. Their introduction brought with it the problem of accommodation and for a while the horses were stabled away from the station. On 31st March 1863 the Assistant Goods

Manager recommended the provision of a stable for three horses at an estimated cost of £150 and the work was subsequently authorised. The stables, located on the Down side of the railway opposite the goods shed, were completed later in the same year. Coal traffic was also increasing rapidly and the company was experiencing problems checking the tonnages and weight of incoming wagon-loads. On 20th October authority was given for the installation of a weighing machine specifically for coal traffic at an estimated cost of £100. On the same date agreement was given for an additional siding at Cole Green at a cost of £167 to obviate complaints from local farmers regarding the lack of accommodation for loading and unloading wagons.

A spate of bad weather, snow interspersed with days of heavy rain, heralded the New Year and on several occasions the branch trains were delayed because of snowdrifts or flooding as thawing snow filled the cuttings with water. GNR passengers from Hertford to London again suffered delays on the morning of Wednesday 23rd March 1864. The 9.45am passenger train was unable to depart from Hertford as the locomotive hauling a preceding freight train failed on the curve near the former Welwyn Junction. A telegraph message was sent from Welwyn Junction signal box to Hatfield and within half an hour an assisting engine had arrived to haul the failed locomotive and its train to Hatfield. Once the single line was clear of the failed train the late running 9.45am train was permitted to depart. Unfortunately the connecting service forward from Hatfield to London departed to time and passengers off the branch train had to wait for a later connecting service, finally arriving at King's Cross shortly after midday. The delays incurred by this and earlier failures cruelly exposed the inadequate communications on both the Dunstable and Hertford branches, especially whenever breakdowns or late running occurred. On 26th April 1864 the GNR finally rectified the deficiency by entering into agreement with the Electric Telegraph Company for the provision of telegraph to stations on both lines.

Welwyn Junction was the scene of a further accident on 4th May 1864 when the rear coach of the three-coach 2.40pm Hatfield to Hertford service became derailed whilst the train was negotiating the points from the main line to the branch. The 4-wheel vehicle overturned resulting in the death of Mark Austin of Hatfield and injuries to other passengers. As late as September claims of up to £1,000 compensation for injuries were being submitted. At the subsequent enquiry the signalman at Welwyn Junction signal box admitted moving the points before the last vehicle had cleared the junction.

After services were extended to Hatfield both Hertford and Dunstable branch trains used the Up and Down main lines from Welwyn Junction to Hatfield. Goods trains to and from Hertford, however, continued to serve the sidings at Welwyn Junction, whilst main-line goods services were also booked to pick up and set down traffic when required. The existing accommodation was considered rather cramped for exchange of traffic and on 30th June 1864 authority was given for the extension of these shunting sidings at a total cost of £2,078 9s 7d.

The actions of the train crew after the accident at Welwyn Junction on 4th May did not go unrewarded for the *Herts Guardian* of 25th February 1865 reported the *'presentation of a slight memorial by certain gentlemen in appreciation of the prudence and care then shown whereby, no doubt, many lives were saved'*. A collection of 10 guineas was apportioned, £6 to Engine Driver Murphy, £3 to Guard Fisher and £1 10s 0d to Fireman Edward Redding.

On Monday 5th June 1865 the Hertford branch dealt with the heaviest passenger traffic since the opening, when the Volunteer Brigade Field Day was held at Panshanger House, the home of Lord Cowper. The Volunteer Company travelled by through train from King's Cross alighting at Cole Green, and so great were the crowds that the GNR ran additional trains to handle the traffic. The *Hertford Mercury* reported: *'Hertford station had to open two windows in the booking office instead of one to handle all the passengers wishing to purchase return tickets to Cole Green'*.

The increasing traffic north of London on the GNR was of constant concern to the company authorities and it was thought expedient to provide a relief to the main line by constructing a line from Hornsey to connect up with the former HL&DR line at Hertford. Plans were drawn up and subsequently on 19th June 1865 the Royal Assent was given to the Great Northern Railway (Hornsey to Hertford) Act 1865 (28 Vic cap cv). The statute authorised the construction of a railway commencing by a junction with the GNR at the north end of the passenger platform at Wood Green station, in the Parish of Tottenham in the County of Middlesex, and passing through Hornsey, Wood Green, Edmonton, Southgate, Winchmore Hill and Enfield, all in the County of Middlesex and then Northaw, Little Berkhampstead, Cheshunt, Goffs Oak, Wormley, Bishop's Hatfield, Bayford, Brickendon, All Saints and St. John's Hertford, St. Andrew's and Hertingfordbury to terminate by a junction with the HL&DR, part of the GNR about a furlong south of the bridge carrying the branch over the River Mimram. Railway No. 2 was a short spur from Railway No. 1 at or about one hundred and fifty yards to the west of Horn's Mill on the River Lea to terminate at a junction with the HL&DR about a furlong south of the junction where the railway crossed the River Mimram. Railway No. 4, entirely in the Parish of Digswell, commenced by a junction on the HL&DR, half a mile from its junction with the GNR at Welwyn Junction and terminated by a junction with the GNR main line, about one furlong south of Welwyn Viaduct. Three years were allowed for the compulsory purchase of land and five years for completion of works. the work was to be self financed by the GNR and the company was authorised to raise £650,000 additional capital, with £216,000 borrowing powers.

Realising the provision of such a line would not obviate the problems of the main-line bottleneck over Welwyn Viaduct and

Coal depot advertisement 1862.

through Welwyn North and South tunnels, a bill was also prepared for another line from Hertingfordbury to join the main line at Stevenage. Then on 10th October 1865 Seymour Clarke, the GNR General Manager, with Cubitt, the Engineer, and Balde, the company architect, met the mayor and corporation of Hertford at Hertford station to explain the routing of another proposed extension to Broadwater, near Knebworth. The applications were not progressed and the Hornsey to Hertford line was eventually reduced as a branch from Wood Green to Enfield, which was subsequently opened in 1871.

The New Year heralded a spate of adverse weather, which culminated in a severe snowstorm on the morning of Thursday 11th January 1866, which brought down the telegraph wires between Hatfield and Hertford and delayed the services on the branch. The conditions were equally as serious on the rival GER system where trains were delayed between Hertford and Broxbourne, whilst the Buntingford branch was totally blocked. Services resumed, however, later the same evening.

Following the serious incident at Welwyn Tunnel on Saturday 9th June 1866, which resulted in total blockage of the main line, the GNR authorities came to an agreement with their GER counterparts at Bishopsgate for certain services in both directions to be diverted via the Hatfield to Hertford branch thence to Broxbourne Junction before reversing and continuing over the GER to Peterborough. The transference of main-line services over the single-track rural branch was not without incident for the *Herts Guardian* reported on 19th June 1866 of '*great excitement at Hatfield when the news of the accident reached the town*'. Inspector Wingate '*went to the spot and was on site all day Sunday and half of the Monday and again at the inquest*'. Mr Cooter the station master '*had to send all the north trains on the single line to Hertford and there was frequently during Sunday and Monday a great accumulation of trains at Hatfield waiting for up trains from the north via Hertford to London*' to clear the single line. '*Mr Cooter's skilful management deserves the highest praise.*' Equally, Mr Kensey, the GER station master at Broxbourne, was a busy man for the *Herts Guardian* continued:

> *the resources of this station were severely taxed on Sunday and Monday by about 80 Great Northern trains, some from Hertford to the north and some from Cambridge and elsewhere, passing through Hertford to London. They all had to be shunted from the up to the down line and vice-versa; the engines were turned when they were not too large for the turntable and they were all sent off without the least delay.*

Several months later, on 5th February 1867 a violent storm caused structural damage in the Hertford area and brought down twigs and boughs on the railway. Services were slightly delayed as permanent way staff had to clear the tracks before trains could continue their journey.

Hertford was the scene of another accident on 7th May 1867, which could have been prevented had block signalling been in operation. The 11.10am passenger train to Hatfield departed to time but on looking back the driver noticed a door open on one of the coaches and brought the train to a stand beyond Port Hill bridge to enable the guard to close the door. On returning to his brake van at the rear of the train the guard was aghast to see the following goods train collide with the rear of the passenger train with such force that the coaches concertinaed as they were pushed forward forcing the vehicle behind the locomotive to break its buffers and partially ride up over the bunker. As a result of the impact several people were injured and at the ensuing local enquiry it was established the guard of the passenger train was at fault for failing to go back and protect his train with detonators on the line, before closing the offending door. In evidence the driver of the goods train admitted he had departed one minute before the booked time. The train had commenced its journey on level gradient near the GER station and this gave him chance to give the locomotive a good run at the gradient beyond Hertford GN station. He had received clear signals but was unaware that the passenger train had halted on the bank as the view ahead was obstructed by Port Hill overbridge and the curvature of the line. The guard of the passenger train was initially suspended from duty but was later reinstated and fined £1 whilst the unfortunate porter/signalman at Hertford was reduced in rank.

Colonel William Yolland was delegated to hold the BOT inquiry into the accident and noted as a result of the collision six passengers were injured, one seriously who was taken to the infirmary and at the time was making a good recovery. The inspector ascertained

Front page of GNR Act for construction of a railway linking Hornsey to the HL&DR near Hertford 19th June 1865.

that the 11.10am Up passenger train from Hertford to Hatfield was formed of a tank locomotive and five vehicles, three of which were: one Carriage Brake, one Composite and one First Class carriage. The train had started to time and as it passed under the overbridge 90 yards from the west end of the station platform, the driver and fireman heard a noise, and, the fireman looking back told the driver they had broken one of the doors, which was swinging open on the offside of the train, the door having come into contact with the abutment of the overbridge. The driver immediately shut off steam and stopped the train, with the engine about 175 yards from the west end of the platform from which the train had started. The driver and the guard of the train proceeded to the Carriage Brake next to the engine for the purpose of closing the door, but had some difficulty as the upper hinge of the door had sprung as a result of hitting the bridge abutment and they had to fasten the door with spun yarn. No person was riding in the compartment at the time. The driver, fireman and guard advised Yolland that as the train was restarting and moving slowly, their train was run into by the goods train booked to leave Hertford station five minutes after the passenger train. All stated the passenger train was not delayed by more than two minutes when securing the door. Immediately after the collision the guard checked his watch and found it was *'hardly 14 minutes past 11 o'clock'*. On challenging the driver of the goods train he had left early, the driver retorted: *'I can't help it; the signal was lowered for me'*.

The inspector could not find any explanation as to the manner in which the door of the carriage had been left open. The guard of the train rode in that compartment on the Down journey of the passenger train due to arrive at Hertford at 10.55am. The guard was adamant that when he got out onto the platform at Cole Green on the Down journey he was certain he closed the door, put out his hand and turned the handle to properly fasten the door. He also advised Yolland that he looked through the carriages from the platform or near side before starting from Hertford and went into a Second Class compartment to shut one of the doors, which had been left open by one of the passengers.

The goods train, formed at the time of the collision of engine and tender, ten wagons and a brake van, started from the Great Eastern station at 9.40am and stopped at the Great Northern station to be formed up and marshalled for its onward journey. The porter responsible for operating the signals then allowed the train to depart at 11.15am according to the station clock, and this was confirmed by an entry in the log-book kept at the station. The Up signal governing the departure of the train was located 110 yards to the east of the west end of the station platform from which it was worked. The goods train stood awaiting departure 176 yards further to the east of this Up signal so that when the signal was lowered for the goods train to start, the driver had a distance of 376 yards for the train to gain speed before reaching the overbridge and supposing he was looking out for obstructions ahead. Yolland ascertained that because of the curvature of the line between the end of the platform and the overbridge, the driver would only have noticed the rear vehicles of the passenger train at a distance of 70 yards. The driver confirmed that as the train was passing the water tank, some 70 yards from the bridge one of the porters signalled to him the stop the train and he immediately reversed the engine and told the fireman to apply the tender brake. He had no time to sound the engine whistle for the guard to apply his brake and 40 yards west of the overbridge the locomotive ran into the back of the passenger train at a speed of between 12 and 13 mph. The collision forced the Carriage Brake next to the engine of the passenger train on to the top of the buffers with the result that one for buffers punctured the tank of the engine.

Colonel Yolland was of the opinion neither the train crew of the passenger train nor the goods train was to blame for the accident. It was probable the passenger train guard was mistaken in supposing he had secured the door of the compartment of the Carriage Brake when stepping out on the platform at Cole Green and it was his responsibility to check that it was secured when he re-entered the brake compartment. From evidence there was no doubt the goods train had been allowed to depart in less than 5 minutes after the departure of the passenger train and the porter was solely to blame for lowering the signal too soon.

In his report William Yolland placed the primary cause of the collision on the dimensions of the overbridge where there was insufficient clearance for double track under the structure. At the time of the original inspection there were short portions of double line at Hertford and at the junction with the GNR at Welwyn Junction, and according to the details furnished by the H&WJR Company engineer to the BOT prior to the inspection, the portion of double line at Hertford station terminated one chain west of the overbridge,

which was not sufficiently wide by about 18 inches to give proper clearance for doors of ordinary sized carriages on either side, if the usual 6 feet be left between the two lines of way.

If these details as to the state of the station when it was inspected be correct, and the double line terminated one chain west of the overbridge, there would not be near so much as a 6 feet space between the two lines under the bridge, and there might have been sufficient space between the rails and the north abutment for an open door of a carriage to pass through without coming into contact with the abutment. I am informed that the station has been altered and rebuilt since I inspected it; the platform has been shifted further to the north, and the view through the bridge has in consequence been limited; the curve has been made sharper, and the double portion of line now extends to more than 4 chains beyond the overbridge; so that there are now two lines of railway through the bridge, occupying the whole space, one of which lines, the proper up line, has been converted into and used as a siding terminating against the west end of the station platform; the up and down traffic passing through the bridge by the north line of railway, which is place too near the abutment.

Yolland concluded:

I cannot speak from recollection as to the exact condition of the Hertford station when I inspected it in 1858, but I have no doubt that the insufficient width of the bridge [22 feet] *for a double line of railway would have attracted my attention, if the lines had been laid as they now are, and that I should have objected to them; and I am confirmed by the fact I had occasion to point out to the Engineer of the line, that the rails were placed 'far too close' to the goods warehouse in Hertford yard, and to the posts of the gates at three level crossings on the line; and in consequence the position of the rails at these places was altered before the line was opened.*

The Hertford branch service was indirectly affected by a further accident, which occurred at Welwyn Junction just before 5pm on Thursday 5th November 1867. An Up main-line freight train arrived at the junction and began shunting duties. Part of the train was detached and set back out of the way via the Hertford branch to an Up-side siding. The engine and some wagons then returned to the main line ready to set back onto the remaining wagons, but unfortunately the under guard inadvertently set the points for the Down main line and the locomotive was struck by the engine hauling the 3.40pm King's Cross to Hitchin train travelling at 40 mph on the Down main line. The Welwyn Junction signalman endeavoured to divert the passenger train onto the Luton branch but in vain and the resultant debris blocked the main lines and the Hertford branch, effectively closing all lines for the rest of the day. Several passengers on the train were injured and some passenger coaches damaged. The accident would have been avoided had all signals and points been interlocked and totally worked from Welwyn Junction signal box.

On 8th November 1867 Lieutenant Colonel C.S. Hutchinson was delegated to conduct the official BOT inquiry into the accident. He subsequently visited the site and interviewed members of staff involved. He observed that at Welwyn Junction, approximately two miles north of Hatfield, the Luton and Hertford branches diverged from the GNR main line. Both were single lines but double for a short distance to form junctions with the main lines. The Luton branch diverged immediately to the west but the Hertford branch ran parallel to and about 10 feet distant from the Up main line for about 300 yards before turning east. There was also a siding running parallel to and on the east side of the branch. The junction was provided with locking apparatus recently provided by Stevens & Sons at a cost of £195, where the double sections of the branches joined the main lines and were worked from Welwyn Junction signal box. However, where the double portions commenced on the respective branches the points were worked by ground frames with point indicators. The Hertford branch points were weighted to lie right for the Up line and the GNR officials at the scene informed Hutchinson it was a most rare occurrence to let any train off the Hertford branch to the Down main line, there being a crossover to the Down main line at the north end of Welwyn Junction yard. The lever for working these points was not fixed, but kept lying on the ground beside the switch box.

On the afternoon of 5th November, as it was getting dusk, a pick Up goods train formed of a tender engine, thirty-five loaded wagons and two guards brake vans, one at the front and the other at the rear of the formation, and both attended by a guard, arrived at Welwyn Junction from the north at 4.48pm and began to shunt under the protection of signals. The leading guards brake van and some wagons were detached from the remainder of the train which was left standing on the Up main line. The engine and wagons then ran forward under the control of the signalman before reversing onto the Hertford branch. Once on the branch the junction porter operated the points leading to the adjacent siding, which ran parallel to the Hertford single line. After shunting was completed the locomotive returned to the Hertford branch hauling the brake van and two wagons, with the intention of reaching the Up main line and reversing onto the remainder of its train. Unfortunately, the under guard held open the points leading to the Down main line as the engine and stock approached. The driver failed to notice the point indicator and immediately the engine had passed through the points he realised the error and took evasive action. He had all but succeeded halting his engine, which was standing foul of the Down main line when it was struck by the locomotive of the Down main-line train travelling at between 35 and 45 mph.

The Down train had departed King's Cross at 3.51pm and was formed of engine and tender, a gas-lit brake van, eleven carriages, a horse box and three other brake vans. The driver of the express advised Hutchinson that he had only seen the goods engine was foul of the Down main line for a few yards before running into it and had no time to moderate the speed of the train. The signalman at Welwyn Junction signal box had also noticed the position of the goods engine when the passenger train was within 50 yards of the box and endeavoured to pull the points to divert the train on to the Luton branch, but the engine was on the points before he could act.

Sturrock '270' series 0-4-2WT, later 'F5' Class No. 275A at Hatfield 13th September 1902. This was one of five built by the Avonside Engine Company in 1867 and was rebuilt with outside frames in 1880. The locomotive has a Stirling 4 feet 5 inches diameter boiler and has double couplings with the centre frame slots filled in. No. 275A was withdrawn from traffic in July 1905. *LCGB/Ken Nunn*

As a result of the collision the buffers of the passenger locomotive struck the buffer plank of the goods engine and both locomotives were driven northwards for a distance of about 40 yards before turning over and blocking both Up and Down main lines. The front brake van crashed into the back of the tender, whilst the Second and First Class carriages behind the brake van were crushed together and it was here that the passenger who suffered broken legs was found under the debris, more than an hour elapsing before he could be extricated. Some of the other carriages in the train suffered minor damage or broken windows. The driver and fireman on the goods engine jumped off the footplate before the collision but the crew of the passenger train engine remained in the cab and suffered shaking and minor injuries.

At the conclusion of the enquiry Hutchinson placed the blame for the accident on the under guard of the goods train improperly meddling with the points and thus diverting the goods engine from the Hertford branch to the Down main line and into the path of the express.

He had always borne an excellent character, and there was not the least suspicion that he was under the influence of drink on the afternoon in question. He was well acquainted with the nature of the points at Welwyn Junction, having often been engaged in shunting there. In explanation of his conduct he stated he had been very much disturbed in mind by having dreamt on the night of the 4th that his train would come into collision with a passenger train the following day, and that he had in consequence felt unfitted for his duties. As to moving the points, he stated he was at the time under the impression that if they opened they would lead to the up, and not the down line, and that by passing the engine through them he would have expedited its return to its train. According to the Company's rules he had no business to have touched the points, that being the duty of the junction porter.

GNR gas lamp case, a survivor on the south-west corner of the station building at Hertford Cowbridge in 1965.   *P. Whitaker*

The Lieutenant Colonel in his report, which was passed to the GNR Secretary on 28th November, required urgent improvements to the working of the points and signals at Welwyn Junction.

While, however, attributing the immediate cause of the accident to the under guard's misconduct, there is no doubt that it could not have occurred had these points been worked from the signal cabin and interlocked with the signals. This alteration the Company is now about to effect, and it is only to be regretted that they should have waited for an accident before adopting a simple precaution of this kind. The points at the commencement of the double portion of the Luton line should also be worked from the signal cabin; and at the north end of the Welwyn Junction yard there should be a low goods signal interlocked with the main signals, and when at danger, locking safety points to protect the main line, there being at present no sufficient safeguard against the driver of a goods train running out and fouling the main line.

The aftermath of the Welwyn Junction incident was still being felt in the early weeks of 1868 when the GNR solicitors received a claim from a Mr Grady against the company for damages accruing as the result of the death of his father Mr P. Grady in the accident. Grady's solicitor advised that the action would be withdrawn if the railway company paid £200 compensation plus costs. At their meeting on 28th January the directors advised their solicitor to settle the claim in the agreed terms.

Panshanger House, the home of Lord Cowper, was the venue for another military field day on Whit Monday 1868 when the 2nd Battalion of the Hertfordshire Rifles and the 1st and 2nd Companies of the 1st Herts Infantry paraded at 10.45am at the GNR station at Hertford, before travelling on the much strengthened 11.10am departure to Cole Green. Needless to say, many of the populace took advantage of the occasion to travel by train and watch the display. The GNR did much to attract patronage by offering return fares for the price of a single ticket.

Since taking over the line, the GNR had brought an improvement in the services but not all welcomed the increased facilities and traffic. In July 1868 William Rolfe of Hertford complained of the nuisance caused by smoke from the company's 'engine house' and asked if it was possible for the engine shed to be moved to the other end of the yard away from the area of housing near the station. Seymour Clarke, reporting the matter to the directors, requested the Way and Works Committee if steps could be taken to moderate the smoke emitted from the locomotives by using coke instead of coal. Instructions were subsequently issued to footplate crews to control the emission of smoke from their engines.

A month later the farmers of the area had a foretaste of what was to become a regular occurrence down the years when the engine of a Hertford to Hatfield train set fire to a field of crops and a hedgerow near Hatfield on 4th August 1868. As well as destroying a considerable acreage of barley the flames, fanned by a strong breeze, also demolished a labourer's cottage, later incurring the company in payment of considerable compensation.

The congestion caused by the operation of all traffic over two running lines between Welwyn Junction and Hatfield was partially eased with the conversion and upgrading of a former ballast line on the western side of the main lines for the use of Dunstable branch traffic, which was completed early in December 1868. Lieutenant Colonel C.S. Hutchinson carried out the BOT inspection of the 2½ mile section on 3rd February 1869 but was far from happy with the signalling arrangements at Hatfield for dealing with traffic emanating from the Luton branch, let alone the existing service on the St. Albans branch. The inspector also criticised the lack of check rails on the sharp 9-chains radius curve where the Luton line veered away from the main line at Welwyn Junction, and because of the incompleteness of works refused to sanction the use of the new line for passenger trains.

The tranquility of the Hertfordshire countryside with ready access by train from the capital was soon exploited by the GNR for staff outings. On Saturday 31st July 1869 the annual excursion for the London District Locomotive Department employees and their families were offered the grounds of Panshanger House for the day by courtesy of Lord Cowper. For most people the attractions offered the only chance of a break from the routine of life in the overcrowded metropolis and so great were the numbers travelling that the train was formed of twenty 4-wheel coaches with almost every seat taken. Hauled by a tender locomotive decorated overall with flags and garlands, the train departed from King's Cross at 8.30am accompanied by the Locomotive Superintendent J. Bridge. After calling at Hatfield to pick up the local staff and those from Hitchin the train traversed the branch arriving at Cole Green at 9.45am. Led by the GNR locomotive department reed band the trippers then walked to Panshanger Park for the recreational day, which included an organised sports meeting. The return special train departed from Cole Green at 8.30pm.

A further accident incurring fatalities occurred at Welwyn Junction on the evening of 24th October 1869. The 8.00pm King's Cross to Peterborough train travelling at speed was derailed at the Hertford branch facing points. The locomotive and leading three coaches passed over the points and continued along the Down main line, but the signalman in placing his signals back to danger altered the points so that the rest of the train swung on to the wrong line and derailed causing considerable damage. Three passengers were killed and a number sustained serious injuries. As a result of the incident the Hertford branch services were curtailed until the afternoon of the next day.

Lieutenant Colonel F.H. Rich subsequently conducted the official BOT inquiry into the accident. He ascertained the Peterborough train departed on time from King's Cross at 8.00pm, formed of engine and tender, two horse boxes, then one First Class carriage, one Second Class carriage and one First Class carriage followed by a guard's brake van occupied by a guard, then one Second Class, one First Class, one Second Class, one First Class, one Second Class and one First Class, then a guard's brake van occupied by a guard at the tail of the train – thirteen vehicles in total. The train subsequently departed Hatfield one minute late at 8.56pm and had an uneventful run to Welwyn Junction where the driver observed the signals were clear for the train to proceed on the Down main line. After the engine and tender, two horse boxes and the First Class carriage had cleared the junction points the remainder of the train derailed except for the last guard's brake van which ran over the points and down the Hertford branch. The two wheels of the First Class carriage in front of this brake van also remained on the rails on the Hertford line. The two horse boxes and the next three carriages remained coupled to the engine and were brought to a stand 500 yards north of Welwyn Viaduct, the couplings between the last of these carriages and the remainder of the train had fractured and the last two vehicles in this front portion were derailed to the right.

Evidence showed that both the trailing springs of the second from last carriage on the front section were broken, one piece about three feet in length was broken out of the top plate of the nearside spring and was found 120 feet north of the junction. It was a fresh fracture and had been sustained after the vehicle passed the junction points, by the jolting caused as the coach derailed. The six bottom plates of the offside trailing spring were also broken; four of these plates showed fresh fractures which were caused by the accident; the bottom plate had an old fracture, and in the plate above it the fracture was half old and half new. Rich was of the opinion the old fractures would not have interfered with the safe running of the carriage. The next carriage had a bent axle, which was sustained at the time of the derailment. The front brake van and the following six carriages and the rear guard's brake van became detached from the front section of the train and came to a stop 150 yards north of the junction. Two of these carriages were thrown on their sides on the Hertford branch, whilst another finished up on the siding east of the Hertford line, the body of this carriage being separated from the frame and wheels. The front guard's brake van and two more carriages were derailed across the Up main line and the Hertford branch. The last carriage of the train stood on the Hertford branch, the front two wheels only were derailed and the rear guard's brake van stood 125 yards from the junction points on the Hertford branch. Most vehicles sustained extensive damage.

The Lieutenant Colonel ascertained there was only slight damage to the permanent way; the right-hand junction point had a slight mark at the right side and from evidence showed that the train had passed over the line for some seconds after the accident without interfering with the points. The rail next to the right-hand point was slightly marked by the flange of a wheel, which had mounted and run along the top of the rail for a short distance. The next mark found was on the ballast 32 yards north of the junction points and from thereon the derailed vehicles had disturbed the ballast. Some of the fishplates were severed and broken. A check rail on the Up main line was fractured and there was a gash in the nearside rail of the Down main line 91 yards from the junction points, and the brick wall of the platform opposite the rail was struck by the leading wheel of the front guard's brake van, which was nearly turned round. The rail on the Up main line was damaged and a rail in the siding on the east side of the Hertford branch about 120 yards north of the junction was fractured. The boundary wall a little to the north of this broken rail was demolished.

Rich concluded from the evidence given that the passenger train had passed Welwyn Junction signal box, located 32 yards south of the junction points, at a speed of 25 mph against an alleged speed of between 15 and 20 mph. The signalman told the inspector that when the engine and two or three vehicles had passed the junction he placed the main-line signal back to danger. The signals and points at Welwyn Junction were rudimentarily interlocked so that when the main-line signals were lowered the points leading from the main line to the Hertford branch were locked. However, as soon as the Down main-line signal was put back to danger the points became unlocked and on this occasion Rich was of the opinion the signalman, without intending to, had pulled the point lever while the train was passing and turned the rear part of the formation down the Hertford branch, whilst the engine and leading section continued along the Down main line. The Welwyn Junction signalman's record book showed that he had telegraphed '*down line clear*' to Hatfield, where a Hertford train was waiting to depart, before the Peterborough train had passed the junction, and it was presumed he would not have sent such a signal after the line was blocked by the derailment. The Hertford train started from Hatfield and was fortunately stopped on the approach to Welwyn Junction by signals.

Lieutenant Colonel Rich was highly critical of the GNR Company for the method of operation and concluded his report:

It is the custom on the Great Northern Railway to put up the signals to danger as soon as the engine and tender have passed a junction. The practice is a most dangerous one, as the signalman, from the force of habit – of constantly moving the points and signals in connection with each other, is almost certain at some point or another to make the mistake of moving the point lever when he should not do so. No signal or point should be moved until after the train has passed clear of the points. Moving the signal while a train is passing incurs also the risk, that if the point lever is not pushed well home, the vibration of the train passing through the junction may move the points, and throw the train off the rails. I do not think this was the case at Welwyn Junction, as the only way to account for the little injury to the points and rails at the junction is by the train having been turned down the Hertford branch. This in my opinion is proved by the position the carriages that had been thrown off the rails were found in, and by the guard's van being on the Hertford branch without having been off the rails. I would strongly urge upon the Great Northern Railway Company, the necessity of altering their system of moving the signals while trains are passing through the junctions, and it would be desirable for the Company to revise their regulations, and strike out such rules as No. 70, which states that 'the speed of a train when approaching any junction must be slackened to 10 to 12 miles per hour'. This regulation is never observed by any of the drivers of the express main line trains, and the services now laid down in the time-tables could not be performed if this regulation was observed. The system of issuing instructions to the servants of railway companies which are not observed, is wrong.

Two local people, residents of Tewin, who were passengers on the doomed train were still recovering from their serious injuries the following January.

Lieutenant Colonel C.S. Hutchinson re-inspected the section of line between Hatfield and Welwyn Junction on 8th November 1869 and found that all signalling was controlled from Hatfield North signal box. All outstanding work had been completed including the fitting of check rails on the Luton branch curve at Welwyn Junction and the inspector had no hesitation sanctioning the use of the former siding between Hatfield and Welwyn Junction as an independent single line for the Luton and Dunstable branch trains.

On Thursday 9th December 1869, GNR passengers for the Hertford branch suffered over an hour and a half delay on their journey when a slip carriage attached to the 5.25pm train from King's Cross, which should have been detached at Hatfield, was uncoupled at New Barnet 8½ miles to the south. Further problems were experienced in taking the carriage forward so that instead of reaching Hertford at 6.20pm, passengers arrived at the county town at 8.00pm. Reporting the incident the local paper was highly critical of the railway company remarking: *'It is not the first time that such delays have been incurred'*.

Panoramic view of Hertford GNR station from Port Hill with McMullen's brewery in the background and showing the extensive length of the goods shed to the east of the station. A line of open wagons stands on the outer siding whilst maltings dominate the background.

D. Dent collection

5

Consolidation

His Royal Highness the Prince of Wales visited the Earl of Fife at his home at Balls Park, Hertford on Tuesday 17th May 1870. The Prince used the GNR route to the county town travelling in a special Saloon attached to the 1.15pm ordinary train from King's Cross as far as Hatfield. The Saloon was then attached to the 1.52pm branch train at Hatfield, which arrived at Hertford at 2.17pm. Both trains were in the charge of J. Alexander, the local District Superintendent, who on arrival supervised the stabling and cleaning of the Saloon by local staff. The Prince was scheduled to return to London in the Saloon attached to the 5.12pm service train but his visit was longer than planned and arrangements were hastily made for a special train to run direct to King's Cross departing Hertford at 6.30pm.

The Hertford branch services were again severely disrupted by the derailment of a goods train just north of Hatfield on 30th April 1871 when wagons blocked the Up main line. Once again, and not for the first time, most travellers from Cowbridge wishing to travel to London were much to the regret of GN staff diverted to the GER Hertford station for their journey. At this time the inhabitants of Hertford were grateful for the duplication of routes to London for on 5th October the GNR came to the rescue after the derailment of two engines near Broxbourne Junction severely delayed the GER Hertford branch services.

Farmers and landowners with fields bordering the railway regularly complained of the inadequacy of fencing and on many occasions branch trains were halted because animals on the line were waiting for farm labourers to usher the beasts back to pasture. The fencing was not, however, at fault on the morning of Tuesday 5th December 1871 when the branch train ran down and killed nine sheep on an occupational crossing near Cole Green. At the subsequent enquiry into the incident the railway company was absolved from blame when it was revealed that the lad employed by J.C. Allen, a farmer of Cole Green, was driving the sheep across the line when the exit gate was blown shut by the strong wind causing the animals to scatter along the track.

Early in 1872 the GNR and GER authorities conferred as to the standardisation of certain fare structures from their respective Hertford stations to London. The initial trial was made on Easter Bank Holiday Monday when the 4s 4d First Class and 2s 2d Third Class fares were common to both systems. Some semblance of competition was retained for these fares were only available on one train: the GNR departure at 8.00am arriving at King's Cross at 9.12am whilst the GER train departed Hertford at 9.30am with a 57 minute run to Bishopsgate. In addition to these excursion fares, Third Class passengers were conveyed by all trains from Hertford on both the GNR and GER routes on and from 1st April.

The Earl Cowper again organised a military gathering at Panshanger Hall in 1872, when on Whit Monday the Metropolitan Volunteer Corps assembled. Several detachments travelled from King's Cross to Cole Green station before marching to the park. During the day cheap fares entitled members of the public to watch the display whilst a special train took members of the Corps back to London in the evening.

Wintry weather during the first few days of February 1873 brought problems to services on the Hertford branch. Heavy snow filling the cuttings along the line forced one train to return to Hertford after running into a drift near Hertingfordbury station, whilst on Monday 3rd a GNR tender locomotive was derailed near the connection with the GER at Hertford Junction. In attempting to start a freight train the wheels had slipped with such violence on the icy rails that two pairs of wheels jumped the track! Re-railing operations took longer than expected as the Hatfield breakdown train was delayed getting to the site of the incident by snowdrifts in several places whilst the GER breakdown facilities at Hertford shed were inadequate.

The failure to construct a railway from Hornsey to Hatfield as authorised in 1865 engendered support for another scheme especially as the area north of London at Palmers Green, Winchmore Hill and Enfield had seen an immediate increase in housing development following the opening of the line from Wood Green in 1871. The possible extension of the existing GNR Enfield branch to Hertford was welcomed by a number of Hertford inhabitants who signed a petition supporting the scheme, presenting it to Henry Oakley, the GNR General Manager, on 15th May 1873. Oakley replying advised the signatories that the memorandum would be brought to the attention of the directors at an early meeting.

On the evening of Sunday 23rd August 1873, between 7pm and 8pm a heavy storm brought torrential rain which resulted in the branch being flooded in several places between Hertford and Hertingfordbury. The Up branch passenger train was forced to run at reduced speed through the floodwater to prevent damage to the track and rolling stock. Further problems were encountered in late January 1874 when the 5.00pm express from Manchester ran into a main-line goods train being shunted onto the Hertford branch at Welwyn Junction. Fortunately the driver of the express had noticed the goods train and applied the brakes so that the resultant collision was at low speed. The branch services were restored within hours after the damaged wagons were lifted clear of the running line.

Just over a month later another accident occurred at Welwyn Junction when at 6.20am in dense fog on Monday 2nd March 1874 the Hatfield to Hertford goods train was crossing from the Down main line to the branch it came into collision with an Up main-line coal train destined for London. Both locomotives were derailed and together with six wagons were damaged. The driver and fireman of the Hertford train and the fireman of the main-line train jumped from the footplate and were uninjured whilst the driver of the coal train remained at his post and fortunately only suffered a sprained hand. At the time of the collision the Up coal train was travelling at 15 mph and the branch train 10 mph. The signals were set clear for the Hatfield to Hertford train to cross the junction but the driver of the coal train admitted he had lost his bearings and consequently passed the Up main-line signal at danger.

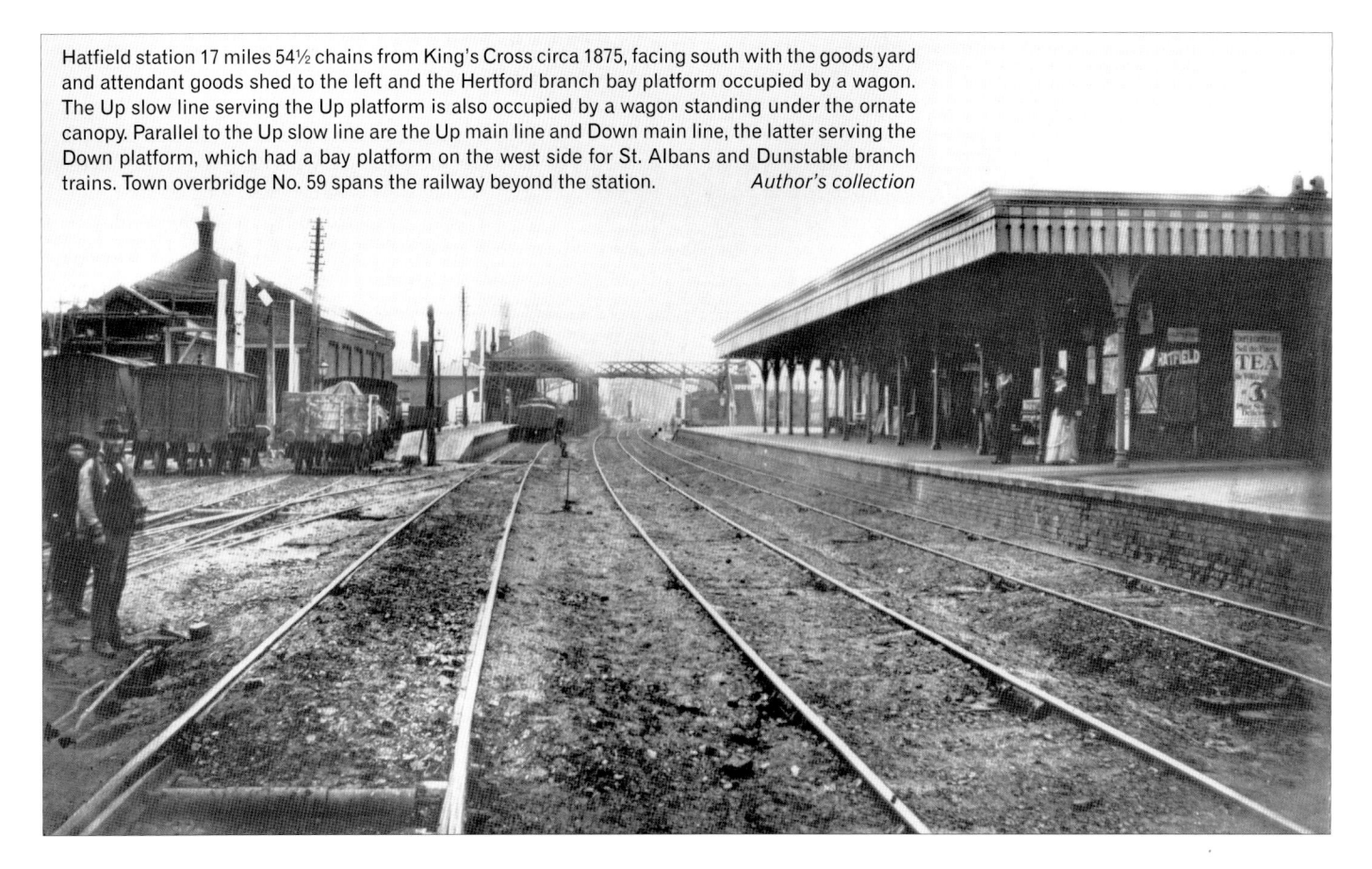

Hatfield station 17 miles 54½ chains from King's Cross circa 1875, facing south with the goods yard and attendant goods shed to the left and the Hertford branch bay platform occupied by a wagon. The Up slow line serving the Up platform is also occupied by a wagon standing under the ornate canopy. Parallel to the Up slow line are the Up main line and Down main line, the latter serving the Down platform, which had a bay platform on the west side for St. Albans and Dunstable branch trains. Town overbridge No. 59 spans the railway beyond the station. *Author's collection*

The line was not fully restored until 1.00pm, but with the help of the breakdown train under the supervision of Frederick Warr from Hitchin shed, Mr Holmes, permanent way superintendent, and his men managed to slew the rails so that some trains could by pass the site of the accident by using one of the parallel sidings. The incident was of such importance – two incidents within a few weeks of each other – that Francis Cockshott, the superintendent and Mr Alexander the district superintendent attended the scene.

Traffic growth from the Hertford line had been increasing steadily over the years with the result that on many occasions siding space was at a premium and wagons had to be held short of their destination until suitable accommodation was available. Farmers and traders also complained of the inadequacies of providing enough empty stock for loading traffic. Matters reached saturation point at the end of 1873 and, after reports from the Goods Agent and General Manager, the directors on 6th February 1874 authorised the expenditure of £1,061 for the provision of additional sidings.

At the end of April 1874 the GER authorities posted a notice in the booking hall at their Hertford station to the effect that the booking office windows would thereafter open 15 minutes before the departure of each train. In reporting the fact the *Hertford Mercury*, without mentioning names, advocated a similar practice at the GNR station remarking '*it was hoped other company's do likewise*'.

Since the opening of the H&WJR, regular calls were made to combine the two Hertford stations located half a mile apart and concentrate traffic on a through route. The attempts to provide a joint GNR/GER station were again resurrected in September 1875 by Hertford Town Council. A letter signed by the Mayor of Hertford to the GNR General Manager was presented to the directors at King's Cross on 18th February 1876, but a decision was deferred pending further enquiries.

The opening of the single line for Luton and Dunstable services alongside the Down main line between Hatfield and Welwyn Junction had certainly eased traffic congestion, but the fact remained that, in the absence of a similar line for Hertford branch services on the Up side of the Up main line, congestion and delays to main traffic increased. The situation deteriorated to such an extent that after years of argument and counter argument the GNR board agreed to the inevitable and authorised the construction of an independent single line for Hertford branch trains between Welwyn Junction and Hatfield. The Hertford branch extension from Welwyn Junction to Hatfield, 2 miles 58 chains of single line alongside the Up main line, was ready for traffic on Monday 28th August 1876. Welwyn Junction signal box was abolished from the 29th August when the points connecting the main line to the branch were removed.

The *Hertford Mercury & Reporter* was enthusiastic, reporting on 2nd September 1876:

On Tuesday last [29th August 1876] *a new line of rails from Hatfield to Welwyn Junction was opened for use of the Hertford trains. This new line is on the east side of the main line, the Luton having a separate line on the west. There will henceforth be no fear of a repetition of the appalling accidents we have had at Welwyn Junction. The Hertford trains will be independent of the main line rails altogether, and the partial and sometimes complete stoppage of Hertford trains at the junction is done away with also. On arrival at Hatfield the trains go alongside the up platform at once instead of onwards, above a quarter of a mile towards Potter's Bar, stopping and then backing as hitherto. A new platform is being made, north of the up platform, especially for the Hertford trains. By these alterations much time will be saved.*

Other alterations included the enhancement of the electric telegraph route on the branch in the spring of 1877 and the abolition of 19th Mile signal box in July of that year.

By kind permission of Earl Cowper, the GNR (London) Locomotive and Carriage Workmen's fete was held at Panshanger Park on Saturday 10th August 1878. The employees, their wives and families, numbering almost 1,000, were conveyed by special train departing King's Cross at 9.15am, with arrival at Cole Green at 10.00am. The company proceeded to the park where a sports programme had been arranged but inclement weather forced postponement until just after 2.00pm, when the rain ceased and the remainder of the day was fine and sunny. Mr Budge, the Locomotive Superintendent, and his family with many others watched the cricket match between the London Locomotive Department and the Peterbrough Locomotive Department, which was won by the latter scoring 67 runs again the 37 runs of the opponents. Races were organised for adults and children and a quoits match played, whilst the Peterborough brass band performed during the afternoon and children enjoyed swings and see-saws. The gathering left the park at about 8.00pm for Cole Green station where the special train returned them to King's Cross shortly before 10.00pm. Mr Campling of the Dimsdale Arms, Hertford served refreshments throughout the day.

On Monday 25th November 1878 the 8.30am passenger train from Hatfield to Hertford had an uneventful run as far as Hertingfordbury but on reaching the connection to Horns Mill siding the engine lurched over the points and ran into the siding. The remaining portion of the train remained on the main single line before the coupling between the engine and leading carriage fractured, whereupon the coaches derailed. Fortunately the derailment was at a slow speed so the vehicles remained upright and although passengers were shaken none complained of injury. The engine, after running along the siding, derailed and juddered to a halt alongside the embankment, leaving the rails torn and twisted over a distance of a hundred yards. Driver Murphy was much shaken by his ordeal necessitating being off duty for two days. The breakdown train was summoned from Hatfield and arrived on site attached to a Down goods service. Traffic was suspended but with commendable speed the derailed coaches were re-railed using portable jacks and the main line was cleared so that normal services resumed with the 1.20pm Hertford to Hatfield service. The locomotive was re-railed and recovered the next day.

For several years fuel supplies to Hertford Gas Works had been offloaded from railway wagons in both the GER and GNR goods yards and carted round to the establishment by road. Early in 1879 the local authorities requested the provision of a siding to the gas works, a suggestion to which the GNR engineer heartily agreed. At the same time a gravel pit was established near the line and, wishing to exploit the market, the GNR Goods Agent requested the provision of a siding. On 2nd May 1879 the Way and Works Committee authorised the expenditure of £200 for the provision of both connections.

The growth of traffic on the branch and the resultant lengthening of formation of passenger trains often meant that either the front or rear vehicles of the branch services were not adjacent to the rather low and short platforms at Cole Green and Hertingfordbury stations. To obviate delays to trains caused by pulling up twice at each location and to prevent accidents, the Traffic Committee on 7th August 1879 sanctioned the extension and raising of platform heights at both stations at a cost of £311. Work was not completed until the following spring.

Having achieved little over the previous decade, in the late spring of 1880 Hertford residents again resurrected the scheme for a joint station at Hertford and presented a memorial to the GNR directors requesting an improvement in facilities. At the board meeting on 4th June the engineer was instructed to report on the condition of the structure at Cowbridge directly to the Chairman, Lord Colville, before any site visit was arranged. A visit was subsequently made in late July when Colville met members of the town council, but the decision of the GNR Chairman could not have satisfied the populace for on 26th October the Town Clerk wrote to King's Cross submitting a petition from the inhabitants of the town for a joint station, a similar document was also presented to the GER directors at Bishopsgate. The matter was fully discussed at the GNR board meeting on 5th November 1880 when the Secretary was instructed to decline the request, it being considered traffic from Hertford was *'not sufficient to warrant the GNR company incurring a share of the cost for the provision of a new station'*.

Although passenger traffic receipts were not to the satisfaction of the GNR authorities, goods traffic on the branch was increasing steadily. The intermediate station goods yards were showing a marked upturn and to deal with the heavier consignments, notably timber exports, authority was given on 7th February 1881 for the provision of a 1-ton capacity crane in the goods yard at Cole Green at a cost of £40.

Increasing traffic on the GNR main line was by 1881 still stretching the essentially double line capacity to its limits. Delays continued to main-line trains between the former Welwyn Junction and Hatfield, although Hertford and Dunstable branch trains were excluded from this bottleneck as they had the use of the parallel independent single line. The sanctioning amongst other sections on 4th November 1881 for the widening of the line from Welwyn Viaduct (north of Welwyn Junction) to Hatfield to include independent Up and Down slow lines promised early improvements. However, this promised an early dawn and several years were to elapse before work was completed.

The subject of a joint station at Hertford was raised yet again at the end of 1881 when the GER authorities intimated they were in the process of obtaining Parliamentary authority for a new station in the town. Heartened by the news the Town Clerk wrote to King's Cross on 21st December asking if it was the intention of the GNR to enter into an arrangement with the GER for the construction of a joint station. The Northern directors were in no mood for endless correspondence with the local authority and tersely replied early in the New Year that the company was in no way committed to the scheme and neither were they considering such proposals.

In September 1880, February 1881 and again on 5th May 1882 the local board of health, the Hertford Rural Sanitary Authority, reported on the repeated complaints made regarding the storage of *'truck loads of putrid matter from slaughter houses in London'*, purportedly manure stored in the sidings at Cole Green before being carted along local roads. The clerk to the authority stated that on 22nd April when Mr Scales, an inspector, had visited the siding he had written to the GNR and the Secretary had passed the matter to the goods manager requesting immediate attention. A further reply stated the complaint had been investigated and that the nuisance was caused by the failure of the consignee Henry Wood to clear the putrid matter promptly on its arrival at Cole Green. The company apologised for the situation stating that there were standing instructions in place, which should have prevented the occurrence. The inspector stated Henry Wood was a tenant farmer at Holwell Hyde Farm and suggested that if he was going to continue to have the material delivered from London, he should make arrangements for a siding to be installed nearer the farm where he could unload the material without causing nuisance to other people. After delicate negotiations, Henry Wood was instructed he could not store the offending material in the ordinary goods yard sidings and that he had to remove any offensive material from the station directly it arrived, and he had undertaken to do so within twenty-four hours. In the event of non-compliance, Wood would be referred to appear before the local magistrates. As a result of the threat the GNR Traffic Committee subsequently sanctioned further improvements at Cole Green on 1st June 1882 after Wood requested the provision of a siding to handle the manure traffic. This new siding at Birchall was located a little way from Wood's farm and situated in a rural area where the material was likely to cause less of a nuisance. After negotiations, Wood agreed to pay 10 per cent as a proportion of the total outlay of £126 and the siding was duly installed later in the same year, the arrangement initially lasting for a period of seven years.

From the opening in 1858 the branch had been worked on a time interval system of train working using the Train Staff only, and then Train Staff and Ticket, with little interlocking of points and signals, a fact that had been all too evident in the incidents which had occurred at Hertford in the early years of operation. The steady increase in the number of passenger and goods trains on the branch meant that services often incurred delays waiting for previous traffic to clear the long section from Hatfield to Hertford. In 1882, along with the St. Albans branch, authority was given for the installation of the block telegraph method of signalling with block posts at Hatfield, Cole Green and Hertford, thus doubling the capacity of the single line (the Hatfield to Dunstable branch had already been provided with block telegraph in 1877). The installation between Hatfield and Hertford, however, took some time to complete and was not finished until late 1883.

The reluctance of the GNR to extend their route beyond Enfield was a source of concern to landowners in the area north of the terminus. Equally, residents of Hertford were forced to take roundabout railway routes to London instead of the direct route which was envisaged in 1865. Frustrated by lack of progress, landowners and gentlemen arranged a private meeting at Hertford on 29th October 1883 to consider plans for a proposed East Hertfordshire Railway from the Enfield terminus of the GNR to Hertford and thence through Walkern to Ashwell and a junction with the GNR Hitchin to Cambridge line. The chairman was W.R. Baker of Bayfordbury Park and at the conclusion of the gathering a resolution was passed to progress the scheme with slight modifications and to present a Bill to Parliament. The *Railway Times* for 10th November 1883 reported on a further meeting held in the Shire Hall, Hertford, where the final plans were approved. Under the chairmanship of the Mayor of Hertford, a committee of eminent local gentry, including the Marquis of Salisbury KG, Abel Smith MP, the Honourable H. Cowper MP, A.J. Balfour MP, Baron Dimsdale, Captain Parker RN and eight others, resolved that immediate steps be taken to present the Bill. The GNR authorities, however, were not in favour of the embryonic HER, which would interfere with their own plans to extend the line from Enfield to Hitchin or Stevenage, whilst the route from Hertford via Walkern would seriously compete for Cambridge traffic. The GNR lodged objections and the added difficulty in raising financial support subsequently doomed the EHR to failure.

The installation of the block telegraph on the three branches from Hatfield proved far from satisfactory and the local District Superintendent and station masters reported inadequacies of the system in a report to the Traffic Committee in the autumn of 1885. After urgent discussion, authority was given on 11th December for £214 to be expended for remedial work on the block system on the Hertford branch to obviate the deficiencies. It was also noted extra signalmen would have to be appointed at Hertford. The short section between Hertford GNR station and Hertford Junction GER was not, however, protected by block signalling.

Agricultural traffic continued its steady growth and farmers of the district were ever keen to dispatch or receive produce by rail. Much delay was also incurred in carting produce as well as sand and ballast to and from the goods yard at the nearest station on the branch, and so to obviate such delay Josiah Smart applied to the GNR authorities for the provision of a siding connecting with the Hertford branch near Hatfield. The application was duly considered on 19th August 1886 when authority was given for the installation of the siding at a cost of £190. Smart, in return, was required to pay an initial 10 per cent and a penalty payment if tonnages did not reach an agreed total.

After block signalling was installed the inadequacies of the existing signalling system on the Hatfield branches became all too evident. It was rumoured that a future Regulation of Railways Act would stipulate tighter controls on signalling and the GNR management anticipating the statute on 6th May 1887 granted authority for the proposed re-signalling of the Hertford branch together with the St. Albans and Dunstable branches and the East Lincolnshire Railway at an estimated total cost of £4,000. To avoid overspending on annual budgets, work was to be spread over four years. The East Lincolnshire scheme was later priced separately at £7,977. The tenders were not immediately awarded and work only commenced in 1890 after the contract was awarded to Saxby & Farmer Limited at a revised price of £7,780 9s 1d for all three branches from Hatfield.

The occupation and public footpath crossings bisecting the railway were a constant source of danger, with animals straying on to the line. Drivers and firemen were always on the alert for trespassers but on the morning of Monday 31st August 1887 the inevitable occurred when James Humberstone, a 55-year-old farm labourer, was taking a plough and pair of horses across the railway near Hertingfordbury station to work in a field alongside the line. Unfortunately he failed to clear the crossing before being struck by the engine of an approaching goods train, receiving such severe injuries that he died shortly afterwards. The horses escaped but the plough was damaged beyond repair.

Pressure from various interested parties continued to be made for the building of a new East Hertfordshire line connecting Enfield with Hertford. On 5th December 1888 Henry Oakley reported to the GNR directors that correspondence had been received from the Town Clerk at Hertford asking for the Proprietors of the Brickendonbury Estate and members of the local National Rifle Association to be associated with the new line and requesting its immediate construction. In the previous month Josiah Smart had opened a new gravel pit alongside the branch at Hertford and during the negotiations he requested the GNR to provide a siding. Whilst acceding to the application for the siding costing £197 on 7th December 1888, the railway company stipulated a guaranteed

7 per cent interest per annum over the next ten years to pay for the installation.

As expected, the 1889 Regulation of Railways Act as well as requiring block working on most lines and the interlocking of points and signals, also stipulated the compulsory provision and use of continuous brakes on passenger trains, and the correct marshalling of mixed trains. Fortunately the GNR had taken action to provide block working on the Hertford Branch but braking was another matter.

The lethargic attitude of the GNR in extending their route beyond Enfield to Hitchin led to the formulation of another scheme in 1890. The plans for the Central Hertfordshire Railway were deposited in the Parliamentary Bill office on 30th November, seeking authority to construct a railway 26 miles 4 furlongs in length. The proposed railway commenced south of Hitchin station and ran via Watton-at-Stone, Hertford (where a junction with the Hatfield branch was planned) then on to Enfield. Clauses 54 and 55 empowered the company to work with the GNR and Midland Railway at Hitchin and the GNR at Wood Green. The CHR was to be constructed in five sections, No. 1 in Hitchin station and yard, No. 2 from Hitchin to Watton, No. 3 Watton to Hertford, No. 4 joined Hertford to Hertingfordbury on the existing GNR branch whilst No. 5 ran from Hertingfordbury to Grange Park, south of Enfield GNR station. The cost of the project was £525,000 in £10 shares with borrowing powers of £175,000. The route envisaged was almost the same as the later GNR scheme and the main-line company officers prepared objections. Their task was obviated when the promoters ran into difficulties raising the first 10 per cent of capital £52,000 as stipulated by the House of Lords before the Bill could be discussed and the CHR met an early demise.

Wintry weather again caused problems on the Hertford branch on the night of 9th March 1891 when a heavy snowstorm effectively blocked cuttings along almost the whole section of line to Welwyn. Permanent way staff were called out to clear the line as soon as the storm subsided but it was the early afternoon of the following day before train services resumed, and even then with some difficulty and delay.

One of King's Cross's most senior and experienced engine drivers admitted misunderstanding instructions from his guard which resulted in an accident at Hatfield station on 30th March 1891. An Up branch train fully fitted with vacuum brake ran into the Hertford bay platform at the station and collided with the buffer stops causing severe injuries to the guard and minor injuries to six passengers. At the subsequent enquiry the guard stated he had earlier advised the driver that the train had through coaches for London and on arrival at Hatfield he was to draw the train well up into the bay instead of stopping outside the station, as was the usual practice to detach the through carriages. The driver, however, under the impression that he was booked to take the train onto the Up slow line, noticed too late that the signals were set for the Hertford bay platform and he was unable to brake the train sufficiently to prevent the locomotive colliding with the buffer stops.

Major F.A. Marindin was delegated to conduct the inquiry into the accident and noted the 9.30am Up passenger train from Hertford consisting of an engine, tender and four passenger vehicles, all fitted with the automatic vacuum brake, when running into the Hertford dock platform at Hatfield at about 9.51am overran the proper stopping place and came into collision with the buffer stops which were broken up. The engine mounted the platform behind the stops, and the whole of the engine wheels and the leading wheels of the tender were derailed over the ruins of the buffer stops or beyond them. No passenger vehicle left the rails and the train was little damaged; engine No. 43 suffering slight damage to the buffer beam, rail guards were broken off, brake hangers and rods bent and the feed pipes slightly damaged. The tender of No. 43 had intermediate buffers broken, left-side trailing buffer head broken off and buffer casing damaged. Brake Third carriage No. 837 had both ends slightly damaged, two buffers bent and damaged, roof cornice damaged and one bottom side split, whilst Composite carriage No. 376 had one buffer bent and one body casting broken. Out of fifty passengers on the train only six complained of slight injuries, although the guard of the train received more serious injuries.

Marindin noted the Hertford branch was a single line running for some considerable distance alongside the main line north of Hatfield station before terminating in a short dock line at the back of the north end of the Up platform at Hatfield. There was no regular running junction between the branch and the main line although there was a set of facing points about 50 yards outside the dock, through which goods trains and through passenger carriages were taken out onto the Up slow line. There was a disc signal at these points, but the only semaphore signals on the branch were an inner home signal, an outer home signal and distant signal. The first of these signals was mounted on a two-arm bracket post on the east side of the line, the right arm of which was the inner home signal for the Up slow line and the left-hand arm the Hertford branch inner home signal. The outer home was one of a group of four home signals upon a gantry, and the distant signal was the upper arm upon a double-armed post. All these signals were worked from Hatfield North or No. 2 signal box which was located on the east side of the line 269 yards north of the buffer stops in the Hertford dock line. It was equipped with 64 working levers working all signals and points on the Up lines north of Hatfield station.

The Hertford single line approached Hatfield on a curve of one mile radius and on a rising gradient of 1 in 200 to a point 100 yards south of No. 2 signal box whence it was level to the station. From the buffer stops in the Hertford dock platform the inspector noted the following distances:

To the outer end of the Up platform	66 yards
To the facing points leading from the branch to the Up slow line	110 yards
To the inner Up home signal	140 yards
To Hatfield No. 2 signal box	269 yards
To the outer Up home signal	406 yards
To the Up distant signal	1,401 yards

The first to give evidence was William Fairhurst, a permanent way inspector who reported he travelled in the front brake van on the 9.30am train from Hertford to Hatfield on the day in question. He did not notice what signal was 'off' as the train approached Hatfield but noticed that as the train was passing Hatfield North signal box it was running at too greater speed to stop in the Hertford branch platform, and he assumed it was going onto the slow road. He estimated speed at 20 to 25 mph and was looking forward but did not notice any signals either semaphore or disc. When about three yards from the points which turn the Hertford branch train onto the slow road he noticed the points were set for the Hertford branch platform road. He immediately realised the driver had made an error and raised the valve of the automatic brake in the brake van. There was no suction and he assumed the driver had already applied the brake. Speed was sensibly reduced between the points and the buffer stops but Fairhurst estimated the engine collided with the buffer stops at about 15 mph. To questioning he advised Marindin that he was holding on the hand brake wheel and was not hurt, save for slight straining of right arm and right leg. He reiterated he had not noticed any signal from the platform and considered there was nothing unusual or irregular in the way the train was worked from Hertford until Hatfield was reached. He was in the front brake van all the way from Hertford and the train stopped in the usual course at Hertingfordbury and Cole Green by the application of the vacuum brake from the engine. He concluded his evidence saying that he had not noticed the position of the vacuum gauge in the brake van, which was past the points when he opened the valve.

Passenger guard William Gaylard advised he had been in the employ of the GNR for near forty years, twenty-six years as a guard and fifteen years on the Hertford branch. He commenced duty on 30th March at 9.10am to first work the 9.30am train from Hertford to Hatfield and was due off duty at 7.45pm. The train comprised engine No. 43, tender, Third Class Carriage Brake, Composite, Third Class and Composite Brake. He rode in the rear brake van and was aware Inspector Fairhurst was riding in the leading brake. Before departure he checked with the driver that he had possession of the Train Staff and, noting he was a *fresh driver*', advised him to go around the sharp curves cautiously, especially at Digswell. He also advised there were no through coaches to London and therefore the train would terminate in the dock platform at Hatfield. The stops at Hertingfordbury and Cole Green were normal, the driver making the correct application of the vacuum brake on the engine. The curve at Digswell was negotiated *'very nicely'* but Gaylard admitted he did not notice the signals as the train approached Hatfield. Near Hatfield No. 2 signal box he thought the train was travelling too quickly and he opened the brake valve in his van. He had difficulty getting the strap off as it fitted tightly on the valve and he was of the opinion the train was near the goods shed when the brake was finally applied. To cross examination he advised Marindin he did not know what effect his action had on the speed of the train as the locomotive hit the buffer stops almost immediately and he was thrown down, stunned and remained unconscious for a short time. His right arm and shoulder were badly bruised and subsequent to the accident he was laid off work as he suffered continuing dizziness. He had no conversation with the driver after the accident but was adamant he was sober and fit for duty when the journey commenced. Gaylard estimated the speed of the train when passing Hatfield No. 2 signal box at between 15 and 20 mph. He was sure that at Hertford he explained quite clearly to the driver that the train would terminate in the dock platform at Hatfield. *'When there are London coaches on, the train stops outside the cross-over road points, and these carriages are detached. The usual speed at No. 2 box is, I should think, 4 or 5 mph.'* To further question, Gaylard concluded it was very unusual for passenger trains to go out onto the slow road as they were always stopped at the points. However, he could not advise as to the procedure for goods trains.

Driver Samuel Lunnis was next to give evidence and advised Marindin he had nearly thirty-two years' service, eighteen of those as a passed driver. He was stationed at King's Cross, taking on King's Cross and Hatfield workings which included regular turns on the Luton branch but not regularly to Hertford, it being nearly nine months since he discontinued taking turns on the Hertford branch. On the day in question he signed on duty at 2.00am after being off duty for twenty-four hours and scheduled to finish at 10.57am, He was booked to work the 2.10am King's Cross to Hatfield goods train but being Easter Monday the train was cancelled and worked his engine light to Hatfield. On arrival he was instructed to take the 6.05am goods train from Hatfield to Hertford in place of Driver Meakin, who had booked off sick. He was aware of this before leaving King's Cross as his booked working was to return from Hertford with the 9.30am passenger train due Hatfield at 9.51am. He reached Hertford with the goods train at 7.22am and carried out shunting and was ready on the Up train at Hertford platform at 9.05am, 25 minutes before scheduled departure time. He confirmed his engine was No. 43 with leading and driving wheels coupled and a 6-wheel tender, with the train consisting of four passenger vehicles, the engine and train fitted throughout with the automatic vacuum brake worked from the engine. At Hertford, guard Gaylard reported *'no London coaches – you can pull right up'* but to questioning he was sure Gaylard did not say *'up to the dock'*. By this he assumed they were to run out onto the Up slow line at Hatfield and draw well up to the platform. He was booked to work the 10.09am train from Hatfield to King's Cross, which started from the south end of the platform back road. He thought the four coaches from the Hertford train would be backed on the coaches standing at Hatfield and that he should take the entire train forward to King's Cross.

Stirling GNR 'F4' Class 0-4-2WT locomotives were regularly used on the Hertford branch for passenger and goods traffic. No. 116A, by this date on the duplicate list, stands at Hatfield on 3rd August 1901. In January 1902 it was rebuilt with a domed boiler and became Class 'F6' before withdrawal from service in September 1918.

LCGB/Ken Nunn

After leaving Hertford *'all went well until the train approached Hatfield'*. No. 2 box Up distant signal was 'off' and the outer home and inner home signals were also clear. He admitted to Marindin he made a mistake as to the latter signal and did not discover until it was too late to stop at the Hertford branch platform. *'I thought at first that this signal was for the slow or platform road'*. When working goods trains on the Hertford branch, *'which he did until nine months ago'* the train was usually turned into the slow or platform road, the disc signal being authority to use the crossover. He thought on this occasion the inner home signal gave similar authority. He again admitted his error and *'am most sorry for it'*. *'It is the first mistake I have made since I have been driving.'* To further question, Lunnis admitted he did not see Mr Vodden or Inspector Worman waving their arms at the north end of the Down platform to stop the train, although his fireman had seen them; he was looking straight ahead. He claimed he was perfectly sober and between leaving King's Cross at 2.10am and the time of the collision he had only drunk tea and one glass of mild ale at Hertford at about 9.15am. He stressed he knew the Hertford branch and the associated signals at Hatfield well but again admitted he had made an error. He had not worked a passenger train across the branch for some years although his fireman Thomas Cooper was well acquainted with the Hertford branch and the Hatfield Yard. Up until nine months ago he had worked the Hertford branch regularly for a period of twenty years. The signals for running into Hatfield were the same on the day of the accident as they were nine months previously. Again pressed, Lunnis stated there was nobody on the footplate except his fireman and himself. The locomotive was running engine first and he was riding on the right-hand side of the footplate. *'I do not think it is the invariable rule for goods trains coming off the Hertford branch on to the up slow line to be stopped dead at the inner home signal before the disc is turned for the train to come out.'* Until recently the points through which the train came out were bolted from the signal box, but worked from the ground. Lunnis stressed the brake was in good order and he passed No. 2 signal box at a speed of about 12 mph with steam shut off, having shut the regulator three-quarters of a mile out. He tried the brake at the signal box but then released it to let the train turnout onto the Up road. When close to the inner home signal he saw that the points were lying for the dock at the back of the Up platform and realised his mistake. The speed at that time was about 10 mph and the driver immediately applied the brake, reversed the engine and put on steam. The brake acted well but the wheels skidded. He thought that if the train had been longer and heavier it would have stopped quickly. As he had been in the habit of working 10- or 11-coach trains he would have been quite able to stop where he intended at the Up platform. To questioning he estimated the speed at which the engine struck the buffer stops was 4 or 5 mph. He remained on the engine as the leading wheels mounted and ran over the stops. He was not hurt neither was the fireman as there was not the slightest rebound after the first shock of the collision. His tea bottle had not shifted off the shelf. He iterated he had not sounded the engine whistle and when he applied the brake near the inner home signal, he had 20 inches of vacuum.

Next to give evidence was Thomas Cooper who stated he had been in the service of the GNR for twenty years, had been a fireman for ten of those years and had recently been passed out as a driver. He advised the inspecting officer he knew the Hertford branch and the layout at Hatfield yard *'very well'*. He had booked on duty to fire to Driver Lunnis on the morning of the 30th March and left Hertford with the 9.30am passenger train. At Hertford he heard the guard advise Lunnis that he was not to stop outside of Hatfield as there were no through coaches, and that he was to run straight up to the Hertford bay platform. He understood that this meant that the train was to run right into the dock, instead of stopping outside, as on other mornings, to detach the through London carriage. The engine and four carriages of the train were fitted throughout with the vacuum automatic brake, which was in good order. The train was worked properly until approaching Hatfield when he noted that all the Hertford dock signals were cleared for the train. In passing under the bridge north of No. 2 signal box he thought the train was travelling too quickly and called upon his mate to apply the brake. He was looking out of his own side of the cab and as the brake was not applied he thought Lunnis had not heard him. He shouted again to him to *'pull her back'* or we would go over the stops. The train was then nearing the north end of the platform when Lunnis finally applied the vacuum brake and reversed the engine. Unfortunately there was insufficient room to stop and the engine struck the buffer stops at an estimated speed of 5 or 6 mph. He was holding on and was not knocked down as a result of the collision. To cross-examining Cooper stated he could not account for Driver Lunnis mistaking the signal and he saw the hand signal from the Down platform to stop. He spoke twice to Lunnis after passing under the bridge, the first to advise *'steady mate'* and when he did not answer he shouted in stronger language to reverse and give her steam or we should be over the stops. He then gave a full brake application and reversed the engine but it was too late. He put the brake on a little when I first spoke to him but only enough to get the blocks in touch with the wheel. I could not have put the brake on myself without pushing Lunnis away as he had his hand on the brake lever. He did not think the speed when passing Hatfield North signal box exceeded 10 to 12 mph. It was before the train reached the inner home signal that he called the driver. It was when they were near to No. 2 signal box that he advised the driver to reverse and he did so and applied the brake. As the brake took hold, Cooper opened the sand boxes but thought he must have shut them again when holding on for there was no trace of sand on the rails when he went back to look after the collision. He reiterated he saw the hand signal from the Down platform after they had done all they could to stop the train. He estimated speed when the locomotive hit the buffers stops at about 6 mph. The usual speed of a train when running into the dock was 4 mph at Hatfield No. 2 signal box. Cooper could not remember a case when a passenger train from Hertford was turned onto the Up slow line. He had been working with Driver Meakin on the branch for about two years. On 30th March he had come on duty at 2.20am after having been off duty for twenty hours.

William Chapman next gave evidence stating that he came on duty on the 30th March at 6.00am for eight hours in Hatfield No. 2 signal box. It was a clear dry morning and the 9.30am train from Hertford passed his box at 9.51am, which was its arrival time in the platform. The Hertford branch signals were cleared for the train and he estimated the speed at between 12 and 14 mph *'much the same as normal'*. He watched the passage of the train but became alarmed when the speed was not reduced when it passed the inner home signal. There was no whistling from the engine. To questioning he said it was very unusual for passenger trains from the Hertford branch to go out onto the Up slow line. *'It does not happen more than once or twice a year. Goods trains go out regularly.'* He added that trains going out to the Up slow line were stopped before the points, for after the home signal was put back to danger the operation required the pulling of six levers. He concluded his evidence advising that when there were through carriages for King's Cross on the branch trains, the service was stopped outside the points to allow the carriages to be detached and then taken out by horse to be attached to the rear of the Up main-line train.

George Worman advised he was the District Traffic Inspector stationed at Hatfield. On 30th March he was standing on the Down side of the line opposite Hatfield No. 3 signal box when the Hertford train was running into the station. He first noticed it passing No. 2 signal box and thought it was travelling too fast at a speed of about 20 to 25 mph. He waved his arms to gain the driver's attention but to no avail. He thought the brake was not applied before the train reached the inner home signal when the speed was reduced to 15 mph. Worman considered the speed was *'not much less'* when the engine collided with the buffer stops. Station Master Vodden was standing with Worman and also waved to the driver. They hurried to the Up platform and arrived just as the many passengers were alighting from the train but none reported any serious injury. The train had not telescoped in any way but the buffer stops were knocked down.

Last to be called to give evidence was Station Master Robert Vodden, who agreed with Inspector Worman's evidence. He added there were between fifty and sixty passengers on the train but only two complained of injury. All the passengers continued their journey on the forwarding connecting service. To questioning Vodden admitted to knowing Driver Lunnis who had told him he thought the train was to go out on the Up slow line. He appeared sober and was a *'very steady man'* who knew *'Hatfield well'*.

After hearing all the evidence Maridin concluded that the collision with the buffer stops was due to the mistake by Samuel Lunnis, the driver of the 9.30am train from Hertford to Hatfield, who had at the time been on duty for 7¾ hours. He was not a regular driver on the branch, although he had frequently driven goods trains but not passenger trains, and had good knowledge of the signals at Hatfield. He misunderstood the guard of the train who advised him at Hertford that as there were no through carriages for London he was to draw the train well up into the dock platform instead of stopping outside as usual to detach the through carriages. Lunnis was under the mistaken impression that his train was to go out on the Up slow line and *'draw well up'* into the Up platform.

Marindin was of the opinion it was *'a most unaccountable mistake for an old and experienced driver to make'* for the signals were off for his train to run into the dock platform and were plain and simple as there was no semaphore signal at all for running out onto the main line. From the evidence, passenger trains only ever ran to the Up platform perhaps *'once or twice'* in a month. Moreover, all trains, whether goods or passenger, before going out to the Up slow line were brought to a stand before the points were set and the disc signal cleared for the movement to take place. The points could not be moved until the inner home signal had been placed back to danger.

There was considerable discrepancy as to the speed of the train, for while the driver, fireman and signalman estimated the speed when passing Hatfield No. 2 signal box, 269 yards from the buffer stops, at 10 to 14 mph, the guard estimated 15 to 20 mph and the station master and two traffic inspectors as 20 to 25 mph. If it was anything like as high as the last estimate, the guard who was riding in the rear brake van and Inspector Fairhurst riding in the front brake van ought to have taken action before they did – checking the speed of the train by the application of the continuous brake. The brake was not applied until the driver, when near the inner home signal or within 150 yards of the buffer stops, realised his mistake but was unable to stop resulting in his engine striking the buffer stops at a speed probably of 8 to 10 mph.

Marindin was of the opinion that Driver Lunnis was a man of excellent character and this was the first occasion in which he had been found responsible for an accident in 32 years' service. The fireman who worked regularly on the Hertford branch expressed his concern as to the speed of the train when passing the signal box and cautioned the driver once when near the box and more emphatically further on when it was too late to do anything. It would have been wiser if, when he found the speed at the box, according to his

An early view of Cole Green station facing east and before the installation of the crossing loop. Wagons are stabled in the goods yard on the Down side of the line and the stop signals for each direction of travel mounted on the same post are to the right.
National Railway Museum

statement, was three times as high than the usual speed, he had taken steps to apply the continuous brake seeing that the driver evidently misunderstood the position.

Clause 5 of the Great Northern Railway Act 1891 (54 Vic cap xix), which received the Royal Assent on 11th May 1891, amongst other new works authorised the widening of the main line between Hatfield and Digswell. The formation work wholly in Hertfordshire commenced in the Parish of Hatfield by a junction with the main line about 143 yards south of the bridge carrying the public road leading from Hatfield to Welwyn over the main line and terminated in the Parish of Digswell by a junction with the main lines 103 yards south of the southernmost end of the Digswell or Welwyn Viaduct. The company was not permitted to use the additional lines until they had constructed and opened to the public a bridge or subway to take public road No. 28 over or under the widened railway. The Act stipulated completion within a period of five years. Clause 26 of the same Act sanctioned the purchase of additional land adjoining the southern boundary of the Hertford branch at Cole Green, in the Parish of Hertingfordbury. The area to be taken was bounded on the west by the public road linking Cole Green to Letty Green.

As both passenger and goods traffic continued to expand on the branch the long single line section between Hatfield and Hertford increasingly proved an operational inconvenience. Delays were frequent and the often slow-moving goods trains fouled up the timetable schedule of passenger trains so that connections were missed at Hatfield. To obviate the problem and negate the ever-rising number of complaints the GNR authorities decided to install a crossing loop at Cole Green. The work, which included the provision of an additional platform with small waiting shelter, and priced at £1,826, had been authorised on 7th November 1890. However, considerable negotiations had taken place between the Cowper Estate and the GNR as to the facilities. As early as 25th April 1890, in response to earlier correspondence, the GNR Surveyor wrote that *'our engineer informs me he would be not unwilling to construct a covering on both platforms for a length of about 75 feet, but that he would require a little more land to do this'*. Evidently Lord Cowper was willing to release the land but with conditions, for on 18th December 1890 Robert Johnson, the GNR Engineer, responded *'I will endeavour to carry out Lord Cowper's wishes and provide covering for the stairs and platforms, so as to enable his Lordship to reach the trains under cover'*. All was not well, for two days later Johnson replied he was *'sorry to find our suggested subway does not meet with Lord Cowper's approval'*. He offered a new scheme for the station with a view *'to carrying out his Lordship's suggestion for forming a carriage way on the Letty Green side of the railway'*. A request for a ticket office on the south side was considered doubtful; *'I will see Mr Cockshott* [General Manager] *but I do not think he would like a ticket office to be on that side of the line.'*

Progress was made on the permanent way during the winter months but little work on the platforms and other amenities, and on 11th April 1891 tracings were made available showing the proposed alterations and additions to buildings, including a small tracing showing the 2 rood 25 perches of additional land required. *'In preparing these plans we have endeavoured to meet your suggestions, so that his Lordship may drive up to the booking office, and be able to enter the train under cover.'* Johnson advised that, *'tenders had*

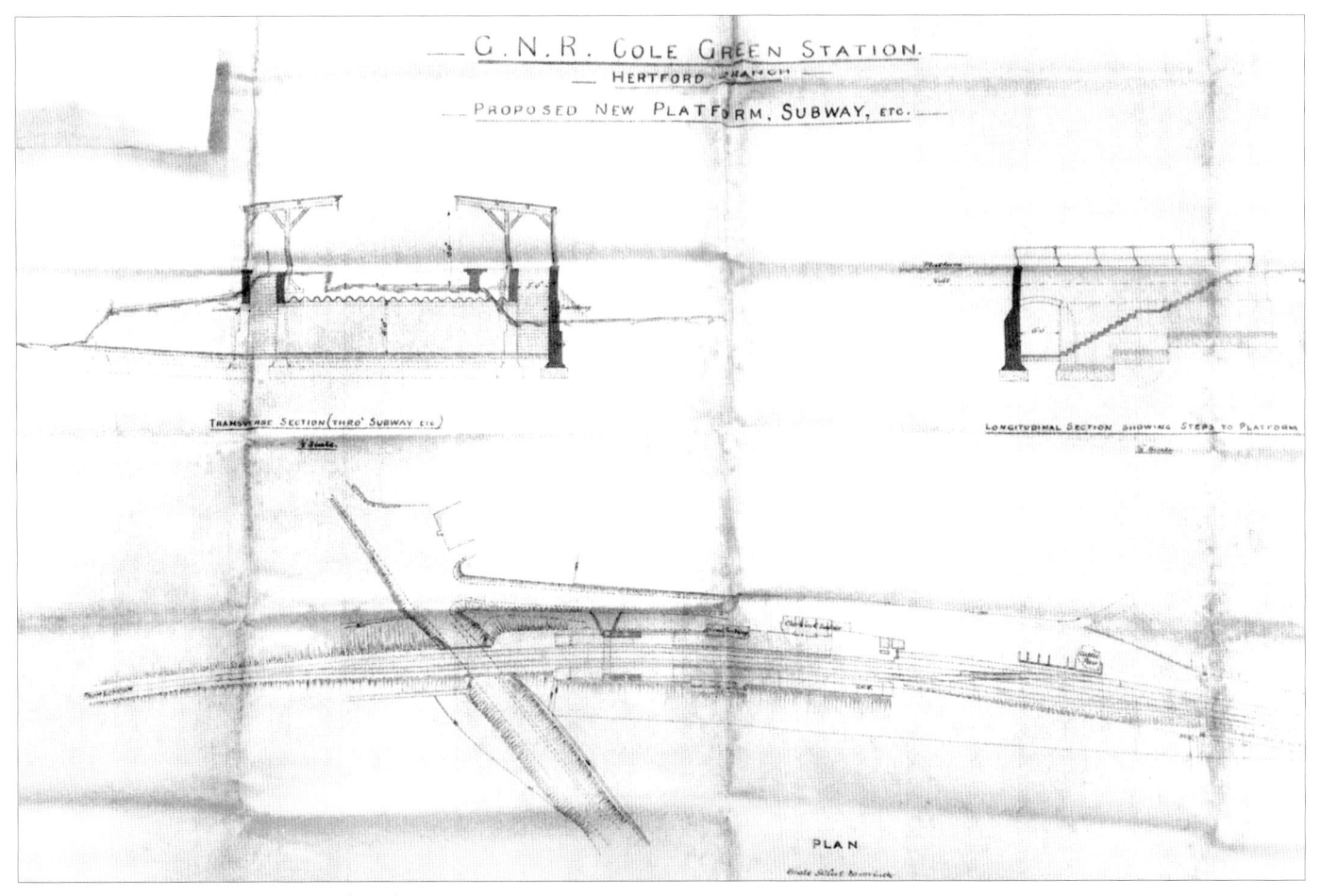

Proposed new platform subway at Cole Green 1891.

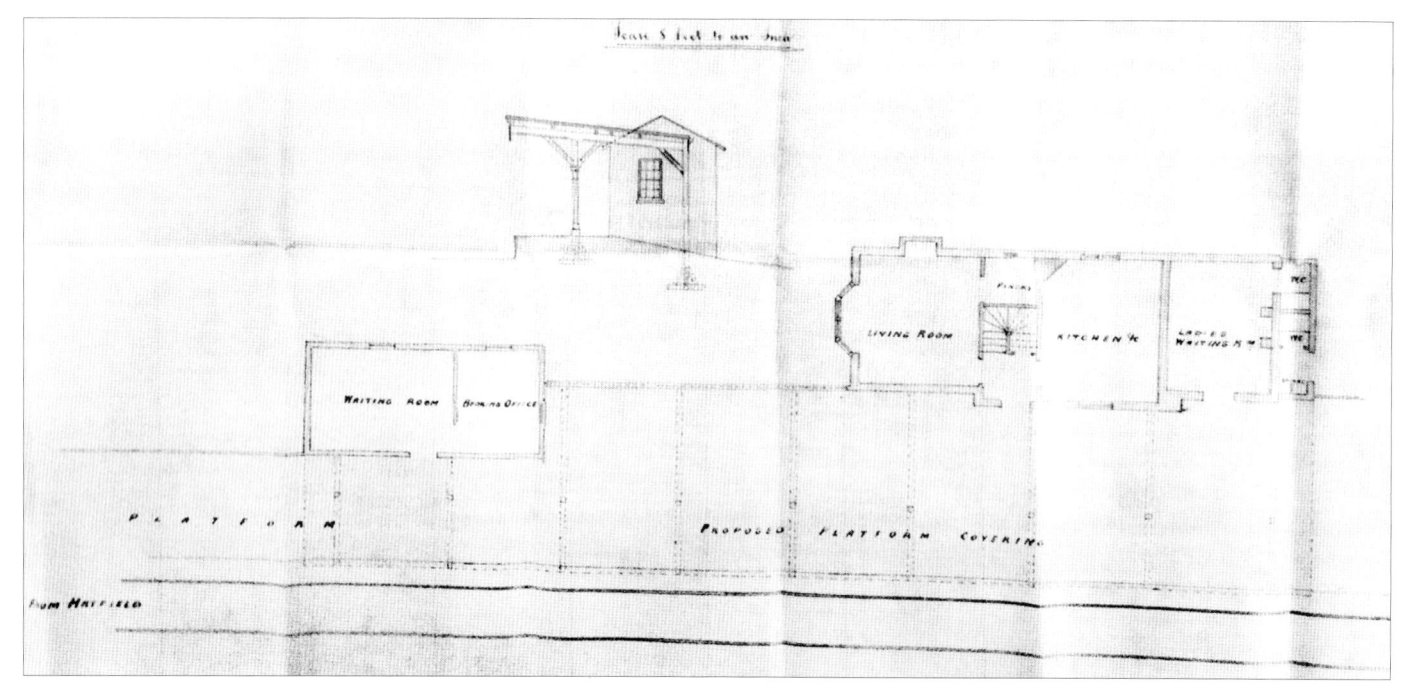

ABOVE: Proposed Up platform, Cole Green, 1891.

LEFT: Underline bridge No. 2 at 24 miles 01¾ chains from King's Cross, immediately west of Cole Green station, was widened in 1891 to accommodate the new crossing loop. This view under the arch looking toward Cole Green carried the lane to Letty Green south of the railway. *D. Dent collection*

been invited and subject to approval they would be sent away to the contractor'.

The situation was not improved when the Down side buildings at Cole Green station were almost totally destroyed by fire on the evening of 26th May 1891. Despite the presence of contractors attending to station improvements a few minutes before 7.00pm station staff noticed smoke coming from the timber section at the east end of the structure used for the storage of paraffin and oil lamps. As soon as the door was opened the resultant draught of air caused the flames to engulf the entire room. The building was connected to the First Class waiting room and the station master's house by another timber building used as an outhouse and it became imperative to contain the fire and stop it spreading. Fortunately some workmen employed by Lord Cowper were on the station and they together with a gang of men from the adjoining brickyard owned by Mr Digby demolished the lean-to building and restricted the fire to the lamp room. In the ensuing excitement a message was sent to Hertford summoning the fire brigade but when the local policeman PC Compton arrived on the scene he quickly realised the flames in the gutted building were subsiding with no further danger of spreading. As the main structure was no longer in danger he instructed a telegraph message be sent to stop the fire brigade. As a result of the inferno the whole stock of signal, platform and waiting room oil lamps were destroyed and replacements had to be obtained from Hatfield. At a subsequent BOT enquiry the inspecting officer stipulated the new lamp room be constructed of brick. The origin of the fire was unknown but the station master in giving evidence stated that at the time thirty gallons of paraffin were stored in the room together with twelve oil lamps. The porter preparing the lamps for the evening had ignited the wicks but left the shed unattended on attending to a train. It was on his return that he noticed the smoke.

By early June, progress on the new facilities were reaching crisis point for on 6th of the month Robert Johnson wrote from King's Cross, *'Mr Cockshott is very anxious to make certain alterations in his timetables for 1st July so as to secure the passing of passenger and freight trains at Cole Green station, and he has requested me to have the new platform ready by the close of the present month'*. He sought urgent help from the estate by arranging for the tenant of the land to release the property so the works may proceed *'without delay'*. Bargaining continued, for on 16th June Johnson acknowledged the fact that:

Lord Cowper is willing to give 1 rood 15 perches of land for the enlargement of the goods yard on the north side of the line in addition to the 2 roods 25 perches on the south side. Next Michaelmas will be a favourable time for taking possession of the land on the north side of the railway [for the goods yard].

The engineer concluded *'we will do all in our power to meet your requirements in carrying out the alterations at Cole Green station'*. The crossing loop, platform and associated signalling were completed and opened for traffic on 27th June 1891.

As part of line improvements between Hatfield and Digswell, two new signal boxes were installed near the 20th milepost from King's Cross to provide closer block sections. Twentieth Mile Up signal box, controlling the Up main line, Hertford single line and future Up slow line, was opened on 29th June 1891, whilst Twentieth Mile Down signal box controlling the Down main line, future Down slow line and Dunstable single line was opened three days earlier on 26th June 1891. Later in the year Second Class fares and accommodation on branch services were withdrawn by the GNR after 31st October 1891.

A bizarre accident occurred on 27th November 1891 when Charles Warren, the 38-year-old driver of the 11.38am Hatfield to Hertford train met his death near Cole Green. Fireman John Gray of Hatfield depot was tidying up on his side of the footplate after firing the locomotive, when he noticed his colleague was missing. Gray quickly applied the brakes and brought the train to a stand before carrying out protection of the line. The guard after protecting the rear of the train walked back along the line and discovered the body of the unfortunate driver lying beside the track with his neck broken. After covering the corpse and returning to the train the guard and fireman took the train on the Cole Green to report the incident and to allow the 11.40am Hertford to Hatfield train to pass. The station master at Hatfield was advised of the matter and after conferring with local staff, Driver J. Constable in charge of the Up service was requested to stop his train and take the body through to Hatfield.

At the coroner's inquest on Monday 30th November the first witness to be called was fireman John Gray who reported the train had left on time at 11.38am from Hatfield and proceeded as far as Hatfield Hyde crossing before he noticed the driver was missing. He was standing on the left side of the locomotive looking out. The engine was running tender first and when he looked round he missed Warren. He went to the driver's side of the cab and applied the brake, the train coming to a stand near the sandpit siding. The guard came and asked the reason for stopping and after noting the driver was missing went back along the line with another man before returning to the train to report they had found the body of the driver. Gray then took the train on to Cole Green where the 11.40am train from Hertford was waiting. He then exchanged footplates and returned on this train to pick up the body of the deceased, which was lying 150 feet on the Hatfield side of the gatehouse. Gray reported there was a slight curve at that spot and he last noticed the driver about thirty seconds before they reached it; he did not notice the engine give an extra lurch and it was the practise to lean over the side of the engine to look out, but there were spectacle glasses in the cab for their use. When leaning out it was the usual stance to hold on to the brake wheel and the lever wheel. There was nothing wrong on the reversing wheel on the driver's side of the cab. Gray explained he examined the engine and found everything *'quite right'*. Nothing had given way that Warren had stood upon, the footplate was not greasy and the weather was fine. Questioned as to the cause of the accident the fireman thought the driver had slipped off the footplate or over-balanced; the speed on the train at the time of the accident was 40 mph. To further questioning Gray was of the opinion Warren was in his usual health.

John Lane, the guard, was the next witness and reported he did not see Warren fall and so when the train stopped he went to ask the fireman the reason. He then went back along the line with Frederick Cross, a passenger on the train, and they found the body about a hundred yards on the Hatfield side of the level crossing. The body lay about 300 yards from the train, on the end of the sleepers clear of the rails with the face doubled up under the body. Lane thought Warren's neck was broken. Cross helped him lift the body on one side of the line and remained there until he went on with the train to Cole Green. Frederick John Cross then advised the court that he was employed as clerk of the works at the new station being built at Cole Green and was a passenger on the train. When the train stopped the guard asked him to go back with him to examine the line. He examined the line and found nothing that would have caused the train to jerk. He remained with the body until the Up train arrived to convey the deceased to Hatfield where it was handed over to the station authorities.

Doctor Lovell Drage stated he was called about 1.00pm on Friday and found the body on a stretcher in the waiting room at Hatfield station. Warren was dead, his neck being sufficiently broken to cause instantaneous death. The doctor stated the deceased was a heavy man but he had never heard of him complaining of heart disease or fits. George Gibson, locomotive superintendent at Hatfield said he inspected the engine on the day of the accident but found nothing wrong. The wheel, which the deceased would hold on to did not move sideways. Warren was an experienced driver and he could not account for the accident. To questioning, Gibson stated the driver would have been standing on boards and not on iron; the boards had no oil on them but were covered with coal dust. *'Drivers need not hang over the side of the engine very far'* and the only way he could account for the accident was that he overbalanced. The fireman on being recalled said the deceased was holding on with his left hand on the side panel and the right hand on the tank. They were both looking out for the crossing gates.

The coroner said he was very sorry indeed as only the week before he had complimented Warren in the way he acted at a fellow workman's death and he was one of the best men in the ambulance class. The jury recorded a unanimous verdict of *'accidental death'*. The funeral the following Wednesday was attended by the family and fifty railwaymen.

For some years the siding on the Up or south side of the main single line, known as Haggar's siding, near Hertingfordbury was out of use, although the points and rails remained in position. In the autumn of 1891 the owner of Horn's Mill tannery applied to the GNR for a siding to serve his premises. On investigating the engineer advised the reinstatement of the former Haggar's siding and the provision of an extension to Horn's Mill tannery would suit the purpose. The work was duly authorised on 4th December 1891 at a cost of £250 after the mill owner agreed to pay interest on the outlay once work was completed.

By now the GNR authorities were keen to provide siding accommodation wherever possible to enhance freight traffic. Early in the new year Mr Peart requested the provision of a siding on the east side of the Hertford branch where it paralleled the main line near Twentieth Mile signal box to facilitate the unloading of manure and loading and forwarding of agricultural products. After due consideration the Way and Works Committee with the agreement of their Traffic counterparts sanctioned the expenditure of £200 on the provision of the siding, with Peart paying interest on the outlay once the connection was installed.

The short Hertford branch bay platform located at the north end of the Up main-line platform at Hatfield had for long been the subject of complaints. Intending passengers, unless resorting to waiting in the main station buildings, were forced to stand on a draughty open platform exposed to the elements. Similarly, staff loading or unloading parcels and mails were critical of the lack of cover. The GNR authorities finally relented and in order to appease the situation on 4th March 1892 sanctioned the provision of a canopy over the branch platform at an estimated cost of £200.

In the closing months of 1891, Henry Wood gave up the tenancy of Holwell Hyde Farm and the stock and machinery was offered for sale. The farm, which was part of the Holwell Estate, was acquired by Earl Cowper of Panshanger and he subsequently entered into a new 7-year agreement for the use of the siding at Birchall on 11th July 1892, the annual rental being fixed at £32 paid in equal half-yearly instalments. Earl Cowper actually assumed responsibility on 25th March and one clause of the agreement stated:

> *The GNR Company shall in consideration of the punctual payment of such rent at the times, and in the manner aforesaid, maintain and keep in good order and repair the said siding and shall supply and furnish at their own expense the pointsmen and other servants necessary for the use of such siding during such period hereafter as the said Earl Cowper, or his licensees shall use and send traffic over the said siding.*

Prior to the signing of the agreement the GNR civil engineer's department carried out repairs including the supply of sleepers, keys, trenails and rails at a cost of £18.

Despite the earlier improvements to the track layout north of Hatfield, with independent parallel single lines for the Dunstable and Hertford branches, the GNR main-line services were still incurring an increasing number of delays because of the bottleneck caused by the necessity to use the Up and Down main lines for all traffic. After several years of frustration, plans were drawn up for widening of the line and on 4th November 1892 authority was given for the provision of additional goods lines at various places between Hatfield and St. Neots at a cost of £82,930. Included within this scheme were the two miles between Hatfield and Twentieth Mile signal box costed at £23,363 and the 1 mile 40 chains thence to the proposed Digswell signal box, to be located south of Welwyn Viaduct, priced at £12,000, both authorised by the GNR 1891 Act.

On the Hertford branch the GNR tidied up some of the outstanding interlocking and signalling works when tenders were invited for the provision of a small signal box to control the signals, gates and points at Dicker Mill Lane crossing, east of Cowbridge station, Hertford. Of the four replies, McKenzie & Holland were awarded the contract on 30th January 1894 tendering at £465 12s 6d.

As predicted, the provision of the various private sidings along the Hertford branch did much to engender additional freight traffic. Farmers and growers regularly used the railway for the conveyance of livestock to local markets and produce to markets in London and provincial centres. Despite the improvements, the facilities at Cole Green were considered far from adequate in the last decade of the nineteenth century. To improve the position the Goods Manager requested additional facilities in the yard and on 5th April 1895 authority was given for the siding to be extended, together with a new loading wharf and carriage dock at a combined cost of £500.

Despite the passing of the 1891 Act, work on the widening of the main line progressed slowly and the GNR directors only sought tenders for the widening on the Up side of the railway between Digswell and Hatfield on 18th February 1895, the contract being subsequently awarded to Baldrey & Yerburgh. To assist with the contract a new signal box had been opened at Digswell south of Welwyn Viaduct on 5th April 1894. During the work the contractors employed their own locomotives to assist with construction and on 14th May 1897 *The Engineer* reported that on completion of the scheme A.T. & E.A. Crow were auctioning on behalf of Baldry & Yerburgh a large amount of plant and two locomotives: a Manning, Wardle 4-wheel tank locomotive with 10-inch cylinders and a 6-wheel tank locomotive with 13-inch cylinders.

The level crossing at Welwyn Junction was also an obstacle in the way of the intended widening of the main line between Hatfield and Digswell, and in 1895 the company obtained the necessary powers for their replacement. The Great Northern Railway Act of 1895 (58 Vic cap xxvi) passed on 30th May 1895 authorised the diversion of the public road crossing the railway on the level about 800 yards north of the 20 mile post from London, such diversion to commence in the said road about 70 yards west of the level crossing and to terminate in the said road about 180 yards east of the level crossing. The company was also required to construct a diversion of the road leading from Stanborough to Hertford, commencing about 50 yards west of the bridge carrying the road across the railway and terminating in the proposed diversion of the road crossing the railway on the level at a point about 40 yards west of the railway opposite a point about 120 yards south of the level crossing. Lastly, the GNR was given powers to construct a new road commencing from a junction with the Stanborough to Hertford road at a point about 40 yards east of the bridge and terminating in the proposed diversion of the road crossing the railway on the level at a point 65 yards east of the railway opposite a point about 120 yards south of the level crossing. Once the road diversions and new road were completed and open to the public the company was authorised to abolish the level crossing and extinguish all rights of way.

Along the line at Hertford the local corporation approached the company early in 1896 seeking approval for a footpath alongside the railway linking North Road and Port Vale. After negotiations the corporation agreed to fund the construction with the GNR providing the land free of charge. At the same time repairs were made to a culvert adjacent to the bridge spanning the River Beane at a cost of £15, and the footpath and bridgework was completed in November of the same year.

A view under the Up platform canopy and the station building and offices at Hatfield, with almost every available space on the walls occupied by railway posters and advertisements.
Author's collection

On 10th October 1896 Lieutenant G.W. Addison inspected the widening of the railway from the north end of Hatfield station to Twentieth Mile signal box. He found that an additional line of rails had been provided for a distance of 2 miles 6½ chains; the new line was to be used for Luton branch traffic, the old Luton line from Hatfield to Twentieth Mile becoming the Down goods line. The permanent way was formed of steel rails weighing 85 lbs per yard and the ballast was of hard burnt clay and pit ballast laid to a depth of 12 inches under the sleepers. The steepest gradient on the line was 1 in 200 and the sharpest curve of 12 chains radius for a distance of 5 chains. The greatest height and depth of embankments and cuttings were 34 feet and 32 feet respectively. The widening work comprised four overbridges with brick arches and brick abutments, the longest skew span being 31 feet 6 inches; each of the bridges had three openings; an additional opening had also been provided but Addison was of the opinion *'a little underpinning was all that was necessary'*. There was one overbridge with wrought iron superstructure on brick abutments and cast iron columns, which remained unaltered together with two underbridges, each with five openings having segmental brick arches on brick abutments which had been added to as necessary. There were also two 3-foot brick culverts with inverts under the line, which had been lengthened. The inspector commented that the works *'appear to be of solid construction and are standing well'*. A new signal box known as Twentieth Mile Down Box was located where the junction of the new line joined the old Luton line, together with a trailing connection on the Down main line forming the present exit from the Down goods line. A short distance north of the signal box were points on the Luton branch facing to Down trains which led to a contractor's siding, the connection being worked by a single lever locked and unlocked by a key on the single line Train Staff. The new signal box contained a 25-lever frame with 18 working and 7 spare levers, which were correctly interlocked. Addison noted a crossover road between the Up and Down main lines worked from Twentieth Mile Down signal box but controlled from a lever in Twentieth Mile Up signal box; this arrangement provided for the release of certain levers and the locking of others when the new signal box was not in use. Addison then inspected the new Up side goods line and associated Twentieth Mile Up signal box which contained a 24-lever frame with 16 working and 8 spare levers. At Hatfield new locking frames had been installed in No. 2 and No. 3 signal boxes but testing could not be conducted when full traffic was so busy. Addison therefore postponed the inspection until a future date, possible a Sunday, when traffic flows were lighter. No's 2 and 3 signal boxes were already in use and if future requirements specified alterations the GNR authorities promised immediate attention as necessary. As a parting comment, the inspector noted the old narrow platform between the Up main and Up slow line at the station had been abolished.

Lieutenant Colonel H.A. Yorke subsequently conducted the official BOT inspection of alterations to Hatfield No. 2 and Hatfield No. 3 signal boxes on 17th November 1896. He explained it had not been possible to carry out the inspection at the same time as his examination of the doubling of the line from Hatfield to the Twentieth Mile but he found that No. 3 signal box was an old structure which had been enlarged and equipped with a new locking frame containing 80 levers with 70 working and 10 spare levers. The interlocking was satisfactory. No. 2 signal box was also an old structure with a new frame containing 85 levers with 77 working and 8 spare levers. The interlocking was correct but No. 77 Up goods signal was to be removed as it appeared to be badly placed to the left of the outside of the three parallel Up lines. Yorke opined *'a signal so placed can only be regarded applying to the road alongside of which it is placed viz the Hertford branch line. Instead of this it is intended to apply to the up goods line which is the central line of the three.'* There was further objection to this signal inasmuch that it was 629 yards from the signal box and was intended to cover shunting operations on the Up goods line. The Lieutenant Colonel stressed:

The goods line is a running line and not a shunting neck and it appears to me undesirable that shunting operations should be permitted upon it at such a great distance from the signal box and on a line which is between two passengers lines, one of which is the up fast to London on which all expresses run. If during shunting operations any wagon was derailed it would foul one or other of the passenger lines and it would take some minutes for the signalman to become aware of the fact a disaster might ensue if a passenger train was approaching. For this reason I am unable to agree to this signal being left in its present position.

Subject to its removal Yorke sanctioned the signalling at the north end of Hatfield station.

Early in the spring of 1897 H. Brazier of Hertford approached the GNR asking for a high loading dock to be built at Hertford to facilitate the loading of gravel. Once Brazier agreed to pay rental for the additional facility the Way and Works Committee authorised construction on 4th June 1897 at an estimated cost of £258; the work being completed in November.

After years of projected and initially fruitless negotiations for a line linking the GNR Enfield branch to the Hatfield to Hertford branch, plans were resurrected for a line running north from the Enfield terminus passing by way of Cuffley and Hertford to Stevenage. The General Manager, Henry Oakley, reported to his directors at a meeting at King's Cross on 1st October 1897 the inclusion of the scheme in a bill for the next session of Parliament, the re-depositing of plans for the railway linking Enfield to Knebworth or somewhere near Stevenage (*sic*) to eliminate the costly widening of tunnels and viaducts on the main line. The estimated cost of the new line was £1,250,000 and the widening of existing tunnels and viaducts £800,000. The new line would however provide an alternative route for trains in the events of blockage of the main line and tap an area of the Home Counties devoid of railway transport.

The loop line from Enfield to Stevenage was authorised by the Great Northern Railway Act 1898 (61 and 62 Vic cap clxv) which received the Royal Assent on 25th July 1898. Clause 5 of the statute sanctioned the construction of Railway No. 1, 10 miles 7 furlongs 0.20 chains in length commencing in the Parish of Enfield in the County of Middlesex by a junction with the Enfield branch of the company at a point about 1,015 yards measured along the branch from the termination and terminating in the Parish of St. Andrew, Hertford in the County of Hertford at a point about ten yards west of the western boundary of the GNR Hertford branch measured along the boundary from a point about 193 yards north of the Hertingfordbury Road. Railway No. 2, 8 miles 0 furlongs 0.70 chains in length commenced at the termination of intended Railway No. 1 and terminated in the Parish of Knebworth in a field adjoining the western side of the Great North Road near the 29 mile post from London. Railways No's 3 and 4 authorised connections with the main line. Of specific concern to the Hatfield

GNR '120' Class later 'G2' Class 0-4-4T 'Back Tank' of the 241 series No. 244 stands at Hatfield during shunting operations on 13th September 1902. The engine was subsequently withdrawn from traffic in April 1913. *LCGB/Ken Nunn*

GNR steam railmotor No. 5 at Hertford North after working a shuttle from Hitchin. Although intended for use on the Hatfield to Hertford and Hatfield to St. Albans branches, the vehicles were never used as such and served on lightly-used branches in East Lincolnshire and North London. No 5, built by Kitson of Leeds, entered traffic in December 1905. *Author's collection*

Hall and Hatfield Hyde, and these were opened for traffic on 1st January 1905. Unfortunately the trials with the petrol railcar were considerd unsuccessful and the halts with ground-level platforms were totally unsuited for normal steam hauled rolling stock. The GNR authorities thus decided to abandon the experiment and subsequently closed Attimore Hall and Hatfield Hyde halts on and from 1st July 1905. The public goods siding at Attimore Hall was unaffected by the closure.

On 22nd July 1905, Lieutenant Colonel E. Druitt, ignorant of the fact that closure had taken place, belatedly conducted the official inspection of the Hertford branch in connection with the introduction of the petrol railcar services. An initial examination of Attimore Hall and Hatfield Hyde halts revealed they were constructed of timber 46 feet in length, 8 feet wide and built to a height of 11 inches above rail level. This was considered adequate for the railcar traffic, as passengers would use the steps attached to the vehicle to join and alight from the train. Druitt noted that each halt was located on the Down side of the single-track railway beside gated level crossings which were hand operated by the resident gate keepers who resided in the adjacent level crossing cottages. The inspector noted that there was no indication available to warn the public of the approach of a train except by the published timetable and was critical of the lack of signals at Hatfield Hyde crossing where there was restricted view in each direction. Although agreeing to the existing method of working, Druitt recommended that in the event of an increase in general traffic or frequency of rail motor traffic, signals were to be provided to protect the crossings operated by the crossing keepers, who would be warned of approaching trains by the provision of an indicator. For the inspection Druitt travelled on and at the same time inspected the rail motor. He concluded his report by noting that the vehicle was driven by petrol engine with the 30 gallons of fuel being carried in two reservoirs under the floor protected by a metal lining. The Dick, Kerr & Company representative assured the inspector that there was no possibility of the petrol in the reservoir accidentally igniting. The car seated thirty-two passengers, all one class, and could travel at 30 mph. It was also noted that the hand brake, when worked, applied the brake blocks on both pairs of wheels and was therefore powerful enough to stop the car moving.

The danger of young children straying onto railway land was fully realised on Wednesday 27th December 1905 when a six-year-old Hertford boy was killed in Dicker Mill yard. Giving evidence at the inquest, John Deamer, a shunter employed by Manson & Company, coal merchants, explained he was shunting wagons with a shunt horse and was unaware of the incident until he found the boy's body after a wagon had hit the child. A verdict of accidental death was recorded.

At about 9.45pm on the evening of 2nd June 1906 the Cole Green station master, relaxing in the station house, was surprised to hear the locomotive of an approaching train whistling continuously and the bells of the telegraphic instruments in the signal box ringing incessantly. On proceeding to the signal box he was astonished to find 23-year-old signalman George Frederick Chevins was missing and the box was empty. The second signalman, who was off duty and lived adjacent to the station, was sent for and signalled the delayed train on its journey. In the meantime the station master advised Police Constable Prior of the matter and a diligent search was made for Chevins but no trace could be found. At a later hour a message was received from Welwyn station on the main line to say that Chevins had been there but was acting strangely. Whilst in Welwyn signal box Chevins had wired through to Twentieth Mile signal box stating that he was Signalman Chevins of Cole Green and had then bolted. A few minutes later he appeared at Digswell signal box, the other side of Welwyn viaduct and the Digswell signalman wired to Cole Green. On receiving the message the station master gave instructions that the errant Chevins was to be detained and he and PC Prior borrowed a horse and trap and drove over to Digswell where they found Chevins in such a violent state that it took several men to hold him. Subsequently he was brought in the trap towards Hertford for medical attention but when at Poplar's Green he jumped out of the vehicle and said he was going to Cole Green. He was then very violent and could not be dissuaded from his purpose, so that PC Gooch and PC Prior forcibly took him to his lodgings at Cole Green. During the night Police Superintendent Foster and Doctor H.S.W. Hall arrived at the scene and Chevins – reported as *'a temperate and steady young man'* – still struggling, was eventually moved to Hertford Infirmary and kept under observation. Later in the week he was well enough to be taken into care by his family.

Chevins, was a native of Lincoln where his father and brother were employed by the GNR.

Royalty again travelled on the Hertford branch on Monday 23rd July 1906 when the Prince and Princess of Wales accompanied by the Lord Mayor of London and other dignitaries visited the town to open the new buildings at Christ's Hospital School. Although the girls' school was almost within sight of the GER station the Prince and his party travelled by special train from King's Cross to Cowbridge station where they arrived at 12.42pm. Their Royal Highnesses were presented with an address at the GNR station by the mayor and corporation, and after the ceremony and lunch the party returned to London by special train departing Hertford at 3.15pm.

As the ballast pits owned by Josiah Smart at Hertford became exhausted, so the workings were transferred to another area on the same site. By September 1906 the existing siding was found to be totally inconvenient for the loading of materials into wagons. Alterations were sanctioned on 5th October at a cost of £105.

The GNR and GER authorities were constantly seeking economies on operating and administration functions, and both Hertford branches were regularly investigated. One cause for concern was the high costs of providing a service to the community at Hertford with two separate terminals located less than half a mile apart. After various meetings the first of several economic measures was introduced at the end of July 1909 when the GER station master retired and both stations were transferred to the control of the GNR station master. In the spring of 1910, further savings were made with the pooling of goods and parcels cartage and delivery services within the town and surrounding area, including ancillary clerical duties resulting in an annual saving to the GER of £223.

The GNR was authorised to purchase a strip of land near Attimore Hall adjoining the south-west boundary of the Hertford branch by the Great Northern Railway Act 1911 (1 and 2 George 5 cap lxxix) which received the Royal Assent on 18th August 1911.

ABOVE: On Monday 23rd July 1906 the Prince and Princess of Wales, accompanied by the Lord Mayor of London and other dignitaries, travelled by Royal Train to Hertford in connection with the opening of the new building at Christ's Hospital School. The chosen route was by the GNR from King's Cross and here the royal party are shown leaving the entrance to the flag bedecked station. *P. Theobald collection*

RIGHT: The ornate archway erected at the approach to Hertford GNR station on the occasion. *P. Theobald collection*

The additional property enabled the extension of the existing siding to cater for increased traffic.

Lieutenant Colonel E. Druitt again visited the branch on 18th June 1913 to inspect alterations made to Paye and Webb's siding at Hertingfordbury where a temporary crossing had been laid between the siding and a contractor's siding, across the main single line. The points and signals on either side of the crossing were worked from a 3-lever ground frame released and locked by the Train Staff for the Hertford to Cole Green section of line. The interlocking was found to be correct and working arrangements satisfactory.

Under the provisions of the GNR Act 1898 the company was empowered to provide land and part costs of a connecting road linking North Road and Port Vale in Hertford. At the time the GNR proportion of the works was estimated at £500. The proposals remained dormant until early 1914 when Hertford Corporation intimated they wished to construct the road at a total cost of £4,500. The matter was placed with the engineer who after negotiating with the local authority agreed the provision of £1,000, provided Hertford Corporation carried out the work and the necessary authority was given on 1st May. The local authority was unhappy at the proposal and the subsequent outbreak of war halted progress.

The outbreak of World War One had an instant impact on Britain's railways, particularly those in the south. The government under the powers of the Regulation of the Forces Act 1871 had taken over control of the railways from 4th August 1914 with the Railway Executive Committee taking overall control. Herbert Walker of the London & South Western Railway became the chairman and all competition ceased as railways set about forming a united front in their wartime role. Most excursion traffic and cheap tickets were suspended. The railway saw the departure of many men who volunteered to serve in the armed forces and on occasions the platforms at Hertford, Hertingfordbury and Cole Green, as well as Hatfield, were crowded as loved ones watched their departure and hoped for an early return. Several railwaymen also joined the colours, and older men continuing in service or the recruitment of women ensured the temporary vacancies were covered. Sadly not all who departed returned to their native Hertfordshire. The war also brought an increase in goods traffic as additional produce from local farms were sent to towns and cities to make up for the loss of imported goods. Training sessions were also arranged locally for troops and extra trains conveyed men and horses to and from manoeuvres.

On 20th January 1916 Lieutenant Colonel E. Druitt visited Hertford to inspect a temporary siding connection laid in the single line facing Up trains connecting to works of the extension of the line from Cuffley to Langley Junction. The new connection enabled materials to be delivered via the branch from Hatfield or via the GER at Hertford and the points were worked from a 2-lever ground frame controlled by the Train Staff for the Hertford to Cole Green section of line. The interlocking and other arrangements were satisfactory and Druitt sanctioned use of the new connection.

On the evening of 28th March 1916 a severe blizzard and snowstorm hit east Hertfordshire. Trees alongside the branch were blown down damaging the telephone and telegraph wires. All communication was lost between Hertford, Hertingfordbury and Cole Green but as only one train had to run across the branch before the line closed for the night, it was decided to allow this to proceed at extreme caution from Hertford to ascertain if any trees were blocking the line. Fortunately only the telegraph wires were affected and the train had an uneventful run to Hatfield.

By December 1916 the strain of the war effort was taxing the resources of all British railways to such an extent that the Railway Executive Committee issued an ultimatum that they could only continue if drastic reductions were made to ordinary services. The Lloyd George Coalition agreed to a reduction of passenger services from January 1917 but with the economic measures the Hatfield to Hertford branch lost only one passenger service in each direction.

Despite hostilities, construction of the new main line continued and on 4th March 1918 the long-promised Hertford loop was finally opened from Cuffley to Langley Junction, south of Stevenage, for freight traffic only. The line was controlled by an absolute/permissive block system using Tyer's No. 5 tablet instruments installed in Cuffley and Langley Junction signal boxes. After passing through Ponsbourne Tunnel, 2,864 yards in length and the longest on the GNR, the single-track railway descended through Bayford and before Hertford crossed twin viaducts: Horns Mill, over the main road and the River Lea, 50 feet high with seven arches, and then Hertford viaduct over the branch from Hatfield on the skew which was 41 feet high. The line then paralleled the branch for a short distance, where a temporary contractor's junction had been installed but which by the time of opening was removed.

The end of hostilities in November 1918 was greeted with great relief and station staff bedecked the branch stations with flags to celebrate the armistice. The branch settled to renewed peacetime operation, which was rudely shattered when a wave of general industrial unrest resulted in a general railway strike from 26th September to 5th October 1919, when the Hatfield to Hertford services were curtailed as the line was closed for most of the time. The cessation of traffic began the gradual exodus of passengers from the railway as local people turned to the embryonic bus services.

On 30th January 1920 sanction was given for expenditure of £238 on alterations to drainage and lavatories at Cole Green station and the station master's house.

Following the success of the Garden City at Letchworth, when Sir Ebenezer Howard called for the creation of planned towns combining the benefits of city and country life but avoiding the disadvantages of both, in 1920 expansion was advocated in an area south of Welwyn and north of Hatfield, where, as with Letchworth, there was access to a main-line railway. Preliminary work had commenced during World War One, for temporary platforms were erected at the site of the former Welwyn Junction on both the Luton and Hertford branches in 1917 essentially for the use of workmen.

At about 2.30am on 6th February 1920 a serious collision occurred between a portion of a Down goods train that had broken away and the following fish train, completely blocking the Up and Down main lines through Welwyn North tunnel. Situated in the *'bottle neck'*, services could not be diverted across the Hatfield to Hertford branch and so a decision was made to divert main-line trains over the new line via Enfield and Cuffley, despite the section between Cuffley and Langley Junction only being single line. No passenger trains had previously operated over the northern part of the route as it had not been inspected by the Ministry of Transport, so early on that day the 4.55am King's Cross mail train to York and Leeds, hauled by Class 'C1' 'Atlantic' 4-4-2 No. 1426, headed north into new territory. In order to avoid the risk of stalling on the 1 in 55 quarter-mile climb over the flyover at Wood Green, 'N1' Class 0-6-2T No. 1572 was attached as far as Palmers Green. Thereafter King's Cross Driver J. Payne, in charge of the 'Atlantic', completed the run to Langley Junction and beyond without a hitch. In the northbound direction up to 4.30pm twelve Down expresses, two milk empties and three goods trains traversed the full length of the line as well as nine southbound trains up to 1.00pm when the Up main line through Welwyn Tunnel was clear.

On 16th April 1920 authority was granted to purchase sixty-nine acres of land from the Second Garden City Estates at a price of £55 per acre for the possible site of a future station to serve the community. The purchase was subject to the Garden City Company agreeing to erect cottages near the site. As the area was to be fully developed, the GNR Company was keen to exploit for new passenger traffic and decided to provide a halt at Digswell for the use of passengers travelling to and from the new development. The halt was authorised on 7th May 1920 but was only provided on the single-track Dunstable branch, and the single wooden platform was opened for public traffic on 16th August 1920. Thus early residents of the Garden City wishing to travel to Hertford by rail had first to go south to Hatfield before changing trains and heading north past the point where their journey commenced.

During the summer months, complaints were received from workmen travelling to the new estate at Welwyn Garden City of the inadequacies of the services on the Dunstable branch to and from Hatfield. The infrequent service on the Luton and Dunstable line was at times which were inconvenient for the starting and finishing times of the workers. In order to nullify the complaints the GNR authorised the Welwyn Garden City Company to build a more substantial workers' halt alongside the Hertford branch almost opposite the halt on the Dunstable branch. Hertford branch trains only called at the new halt when required to pick up or set down workers but complaints were soon forthcoming from the new residents who wished to use the additional facility. After due discussion over the legalities of allowing ordinary passengers to use what was essentially a private station, the GNR solicitor advocated the outright purchase and on 3rd December 1920 arrangements were made to purchase the halt for £100. At the other end of the branch, double line working was introduced between Cuffley and Langley Junction on and from 23rd December although only goods services were permitted to use the new line.

On 14th July 1921 the first inroads were made into the monopoly enjoyed by the GNR when Harvey & Burrows began a joint operation of motor-bus services between St. Albans, Hatfield and Hertford, with Road Motors of Luton serving the intermediate villages of Hertingfordbury, Letty Green and Cole Green. The London General Omnibus Company, who had considerable ambitions in Hertfordshire with an interest in the National Bus Company, diplomatically persuaded Harvey & Burrows to withdraw from the St. Albans to Hertford service and National took over the joint operation with Road Motors on 8th September 1921. In the meantime the line between Cuffley and Stevenage had been fully open for goods traffic from February 1921. The road works at Hertford, initially raised in 1914, were resurrected on 6th January 1922 when £1,000 was transferred to Hertford Corporation for the new road together with 227 square yards of land to enable Sandy Lane to be widened.

Originally the halt near the site of Welwyn Junction on the Dunstable line and later the halt on the Hertford branch came under the control of the station master at Hatfield. The station on the Dunstable line consisted of a timber platform and a timber hut for office purposes; the first member of staff commented *'when the station was opened the total stock-in-trade consisted of 50 blank tickets and the added facility of a broom'*. Fourteen weekday trains stopped daily. The timber platform on the Hertford branch had no facilities

A general view of Hertford GER terminus in 1911 with the goods shed to the left, Station signal box to the centre and the headshunt running behind the signal box. The GNR single line to the right is separated from the GER by post and rail fencing. Empty wagons are stabled in the lengthy Gray & Miles siding whilst in the background is Brazier's Gas Works siding also occupied by wagons. Beyond that siding is Dicker Mill level crossing.

GERS/Windwood 612

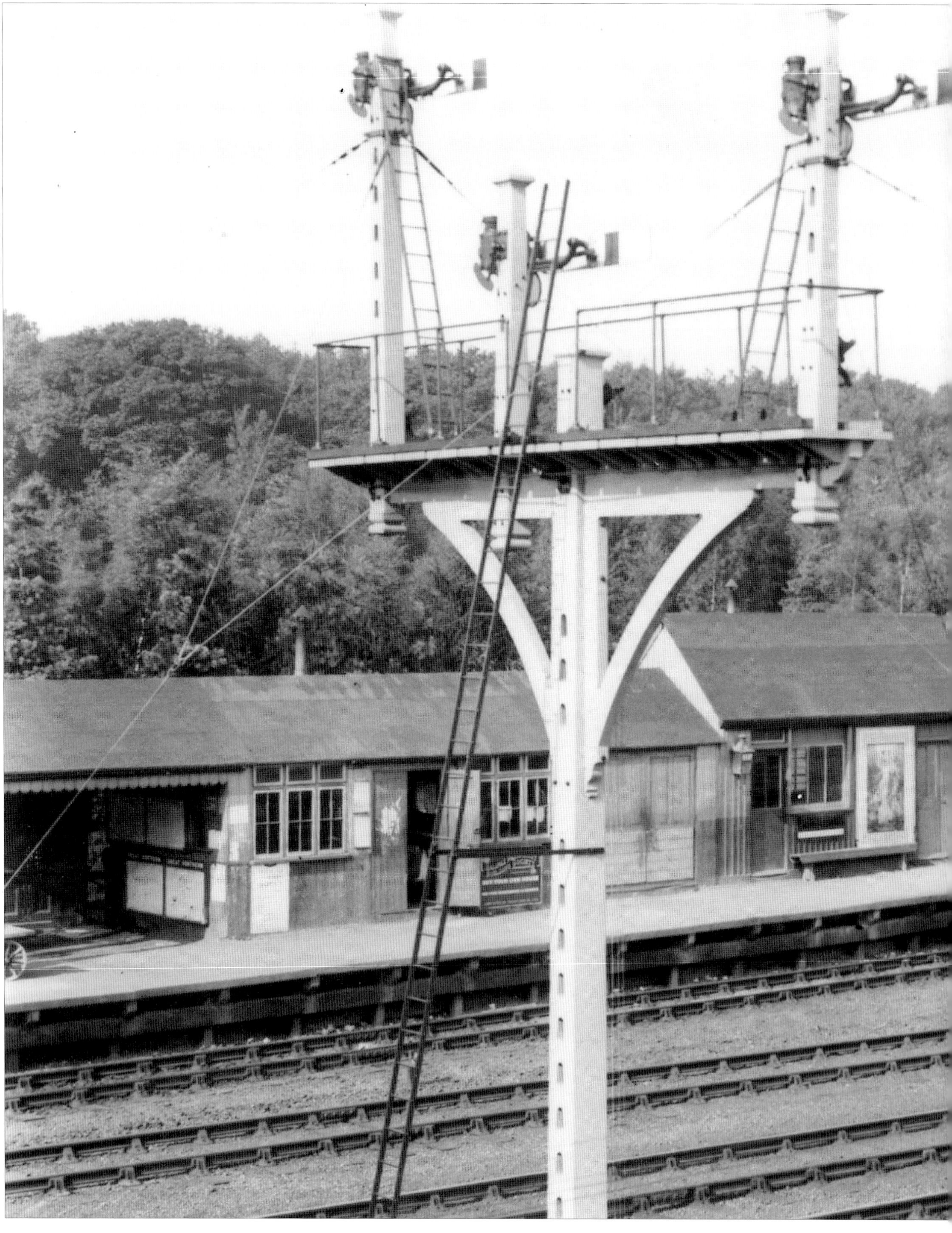

The temporary station provided on the Luton and Dunstable branch at Welwyn Garden City on 16th August 1920. Passengers wishing to travel to Hertford from the expanding new town complained to the GNR and L&NER management that they had first to travel to Hatfield to join the Hertford branch service. *Author's collection*

and was open to the elements. As the new Welwyn Garden City developed, so traffic increased and plans were prepared for a new station once the volume of traffic was sufficient to warrant the large outlay. Anticipating such growth the GNR authorities decided to appoint a station master to the halts pending the development and tenders were invited for the construction of a station master's house. On 27th January 1922 the contract was awarded to W. Pattison & Son who tendered at £1,039.

The GNR in their last year of independence made the initial moves to develop the new station and facilities at Welwyn Garden City when they obtained Parliamentary authority to purchase additional land. Clause 8 of the Great Northern Railway Act 1922 (12 and 13 George 5 cap lix) sanctioned the purchase of property in the Parish of Welwyn Garden City:

a   an average width of twelve yards or thereabouts adjoining and on the western side of the main line and extending between four chains and forty two chains or thereabouts measured in a north easterly direction along the main line from the 19¼ mile post from London.

b   an average width of twelve yards or thereabouts adjoining and on the eastern side of the main line and extending between four chains and twenty chains measured in a north easterly direction along the main line from the 19¼ mile post.

c   an average width of twenty five yards or thereabouts adjoining and on the eastern side of the main line and extending between two and a half chains measured in a south westerly direction and four and a half chains measured in a north easterly direction along the main line for the 19¾ mile post.

d   an average width of seventy yards adjoining and on the western side of the main line and extending between sixteen chains measured in a south westerly direction and thirty seven chains in a north easterly direction from the 20 mile post from London.

e   an average width of one hundred and two yards adjoining and on the eastern side of the main line extending between thirty five chains measured in a south westerly direction and sixteen and a half chains measured in a north easterly direction along the main line from the 20¼ mile post.

f   an average width of seventy yards adjoining and on the eastern side of the main line extending between one and a half chains measured in a south westerly direction and ten and a half chains measured in a north easterly direction from the 20½ mile post.

g   an average width of one hundred and fifteen yards adjoining on the western side of the main line and extending between seven and a half chains measured in a south westerly direction and nine and a half chains measured in a north easterly direction along the main line from the 20¾ mile post from London.

h   an average width of fifteen yards adjoining and on the western side of the main line and extending from ten chains in a south westerly direction along the main line from the 21 mile post to a point near the 21½ mile post.

j   an average width of twelve yards adjoining and on the eastern side of the main line and extending three chains in a south westerly direction along the main line from the 20¾ mile post to a point nearly opposite the south end of Welwyn Viaduct.

GNR 'G2' Class 'Back Tank' 0-4-4T No. 531 pauses at Cole Green with a five coach Hatfield to Hertford train in 1910. Locomotives of this class were regularly diagrammed on both passenger and freight duties. The coaching stock is a mixture of four and five compartment 6-wheel stock including two brake thirds. The locomotive was later placed on the duplicate list as No. 531A and was withdrawn from service in June 1919.

Author's collection

Ivatt 'G2' Class 0-4-4 Back Tank No. 245 spins along the GNR main line near Potters Bar with a through King's Cross to Hertford train in 1913. Note the engine is displaying the correct destination indicator on the smokebox door. *Author's collection*

k an average width of sixteen yards adjoining and on the western side of the main line and extending between two chains and nineteen and a half chains in a north easterly direction from the south end of Welwyn Viaduct.

l a strip of land maximum width of ten yards and minimum width of two yards adjoining and on the south western and southern side of the Luton and Dunstable branch and extending from the north side of the bridge over the main line, known as Hunter's Bridge near the 20½ mile post to a point nearly opposite the 21 mile post.

m an average width of eleven yards adjoining and on the southern side of the Luton and Dunstable branch extending from the 21 mile post for a distance of seven and a half chains in a westerly direction.

n a strip of land of an average width of three and a half yards adjoining and on the northern and eastern side of the Luton and Dunstable branch extending from a point eleven chains measured in an easterly direction from the 21 mile post from London to a point seven chains measured in a north easterly direction from the 21½ mile post.

o land with a maximum width of twelve yards and a minimum of four yards adjoining and on the south western side of the Luton and Dunstable branch extending in a north westerly direction from a point six and a half chains measured in a northerly direction along the branch from the 21½ mile post to a point on the south eastern side of the road crossing the branch and leading from Hatfield to Hitchin and known as the Great North Road.

p land with a maximum width of seventy yards and a minimum width of five yards adjoining and on the eastern side of the Hertford branch and extending from ten and a half chains measured in a north easterly direction along the branch from the 20½ mile post from London to a point nine chains measured along the branch in a south easterly direction from the 21 mile post.

q land with average width of six yards adjoining on the south western side of the Hertford branch and extending seven chains in a north westerly direction and one chain in south easterly direction along the branch from the 21¼ mile post.

r land with average width of five yards adjoining and on the south western side of the Hertford branch and extending between two chains and eight chains measured in a south easterly direction along the branch from the 21½ mile post.

s land partly in the Parish of Hatfield and partly in the Parish of Tewin of an average width of five yards adjoining and on the south western side of the Hertford branch and extending between eleven and a half chains measured in a north westerly direction and seven chains in a south easterly direction from the 21¾ mile post from London.

The industrial dispute of 1919 began the decline in railway freight. Farmers and growers realised for the first time that with improving roads, goods could be sent by motor lorry, using in some cases vehicles purchased second hand from the military, thus making short haul journeys cheaper than the rates charged by the GNR. The door-to-door service was more convenient than the double handling caused by loading and unloading into and out of railway wagons. The primitive commercial road vehicles of the day were not capable of continuous long hauls, however, and the middle and long distance freight traffic remained safely in the hands of the railway company. Fortunately, the same problem was less severe with passenger traffic – few local people owned cars and most were still reliant on the branch for some journeys. The GNR did not have the complete monopoly, for infrequent bus services were soon re-established. Under persuasion or pressure, Road Motors of Luton withdrew from the fray in September 1922 leaving National a free rein. From 1st October the route N10 was established between St. Albans, Hatfield, Cole Green, Hertingfordbury and Hertford, whilst N10A, the old Road Motors route, ran from St. Albans to Hatfield, Essendon Mill and Hertford. Little concern was felt at the time but these services formed the nucleus of a cancerous growth which three decades later finally destroyed the branch.

Although peace had been declared, the Government retained control of the railways until 15th August 1921 as the war effort

Stirling GNR 'G1' Class 0-4-4T No. 767, departing from Hatfield with a mixed train for Hertford in 1921. The locomotive was allocated number 3767 at grouping but this was never carried before withdrawal from traffic in January 1924. *Kidderminster Railway Museum*

had seriously debilitated the concerns, with little or minimal maintenance of rolling stock and infrastructure. In 1918 the Coalition Government had hinted at support for nationalisation, a thought that had been festering since the formation of the Railway Nationalization League in 1895, and with later support of the railway unions and the formation of the Railway Nationalisation Society in 1908. A number of industrialists and traders were sympathetic, saying the railways should be a public corporation rather than a profit making concern. Nationalisation was even proposed by the *Railway Gazette* in 1919. In the event the Government fell short of full nationalisation and formed the over 100 individual companies into four groups. The impending grouping of the railways meant the problem of road competition was of little concern to the GNR management in the last months of their administration.

Stirling 'G1' Class 0-4-4Ts were used on the Hatfield to Hertford and Dunstable branch services in the early 1920s. Here regularly allocated locomotive No. 767 is waiting to depart from King's Cross with a train for Hatfield. *Author's collection*

6

L&NER Operation

As a result of the 1921 Railways Act, from 1st January 1923, the GNR was amalgamated with the Great Eastern, Great Central, North Eastern, North British and several smaller railways to form the London & North Eastern Railway. The new management made few initial changes to the branch, save some of the locomotives and rolling stock working the line showed the ownership of the new company. Then on 1st July 1923 the L&NER renamed the Hertford GN station at Cowbridge 'Hertford North', whilst the former GER station became 'Hertford East'.

On 1st November 1923 the L&NER Company entered into a fresh agreement with H. Brazier for the siding and loading dock at Hertford. Under agreements of 18th September and 31st December 1897 the GNR company had provided a siding and loading dock for sand and gravel traffic but the agreement had been terminated in 1921. The trader now wished to use the facilities and under the revised agreement the L&NER authorities sanctioned the construction of a new loading dock, with the trader paying the full cost of £80, exclusive of the gravel provided. Brazier was also responsible for future maintenance of the platform. The trader was to pay an annual rent of £20 with a £2 rebate for every 1,000 tons of gravel dispatched in excess of 5,000 tons per annum, the total rebate not exceeding £20 per annum.

The equipping of the Cuffley to Stevenage new line authorised by the GNR board on 22nd December 1922 had surprisingly made no provision for connecting the Hatfield to Hertford branch with the new line. Consequently, it had been necessary to retain the old GNR Hertford station in addition to the new station. This was obviously undesirable as in future passengers could not readily interchange trains and connections could not be made. Thus on 21st February 1924 the L&NER Traffic Committee recommended

The new Hertford North station under construction with the Hatfield to Hertford branch in the foreground with path of the Cuffley to Langley Junction line passing between the platforms.

Author's collection

the closure of 'Hertford Old' station for passenger traffic and provision of a connection to bring the Hatfield branch traffic into the new station. The estimated cost of providing the connection line and associated signalling, sidings, adjacent shed, waiting room accommodation and a lift on the Down platform together with lighting was estimated at £16,697. The scheme also necessitated the provision of block signalling huts at Bayford to the south of Hertford as well as Stapleford and Watton to the north. It was also envisaged the portion of line north of Hertford North new station towards Hitchin would be worked by shuttle rail-motor train. An increase in costs to staff the new station estimated at £1,036 per annum brought the total expenditure to £16,898. The following month, on 13th March the contract for the construction of the buildings at Hertford North was awarded to Ekins & Company at a cost of £5,345.

Along the branch at Welwyn Garden City, the Welwyn Garden City Company Limited were keen to develop a factory area to the east of the main line and a major breakthrough came early in 1924 when a portion of land was leased to the Shredded Wheat Company, formed in America in 1898 as the National Biscuit Company. The Welwyn Garden City Company Limited approached the L&NER for the provision of sidings to the factory then in the course of construction, with connections from the single line Hertford branch together with two gates. After several site meetings, agreement was reached and the work costing £2,475 was authorised on 26th June. The Garden City Company agreed to pay the full amount estimated at £1,780 on their land and £695 on railway company property. The L&NER in return would pay a rebate of 10 per cent over a period of fourteen years, calculated on the portion of receipts, the rebates ceasing when the amounts reached the cost of work on the L&NER land.

The seven-day strike of railwaymen commencing on 26th January 1924 hastened the serious decline in passengers using the branch. Would-be travellers turned to road transport and many of those journeying short distances were never to return. The mails were dispatched twice daily by road using private cars and a local publican operated a commuter service to London using a converted char-a-banc.

Before the 'new line' from Wood Green via Enfield and Cuffley to Langley Junction could officially open for passenger traffic the Board of Trade inspection was made on 27th May 1924, when Gresley 'A1' Class 4-6-2 tender locomotive No. 1474 (later No. 4474 *Victor Wild*) and three 4-4-2 'C1' Class 'Atlantic' tender locomotives No's 1400, 1418 and 1443 ran down separately as light engines to stand and then travel slowly to test underbridges and other structures during the inspection. Thereafter some suburban trains were extended beyond Cuffley to Hertford North before the official opening date to provide locomotive crews with adequate route knowledge.

The most important change made to the Hatfield to Hertford branch services came with the official opening of the much vaunted Wood Green to Stevenage loop line to passenger traffic on 2nd June 1924, when services from King's Cross via Enfield Chase were introduced, terminating at the new Hertford North station located a mile west of the centre of the town. On the same day the former Cowbridge station, renamed North in 1923 and subsequently referred to as 'Hertford Old', lost its passenger traffic as all services from Hatfield also terminated at the new station. The first section of the loop, between Enfield and Cuffley, had been used for passenger and goods trains from 1909. The new section from Cuffley by way of Bayford, Hertford, Stapleford and Watton thus provided a new route between Hertford and King's Cross and the main service was given by extending to Hertford some of the trains which heretofore terminated at Gordon Hill or Cuffley on both weekdays and Sundays. A new service of four trains in each direction was also operated north of Hertford to Hitchin via Stevenage, worked by a rail-motor on weekdays only. As a result of these improvements the Hatfield to Hertford branch passenger services were reduced, for with two alternatives routes to London local residents were unlikely to choose the third and most circuitous route with a change of trains at Hatfield. The opening of the new station coincided with the erection of new houses within a short distance of the railway.

Although Hatfield Hyde was recorded in the HMSO list of quarries in 1920 as a sand and ballast pit it was being used from 1924 for the dumping of rubbish from London. This was brought and tipped from standard gauge wagons into narrow gauge wagons and then hauled by diesel mechanical locomotives for distribution around the site. The narrow gauge system was relaid as and when required and as well as rubbish the wagons were used to convey overburden to cover the rubbish.

With a view to rationalisation and saving on operating costs the Traffic Committee agreed on 30th October 1924 to the abolition of the former GER Hertford Junction signal box. The points controlling the connection to the former GNR route and associated signalling were to be controlled from Hertford East Station signal box. The cost for alterations, including track circuitry and electric signal repeaters, was £1,606 but after allowing for the saving of three signalmen, the regrading of the signalmen in the Station signal box and cost of additional maintenance the savings amounted to £396 per annum. The signal box was subsequently abolished in January 1925.

On 19th January 1925 the Chief General Manager reminded the directors that in connection with the development of Welwyn Garden City Estate the late GNR had under agreement with the Garden City Company constructed a halt on the Luton branch for passenger traffic to and from the Garden City. In return the developers had conveyed 65½ acres of land to the railway company for the provision of a permanent passenger station and sidings if and when the volume of traffic warranted such action. Because of the rapid growth in population of the town and the erection by the Shredded Wheat Company of the large factory to the east of the railway, the existing facilities were now considered totally inadequate. It was therefore proposed to build the new station and associated goods yard, which would be served by trains on the Luton and Hertford single lines as well as the main lines. The cost including lighting and signal and telegraph work was estimated at £35,341. The contract for the construction of the new station was awarded to H. Arnold & Sons Limited on 30th July 1925, after the firm tendered at £23,672, subject to completion within nine months.

In the meantime Major G.L. Hall inspected the new facilities at Hertford North on 22nd February 1925. Before commencing his examination of the buildings, the inspector viewed the signalling arrangements. He noted the single line from Hatfield joined the Down main line of the Cuffley to Langley Junction branch a short distance north of the new Hertford North signal box. Nearby this connection was the junction between the goods line from the old station at Hertford and the loop line off the Up main line. There was also a short connecting line between the goods line and the Hatfield line east of the signal box. Complete signalling had been installed including outer home and advance starting signals in both directions on the double-track main line. Direction indicators for various routes were given at only one signal in each case. Track circuits were provided in the Up and Down main lines as follows:

1. On the Down main line from a point 200 yards in the rear of the Down outer home signal to a point in advance of the Down main inner home signal.
2. On the Down main line from a point in advance of the Down main inner home signal as far as the fouling point of the junction between the Down main line and the single line from Hatfield.
3. On the Down main line for a distance of 668 yards in the rear of the Down main advance starting signal which is 740 yards from the starting signal.
4. On the Up main line from the points 200 yards to the rear of the Up main outer home as far as the Up main inner home.
5. On the Up main line from the points approximately opposite the Down main inner home to the Up main advance starting signal which is 800 yards from the signal box.

The condition of all track circuits was indicated in the signal box and the usual controls, either block control or lever in the signal box in the rear, were provided. Certain special electrical interlocking was also provided to prove the position of the signal arms, track circuits and block instruments. The points and signals on the main line and leading to the yard were worked from the new Hertford North signal box, located south of the station and containing a 65-lever frame with 56 working and 9 spare levers. Because of the complexity of the layout and number of crossings and facing points, the locking in the frame was considered *'intricate but satisfactory'*.

Hall then turned his attention to the new Hertford North station, which had been provided with two island platforms for Down and Up line traffic. The Down side platform located west of the double line lay between the Down main line and the bay platform road onto which both Down trains from Cuffley on the double line or from the Hatfield single line could be signalled. Trains departing both from the bay or Down main line could be signalled to the Up main line or to the Hatfield branch. The Up platform line east of the double lines was served only by trains on the Up main line, although it was contemplated a further alteration in permanent way would include the installation of another platform line to the east of this platform. Both of the island platforms were 500 feet in length with width of 36 feet at the centre. They were formed of a brick wall and concrete coping-stones with the requisite overhang. Hall found the platform surface between the coping stones was of gravel south of the station buildings and asphalt under the canopy. Electric lighting had been provided with transparent nameplates on the front of each lamp. Wooden nameboards bearing cast letters and mounted between concrete posts were also erected on the platforms outside the canopy. A verandah roof 156 feet in length was erected over the Down island platform with a double row of supports located 12 feet from the platform edges. The permanent station buildings erected on the Down platform contained a gentlemen's lavatory, porters' room, ladies' waiting room and lavatory and general waiting room, all illuminated by electric lights. On the Up platform the inspector found neither permanent buildings erected nor the platform covered over, pending the rearrangement of the track to the back of the platform. A temporary waiting shed measuring 20 feet by 9 feet had, however, been provided. A subway connected the two island platforms, with steps leading up to the centre of both platforms. The booking office was provided just inside the entrance from the road, which ran in a north-easterly to south-westerly direction on the east side of the station. A luggage lift with automatic electric operation was provided leading from the subway up to both platforms. At the conclusion of the inspection the Major made the following observations.

1. The company in due course will submit a proposal for the rearrangement of the permanent way and permanent station buildings on the Up side platform.
2. The long brick viaduct south of the Down main outer home signal is so placed that a train stopping at the signal would overlap the viaduct. In that case the top of the parapet wall is 5 feet above rail level and its distance 5 feet 6 inches from the gauge line, no additional protection is therefore necessary against passengers leaving the train under the impression they had arrived at the station.

L&NER notice of the opening of the new line between Guffley and Stevenage and Hertford North station and closure of Hertford Cowbridge station to passenger traffic; 2nd June 1924.

3. Trap points are provided on the Up siding very close to the Hertford to Hatfield single line as it approaches the junction with the Down main line. Improvements are called for to make sure movements detached here are thoroughly clear of the passenger line. A trap of the double switch type and the necessary improvements could be effected by altering the lead of the right-hand switch and possible additional lengthening.
4. There are no trap points at the south end of the both ways goods line between the Old Station single line and the Hatfield single line. At the north end of this goods line traps have been provided by staggering the switches of the facing points between the Old Station line and the connection therefrom towards the Up main line.

Railway officials advised Hall that no movement was allowed in the direction of Hatfield past the facing points unless the driver was in possession of the single line Train Staff. Moreover, the goods line was used as a running line and in no circumstances were vehicles allowed to be stabled thereon. On this understanding, and subject to confirmation in writing, the inspector waived the necessity for trap points at the south end. Before sanctioning full use of the station the inspector reminded railway officials that no clocks had been provided on either platform.

On the same day as he visited Hertford North, Major Hall inspected the new works at Cole Green where he found alterations had been made to enable the signal box to be switched out, when required, and a Long Section Staff introduced for the Hatfield to Hertford single line section as a substitute for the short section Train Staffs from Hatfield to Cole Green, and Cole Green to Hertford. When the short section working was in operation the Long Section Train Staff was retained in a locked box in Cole Green signal box and trains were signalled through Cole Green using the Up and Down loop lines according to the direction of travel. When it was desired to bring the Long Section working into use, the last train carrying the Short Section Staff was admitted to the Down loop line. Both Short Section Staffs were then placed in the locking box and various points pulled to allow through running via the Down loop line. A King Lever was then pulled halfway to release mechanically the interlocking between the conflicting signals, which were then pulled over. The King Lever when fully pulled back locked or locked normally all the levers when the frame was in condition for through running and the signals pulled off for both directions. When the frame was correctly set the Long Section Staff was withdrawn from the box and the Short Section Staffs locked in the box and the block circuit switched through. Special Ticket boxes for the Long Section Working were provided at both Hatfield and Hertford, which could only be interlocked by a Yale key attached to the Long Section Staff. Having tested the equipment and interlocking and found both satisfactory, Major G.L. Hall sanctioned use of the revised working.

The affairs of the branch were again disrupted by the General Strike in early May 1926. Railway union members withdrew their labour in support of the miners and subsequently train services could not be guaranteed. On several days the Hatfield to Hertford North branch, and indeed outer suburban services, were suspended. Fortunately within a week regular railwaymen returned to duty and services resumed. The impact of the continuing miners' strike meant reduced coal stocks available to the railway companies and the L&NER authorities decided on the only course of action available to conserve stocks by reducing train services. Thus from 31st May a much reduced service, initially two trains in each direction, operated across the branch until the situation improved some weeks later.

For the last full year of Hertford passenger rated traffic travelling via the branch to King's Cross the station receipts were:

	Passengers	Passenger Receipts	Parcels Receipts	Season Ticket Receipts	Total
1923		£	£	£	£
Hertford North	88,593	6,335	619	2,509	9,463
Hertingfordbury	8,957	410	50	257	717
Cole Green	19,900	598	254	346	1,198

From 2nd June 1924, when Cowbridge station closed to passenger traffic, most Hertford passengers used the newly opened loop line to London via Enfield Chase and although Hertford receipts are given below only a small percentage could be credited to the full branch takings which, reliant only on Cole Green and Hertingfordbury, reduced considerably.

	Passengers	Passenger Receipts	Parcels Receipts	Season Tickets Receipts	Total
1924		£	£	£	£
Hertford	98,547	6,287	563	2,659	9,509
Hertingfordbury	3,868	282	56	239	577
Cole Green	12,403	382	193	420	995
1925					
Hertford	117,119	6,705	702	3,205	10,612
Hertingfordbury	2,573	77	16	249	442
Cole Green	8,939	310	277	259	846

With the opening of the new Welwyn Garden City station, designed by Garden City architect Louis de Soissons, on 20th September 1926, the temporary wooden station on the Dunstable branch and the workers' halt on the Hertford line were closed on the same day. Hertford branch trains were accommodated at the back of the Up platform at the new station. The Right Honourable Arthur Neville Chamberlain, Conservative MP for Birmingham Ladywood and the Minister of Health, officially opened the new Welwyn Garden City station on 5th October 1926. At the ceremony the L&NER Chairman, William Whitelaw, recorded a vote of thanks to the minister. Chamberlain had travelled with other L&NER officials from King's Cross by special train for the event hauled by an immaculate 'C1' Class 4-4-2 tender locomotive No. 4436. Following the ceremonial opening of the door to the main entrance of the station the ensemble returned to King's Cross on the special train.

The opening of the new station at Welwyn Garden City had a drastic effect on the Hertford branch as only a minor proportion of receipts could be credited to the local line. The combination of the new station together with the opening of the new Hertford North brought a considerable reduction in the number of passengers travelling across the branch, as the L&NER also increased the service to London via Enfield Chase. In the following totals for the years 1926 to 1928 the Welwyn Garden City and Hertford North figures are only quoted to show the traffic increases compared with the reductions recorded at the intermediate stations of Hertingfordbury and Cole Green.

	Passengers	Passenger Receipts £	Parcels Receipts £	Season Tickets Receipts £	Total £
1926					
Hertford North	90,276	5,932	664	2,881	9,477
Hertingfordbury	2,272	153	68	202	423
Cole Green	7,142	266	366	242	774
Welwyn G.C.	94,207	6,584	263	9,327	16,174
1927					
Hertford North	90,986	6,316	752	3,319	10,387
Hertingfordbury	2,478	160	17	227	404
Cole Green	5,851	276	291	223	790
Welwyn G.C.	146,551	9,592	343	14,576	24,511
1928					
Hertford North	98,552	6,384	696	3,239	10,319
Hertingfordbury	2,379	139	35	166	340
Cole Green	5,849	266	131	294	691
Welwyn G.C.	176,503	10,896	5,811	16,178	27,575

The reduction in importance of the branch can be gauged by the loss of effective receipts between 1923 and 1928. Before the loss of Hertford traffic to the more direct route via Cuffley, 117,540 passengers travelled on the branch services paying £7,343 and this, together with parcels traffic and season tickets, brought receipts to £11,378. Five years later with just two intermediate stations offering full credit to the branch receipts, totals had reduced to 8,228 passengers offering a mere £405 in receipts. Full receipts for all traffic only totalled £1,031. To this could be added minor proportion of receipts from the larger stations. The effect of the introduction of local bus services also had a drastic impact on the smaller stations. In 1923 Cole Green was booking an average of 382 passengers each week but by 1928 this had reduced to 112. The close proximity of Hertingfordbury to the new Hertford North also caused a drastic loss of traffic for in 1923 the average number of passengers booking from the station each week was 172 but five years later it was only forty-six. The general strike of 1926 also started the decline in railway freight when many local farmers and growers realised for the first time that goods could be sent by road instead of rail, using in some cases old army vehicles.

Alterations were made to the branch connection to the former GER Hertford branch when the Junction signal box was abolished and the workings transferred to Hertford East signal box (the former Station signal box). Major G.L. Hall inspected the alterations on 16th July 1926 and found that the whole of the connections at

Hertford North station 19 miles 48 chains from King's Cross via Cuffley and 9 miles 04 chains from Hatfield opened for traffic on 2nd June 1924. This early view shows a line of GNR 6-wheel coaches standing at the Down side back platform. To the right are the Down and Up main lines with the branch to Hertford Cowbridge and Hertford East curving away to the right protected by Hertford Cowbridge Down distant signal. The engine release road is to the left of the coaching stock whilst the parachute water tank dominates the near view. In the far distance on the double-track line to Langley Junction is Molewood tunnel. *D. Dent collection*

the station, including the junction with the single line to Hertford North, were now worked from Hertford East signal box; those at the west end of the yard were previously controlled from the East signal box and those at the east end transferred from the former Junction signal box to Hertford East. Track circuits were laid on the Down line from a point in the rear of the Down outer home signal as far as the Down inner home signal and on the Up road from the Up starting signal as far as the Up advance starting signal. Track circuits were also laid in the single line as far as a point just west of Hertford East signal box, near which was erected a notice lettered *'No Engine to Pass This Board Without The Train Staff'*. Signal 43, which gave access from the Up main line to the single line, was controlled by Annett's Key on the single line Train Staff. Hall noted that a path was provided over the adjacent siding to enable the signalman in the East signal box to hand the single line Train Staff Token to the driver near the notice board. Hertford East signal box containing a 46-lever frame now had 45 working levers and 1 spare lever.

The construction of the new station at Welwyn Garden City, together with the altered track layout, required centralised control and a new signal box had been erected immediately north of the Down platform between the Dunstable single line and the Down main slow line. This signal box formed a new block post on the main line between Hatfield No. 2 and Hatfield No. 3 signal boxes to the south and Welwyn North signal box to the north and replaced the former Twentieth Mile Up and Down signal boxes which were abolished.

South of the new station, new facing crossovers from the Down fast to the Down slow main line and from the Up slow to the Up fast main line replaced connections located further south previously worked from Twentieth Mile signal boxes, and these were abolished. North of the station a facing crossover from the Down slow line to the Down main fast line and from the Up fast to the Up slow main line were installed. Other installations included a pair of trailing trap points in the Down goods line which formed the northerly continuation of the Down slow line, a trailing crossover between the Up and Down main fast lines and a facing sand drag in the Up goods line, the southerly continuation of which was the Up slow line. The sand drag was of the parallel type about 230 feet in length from the facing points which were equipped with a bolt lock and 40 feet long locking bars.

The station and yard was completely signalled for all main lines and the single branch lines to Dunstable and Hertford, but in the case of the branches the station was not a Train Staff station and the single line sections remained Hatfield to Cole Green on the Hertford branch and Hatfield to Ayot on the Dunstable line.

Track circuiting was provided on the Up fast line from the trailing points of the facing crossover from the Up slow line, as far as the Up slow advance starting signal. This track circuit when occupied locked the levers of the signals in the rear giving access to that portion of line. On the Down fast line a track circuit extended from the trailing points of the crossover between the main lines as far as the Down main advance starting signal and a second for 200 yards in the rear of the Down fast home signal, and when occupied controlled block working to the signal box in the rear, Hatfield No. 3. A third track circuit extended from the rear of the Down main slow outer home signal as far as the Down main slow inner home and when occupied controlled the block working to the signal box in the rear. On the Up slow line a track circuit extended from the fouling point of the crossover from the Up slow to the Up fast line, as far as the Up slow advance starting signal. This track circuit when occupied locked the lever of the signal in the rear giving access to that section of line. The condition of the track circuits was indicated in the signal box, the indicators being grouped to indicate a lever 'locked' or 'free' position, thus the whole of the track circuit affecting the lock on any given lever was grouped on one indicator.

Lieutenant Colonel G.L. Hall conducted the BOT inspection of the new arrangements on 5th January 1927. He noted the new Welwyn Garden City signal box was equipped with a 65-lever frame with 44 working and 21 spare levers. In addition, luggage barriers located at the north end of each platform, giving access to the sleeper crossing connecting Down and Up side platforms, were worked by the signalman and interlocked with the Up and Down main fast home signals. The arms and lights of all signals were visible from the signal box and including all distant signals were repeated by means of indicators.

The inspector was generally satisfied with the new arrangements but required certain alterations and amendments. The spacing of the signal arms on the bracket post carrying the Down inner home signals was not clear and the L&NER company officials were requested to reposition the arms to increase the space between the Down inner home and the Down fast to Down slow inner home signal. Hall found the facing point equipment was of the GNR standard type and thus not strictly in accordance with the latest revised requirements. He was informed that the standard facing point equipment was available and ready to replace the dated items. On the understanding the GNR equipment was withdrawn and not utilised elsewhere the inspector agreed a re-inspection was unnecessary. The disc signals in the station yard were also found to be displaying the white aspect formerly used by the GNR. Again the railway officers advised Hall a conversion programme to more modern equipment was underway and no further inspection was deemed necessary. The inspector was critical of the treads of the footbridge steps giving access to the footways to the platforms, which were found to be of plain oak, which as long as they were kept dry formed a satisfactory foothold. The roof of the footbridge and staircase helped to maintain the condition but Hall was of the opinion when the treads became damp or wet they would become slippery and dangerous for passengers. As a safeguard the L&NER officers were recommended to install a special form of non-slip metal tread.

On the same day Hall inspected the new passenger lines converted from the former goods lines between Welwyn Garden City and Hatfield. In the Down direction the section ran from the site of the former Twentieth Mile signal box to a point a few yards north of the new station, a distance of 56.54 chains, whilst in the Up direction the section commenced a few yards south of Welwyn Garden City station to Hatfield, a distance of 2 miles 51.46 chains. The inspector found the permanent way on both sections had been overhauled, reballasted and retimbered where necessary. Where the old timbers existed two spikes and two trenails held the chairs and where new sleepers were laid coach screws were used instead of trenails. The rails were generally in 30-foot lengths with twelve sleepers to each rail length. The original ballast of ash was reinforced with slag and stone, Hall noting particularly that on the Up line near Hatfield total reballasting had taken place. The bullhead rails were steel weighing 77 lbs per yard. The alignment and curvature of the converted lines ran adjacent to the existing main lines with no serious gradients or sharp curves. The new lines were protected from the adjacent Up and Down goods lines at Welwyn Garden City by

Welwyn Garden City new passenger station booking hall from the approach road on 7th October 1926. Passengers passing through the booking hall then had to negotiate the steps of footbridge No. 67C linking the platforms to join their trains. *D. Dent collection*

trailing trap points and a facing sand drag respectively. The existing trailing trap point south of the station was left in temporarily as it was not intended to use the lines for passenger trains until the rush of excessive goods traffic was over. The facing trap point at the Hatfield end of the Up slow line was temporarily retained for the same reason. Hall was satisfied with the works and authorised the converted lines to be brought into use.

Lieutenant Colonel G.L. Hall then conducted the official BOT inspection of the siding installed for the Shredded Wheat Company at Welwyn Garden City. He found that the siding connection had been made from the single line Hertford branch a few yards north of the station platform. The points were operated from a 2-lever ground frame, one lever working the points and the second the bolt lock. The single line Train Staff for the Cole Green to Hatfield section released the ground frame. Hall found the interlocking to be correct and sanctioned use of the siding.

On the Hatfield to Hertford North branch the competitive bus services running on roads paralleling the railway had seen further improvements. During the summer months of 1927 and 1928 both the N10 and N10A routes had been extended beyond Hertford to Rye House. At a special board meeting it was resolved to stem the loss of receipts by introducing twenty railway-operated bus services entailing the purchase of sixty motor buses. One of the centres for the new services was Hertford where it was envisaged a route would operate to St. Albans via Hatfield using six 32-seater vehicles, in competition with the existing services. Allocations would, however, be varied in the event of the L&NER coming to terms with local bus proprietors. The engineer estimated the cost of providing garage accommodation at Hertford at £4,000 exclusive of lighting and petrol pumps. On 29th November 1928 authority was given for the outlay on the garage at Hertford, but no further developments were forthcoming pending negotiations with road operators.

Yet further sidings were added at Welwyn Garden City and were inspected by Lieutenant Colonel A.H.L. Mount on 4th July 1927. He found that a connection from the Hatfield to Hertford single line had been laid on the south side of the branch to serve premises of the Welwyn Garden City Limited. The points facing traffic from Hertford were worked by a 2-lever ground frame controlled by the single line Train Staff. The siding had been laid using new 85 lbs per yard rail where the loop line was equipped with catch points. Cole Green station was awarded a First Class certificate for Best Kept Station in 1927 by the L&NER directors after a tour of inspection, earning the station master and staff the prize of £7 10s 0d. This followed a Best Kept Station award to Hertingfordbury in 1924.

By 1928 between sixty and seventy trains called at the new Welwyn Garden City station, several running non-stop to and from King's Cross. Compared with the original station opening on a green-field site, the new structure served a growing community of 7,000 with an area of 4 square miles. Comparison between 1921 and 1928 were eye-watering to the L&NER authorities:

	1921	1928
Number of passengers booked	18,859	177,009
Receipts	£1,756	£10,959
Season ticket receipts	£1,062	£16,334

Goods tonnage totalled nearly 50,000 tons for the 12 months ending 31st December 1928, whilst coal and coke tonnage was

Hatfield Railway Station

Hatfield station from the south with a Gresley 2-8-0 locomotive hauling a freight train on the Up main line. Note the lack of connection to the Down back platform and the several sidings used for the berthing of coaching stock. The deficiency was rectified in World War Two when a facing connection was provided off the Down main line to the St. Albans and Dunstable platform.

Author's collection

11,000 tons, and 9,000 wagons of goods was handled. Royal Mail traffic delivered by rail amounted to 30,000 letters and 750 parcels weekly, with dispatch of up to fifty mailbags each night.

In a memorandum of 16th May 1929 the Divisional General Manager (Southern Area) reported that the only entrance and exit at Welwyn Garden City station was on the west side of the railway and consequently residents on the east side of the line had to make a detour of over half a mile to get to or from the station. As a result of negotiations with the Welwyn Garden City Company it was proposed to erect a steel girder and concrete footbridge, 6 feet in width, which would then become a public thoroughfare linking both east and west side of the railway and would afford access to and from the station from the Up and Down sides. The cost of the structure, estimated at £6,700, was to be borne by Welwyn Garden City Urban District Council, the L&NER paying a sum of £250 per annum for twenty years. The Traffic Committee discussed the matter on 6th June 1929 and it was agreed to the work progressing subject to the L&NER Company granting the necessary easement for the footbridge free of charge and to contribute no more that £250 per annum. The Welwyn Garden City Urban District Council and Welwyn Garden City Company were to provide the basis of interest and sinking fund charge and to bear the whole cost for maintenance, repairs and lighting of the footbridge. If the UDC so desired the footbridge to be 9 feet wide with additional costs of £890, they were to be responsible for such costs.

A further blow to the well being of the Hertford to Hatfield branch passenger service came in August 1929 when National bus route N10 was extended beyond Hertford to run through to Bishop's Stortford. The service was augmented by route N11, which originally connected Bishop's Stortford to Hertford via Little Hadham, Much Hadham and Ware, being extended via Horns Mill to Hatfield and St. Albans from the same date. At this time much thought was given to the withdrawal of the branch passenger services but as the railway required to be fully operational for the lucrative freight services with full signalling the decision was deferred.

In 1930 Norton Grinding Wheel Company Limited, a subsidiary of an American firm founded in February of the same year, established a factory on the eastern outskirts of Welwyn Garden City and the company approached the L&NER management for a siding connection to their works. Plans were duly prepared to use an existing siding connection and the new facility served by Down trains on the Hertford branch was opened in 1931.

On 18th June 1931, T. Blackwell, a groom in private employment, suffered fatal injuries in an accident at Hatfield. J.L.M. Moore subsequently conducted the official BOT inquiry into the incident and after investigation discovered that Blackwell had taken it upon himself to accompany two horses from the Hertfordshire Agricultural Show, which were loaded into a horsebox for dispatch to Olympia. When these and a dozen other horses had been loaded at the cattle dock shortly after 5.00pm, the train of horseboxes was propelled along the goods shed road to pick up two additional vehicles which had been loaded in the carriage dock beyond the goods shed. Blackwell was in one of the horseboxes, which came to rest within the goods shed during the time the additional vehicles were being attached but unfortunately he put his head out of the window of the horsebox as the vehicle was passing through the doorway. As there was only a clearance of 4 inches between the doorway and the side of the horsebox Blackwell's head was crushed. The guard of the train walked alongside the cattle dock before any shunting took place and did not notice anyone in the vehicles but admitted to Moore that he did not look deliberately into each horsebox. Had he seen anyone he would have warned of the lack of clearance, as he was thoroughly conversant with the danger having worked at Hatfield as a shunter for twenty-five years. The inspector noted that Blackwell should not have been in the horsebox and understood he had only joined the vehicle as it was moving out of the cattle dock. A groom was already in charge of the horses and Moore surmised that this man, knowing that the deceased was to join him, deliberately kept out of sight of the guard. In his conclusion Moore placed the cause of the accident on the lack of clearance of the goods shed doorway and asked the L&NER officials to improve the clearance as soon as possible. No blame was attached to members of the railway staff but the inspector concluded:

It appears desirable, however, that in similar circumstances in future when horseboxes, or any other vehicles, which are likely to contain passengers, are known to pass a point where the clearance is so inadequate, it should be the definite duty of somebody to warn the occupants of their danger.

Whilst all attention had been placed on passenger traffic the Chief Goods Manager reported the accommodation at Welwyn Garden City consisted of only one siding, installed in 1920 and capable of holding thirteen wagons. With the development of the new town these facilities were totally inadequate for the goods and coal traffic, there was dissatisfaction amongst traders and the Chamber of Commerce was pressing strongly for immediate improvements. As there was no covered accommodation the forwarding of cartage traffic was dealt with at the passenger station where it was barrowed across the main line to the Up side to be loaded into a pick up goods train. The road approach to the existing single siding was also in very poor condition, being only 10 feet wide. As Welwyn Garden City continued to expand as both residential and industrial centres, designed ultimately to accommodate 40,000 to 50,000 people, it was imperative to have proper goods handling facilities. The Traffic Committee addressed the problem on 23rd July 1931, when authority was given for the provision of three sidings to hold fifty-four wagons together with a cart road and stacking ground, a new goods shed 80 feet in length to hold six wagons under cover, with an office to accommodate six clerical staff and one second-hand fixed crane of 10 tons capacity in the Up side yard, with connections from the Hertford branch. The original estimate of £11,289 was reduced to £10,980 by the time tenders were invited. It was considered the adoption of the scheme would secure to the railway additional traffic which could not have been dealt with and retain traffic which would have otherwise gone by road. In September 1931 it was announced that around fourteen firms were requesting the provision of private sidings.

On 28th January 1932 it was announced the contract for the construction of the new goods shed at Welwyn Garden City had been awarded to Fisher & Sons at a vastly reduced cost of £6,812 7s 6d, subject to the period for completion being satisfactorily arranged with the railway company engineer. The new depot was opened by George Shaw, the goods manager, on 27th July 1932, with 800 square yards of coal stacking ground and the goods yard designed for extension, if necessary. A 10 tons capacity fixed crane was available for lifting heavy loads.

The decline in passenger traffic receipts on the branch was halted momentarily from the early 1930s when holidays and rambles in the country were the fashion. The L&NER issued a booklet *Rambles in*

Hertfordshire to encourage walkers, with a description of moderate routes accompanied by maps with walks starting and terminating at stations including Cole Green. Ramble No. 10, entitled 'The Uplands of Hertfordshire from Cole Green to Welwyn North', enticed participants stating:

> *The countryside covered by this walk is remote and full of quiet charm. For the most part building development is confined to areas near the railway stations. For this reason the blackberry-gatherer will find that the harvest of the autumn hedgerows is abundant and except close to the villages, is often practically ungathered.*

Ramble No. 6 from Bayford to Hertford took walkers close to Cole Green and Hertingfordbury stations so that ramblers desiring to shorten their walk could catch the train, whilst walkers on Ramble No. 9 from Welwyn North to Hatfield could halve their 10-mile hike by catching the train at Cole Green to return to Welwyn Garden City or Hatfield. In 1932 and 1933, large numbers of passengers used the branch trains at weekends, bank holidays and when taking advantage of their days off from work.

On 18th January 1933, Lieutenant Colonel E.P. Anderson belatedly inspected the new siding installed to serve Norton & Company's factory. He found the connection had been made in the single line at 21⅜ miles facing trains going towards Welwyn Garden City. The arrangements were as shown in the original plan for the scheme dated 29th January 1931. The permanent way in the siding was formed of 85 lbs per yard track laid on stone ballast. Full facing point equipment had been installed and trap points laid away and well clear of the main single line. Although the gradient in the sidings fell towards the points, the arrangements were considered adequate. The points were worked from a 2-lever ground frame controlled by Annett's key attached to the Train Staff, and as the locking was correct the inspector sanctioned use of the sidings.

The Divisional General Manager (Southern Area) reported on 1st October 1934 that the agreement for a footbridge negotiated with Welwyn Garden City Company and Welwyn UDC in 1929 had foundered. Despite repeated negotiations and alternative proposals it had not been possible to come to any satisfactory arrangements with the two parties and there was no probability of the scheme being completed. On 25th October the agreement for the footbridge across the railway was rescinded.

In the meantime the local bus services were taken over by the London General Omnibus Company and then the London Passenger Transport Board. New route numbers were introduced from 3rd October 1934, and all journeys between St. Albans and Bishop's Stortford via Hertford were renumbered 340 whether running via Cole Green or Bayford Turn. The 341 bus route was used for short workings between St. Albans and Hertford via Bayford Turn.

Complaints were regularly received from people using the eastern approach to Welwyn Garden City station of the lack of booking facilities. Much time was lost as intending passengers had to use the ticket office on the west side of the station. On 20th March 1935 the Divisional General Manager (Southern Area) reported that passengers from the east side of the line were reluctant to make the half-mile detour to reach the station with the result that many, instead of using the authorised route, made their way across the railway and trespassed on company property. He reminded the directors that the question of providing booking accommodation on the east side of the railway had been under consideration for some time and in 1929 the company recommended a scheme, which subsequently failed to reach fruition. Negotiations with the Welwyn Garden City Company and Welwyn Garden City UDC had continued, and a revised and less expensive scheme had been formulated. Agreement had been reached to the formation of a footpath, six feet in width with post-and-wire fence on either side between the L&NER boundary to a point where it joined up with the existing station footbridge, which itself was to be extended. There was also to be a footpath to connect with the goods yard roadway. The goods yard roadway was, however, not available for use at certain times when shunting was in progress but necessary notices would be placed to advise the public. Finally, a passimeter booking office was to be located at the foot of the staircase leading to the footbridge.

The current for heating and lighting the footpath and new booking office was to be provided by the Welwyn Garden City Electric Light Company, who already supplied the station lighting. In consideration of the L&NER Company incurring the expense of construction, maintenance and lighting of the footpaths on their property and the extension of the footbridge, the Welwyn Garden City Company had agreed to pay £200 towards the initial outlay, thereby reducing the amount to £1,118. The company would also dedicate a strip of land outside the L&NER boundary for the forming of public footpaths to join up with the footpath on L&NER property. The Council was also prepared to bear the cost, estimated at £200, to make up the footpaths on the dedicated land and provide the necessary lighting. The Divisional General Manager explained that the scheme would involve additional annual charges of £499 for the employment of two clerks, £36 for maintenance and renewals, and £35 for electric lighting and heating. He reiterated that extensive trespassing continued with an average of 1,000 people crossing the main lines and Hertford and Dunstable branch line on a daily basis, with danger to life and limb. Under such conditions prosecution for trespassing was considered futile. He considered the adoption of the scheme would enable the company to deal with any trespassing and reduce the risk of passengers travelling by train without a ticket. It was proposed the footpaths would be made available for any person wishing to cross from one side of the railway to the other but if not travelling by train they would be required to purchase a 1d platform ticket which would be handed in as they left the station. The Traffic and Works Committees considered the report on 28th March 1935 and noted that, although originally estimated at £1,318, the costs were now revised to £1,118, and authorised the work. Later the costs were again revised to £1,086. As the scheme progressed the Cleveland Bridge & Engineering Company Limited were awarded the contract to supply the ironwork for the footbridge extension on 26th September 1935 at a cost of £434 19s 6d, against an original estimate of £385.

On the competitive bus routes, the long through workings were found unsatisfactory by the LPTB and from 27th November 1935 routes 340 and 341 were rationalised to run between St. Albans and Hertford only, via Cole Green and Bayford Turn respectively. At this time, apart from the sundry short workings between St. Albans and Hatfield, single-deck buses worked all services. As a light relief from the dwindling trade in 1936, Hertingfordbury station was used for the filming of the musical *When Knights Were Bold* starring Jack Buchanan and the Canadian-American actress Fay Wray, who had starred three years earlier in the epic film *King Kong*. The station assuming the title of Little Twittering featured in the first scenes when Buchanan playing Sir Guy de Vere arrives home upon

'N7/3' Class 0-6-2T No. 2651 running into the Down platform at Cole Green with a Hatfield to Hertford North train in 1938. To the left is the Up side platform with canopy fronting the brick and timber waiting room. *Stations UK*

inheriting his father's estate to be met by all the inhabitants of the fictional village. Fay Wray played Lady Rowena.

The L&NER issued an official notice at the end of January 1936 stating that:

On and from Monday, February 3 next, the LNER are providing by means of bridge extensions, direct access to Welwyn Garden City station from the east side of the town, the new entrance being served by footpaths, one through the goods yard at the north end and one leading from Broadwater Road at the south end. The provision of the additional entrance is designed to obviate the trespassing and irregular access to the station which has occurred in the past and it is expected that passengers and others approaching the station from the East side will adhere strictly to the routes indicated.

The *Welwyn Times* for 6th February reported the eastern entrance to the railway station, *'which has been patiently waited for by residents by the east side for over 10 years'*, was opened to the public in the dark hours of Monday morning, 3rd February, without ceremony; the first passengers buying their tickets and entering the station about 6.00am. It facetiously added the occasion should have been marked by the Chairman of the Council of the Tenants' Association ceremonial purchase of the first ticket from the new booking office to the accompanied playing of the town band. The new booking office proved popular *'with several hundred tickets being issued on the opening day'*.

The increasing industrial activity on the eastern side of the line at Welwyn Garden City exceeded all forecasts; by 1937 railway facilities to handle the growth were totally inadequate and if the L&NER company was to benefit with additional traffic urgent alterations were required. After negotiations with the Welwyn Garden City Company, the Divisional General Manager (Southern Area) submitted a report to the directors on 18th June. It was apparent that almost all land originally scheduled for industrial development had been exhausted. The Company had earmarked a further area of almost a hundred acres to the east of the main line and immediately north of the Hertford branch. The Welwyn Garden City Company had already come to terms with the Imperial Chemical Industry regarding fifteen acres where the firm intended to concentrate one of their subsidiaries, Mouldrite Limited. This firm produced the powder used to make bakelite and their existing premises at Welwyn Garden City would be closed and concentrated at the new plant. The Divisional General Manager advised that the existing rail traffic for Mouldrite Limited was mostly clay worth £650 per annum. He was of the opinion that with fifteen acres of land, ICI would transfer other subsidiaries to the site and not limit the area to Mouldrite Limited. Negotiations had been made with the Welwyn Garden City Company regarding the provision of rail facilities to the new industrial estate but because of the sharp curve of the Hertford branch it was found impracticable to lay in direct siding connections. As the ICI site was being developed a considerable quantity of construction material was shortly to be delivered; it was therefore considered necessary to provide two reception sidings capable of accommodating sixty-five wagons, with points leading from the Hertford branch, together with a siding for Mouldrite Limited leading from the reception siding and with capacity for thirty-five wagons. The estimated cost of the reception sidings was £1,617 and the private siding £684, giving a total of £2,301. The earthworks and formation outside the L&NER company boundary and owned by the Garden City Company was £1,519, whilst the maintenance of the junction points was £47 per annum. The Garden City Company had agreed to pay £150 for ten years to cover the cost of works on their land. The Traffic and Works Committees authorised the expenditure on 24th June 1937, subject to ICI paying £684 as a proportion of that sum for their exclusive facilities. During the later negotiations over the wording of the agreements between the L&NER, Welwyn Garden City Company and ICI, the Garden City Company agreed to transfer to the L&NER company free of charge the ownership of the land required for the two reception sidings. If the sidings were later removed the land would revert to former ownership. The sidings

'N7/2' Class 0-6-2T No. 2649 departing from the Hertford branch bay platform at Hatfield with a passenger service to Hertford North on Saturday 3rd June 1939. No. 2649 later became 9689 in the 1947 renumbering programme and as BR 69689 was the first 'N7' Class locomotive to be withdrawn in March 1957.
Canon C. Bayes

were completed in 1938, when Lord Cowper's sidings were replaced by the Imperial Chemicals Industry's siding.

The ever increasing industrial development and subsequent large increase in traffic brought additional work to the goods department at Welwyn Garden City and necessitated the employment of additional staff. The Divisional General Manager (Southern Area) reported to the Traffic Committee on 26th January 1939 that the existing goods office was too small to accommodate the clerical staff whilst the messroom for outside staff was totally inadequate. He advised it was proposed to extend the existing brick building to provide additional accommodation for clerks and convert the book room as an addition to the mess room for outside staff. Authority was duly given for the work to be executed at a cost of £732 and the contract awarded to J. Willmott & Sons (Hitchin) Limited on 25th May 1939 after they tendered at £868.

The development of industrial premises alongside the Hertford branch at Welwyn Garden City and to a lesser extent at Hertford Old station offered scope for increasing freight traffic, but to the concern of the L&NER authorities at King's Cross the single line working arrangements on the Hatfield to Hertford branch were totally inadequate to handle the increased train services. It was evident that improvements were required to increase the capacity of line occupation and after investigation into various methods of working the Divisional General Manager Southern Area advised the Traffic Committee on 29th June 1939 that the Train Staff and Paper Ticket method of working would be replaced by the Train Staff and Metal Ticket fitted with Annett's key enabling goods trains travelling with a Metal Ticket to shunt at intermediate sidings. An Occupational Key would enable trains to be shut in on any of four intermediate sidings, to permit other trains to pass. An outer home signal was to be provided at Hatfield No. 2 signal box to relieve Welwyn Garden City signal box of signalling the Hertford branch, whilst the Hertford to Cole Green telephone circuit was to be extended to Hatfield with connections to intermediate points. A shunt spur to accommodate eleven wagons was to be provided at Welwyn Garden City to enable the yard to be shunted independently of and without interference with the branch. The new method of working together with other signalling alterations, estimated at £1,656, was duly authorised, the total cost of the scheme being slightly offset by £30 earned from the sale of recovered materials and £119 for renewal work which would no longer be required.

In the autumn of 1939 London Passenger Transport Board advised Hertfordshire County Council and Hertford Council they proposed to operate double-deck buses between Ware and Bengeo via Hertford. They could not introduce the vehicles because Port Hill bridge, spanning the railway, was unable to take the additional weight. Hertfordshire County Council approached the L&NER authorities asking the railway company to undertake the work provided the council fully paid for the rebuilding. After the necessary negotiations the Engineer (Southern Area) advised the Works Committee that his department would undertake the rebuilding work on bridge No. 17, estimated at £2,264. On 23rd November the work was authorised, subject to Hertfordshire County Council paying an initial sum of £840 when the contract was awarded and then further regular payments as the work progressed. If the accounts remained unpaid two months from the invoice date, the Council was required to pay 5 per cent interest on the outstanding sum. The Council was also to take full responsibility for future maintenance of the bridge. Double-deck STL-type buses were also introduced in 1939 on the 341 route, whilst the 340 was abandoned as a through route, the low bridge at Cole Green limiting the road to single-deck vehicles.

The deterioration of relationships between the nations of Europe, had allowed the military and other authorities, including railway companies, to place themselves on a war footing. The advancement of the aeroplane and other military technology would be brought to the experience of every person in the land for air raids would cause loss of life and untold destruction to railways and other properties. Prior to the outbreak of war the L&NER merged with the other major railway companies under the Railway Executive Committee from 1st September 1939. A number of schemes, including blackout precautions, were introduced and an immediate reduction of road traffic came with the enforcement of petrol rationing from 16th September 1939. The branch services were not drastically reduced and soon evacuees began to arrive from the East End of London and from the south coast by special trains. As late as 1940 and 1941, Hackney, Islington and Clapham children arrived at Hertingfordbury and Cole Green, some staying in the countryside for the first time in their lives. Many cheap day facilities were withdrawn and all excursion traffic was curtailed, but with most of the local bus services removed from the roads because of the shortage of fuel caused by rationing, the railway once again came into its own. Most trains ran with a reasonably full complement of passengers and for those workers not called up to serve with the armed forces or work on the land, regular commuting took place between the branch stations and the munitions factories in the Lea Valley via Hertford East, and to Hatfield and stations on the St. Albans branch. Various precautions were taken to guard against air raids, especially at night when station lamps remained unlit or dimmed to provide minimum illumination and staff used shielded hand lamps to attend to trains and for shunting duties. To assist passengers in the hours of darkness the platform edges received a coating of whitewash. The agricultural nature of the local freight handled by the branch was of the utmost importance as the vital provisions of home-grown food, grain, vegetables and fruit traffic were dispatched away to markets. In addition to the outward flow of produce, the war years brought an influx of tinned food by rail to the many Ministry of Food storage depots in the area.

With the reduction in passenger leisure travel and growth of freight traffic brought about by the increase in the number of private sidings on the branch, the L&NER operating authorities soon found the Train Staff and Metal Ticket system of working, introduced as recently as 1939, to be totally inadequate. In 1941 it was decided to alter the system of working the western end of the branch, which had the greater number of sidings, so as to make it more flexible. To achieve greater capacity, Key Token working was introduced between Hatfield and Cole Green, with intermediate token instruments at four outlying sidings. The existing Train Staff and Metal Ticket system was retained between Cole Green and Hertford North, whilst at the same time alternative Long Section working with suitably interlocking arrangements at Cole Green was introduced between Hatfield and Hertford. In the same year improvements were made to the Down side of Hatfield station, the dead end platform siding previously used by only St. Albans and Dunstable branch trains being converted to a through running line with connections to the Down main and Down slow lines at the south of the station.

By 1943 the increasing difficulties handling heavy war-time traffic Up the former GNR main line through Welwyn Garden City and Hatfield were giving cause for concern. The situation was especially critical at Hatfield where wagons passing to and from the Dunstable, St. Albans and Hertford branches were sorted and marshalled for onward transit. The additional traffic movements generated as the result of hostilities, with as many as sixteen special freight trains working into the junction from the Dunstable branch alone, meant the situation was far beyond the capacity of Hatfield yards to handle. It was impracticable to transfer the shunting work to Hitchin, which was already overtaxed, whilst Peterborough was too far distant. Occasionally as many as 400 wagons had to be held back at various points as there was no room for them at Hatfield. It was therefore of the utmost necessity that improvements in freight handling facilities be made at both Hatfield and Welwyn Garden City and in September 1943 the necessary authority costing £62,325 and financed by the Ministry of War Transport was given. At Welwyn Garden City a new Up-side marshalling yard was laid out on the east side of the main line, immediately south of the station. It was formed of five double-ended sidings capable of holding 162 wagons, so arranged that southbound freight trains could run directly into the yard, and when the wagons had been sorted, continue on their journey without delay. The existing goods yard, then consisting of three short dead-end sidings and capable of holding fifty-one wagons, was extended and converted into through lines to accommodate a further eighty-one wagons, giving a total of 132 wagon capacity. Additional loading facilities, loading docks, cart roadways and office accommodation was also included in the scheme. The scheme also provided for a 30-foot-long engine inspection pit and water column. The construction of the marshalling yard and extension of the goods yard necessitated closing the footpath used by passengers approaching the station from the east side of the railway. The footbridge was therefore extended to about three times its previous length and gave direct access via Hyde Way to that side of the Garden City. A new booking office was also constructed at the east end of the bridge.

To cater for the new arrangements and give greater capacity on the main line, the single line Hertford branch was terminated at Welwyn Garden City and the section onwards to Hatfield converted into a new Up goods line. The former Up goods line between the two points was converted into the Up slow line. At the north end of Welwyn Garden City new yard access was provided into the Up slow line and in the Hertford branch, whilst at the south end by a trailing connection into the Up slow line. An additional outlet from the ICI siding north of the station provided access directly into the Up slow line. The new connections were brought into use on 17th September 1944. At Hatfield the former Hertford branch platform line was connected to the Up slow through a trailing connection at the south end of the platform. To complete the conversion new facing connections were made at the north end of Hatfield station between the new Up goods line and the new Up slow, and between the new Up slow and the existing Up main line, the works costing £8,528 and financed by the Ministry of War Transport.

With the conversion of the former Hertford branch into the new Up goods line south of Welwyn Garden City and the termination of the branch at the station certain signalling alterations were necessary. The Key Token instruments at Hatfield were transferred to Welwyn Garden City signal box and the number of intermediate Token instruments reduced to two. The release of the points to the ICI siding was also transferred to Welwyn Garden City signal box as they were within signal limits. The starting signals on the Welwyn Garden City to Cole Green section were released by the appropriate Token but those between Cole Green and Hertford required 'Line Clear' in addition so that Train Ticket working could operate if necessary.

On several occasions the branch from Hertford East to Hatfield, and later Welwyn Garden City, was used as a diversionary route by troop trains from and to Peterborough to avoid problem areas closer to London. Most movements were arranged at short notice and usually a 'J3' or 'J4' Class 0-6-0 tender locomotive or an 'N7' Class 0-6-2 tank locomotive was diagrammed for the special. Fortunately, enemy action caused few problems for the former Hatfield to Hertford branch line during the hostilities; however, at 4.55am on 10th October 1944 a 'V1' flying bomb fell near Hatfield No. 3 signal box causing only slight damage to the structure and superficial damage to the station buildings. There were no casualties but the block telegraph and other communications were destroyed between Hatfield and Welwyn Garden City. Trains on all lines were worked by the time interval system until 8.10am when all communications were restored and normal block working of trains resumed. Then on 17th January 1945 at 11.45am a 'V2' rocket fell in the vicinity of Molewood tunnel just to the north of Hertford North station, followed by a second at 12 noon. All communication between Hertford North and Watton-at-Stone were severed but the Hatfield to Hertford North branch service was unaffected.

Peacetime returned and a further extension to the buildings on the Down platform at Welwyn Garden City was sanctioned on 27th September 1945, to provide two separate offices, one for the station foreman and the other for the station master's clerk. The period after the war, however, found the railways resuming peacetime activities with run-down rolling stock and equipment, and dilapidated stations and buildings. Lack of proper maintenance during the hostilities had left affairs in a sorry plight. As late as November 1946 Derek Walker Smith, the MP for Hertfordshire, asked the Minister of Transport when an improvement could be expected in the L&NER services from Liverpool Street to Broxbourne, Bishop's Stortford, Buntingford and Hertford. Fellow MPs quickly added their concerns about the branch services radiating from Hatfield.

The severe weather early in 1947 brought problems, initially with heavy snow and then in February when thawing caused the local rivers to rise and break their banks to flood the surrounding land. The Hertford to Welwyn Garden City branch suffered from minor flooding during this period when water flushed off the surrounding fields and washed away some of the ballast. As the water subsided, so permanent way staff quickly replaced the clinker and ashes but speed restrictions were enforced for over a month until the trackbed consolidated. The branch services continued to serve the locality but as petrol rationing eased so bus services improved and passengers once again turned to the competitor who could offer an almost door-to-door service. The poor state of Britain's railways could not be disguised and with nationalisation on the horizon the future of the Welwyn Garden City to Hertford North branch passenger service looked none too secure.

The entire railway network was still under Government control and the post war political mood did little to encourage investment. It was the declared intention of the Labour Government to nationalise the majority of public utilities and associated industries, including railways, which they had announced in their 1945 election manifesto. The Royal Assent was given on 6th August 1947 to the Transport Bill establishing the British Transport Commission for the purpose of setting up a publicly owned system of inland transport, other than by air. From 1st January 1948 the intention was to take over the railways and canal undertakings – including the London Passenger Transport Board – specified in a schedule of all main-line railways, their joint committees and smaller undertakings at that time under the control of the Railway Executive Committee. The scene was thus set for further changes to this Hertfordshire branch line.

Close up view of the ornate buildings at Hertingfordbury station with from right to left the goods transit shed, booking office and porter's room and station master's house with its unusually tall chimneys. Although the advertising boards are headed LNER, the posters are promoting travel by British Railways; the one on the transit shed is for Bridlington. *D. Dent collection*

7

Nationalisation and Closure

THE NATIONALISATION OF THE RAILWAYS from 1st January 1948 initially brought few changes to the Hertford to Welwyn Garden City branch, which except for locomotives and rolling stock retained the GNR/L&NER atmosphere until the withdrawal of steam traction from the line. Most stocks of L&NER tickets remained in use until the branch closed for passenger traffic, although tickets in constant demand were replaced by those bearing the legend 'Railway Executive' or 'British Railways'. Locomotives working the line soon lost the 'NE' or 'LNER' on the side tanks or tenders and 'BRITISH RAILWAYS' was substituted, whilst varnished teak or brown paint remained on the branch coaching stock until the withdrawal of passenger traffic.

British Railways (BR) made few alterations to the timetable and although a through service was operated to London from the branch stations, passenger numbers continued to dwindle. With the ever increasing competition from local bus routes – especially London Transport route 341 which ran from Hertford to St. Albans via Hatfield, the 350 Hertford to New Barnet via Cole Green and another route from the county town to Welwyn Garden City – the passenger trains ran almost empty. The cost-conscious Railway Executive had directed the railway regions to investigate unremunerative lines and the new British Railways Eastern Region management at King's Cross was soon seriously investigating loss-making services when it became all too evident from the poor traffic receipts that the Hertford North to Welwyn Garden City passenger service was a prime suspect for pruning.

Thus early in January 1951 the Railway Executive advised the county and parish councils of the possible closure of the branch to passenger traffic. It appeared to British Railways that a bus running on a similar route to the railway and serving the same villages was a more convenient method of transportation as it ran nearer to the centres of the rural population of Hertingfordbury, Cole Green and Letty Green. The Executive stressed it had no obligation to keep the line open for those people who did not live near the route.

The proposed closure immediately became the main topic of discussion at the various council meetings. At the North Hertfordshire Joint Transport Conference held at Letchworth the delegates resolved that BR was under a moral obligation to maintain the service and suggested running services during the morning and evening peak periods only. Replying to the subsequent petition the BR Eastern Region management statement said economies had to be effected and the suggested arrangements would still require the employment of guards and porters.

With all attention focused on possible withdrawal of passenger services, Cole Green station and the branch were used on Sunday 7th January 1951 by the BBC TV crew to shoot scenes for the filming of Enid Nesbit's classic *The Railway Children*. Former GER 'T26' Class, L&NER 'E4' Class 2-4-0 tender locomotive No. 62791 was brought out of store at Stratford for the event and specially cleaned for the filming, although the BRITISH RAILWAYS on the tender sides was obliterated with grease. No. 62791 worked via Hertford East and Hertford North to Cole Green with four Eastern Region coaches and spent most of the restricted daylight hours steaming up and down the branch and pulling to a halt at Cole Green. By 13th January the 'E4' Class locomotive was back in store at Stratford shed.

Despite the vigorous opposition to closure, at the beginning of May BR announced the withdrawal of passenger train services from the Welwyn Garden City to Hertford North line on and from Monday 18th June 1951. It was considered London Transport Country bus service 372, operating between Welwyn Garden City and Hertford and serving Cole Green and Hertingfordbury, provided an adequate alternative service and no hardship would ensue. Cartage for parcels traffic was to be operated from Hatfield to Cole Green and Hertford to Hertingfordbury.

Hertford Cowbridge station in 1951 showing the relatively short low platform. After the withdrawal of passenger services the building was used as a goods office and accommodation for a railwayman and his family.
Author's collection

Hatfield station in the latter year of branch traffic viewed from the Up platform looking north showing the Up platform and connecting footbridge No. 60 at 17 miles 55¾ chains ex King's Cross. Note the mail being trollied across the main lines on the barrow crossing. *Author's collection*

0-4-2 locomotive *Lion* standing at the Down platform at Cole Green station during the filming of *The Lady with the Lamp* on 4th June 1951. The locomotive is hauling replica 4-wheel Liverpool & Manchester Railway coaches built by the London Midland & Scottish Railway in 1930 for the centenary of the Liverpool & Manchester Railway celebrations. Hatfield shed provided a footplate crew in period costume, whilst *Lion* had to have wheel flanges specially profiled to work through the station during filming.
LCGB/Ken Nunn

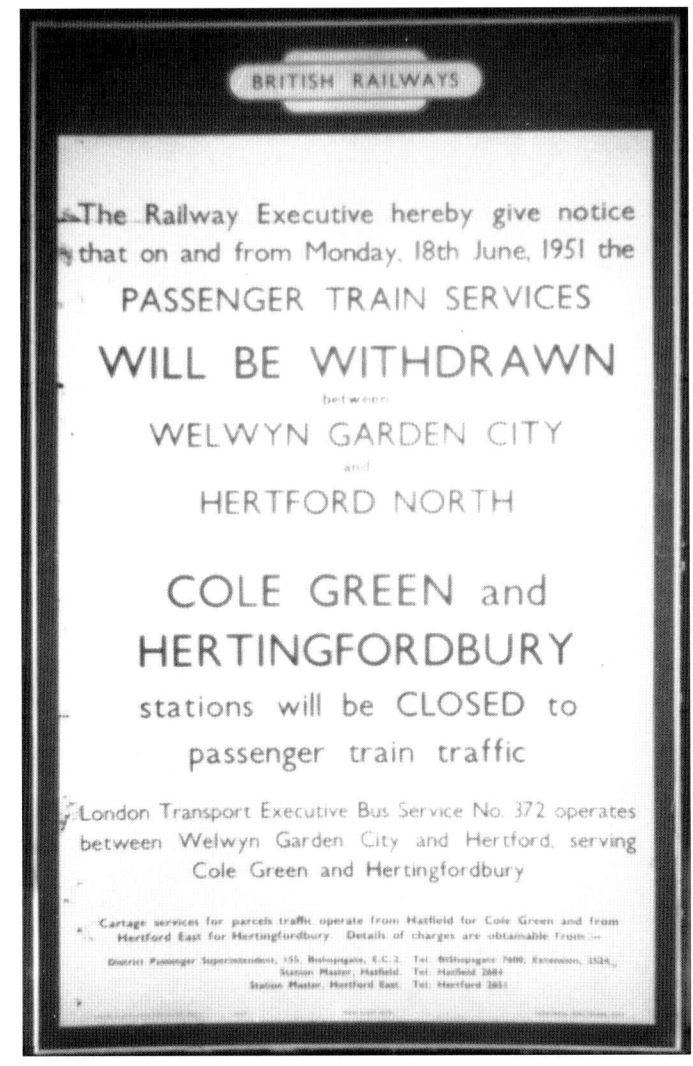

Notice of the withdrawal of passenger services from the Welwyn Garden City to Hertford North branch on and from Monday 18th June 1951. *Author's collection*

Early in June 1951 the branch again gained fame when Cole Green station was used for filming scenes for the film *Lady with the Lamp* starring Anna Neagle as Florence Nightingale. Cole Green was renamed Whatstandwell for the occasion. The former Liverpool & Manchester Railway 0-4-2 tender locomotive *Lion* was brought out of retirement to work with three coaches specially built by the London Midland & Scottish Railway at Crewe Works for the 1930 centenary celebrations. The locomotive and coaches departed from Crewe Works and were delivered by rail to site on 30th May on Crocodile wagons before being unloaded by crane. Before working on the branch the locomotive tyres and flanges had to be correctly profiled. *Lion*, crewed by Hatfield footplatemen suitably attired in period dress, steamed with its train into and out of the platform on 3rd and 4th June until scenes were finalised; the stock was returned from Cole Green to Crewe loaded on wagons the following day.

This was the swansong of the branch for the announcement was made that the passenger services would be withdrawn on and from Monday 18th June 1951; there being no Sunday service, the last operational day was the previous Saturday. As the final day of passenger train operation approached the numbers of regular travellers was augmented by railway enthusiasts taking the opportunity to ride between Welwyn Garden City and Hertford North for the last time. The final Up passenger train, the 7.18pm Hertford North to Welwyn Garden City on Saturday 16th June 1951, was formed of two 2-coach articulated sets hauled by 'N7/2' Class 0-6-2 tank locomotive No. 69695 running bunker first. The platform was crowded with people and one coach was occupied by members of the Hertford Dramatic & Operatic Society with men dressed in top hats and frock coats and the women in tight laced Victorian costumes together with two small boys in sailor suits. Two Gladstone bags and a tin trunk were placed on board the train as the station master and Counsellor W.V. Proctor shook hands with the Hatfield train crew: Driver J. Warner, Fireman A. Hill, accompanied by King's Cross Locomotive Inspector Maynard and Guard W.A. Hancock. Sharp to time, Guard Hancock gave 'right away' and the train departed over the points to join the single line branch exploding detonators in its path. The well-filled train was scheduled

Hatfield goods yard view facing north in early BR days, with the goods shed to the left. All sidings appear to be occupied by wagons which must have proved a shunter's nightmare when empty wagons by the buffer stops required to be moved to make way for arriving vehicles. *Author's collection*

'N7/2' Class 0-6-2T No. 69695 at Hertford North with the last regular passenger service on the branch, the 7.18pm train to Welwyn Garden City on 16th June 1951. Passengers in period costume are conversing with the engine crew before departure. *Author's collection*

to run non-stop and duly passed the deserted Hertingfordbury station but a call was made at Cole Green at 7.24pm for 1½ minutes where a large contingent joined the train. On the approach to Welwyn Garden City more detonators were exploded and as the train pulled into the platform at 7.33pm, after its sixteen-minute journey, it was met by Station Master T. Saunders.

The Rector of Hertingfordbury, the Reverend W.E. Woosnam Jones penned the following poem to record the passing of the passenger traffic.

Along our glebe
The old trains go,
Wheezy and wan,
And terribly slow.

Only three or four
Go by all day,
There used to be more
The old folks say.

Back a hundred years
When trains were new,
And folks came a running
When the whistle blew.

And the engine roared past
Going like the wind,
With trucks and carriages
Rumbling behind.

And the passengers all cheery
And the guard so bold,
Sitting on the tops
So I've been told.

And the speed it went
Made folks feel queer,
And scared all the horses
And Lord Cowper's deer.

But now they reckon
The old train's slow,
And in buses and cars
The folks all go.

A shopping and a marketing
Up to the town,
So they're going to close
The old line down.

But many will sigh,
When naught remains
Of our old railroad,
And its little trains

For down in the village
The old folks moan,
Those days were happier
Long ago.

From Monday 18th June 1951, to coincide with the official withdrawal of passenger traffic, Cole Green and Hertingfordbury goods yards were downgraded to un-staffed public sidings. For some time following closure an empty coaching stock train worked across the branch, the 4.57pm arrival at Hertford North via Enfield Chase, then ran to Welwyn Garden City via Cole Green to form the 5.58pm passenger train to King's Cross.

The BOT inspection of various installations on the branch, which had been delayed by World War Two and other pressing matters, was belatedly carried out by Brigadier C.A. Langley on 26th June 1951. At Welwyn Garden City he found the private sidings installed for ICI in 1938, with connections from the Hertford branch, were originally worked by a ground frame controlled by Annett's key attached to the Train Staff or Train Staff Metal Ticket. By the time of the inspection the ground frame was released electrically from Welwyn Garden City signal box. The extensive alterations at Welwyn Garden City had involved considerable signalling and track alterations and Langley noted that all running lines within station limits were track circuited. The controls were in accordance with Eastern Region standard practice, whilst the crossings in the running lines were formed of 95 lbs per yard track, with second-hand materials in the sidings. Brigadier Langley noted the Hertford branch was closed for passenger traffic but that the signalling facilities installed in 1943 were being retained in case any special or excursion trains were worked across the branch.

Along the line the crossing work at Hatfield was the same as at Welwyn Garden City and generally in good order, but at the time of the inspector's visit clay had worked up through the ballast on the

In 1954 the engine turntable at Hatfield shed was removed as surplus to requirements, not being necessary for turning the tank engines allocated to the depot. On 24th May, however, before the pit could be filled in the driver of 'N7/5' Class 0-6-2T No. 69638 failed to control the locomotive which did not stop, resulting in the engine falling into the gap. *Peter Townend*

'N7/5' Class 0-6-2T No. 69635 heads a train of 16-ton all steel mineral wagons across Mill Tail underbridge No. 20 in 1955 en route to industrial sidings east of Dicker Mill crossing. Note the goods brake van and a tar tank wagon behind the engine.
Ed Graves

Up slow line and pushed the track out of alignment on the facing connection leading to the Up main. There were also problems with the Down side facing connections and he was advised of the serious shortage of permanent way staff in the Hatfield District with the local permanent way inspector experiencing great difficulty maintaining the passenger lines in first class condition. He had rightly concentrated on the main lines but Langley required immediate action on the problem areas. Langley tested the interlocking at various signal boxes as far as time and traffic would permit and found it satisfactory. None of the signalmen had any comments to make.

With the run-down of the branch and the reduction in freight traffic, further rationalisation took place when the Up loop line at Cole Green station was lifted in 1953. At the same time the redundant timber buildings on the Down side platform were demolished leaving only the brick buildings extant. Thus the branch entered into a somnolent state with the goods yards at Cole Green and Hertingfordbury receiving little traffic other than supplies of

RIGHT: 'B12/3' Class 4-6-0 tender locomotive No. 61576 stands at Hatfield after hauling the Railway Correspondence & Travel Society's 'Hertfordshire Railtour' train consisting of six ex-LM&SR coaches from St. Pancras via Hertford East Junction, Hertford North and the branch to Welwyn Garden City and Hatfield on 30th April 1955. The locomotive was replaced by 'J52' Class 0-6-0 saddle tank No. 68878 for the continuation of the tour to St. Albans Abbey. *Author's collection*

BELOW: Hertford North station on 17th July 1955 with 'L1' Class 2-6-4T No. 67793 waiting in the Down back platform to depart with a train for King's Cross. An engineering train headed by a 'B1' Class 4-6-0 stands on the Up main line. The branch to Hertford Cowbridge and Hertford East can be seen curving away to the east.
J.F. Aylard

Craven 2-car diesel multiple unit forming the Stephenson Locomotive Society special on 21st November 1959 pausing at the Down platform at Cole Green, where only the station building is extant on the former Down platform. *Author's collection*

The same special train as above stands at Hertingfordbury on 21st November 1959 to allow railtour passengers to inspect the station and take photographs. Participants arrived by service train from King's Cross to join the special at Welwyn Garden City for the journey across the branch to Hertford East. From there passengers were booked to return via Broxbourne to Liverpool Street on service trains. The train was not advertised and was for SLS members only. *Author's collection*

domestic coal and coke. In contrast, the sidings at Holwell Hyde saw a vast increase in rubbish from London Boroughs which was used as landfill for the exhausted ballast pits, although even this declined from a train every weekday to often only two trains a week.

As the decade progressed, railway enthusiasts increasingly became interested in minor branch lines especially where passenger services had been withdrawn. The first of these special trains – the 'Hertfordshire Railtour' organised by the Railway Correspondence & Travel Society – ran on 30th April 1955, departing from St. Pancras at 1.55pm hauled by 'B12/3' Class 4-6-0 tender locomotive No. 61576. The train was routed via Kentish Town, South Tottenham and the former GER main line along the Lea Valley to Broxbourne, from whence it ran to Hertford East and the junction to Hertford Old, then on via Cole Green and Welwyn Garden City to Hatfield. The train, formed of six ex-LM&SR corridor coaches, then reversed and, hauled by 'J52' Class 0-6-0ST No. 68878, ran to St. Albans Abbey from where it was worked forward onto the London Midland Region. For the record, ex-L&NWR 0-8-0 No. 49431 hauled the train from St. Albans to Watford Junction where Stanier 0-4-4T No. 41909 worked separate stock on two round trips to Rickmansworth Church Street. No. 49431 then hauled the main train to St. Pancras sidings where No. 68878 hauled the special via King's Cross Goods and Mineral Junction and Copenhagen Junction to terminate at Finsbury Park.

On 27th April 1958 the Railway Correspondence & Travel Society organised their 'Hertfordshire Railtour No. 2', commencing at London Fenchurch Street at 12.00 noon and terminating at Broad Street at 6.55pm. The train, formed of eight coaches, commenced its journey behind 'N7' Class 0-6-2T No. 69614, the highly polished Liverpool Street West Side Pilot engine which suffered a defective steam joint en route to Harrow and Wealdstone before failing completely at Watford Junction. Sister engine No. 69632 from Hatfield, in surprisingly clean condition, was sent to St. Albans Abbey, where it took over from ex-LM&SR Stanier 0-4-4T No. 41901 which had worked a separate 4-coach push-and-pull special from Harrow and Wealdstone to Stanmore and return to Watford Junction before hauling the 8-coach train to St. Albans Abbey. Here Class 'N7' No. 69632 took over the train for the run to Hatfield before continuing from Hatfield: depart 4.08pm for Welwyn Garden City 4.13pm to 4.28pm, thence to Hertford North signal box 4.52pm to 4.54pm, and on to Hertford East junction 4.49pm to 5.09pm, before the run thence via Broxbourne, Bury Street Junction, Stratford and Lea Junction to Broad Street, arriving at 6.55pm.

The Stephenson Locomotive Society (London & Southern Area) organised a special 2-car Craven diesel multiple unit to work across the branch from Welwyn Garden City to Hertford East via Hertford Cowbridge on 21st November 1959. Participants travelled by normal service train from King's Cross to Welwyn Garden City, where they joined the special train which departed at 1.52pm. After arrival at Hertford East the passengers returned to Liverpool Street by normal service train. During the course of the journey across the branch the multiple unit called at all the closed stations to allow photographs to be taken. Then on 16th September 1961 preserved former GNR 'J52' Class 0-6-0ST No. 1247, ex 68846, worked a South Bedfordshire Locomotive Club 'Lea Flyer' special train across the branch. Formed of BR Mark 1 corridor stock the train commenced its journey at Welwyn Garden City, departing

Former 'J52' Class 0-6-0ST preserved at GNR No. 1247 standing at Cole Green with the South Bedfordshire Locomotive Society 'Lea Flyer' rail tour train on 16th September 1961.
R.C. Riley

The remains of Cole Green station facing towards Welwyn Garden City on 5th February 1959. Only the former Down loop line remains whilst the timber and brick building on the Up platform are extant. The canopy has, however, been removed from the front of the Down side station buildings. *Author's collection*

The coal depot located on the site of the former sidings east of Dicker Mill Lane, Hertford in 1961. The level crossing is in the background protected by Hertford Old fixed distant signal. *Author's collection*

Demolition of North Road underbridge No. 12 on Sunday 2nd April 1967. *P. Whitaker*

2.15pm, and called at all stations for photographic stops: Cole Green 2.37pm to 2.50pm, Hertingfordbury 2.56pm to 3.10pm and Hertford Cowbridge arriving at 3.26pm. After reversing, the train departed Hertford Cowbridge at 4.15pm and returned to Welwyn Garden City. The train then continued, departing Hatfield at 5.15pm to terminate at Luton Bute Street at 6.00pm.

Two goods workings ran across the branch on weekdays between Welwyn Garden City and Hertford, but when goods facilities were withdrawn from Hertingfordbury on and from 5th March 1962 the working was terminated at Cole Green. When freight traffic was withdrawn from the intermediate station on and from 1st August 1962 the service terminated at Welwyn Garden City except for the rubbish trains destined for Holwell sidings. In 1963 the timber buildings and canopy on the Up platform at Cole Green were demolished leaving a desolate site compared to Hertingfordbury, where the former station became a private dwelling.

From the end of 1963 the section of line from Hertford North to Hertford Cowbridge station was abandoned as traffic for the latter was worked direct from Hertford East, and the GER section took over responsibility for providing shunting power for the yard. The track remained in-situ for over a year, gradually disappearing under a sea of weeds and brambles. In April 1965 it was expected a contract would soon be awarded for removal of the permanent way. The connection was finally severed on the weekend of 23rd and 24th October 1965, when buffer stops were erected on the west side of Hertford Cowbridge station.

After the closure of Cole Green, trains continued to bring refuse to Holwell ballast pit as well as serving the remaining intermediate sidings. Attimore siding closed on 4th May 1964 and Luton Council rubbish continued to be offloaded at Holwell siding until the last train ran on 30th April 1966. Traffic was officially withdrawn on and from 23rd May 1966, leaving a short section near Welwyn Garden City open to serve the premises of Guest, Keen & Nettlefold and Norton Abrasives. Goods facilities were finally withdrawn from Hertford Cowbridge on 18th April 1966, the station having dealt only with coal traffic from 3rd January of that year.

Lifting of the branch track commenced in July 1967 and all permanent way was removed except for a short 1½ mile section at the Welwyn Garden City end of the line, retained to serve the Guest Keen & Nettlefold Limited Works and Norton Abrasives Limited. Curiously, Hertingfordbury station was used for the filming of the BBC children's television programme *Catweasle* in 1970. During excavation work for electrification on the Great Northern main line the former Hertford branch was severed just south of Welwyn Garden City during construction of a flyover. The only access to the two sidings was via Welwyn Garden City goods yard

The trackbed of the branch was the subject of controversy for some time. In March 1972 Hertfordshire County Council announced plans to acquire part of the route for conversion to a bridleway and cycle track, whilst the New Towns Commission and gravel companies had purchased sections of the line between Cole Green and Welwyn Garden City. The County Council planned the walkway from the outskirts of Hertford to the A414 Hatfield to Hertford road in connection with the recreational use of Cole Green station as a car park and picnic area. The concept was unpopular with local residents who formed 'The Green Action Group' to fight

From the end of 1963 the section of line between Hertford North and Hertford Cowbridge exclusive was abandoned and traffic for intermediate sidings was handled by trip workings from Hertford East. Gradually this section saw closures and when Cowbridge coal traffic ceased on and from 18th April 1966 the buffer stops edged ever nearer to the former Hertford Junction as only a few intermediate sidings were served. In this view facing east, the buffer stops are a few yards short of the former Dicker Mill crossing. *Ed Graves collection*

Contractors dismantling the railway on the Hertford side of Hertingfordbury station on 10th July 1967; view facing towards Welwyn Garden City. Much of the trackbed of the branch has been converted into a walking and cycle path known as the 'Cole Green Way' with parking facilities at the site of Cole Green station.
R. Hummerston

the threat of increased traffic and pollution of the countryside. The walk is now known as the 'Cole Green Way'.

Welwyn Garden City goods yard was closed on 5th April 1975 except for private sidings, the same year as the dilapidated buildings at Cole Green station were demolished. Traffic to Guest, Keen & Nettlefold's siding had continued irregularly until the summer of 1970, although the siding remained extant until 1981. Until the late 1970s, Welwyn Garden City was allocated a Class '08' diesel electric shunting locomotive and this took daily trips along the truncated Hertford branch to deliver and clear wagons from the two remaining sidings.

Gradually the GKN factory ceased to provide traffic and the mainstay of the line was goods to Norton Abrasives Limited which required two or three trips a week, normally departing Welwyn Garden City at 10.30 hours, the round trip taking some 30 minutes. In April 1980 a Class '31' Brush Type 2 diesel electric locomotive made a trial trip on the branch to ensure it could negotiate the 8 chains radius curve away from the main line. All was successful and thereafter Class '31' locomotives took over the branch duties and the Class '08' was transferred away.

The amount of traffic declined further: Norton Abrasives received one train per week, when four to six wagons were usually sufficient. The train was usually formed of 21-ton hopper wagons covered in tarpaulin and lettered 'Electro-Furnace Products Hull'. After arriving at Welwyn Garden City from the north, the Class '31' ran round its train and took the wagons Down the branch, returning shortly after with the brake van. The empty wagons were usually recovered several days later. With the termination of the contract with BR, traffic ceased and the last working was on 12th November 1981 when the Brush Type 2 Class '31', with several short wheelbase wagons and a brake van, made the short journey to pick up empty wagons for the last time. Two weeks later, two short sections of rail were removed from a point just before the curve away from the main line and a sleeper was placed across the track to mark the new end of the line. Thereafter for a short period the siding was used for storing empty coaching stock before the remaining track was lifted and the former H&WJR was consigned to history.

Much of the former railway between the outer fringes of Welwyn Garden City and Hertingfordbury forms part of the Cole Green Way, a cycle and bridleway with parking and picnic facilities at the site of Cole Green station. Hertingfordbury station is now a private dwelling. Elsewhere the trackbed has disappeared under farm fields, but at Hertford, where Cowbridge station building was demolished in December 1990, much of the railway land has been redeveloped, including most of the station site, which is now part of Sainsbury's supermarket and associated car park and council car park. In 2008 the derelict track bed in the deep cutting between Port Hill bridge and Port Vale bridge was offered for sale by British Railways (Subsidiary) Board, later Railtrack, and was subsequently sold to a purchaser from Mill Hill in North London. With restricted access, to date the land has not been developed.

The county town still enjoys the luxury of two railway routes – from Hertford East and Hertford North – but few now remember the single-track railway which connected the community to Hatfield. Fortunately cyclists, joggers, ramblers and walkers using the Cole Green Way can enjoy the rural surroundings of the former line where once 0-4-4, 4-4-2 and 0-6-2 tank locomotives in apple green or austere black livery, hauling teak or brown painted carriages, roused the echoes and disturbed the wildlife for a few brief seconds on their journey.

8

The Route Described

BEFORE EMBARKING ON THIS CHAPTER, the reader must be made aware that the GNR Hatfield to Hertford branch, although under 10 miles in length, was endowed with a plethora of sidings installed and removed at various times over the life span of the railway. For clarity the first part of the chapter describes the route of the branch and its terminal and intermediate stations, with only basic reference to sidings, whilst the second part provides a fuller description of the many connections off the main single line. A further complication was that initially the mileage quoted was from zero at King's Cross and most railway departments used this measurement. However, at various times zero was recorded from Hatfield as shown on the GNR gradient diagram, and then again zero from the junction at Welwyn. For clarity the mileage in this chapter is zero from King's Cross, although there is reference to the alternative mileage as necessary.

For 68 years Hatfield station was the junction for the Hertford branch. Located 17 miles 54½ chains from King's Cross, the station was originally the fifth when the GNR line from Maiden Lane to the North opened on 7th August 1850. The station served a small community of 3,800 inhabitants who mostly lived to the west of the Great North Road. The town was a staging post for horse drawn coaches and over seventy called daily at the various establishments in the town. With the advent of the railway, road traffic declined.

Hatfield had already secured a place in history with its close association with the first Queen Elizabeth who was imprisoned at the Great House built in the late 15th century by Bishop Morton of Ely. It was during this period, in November 1558, that Elizabeth was informed of her succession to the throne of England on the death of Queen Mary. In later years Hatfield House was enlarged and rebuilt by members of the Cecil family, and the third Marquis of Salisbury was thrice Prime Minister of England.

When the railway was first constructed, agreement had been reached with Lord Salisbury for the GNR to build a station convenient for Hatfield House. The railway thus swung in a large arc around the estate on its route to where a station was provided directly opposite the main gates to the house. The siting of the

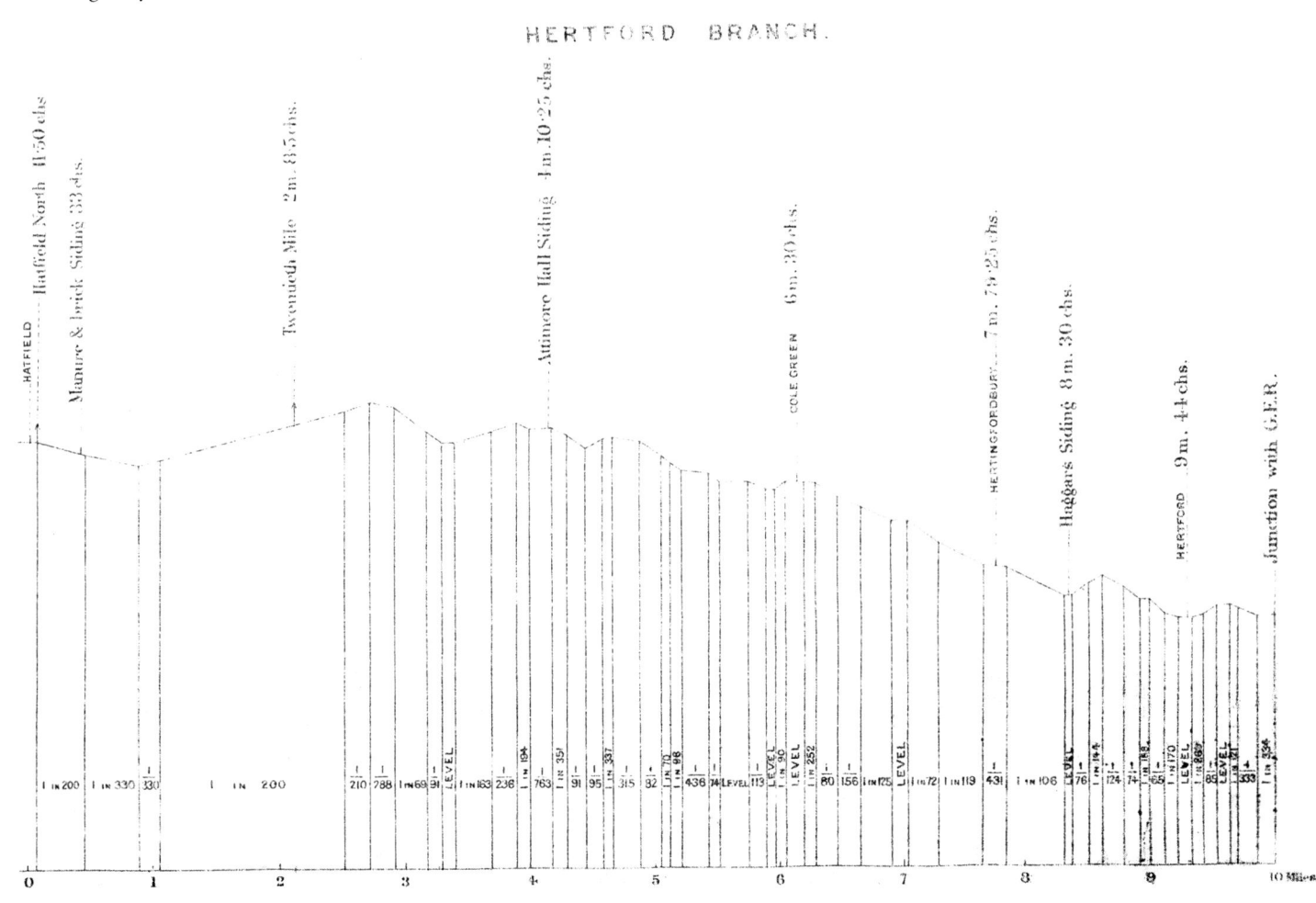

GNR Hatfield to Hertford GE Junction gradient chart.

Hatfield Station 1903

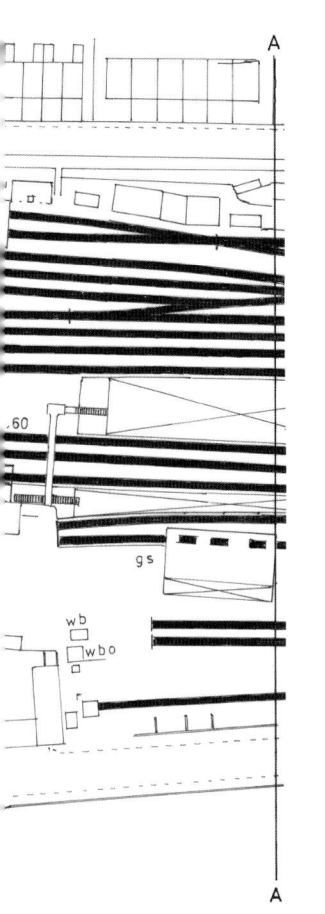

Key to Track Diagrams

BO	BOOKING OFFICE
CD	CATTLE DOCK
CP	CATTLE PENS
CS	COAL STAGE
FB	FOOTBRIDGE
FP	FOOTPATH
GKC	GATE KEEPER'S COTTAGE
GO	GOODS OFFICE
GS	GOODS SHED
LC	LEVEL CROSSING
LD	LOADING DOCK
LG	LOADING GAUGE
MP	MILE POST
OB	OVERBRIDGE
OC	OCCUPATION CROSSING
PWH	PERMANENT WAY HUT
RR	REFRESHMENT ROOM
SB	STATION BUILDINGS
SC	SIGNAL BOX
SMH	STATION MASTER'S HOUSE
SMO	STATION MASTER'S OFFICE
SP	SIGNAL POST
UB	UNDERBRIDGE
WB	WEIGHBRIDGE
WBO	WEIGHBRIDGE OFFICE
WC	WATER COLUMN
WPH	WATER PUMPHOUSE
WR	WAITING ROOM
WT	WATER TANK

station also entailed a slight deviation of the Great North Road, which passed immediately between the station entrance and the gates to the house.

Hatfield station, in its final form before complete rebuilding for electrification of the main line, had some grand features. The two platforms in staggered formation were connected by Station footbridge No. 60 at 17 miles 55¾ chains. Both the Up side and Down side island platform had waiting rooms, whilst the Up side also had a refreshment room. The eastern face of the Down island platform served the Down fast line, at which all trains from London arrived and departed. The outside or western face was used by both St. Albans and Dunstable branch services. As the back platform line initially had no facing connection from the Down fast line, through trains from King's Cross to Dunstable had to run through the station and set back into the platform before continuing the journey. At other times the two branch trains were positioned at the back platform awaiting arrival of the London train, the St. Albans in front and the Dunstable in the rear. This arrangement remained until 1941 when a connection was made from the Down goods line to the back platform road, which had hitherto not carried passenger trains, between Red Hall signal box, located just over one mile south of Hatfield and the station.

The eastern or Up side platform was served by the Up slow line and originally had bay platforms to the north and south. London local trains used the latter whilst Hertford branch trains were accommodated at the north end bay. Until 1935 the Up platform possessed an early GNR awning roof which extended over the running line. Adjacent to the southern bay was the small waiting room built especially for Lord Salisbury, which in L&NER days housed the District Signalling School.

The goods yard located to the east of the Hertford branch contained a goods shed and nine sidings, one of which served Sheriff's grist mill, opened in 1905 with its four associated cottages The Sheriff family had arrived at Hatfield in 1872 from Northampton to take over a brewing, corn and coal business. The mill, used for the grinding of flour as well as storing seed corn and animal foodstuffs, burnt down in the 1960s.

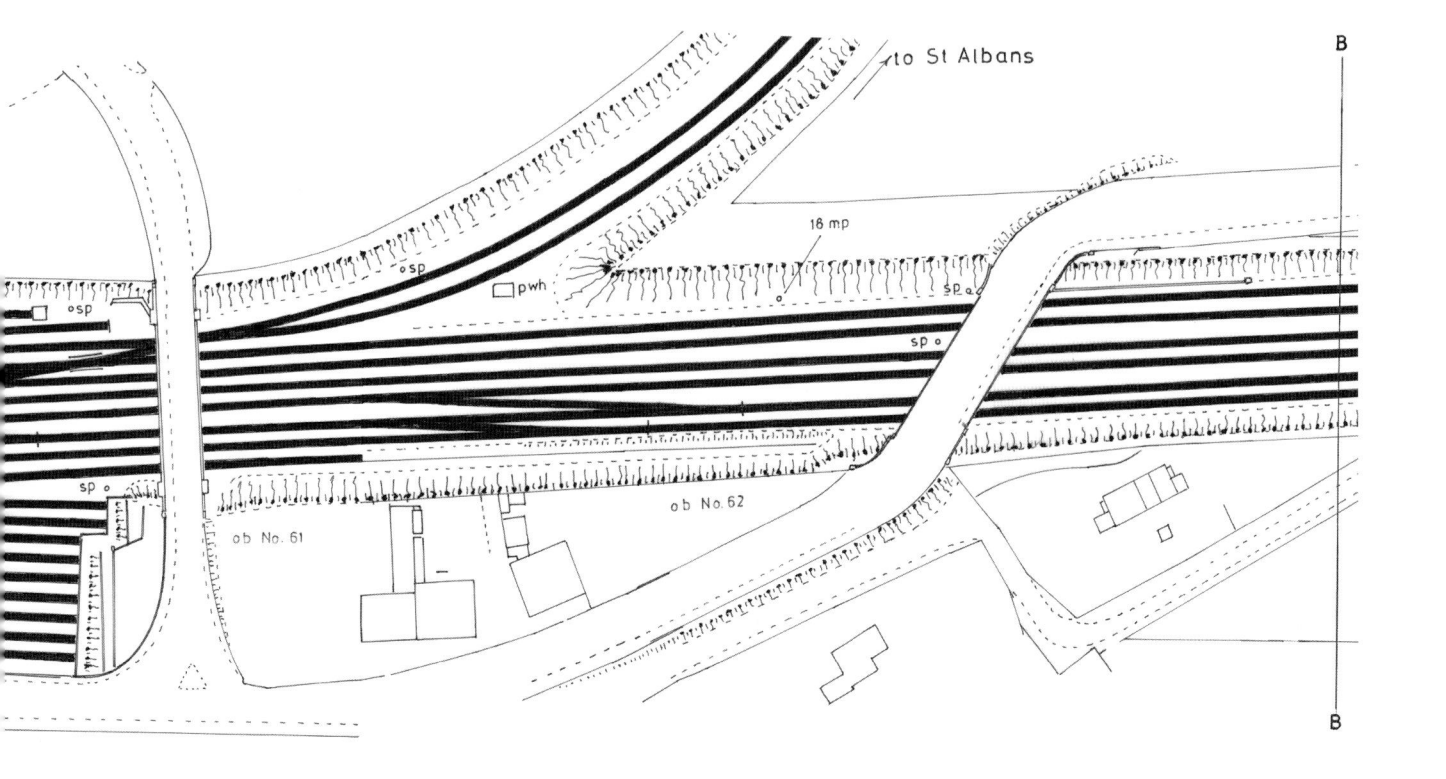

Hatfield station, 17 miles 54½ chains from London King's Cross, facing north showing from the left the railway cottages, then the Down side yard, the Down main line serving the Down platform, the Up main line and then the Up slow serving the Up platform, with its overall canopy. Footbridge No. 60 at 17 miles 55¾ chains connects the Up and Down platforms. *Author's collection*

The rather austere frontage to Hatfield station from the approach road. The glass-covered canopy protecting the Up platform and the Up slow line dwarfs the building. The station master's accommodation was on the first floor. *Author's collection*

A general view of Hatfield station showing Down and Up main lines in the centre. On the right the Up slow line serves the Up platform. The sorting yard is to the left of the Down island platform and the locomotive shed beyond. *Author's collection*

Town footbridge No. 59 spans the railway south of Hatfield station as Stirling 2-4-0 tender locomotive No. 884, as rebuilt by Ivatt, departs on the Up slow line with a train for King's Cross. The large water storage tank served the station and also provided a supply to the engine shed. The chimney of the steam pump house dominates the scene. To the side of the water tank is the VIP waiting room. *Author's collection*

The Up platform at Hatfield served by the Up slow line viewed from the Down side platform served by the Down main line, with the connecting footbridge in the foreground. In the far background is Town footbridge No. 59. The signal in the foreground is Hatfield No. 2 starter for the Up main line. *Author's collection*

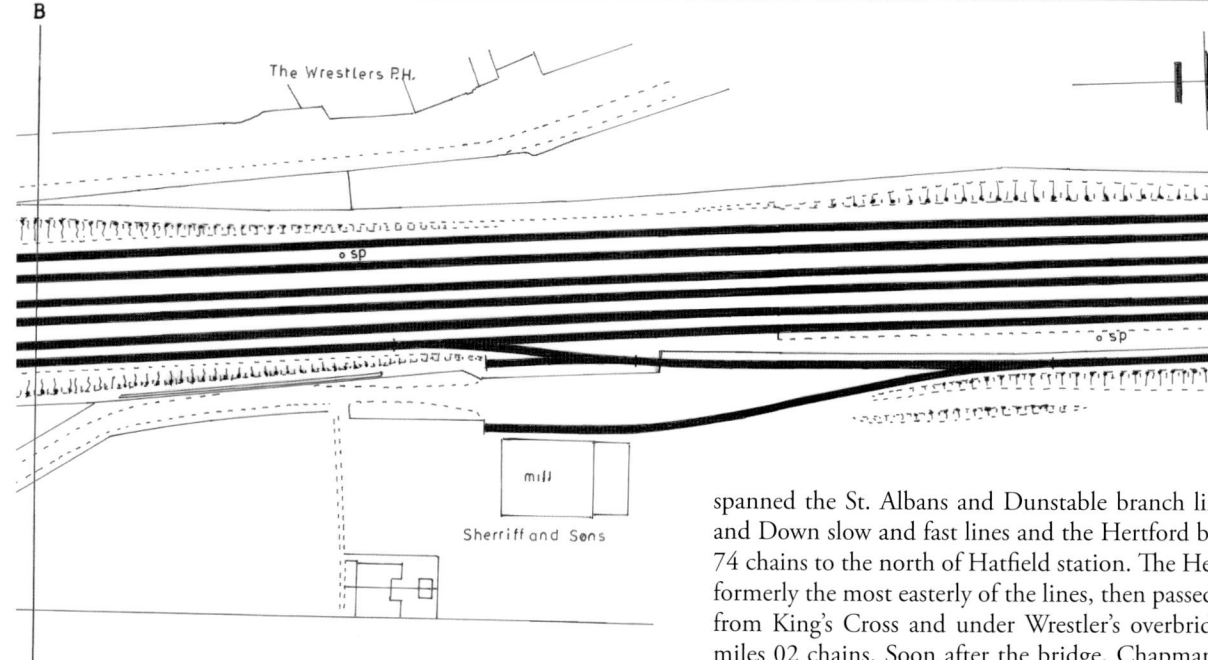

On departing from the Hertford bay platform, 200 feet in length with the buffer stops 17 miles 56 chains from King's Cross or the Up main platform 570 feet, the Hertford branch trains negotiated the points of the junction between the branch and the Up slow line before curving to the left, passing Hatfield No. 2 signal box at 17 miles 68 chains located on the Up side of the railway, responsible for signalling trains on the Up main and Up slow lines as well as to and from the Hertford branch. The line then descended at 1 in 200, before passing under St. Albans Road overbridge No. 61 which spanned the St. Albans and Dunstable branch lines as well as Up and Down slow and fast lines and the Hertford branch at 17 miles 74 chains to the north of Hatfield station. The Hertford single line, formerly the most easterly of the lines, then passed the 18 mile post from King's Cross and under Wrestler's overbridge No. 62 at 18 miles 02 chains. Soon after the bridge, Chapman's, also known as **Mount Pleasant Brick sidings**, was located on the Up or east side of the single line with facing access points at 18 miles 09½ chains (33 chains from Hatfield).

Beyond the siding connection the railway followed as easy right-hand curve descending at 1 in 330 to pass under Blue Bridge No. 63 at 18 miles 39¼ chains before rising at 1 in 330 over the River Lea by underbridge No. 64 at 18 miles 58 chains. The branch, associated main lines and Dunstable branch then followed a straight course climbing at 1 in 200 in a northerly direction over Pearts, also known as Townsends, underbridge No. 65 at 18 miles 74 chains and

ABOVE: Hatfield station, view facing south from the Up fast platform. To the left is the goods shed and beyond that the short rump of the former Hertford branch bay platform. The Up platform is served by the Up slow line, whilst Station footbridge No. 60 spans the railway at 17 miles 55¾ chains and connected the Up and Down sides of the station.
Author's collection

FACING PAGE: The north end of Hatfield station with Hatfield No. 3 signal box on the left containing a 80-lever frame which controlled the Down main line and connections to the St. Albans and Dunstable branches. To the right, partially obscured, is Hatfield No. 2 signal box which signalled trains on the Up lines as well as the Hertford branch before services were cut back to Welwyn Garden City in 1944. No. 2 signal box contained a 75-lever Railway Signal Company tappet frame with 65 working and 10 spare levers. By 1915 this was increased to an 85-lever frame with 76 working and 9 spare levers. The box was abolished on 20th May 1973.
Author's collection

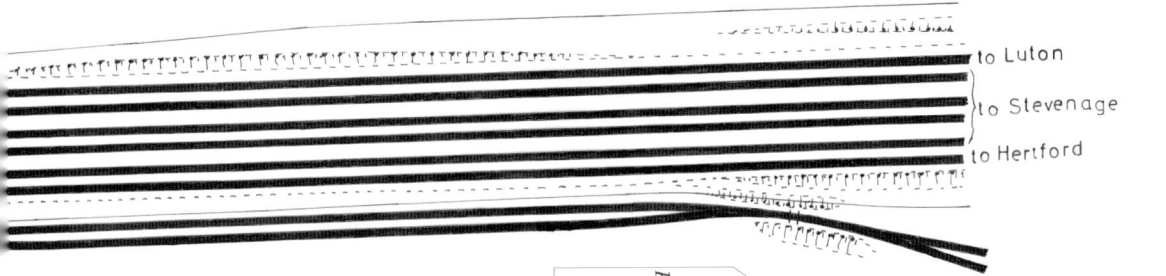

the 19 mile post. After passing over footpath crossing No. 4 at 19 miles 09¾ chains the branch continued climbing at 1 in 200 under Titmus, also known as Farr's, overbridge No. 66 at 19 miles 36½ chains and the junction facing points leading to **Smart's siding** at 19 miles 39 chains Because of the close proximity of the entry points off the main Hertford single line to the Up goods line drivers of trains on that line were instructed to sound the engine whistle whenever a branch train was working the siding.

RIGHT: Track Plan, Mount Pleasant siding Hatfield.

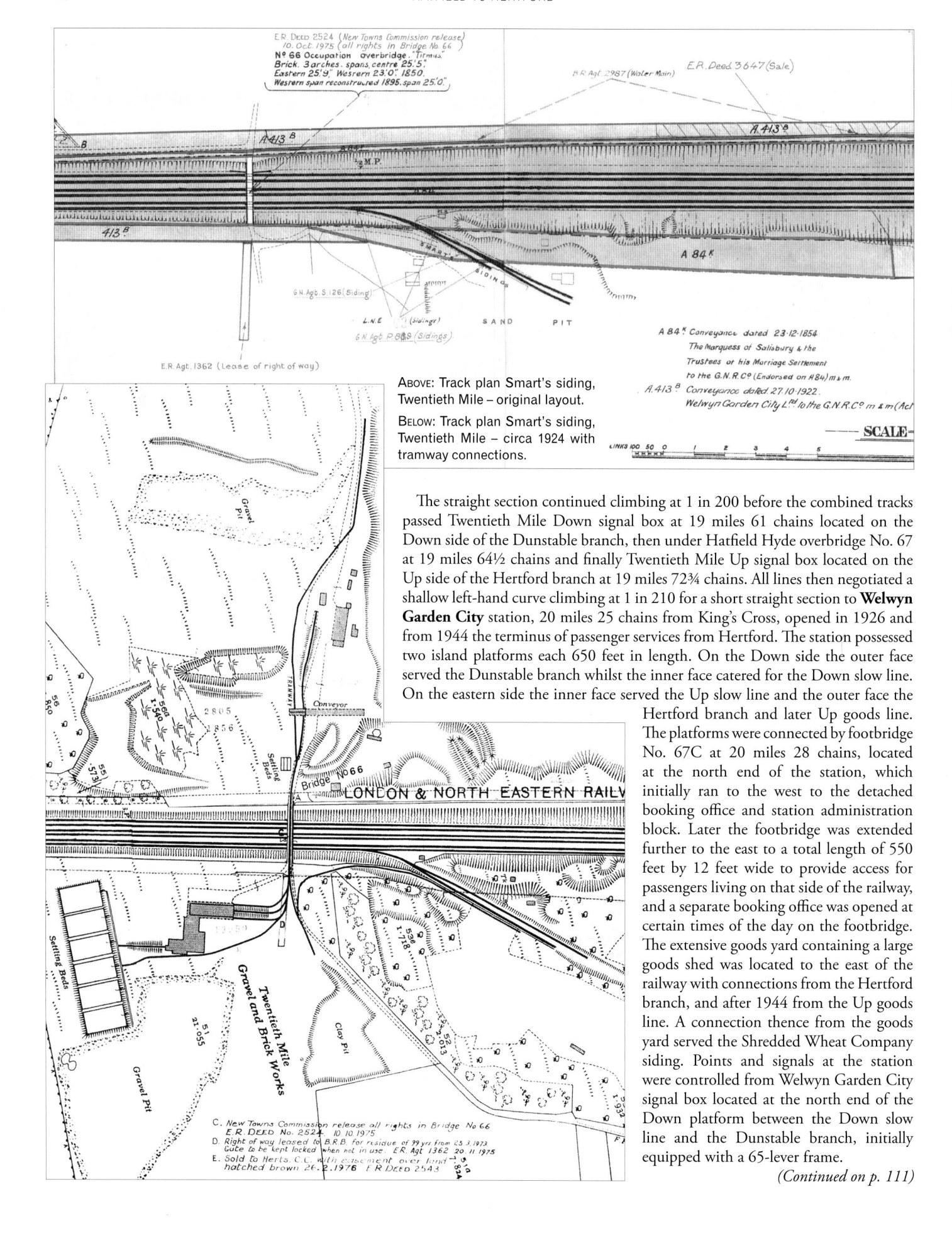

ABOVE: Track plan Smart's siding, Twentieth Mile – original layout.

BELOW: Track plan Smart's siding, Twentieth Mile – circa 1924 with tramway connections.

The straight section continued climbing at 1 in 200 before the combined tracks passed Twentieth Mile Down signal box at 19 miles 61 chains located on the Down side of the Dunstable branch, then under Hatfield Hyde overbridge No. 67 at 19 miles 64½ chains and finally Twentieth Mile Up signal box located on the Up side of the Hertford branch at 19 miles 72¾ chains. All lines then negotiated a shallow left-hand curve climbing at 1 in 210 for a short straight section to **Welwyn Garden City** station, 20 miles 25 chains from King's Cross, opened in 1926 and from 1944 the terminus of passenger services from Hertford. The station possessed two island platforms each 650 feet in length. On the Down side the outer face served the Dunstable branch whilst the inner face catered for the Down slow line. On the eastern side the inner face served the Up slow line and the outer face the Hertford branch and later Up goods line. The platforms were connected by footbridge No. 67C at 20 miles 28 chains, located at the north end of the station, which initially ran to the west to the detached booking office and station administration block. Later the footbridge was extended further to the east to a total length of 550 feet by 12 feet wide to provide access for passengers living on that side of the railway, and a separate booking office was opened at certain times of the day on the footbridge. The extensive goods yard containing a large goods shed was located to the east of the railway with connections from the Hertford branch, and after 1944 from the Up goods line. A connection thence from the goods yard served the Shredded Wheat Company siding. Points and signals at the station were controlled from Welwyn Garden City signal box located at the north end of the Down platform between the Down slow line and the Dunstable branch, initially equipped with a 65-lever frame.

(Continued on p. 111)

The ornate frontage of Welwyn Garden City station, opened to the public on 20th September 1926, is seen here in British Railways ownership. The official opening, by the Right Honourable Arthur Neville Chamberlain MP, was made a few days later on 5th October. *D. Dent collection*

ABOVE: The road approach to Welwyn Garden City with the main entrance on the Down side of the railway and the island platforms beyond connected by footbridge No. 67C at 20 miles 28 chains. *D. Dent collection*

RIGHT: Former L&NER bogie-bolster wagons in the goods yard at Welwyn Garden City. The Shredded Wheat factory, also rail served, dominates the scene in the left background. *P. Whitaker*

to Hatfield

Welwyn Garden City

chemical works

THE ROUTE DESCRIBED — 107

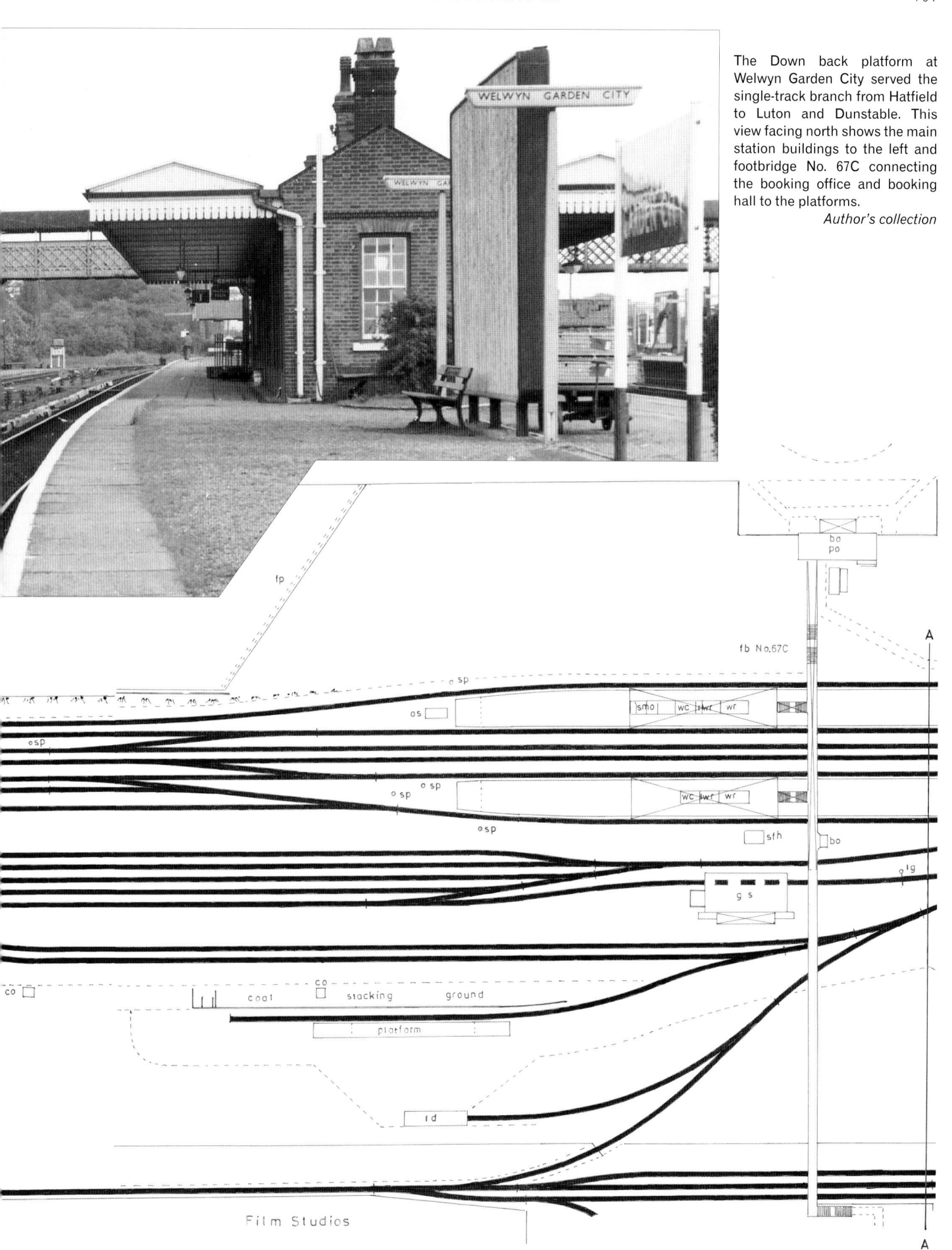

The Down back platform at Welwyn Garden City served the single-track branch from Hatfield to Luton and Dunstable. This view facing north shows the main station buildings to the left and footbridge No. 67C connecting the booking office and booking hall to the platforms.
Author's collection

The Up side platform and buildings at Welwyn Garden City in May 1969. The nearest platform served the Up slow line, whilst from 1944 until 1951 the back platform was the terminal point for the Hertford branch passenger train. In the background is the substantial goods shed provided when the goods yard was enlarged in 1932. *Author's collection*

THE ROUTE DESCRIBED

Looking north from the Down slow line at Welwyn Garden City in 1969. To the left is the Down platform and to the centre are the Down and Up main lines. On the right, the Up slow line serves the Up platform. Footbridge No. 67C connected the platforms whilst in the distance beyond the station is Digswell Lodge Farm overbridge No. 67A spanning the railway.
Author's collection

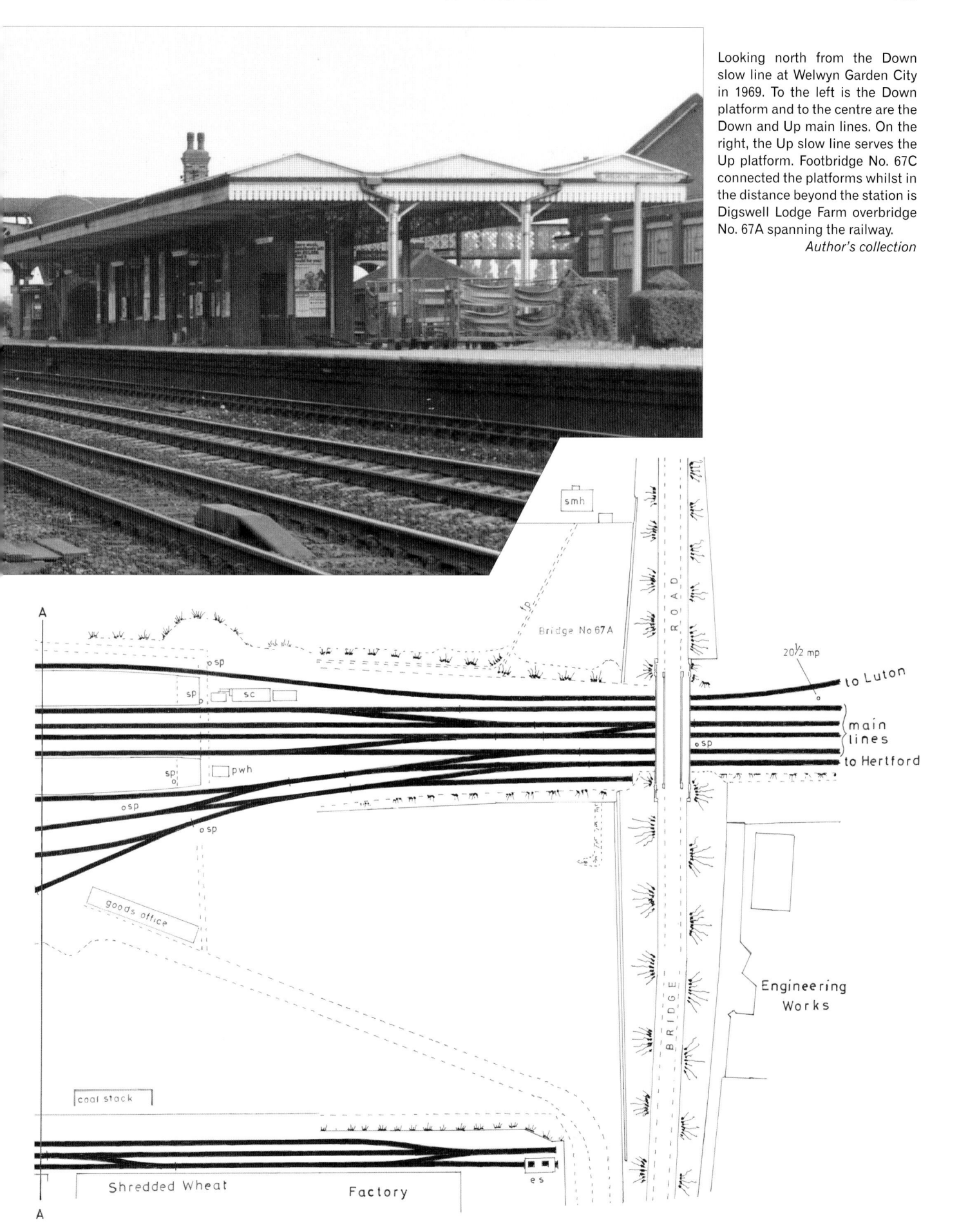

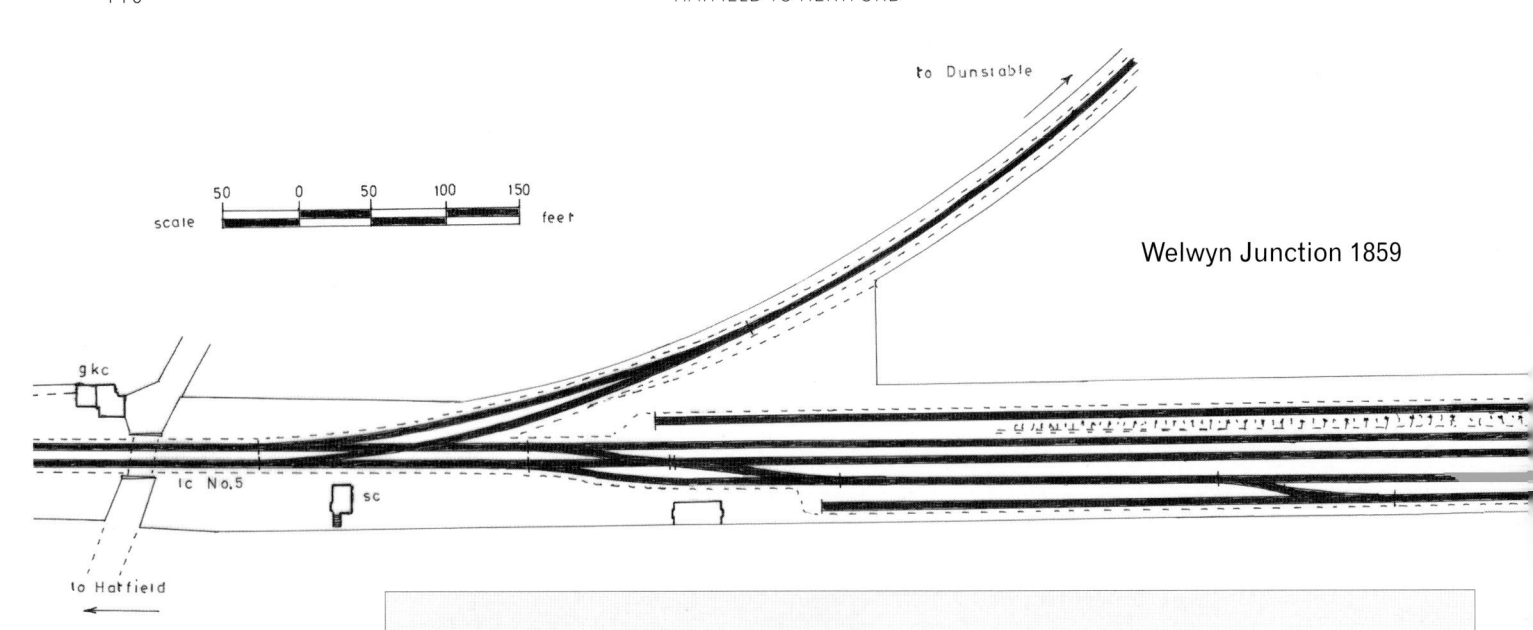

Welwyn Junction 1859

Two halts were provided at Welwyn Garden City. On the left is the platform serving the Luton and Dunstable branch, opened on 16th August 1920, whilst to the right is the halt provided for contractor's workers on the Hatfield to Hertford branch. It was not unknown for bona fide passengers to use the latter with the knowledge of a friendly and understanding guard.
Author's collection

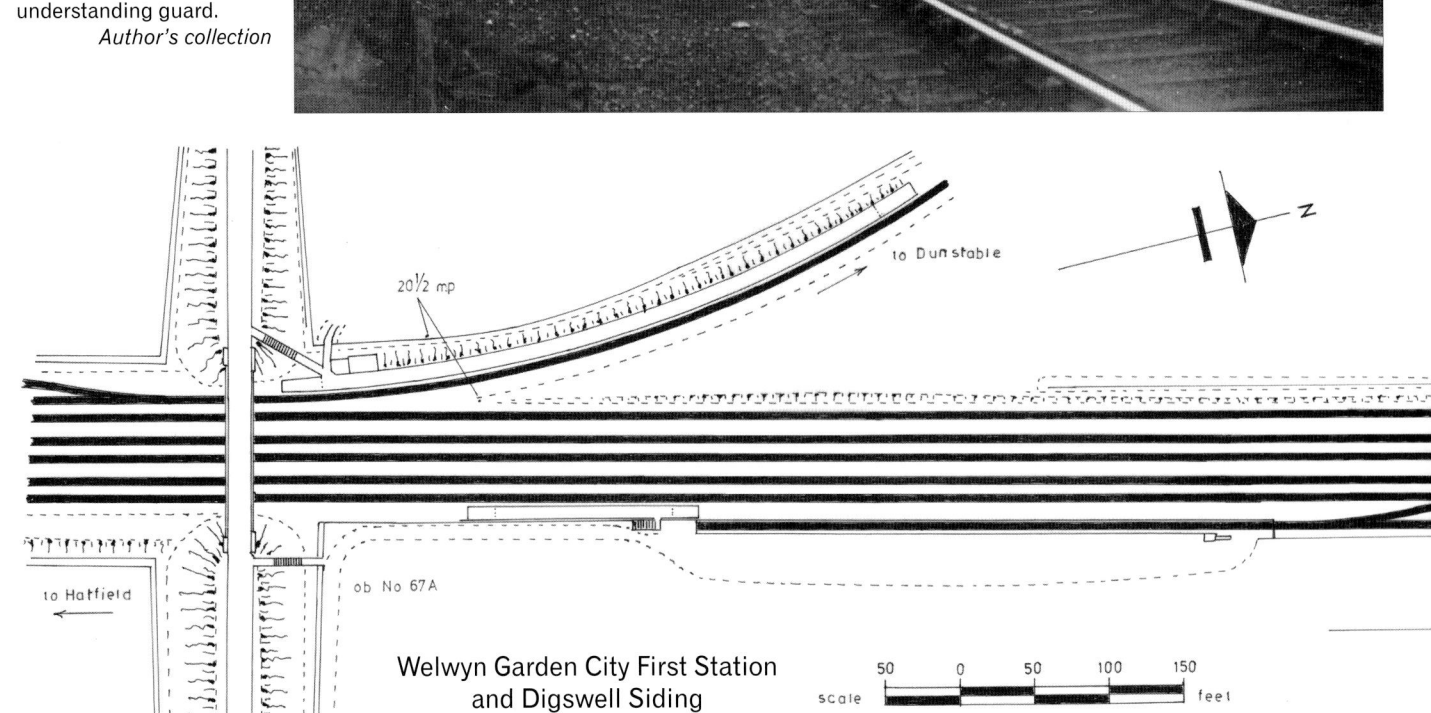

Welwyn Garden City First Station and Digswell Siding

(Continued from p. 104)

Before 1896 and the subsequent construction of Welwyn Garden City station, the main line and the Dunstable and Hertford branches bisected Digswell Lodge level crossing No. 5 at 20 miles 36 chains with its attendant gate keeper's lodge on the Down side of the railway, and later under the replacement Digswell Lodge Farm overbridge No. 67A at 20 miles 37½ chains. The gradient then descended for a short distance at 1 in 788, as the Hertford branch paralleled the Up slow line past the site of the former contractor's halt. Immediately beyond the structure were the entry points to **Digswell siding** to the east of the single line at 20 miles 51 chains (2 miles 76¼ chains from Hatfield) and the later connection to **Dawnays siding**.

The temporary timber platform alongside the Hatfield to Hertford line at the embryonic Welwyn Garden City. Essentially provided for the use of workmen it was not unknown for passengers to use the halt when trains picked up or set down workers. The large notice advises enginemen working branch services to reduce speed for the curve (at one time 10 mph but later raised to 15 mph). To the extreme left is the Luton and Dunstable branch and then heading north the Down slow or goods line, Down fast line, Up fast line, Up slow or goods line and then the Hertford branch. *Author's collection*

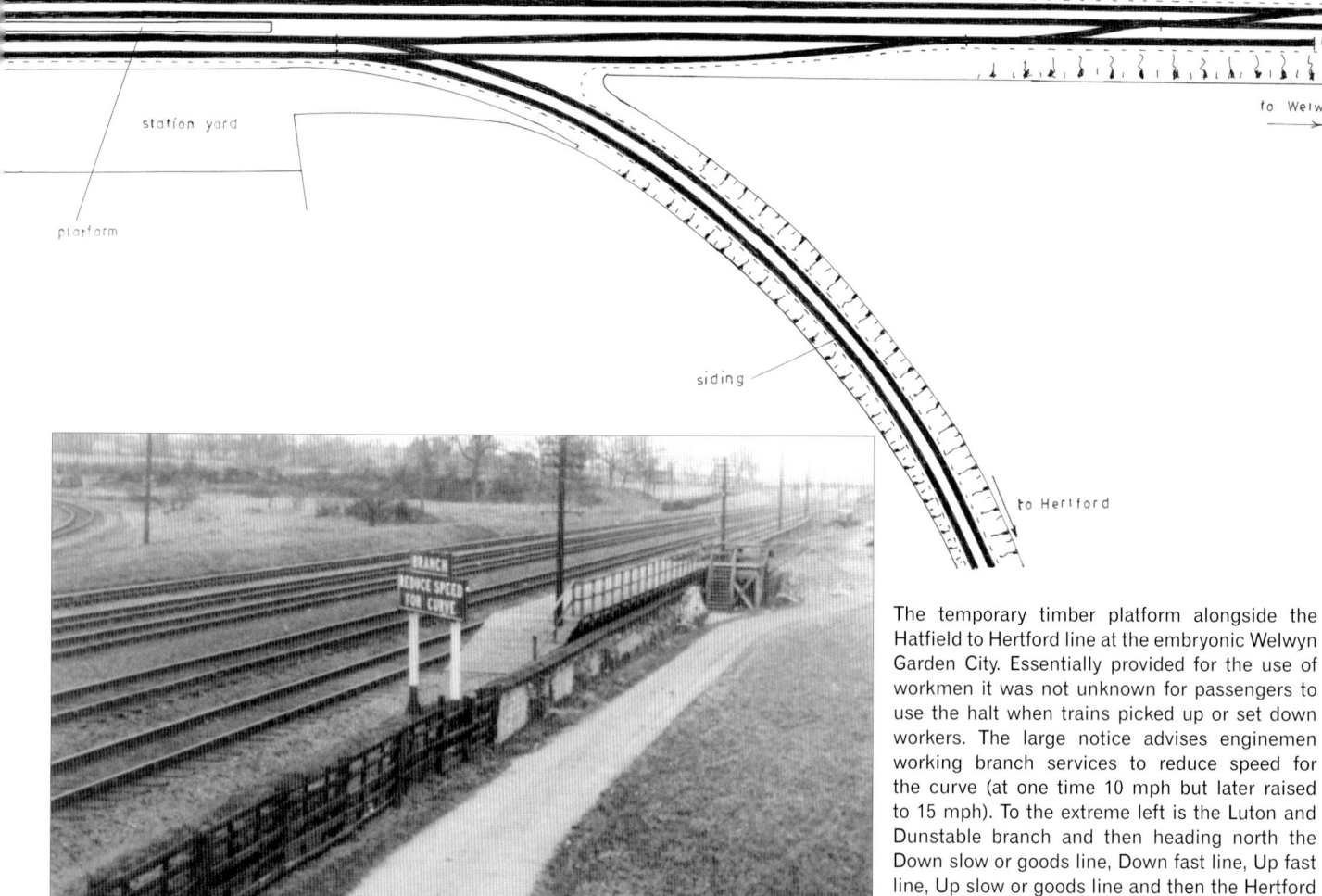

Falling at 1 in 69/98 the branch curved sharply to the south east on an 8 chains radius curve with 10 later 15 mph speed restriction. Boards were erected about 300 yards from each approach to the curve worded 'REDUCE SPEED FOR CURVE'. On exit from the curve the trailing points to **Lord Cowper's siding** were located on the Down side of the railway at 20 miles 68 chains. After the removal of Lord Cowper's siding, later used by Hall & Bartholomew, a connection was provided from the curve to sidings on the Down side of the railway serving the premises of **Imperial Chemical Industries**. A few chains round the curve on the Up side of the railway with trailing points for Down trains at 20 miles 62 chains was Welwyn Garden City No. 2 siding.

The branch continued passing Gutteridge Grove on the Down side and over footpath level crossing No. 1 at 20 miles 78½ chains before levelling out soon after the 21 mile post where the branch negotiated a left-hand curve at the 21¼ milepost, climbing at 1 in 238 and over Crossley Hill, also known as Bramley Hill occupational crossing No. 2 at 21 miles 34 chains, later converted to a public level crossing before climbing at 1 in 163 past milepost 1 (from Welwyn Junction) at 21 miles 43¼ chains.

In later years the area from the curve away from the main line to the crossing was converted to a factory complex for the New Town with connections at 20 miles 59½ chains to the **ICI plastic powder works** on the Down or north side of the single line and an **iron foundry** to the south. As part of the industrial development, underbridges were provided at Bessemer Road (No. 1B at 20 miles

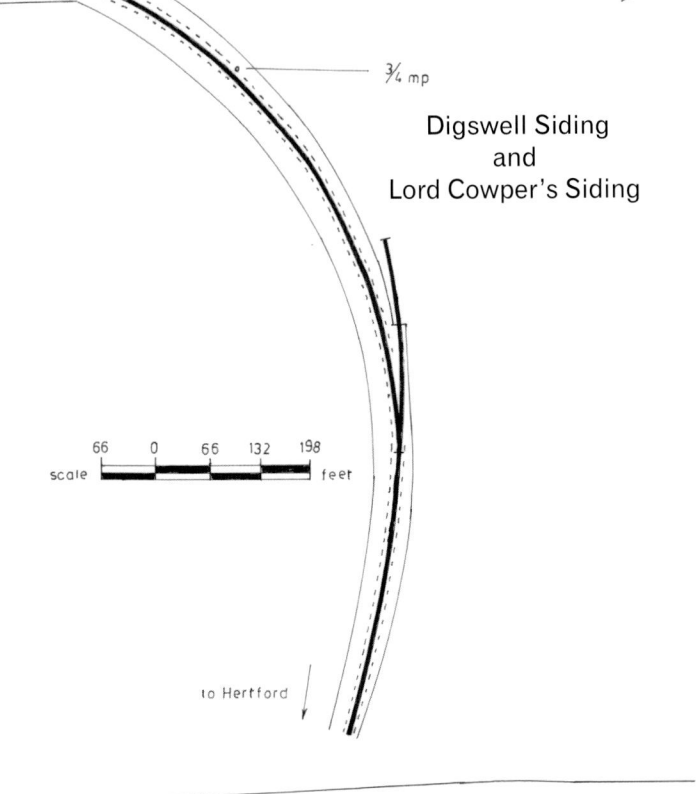

Digswell Siding and Lord Cowper's Siding

ICI Siding, Welwyn Garden City

Lord Cowper's footpath crossing No. 1 at 20 miles 78½ chains showing the rural scene before the development of Welwyn Garden City. In the background can be seen steam from a Down train on the main line. *D. Dent collection*

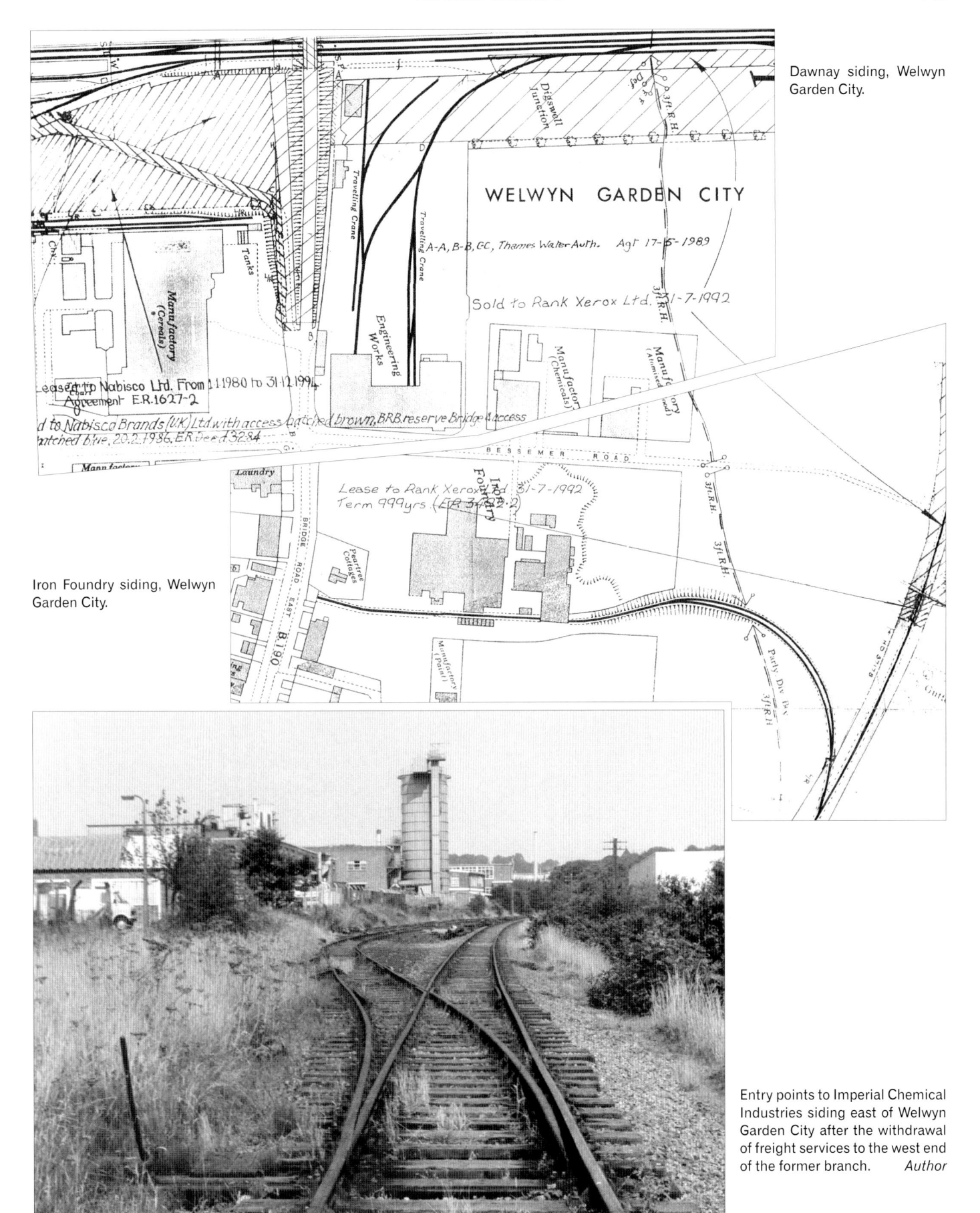

Dawnay siding, Welwyn Garden City.

Iron Foundry siding, Welwyn Garden City.

Entry points to Imperial Chemical Industries siding east of Welwyn Garden City after the withdrawal of freight services to the west end of the former branch. *Author*

Looking east along the branch towards Attimore Hall level crossing with the sidings serving Imperial Chemical Industries to the left. The post of the former Attimore Hall distant signal is to the centre. *Author*

Tewin Road underbridge No. 1A at 21 miles 01 chains was a later addition to the branch infrastructure being constructed in 1925 to cater for the development and expansion of the embryonic Welwyn Garden City. This view facing west shows the single-track curving towards the main line. *Ed Graves collection*

Despite the creation of the second Garden City, the branch line approach to Welwyn Garden City from Hertford maintained a rural character. *Ed Graves*

THE ROUTE DESCRIBED

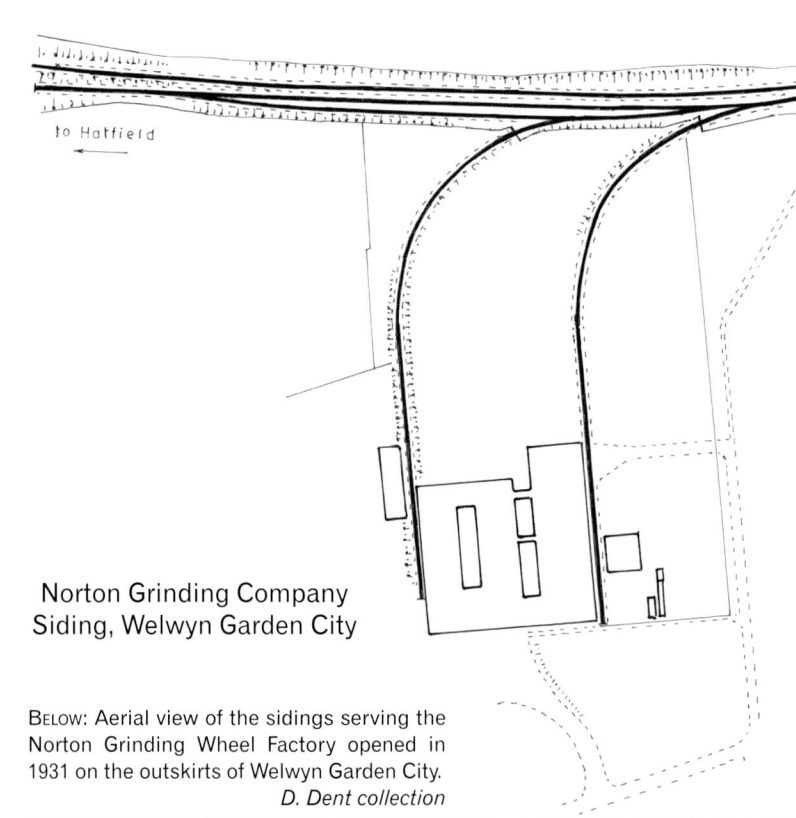

75 chains) and Tewin Road (No. 1A at 21 miles 01 chains). An agricultural siding on the Up side of the line at 21 miles 11 chains, with points facing Up trains, was from 1931 used to serve the **Norton Grinding Wheel Company** factory.

After passing Attimore Hall crossing Down gate distant signal on the Up side at 21 miles 48 chains, and level crossing No. 3 at 21 miles 55 chains, Herns Wood was located on the Up side of the line. Here a siding with facing points for Down trains was installed on the Down or north side of the railway in 1957 to serve the premises of the **Lincoln Electric Company Limited**. Beyond No. 3 level crossing the single-track branch followed a straight section before curving to bisect Attimore Hall level crossing No. 4 at 21 miles 66¾ chains with its attendant gatekeeper's lodge on the Up side of the railway, east of the crossing, with Bushey Leys Wood on the Up side. Also east of the crossing was the 330 feet Attimore Hall siding on the Down side of the branch with facing points for Up trains at 21 miles 70 chains (4 miles 10¼ chains ex Hatfield).

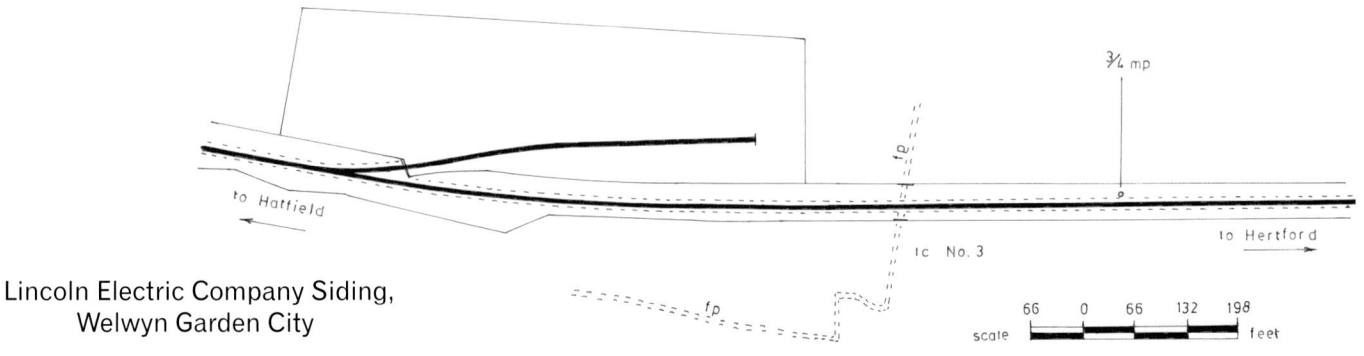

Norton Grinding Company Siding, Welwyn Garden City

BELOW: Aerial view of the sidings serving the Norton Grinding Wheel Factory opened in 1931 on the outskirts of Welwyn Garden City.
D. Dent collection

Lincoln Electric Company Siding, Welwyn Garden City

Attimore Hall Siding and Halt

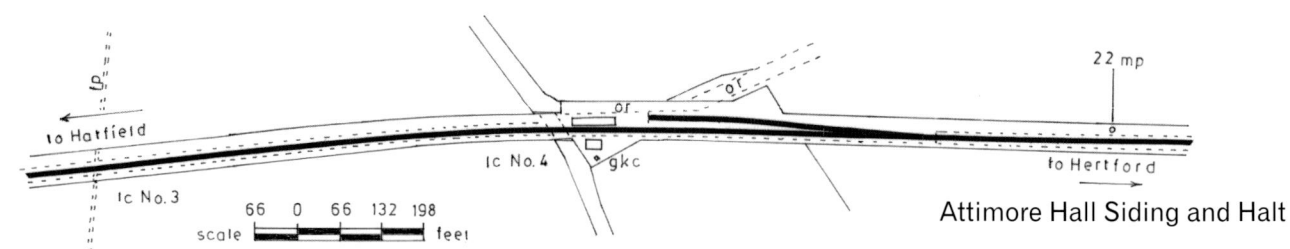

Between the crossing and the points leading to the siding was the site of short-lived **Attimore Halt** with its 46 feet long platform on the Down side of the line. After the withdrawal of passenger services, trainmen were responsible for opening and closing of the level crossing gates at Attimore Hall and Birchall level crossings, and crossing keepers were withdrawn. The railway then passed through undulating Hertfordshire pasture and woodland curving gently to the east past the 22 mile post and bisecting occupational crossing No. 5 at 22 miles 07 chains and past Attimore Hall crossing Up gate distant signal on the Down side of the railway at 22 miles 13 chains. The single branch then negotiated a right-hand curve which led to another straight section over Hatfield Hyde level crossing No. 6 at 22 miles 38 chains with the gatekeepers' cottage on

ABOVE: 'N5' Class 0-6-2T No. 5930 departing Attimore Hall level crossing with a Hertford North to Hatfield train in 1936. *J.L. Kite*

ABOVE: Attimore Hall level crossing No. 4 at 21 miles 66¾ chains from King's Cross with the remains of the short platform 46 feet in length opened on 1st January 1905 for use with the experimental petrol railcar service. The experiment was unsuccessful so the halt had a short life and was closed on 1st July of the same year.
Author's collection

LEFT: Attimore Hall level crossing, 15th June 1951.
Robert Kirkland, Lens of Sutton

Level crossing No. 6 and crossing keeper's cottage at Hatfield Hyde, 15th June 1951.
Robert Kirkland, Lens of Sutton

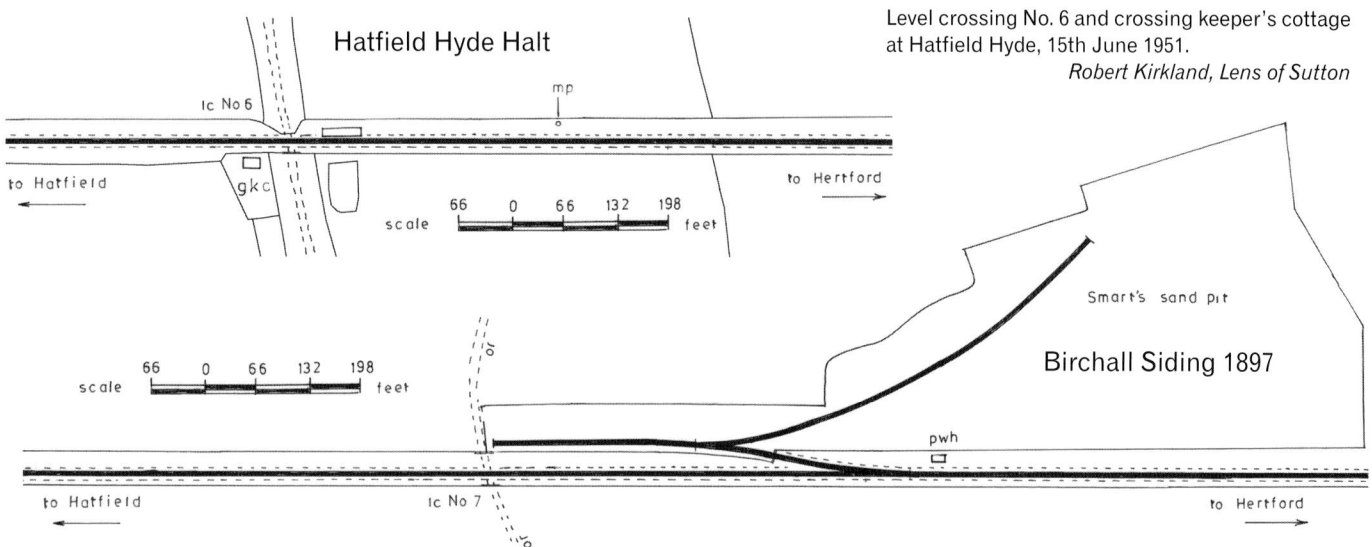

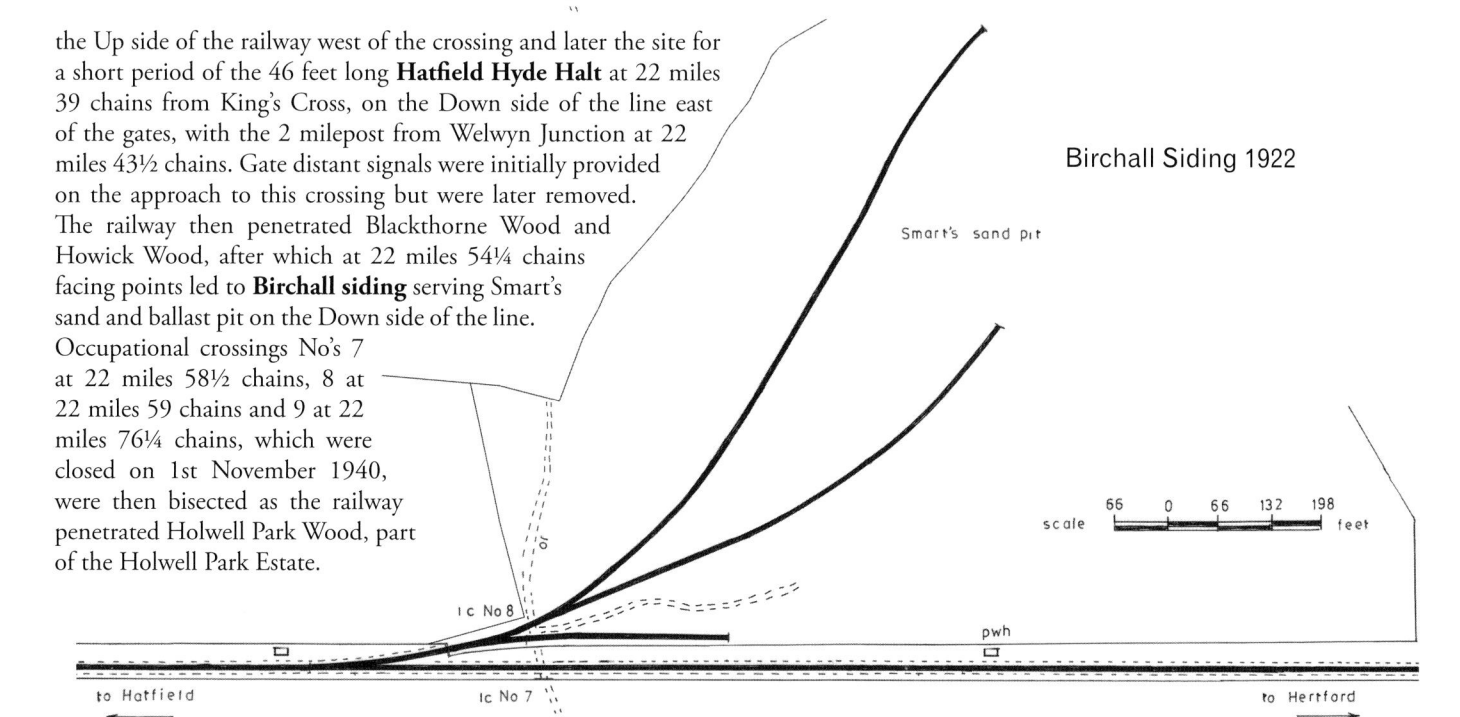

Hatfield Hyde Halt

Birchall Siding 1897

Birchall Siding 1922

the Up side of the railway west of the crossing and later the site for a short period of the 46 feet long **Hatfield Hyde Halt** at 22 miles 39 chains from King's Cross, on the Down side of the line east of the gates, with the 2 milepost from Welwyn Junction at 22 miles 43½ chains. Gate distant signals were initially provided on the approach to this crossing but were later removed. The railway then penetrated Blackthorne Wood and Howick Wood, after which at 22 miles 54¼ chains facing points led to **Birchall siding** serving Smart's sand and ballast pit on the Down side of the line. Occupational crossings No's 7 at 22 miles 58½ chains, 8 at 22 miles 59 chains and 9 at 22 miles 76¼ chains, which were closed on 1st November 1940, were then bisected as the railway penetrated Holwell Park Wood, part of the Holwell Park Estate.

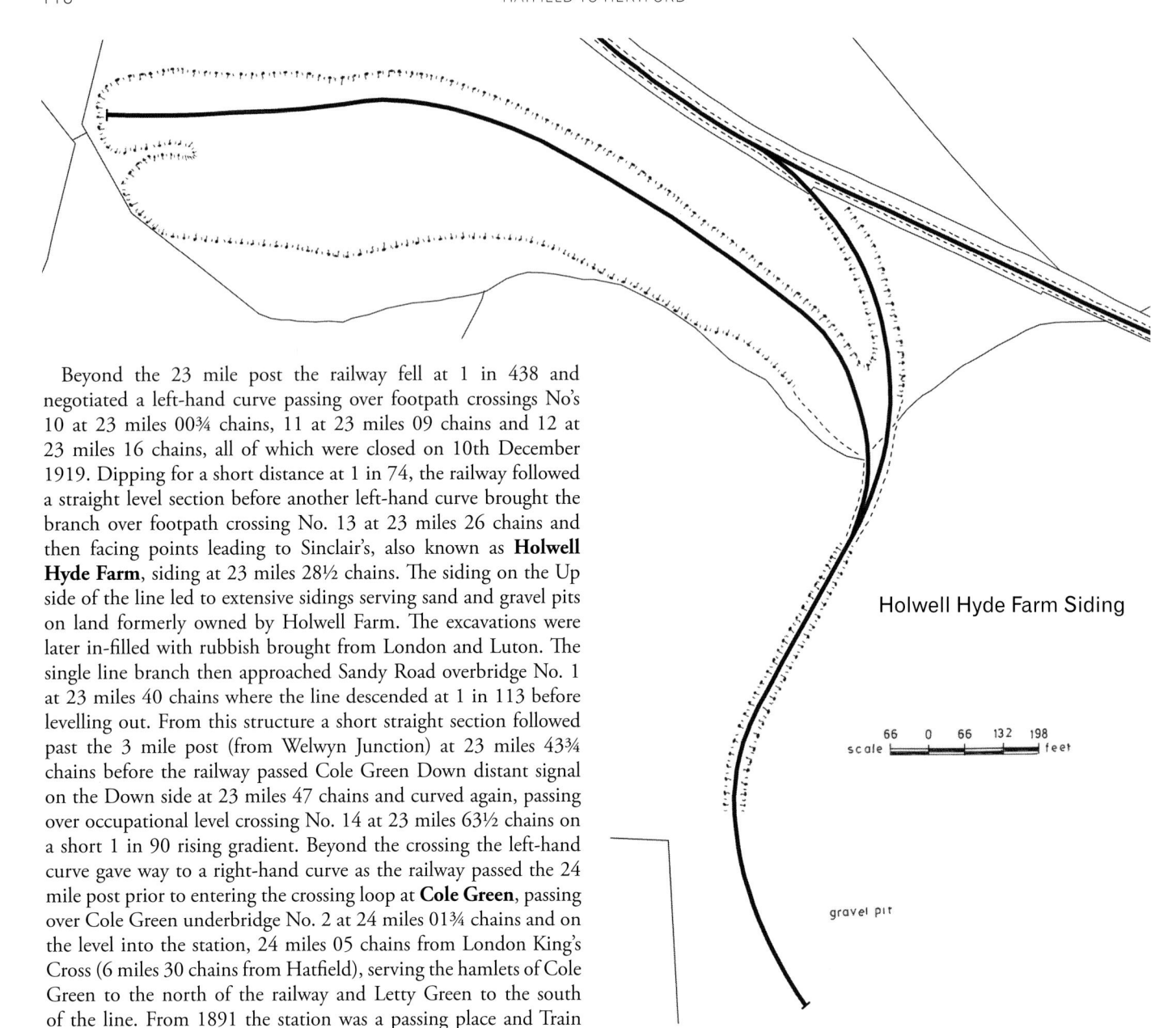

Beyond the 23 mile post the railway fell at 1 in 438 and negotiated a left-hand curve passing over footpath crossings No's 10 at 23 miles 00¾ chains, 11 at 23 miles 09 chains and 12 at 23 miles 16 chains, all of which were closed on 10th December 1919. Dipping for a short distance at 1 in 74, the railway followed a straight level section before another left-hand curve brought the branch over footpath crossing No. 13 at 23 miles 26 chains and then facing points leading to Sinclair's, also known as **Holwell Hyde Farm**, siding at 23 miles 28½ chains. The siding on the Up side of the line led to extensive sidings serving sand and gravel pits on land formerly owned by Holwell Farm. The excavations were later in-filled with rubbish brought from London and Luton. The single line branch then approached Sandy Road overbridge No. 1 at 23 miles 40 chains where the line descended at 1 in 113 before levelling out. From this structure a short straight section followed past the 3 mile post (from Welwyn Junction) at 23 miles 43¾ chains before the railway passed Cole Green Down distant signal on the Down side at 23 miles 47 chains and curved again, passing over occupational level crossing No. 14 at 23 miles 63½ chains on a short 1 in 90 rising gradient. Beyond the crossing the left-hand curve gave way to a right-hand curve as the railway passed the 24 mile post prior to entering the crossing loop at **Cole Green**, passing over Cole Green underbridge No. 2 at 24 miles 01¾ chains and on the level into the station, 24 miles 05 chains from London King's Cross (6 miles 30 chains from Hatfield), serving the hamlets of Cole Green to the north of the railway and Letty Green to the south of the line. From 1891 the station was a passing place and Train Staff station, although in latter years of regular passenger traffic

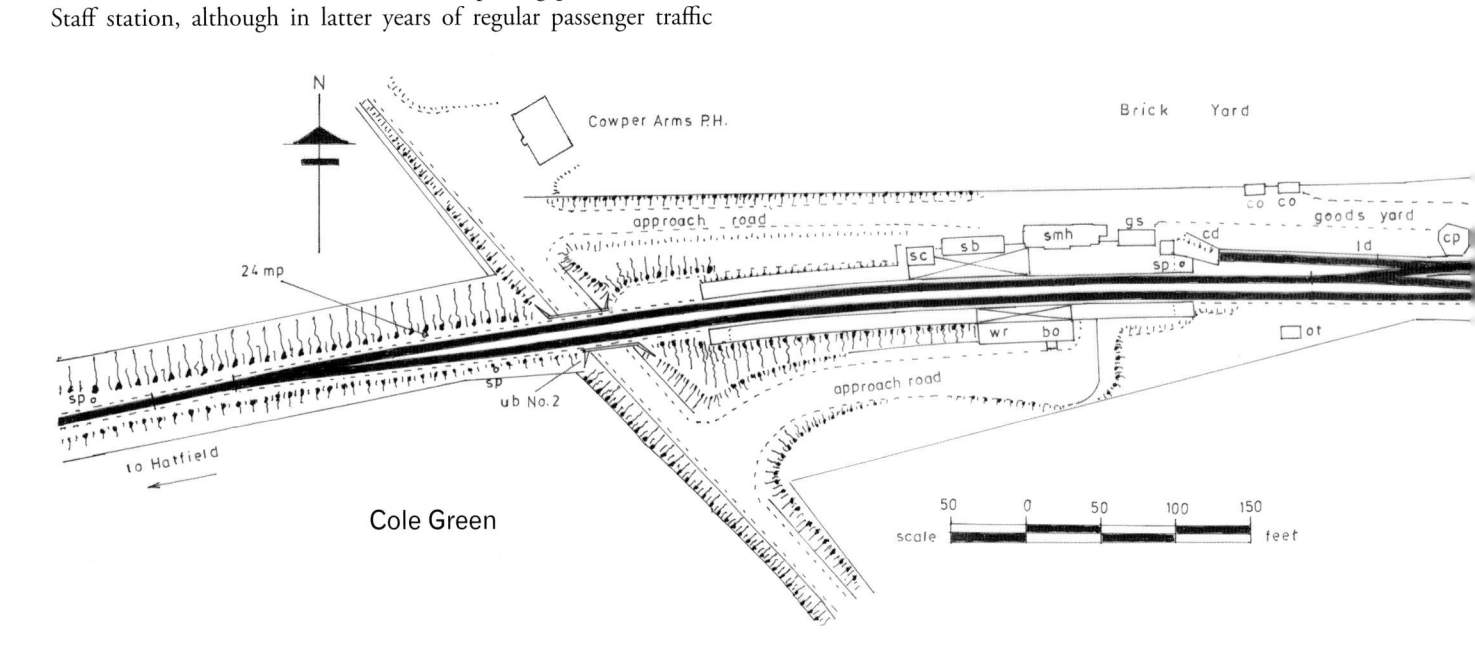

Holwell Hyde Farm Siding

Cole Green

most trains used the Down side platform as the Down line was signalled for bi-directional working. The 1,056 feet long crossing loop served the Down platform 312 feet in length, which was host to the main station buildings including booking office, waiting room, staff rooms and the attendant station master's house. The Up side platform, 310 feet in length, was occupied by a covered waiting room fronted by an ornate canopy. Originally it was planned that the platforms would be connected by an under-track subway but this was not provided.

It is interesting to quote the synopsis issued by the GNR Estate Office of facilities at Cole Green station prior to and post 1891 in a document dated 20th November 1891.

Prior to 1891	Approach road and footpath
	Station master's house
	Ladies' waiting room and WC
	Gentlemen's WC and urinal
	Booking office
	General waiting room
1891 South side	The GNR Company's bridge over public road widened
	New loop line through the station
	New platform
	New booking office and part roof at entrance
	New general waiting room
	New ladies' waiting room and WC
	New gentlemen's WC and urinal
	New pump room
	New covering (canopy) over part of the platform for the length of the building on south side
	New approach road and footpath
	New palisade fence and post and rail fence
1891 North side	Approach road and footpath
	Station master's house
	Gentlemen's WC and urinal
	Ladies' waiting room and WC
	General waiting room
	Covering (canopy) over part of the platform and part roof at entrance
	Signal box
	Tranship shed

TOP OF PAGE: Cole Green station, 24 miles 05 chains from King's Cross and 6 miles 10¾ chains from Hatfield, viewed from the Down platform facing east in the 1930s with the goods yard beyond the Down starting signal. The signal box is shrouded by the shadow cast by the Down side platform canopy. *Author's collection*

The Down side platform at Cole Green with the signal box barely visible behind the canopy. The main station building and transit shed are at the far end of the platform. Note the small station running in or nameboard to the left. The GNR-style somersault Down starting signal at the end of the platform is cleared for the passage of a train. *D. Dent collection*

Close up view of the station master's house and goods transit shed on the Down platform at Cole Green. *D. Dent collection*

A small goods yard was located on the Down or north side to the east of the station, with entry facing points in the Down direction. Three sidings were available: the 112 feet dock siding at back of the Down platform, the 350 feet back road serving the 119 feet coal ground siding, and the 350 feet front road running parallel to the Down loop line. Points and signals at the station were worked from Cole Green signal box located near the west end of the Down platform and equipped with a Saxby & Farmer 30-lever frame. Catch points were provided in the Down loop, 80 yards after passing the home signal on a 1 in 90 gradient and 58 yards east of the platform on a level gradient. To the north of the railway, at one time a small brickworks abutted the property but was not rail served. Passengers seeking refreshment could quench their thirst or sate their appetite in the adjacent Cowper Arms public house.

Away from Cole Green the railway followed a meandering course, initially bisecting footpath crossing No. 15 at 24 miles 12 chains before falling at 1 in 252/80/156 to follow a short straight section of line over Letty Green footpath crossing No. 16 at 24 miles 27

The Up side buildings at Cole Green with their ornate canopy were provided in 1891 when the station became a crossing place. Initially a booking office was provided but it was soon closed, as with the small amount of passenger traffic all transactions could be handled by the original booking office on the Down platform. *D. Dent collection*

Looking west from Cole Green Down platform towards Welwyn Garden City, with the double-track crossing loop passing over underbridge No. 2. Note the ornate platform lamps and the GNR somersault Up starting signal at danger. *D. Dent collection*

chains. A left-hand curve then took the branch over Letty Green underbridge No. 3 at 24 miles 37¼ chains and past Cole Green Up distant signal at 24 miles 43 chains, followed by occupational crossing No. 17 at 24 miles 52 chains. Another short straight section past the 4 mile post (from Welwyn Junction) at 24 miles 44 chains took the railway on a 1 in 125 falling gradient over footpath crossing No. 18 at 24 miles 58½ chains before the branch negotiated a 30 chains radius right-hand curve to pass Hazeldene Farm on the Up side and then under Birch Green (also known as Staines Green) overbridge No. 4 at 24 miles 68½ chains on the level, beyond which was the

The former station master's house at Cole Green, standing at the rear of the former Down platform, is seen after demolition of the wooden buildings. This view, taken from the former Up platform, shows the loading dock in the goods yard. *Author's collection*

Cole Green station seen from a Down train on 3rd June 1951, showing the Up side platform, with 0-4-2 locomotive *Lion* and the 4-wheel coaches stabled in the goods yard ready for filming *The Lady with the Lamp*. *Author's collection*

An unidentified 'N7' Class 0-6-2T standing with the 2-coach Welwyn Garden City to Hertford North train at Cole Green in 1950. The lower quadrant Down starting signal protects the route ahead whilst the station master's house and other station buildings are in the background. *Author's collection*

Cole Green station facing west, circa 1950, with the Up platform and buildings fronted by an ornate canopy on the left, and the main station buildings with an equally ornate canopy on the Down side. *Author's collection*

ABOVE: The eastern end of Cole Green station showing the Up platform and the running in nameboard. In this 1930s view the rural location of the station is evident. *S. Ruff collection*

LEFT: Cole Green station from the Up platform looking east with the goods yard on the Down side of the line. *Author's collection*

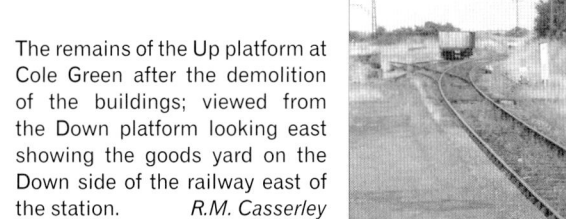

The remains of the Up platform at Cole Green after the demolition of the buildings; viewed from the Down platform looking east showing the goods yard on the Down side of the railway east of the station. *R.M. Casserley*

25 milepost adjacent to occupational crossing No. 19 as the line fell at 1 in 72. Meandering through rolling Hertfordshire terrain, at first curving to the right before swinging left and falling at 1 in 119 over occupational crossing No. 20 at 25 miles 21 chains, the branch negotiated a right-hand curve past the 5 mile post (from Welwyn Junction) at 25 miles 44 chains then over the trailing connecting points to **Smart's Hertingfordbury gravel siding** located on the Up side of the line at 25 miles 49¾ chains. The siding was removed by 1907.

Immediately beyond the siding connection the line passed over Hertingfordbury underbridge No. 5 at 25 miles 50½ chains and into **Hertingfordbury** station 25 miles 56 chains (7 miles 79¼ chains from Hatfield) on a 1 in 491 falling gradient, where the 225 feet platform was located on the Up or south side of the line.

The station was located over half a mile south of the village it was supposed to serve, with its spiritually protective church of St. Mary – and the railway property bordered Hertingfordbury House and Park, the home of the Cowper family, to the north of the railway. Hertingfordbury was mentioned in Domesday as Hertfordingberie, meaning the stronghold of the people of Hertford. The platform was extended at the west end in 1902 from 225 feet to 312 feet in length. The station buildings contained the two-storey station master's house and usual single-storey station offices including booking office, waiting room and staff rooms, which were considered of a better quality than those at Cole Green. Beyond the platform on the Up side of the line was a single siding with facing points in the Down direction, later converted to a 245 feet loop goods siding entered by facing and trailing points, with a 200 feet headshunt

Hertingfordbury station, 7 miles 79¼ chains from Hatfield and 25 miles 56 chains from King's Cross, with its massive chimneys aloft the station buildings. This view of circa 1955, looking towards Hertford, shows the Up goods loop siding beyond the platform with its attendant loading gauge in the background. The station master's house has a bow-fronted window facing the platform whilst the station offices are more modest in size. *Author's collection*

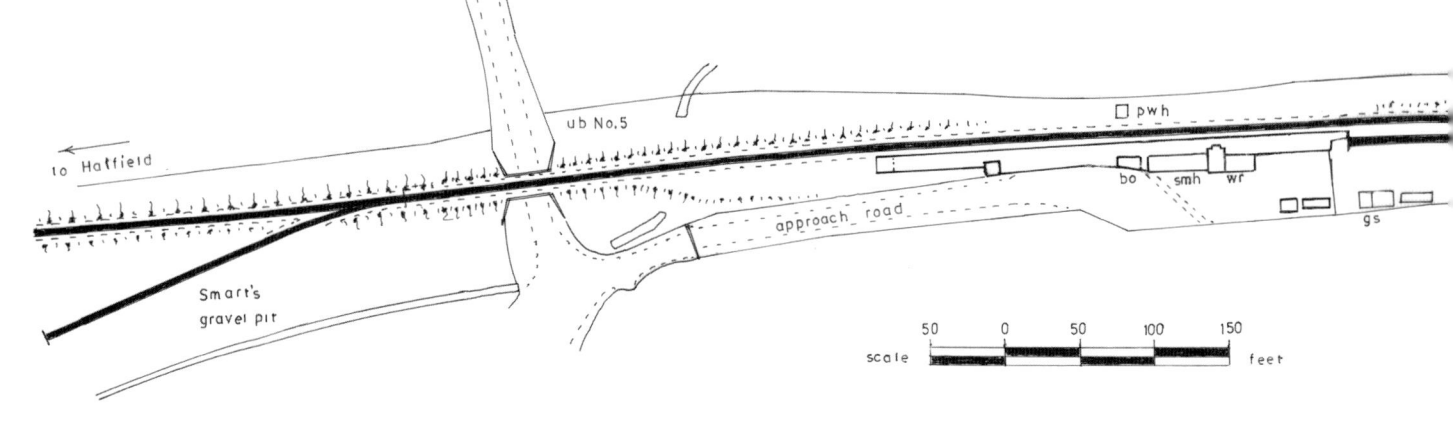

ABOVE: The road approach to Hertingfordbury station on 9th September 1962, eleven years after withdrawal of the passenger train service. The gate at the far end of the drive leads to the small goods yard. *R.M. Casserley*

A close up view of the northern aspect of Hertingfordbury with the station master's house to the left and station offices and transit shed to the right.
Author's collection

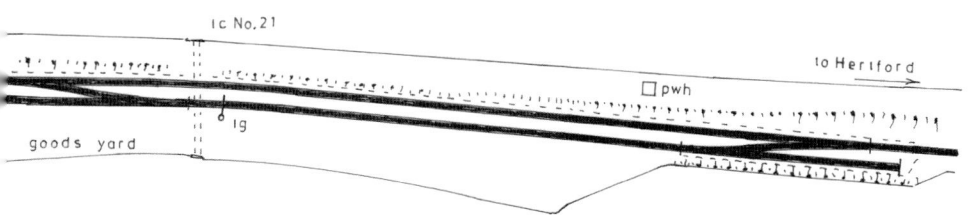

Hertingfordbury and Smart's Siding

at the east end and 210 feet headshunt at the west end. In the absence of a signal box the points were released and locked by Annett's key on the Train Staff. The towing of vehicles by rope for shunting purposes was permitted at Hertingfordbury.

From the station, a right-hand curve falling at 1 in 106 took the railway over Hertingfordbury footpath crossing No. 21 at 25 miles 62 chains, which gave way to a left-hand bend south of Hertingfordbury Park as the line passed under Wells occupational overbridge No. 6 at 25 miles 78½ chains, and then the 26 mile post on a rising 1 in 76/144

Hertingfordbury station from the east showing the entrance to the loop siding. To the left of the station is the road access to the goods yard. *Author*

BELOW: Hertingfordbury station platform and station building viewed from the passing 'Hertfordshire No. 2' railtour train headed by 'N7' Class No. 69632 on 27th April 1958.
D. Dent collection

Hertingfordbury station, built to serve a small population of between 600 and 700 souls, was only provided with a single platform, latterly 312 feet in length on the Up or south side of the railway. Following the opening of the Cuffley to Stevenage line in 1924 it saw little traffic, as Hertford North station, with a vastly superior passenger service, was less than a mile distant. Beneath the running in board, where the original cast letters have been removed and replaced by an enamelled sign, a bed of lupins adds some colour to the platform. *D. Dent collection*

LEFT: Hertingfordbury station facing west in 1963, with the buffer stops of the loop siding head shunt at the east end of the 312 feet long platform.
Author's collection

Soon after leaving Hertingfordbury station the railway curved towards Hertford and passed under Wells occupational bridge No. 6 at 25 miles 78½ chains, built for the owners of the adjacent Hertingfordbury Park.
D. Dent collection

gradient. The branch passed under another occupational footbridge No. 7 at 26 miles 06 chains, beyond which facing points on level track led to **Haggar's, later Webb, Paye and Welch's, sidings** at 26 miles 07¼ chains located on the Up side of the railway. Beyond the siding complex, the single branch line continued following the left-hand curve over occupational crossing No. 22 at 26 miles 13½ chains and Cattle Arch underbridge No. 8 at 26 miles 15½ chains. Falling at 1 in 126, the branch passed under the Wood Green to Stevenage line carried on Hertford Viaduct (bridge No. 39 at 19 miles 01¼ chains to 19 miles 15 chains from King's Cross via Enfield Chase) and then over the River Mimram on underbridge No. 9 at 26 miles 24 chains before climbing at 1 in 200 to run parallel with the loop line. Initially the branch trains passed the

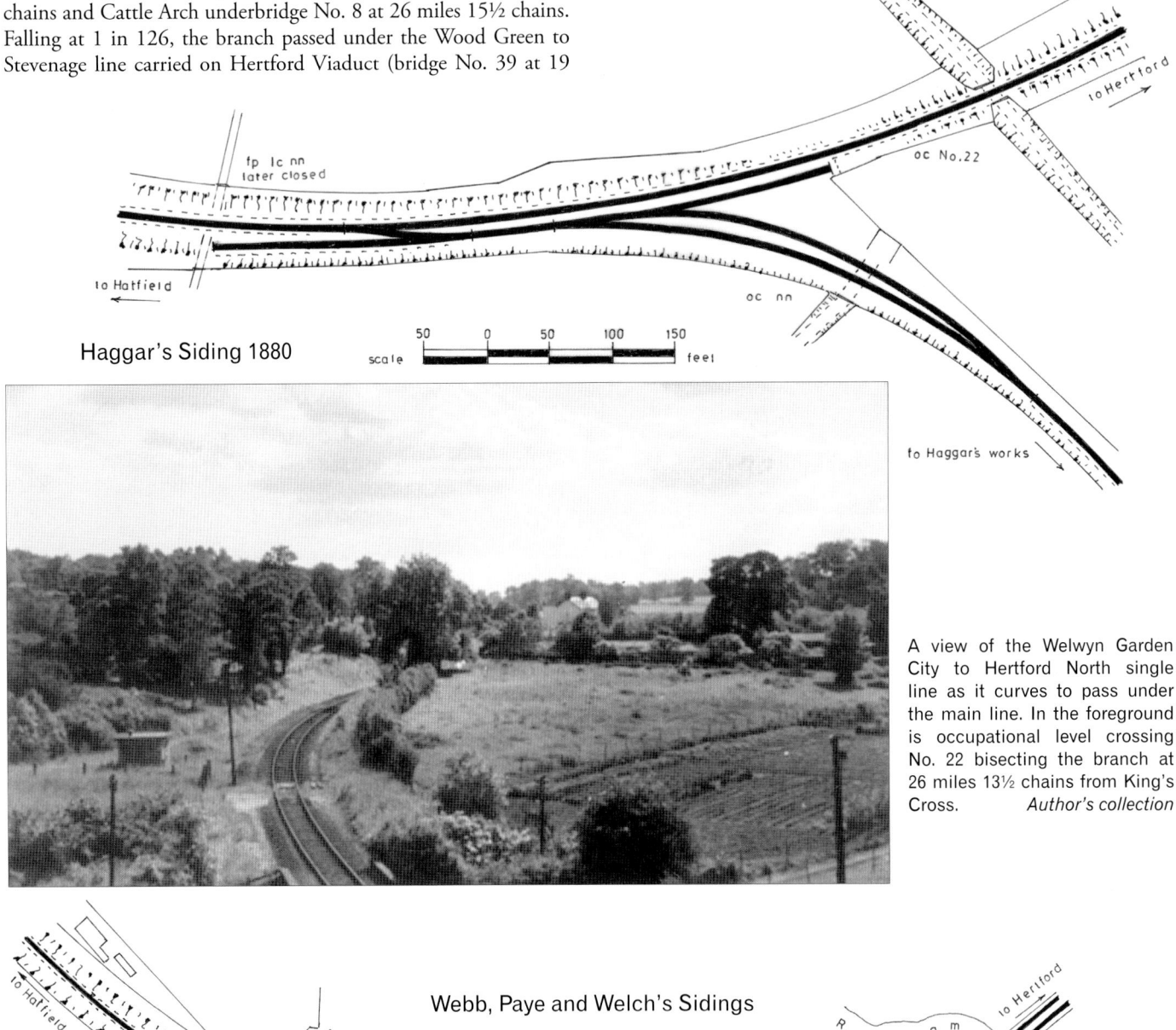

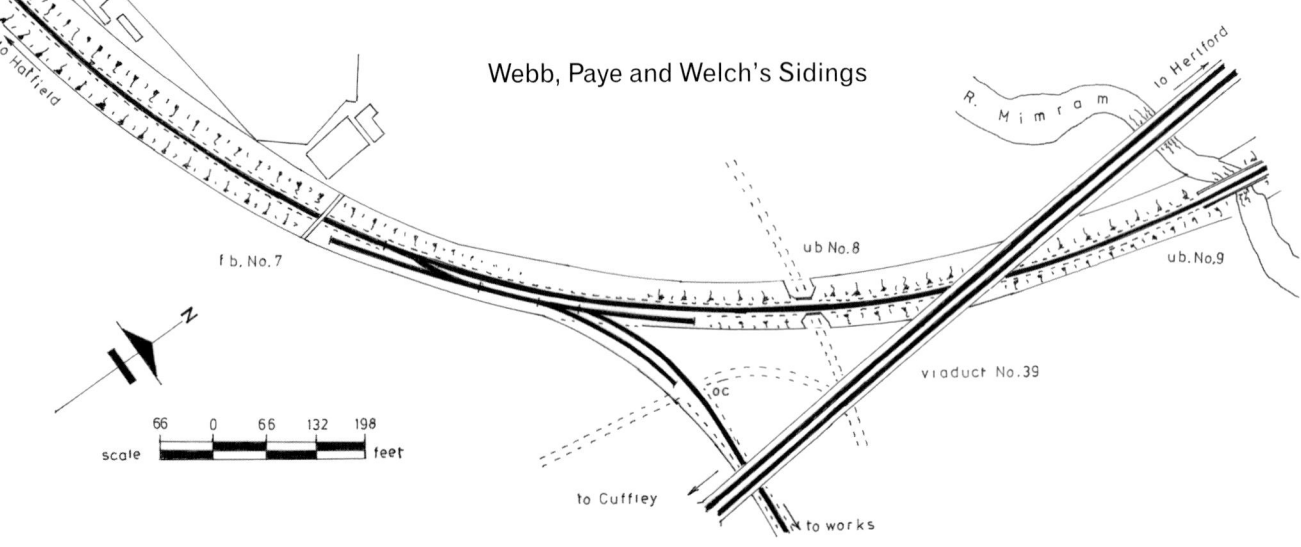

Haggar's Siding 1880

A view of the Welwyn Garden City to Hertford North single line as it curves to pass under the main line. In the foreground is occupational level crossing No. 22 bisecting the branch at 26 miles 13½ chains from King's Cross. *Author's collection*

Webb, Paye and Welch's Sidings

Webb, Paye and Welch's sidings on the south side of the main single line east of Hertingfordbury station. In the background is the viaduct carrying the Wood Green to Langley Junction line over the single-track branch.
Author's collection

Left: 'N7/3' Class 0-6-2T No. 69691 passing Webb, Paye and Welch's siding connection with a Hertford North to Welwyn Garden City train in 1951. In the background, Hertford viaduct carrying the Wood Green to Langley Junction line spans the branch.
Author's collection

Hertford viaduct No. 39, located at 19 miles 01¼ chains to 19 miles 15 chains and carrying the Wood Green to Stevenage line, forms a backcloth as 'N7/2' Class 0-6-2T No. 69695 hauls a 4-coach Hertford North to Welwyn Garden City towards Hertingfordbury on 16th June 1951. The train had been strengthened in anticipation of a larger number of passengers wishing to travel on the branch on the last day of passenger services.
Author's collection

The connection on the main single line at 26 miles 07¾ chains, as well as serving Paye and Welch's sidings also led to Webb & Company's Horn's Mill leather factory by a long 1,875 feet connection, shown on some plans as a tramway. Locomotives were not permitted beyond the entry gates and therefore the siding used horse power and later Simplex tractor units for wagon movements. The siding crossed the River Lea by an unnumbered bridge, which is shown in this view long after the track had been lifted. *Barry Gray collection*

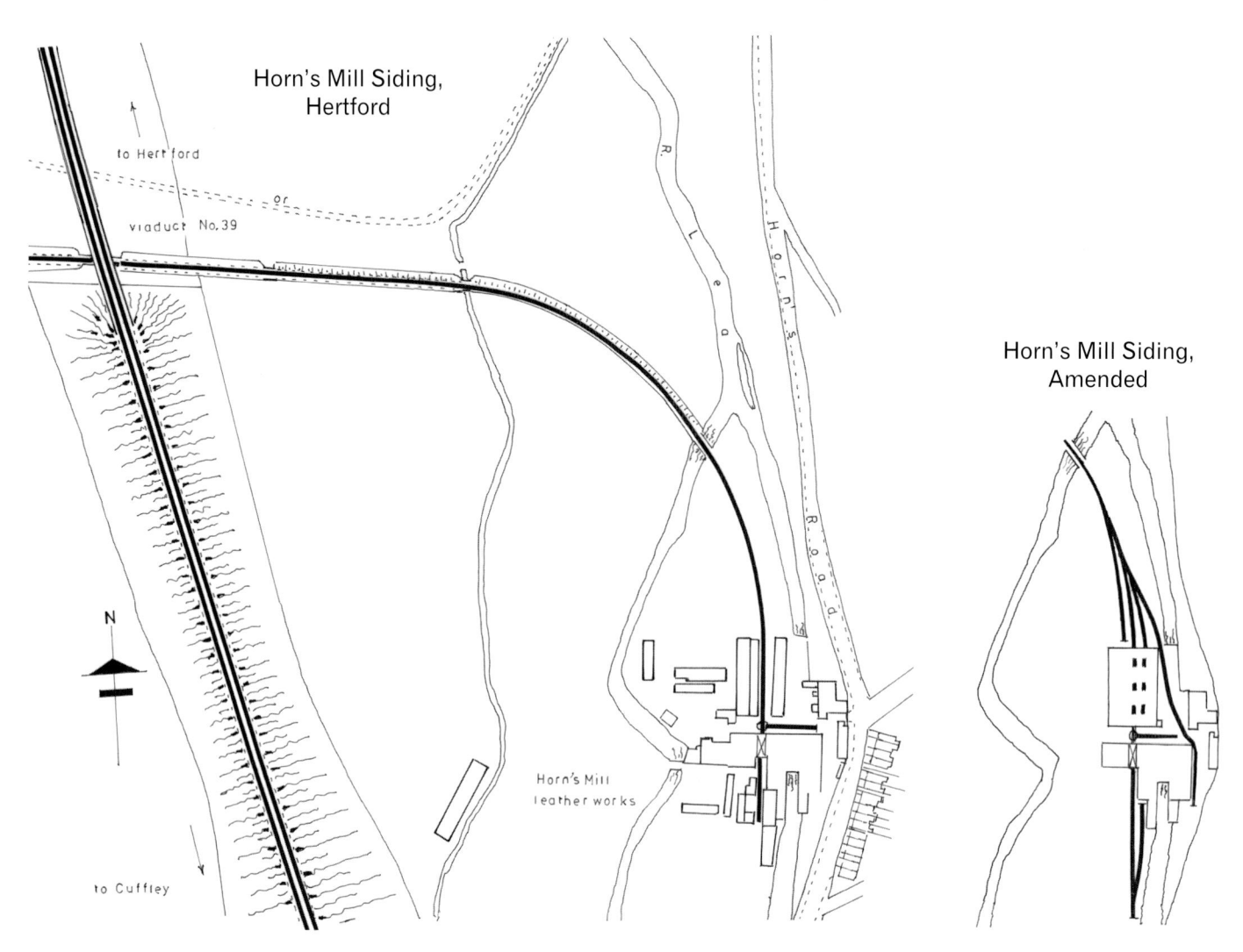

Horn's Mill Siding, Hertford

to Hertford or viaduct No. 39

R. Lea

Horn's Road

Horn's Mill leather works

to Cuffley

Horn's Mill Siding, Amended

Underbridges No. 40 on the Wood Green to Stevenage line and No. 10 on the Hatfield to Hertford branch line were at the junction from the branch to Hertford North station; 15th June 1951.
Robert Kirkland, Lens of Sutton

The physical junction between the former Hatfield to Hertford Cowbridge line and the Wood Green to Stevenage at Hertford North was made just east of the station. Hertford North signal box, containing an 65-lever Saxby & Farmer double tappet frame, controlled the connections from the main line in the foreground, with the route to Hertford East dropping away to the right and the connection to Welwyn Garden City curving Down to the left.
D. Dent collection

The junction between the main line and the branch to Hertford Cowbridge on 15th June 1951. Hertford North station can be seen above the branch line.
Robert Kirkland, Lens of Sutton

new **Hertford North** station, 19 miles 48 chains from King's Cross via Enfield Chase and 26 miles 37 chains from King's Cross via Hatfield, but in 1924 two connections were made from the north and south to the new station to enable trains from Hatfield and Welwyn Garden City to terminate there.

Hertford North station was provided with two island platforms on an elevated embankment, the Down side 530 feet and Up side 550 feet in length. The main station buildings and offices were on the Down side and terminating trains from London and branch trains from Hatfield or Welwyn Garden City terminated at or started back from the Down bay platform or Down main platform. The Up side platform had few facilities save for a waiting shed and was never provided with a back platform road. It was rarely used except for the short-lived train services between Hitchin or Stevenage to Hertford North operated by steam railcars until World War Two and saw little regular use until the loop line was electrified. The booking office was at ground level and platforms were accessed by a subway passing under the line and steps to the platform or by lift from the ground floor tunnel to the platform level. The sidings to the south of the station used for stabling coaching stock were rarely used by the branch trains as most workings were to and from Hatfield and goods was dealt with at Hertford Cowbridge. Points and signals at Hertford North were controlled from Hertford North signal box containing a 65-lever Saxby & Farmer frame located on the Up side of the line at the entrance to the sidings.

As the left-hand curve ended, the branch from Hatfield passed over the Hertingfordbury Road by underbridge No. 10 at 26 miles 36½ chains before curving to the right falling at 1 in 74 past the 6 mile post (from Welwyn Junction) at 26 miles 44½ chains, then

(Continued on p. 139)

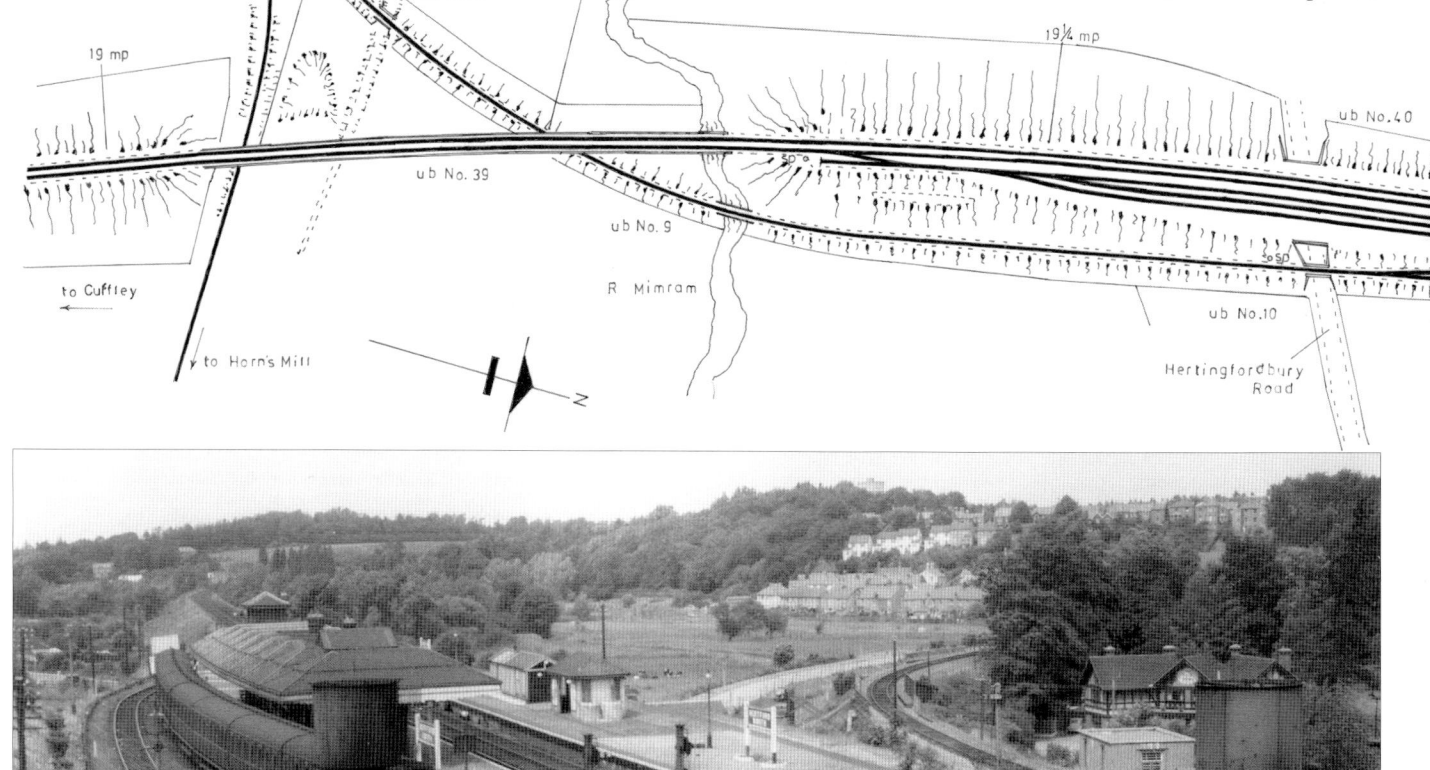

The view from overbridge No. 41 looking north on 28th June 1955. 'N2/4' Class 0-6-2T No. 69584 was waiting to depart Hertford North with a train for Moorgate. The sparseness of the Up platform can be compared with the Down side platform with it fine array of buildings. The line to Hertford Cowbridge and Hertford East curves away to the right beyond the parachute water tank. *J.F. Aylard*

The Welwyn Garden City branch approach to Hertford North is being used by a Down train formed of four coaches hauled by 'N7/2' Class 0-6-2T No. 69695 on 16th June 1951. To the left the Hertford North signalman stands waiting to collect the single line train staff from the engine crew. *Author's collection*

Hertford North

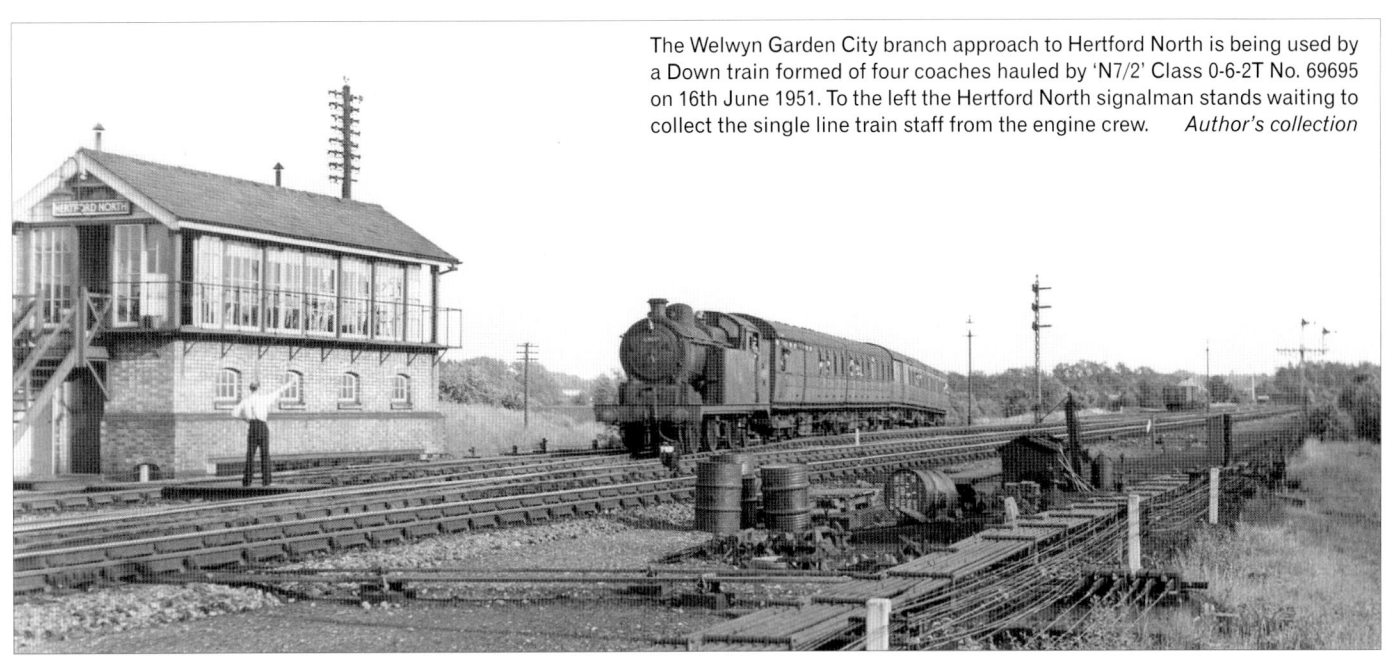

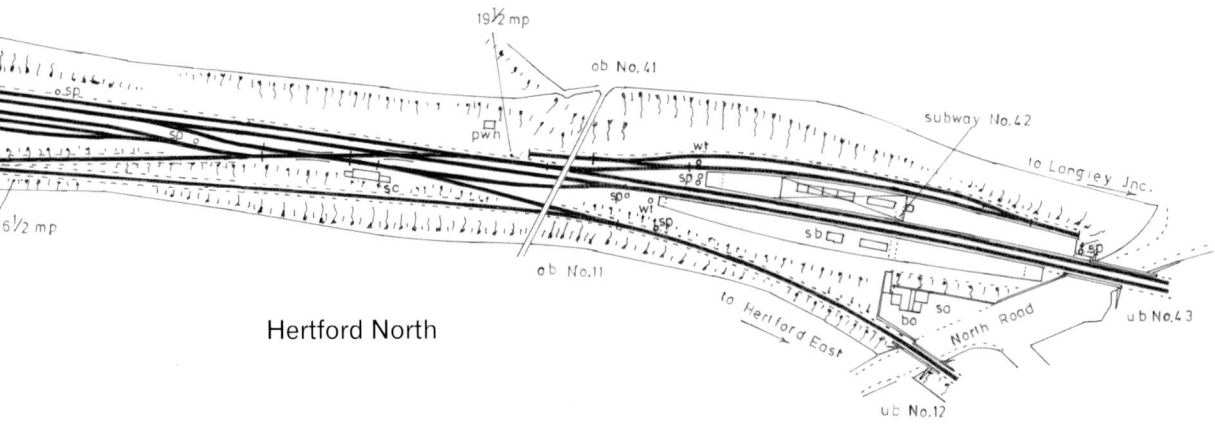

Looking south from overbridge No. 41, the southern approach to Hertford North, 19 miles 48 chains from King's Cross via Cuffley, is seen with 'J39' Class 0-6-0 No. 64796 approaching with a Down permanent way train on 17th June 1955. To the left is Hertford North signal box controlling signals at the station and the junction with the branches to Welwyn Garden City and Hertford East. *J.F. Aylard*

LEFT: Front aspect of Hertford North signal box, which controlled the connection from the Welwyn Garden City to Hertford Cowbridge goods line with the Wood Green to Langley Junction main line.
P. Whitaker

FACING PAGE TOP: Hertford North station facing north in 1969 showing the building provided on the Down side platform and the sparse facilities on the Up side. Although the eastern face of the Up platform was provided with edging slabs no track was installed. *British Railways*

ABOVE: An April 1969 view of the station entrance at Hertford North showing the corrugated iron building at street level and steps rising to the subway that led to the platforms. The rear of the simple building provided on the Up platform partly obscures the ornate buildings on the Down side platforms. *Author's collection*

FACING PAGE BOTTOM: Two-car Craven diesel multiple unit approaching Hertford North with a train from King's Cross as 'N7/5' Class 0-6-2T No. 69640 waits to depart with the branch goods train to Welwyn Garden City on 4th April 1959. To the left is the parachute water tank used to provide replenishment to locomotives on the Up main line. *Author's collection*

THE ROUTE DESCRIBED 135

Hertford North station, 19 miles 48 from King's Cross via Cuffley and 9 miles 04 chains from Hatfield via Cole Green, the view facing south from the Down main platform. The Down bay, used for terminating trains from King's Cross and Hatfield, is to the right. The Up side platform serving the Up main line is devoid of buildings except for a waiting shed.
Author's collection

RIGHT: Looking south from the Down platform at Hertford North with the Down and Up lines in the foreground. Beyond the overbridge are the goods and carriage sidings, whilst the signals to the left are the home signals from Hertford Cowbridge, the left-hand arm denoting the route to Welwyn Garden City whilst the right-hand arm denotes the connection to the Up main line and yard sidings.
Author's collection

LEFT: A similar view to those above. To the right the line serving the Down back platform ended in buffer stops and was only available for turn-back facilities. The tall tower holds the lift stage to the subway under the main lines. *Author's collection*

Hertford North station facing north from the Down platform looking towards Molewood Tunnel. On the right is the Up platform provided with a simple waiting shelter and building covering the staircase to the booking hall.
Author's collection

LEFT: Hertford North station facing north from the Up platform with the stock of a Hatfield branch train waiting at the Down main-line platform and a King's Cross train at the Down back platform.
Author's collection

LEFT: The fireman on 'N7/2' Class 0-6-2T No. 69695 is trimming coal in the bunker at Hertford North before the locomotive sets out from the Down main platform with the 7.18pm train to Welwyn Garden City on 5th June 1951. Because of the sparse service this was the last passenger train of the day on the branch.
J.F. Aylard

LEFT: The span of North Road underbridge No. 12 at 26 miles 59¾ chains from London King's Cross via Hatfield.

BELOW: View looking west from River Beane underbridge No. 13 at 26 miles 66¾ chains from King's Cross, showing the curve leading towards the junction at Hertford North. *P. Whitaker*

BOTTOM LEFT: Underbridge No. 13 spanning the River Beane. The span was removed in 1971.
P. Whitaker

BOTTOM RIGHT: View of the same bridge facing towards Hertford Cowbridge.

(Continued from p. 132)

under footbridge No. 11 at 26 miles 51 chains and over North Road underbridge No. 12 at 26 miles 59¾ chains in quick succession, the last bridge being adjacent to Hertford North station booking office.

The single line continued descending at 1 in 68/170 whilst continuing to circuit the environs of the county town of Hertford, initially on an embankment crossing the River Beane by underbridge No. 13 at 26 miles 66¾ chains on the level and passing over Molewood underbridge No. 14 at 26 miles 76 chains. Soon after the 27 mile post the railway ran under the lee of the hill in a cutting before passing under Port Vale bridge No. 15 at 27 miles 04½ chains followed by Thompson's occupational overbridge at 27 miles 06½ chains. This bridge had been built to provide access to two large houses which had been isolated by railway construction. In the course of construction, six houses at the end of George Street had to be demolished with more houses demolished at the end of

ABOVE AND ABOVE RIGHT: The remains of Molewood underbridge No. 14 at 26 miles 76 chains during removal of the structure in 1966.

RIGHT: Thompson overbridge No. 16 between Hertford North and Hertford Cowbridge, facing west. The company was forced to provide this occupation bridge as the course of the railway severed the original right of way to two houses.

The western approach to Port Hill overbridge No. 17 at 27 miles 16 chains; the original side arches were filled in to strengthen the structure and permit London Transport Country Area double-deck buses to pass over the span en route from Hertford to Bengeo. The site of the former cattle dock is to the right.

Russell Street. The right-hand curve gave way to a left-hand bend as the railway passed on level track under Port Hill overbridge No. 17 at 27 miles 16 chains and once again over the River Beane by underbridge No. 18 at 27 miles 18¾ chains, before bisecting Port Hill occupational level crossing No. 23 at 27 miles 20 chains and passing Hertford signal box to enter **Hertford** station 27 miles 21½ chains from King's Cross and 9 miles 44 chains from Hatfield. The single platform, 210 feet in length, was located on the Up or south side of the railway with ornate station buildings containing station master's accommodation, booking and parcels offices, waiting room and staff rooms.

A long passing loop, 485 feet in length, ran to the north of the platform line and connections led to the goods yard sidings: back road 400 feet in length, middle road 380 feet and inside road 325 feet. The former engine shed road, 130 feet, was used as a head shunt at the west end of the run round loop but was later removed. From the run round extension road, facing points in the Down direction led to the 270 feet Hartham road which at one time served the second engine shed. To the south of the station and east of the platform, the 95 feet by 35 feet goods shed initially containing three 1-ton capacity fixed cranes (later removed) was served by the 260 feet shed road, which terminated at the west end with a wagon turntable connection with the 140 feet shed short road running north of the building. The goods yard was served by the 270 feet crane road serving the associated 5-ton capacity fixed crane and 225 feet yard road. To the west of the station on the south side of the line the 240 feet dock road served the cattle dock. Points and signals at the station were controlled by Hertford signal box equipped with a 26-lever, later 30-lever, Saxby & Farmer frame located at the west end of the station platform.

Away from Hertford station the left-hand curve ended just before the line climbing a short 1 in 66 crossed Cattle Arch underbridge No. 19 at 27 miles 26¾ chain, which also served as a public access to Hartham Common from Hartham Lane if the gates of occupational crossing No. 24 at 27 miles 27 chains were closed. Beyond the crossing were connections leading to the group of

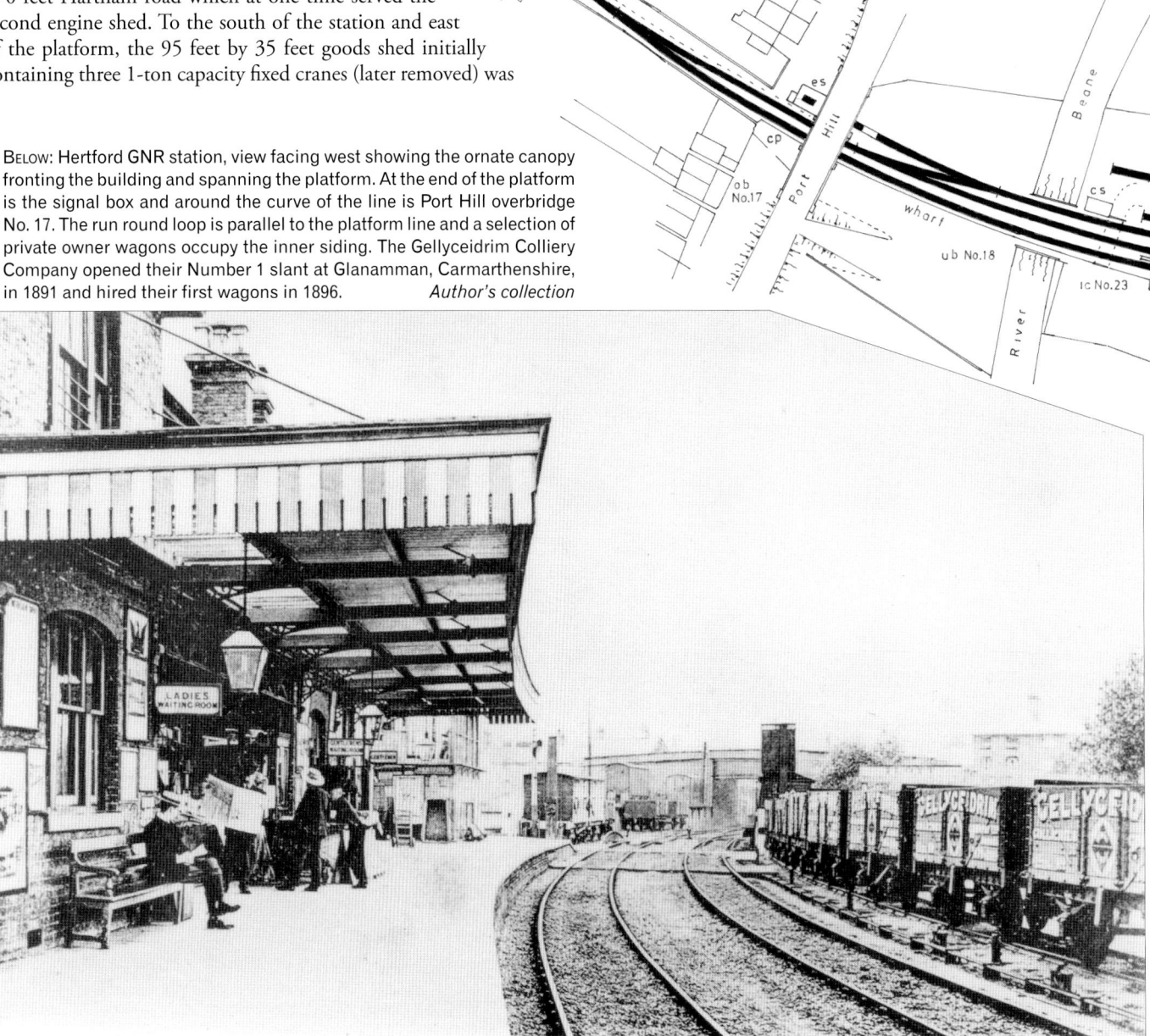

BELOW: Hertford GNR station, view facing west showing the ornate canopy fronting the building and spanning the platform. At the end of the platform is the signal box and around the curve of the line is Port Hill overbridge No. 17. The run round loop is parallel to the platform line and a selection of private owner wagons occupy the inner siding. The Gellyceidrim Colliery Company opened their Number 1 slant at Glanamman, Carmarthenshire, in 1891 and hired their first wagons in 1896. *Author's collection*

The road approach to Hertford station with a horse draw bus awaiting prospective customers. Beyond the station building is the rear view of the signal box and, to the extreme left, three cattle wagons stand on the cattle dock siding. *Author's collection*

Hertford GNR 1880

sidings on the Down side of the railway and the Up goods yard, and at 27 miles 31¾ chains the trailing points leading to McMullen & Sons brewery and maltings sidings on the Up side. The railway as double track then crossed Mill Tail underbridge No. 20 at 27 miles 32¾ chains, which of timber construction was rebuilt in concrete in 1926, and then crossed the River Lea by underbridge No. 21 at 27 miles 41 chains. Immediately beyond the structure was the facing connection to Manser's siding on the Down side at 27 miles 41½ chains, leading to the canal-side wharf and gravel quay by the Lea Basin, which was equipped with a 10-ton capacity fixed crane. From this siding a long connection ran between the Mill Tail and the River Lea to Dicker Oil and Cake Mill crossing in its course an un-numbered bridge with 22 feet span and height above the waterway of 7 feet.

The 7 mile post (from Welwyn Junction) was passed at 27 miles 43 chains before trailing points brought the connection from Ewan & Tomlinson's, later Andrew's saw mill, siding which joined on the Up side at 27 miles 45¾ chains prior to the line bisecting on the level Dicker Mill crossing No. 25 at 27 miles 46 chains. The gates were controlled between 1894 and 1929 from a small signal box located on the Up side of the railway at 27 miles 47½ chains, the gates for the crossing being interlocked with the signals. The signal box also controlled entry to Gray & Miles siding on the Down side at 27 miles 55¼ chains and a connection on the Up side at 27 miles 49 chains serving Brazier's siding, also known as Gas Works siding in Railway Street. A slight left-hand

(Continued on p. 150)

Hertford station and signal box showing the 210 feet long platform. To the left is the goods shed and beyond the station is McMullen's brewery and maltings. Port Hill occupational crossing No. 23 bisects the railway at the west end of the platform, whilst underbridge No. 18 spans the River Beane. Dominating the scene is the parachute water tank in the goods yard, which also supplied the water crane at the end of the station platform. *Author's collection*

THE ROUTE DESCRIBED

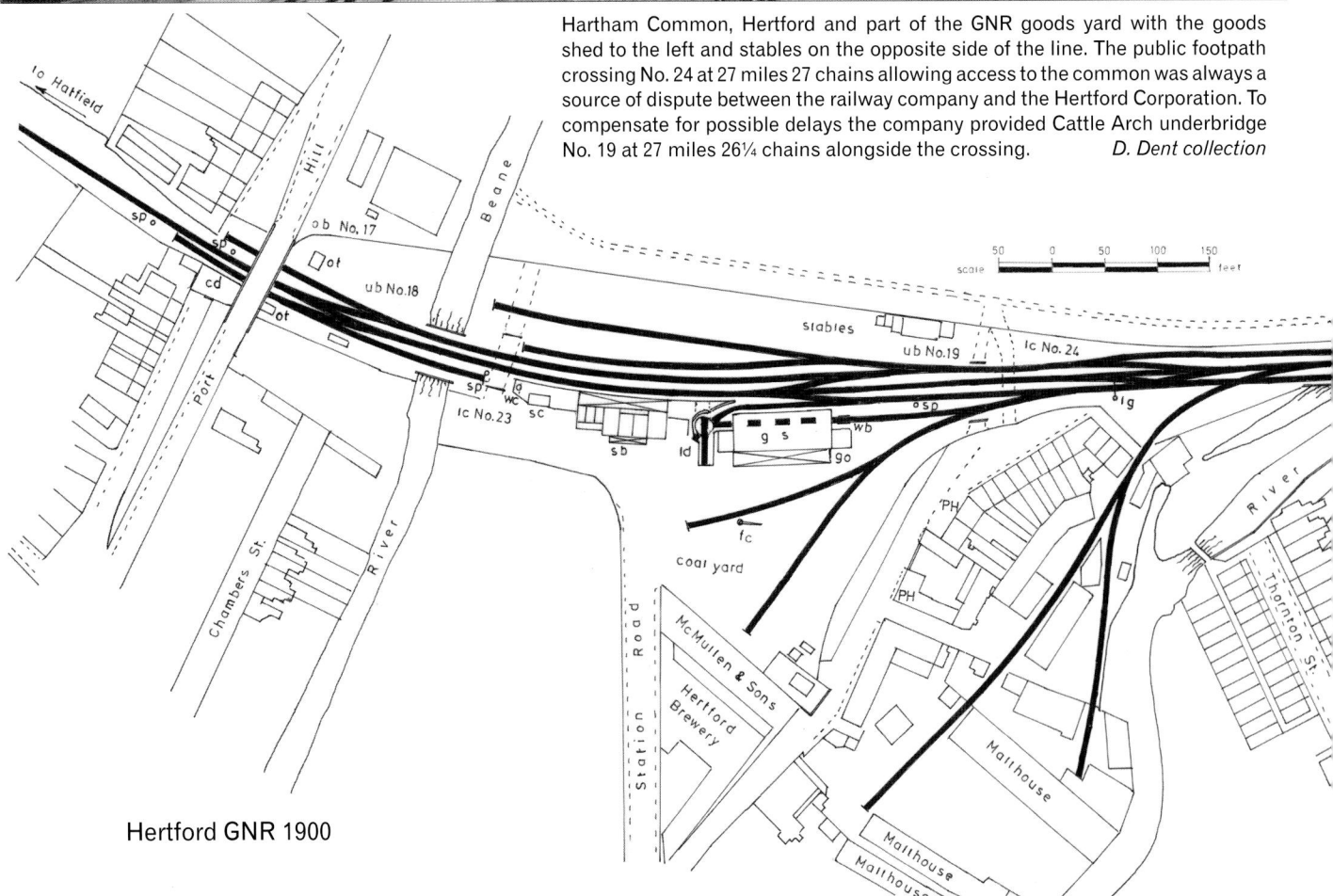

Hartham Common, Hertford and part of the GNR goods yard with the goods shed to the left and stables on the opposite side of the line. The public footpath crossing No. 24 at 27 miles 27 chains allowing access to the common was always a source of dispute between the railway company and the Hertford Corporation. To compensate for possible delays the company provided Cattle Arch underbridge No. 19 at 27 miles 26¼ chains alongside the crossing. *D. Dent collection*

Hertford GNR 1900

Aerial view of Hertford town centre in the 1950s with the ex-GNR goods shed and associated goods yard in the foreground. Traffic is brisk, for the coal grounds are full and the sidings are occupied by many open wagons and covered vans. *Barry Gray collection*

General view of the approach to Hertford Cowbridge facing west, with the parapet rails of Mill Tail underbridge No. 20 to the left and Dicker Mill crossing Down distant signal to the right. The siding to the left served the premises of McMullen's brewery. *P. Whitaker*

Goods office at the west end of the goods shed at Hertford Cowbridge. In its heyday the GNR employed six clerks in the goods department at Hertford.
P. Whitaker

Site of the former wagon turntables and loading dock west of the goods shed at Hertford Cowbridge. The goods office is to the left and McMullen's brewery in the background.
P. Whitaker

Goods office at the east end of the goods shed at Hertford Cowbridge. This building also contained the weighbridge office with the weighbridge located in the track in front of the building. The photographer recorded the main building as being constructed of yellow stock bricks, with doors and windows painted green, window frames cream, and gutters and pipe work green. The coal store alongside the office was constructed of orange/red bricks and the capping was blue engineer brickwork.
P. Whitaker

ABOVE: Hertford Cowbridge station viewed from the west on 17th July 1955. In the foreground is underbridge No. 18 spanning the River Beane and then Port Hill occupational level crossing No. 23. Beyond the parachute tank are three reception roads in the Down side yard whilst to the right of the building wagons are stabled in the goods yard and McMullen's siding.
Author's collection

The road approach to Hertford GNR station with the McMullen Brewery to the right.
D. Dent collection

Hertford Cowbridge station frontage seen on 15th June 1951.
Robert Kirkland, Lens of Sutton

BELOW: Hertford Cowbridge showing the short 210 feet long low level platform. The canopy has been removed and 16-ton all-steel mineral wagons are stabled in the siding adjoining the goods shed.
Author's collection

LEFT: General view from the east end of Cowbridge station platform facing towards the junction with the GER lines, with the goods shed to the right and former stable block to the left. A tar wagon has been deposited on the former run round loop line in this 1962 view. *P. Whitaker*

ABOVE: Platform aspect of Hertford Cowbridge station building with additional external wooden stairs leading to the first floor. The building was demolished in 1990.
P. Whitaker

RIGHT: The west end of the station platform at Cowbridge formerly occupied by the signal box. Note the alteration in platform height and the ornate entrance pillars.
P. Whitaker

Hertford Cowbridge station from the west with No. 18 underbridge spanning the River Beane and beyond that Port Hill occupational level crossing No. 23. *Author's collection*

(Continued from p. 141)
curve brought the line to the connection to Smart's Kingsmead sidings on the Down side at 27 miles 70 chains, the connection also in later years serving Tottenham & District Gas Company, later Eastern Gas Board, Permanite and Regent Tar Distillers sidings. The **end of GNR maintenance** was reached at 27 miles 74 chains 59 links, as the line falling at 1 in 333 formed a trailing connection with the GER Up line from Hertford to Broxbourne at 27 miles 77 chains and 9 links from London King's Cross. The connection was controlled by the GER Hertford Junction signal box, and after the abolition of that box by Hertford East signal box. Hertford East GER station was 10 miles 27¾ chains from Hatfield.

Authority was given to propel up to twenty wagons in daylight and clear weather at a speed not exceeding 15 mph between Hatfield No. 2 signal box and Smart's siding. If necessary a train with brake van accompanied by a guard could at the same time be

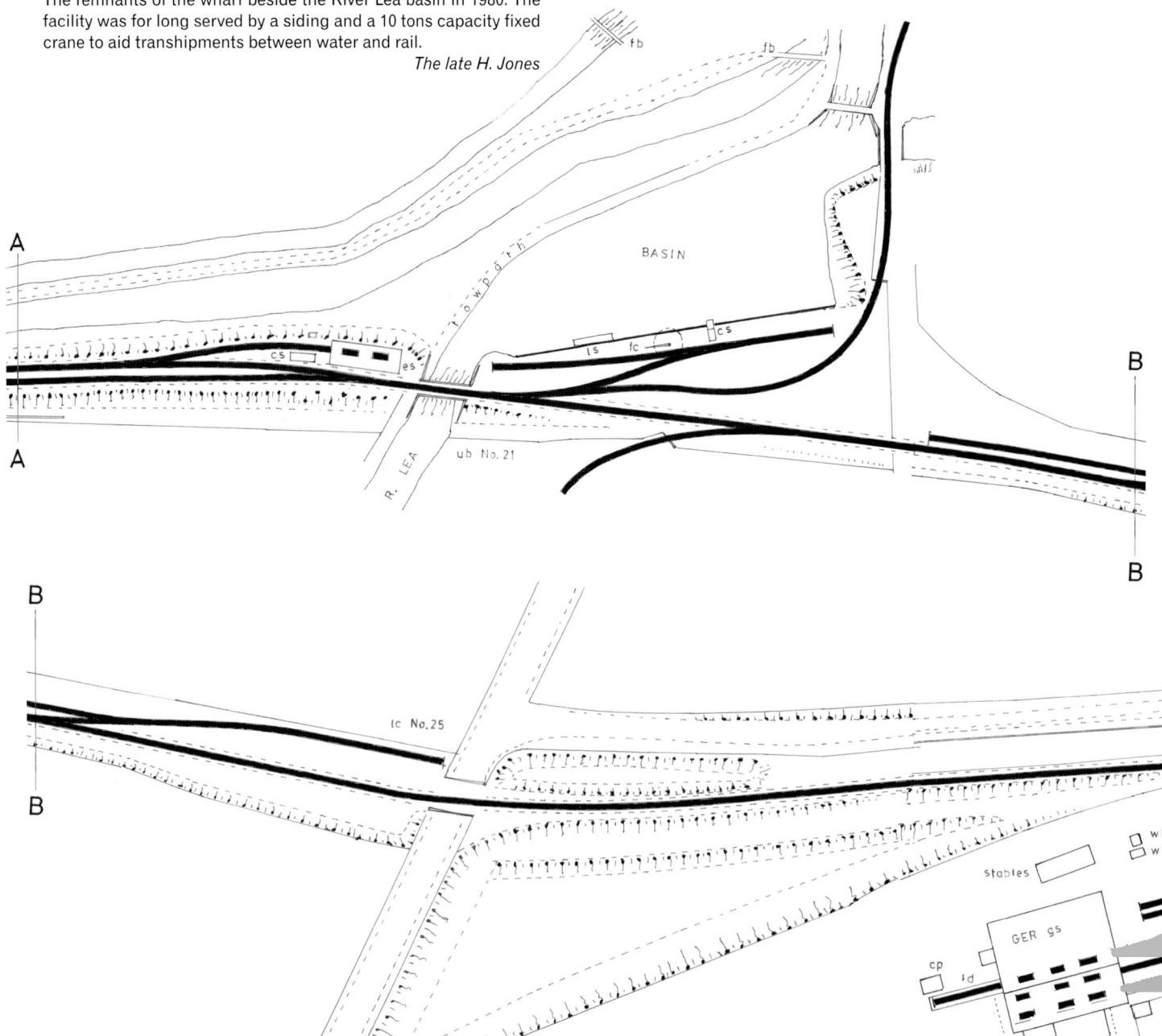

The remnants of the wharf beside the River Lea basin in 1980. The facility was for long served by a siding and a 10 tons capacity fixed crane to aid transhipments between water and rail.
The late H. Jones

View looking west from Hertford Junction signal box in 1911 showing the physical connection between the GNR and the GER centre right, with the single branch line running behind the engine shed. The GER goods shed and yard are to the left, as the Down and Up main lines curve round the structure to access the station. Note the close proximity of the engine shed to the GNR line; in later years it was not possible to turn a long GER locomotive whilst a train was operating on the branch because of restricted clearance. The buffer stops to the right have been strengthened by the addition of a ballast compound. *GERS/Windwood 614*

drawn by the engine propelling the wagons but the total number of wagons propelled and drawn was not to exceed the load laid down in the loading circular. It was also permitted to propel wagons over the single line between Sherriff's and Hatfield Manure siding to Hatfield No. 2 signal box.

It was permitted to propel not more than twenty-five wagons including horse boxes and similar vehicles from Hertford Goods to Hertford North passenger and between Hertford Goods and Hertford North sidings but such movements, when consisting of more than ten wagons, were not to commence until the shunter in charge had been informed by the signalman in Hertford North signal box that the road was set and the home signal was in the 'off' position. Between Hertford East Junction and Hertford Goods wagons could be propelled but the driver had to stop the train with the leading vehicle clear of Dicker Mill Lane level crossing and await the gates to be closed across the public road before proceeding.

Propelling of trains or vehicles was also permitted in the latter years as under: from Welwyn Garden City yard to Lincoln Electric Company' private siding where a freight train composed of not more than twelve wagons could also propel up to ten wagons. In the reverse direction between the Lincoln Electric Company's private

Hertford GER 1880

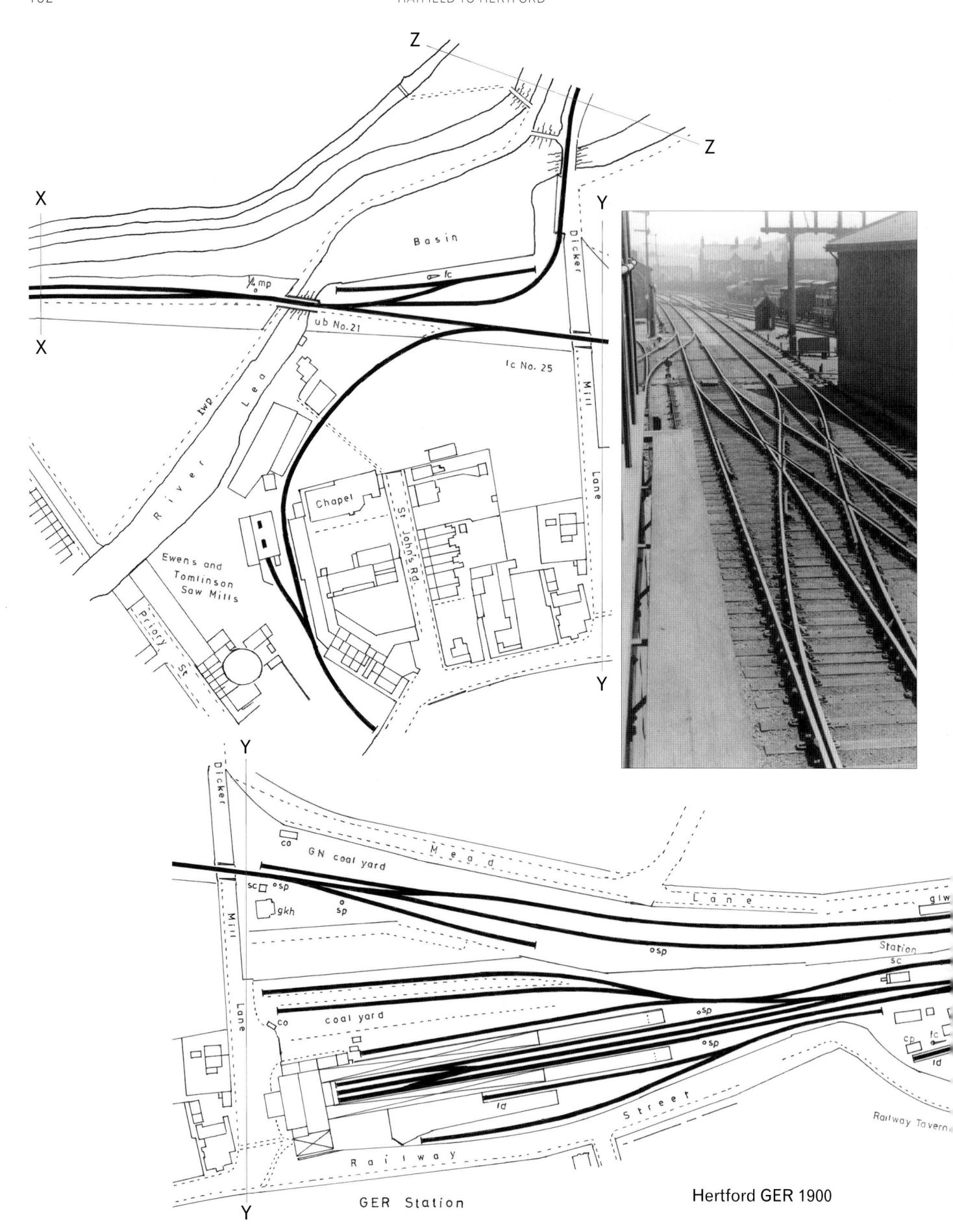

Hertford GER 1900

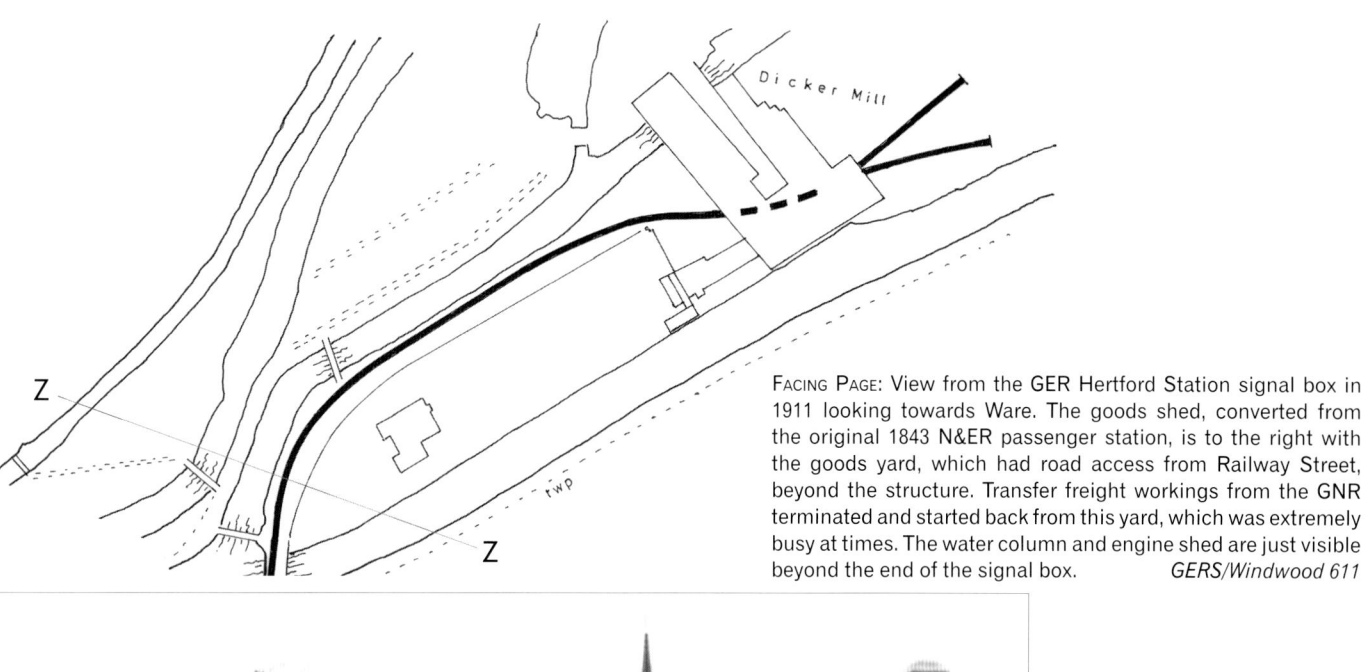

FACING PAGE: View from the GER Hertford Station signal box in 1911 looking towards Ware. The goods shed, converted from the original 1843 N&ER passenger station, is to the right with the goods yard, which had road access from Railway Street, beyond the structure. Transfer freight workings from the GNR terminated and started back from this yard, which was extremely busy at times. The water column and engine shed are just visible beyond the end of the signal box. *GERS/Windwood 611*

LEFT: The remains of Dicker Mill level crossing gates (No. 25 at 27 miles 46 chains) shortly before removal of the barriers and the track.

siding to Welwyn Garden City goods yard a freight train composed of not more than twelve wagons was permitted to propel not more than twenty-five wagons over the single line. It was also permissible to propel wagons from Foundry sidings, Norton's sidings and Attimore siding to Welwyn Garden City goods yard, as well as a rake of up to thirty wagons from Felt & Damp Course siding at Attimore Hall to Welwyn Garden City yard.

The speed limit of trains on the branch between Hatfield and Hertford, later Welwyn Garden City and Hertford North, was 50 mph, but was then reduced after the withdrawal of the passenger service as a consequence of the reduction in permanent way maintenance to 40 mph between Hatfield and Hertford North and Hertford East with 10 later 15 mph round the sharp curve between Welwyn Garden City and Cole Green.

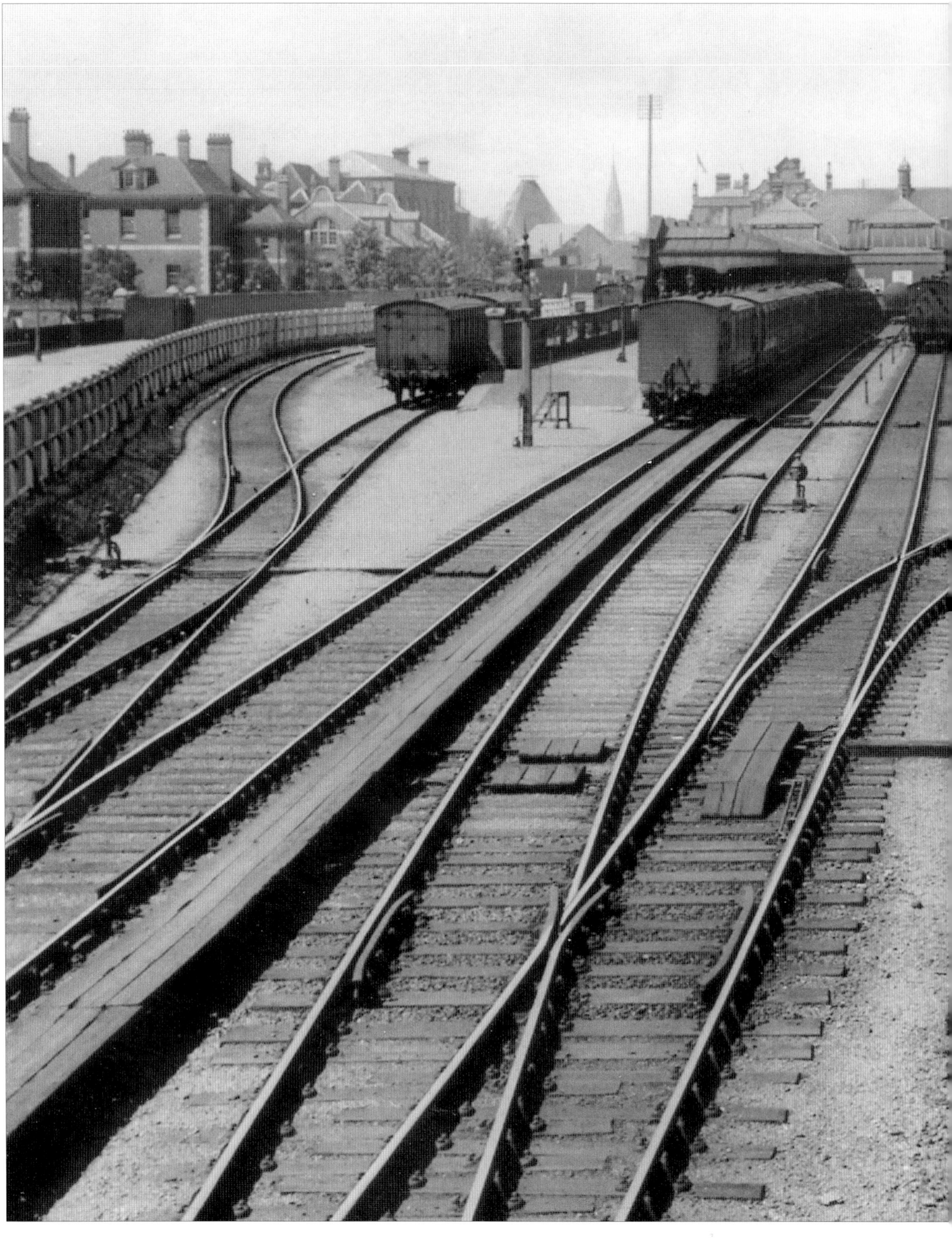

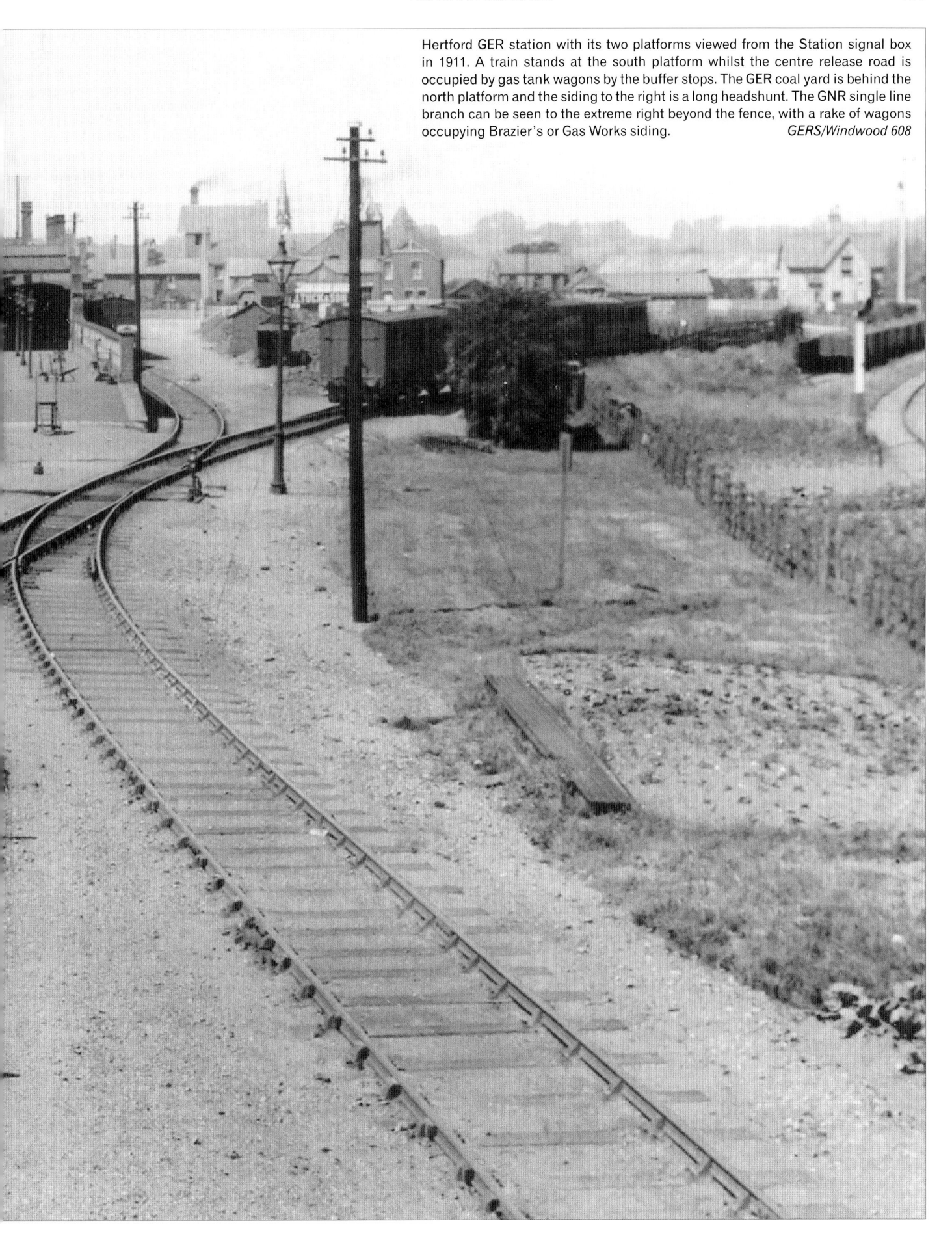

Hertford GER station with its two platforms viewed from the Station signal box in 1911. A train stands at the south platform whilst the centre release road is occupied by gas tank wagons by the buffer stops. The GER coal yard is behind the north platform and the siding to the right is a long headshunt. The GNR single line branch can be seen to the extreme right beyond the fence, with a rake of wagons occupying Brazier's or Gas Works siding. *GERS/Windwood 608*

Exterior of Hertford GER station dating from 1888, the construction of which as a terminal station effectively dashed all hopes of providing a joint GNR/GER facility for the town.
Author's collection

Facing west from Hertford Junction with the GER goods yard to the left, the two-road engine shed and the neatly stacked coal to the right, with the Down and Up main line leading to the terminus in the centre. Note also the close proximity of the engine shed to the GNR single line, where the connection to the extreme right leads to Smart's Kingsmead ballast sidings.
GERS/Windwood 616

Sidings

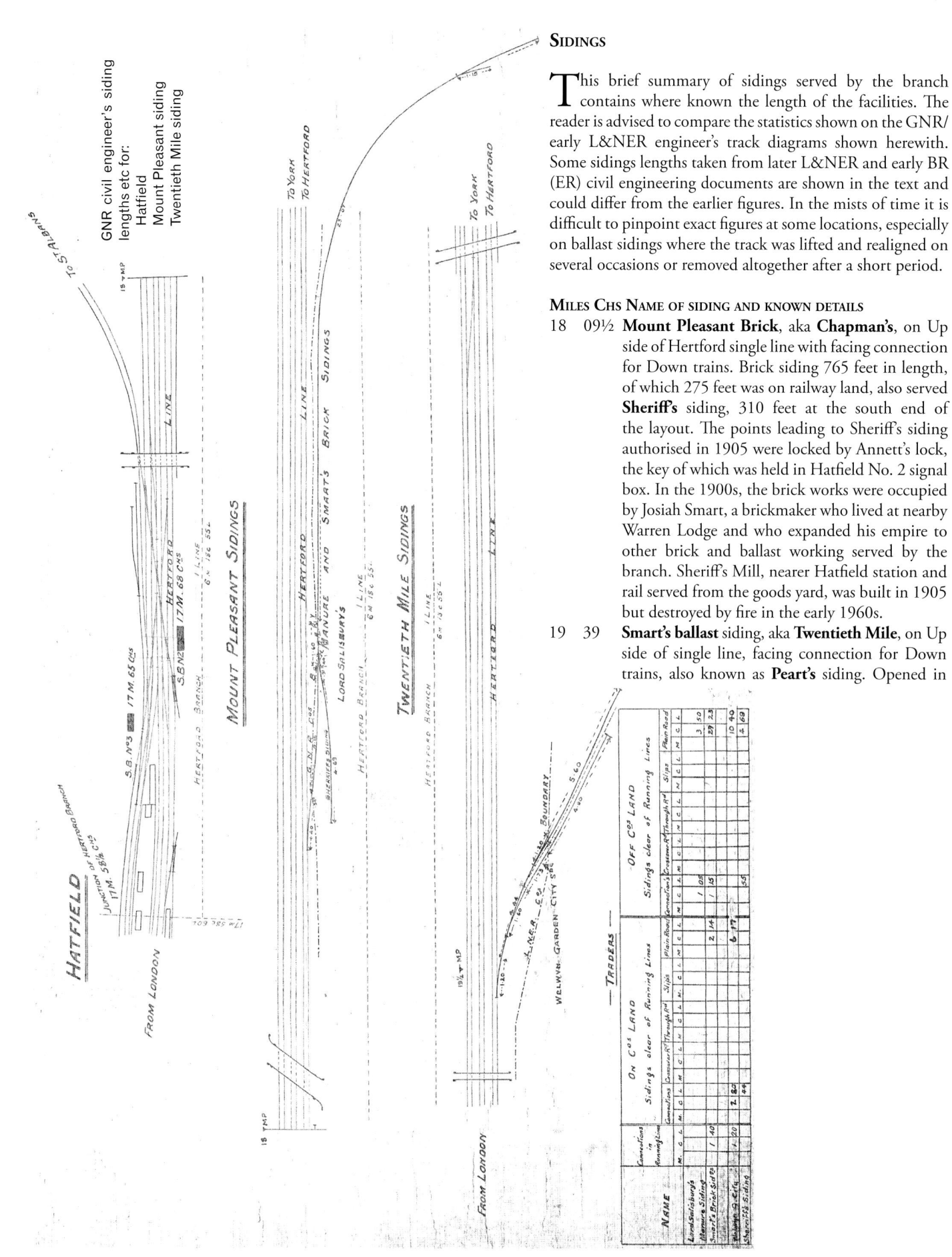

This brief summary of sidings served by the branch contains where known the length of the facilities. The reader is advised to compare the statistics shown on the GNR/early L&NER engineer's track diagrams shown herewith. Some sidings lengths taken from later L&NER and early BR (ER) civil engineering documents are shown in the text and could differ from the earlier figures. In the mists of time it is difficult to pinpoint exact figures at some locations, especially on ballast sidings where the track was lifted and realigned on several occasions or removed altogether after a short period.

Miles Chs Name of siding and known details

18 09½ **Mount Pleasant Brick**, aka **Chapman's**, on Up side of Hertford single line with facing connection for Down trains. Brick siding 765 feet in length, of which 275 feet was on railway land, also served **Sheriff's** siding, 310 feet at the south end of the layout. The points leading to Sheriff's siding authorised in 1905 were locked by Annett's lock, the key of which was held in Hatfield No. 2 signal box. In the 1900s, the brick works were occupied by Josiah Smart, a brickmaker who lived at nearby Warren Lodge and who expanded his empire to other brick and ballast working served by the branch. Sheriff's Mill, nearer Hatfield station and rail served from the goods yard, was built in 1905 but destroyed by fire in the early 1960s.

19 39 **Smart's ballast** siding, aka **Twentieth Mile**, on Up side of single line, facing connection for Down trains, also known as **Peart's** siding. Opened in

1886 by Smart, Peart had connection from 1891 for manure traffic. Closed by 1937. North siding 370 feet on railway land plus 370 feet on private land. South siding 217 feet on railway land, 320 feet on private land. Connection with extensive 2 feet gauge **Welwyn Garden City Light Railway** in the 1930s when gravel was conveyed from Digswell pit to the washing plant at Twentieth Mile complex. The system, which had no other connection with the GNR/L&NER, closed entirely in May 1940.

20 51 **Digswell**, located on Up side of line trailing connection for Down trains, straight siding 396 feet at south end with 290 feet headshunt north of connecting points. Connection later led to **A. Dawnay's** siding curving away from the above with 1,180 feet main siding and 570 feet siding serving a travelling crane connected by crossover. Connection from Welwyn Garden City goods yard to **Shredded Wheat** siding installed 1924 for Shredded Wheat Company, founded in USA in 1898, Nabisco Foods Limited from July 1956. Siding 2,000 feet in length, also served other premises including 260 feet siding curving into electric heating manufacturing company. Shredded Wheat siding operated by 0-4-0 diesel mechanical shunting locomotive built in 1934,

			HATFIELD AND HERTFORD BRANCH.	
NO BLOCK.	..	..	Hatfield Station	
	..	11½	" North Box	
	..	33	Manure and Brick Siding (Signals worked by Hatfield Porter.)	¶
	2	76¼	Digswell Siding .. ... (~~Signals worked by Gateman.~~)	¶
	4	10¼	Attimore Hall Siding .. (Signals worked by Digswell Gateman on Down and by Guard on Up Journey.)	¶
	6	30	Cole Green Station ..	¶
	7	79¼	Hertingfordbury Station	¶
	8	30	Haggers Siding .. .. (Signals worked by Hertingfordbury Porter.)	¶
	9	44	Hertford, G.N. Station ..	..
	..	..	Mansers and Gas Works Sidings.	
	10	27¾	Hertford, G.E. Station ..	¶

ABOVE: Branch mileage and signalling from GNR Appendix to Working Timetable, 1881.

BELOW: Branch mileage and signalling from GNR Appendix, 1905.

FACING PAGE TOP: Instruction for working branch stations 1881.

FACING PAGE BOTTOM: Branch mileage and signalling from GNR Appendix, 1912, showing Attimore and Hatfield Hyde halts.

Block working.	Distance from King's Cross passenger station. Miles	Chns	Stations, sidings and signal boxes.	Distance from point to point. Miles	Chns.	Shunting sidings. Down.	Up.	Closed	Stations to which the signal boxes and sidings are attached.
			HERTFORD BRANCH.						
	17	64½	**Hatfield station & junction**	..	..	..	..	See main line	Hatfield.
Absolute.	17	58½	" junction with main line	..	4	..	..		
	17	68	" box 2	..	9¼	..	..		
	18	9½	Mt. Pleasant manure & brick sidng	..	21½	..	..		
	19	39	Smart's siding	1	29¼	..	..		
	19	72¾	Twentieth mile up box	..	33¾	..	..		
	20	51	Digswell siding	..	58¼	..	..	.. ..	
	20	68	Lord Cowper's siding	..	17	..	..	.. ..	
	21	66¾	Attimore Hall crossing .. *	..	78¾	..	..	.. ..	
	21	74¼	" " siding	..	7½	..	..	.. ..	
	22	38¼	Hatfield Hyde crossing .. *	..	44	..	..	.. ..	
	22	66½	Birchall's siding	..	28¼	..	..	.. ..	Cole Green.
	23	28½	Holwell Hyde Farm siding ..	..	42	..	..	.. ..	
	24	5	Cole Green box	..	56½	..	..	After last train is out of section Saturdays to 6.40 a.m. Sundays; after up goods train is out of section Sundays to 4.50 p.m.; and after last train is out of section, Sundays to 5.50 a.m. Mondays	
	24	5¼	**Cole Green station**	..	¼	..	..	.. ..	
	25	50	Smart's Hertingfordbury gravel siding	1	44¾	..	..	.. ..	Hertingfordbury.
	25	56½	**Hertingfordbury station** ..	..	6¼	..	..	.. ..	
	26	7¼	Webb's and Paye & Welch's siding	..	31	..	..	.. ..	
	27	20¼	Hertford box	1	13	..	..	After last train is out of section Saturdays to 6.45 a.m. Sundays; Sundays after up goods train is out of section to 5.0 p.m.; and after last train is out of section Sundays to 6.0 a.m. Mondays	Hertford (G.N.)
	27	21½	**Hertford G.N. station** ..	..	1¼	..	..	.. ..	
Nil.	27	31¾	McMullen's siding	..	10¼	..	..	.. ..	
	27	41½	Manser's siding	..	9½	..	..	.. ..	
	27	45¾	Andrew's siding	..	4¼	..	..	.. ..	
Nil.	27	47	Dicker Mill crossing .. *	..	1¼	..	..	.. ..	Hertford (G.N.).
	27	47¾	" " box .. .. *	..	0¾	..	..	.. ..	
	27	47¾	Brazier's sidings	..	..	..	..	.. ..	
	27	49¼	Gasworks siding .. / Gray & Miles' siding / Barber's siding ..	..	1½	..	..	.. ..	
	27	69¾	Smart's siding (Kingsmead) ..	..	20½	..	..	.. ..	
	27	77	Hertford, G.E. junction ..	..	7¼	..	..	.. ..	Hertford (G.E.).
	28	25	**Hertford G.E. station** ..	.	28	..	..	.. ..	

39

Special Instructions as to the working of certain Stations, Sidings, &c.—*continued.*

HATFIELD AND HERTFORD BRANCH.

Manure and Brick Siding, Hatfield.—The signals will be worked by a Hatfield porter, who must attend all train stopping at this siding. No train or engine must stop unless the single line staff be on the engine. An Arnett's patent safety lock has been fixed to the points of this siding. The Hatfield North Box signalman has charge of the key to unlock the points, which he cannot give to the porter until the signals controlling the Hertford line have been placed to "danger." The signals remain at "danger" until the porter returns the key, which he cannot do until he has locked the siding points.

* **Digswell Siding and Lord Cowper's Siding.**—The signals controlling these sidings are worked by the porter in charge of the Digswell crossing gates, who must attend all trains stopping at the siding. No train must stop after dusk or in foggy weather.

* **Attimore Hall Siding.**—The signals must be worked by the Digswell gateman on the down, and by the guard on the up journey, and before leaving the siding the points communicating with the main line must be securely locked by the Digswell gateman or guard as the case may be, so that the points may remain in the proper position for the passage of trains on the running line. No train must stop after dusk or in foggy weather.

* **Hagger's Siding.**—Certain trains only, as per monthly working book, will stop at this siding. A porter from Hertingfordbury will meet such trains and work the signals during the time the trains stop at and use the siding.

* *The guard must leave word at the preceding station that he is going to stop at either of these sidings, in which case the station master is to stop and caution any train following within twenty minutes.*

Block working.	Distance from King's Cross passenger station. Miles	Chns	Stations, sidings and signal boxes.	Distance from point to point. Miles	Chns	Shunting sidings. Down.	Up.	Closed	Stations to which the signal boxes and sidings are attached.
			HERTFORD BRANCH.						
Absolute.	17	54½	**Hatfield station & junction**	..	..	..	..		
	17	58½	,, junction with main line	..	4	..	..		
	17	68	,, box 2	..	9½	..	..		
	18	9½	Hatfield manure, Sherriff's and Mount Pleasant sidings	..	21½	..	..	See main line	
	19	39	Peart's and Smart's sidings ..	1	29½	..	..		
	19	72¾	Twentieth mile up box	..	33¾	..	..		Hatfield.
	20	51	Digswell siding	..	58¼	..	..	.. ..	
	20	68	Lord Cowper's siding	..	17	..	..	.. ..	
	21	66¾	Attimore Hall crossing .. *	..	78¾	..	..	.. ..	
	21	67½	**Attimore Hall "halt"** ..	..	¾	..	..	.. ..	
	21	74¼	,, ,, siding	..	6¾	..	..	.. ..	
	22	38¼	Hatfield Hyde crossing .. *	..	44	..	..	.. ..	
	22	39	**Hatfield Hyde "halt"** ..	..	¾	..	..	.. ..	
	22	54½	Birchall siding	..	15½	..	..	.. ..	
	23	28½	Holwell Hyde Farm siding .	..	54	..	..	.. ..	
	24	5	Cole Green box	..	56½	..	..	After last train is out of section Saturdays to 6.40 a.m. Sundays; after up goods train is out of section Sundays to 5.25 p.m.; and after last train is out of section, Sundays to 6.0 a.m. Mondays	Cole Green.
	24	5¼	**Cole Green station**	..	¼	..	..	.. ..	
	25	50	Smart's Hertingfordbury gravel siding	1	44¾	..	..	.. ..	
	25	56¼	**Hertingfordbury station** ..	..	6¼	..	..	.. ..	Hertingfordbury.
	26	7¼	Webb's and Paye & Welch's siding	..	31	..	..	.. ..	
	27	20¼	Hertford box	1	13	..	..	After last train is out of section Saturdays to 6.45 a.m. Sundays; Sundays after up goods train is out of section to 5.40 p.m.; and after last train is out of section Sundays to 6.0 a.m. Mondays	
Nil.	27	21½	**Hertford G.N. station** ..	..	1¼	..	..	.. ..	Hertford (G.N.)
	27	31¾	McMullen's siding	..	10¼	..	..	.. ..	
	27	41¼	Manser's siding	..	9½	..	..	.. ..	
	27	45¾	Andrew's siding	..	4½	..	..	.. ..	
Nil.	27	47	Dicker Mill Lane crossing *	..	1¼	..	..	.. ..	
	27	47¾	,, ,, box .. .. *	..	0¾	..	..	.. ..	
	27	47¾	Brazier's siding	..	..	..	..	.. ..	Hertford (G.N.).
	27	49¼	Gasworks siding .. / Gray & Miles' siding / Barber's siding ..	..	1½	..	..	.. ..	
	27	69¾	Smart's siding (Kingsmead) ..	..	20½	..	..	.. ..	
	27	77	Hertford, G.E. junction ..	..	7¼	..	..	.. ..	
	28	25	**Hertford G.E. station** ..	.	28	..	..	.. ..	Hertford (G.E.).

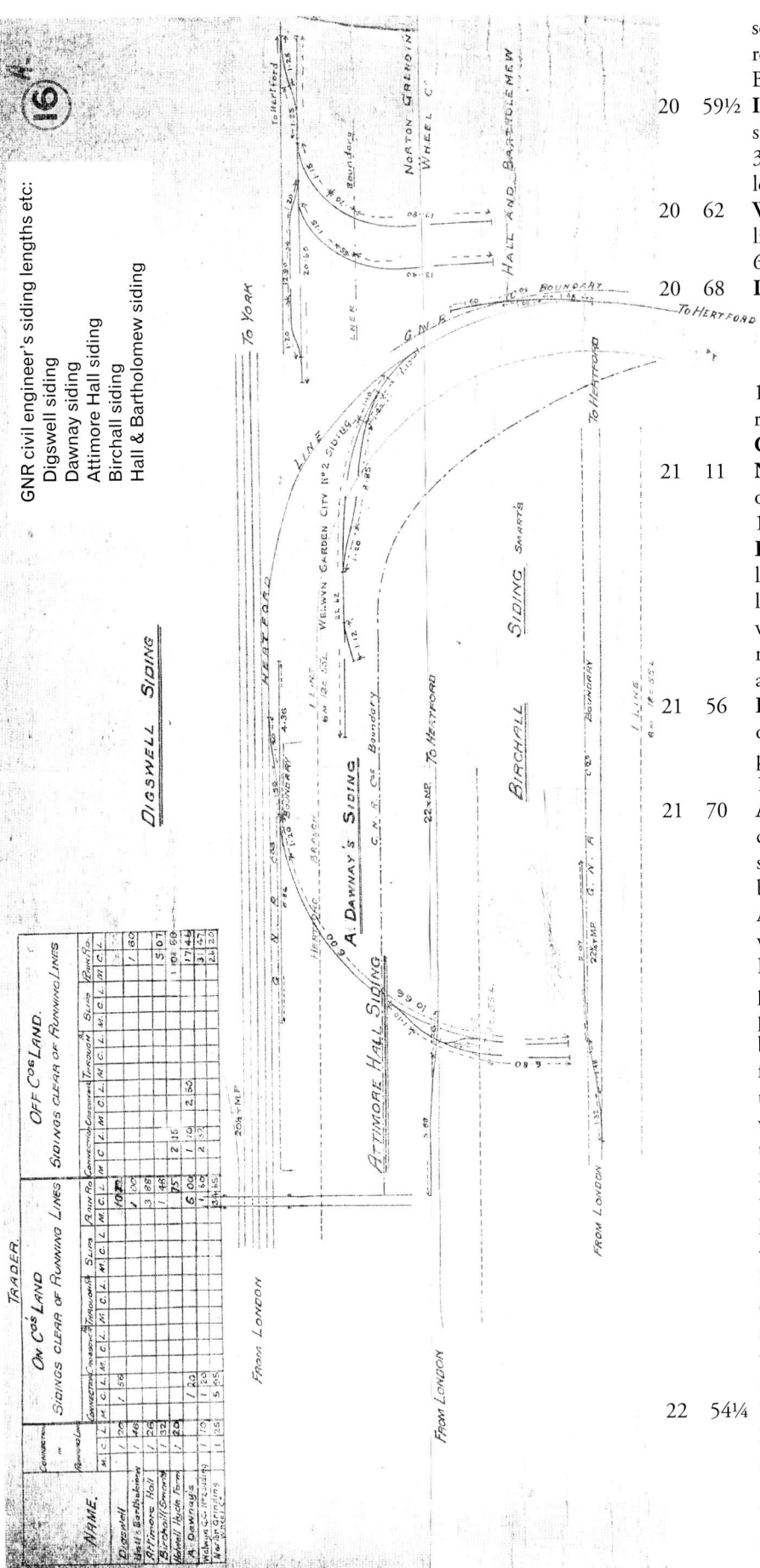

20	59½	**Imperial Chemical Industries** siding Down side serving a plastic powder works; main siding 350 feet in length, with 280 feet run round loop; opened 1937.
20	62	**Welwyn Garden City No. 2** on Up side of single line, installed 1927. Main siding 1,600 feet with 630 feet loop and 75 feet offshoot headshunt.
20	68	**Lord Cowper's** private siding for agricultural traffic, taken over by **Hall & Bartholomew**, on Down side of line with trailing connection for Down services 110 feet on railway land, 110 feet on private land. Closed by 1937 and removed 1938; replaced by **Welwyn Garden City Transport** siding for a short period.
21	11	**Norton Grinding Wheel Company** was opened 1931 by subsidiary of US firm registered 12th February 1930, became **Norton Abrasives Limited** in 1963; operated by one 4-wheel locomotive; trailing connection on Up side of line points leading to 1,360 feet straight road with 1,005 feet loop at the western end – all on railway land – points led to two sidings 960 feet and 965 feet.
21	56	**Lincoln Electric Company Limited** siding on Down or north side of the line with facing points in the Down direction. Agreement dated 19th October 1957. Siding 250 feet in length.
21	70	**Attimore Hall**, Down side of line trailing connection for Down trains, 260 feet straight siding. It is recorded that this siding was used between April 1893 and November 1894 by Arthur Christopher William Hobman, who was the owner or possible tenant of Ludwick Hall Stud Farm. He was a successful tar paving contractor based in South London with probable connections with Josiah Smart. The business appears to have provided him with funds to invest in the breeding of horses at the stud farm. According to tonnage returns, which survive in the Panshanger Estate Archive, the GNR delivered 723 tons 12 cwt of mixed materials (oats, carrots, white lead, timber) to the siding for him. His association appears to have ended in 1895 after a number of auctions were held to dispose of the horses. Attimore Hall Farm was at the same period in the tenancy of William Pigg who also used the siding, but about 1903 the tenancy passed to John Masson who was also permitted to use the siding as part of the tenancy.
22	54¼	**Birchall**, Down side with facing points in Down direction, 495 feet of which 330 feet was outside of railway property. Initially opened in 1882 for manure traffic for Henry Wood. On Wood's departure Earl Cowper leased siding from GNR then leased to Josiah Smart January 1892. Josiah Smart granted further permission

sold to Knebworth Park July 1986, now restored and with Mid Suffolk Light Railway at Brockford.

to extract sand and ballast from lands at Holwell, part of Birchall Farm for 14 years on 20th September 1892.

23 28½ **Sinclair's**, aka **Holwell Hyde Farm**, Up side facing points in Down direction; agreement signed 2nd June 1904 between GNR and Lord Cowper. Sidings developed and expanded over the years. Listed as a sand pit in Government returns for 1920. Main siding 1,465 feet plus 1,190 feet south of siding facing points, 1,850 feet off trailing connection, later extended to 2,820 feet. Taken over by Inns & Company; contract signed 5th September 1935; still recorded for sand and gravel excavation in 1948, also used from 1924 for tipping of London and Luton rubbish. Rail traffic ceased in 1968. From 1924 a 2 feet narrow gauge system was developed with rubbish tipped from standard gauge wagons to narrow gauge vehicles for conveyance to convenient sires for dumping and infilling where ballast had been removed. The system was also used to convey ballast to load on to standard gauge trucks. The track system was very flexible being lifted and relaid as required. As the site developed the narrow gauge line was used for conveyance of overburden or top-soil to cover the rubbish. It was not unknown for rats to infest the site and the pest control authorities were frequently called to administer the culling of vermin. At least three 4-wheel diesel mechanical locomotives worked on site in the latter years: MR No. 5932 transferred from Wheathampstead rubbish tip in May 1953 and sent on to Broxbourne pits in 1966; MR 5931 ex Sundon rubbish tip, Bedfordshire by May 1953 sent on to Sawbridgeworth pits in 1962 and MR 4806 received from Denham Pits Harefield, Middlesex in 1963 and moved on to Farnborough, Hampshire pits in May 1965.

25 49¾ **Smart's Hertingfordbury**; authorised in 1903 opened 1904, used for extraction of gravel, closed and removed by 1907.

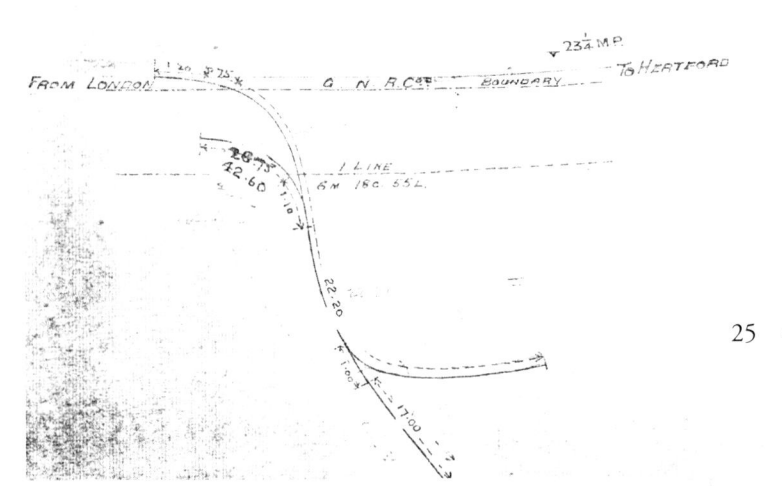

GNR civil engineer's siding lengths etc:
  Holwell Hall Farm siding
  Cole Green station

GNR Appendix instructions applicable to the branch 1912.

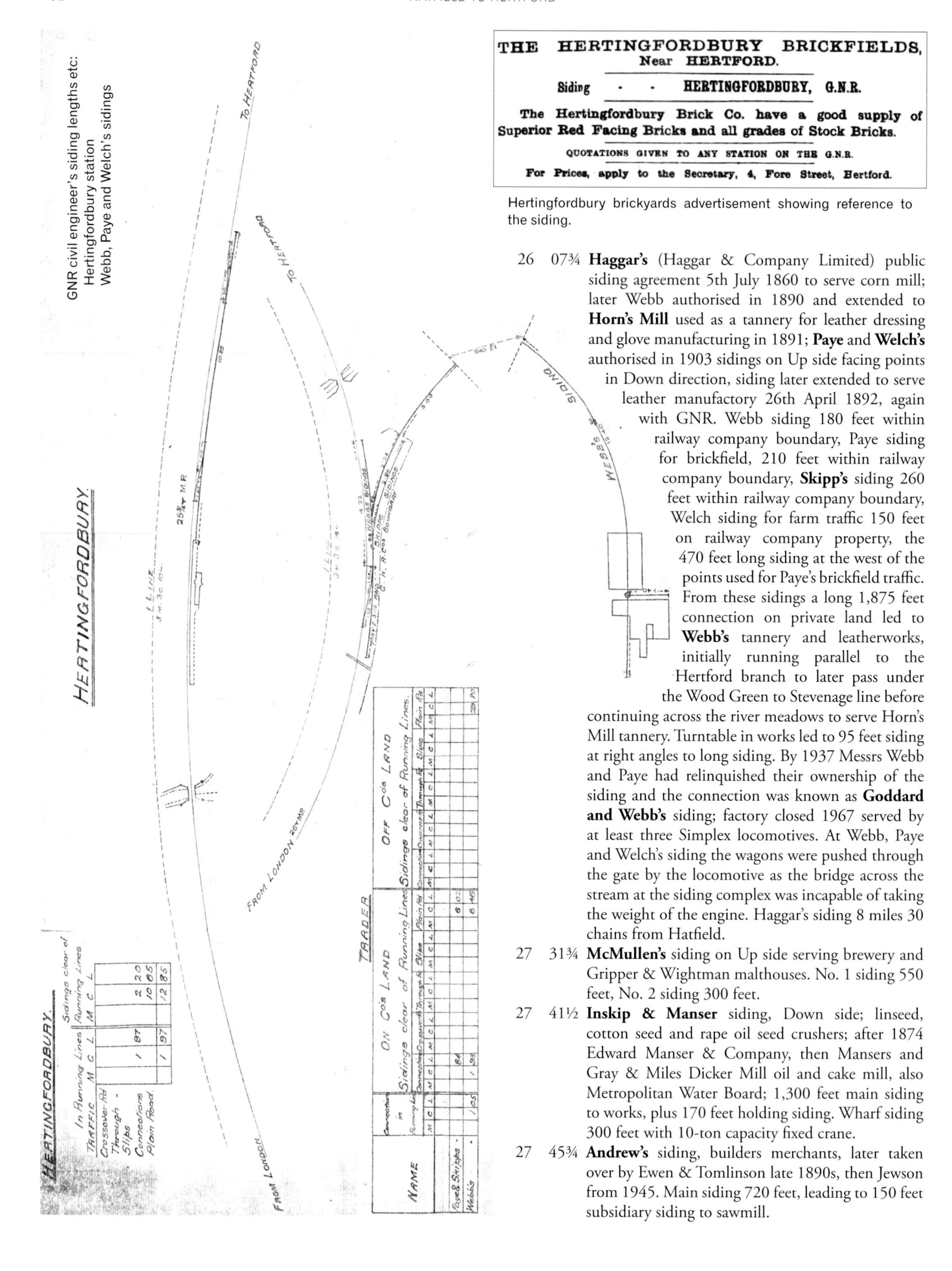

THE HERTINGFORDBURY BRICKFIELDS, Near HERTFORD.

Siding - - **HERTINGFORDBURY, G.N.R.**

The Hertingfordbury Brick Co. have a good supply of Superior Red Facing Bricks and all grades of Stock Bricks.

QUOTATIONS GIVEN TO ANY STATION ON THE G.N.R.

For Prices, apply to the Secretary, 4, Fore Street, Hertford.

Hertingfordbury brickyards advertisement showing reference to the siding.

26 07¾ **Haggar's** (Haggar & Company Limited) public siding agreement 5th July 1860 to serve corn mill; later Webb authorised in 1890 and extended to **Horn's Mill** used as a tannery for leather dressing and glove manufacturing in 1891; **Paye** and **Welch's** authorised in 1903 sidings on Up side facing points in Down direction, siding later extended to serve leather manufactory 26th April 1892, again with GNR. Webb siding 180 feet within railway company boundary, Paye siding for brickfield, 210 feet within railway company boundary, **Skipp's** siding 260 feet within railway company boundary, Welch siding for farm traffic 150 feet on railway company property, the 470 feet long siding at the west of the points used for Paye's brickfield traffic. From these sidings a long 1,875 feet connection on private land led to **Webb's** tannery and leatherworks, initially running parallel to the Hertford branch to later pass under the Wood Green to Stevenage line before continuing across the river meadows to serve Horn's Mill tannery. Turntable in works led to 95 feet siding at right angles to long siding. By 1937 Messrs Webb and Paye had relinquished their ownership of the siding and the connection was known as **Goddard and Webb's** siding; factory closed 1967 served by at least three Simplex locomotives. At Webb, Paye and Welch's siding the wagons were pushed through the gate by the locomotive as the bridge across the stream at the siding complex was incapable of taking the weight of the engine. Haggar's siding 8 miles 30 chains from Hatfield.

27 31¾ **McMullen's** siding on Up side serving brewery and Gripper & Wightman malthouses. No. 1 siding 550 feet, No. 2 siding 300 feet.

27 41½ **Inskip & Manser** siding, Down side; linseed, cotton seed and rape oil seed crushers; after 1874 Edward Manser & Company, then Mansers and Gray & Miles Dicker Mill oil and cake mill, also Metropolitan Water Board; 1,300 feet main siding to works, plus 170 feet holding siding. Wharf siding 300 feet with 10-ton capacity fixed crane.

27 45¾ **Andrew's** siding, builders merchants, later taken over by Ewen & Tomlinson late 1890s, then Jewson from 1945. Main siding 720 feet, leading to 150 feet subsidiary siding to sawmill.

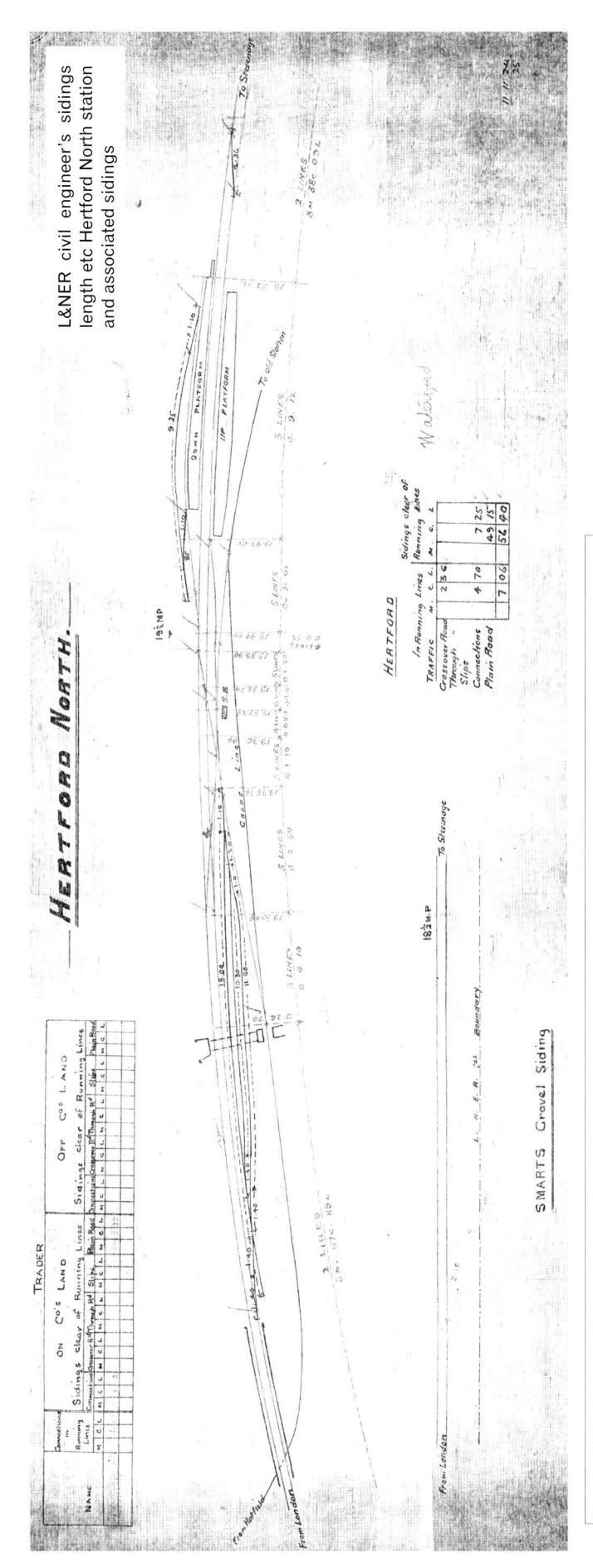

27	49	**Brazier's** siding, also known as **Gas Works**, 390 feet, opened in 1879, high loading dock for gravel 1897. New agreement 1923.
27	55¼	**Gray & Miles** siding, Down side; sand and ballast, building materials.
27	70	**Josiah Smart's Kingsmead** sand and gravel merchants, Gashouse Lane; opened in 1888, extension across Mead Lane 1900, exhausted 1906, track realigned to new site; siding 1,400 feet; also **Hertford Gas & Light Company**, then Tottenham & District Gas Company, later Eastern Gas Board, Tottenham Division Board, 650 feet siding. **Permanite** roofing manufacturer, Gashouse Lane; 300 feet siding. **Smart's Tar Distillery** Limited, The Distillery Works Mead Lane, later P**rince Regent Tar Distillers**, 450 feet siding.
27	74	End of GNR maintenance.
27	77	Junction with GER.

Sale brochure, 1880, showing Webb's siding as a tramway.

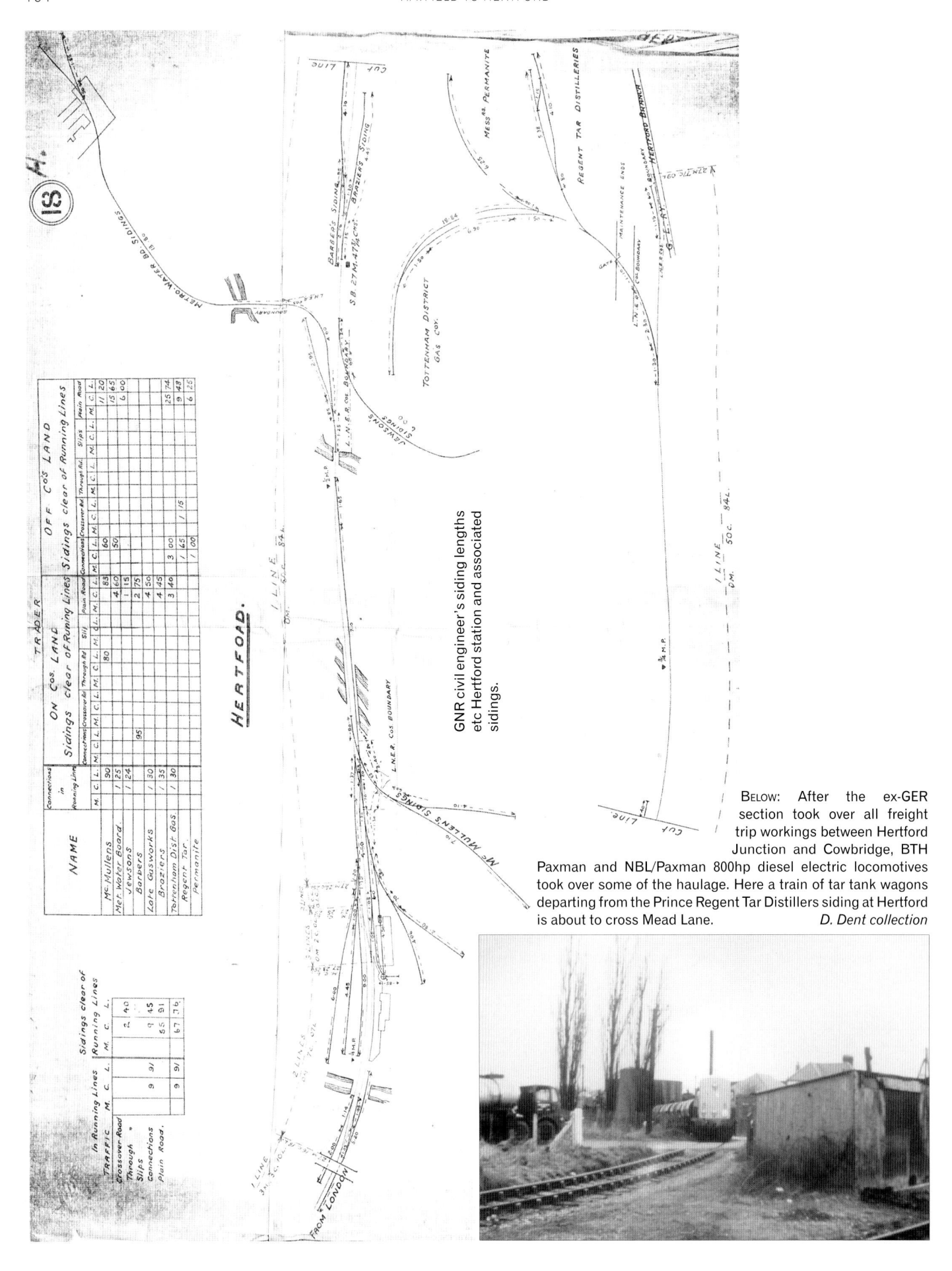

GNR civil engineer's siding lengths etc Hertford station and associated sidings.

BELOW: After the ex-GER section took over all freight trip workings between Hertford Junction and Cowbridge, BTH Paxman and NBL/Paxman 800hp diesel electric locomotives took over some of the haulage. Here a train of tar tank wagons departing from the Prince Regent Tar Distillers siding at Hertford is about to cross Mead Lane. *D. Dent collection*

9

Permanent Way, Signalling and Staff

Permanent Way

The initial permanent way of the H&WJR was formed of 'T' rails weighing 65 lbs per yard in 28 feet lengths, fastened by oak keys to cast iron chairs each weighing 22 lbs. The rails were joined by wrought iron fishplates, each weighing 28 lbs and secured by four bolts, two in each rail. The chairs were fastened to transverse sleepers of creosoted larch or memel; the sleepers being 9 feet in length by 10 inches by 5 inches were half rounded and laid 3 feet apart at the rail joints and 4 feet 6 inches apart intermediately. Lieutenant Colonel W. Yolland, during the initial inspection of the railway on 15th February 1858, remarked: *'It is intended that this form of rail makes the road as good as ordinary 75 lbs per yard rail laid on sleepers placed 3 feet 6 inches apart'* and concluded: *'I should very much prefer the latter'*. The ballast was laid to a depth of one foot under the sleepers and was formed of a mixture of gravel and sand; the formation was 18 feet wide, enough for a second line of rails to be laid if traffic increased.

As early as the summer of 1860 the permanent way was reported in poor condition and the GNR authorities wrote to the HL&DR board requesting urgent remedial action to bring the line up to satisfactory standard. Following discussions it was agreed the GNR would take over maintenance from 1st September 1860, subject to remedial work being carried out before transfer of responsibility. Both parties required certain modifications to the contract so that the agreement was sanctioned for a period of ten years. On 25th September it was reported the condition of the line continued to deteriorate and the GNR Engineer was adamant such agreement would only be acceptable if the HL&DR at first brought the line up to the required standard.

The permanent way was improved to a degree so that the GNR engineer accepted maintenance, but it only remained in use for a few years and by the early 1870s the branch was extensively laid with 75 lbs per yard bullhead rails in 30 feet lengths with thirteen sleepers under each rail length, the rails being affixed to the sleepers by cast or wrought iron chairs weighing 35 to 40 lbs each. In the 1880s, 80 lbs per yard bullhead rails, in 40 feet and 45 feet lengths were in use. These were joined by fishplates weighing 40 lbs per pair and supported on chairs weighing 38 lbs each, the chairs were secured to the sleepers by iron spikes and wooden trenails. Each

Vegetation covers the 312 feet long platform at Hertingfordbury with the ornate station buildings at the east end. By this date the passenger train service was but a memory although the permanent way appears to be in good order for a freight line. *Author's collection*

sleeper was creosoted and measured 9 feet by 12 inches by 5 or 6 inches. Around the turn of the century 85 lbs per yard rails replaced the lighter bullhead track and these sufficed, with the replacement of worn rails, until just before the grouping.

From 1923 the L&NER began replacing the remaining 30-foot lengths of rail used on the branch, with lengths of 40 and 45 feet rails weighing between 85 and 97 lbs per yard. From the 1930s bullhead rails of 90 to 97 lbs per yard rail in lengths of 45 to 60 feet were installed. Of late GNR and L&NER vintage, they were laid on chairs of similar origin. Further sections received 60-foot lengths of rail as replacements became due, but even so considerable lengths of 45 feet long rails remained when the branch closed. In the latter years nearly all the track used on the Hertford to Welwyn Garden City branch was second hand, having initially served on the main line.

The original gravel ballast used when the line opened was found suitable for the moderate traffic carried but within a decade the GNR introduced ashes and clinker. The GNR found ashes were adequate for the ballasting of many of their branch lines and supplies were readily available from the motive power depots on the system. Ashes and clinker remained the staple formation of ballast until after World War Two. When supplies of ashes were not available from locomotive sheds, wagon loads were obtained from Tate & Lyle's sugar refinery at Silvertown and after the early 1920s from the British Sugar Corporation factories at Peterborough and Spalding. Only at the last were supplies of spent ballast removed from the main line made available to supplement the ballasting between Welwyn Garden City and Hertford Old.

The permanent way and civil engineering on the branch came under the control of the District Engineer King's Cross, with gangs initially based at Hertford, Cole Green and Welwyn, although individual lengthmen were responsible for patrolling sections of line. The section between Hatfield and Welwyn Junction was the responsibility of a gang based at Hatfield, whilst after the opening of the Cuffley loop line the Hertford gang was responsible for the section of line from Hertford Old to Cole Green, and the Hatfield gang with a sub gang at Welwyn Garden City responsible for the section from Cole Green exclusive to Welwyn Garden City.

As well as attending to the day-to-day track maintenance, the permanent way gangs on the branch were responsible for cleaning the toilets at stations and crossing gate cottages where no mains sewerage existed, and on hot summer days, especially during harvest time, they acted as beaters to extinguish any small fires caused by stray sparks emitted by passing locomotives. They also cut the grass on the side of the embankments and cuttings, and this was used as fodder for railway horses, or in World War One sent to London and other provincial centres for feeding military horses.

Of the permanent way staff, ganger S. Wrangles of Cole Green retired on 26th April 1933 followed by underman A.J. Andrews on 3rd September 1934; both had spent many years at the station. Along the line at Hertford North, ganger H. Parsley retired on 3rd August 1948.

The country or eastern end of Cole Green station in the 1930s looking towards Hertford showing the goods yard to the left and main single line to the right. On the extreme left open wagons are stabled on the dock road whilst permanent way staff are greasing the points.

S. Ruff collection

PERMANENT WAY, SIGNALLING AND STAFF

Entry points to the Down side yard at Hertford Cowbridge, with the goods shed to the left and the parapet to Cattle Arch underbridge No. 19 in the foreground.
P. Whitaker

Signalling

The original signalling on the line was formed of semaphore signals with coloured aspect glasses rotating by the action of a connecting rod attached to bell crank levers and operated from station platforms. Each station and Welwyn Junction (for the branch) had a stop signal for each direction of travel mounted on the same post on the platform, and auxiliary signals located 800 yards in the rear of the stop signal. At a date soon after opening to traffic, stops signals were also provided at Attimore Hall and Hatfield Hyde level crossings, mounted on one post by the gates for each direction of travel; they denoted to the driver whether the gates were open for the passage of a train but without the auxiliary signals. Station staff or the resident gatekeepers operated these signals.

Gradually other signals were introduced at strategic points. The signal controlling entry to the Manure & Brick siding located 33 chains from Hatfield were operated by a designated porter from Hatfield; no engine or train was permitted to stop unless the single line Train Staff was on the engine; an Annett's patent safety lock was fixed to the points of the siding; the Hatfield North signalman had charge of the keys to unlock the points, which he could not give to the porter until the signals controlling the Hertford line had been placed to danger; the signals were to be maintained at danger until the porter had locked the siding points for the main single line and returned the key to the signalman. At Digswell siding, 2 miles 76¼ chains from Hatfield, the signals were worked by the gatekeeper from the adjacent level crossing. At Attimore Hall siding the signals were worked by the Digswell gatekeeper for Down trains whilst for Up services the signals were worked by the guard. At Haggar's siding, 8 miles 30 chains, the Hertingfordbury station porter was responsible for operating the signals.

Initially the branch was worked by the Train Staff only method of single line working, with the Train Staff stations at Welwyn Junction and Hertford. When services were extended to Hatfield from 28th August 1876, Hatfield became the new Train Staff station. To permit greater occupancy of the line Train Staff and Ticket working

Hertford North Down fixed distant somersault signal located on the Up side of the railway just before the connection to Webb, Paye and Welch's sidings. In the background is the viaduct carrying the Wood Green to Langley Junction double-track line across the valley over the branch.
Author's collection

Somersault Up home signal at Cole Green, 15th June 1951.
Robert Kirkland, Lens of Sutton

was introduced from 1877, the line being worked under 'no block' regulations. In 1881 the single line Train Staff for the Hatfield to Hertford branch was circular in shape whilst the colour of Train Staff Tickets was white for Down workings and blue for the Up direction. After the opening of Cole Green as a crossing station in 1891, the Train Staff and Tickets were: Hatfield to Cole Green, circular Staff with white tickets for Down workings and blue tickets for Up trains; Cole Green to Hertford GNR, triangular staff with red tickets for Down workings and yellow tickets for Up services, and Hertford GNR to Hertford GER, a square staff with white tickets with red lettering for Down trains and green tickets for Up services. Later, to increase track occupancy, Welwyn Garden City to Hertford North was worked by Electric Token, whilst Hertford North to Hertford East retained Train Staff and Ticket working. Train Staff and Metal Ticket working was introduced in 1939 to increase occupancy of the branch and enable trains to be shut in at intermediate sidings.

Block signalling was authorised for the Hertford branch in June 1882 with an additional £214 authorised on 11th December 1885. The GNR commenced a programme of installation of block instruments where none was already provided. A sum of £3,299 7s 1d for further signalling works to completely revise Hatfield was authorised on 4th October 1889, to be followed by a further £541 on 29th July 1890. Resignalling of the Hertford branch along with the lines to St. Albans and Dunstable was authorised on 6th May 1887 at a cost of £4,000, the work to be undertaken as required but completed within four years in order to spread the budget. As a result of the Regulation of Railways Act 1889 the GNR authorities were required to renew most of the signalling equipment as a matter of urgency, and so work was rescheduled. The statute also made block working mandatory on all lines except those worked on the One Engine in Steam or Train Staff without Tickets principle. The BOT having stipulated all work was to be completed within twelve months of 20th November 1890 also required the interlocking of points and signals within eighteen months. Saxby & Farmer received the contract for resignalling on Hertford, St. Albans and Dunstable branches in 1890, after tendering at £7,780 9s 1d, and work started almost immediately. To increase line occupancy Cole Green was created a crossing loop, the work being authorised on 7th November 1890 and installation was completed the following year at a cost £1,826. The sum of £936 was awarded for further alterations at Hatfield station on 7th June 1895 following a collision at the station on 6th February. The work included remodelling the track layout and the interlocking of the additional points and signals,

By 1892 the old style semaphore signals were replaced with lower quadrant home and distant signals with pitch pine posts, cedar arms, and cast and wrought iron fittings. The Regulation of Railways Act also required the interlocking of signals and points, and the new signals were provided to GNR somersault design. As a result of an

Hertford Old (Cowbridge) GNR fixed somersault distant signal near Dicker Mill crossing between Hertford East and Hertford (Cowbridge) on 9th December 1958. The notice affixed to the post advised *'Trains must not pass this board until drivers are in possession of the Train Staff'*. Author's collection

Rear view of the GNR Hertford North Up distant signal mounted on a concrete post near the west end of Hertford Cowbridge platform. The notice attached to the post advised drivers that they should be in possession of the Train Staff or Train Staff Ticket before proceeding towards Hertford North. D. Dent collection

accident at Abbot's Ripton where the signal arm was clogged with snow, the new centrally balanced signal arm was proof against such problems, for the arm hung clear of the post in the clear position and dropped back to danger in the event of a wire breaking.

Hertford station was provided with distant, home and starting signals for each direction of travel, whilst Hertingfordbury station was now devoid of any signalling. At Cole Green distant, home and starting signals were also provided for each direction of travel; initially Attimore level crossing and neighbouring Holwell level crossing were provided with distant signals for each direction of travel, operated by the resident gatekeeper, but these were later fixed at caution, and then removed altogether from the latter. At Hatfield station, distant and splitting home signals were provided on the branch approach to the station, the left-hand arm denoting access to the branch platform and the right-hand arm giving authority for a train to run into the Up slow line platform. In the Down direction a starting signal was provided at the north end of the bay platform and at the north end of the Down slow platform, leading to an advance starting signal on the branch single line for departing trains. With the opening of Welwyn Garden City station, distant, home and starting signals were provided for each direction of travel. At Hertford North, at the junction between the single branch and the main line in the Down direction a distant signal led to splitting home signals, the left-hand arm denoting access to Hertford North station and the right-hand arm authority to proceed to Hertford Cowbridge. In the Up direction a distant signal from Hertford Cowbridge led to splitting home signals, the left-hand arm giving authority to proceed along the branch whilst the right-hand arm gave permission to proceed to Hertford North goods yard. Advance starting signals were provided on the branch in both Up and Down directions. Access to the branch from the station was given by splitting starting signals applicable to the Up main line: the left-hand arm giving access to the branch and the right-hand arm the Up main line. Starting signals were also provided for branch trains departing the Down main platform or the Down back platform. With the advent of the L&NER the distant signals were gradually repainted the familiar yellow with a black >, and as a result of the 1923 rationalisation programme the gate distant signals at Attimore Hall and Holwell Hyde level crossings were abolished.

In GNR and L&NER days the points leading to the undermentioned sidings on the branch were secured by a lock, the key of which was on the single line train staff. Guards of trains having to call at these sidings were also to have the key to the siding gate, spare keys being kept at both Hertford and Hatfield. The gates were to be closed and locked across the siding when shunting was completed.

- Hatfield manure
- Sheriff's and Mount Pleasant siding
- Smart siding
- Peart's siding
- Digswell siding
- Lord Cowper's siding
- Attimore Hall siding
- Birchall siding
- Holwell Hyde Farm siding
- Hertingfordbury gravel siding
- Hertingfordbury siding east
- Hertingfordbury siding west
- Webb, Paye and Welch's siding

Revised arrangements for fog signalling on the branches radiating from Hatfield was introduced from 20th December 1897, including the introduction of fog signalmen at the following signals during fog or falling snow:

Hatfield No. 2 signal box	Up main, Up goods and Hertford branch distant signals
Twentieth Mile signal box	Up Hertford distant signal
Cole Green	Down and Up distant signals
Hertford	Down distant and Up home signals

In 1927 the points connecting the running line with Hatfield, Sheriff's and Mount Pleasant sidings, Smart and Peart's sidings, Digswell siding, Shredded Wheat siding, Lord Cowper's siding, Welwyn Garden City No. 2 siding, Attimore Hall siding, Birchall siding, Holwell Hyde Farm siding, Hertingfordbury siding West, Hertingfordbury siding East and Webb, Paye and Welch's sidings were secured by a lock, the key of which was on the single line Train Staff. Guards of trains requiring to call at the sidings to attach or detach wagons were required to also have the key of the siding gates. Spare keys were kept at both Hatfield and Hertford North. The gate was to be left locked across the sidings before the departure of the train. At Webb, Paye and Welch's siding, engines were not permitted to pass the gate leading to the sidings. Brazier's siding, also known as Gas Works siding, at Hertford was entered by facing points in the main line immediately east of Dicker Mill lane crossing. There were no signals and the points were hand operated.

Specific instructions were issued regarding the shunting of Smart's siding at Kingsmead between Hertford North and Hertford East. The points were secured by a lock, the key of which, when not in use, was kept by the station master. Traffic to and from the siding was worked by a pilot engine at about 10.30am, and again at about 2.40pm by No. 16 Up goods, or with the engine working the latter

Dicker Mill crossing Down distant signal. *P. Whitaker*

train from Hertford North in the event of No. 14 Down and 16 Up trains not operating to and from Hertford East. The gates across this siding were to be closed and padlocked when not required for shunting purposes. Trains calling at this siding to attach or detach wagons were not to exceed thirty wagons in length and in each case a 20-ton brake van was to be attached at the rear. The shunting of the siding was to be carried out during daylight hours only. The driver of any engine working the siding was required to be in possession of the single line Train Staff for the section Hertford North to Hertford East. This instruction was superseded in 1942 by the following:

The points for Smart's Kingsmead and Tottenham and District Gas Company siding are secured by a lock, the key of which, when not in use must be kept by the Station Master at Hertford North. Traffic to and from the siding is worked by the pilot engine from Hertford North and the gates across the siding must be closed and padlocked when not required for shunting purposes. Trains calling at this siding to attach or detach traffic must not exceed 30 wagons, and in each case a 20-ton brake van must be attached in the rear. The shunting of the siding must, in all circumstances be carried out during daylight only. Engines having work to do at this siding must carry the Train Staff for the section.

Hertford North to Welwyn Garden City single line token.

After grouping, the GER section took over much of the shunting movements between Hertford Junction and Hertford Old, but much care had to be taken when propelling and shunting for with a slightly falling gradient in the holding sidings opposite the former GNR station a slight tap was all that was needed to push the wagons into the sidings. Many a driver learnt the hard way with a verbal reprimand from the shunter or even a caution from the Hertford or Hatfield shed foreman after a hard propelling movement resulted in derailed wagons after a hard knock against the buffer stops or as in some cases the buffer stops being up-ended as wagons overran the stop block! Locomotives could take water at Hertford Old and soon some crews also used the time to clean the fire and smokebox and, if time, the ashpan. Unfortunately, on some occasions the exercise resulted in the sleepers catching alight.

After the withdrawal of Hertford branch services between Hatfield and Welwyn Garden City, Smart's siding was connected with the Up goods line and the points were controlled by Annett's key kept in Welwyn Garden City signal box; guards of trains calling at the siding were instructed on completion of the work to deliver up the key to Hatfield station from which place it was returned by the first available train to Welwyn Garden City. Drivers of trains on the Up slow line had still to sound the engine whistle on approaching whenever a train was working the siding.

When the Enfield branch was extended beyond Cuffley to Langley Junction on and from 4th March 1918 it operated as a single line for goods traffic only. No intermediate signal boxes were provided and a special form of absolute/permissive block system was provided over the 14¾ miles section using Tyer's No. 5 tablet instruments installed in Cuffley and Langley Junction signal boxes. Once a tablet had been withdrawn for a train to proceed over the single line section, if another train was to travel behind it in the same direction another tablet could be withdrawn, placed in a 'permissive' pouch and given to the crew of the second train who were cautioned as to standard permissive regulations. A tablet could not be withdrawn from the instrument at the other end of the section for a train travelling in the opposite direction until all tablets were placed in the receiving instrument. This method of working continued for a little over two and a half years until double line working began on and from 23rd December 1920.

After the opening of the Enfield to Langley Junction line and the transfer of passenger services to the new Hertford North station, the single line branch from Hertford North to Hertford East was worked under the instruction shown in Railway Clearing House Appendix 1. Train Staff tickets were only issued by the foreman at Hertford Goods yard for Up trains to proceed to Hertford North signal box and he was entirely responsible for the line being clear at Hertford Goods yard before the Train Staff was taken to Hertford North signal box and for the Train Staff to be at that signal box when required.

In 1941 important alterations were made to the single line working between Hatfield and Hertford North with the introduction of Long Section and Short Section Key Token Working. In normal circumstances Short Token working was in operation between Hatfield and Cole Green with the existing Train Staff and Metal Tickets from Cole Green to Hertford North. When it was desirable to close Cole Green signal box the Long Section Token working was introduced between Hatfield and Hertford North. To cater for freight services serving some intermediate sidings an Intermediate Key Token was available for use at all intermediate sidings between Hatfield and Cole Green. To enable a train to leave a siding the Short Section Main Line Token had to be inserted into the Intermediate Token Instrument at Hatfield before an Intermediate Token could be withdrawn at any of the sidings. To shut in the siding, the insertion of the Token at any of the sidings enabled the Main Line Token to be withdrawn at Hatfield after which Short section working could resume. The table of control at Hatfield No. 2 signal box was:

Signal 81	Controlled by 82-lever normal (mechanical).
Signal 82	Track circuit B and withdrawal of Long or Short section Key Token.
Signal 85	Track circuit A and 84-lever normal.
Key Token Instrument, Long or Short Section	Withdrawal of Key Token or release to Cole Green or Hertford subject to track circuit B being clear, 85 arm normal and 82 and 85 levers locked normal.

All sidings between Hatfield and Cole Green were fitted with Key Token point locks, except Sheriff & Company siding and these locks could be released by Long or Short Section Key Tokens. Sheriff & Company siding was released by Annett's key held in Hatfield No. 2 signal box. One Short Section Key Token was fitted with a Staff end to fit the existing Token Box at Cole Green. This Token was chained to the instrument and was only used for switching out operations. All Long Section Key Tokens were fitted with a Staff end to fit the existing Token Box at Cole Green.

Under the new arrangements block working was dispensed with between Hatfield and Cole Green, and Welwyn Garden City signal box ceased to be a block post on the Hatfield to Hertford line. To assist with the smooth working the telephone was improved, with connections between: Hatfield Inspector's Office – Hatfield No. 2 signal box – Welwyn Garden City Goods Yard ground frame – Welwyn Garden City signal box – ICI siding ground frame – Norton's siding ground frame – Attimore Hall gate hut – Birchall gate hut – Holwell siding ground frame – Cole Green signal box – Hertingfordbury station – Hertford North signal box.

At Cole Green the switching out arrangements required the Long Section Staff normally locked in a special box to be withdrawn only when a Short Section Token and the Train Staff had been inserted. These were then locked in when the Long Section Token was withdrawn. A small lever on the Token Box effected the interlocking between the Token and also interlocked with the signalling frame as below:

Signal No. 7	Released by withdrawal of the Short section Key Token.
Signal No. 19	Released by withdrawal of the Short Section Key Token.
Signal No. 25	Line clear from Hertford North (one movement only) and withdrawal of Train Staff from Ticket Box.
Signal No. 18	Released by 20 in mid position (mechanical locking).
Signal No. 19	Locked by 3, 25, 26 and 29 when 20N to mid position (mechanical locking).
King Lever No. 20	Released by SL reversed. Released mid position to reverse by No. 17 reversed (mechanical locking).
Small lever SL	Released by 3, 23, 24, 27, 28, 30 reversed. Locks 13 (mechanical locking).
Key Token to Hatfield No. 2	Withdrawal of Key Token or release to Hatfield No. 2 subject to 30 arm normal, 29 lever normal and 7 and 19 levers locked normal.
Block to Hertford North	17 arm normal, 2, 18, 26 levers normal, 25 lever locked normal.
Signal No. 26	25 lever normal (mechanical).
Signal No. 29	26 lever normal (mechanical).
Signal No. 2	7 lever normal (mechanical).

The procedure for switching out at Cole Green was that if a train arrived from Hatfield the Key Token was placed in the Short Section instrument and the section cleared then:

1. The Special Key Token with Staff was withdrawn from the Short Section instrument and inserted in the Token box.
2. The Cole Green to Hertford Train staff was turned and withdrawn from the Ticket Box and inserted in the Token Box.
3. Hertford asked for line clear on short section block.
4. The through roads were set by reversing levers 9, 24, 23, 28 and 27.
5. Down line signals pulled off 29, 26, 25 and 30.
6. The small lever on the token box was reversed and the long section staff was now free.
7. Lever 20 pulled to half stroke and the Up road signals 19, 18 and 17 pulled off.
8. No. 20 lever was then pulled to full stroke.

If the train arriving from Hertford was drawn into the Down platform with disc No. 10 and the Train Staff was placed in the Ticket Box then the procedure was as for a train from Hatfield.

The procedure for switching in was:

1. On the arrival of a train the Long Section Staff was placed in the Ticket Box.
2. Lever No. 20 was put back to mid position.
3. Up road signals 17, 18 and 19 were replaced.
4. No. 20 pulled to normal.
5. The small lever on the Token Box was put to normal leaving the Short Section Token and Train Staff free.
6. The Down road signals No. 30, 25, 26 and 29 were replaced.
7. The Short Section Token placed in the instrument, the Train Staff placed in the Ticket Box and normal short section working resumed.

All sidings between Cole Green and Hertford were fitted with Staff locks which could be released by the Short Section Staff or Metal

It was possible to close Cole Green signal box for certain periods and operate the line from Welwyn Garden City to Hertford North as one single line section. In this view facing west the Up starting signal for the Up loop line is at danger as all services were being operated over the Down loop line. Thus the Down home signal and Up starting signal for the Down loop are in the clear position; the Up side starting signal is at danger.
Author's collection

Ticket or by the Long Section Token fitted Staff end. At Hertford North the table of controls were as under:

Signals No. 14, 59, 60 and 61	Line clear from Cole Green (movement only) and removal of Train Staff from the Ticket Box or withdrawal of the Long Section Key Token.
Key Token to Hatfield No. 2	Withdrawal of Key Token to release to Hatfield No. 2 subject to levers 11, 15 and 18 normal and levers 14, 59, 60, 61 locked normal.
Block to Cole Green	Track circuit C and 11, 15 and 18 levers normal (acceptance only).

By 1942 the instruction for operating the single line between Hertford North and Hertford East was amended; the line being worked in accordance with the Regulation for Working Single Lines by Train Staff and Ticket, but tickets were only issued by the shunter at Hertford North Goods Old Station for Up trains proceeding from Hertford Old to Hertford North. The shunter was then responsible for ascertaining the single line was clear to Hertford North before allowing a train to follow a train carrying the Ticket, and also for ensuring the Train Staff was at Hertford North signal box when required. Trains proceeding from the main line at Hertford East in the direction of Hertford North could pass as far as the Hertford East Station signal box without the single line Train Staff. On reaching the stop board adjacent to the signal box the driver was to bring his train to a stand and take the single line Train Staff from the signalman. Trains proceeding from Hertford North towards Hertford East were to stop at the board and hand the Train Staff to the Hertford East signalman. The Hertford East and Hertford North signalmen were to advise each other of the departure of trains along the single line, communicating as necessary with the shunter at Hertford North Goods Old station.

In 1960 it was permissible for trains to be shunted at three of the intermediate sidings between Welwyn Garden City and Cole Green. At Imperial Chemical Industries siding the ground frame was electrically released from Welwyn Garden City signal box, whilst at Norton's siding and Holwell siding an Electric Token intermediate token instrument controlled entry to the siding. Should the guard of a freight, ballast or officer's special train calling at Foundry, Norton's, Attimore Hall or Holwell intermediate sidings require his train to return the Token to the staff station in the rear instead of going forward to the Token or staff station in advance, he was required to obtain the permission of the signalman before the train entered the single line section.

SIGNAL BOXES

Hatfield North signal box, authorised in November 1867 and opened in June 1868, was equipped with a Saxby & Farmer frame but a new frame was provided on 13th November 1869. This frame was obviously too small for a growing junction station with its increasing traffic from the branches, so two new frames were ordered from McKenzie & Holland and installed on 2nd October 1875. Yet further alterations were made the following year when the box had a 75-lever frame with 65 working and 10 spare levers. In 1882 the north end of Hatfield station was resignalled and the following year the Up goods line from Digswell was opened.

The existing signalling was again totally inadequate for the increasing traffic and on 3rd October 1889 authority was given for the provision of four new signal boxes: Hatfield No. 1 to the south of the station, Hatfield No. 2 on the Up side north of the station, Hatfield No. 3 on the Down side north of the station and Hatfield No. 4. Hatfield No. 2, which signalled the Hertford branch services, was equipped with a 75-lever Railway Signal Company Tappet frame with 65 working and 10 spare levers. By 1915 the frame was increased to 85 levers, with 76 working and 9 spare, and this remained almost unaltered until the Hertford branch services

Looking west towards Welwyn Garden City from the Up platform at Cole Green. The Down line is signalled for bi-directional working; the Down home signal is clear and the Up starting signal is cleared for a train as the signal box is switched out and long section working is in operation between Hertford North and Welwyn Garden City. *Author's collection*

were curtailed at Welwyn Garden City and the branch single line converted to the Up goods line with trains worked only in the Up direction. By 1940 Hatfield No. 2 signal box still boasted the 85-lever frame but now with 64 working and 21 spare levers. This signal box was abolished on 20th May 1973. Of the other signal boxes at Hatfield: Hatfield No. 1, of timber construction, contained a 30-lever, later 60-lever, frame; it closed on 4th November 1920 when work was transferred to Hatfield No. 4 signal box which confusingly was renamed Hatfield No. 1. The work was authorised on 30th January 1920 at a cost of £976 and resulted in a saving of £250 per annum on signalmen's wages after providing additional lads for train recording duties. Then on 23rd July 1921 a sum of £243 was authorised for alterations to Hatfield No. 1 signal box to allow it to close on Sundays, resulting in a saving of £106 per annum. Hatfield No. 3 signal box opened in 1890 and contained an 80-lever Railway Signal Company frame with 4-inch centres.

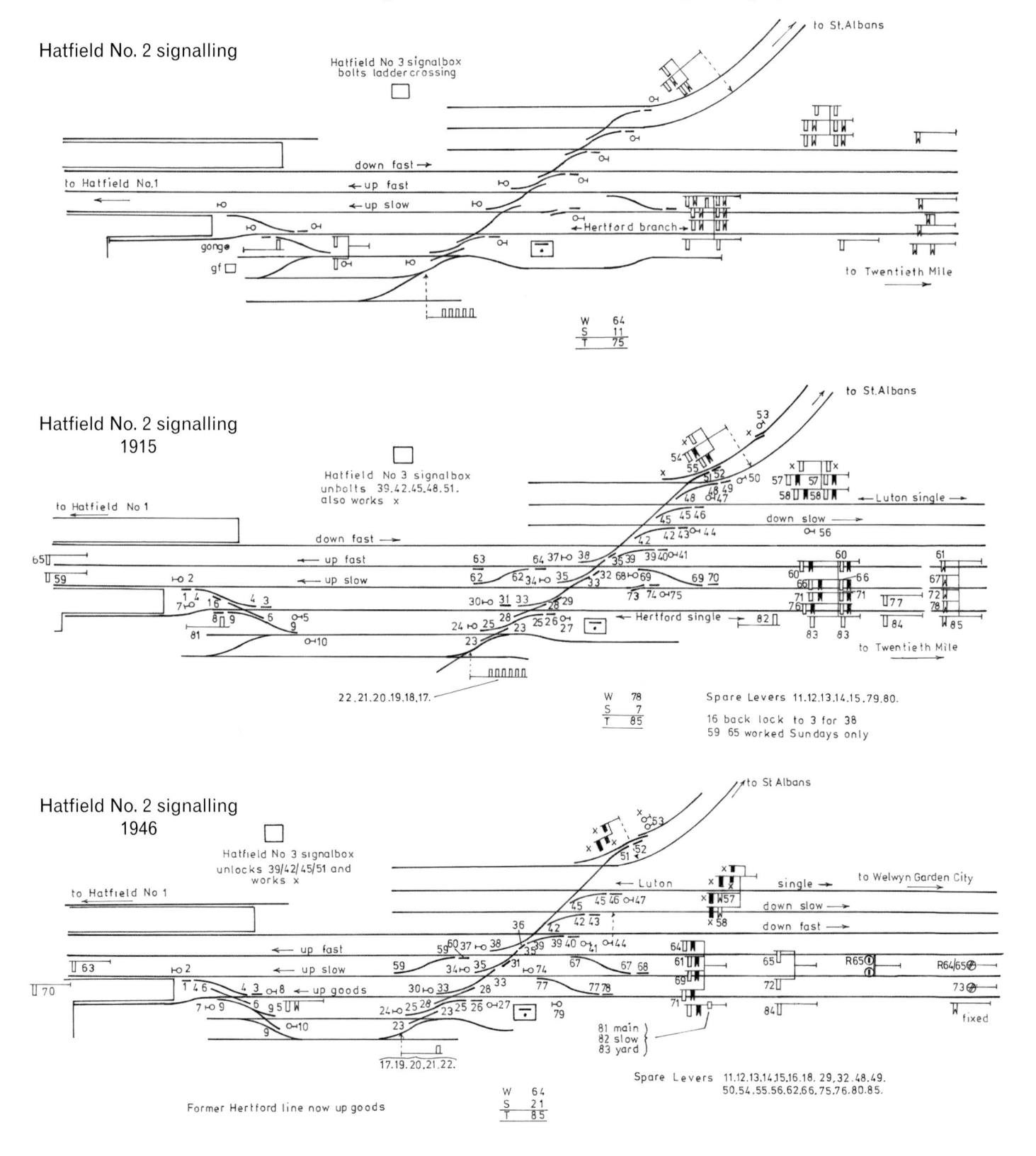

Hatfield No. 2 signalling

Hatfield No. 2 signalling 1915

Hatfield No. 2 signalling 1946

Hatfield No. 3 signal box located north of the station on the Down side of the railway signalled trains on the Down main and slow lines as well as branch services to St. Albans and Dunstable. It was also with Hatfield No. 2 signal box involved with shunting movements to the Hertford branch. No. 3 signal box contained an 80-lever Railway Signal Company frame with 4-inch centres. *Author's collection*

Around the turn of the century indicators were placed in signal boxes at Hatfield, worked by levers on or near the station platforms. Where these were provided the person in charge of the station was held responsible for seeing that the indicator in the signal box was placed at 'danger' when a vehicle or vehicles were detached from trains or had to be set back on the line on which the indicator applied, and for maintaining the indicator in that position until the vehicle or vehicles had been shunted clear of the running line; after which the indicator was to be placed in the 'clear' position. The signalman for his part was not to admit a train when the indicator showed 'line blocked'.

On the main line north of Hatfield, Nineteenth Mile signal box dating from 1860 closed in 1875, whilst the initial Twentieth Mile Up signal box – opened in 1882 and closed on 29th June 1891 – contained a Railway Signal Company 18-lever frame. This was replaced by a second signal box, opened on 29th June 1891 and closed 19th September 1926. Twentieth Mile Down signal box dating from 1874 closed on 29th June 1891, being replaced by a second structure on the same date, which had a 22-lever Railway Signal Company frame dating from 1882, also closing on 19th September 1926. Both these signal boxes were provided to reduce the length of the block section north of Hatfield, the former

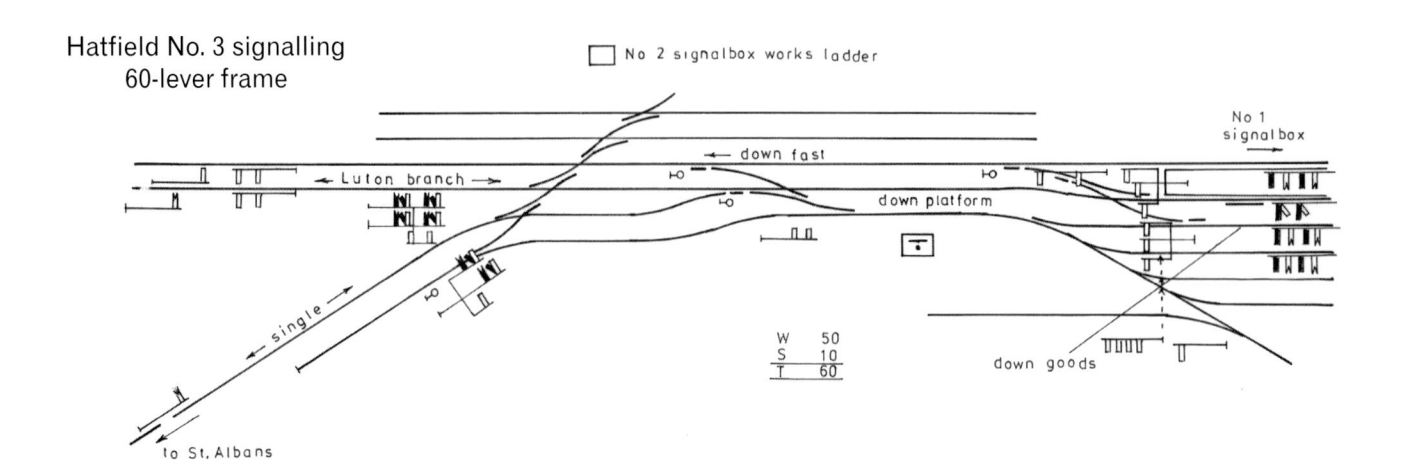

Hatfield No. 3 signalling 60-lever frame

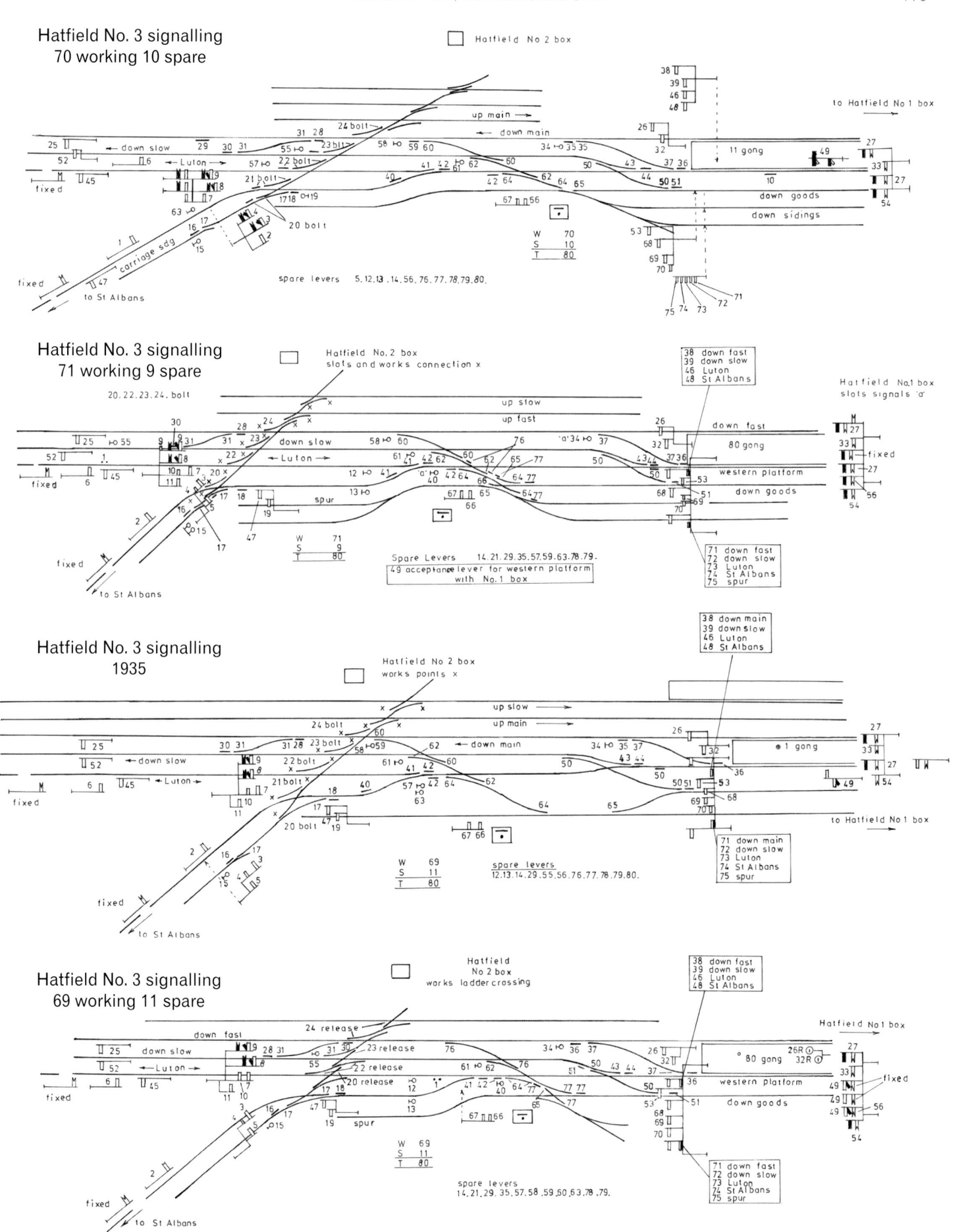

PERMANENT WAY, SIGNALLING AND STAFF

175

Hatfield No. 3 signalling
70 working 10 spare

Hatfield No. 3 signalling
71 working 9 spare

Hatfield No. 3 signalling
1935

Hatfield No. 3 signalling
69 working 11 spare

Welwyn Junction signalling 1878

Welwyn Junction signalling 1885–1893

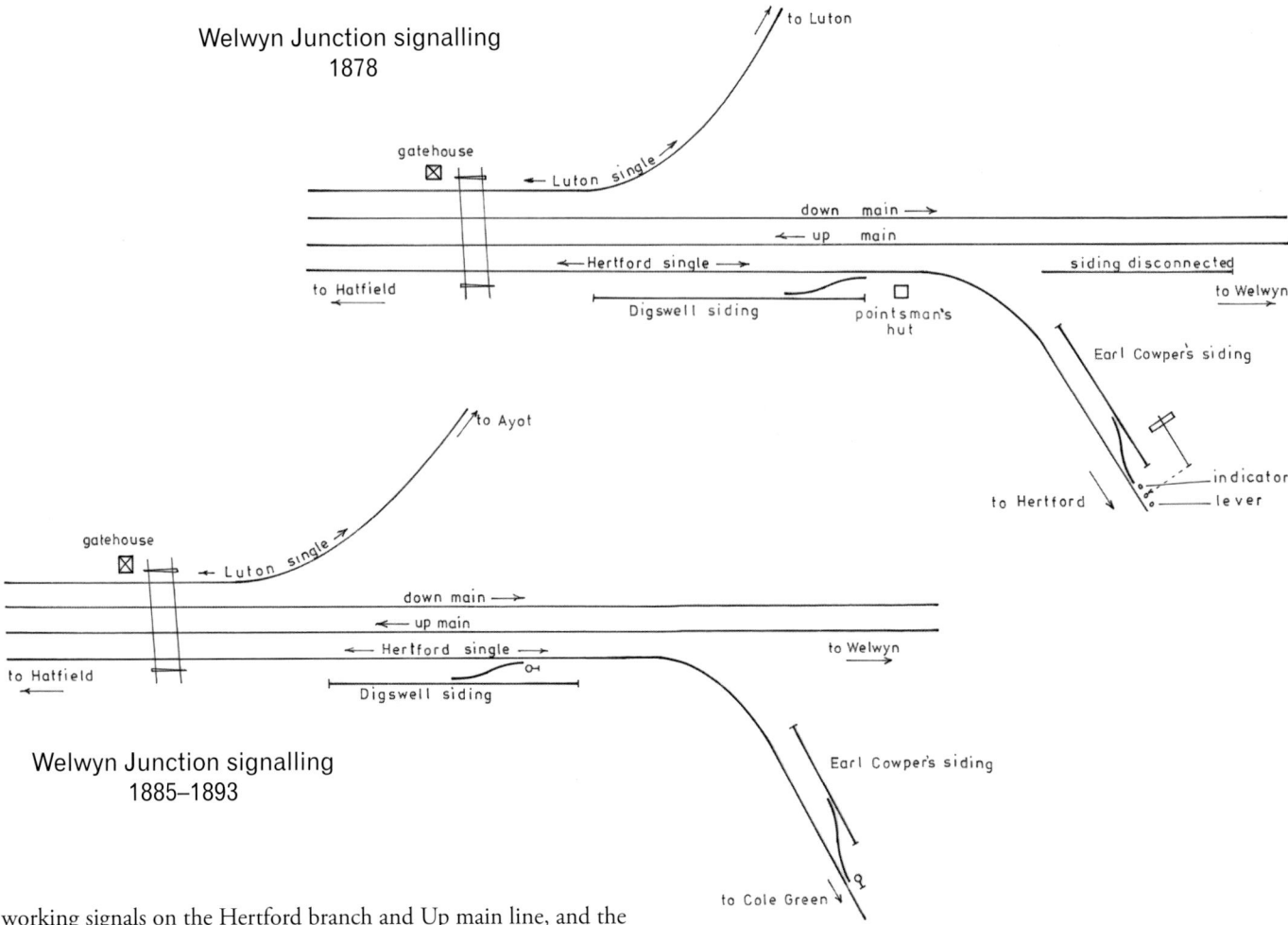

working signals on the Hertford branch and Up main line, and the latter the Dunstable branch and the Down main lines. Welwyn Junction signal box, equipped with a Steven's frame, opened with the Hertford branch on 1st March 1858 and closed on 29th August 1876 when Hertford branch services were extended to Hatfield.

Welwyn Garden City signal box was opened on 19th September 1926 and was provided with a 65-lever Saxby & Farmer Duplex Tappet frame with 4-inch centres initially with 45 working and 20 spare levers. As facilities at the station expanded, so the frame was enlarged to 85 levers, with 81 working and 4 spare. Later, after the Hertford branch single line was terminated at Welwyn Garden City, a separate 19-lever Luton line frame was added to the 85-lever frame making a total of 104 levers, although they were always regarded as separate. Of the total, 2 levers on the Luton frame and 7 levers on the main frame were spares. The signal box was abolished on 26th September 1976.

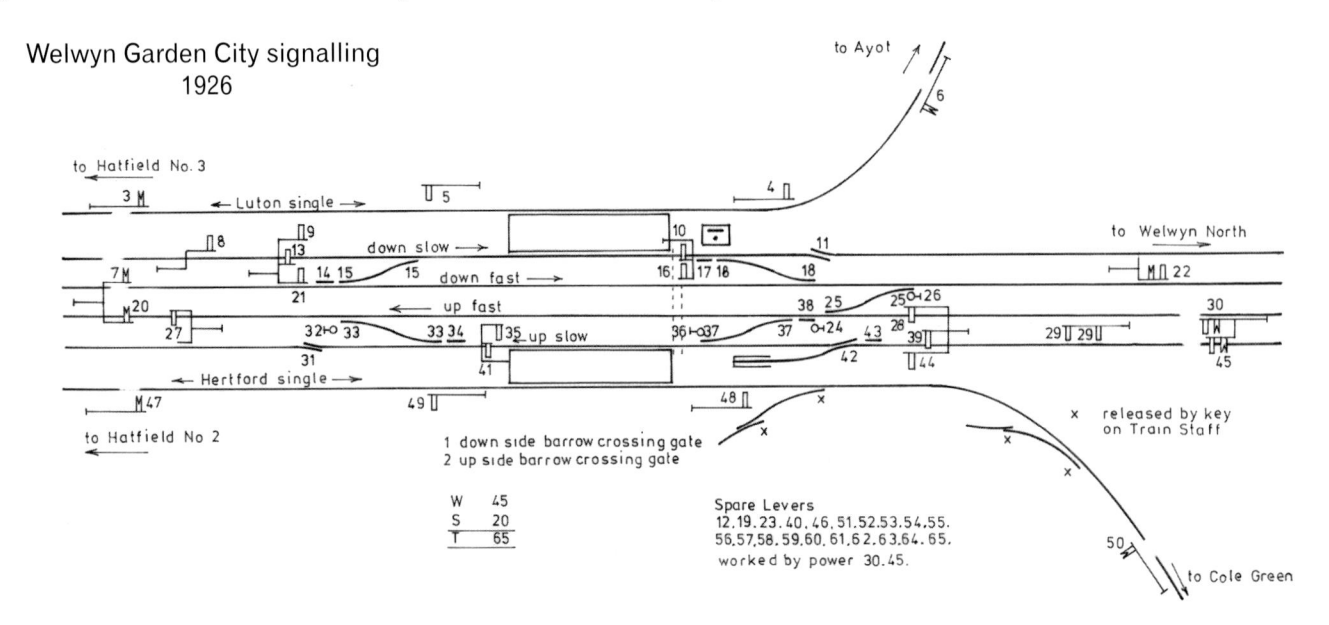

Welwyn Garden City signalling 1926

PERMANENT WAY, SIGNALLING AND STAFF

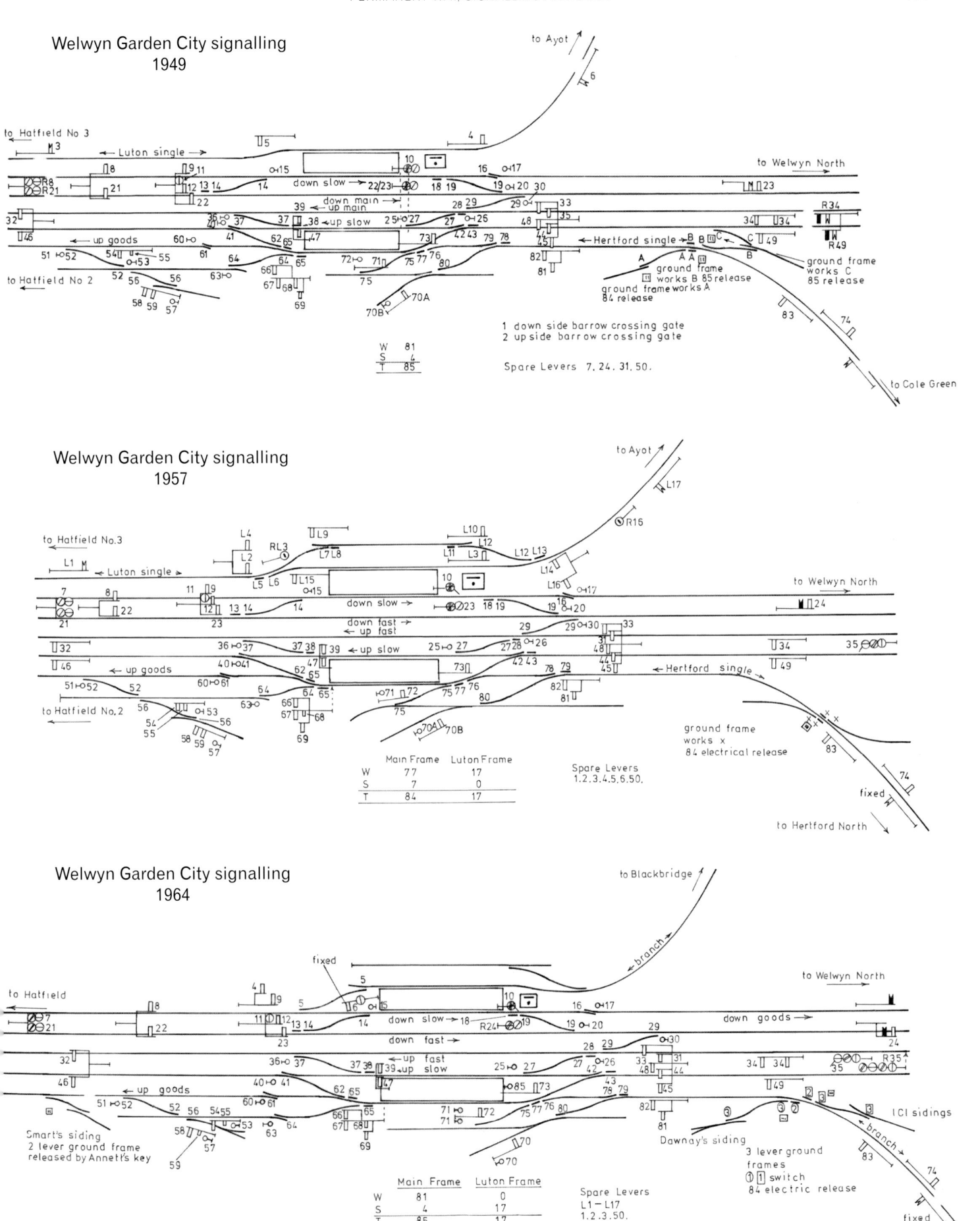

Welwyn Garden City signalling 1949

Welwyn Garden City signalling 1957

Welwyn Garden City signalling 1964

Welwyn Garden City station from the north with the goods yard to the left and station buildings to the far right. Footbridge No. 67C spans all lines and connects the platforms with the Down side and Up side entrances. Welwyn Garden City signal box, opened in 19th September 1926, was located at the north end of the Down island platform and was provided with a 65-lever Saxby & Farmer Duplex Tappet frame. As traffic increased the frame was enlarged to 85 levers, with 81 working and 4 spare; the box was abolished on 26th September 1976. *Author's collection*

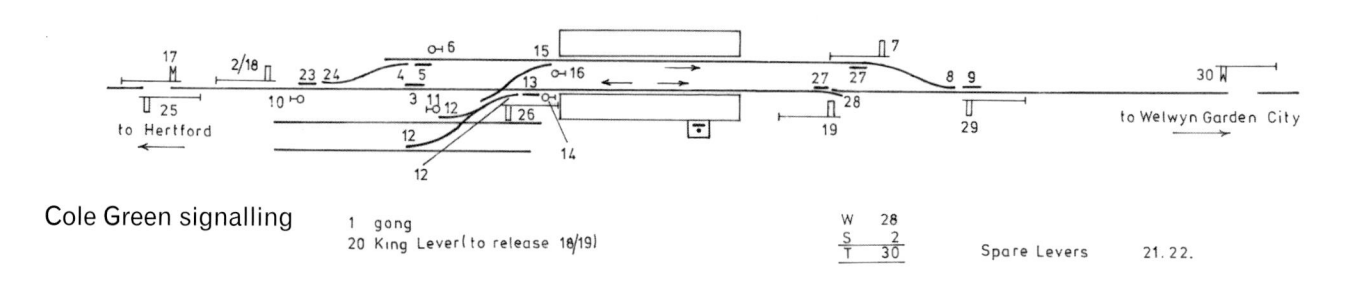

Cole Green signalling

1 gong
20 King Lever (to release 18/19)

W 28
S 2
T 30

Spare Levers 21. 22.

The Down platform at Cole Green view facing east, with the signal box located behind the ornate awning beside the waiting room and former booking office.
Author's collection

Hertingfordbury signalling 1880

Diagram showing: to Cole Green ← up — 1-lever — down → to Hertford

Hertingfordbury signalling 1904

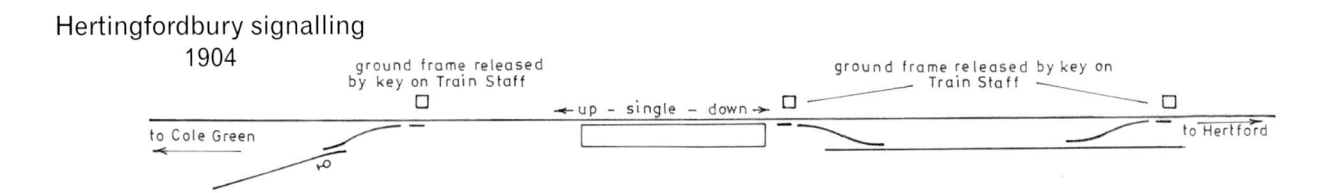

Diagram showing: to Cole Green ← — ground frame released by key on Train Staff — up – single – down → — ground frame released by key on Train Staff — to Hertford

Cole Green signal box opened on 27th June 1891 and was provided with a 30-lever Saxby & Farmer Duplex frame with 4-inch centres with 28 working and 2 spare levers. In 1925, for long section working a King lever was installed. The box was abolished on 19th March 1953 and a 3-lever ground frame provided, this being abolished on 20th October 1965.

Hertingfordbury station was originally provided with a small frame to operate signals for each direction of travel mounted on the same post, and the points and an associated ground signals for the single siding at the east end of the layout. By 1904, three ground frames were provided to control points leading to a new siding to the west of the station and for the two sets of points leading to the loop siding serving the small goods yard at the east end.

Hertford station was provided with a signal box on 27th March 1890, which contained a 26-lever Saxby & Farmer frame with 23 working and 3 spare levers. The frame was later increased to 30 levers as the yard expanded, with 26 working and 4 spare levers. On 2nd June 1924 the box was abolished and replaced by four ground frames as a result of the opening of the new Hertford North station signal box. The old Hertford station signal box was subsequently

Hertford, later Cowbridge, signal box was opened on 27th March 1890 and contained a 26-lever Saxby & Farmer frame with 23 working and 3 spare levers, later increased to 30 levers with 26 working and 4 spare levers. The signal box was abolished on 2nd June 1924 when passenger train services terminated at the new station. The structure was subsequently transferred to serve as a signal box at Palmers Green on the Wood Green to Langley Junction line, opening on 12th May 1925.
Author's collection

Hertford Cowbridge signalling 1890

Hertford Cowbridge signalling 1909

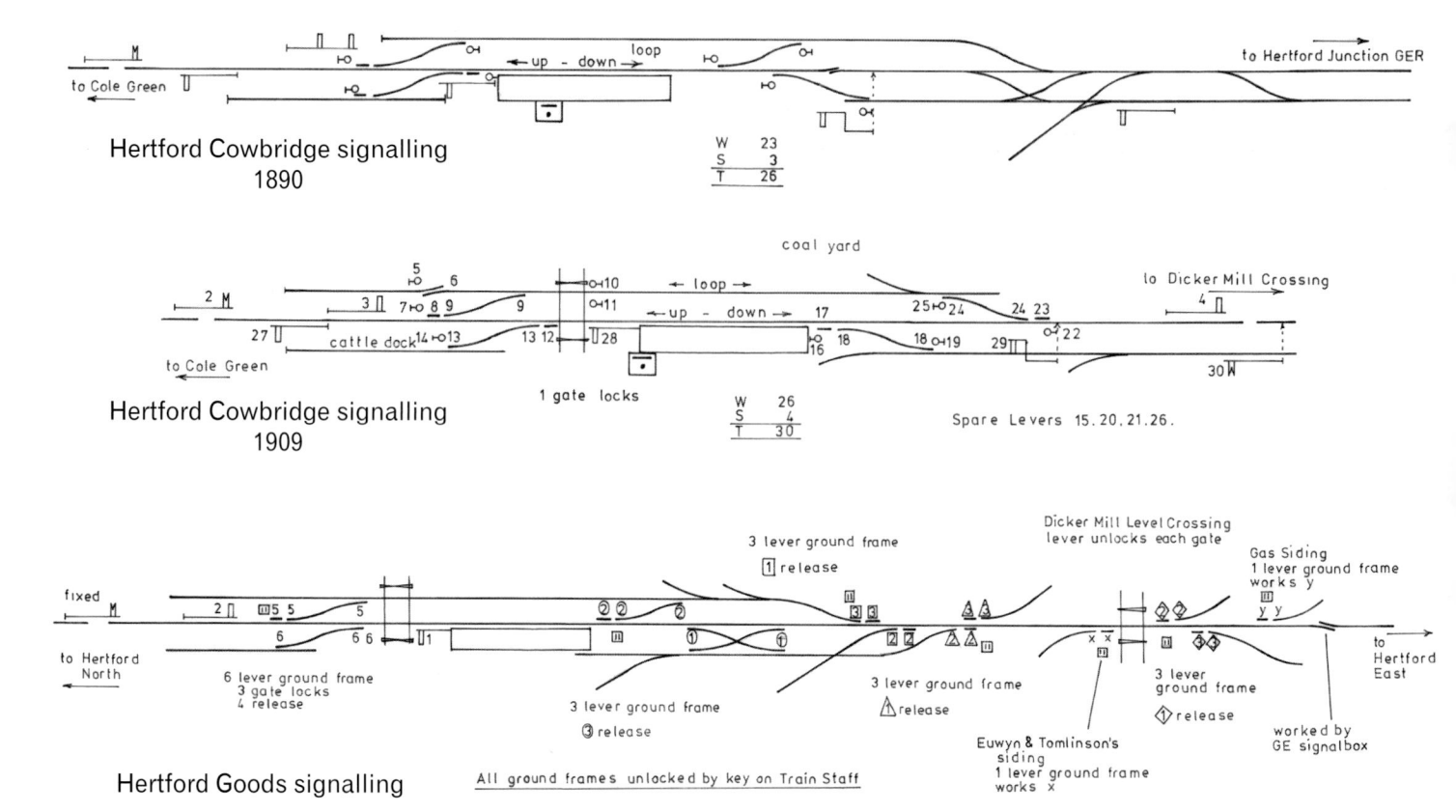

Hertford Goods signalling

transferred for further use at Palmers Green on the Wood Green to Langley Junction loop line, replacing the previous signal box there with effect from 12th May 1929.

Tenders for the provision of a signal box at Dicker Mill Lane crossing east of Hertford were invited in the autumn of 1893 with the following tendering: McKenzie & Holland £465 12s 6d, Railway Signalling Company £477 6s 8d, Saxby & Farmer £479 11s 2d, Dutton & Company £486 11s 8d. McKenzie & Holland were subsequently awarded the contract on 30th January 1894. Dicker Mill Crossing was provided with a 5-lever McKenzie & Holland Cam and Tappet frame with 6-inch centres, controlling the gates and associated signals. When the small box burnt down on 13th May 1929 it was not replaced but the gates and associated sidings were controlled from the growing number of individual ground frames.

The normal position for the Dicker Mill crossing gates was open for road traffic and closed across the railway. After the loss of the signal box in 1929, drivers of engines travelling to or from Hertford East were required to bring their engine to a stand well clear of the crossing and wait for the shunter who had to accompany the engine to open the gates. The shunter was then required to close the gates across the railway after the engine had passed and the crossing was clear. Later the instruction required the engine or train to be brought to a stand well clear of the gates, after which the fireman opened the gates for the passage of the train over the crossing. When the train had passed over the crossing, the guard (or fireman in the case of a light engine) was required to close the gates across the railway and relock them, the driver taking care not to again proceed on the journey until he had received the 'all right' signal from the guard. Enginemen and guards were to ensure they were supplied with keys to open and close the gates.

The junction with the GER at Hertford was controlled by Hertford Junction signal box equipped with a 28-lever McKenzie & Holland frame with 5-inch centres, the building measuring 22 feet by 11 feet 6 inches with operating floor 10 feet above rail level, the box closing in 1925. Thereafter the junction was controlled from Hertford East signal box, originally measuring 20 feet by 11 feet 4 inches with operating floor 12 feet above rail level and equipped with a 36-lever McKenzie & Holland frame with 5-inch centres, but in 1925 extended to a length of 26 feet to accommodate an additional 9 levers.

Hertford, later Hertford North, signal box on the loop line opened with the extension to Langley Junction on 4th April 1918. Although the line was initially single, the route was doubled from

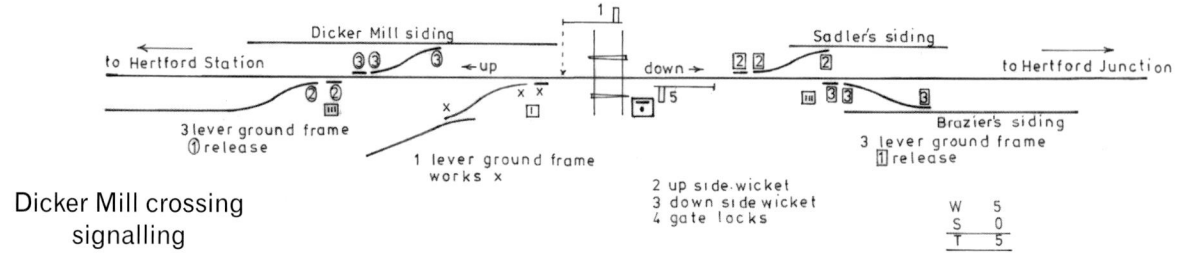

Dicker Mill crossing signalling

LEFT: **GNR** 3-lever ground frame located near the goods shed at Hertford Cowbridge in July 1954. The former stables can be seen on the left.
RIGHT: **GNR** 2-lever ground frame located west of the station on the same day. After the abolition of the Station signal box all points at the goods station were converted to ground frame operation, the frame being released by Annett's key on the single line Train Staff. *Both P. Whitaker*

Dicker Mill level crossing No. 25 at 27 miles 46 chains from Hatfield with its attendant signal box containing a 5-lever McKenzie & Holland Cam and Tappet frame with 6-inch centres. The crossing keeper's cottage is in the background. The signal box was opened in 1894 and was destroyed by fire in 1929, after which it was replaced by ground frames operating the gate release and points to various sidings, the levers released and locked by Annett's key on the single line Train Staff. *Author's collection*

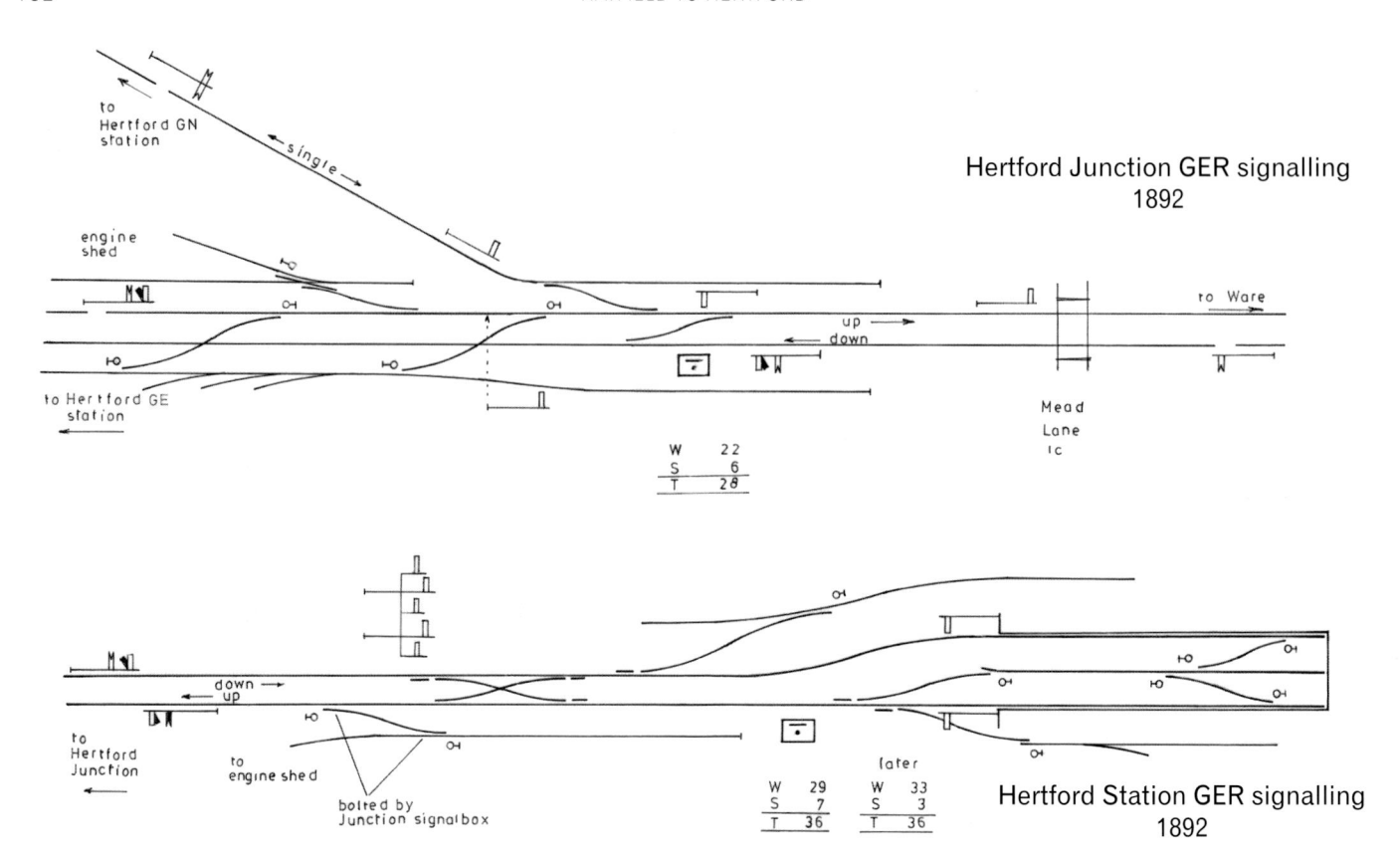

Hertford Junction GER signalling 1892

Hertford Station GER signalling 1892

Hertford East signalling 1926

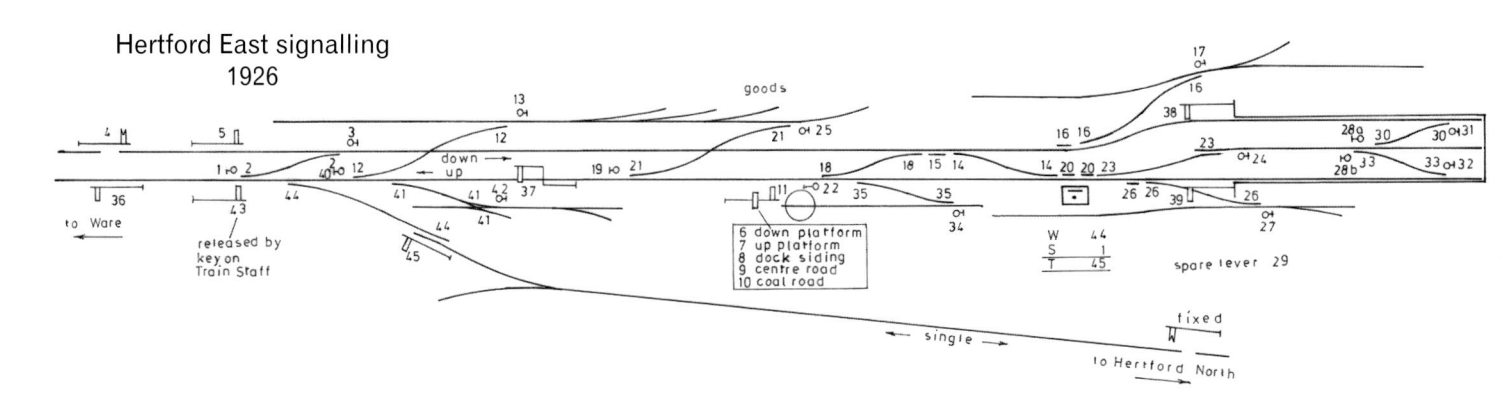

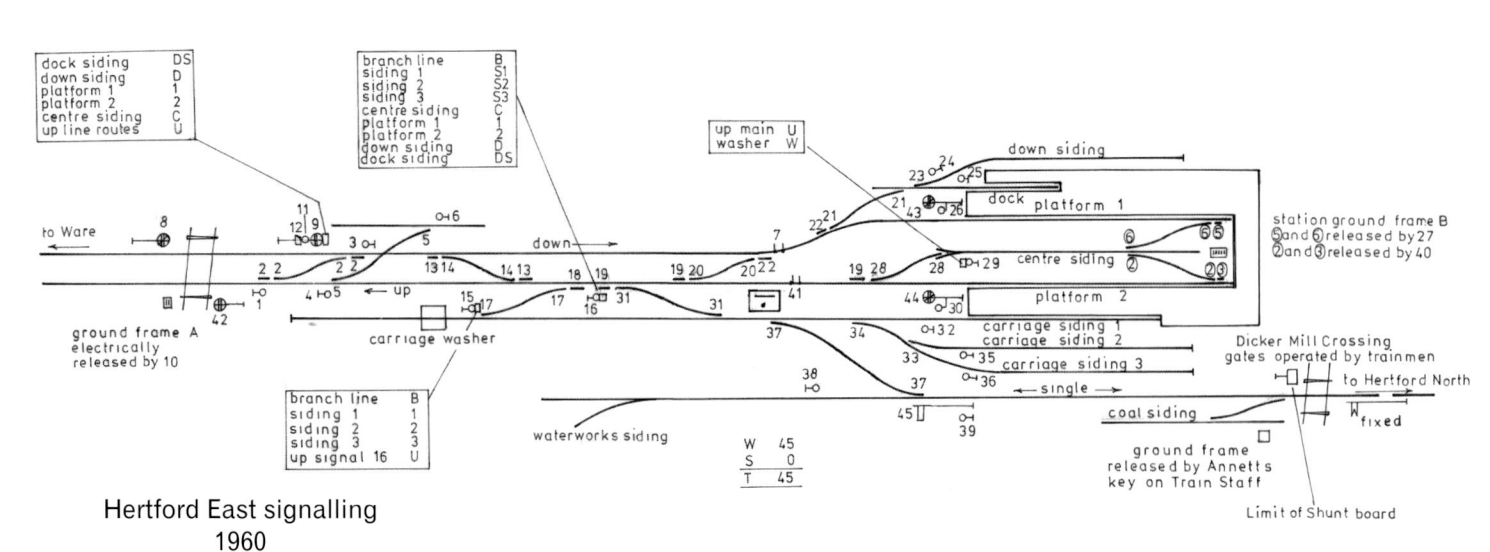

Hertford East signalling 1960

Hertford North signal box opened in April 1918, extended in 1924 and was equipped with a 65-lever frame with 57 working and 8 spare levers. The signal box was abolished on 18th April 1971 when control of the Wood Green to Langley Junction line was taken over by King's Cross Power Signalling Centre. *D. Dent collection*

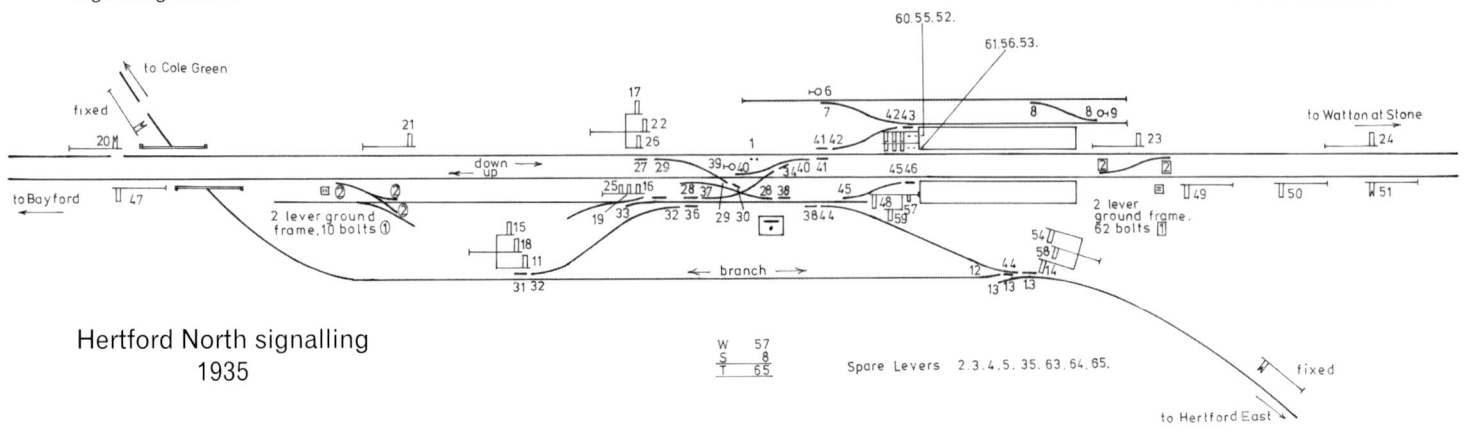

Hertford North signalling 1935

23rd December 1920 and, fortuitously, provision had been made for growth as the box was subsequently equipped with a Saxby & Farmer 65-lever Double Tappet frame, some of the frame being transferred from Foxton signal box on the Hitchin to Cambridge branch, and ready for use on 4th May 1924. Initially the box had 57 working and 8 spare levers. The signal box was abolished on 18th April 1971.

In 1905 Hatfield No. 2 and No. 3 signal boxes were open continuously. Cole Green signal box was closed after the last train was 'out of section' on Saturdays until 6.40am on Sunday, after the Up goods train was 'out of section' on Sunday to 4.50pm, and then after the last train was 'out of section' Sundays until 5.50am on Monday. Hertford box closed after the last train was 'out of section' on Saturdays to 6.45am on Sunday, then closed after the Up goods train was 'out of section' to 5.00pm, and then after the last train was 'out of section' on Sundays to 6.00am on Monday.

By 1927 Welwyn Garden City signal box was open continuously. Cole Green box was closed on weekdays after No. 26 Up goods was 'out of section' to 6.55am, Saturdays after 'out of section' received for No. 27 Up goods to 6.55am on Mondays. Hertford North was closed on Sundays after 'out of section' for No. 1 Up goods (about 1.40am) to 9.30am, then 1.05pm to 3.00pm, then after 'out of section' received for No. 186 Up passenger (about 9.32pm) to 5.45am on Mondays.

In 1933 Hatfield No. 2 and No. 3 signal boxes and Welwyn Garden City were open continuously. Cole Green signal box was closed after No. 20 Up goods had departed to 4.55am; on Saturdays the box was closed after No. 27 Up goods train had left until

6.30am on the following Monday. Hertford North signal box was closed after 'out of section' had been received for No. 1 Up goods on a Sunday (about 1.40am) to 9.30am, and then after 'out of section' was received for No. 206 train (about 10.30pm) until 5.45am on Monday

By 1942 Hatfield No. 2 and No. 3 signal boxes and Welwyn Garden City signal box were open continuously. Cole Green signal box was closed on weekdays from 9.15pm or after the departure of No. 26 Up goods train until 6.00am, and on Saturdays from 9.15pm or after the departure of No. 26 Up goods until 6.00am on Monday. Hertford North signal box was open continuously.

After nationalisation in 1948, Hatfield No's 2 and 3 signal boxes were open continuously, as was Welwyn Garden City. Cole Green signal box was open on weekdays from 6.00am until 8.40pm, whilst Hertford North signal box was open continuously. In 1963 Welwyn Garden City and Hertford North signal boxes were open continuously.

The maintenance of signalling on the main line in the Hatfield area and the Hertford branch was the responsibility of signal fitters and linemen based at Hatfield, with an additional lineman based at Hertford. The establishment at Hertford North was increased with the opening of the new line, when their sphere of operation included the section south to Cuffley and north to Langley Junction, south of Stevenage.

The junction between the GER and GNR at Hertford in 1911. Hertford Junction signal box located on the Down side of the double-track branch from Broxbourne controlled all movements over the junction. This structure replaced an earlier signal box in 1888 and was equipped with a 28-lever McKenzie & Holland frame with 22 working and 6 spare levers. As a result of rationalisation the signal box was abolished in 1925 when all control was passed to Hertford East, previously Hertford Station, signal box. Note the well-tended allotments on the Up side of the railway.
GERS/Windwood

Superintendence

The commercial aspects of the GNR were rearranged as a result of the working of the Hertford and Luton sections of the HL&DR. On 6th August 1860 the General Manager advised the board of the proposed rearrangements of the districts. Charles Plaskett was subsequently appointed District Agent for the area Holloway to Hitchin as well as Dunstable to Hertford inclusive at the same salary at the Nottingham District agent, earning £180 per annum together with £40 housing allowance and £20 travelling expenses. At the same time, from a list of fourteen applicants William Bradley, formerly clerk-in-charge at Boston, was appointed agent for the Luton District on the same salary. Four months later Doctor Drage of Hatfield offered his services as Medical Officer to the GNR Sick Fund for the Hatfield to Hertford line. At their meeting on 16th October 1860 his offer was readily accepted by the directors.

Station Masters

When the line first opened the initial Hertford station was a temporary structure when Anthony Hamilton was station master. It was not until 1862 that a contract was awarded to Kirk & Parry for a permanent station costing £3,500 and at this stage William Cook was in charge. The facilities were completed early in 1863 when station master's accommodation was provided; by 1867 Frederick Carpenter was station master and he remained in charge until his untimely death in 1874. Richard Croft Rowe, who transferred from the position of station master at Spilsby, was appointed to the vacancy and he was still in the position in 1890, at which time he was replaced by Richard Charles Gaylard who had transferred from nearby Hertingfordbury. Gaylard's tenure was short, for by 1908 Frederick Reed Beavis was in charge. With a view to economy of working, the GNR and GER authorities arranged for their respective Hertford stations to be under the supervision of one station master. The imminent retirement of the GER station master at the end of July 1909 offered an opportune time for the merger of the two posts. The GER man had received a salary of £190 per annum including house rent but his successor, Frederick Reed Beavis, only received £180 per annum plus free lodging in the station house for taking control of the two stations. Under these arrangements the GER saved £90 per annum. Beavis stayed

RIGHT: Richard Croft Rowe, the GNR station master at Hertford from 1874 until 1890. *D. Dent collection*

until 1916, to be replaced by Henry Dennick who served until 1921 when Charles Henry Wood was appointed as joint station master for the GNR and GER stations. John George Hurst gained promotion from Potters Bar and South Mimms in March 1924 but died on 27th May 1928. Henry Clark, station master at Crouch Hill and Stroud Green, gained promotion to take charge of the two Hertford stations including Stapleford and Watton-at-Stone in September 1928 before retiring in June 1934. The next incumbent was W. Rains who came from Widnes in October 1934 and served the two stations until April 1936, when he transferred to take charge at Tottenham. He was succeeded by J.F. House who had earlier served at Welwyn Garden City, and transferred on promotion from Muswell Hill and served the town until 15th April 1945. H.J. Crick, 5½ years as station master at Sudbury, gained promotion to Hertford North and East in February 1946. During his tenure at Sudbury he had the privilege of shaking the hand of His Majesty King George VI twice in one day when he escorted the king from the royal train to royal car during a visit to D-Day troops massed in the area of Suffolk. Crick died on 6th February 1948.

Along the line at Hertingfordbury the initial station master was Edmund Redrupp, who served at the station until 1863 when he was succeeded by William Henry Smith. Thomas R. Wharam then took over the position in 1869 but by 1874 he was replaced by William Perkins who served until 1881. Richard Charles Gaylard was appointed to the vacancy but his tenure was short, for by 1886 he had been succeeded by George Wheatley who was station master until 1890 when George Currell was recorded as station master. By 1895 Francis Martin was in charge but from 1902 Arthur Bidnell assumed responsibility, serving until early 1920 when the position fell vacant. However, Henry Richardson, a clerk at Knebworth, was appointed station master in July 1920 but his stay was short for he was promoted to take charge at Corby in January 1922 before resigning from the L&NER on 29th December 1928. A. Giddins then became station master and achieved a Best Kept Station award in 1924. By the mid 1930s, under a rationalisation programme Hertingfordbury came under the jurisdiction of the station master at Cole Green.

William Gresham was the first station master appointed to Cole Green, serving until 1867 when Henry Wallis was appointed to the post. His tenure was short for in 1870 William Henry Smith – whose wife three years his senior went by the unusual name of Appolonia – had charge of Cole Green station; he remained there until 1902 when he was succeeded by Edwin Hawes who served at the station until 1924, when he was promoted to station master at Winchmore Hill from where he retired on 3rd December 1931. G. Dobson took over the vacancy and served until August 1937 when he was promoted as station master at Stevenage. Ernest C. Blagg became the new incumbent but he died on 20th August 1943; he was not replaced until January 1944 when H. Scampion transferred from New Southgate on a temporary tenure until he was transferred to Welwyn Garden City. From the 1940s, at Cole Green the station master was responsible for issuing tickets. W.G. Peacocke transferred to Cole Green including Hertingfordbury in February 1944, having served in a similar capacity at Great Bentley, but his stay was short as he transferred to Tallington in August 1945. The new incumbent also had a short reign, for G.H. Mitten only served the two stations until April 1946, when he transferred to Finmere on the ex-GCR main line.

At the embryonic Welwyn Garden City, J.F. House transferred to Daybrook in October 1928 and was replaced by H.F. Hodson who had been in charge at Yaxley, south of Peterborough. He stayed until retirement on 11th September 1943 and at a ceremony on 27th October he was presented with a cheque for £166 7s 6d, collected by local businessmen and present and past season ticket holders, by the president of the Welwyn Garden City Chamber of Commerce.

Traffic Staff

From the early 1940s, Hertingfordbury station was manned by a leading porter between the hours of 6.30am and 4.00pm, after which a lad porter was sent from Hertford North until the station closed at 7.00pm. The leading porter's duties included the issuing of tickets and shunting duties for trains calling at the station siding. At Cole Green, platform and signal box duties were handled by two porter signalman, one working early turn and the other late turn. The three signalmen at Hertford North in the latter years of the branch working were George Geraldine, Alfred Pacey and Reuben Waldock. Percy Lee was the District Signalling Inspector based at Hatfield. Earlier signalmen at Hertford North included W.V. Proctor, who had been mayor of the town in 1933 and who later became a district signalling inspector, and A.H. Medcalf who retired on 9th November 1938 after thirteen years' service in the box. H.W. Hebblethwaite, a signalman at Cole Green, won a prize in the L&NER staff suggestion scheme in August 1934.

Lad porter Reuben Arthur Waldock at Hertingfordbury station in 1910. Note the ornate painted station nameboard and the metal cast name on the seat back. Waldock later became a signalman at Hertford North. *Barry Gray collection*

10

Timetables and Traffic

The building of the railway west of the county town of Hertford to connect up with the Great Northern Railway at Welwyn, and later Hatfield, was essentially to open up new spheres of trade in competition with the Eastern Counties and later Great Eastern Railway. The promoters had little thought for the local populace and in fact stations at Hertingfordbury and Cole Green were only provided as an afterthought. Although the local company ultimately changed its name and extended to the manufacturing centre of Luton and on to Dunstable to join up with the London & North Western Railway, it had little effect on the local populace. However, once the Great Northern Railway had taken over, traffic improved as commodities were transported to and from the North of England and the Midlands without having to travel the roundabout route via Cambridge and Ely to Peterborough. A good passenger service was operated from London to Hertford in competition with the GER, which benefited the commuters from Hertford but did little to increase the population of the intermediate locations served by the branch as the figures below show. Once the new line from Wood Green was extended beyond Enfield to Stevenage via the new Hertford North station, and despite the development of the new town of Welwyn Garden City, the branch to all intents and purposes became almost surplus to requirements to the new L&NER in the mid-1920s. Direct services by the main line and the new line to London condemned the branch to a domiciled fate, as competitive bus services had increased and train services were reduced accordingly. Passenger services were withdrawn as early as 1951 but could have closed earlier had it not been for munitions workers using the branch during World War Two. Freight traffic survived for over another decade as the GNR had wisely opened many sidings, which continued to be served until the end of petrol rationing found traders turning to motor transport and forsaking the railway.

The initial timetable operative from **March 1858** for the branch and connections to and from the GNR ran on weekdays only. The fastest journey time for the 27¼ miles from King's Cross to Hertford of 57 minutes compared favourably with the ECR best timing of 65 minutes for the 26 miles from Bishopsgate via Stratford. On the branch all trains conveyed First, Second and Third Class passengers.

From **1st April 1858** the following timetable was advertised with an increased number of trains including two Sunday services in each direction from 4th April.

The ECR also commenced working the goods services on the H&WJR from the same date with two services in each direction.

Timetable from March 1858

Up		123P am	12 am	12 am	123 pm	123 pm
Hertford	dep	8.15	9.10	11.40	3.10	7.30
Welwyn Junction	arr	8.33	9.30	12.00	3.30	7.50
Welwyn Junction	dep	8.47	9.35	12.03	3.35	7.57
Hatfield	arr	8.52		12.10	3.40	8.05
King's Cross	arr	9.30	10.15	12.45	4.15	9.55

Down		123P am	123 am	12 pm	12 pm	123 pm
King's Cross	dep	6.50	10.15	1.45	5.03	7.45
Hatfield	dep	7.40	11.03		5.32	8.35
Welwyn Junction	arr	7.44	11.07	2.19	5.36	8.39
Welwyn Junction	dep	8.38	11.10	2.25	5.40	8.45
Hertford	arr	8.55	11.30	2.45	6.00	9.05

Timetable From 1st April 1858

		Weekdays							Sundays	
		am	am	am	pm	pm	pm	pm	am	pm
Hertford	dep	7.30	9.25	10.50	12.50	3.55	5.03	7.30	8.10	7.10
Welwyn Junction	arr	7.45	9.45	11.10	1.09	4.12	5.23	7.50	8.30	7.29
		am	am	am	pm	pm	pm	pm	am	pm
Welwyn Junction	dep	8.45	9.55	11.18	1.22	4.28	5.40	8.45	9.00	8.45
Hertford	arr	9.05	10.15	11.38	1.40	4.48	6.00	9.05	9.20	9.05

Population Figures

Year	1851	1861	1871	1881	1891	1901	1911	1921	1931	1951	1961
Hertford	5,703	5,747	6,206	6,595	9,023	9,332	10,384	10,702	11,378	13,884	15,787
Hertingfordbury	752	799	828	823	797	733	667	815	738	640	746
Digswell	239	243	255	227	249	285	401	423	644	—	—
Welwyn Gdn City	—	—	—	—	—	—	—	767	8,586	18,314	35,179
Hatfield	3,862	3,871	3,998	4,059	4,330	4,754	5,306	5,054	6,187	13,834	21,019
Total*	6,694	6,789	7,289	7,645	10,069	10,350	11,452	12,707	21,346	32,838	51,662
Total+	6,694	6,546	7,034	7,418	9,820	10,065	11,051	12,707	738	640	746

* Total excluding Hatfield.
+ Effective catchment area of branch stations.

ECR Goods Service From 1st April 1858			
Up		am	pm
Hertford	dep	4.00	9.35
Welwyn Junction	arr	4.25	10.05
Down		am	pm
Welwyn Junction	dep	5.15	10.30
Hertford	arr	5.40	10.55

The April timetable was considered too ambitious and in **May 1858** a reduced service operated. In the same month the ECR also reduced the service to the 4.00am Up and 5.15am Down goods workings only.

The Hertfordshire election on Tuesday 8th June 1858 was important enough to warrant the company to run an extra train departing Welwyn Junction at 9.55am providing a connection from Hertfordshire stations to the north and arriving at Hertford at 10.15am. The company also advised the extra train would run every Tuesday until further notice.

Evidently the enhanced service proved over ambitious for the sparse traffic, for from **July 1858** the working timetable showed the GNR operating three passenger services in each direction on weekdays only, departing Hertford at 9.25am, 3.55pm and 7.30pm, returning from Welwyn Junction at 11.18am, 5.40pm and 8.45pm, with two trains each way on Sundays departing Hertford at 8.10am and 7.10pm, returning from Welwyn Junction at 9.00am and 8.45pm The solitary goods train worked by the ECR on weekdays only departed Hertford at 4.00am, returning from Welwyn Junction at 5.15am, with a 25-minute timing in each direction.

Complaints were made in November 1858 after the GNR withdrew the Welwyn Junction stop by the 5.05pm Down train from King's Cross resulting in a 6-hour gap in services from the capital to Hertford. A letter sent by the H&WJR Secretary was considered by the GNR Traffic Committee on 30th November and the General Manager replied the company would review the situation although it was not possible to alter the timetable for December 1858.

By **November 1859** services were sparse and hardly conducive to attracting patronage, with the ECR working all trains. The weekday passenger services departed Hertford at 9.35am and 5.38pm, returning from Welwyn Junction at 9.35am and 4.05pm, being allowed between 17 and 20 minutes for the journey. The goods services departed Hertford at 7.00am and 8.00pm, and returned from Welwyn Junction at 7.45am and 9.00pm, with 25 and 35 minutes respectively allowed for shunting and interchange of traffic. On Sundays two passenger trains continued to run in each direction, departing Hertford at 8.05am and 7.05pm, returning from Welwyn Junction at 8.50am and 8.50pm. Although Cole Green and Hertingfordbury stations had been open for almost a year there was no reference to them in the working timetable and trains called by request only.

The working timetable for **July 1860** showed the GNR responsible for three passenger trains in each direction on weekdays and two each way on Sundays, with timings varying from 17 to 20 minutes. On weekdays the ECR operated two goods trains each way between Blackwall and Welwyn Junction, with a uniform 20-minute running time between Hertford and Welwyn Junction.

Timetable from May 1858		Weekdays					Sundays	
		am	am	pm	pm	pm	am	pm
Hertford	dep	7.30	9.25	12.40	3.55	7.30	8.10	7.10
Welwyn Junction	arr	7.48	9.45	1.00	4.12	7.50	8.30	7.29
Welwyn Junction	dep	8.00	9.50	1.01	4.20	7.57	8.52	7.30
Hatfield	arr	8.10		1.10	4.26	8.05	8.59	7.36
King's Cross	arr	9.00	10.25	2.00	5.30	8.55	9.55	8.40
		Weekdays					**Sundays**	
		am	am	pm	pm	pm	am	pm
King's Cross	dep	7.45	10.15	12.25	5.03	7.45	7.30	7.45
Hatfield	dep	8.35	11.03	1.13	5.32	8.35	8.22	8.35
Welwyn Junction	arr	8.40	11.11	1.18	5.35	8.40	8.31	8.40
Welwyn Junction	dep	8.46	11.18	1.20	5.40	8.45	9.00	8.45
Hertford	arr	9.03	11.40	1.40	6.00	9.05	9.20	9.00

GNR working timetable July 1858.

GNR working timetable November 1859.

By **November 1860** the situation had drastically improved with passenger services working through to Hatfield and the working timetable advising that the stoppage of passenger trains at Welwyn Junction would be discontinued, but goods and coal wagons were to be left at the siding until further notice. Goods and coal wagons to and from the Luton and Dunstable branch were to be worked to and from Hatfield. All services were worked by the GNR, with a Hertford-based engine working the passenger services and a Hatfield locomotive on the freight turns. The working timetable showed six passenger and three goods train in each direction on weekdays and two passenger trains each way on Sundays. Passenger services were allowed 20 minutes running time on both Up and Down journeys, except the 9.08am Down train from Hatfield which ran in the accelerated time of 17 minutes. Goods services were allowed between 30 and 40 minutes for the journey and all called at Welwyn Junction.

Almost a decade later, in **June 1869** the passenger timetable showed the following service on the Hatfield to Hertford branch, which continued unchanged the following year.

In comparison, the GER was offering a total of nine Up and twelve Down trains

Right: GNR working timetable July 1860.

Below: GNR working timetable November 1860.

Above: GNR working timetable 1861.

Timetable June 1869									
Up		**Weekdays**						**Sundays**	
		123	12	123	12	123	123	123	123
		am	am	am	pm	pm	pm	pm	am	pm
Hertford	dep	8.00	9.55	11.10	1.15	4.00	5.12	7.40	7.50	6.30
Hertingfordbury	dep	*	*	*	*	*	*	*	*	*
Cole Green	dep	*	*	*	*	*	*	*	*	*
Hatfield	arr	8.23	10.20	11.33	1.38	4.23	5.33	8.03	8.10	6.55
Down		**Weekdays**						**Sundays**	
		123	123	123	123	123	123	123	123
		am	am	pm	pm	pm	pm	am	pm
Hatfield	dep	8.58	10.32	12.00	1.53	4.42	5.57	8.52	8.47	9.01
Cole Green	dep	*	*	*	*	*	*	*	*	*
Hertingfordbury	dep	*	*	*	*	*	*	*	*	*
Hertford	arr	9.23	10.55	12.25	2.15	5.05	6.18	9.15	9.10	9.21
* Trains call at Cole Green and Hertingfordbury by signal only when there are passengers to pick up or set down. Notice must be given to the guard at the previous station.										

Branch timetable from Bradshaw's 1869.

to and from Bishopsgate, with four trains each way on Sundays. From 1st August 1870 St. Pancras station became an alternative London terminus for GER trains. The branch suffered a further setback in the timing competition from Hertford to London when from August 1872 the GER services from the county town were accelerated with the opening of the direct line via Clapton and Hackney Downs. Then from 2nd February 1874 GER trains were diverted to Liverpool Street half a mile nearer the city than Bishopsgate.

Meanwhile the **December 1873** GNR public timetable showed a service of eight SX and nine SO passenger trains in the Down direction and seven SX and eight SO trains on the Up road. The additional SO services departed Hatfield at 11.10am, returning from Hertford at 12.00 noon. On Sundays two trains ran each way. All trains called at Cole Green and Hertingfordbury by signal only when there were passengers to pick up or set down, passengers alighting being required to advise the guard at the preceding station. All the passenger services were worked by Hertford-based engines and were allowed 23 to 25 minutes for the journey. An identical service operated in 1874 with only minor timing alterations to two trains.

The working timetable for **1875** showed a weekday service of seven SX and eight SO passenger trains and four goods trains in each direction. Passenger services were worked by a Hertford engine, outbased from Hatfield, with all trains calling at Cole Green and Hertingfordbury by signal only when there were passengers to take up or set down. The additional Saturday trains departed Hatfield at 11.30am, returning from Hertford at 12.00 noon. Trains were allowed between 23 and 25 minutes running time for the journey. On Sundays two passenger services ran in each direction, again calling at Cole Green and Hertingfordbury only if required. The

GNR working timetable 1875.

goods and cattle trains were worked by Hatfield-based engines, the 6.00am ex Hatfield conveyed through goods to Hertford GE arriving 7.00am, returning at 7.20am with 10 minutes allowed for stopping at Cowbridge and Haggar's siding before reaching Hatfield at 8.34am. The afternoon Down goods departed Hatfield at 2.45pm and served the sidings at Welwyn Junction, Attimore Hall, Cole Green and Hertingfordbury when necessary and called at Haggar's siding; it departed Hertford GN at 3.45pm before terminating at Hertford GE. The train returned at 4.15pm with the same stopping pattern as the outward journey save that a mandatory call was made at Welwyn Junction before the train terminated at Hatfield at 7.40pm. A further goods train departed Hatfield at 8.30pm for Cowbridge and Hertford GE arriving at 9.10pm, returning 15 minutes later calling at Cowbridge and conveying GER through goods and arriving back at Hatfield at 10.15pm. The final goods train of the day departed Hatfield at 11.00pm and after calling at Cowbridge ran through to Hertford GE arriving at 11.40pm, returning thence at 11.50pm conveying GER through goods when necessary, calling at Cowbridge 10 minutes later and arriving at Hatfield at 12.35am. The 8.30pm Down goods and cattle train ex Hatfield was permitted to run earlier, departing at 6.15pm, if there was insufficient traffic for the 2.45pm goods and cattle train to run, in which case the balancing 4.45pm Up goods from Hertford GE was cancelled.

The **1882** working timetable showed a weekdays service of nine passenger trains in each direction with three MO and four MX goods trains each way. Passenger services were worked by a Hertford-based engine and goods services by Hatfield locomotives. In the Down direction the 8.25am and 11.35am passenger services ex Hatfield made mandatory calls at Cole Green and Hertingfordbury, but the remaining services only called at Hertingfordbury if required to pick up or set down passengers. In addition the 8.25am, 7.33pm and 10.05pm from Hatfield could convey not exceeding five wagons of cattle. In the Up direction the 9.30am, 10.45am and 8.15pm ex Hertford passenger trains called at both Hertingfordbury and Cole Green, but the remaining services only called at Hertingfordbury if required. The freight traffic in the Down direction was handled by the 1.00amMX ex Hatfield to Hertford GN and Hertford GE, which returned at 2.00am calling at Hertford GN for 15 minutes before arrival back at Hatfield at 3.05am. A goods train operating only when necessary departed Hatfield at 4.00am running directly to Hertford GN arriving at 4.25am, returning at 5.00am directly to Hatfield arriving at 5.25am. This was followed by the 5.50am ex Hatfield, which ran directly to Hertford GN arriving at 6.15am and returning at 7.10am with a 30-minute run to Hatfield. This train when necessary could run on to and start back from Hertford GE, and called when required at Cole Green on Mondays and Tuesdays to collect cattle traffic for Luton and Hitchin markets respectively. The final weekday goods working departed Hatfield at 2.40pm with mandatory calls at Cole Green and Hertingfordbury, Haggar's siding, Hertford GN and Manser's and Gas Works sidings before arrival at Hertford GE at 5.40pm. This train also served Digswell siding, Attimore Hall and Holwell Hyde sidings only if required. The last Up working departed Hertford GE at 6.00pm serving Manser's and Gas Works sidings to arrive at Hertford GN at 6.23pm. After shunting and outsorting wagons the train departed for Hatfield at 8.25pm, serving Haggar's siding if required and made mandatory calls at Hertingfordbury, Cole Green and Digswell siding to arrive at the junction at 9.40pm. The Sunday branch service consisted of one goods and two passenger trains in each direction. The goods service departed Hatfield at 1.00am calling at Hertford GN for 10 minutes and terminating at Hertford GE at 1.45am. The train returned 15 minutes later with a 20-minute stopover at Hertford GN, arriving back at Hatfield at 3.00am. The passenger service, worked by a Hertford engine, departed Hertford at 8.28am and calling at both intermediate stations arrived at Hatfield at 8.53am. The service returned at 9.00am, again serving both intermediate stations and arrived back at Hertford at 10.03am. In the afternoon the engine and stock worked up from Hertford at 6.17pm, calling at Hertingfordbury only if required and Cole Green, reaching Hatfield at 6.42pm. The train returned at 7.50pm, again with mandatory calls at Cole Green and only as required at Hertingfordbury, terminating at Hertford at 8.15pm. Both the 8.28am and 6.17pm Up services were permitted to take not exceeding five wagons of cattle.

By **1883** the service of passenger trains shown below operated across the branch, with connections to King's Cross.

In **1885** the working timetable for weekdays showed a service of ten passenger trains and two MO and three MX goods trains in each direction. Passenger services were allowed 23 minutes running time and in the Down direction the 8.23am and 3.23pm ex Hatfield

Passenger Timetable 1883												
Up		**Weekdays**									**Sundays**	
		am	am	am	pm	pm	pm	pm	pm	pm	am	pm
Hertford	dep	7.45	9.28	10.32	12.08	1.25	4.05	5.30	6.49	8.15	8.28	6.17
Hertingfordbury	dep	*	9.34	*	*	*	*	*	*	8.21	8.35	*
Cole Green	dep	7.55	9.39	10.43	12.17	1.34	4.16	5.39	6.58	8.26	8.40	6.28
Hatfield	arr	8.08	9.53	10.57	12.29	1.46	4.30	5.53	7.10	8.38	8.53	6.42
King's Cross	arr	9.03	10.27	11.30	1.20	2.45	5.14	6.47	7.45	9.15	9.57	7.50
Down		**Weekdays**									**Sundays**	
		am	am	am	pm	pm	pm	pm	pm	pm	am	pm
King's Cross	dep	7.45	9.15	11.10	12.00	1.10	4.20	5.45	7.00	9.30	8.35	6.50
Hatfield	dep	8.25	10.03	11.38	12.35	2.02	5.00	6.20	7.33	10.05	9.40	7.50
Cole Green	dep	8.39	10.17	11.52	12.49	2.16	5.14	6.34	7.47	10.19	9.52	8.04
Hertingfordbury	dep	8.44	*	11.57	*	*	*	*	*	*	9.57	*
Hertford	arr	8.50	10.26	12.03	12.58	2.25	5.23	6.43	7.56	10.28	10.03	8.15
* Stops by signal to take up, and set down on informing the guard at the preceding stopping place.												

HATFIELD AND HERTFORD BRANCH.
SINGLE LINE. TRAIN STAFF STATIONS:—HATFIELD AND HERTFORD, G.N.

DOWN.			WEEK DAYS.													SUNDAYS.			
		1	2	3	4	5	6	7	8	9	10	11	12	13	14	1	2	3	4
		Gds.	Gds.	Gds.	Pass	Pass	Pass	Pass	Pass	Pass	Pass	Pass	Pass	Pass	Pass	Gds.	Pass	Lgt. Eng.	Pass
										E			A	A					
		a.m.	a.m.	a.m.	a.m.	a.m.	a.m.	a.m.	p.m.	p.m.	p.m.	p.m.	p.m.	p.m.	p.m.	a.m.	a.m.	p.m.	p.m.
HATFIELD	dep.	1 15	4 0	3 50	9 33	10 0	11 37	12 37	1 55	3 23	5 0	6 23	7 33	10 5	...	6 45	9 40	5 0	7 30
Manure & Brick Sg.		...	...		...	...	...	...	...	...	...	...	...	...		...	...	...	...
Digswell Siding	arr. dep.	...	...		...	...	...	...	...	...	...	...	...	...		...	...	...	...
Lord Cowper's Sdg.	,,	...	...	X	...	...	...	...	...	...	...	...	...	...		...	...	...	...
Attimore Hall S.	arr. dep.	Mondays excepted	...	X	...	...	...	...	...	...	...	...	...	...		...	...	...	...
Holwell Hyde Sdg.	,,		...	X	...	...	...	...	...	...	...	...	...	...		...	...	...	...
Cole Green	arr. dep.		...	X	8 33 8 34	10 13 10 14	11 50 11 51	12 50 12 51	2 8 2 9	3 33 3 34	5 13 5 14	6 35 6 36	7 46 7 47	10 18 10 19		...	9 51 9 52	...	7 42 7 42
Hertingfordbury	arr. dep.		...		8 38 8 39	*	*	*	*	3 38 3 39	*	*	*	*		...	9 57	...	*
Horn's Mill Siding	,,		...		...	...	...	...	...	...	...	...	...	...		...	...	...	...
HRTFD (G.N.)	arr. dep.	1 46 1 50	4 25 5 30	7 0	8 45	10 23	12 0	1 0	2 13	3 45	5 23	6 45	7 56	10 28		7 10 7 25	10 3	5 20	7 55
Manser's & Gas Works Sdngs.	arr. dep.	...	...		...	...	...	...	...	...	...	...	...	...		...	...	...	...
HRTFD (G.E.)	arr.	2 0	6 40		...	...	...	...	...	...	...	...	...	...		7 35	...	...	...

A May take not exceeding Five wagons of cattle.   B May take one wagon of important goods from Hatfield to Hertford.

GNR working timetable 1885.

UP.			WEEK DAYS.													SUNDAYS.			
		1	2	3	4	5	6	7	8	9	10	11	12	13	14	1	2	3	4
		Gds.	Gds.	Pass	Pass	Pass	Pass	Pass	Pass	Gds.	Pass & Cttl.	Pass	Pass	Pass	Gds.	Gds.	Pass	Pass	Lgt. Eng.
				C													A	A	
		a.m.	a.m.	a.m.	a.m.	a.m.	a.m.	noon	p.m.	p.m.	p.m.	p.m.	p.m.	p.m.	p.m.	a.m.	a.m.	p.m.	p.m.
HRTFD (G.E.)	dep.	2 25	6 50	...	...	...	...	...	1 02	...	...	...	...	...	...	7 50	...	...	...
Manser's & Gas Works Sidings	arr. dep.	2 29 2 33	...	...	...	...	...	...	...	...	...	...	...	...	...	...	...	...	...
HRTFD (GN)	arr. dep.	2 35 2 55	7 0	7 45	6 50	9 30	10 45	12 5	1 25	2 24	4 5	5 42	6 50	8 15	11 0	X	8 0 10 15	8 23	6 17 X	8 10
Horn's Mill Siding	,,			...	...	...	...	...	...	...	...	...	...	...			...	...	...
Hertingfordbury	arr. dep.	Mondays excepted		*	8 55	9 35	10 50	*	*	X	4 15	*	*	8 21	...		...	8 25	*	
Cole Green	arr. dep.			7 53 7 54	8 59 9 0	9 39 9 40	10 44 10 55	12 13 12 14	1 33 1 34	X	4 15 4 16	5 51 5 52	6 58 6 59	8 25 8 26	...	X	...	8 39 8 40	6 27 6 22	
Holwell Hyde Sdg.	,,			...	...	...	...	...	...	...	...	...	...	...		X	...	...	...	
Attimore Hall S.	arr. dep.			...	...	...	...	...	...	...	...	...	...	...		X	...	...	...	
Lord Cowper's Sdg	,,			...	...	...	...	...	...	...	...	...	...	...		X	...	...	...	
Digswell Siding	arr. dep.			...	...	...	...	...	...	...	...	...	...	...		X	...	...	...	
Manure and Brick S.	,,			...	...	...	...	...	...	...	...	...	...	...			...	...	...	
HATFIELD	arr.	3 25	...	8 6	9 11	9 51	11 8	12 26	1 46	3 14	4 30	6 5	7 12	8 38	11 55	10 40	6 33	6 48	9 30

C May take from Cole Green on Mondays one wagon of cattle for Luton, and on Tuesdays one wagon for Hitchin.

called at Cole Green and Hertingfordbury, whilst all other trains called at Hertingfordbury only if required. The 3.23pm was also permitted to take one wagon of important goods from Hatfield to Hertford, whilst the 7.33pm and 10.05pm ex Hatfield could take not exceeding five wagons of cattle. On the Up road the 8.50am and 9.30am ex Hertford called at both Hertingfordbury and Cole Green, whilst all other services only called at Hertingfordbury if required. The 7.45am ex Hertford was permitted to take from Cole Green on Mondays one wagon of cattle destined for Luton, and on Tuesdays one wagon of cattle for Hitchin. The 4.05pm from Hertford was designated as a passenger and cattle train, and was allowed 25 minutes for the run to Hatfield. Of the goods services, the 1.15amMX ex Hatfield was a through working to Hertford GE with a 10-minute stand at Hertford GN. The 4.00am Down working from Hatfield arrived at Hertford at 4.25am and spent 2 hours 5 minutes shunting and outsorting wagons before continuing to Hertford GE, arriving at 6.40am. The remaining Down goods working actually departed Hatfield at 3.50am and called at Digswell, Lord Cowper's, Attimore Hall, Holwell Hyde, Cole Green, Hertingfordbury and Horns Mill sidings if required, arriving at Hertford GN at 7.00am. On the Up road the 2.25amMX ex Hertford GE called at Manser's and Gas Works sidings if required, arriving Hertford GN at 2.35am before departing 20 minutes later for Hatfield arriving at 3.25am. The 6.50am ex Hertford GE was a short working to Hertford GN. The next Up goods train departed Hertford at 2.24pm serving Hertingfordbury and Cole Green with arrival at Hatfield at 3.14pm. The final Up goods working departed Hertford at 11.00pm and served Horns Mill, Holwell Hyde, Attimore Hall, Lord Cowper's and Digswell sidings if required, arriving at Hatfield at 11.55pm. On Sundays the 6.45am Down goods ex Hatfield worked through to Hertford GE arriving at 7.35am, before returning at 7.50am to Hertford GN arriving at 8.00am for the engine to work the 8.28am passenger train to Hatfield calling at both Hertingfordbury and Cole Green, arriving at 8.53am. The engine and stock returned to Hertford, departing Hatfield at 9.40am calling at both intermediate stations with arrival

Sheriff's granary, at the north end of Hatfield station, provided much traffic for the railway and forms the background to this scene. 'J67/2' Class 0-6-0T No. 8572, carrying the rather austere NE on the side tank, is shunting on 28th September 1946.
H.C. Casserley

at 10.03am in time for the locomotive to work the 10.15am goods train back to Hatfield, arriving at 10.40am. In the afternoon a light engine departed Hatfield at 5.00pm to work the 6.17pm Up passenger train ex Hertford, calling at Horns Mill siding if required, Hertingfordbury only if required and Cole Green, with arrival at Hatfield at 6.42pm. The last Down passenger working departed the junction at 7.30pm calling at Cole Green, Hertingfordbury only if required with arrival at Hertford at 7.55pm, after which the engine ran light back to Hatfield departing 8.10pm. It is interesting to note that the 8.28am and 6.17pm passenger services from Hertford were both permitted to take not exceeding five wagons of cattle.

From the early 1890s the GNR introduced a through afternoon express from King's Cross to Hertford. Departing at 4.30pm the train called at Finsbury Park and was then allowed 14 minutes for the 10 miles non-stop run to Potters Bar. The service then called at Hatfield from 4.59pm until 5.04pm and arrived at Hertford at 5.27pm.

The **1896** working timetable showed twelve FX and thirteen FO weekday passenger trains in the Down direction, all calling at Cole Green and Hertingfordbury except the 12.57am ex Hatfield which only called at Cole Green. Services were allowed between 21 and 24 minutes for the run to Hertford and the 8.23am ex Hatfield was permitted to convey cattle wagons if fitted with vacuum brake pipes. In the Up direction twelve passenger trains ran each weekday with the 7.45am ex Hertford allowed to take cattle trucks from Cole Green on Mondays for Luton and Tuesdays for Hitchin if the wagons were fitted with brake pipes. On Saturdays the service was augmented by the 4.20pm mixed train ex Hertford which called at Hertingfordbury and Cole Green with a 27-minute timing to Hatfield. Freight traffic was handled by four MO and five MX workings in the Down direction: the 1.30am ex Hatfield called at Cole Green and Hertingfordbury and ran through to Hertford GE; the 4.40am ex Hatfield was a short working to the Manure & Brick Company siding, whilst the 5.57am ex Hatfield conveyed wagons for both Hertford GN and Hertford GE only. The 6.20am ex Hatfield served Smart's siding and Cole Green, and called at Hertingfordbury and Webb's siding only if required; this train did not continued beyond Hertford GN if the engine worked

A combined GNR/GER loading gauge spans three wooden-bodied ex private owner open wagons in Hertford Cowbridge yard in July 1952. *P. Whitaker*

the 7.55am Up goods to Cole Green calling at Webb's siding and Hertingfordbury and the 8.20am engine and brake van return from Cole Green. The 12.35pm ex Hatfield was a short trip working to Cole Green arriving 1.25pm and calling at Digswell, Lord Cowper's, Attimore Hall and Birchall sidings if required. On the Up road the 2.45amMX ex Hertford GE made only a short stop at Hertford GN and served Webb's siding, Birchall siding and Smart's siding if required, with arrival at Hatfield at 4.00am. The 7.05am ex Hertford GE short working was allowed 30 minutes to Hertford GN serving the Gas Works and Manser's siding if required. The short Down working from Hatfield returned from Cole Green at 1.38pm serving Smart's siding if required, whilst the last Up working for the day, 11.12pm ex Hertford, called at Webb's siding and Hertingfordbury SO and served Birchall, Smart's and Manure & Brick Company sidings only if required. On Sundays the locomotive working the 6.45am goods ex Hatfield through to Hertford GE returned at 7.50am with a goods train to Hertford GN station arriving at 8.00am, in time to work the 8.25am passenger train to Hatfield calling at Cole Green only and arriving at 8.46am. The engine then returned with the 9.53am passenger train ex Hatfield calling at Cole Green and Hertingfordbury arriving at Hertford GN at 10.14am before returning with the 10.35am Up goods working calling at Birchall siding, Smart's siding and Manure & Brick Company siding only if required, with arrival at Hatfield at 12.00 noon. For the Sunday afternoon service a light engine departed Hatfield at 5.00pm with a 22-minute run to Hertford from whence it returned with the 5.25pm Up passenger train to Hatfield. The locomotive then returned with the 7.30pm Down passenger train before returning with the 8.20pm Up mixed train from Hertford calling at Hertingfordbury and Cole Green with Hatfield arrival at 8.48pm.

The **1897** working timetable showed a weekdays service of thirteen passenger FO and twelve FX augmented by four MX and three MO goods trains in the Down direction. The locomotive working the 11.12pm Up goods from Hertford worked the 12.57amFO passenger service ex Hatfield to Hertford, which called at Cole Green before the engine returned light to Hatfield shed. Of the other Down passenger services, the 8.23am ex Hatfield was permitted to take cattle wagons if fitted with brake pipes, whilst all trains called at Cole Green and Hertingfordbury. The first Down goods working departed Hatfield at 1.30amMX and worked through to Hertford

GNR working timetable 1897, Down direction.

GE, whilst the 5.57am ex Hatfield conveyed newspapers and mail to Cole Green and Hertford, and also conveyed wagons destined for Hertford GN and Hertford GE only. The 6.20am ex Hatfield made mandatory calls at Smart's siding and Cole Green, and also Hertingfordbury and Webb's siding only if required, and only ran between Hertford GN and Hertford GE when necessary. If required the engine worked the 7.55am 'Q' 'as and when required' goods train from Hertford to Cole Green calling at Webb's siding and Hertingfordbury, with the engine then returning light with its brake van, departing Cole Green at 8.20am. This train only ran if the 6.20am ex Hatfield omitted calling at Webb's siding and Hertingfordbury on the Down run. The final Down goods of the day departed Hatfield at 12.25pm for Cole Green, calling at Digswell siding, Lord Cowper's siding, Attimore Hall and Birchall siding only if required. On the Up road twelve passenger services operated each weekday with an added mixed train 4.20pmSO ex Hertford. All trains called at Hertingfordbury and Cole Green. The branch was served by five freight trains MSX and four trains MSO. The 2.45amMX ex Hertford GE served Hertford GN and called at Webb's, Birchall and Smart's sidings only if required and arrived at Hatfield at 4.00am. A short trip working departed Hertford GE to Hertford GN serving Gas Works, Manser and Gray & Miles sidings if required. The return working of the 12.25pm Down goods ex Hatfield departed Cole Green at 1.38pm calling at Smart's siding if required, with arrival back at Hatfield at 2.07pm. The next Up goods train departed Hertford GN at 4.05pmSX serving Webb's siding if required and, with mandatory calls at Hertingfordbury and Cole Green, arrived Hatfield at 5.32pm. The final working of the day, the 11.20pm ex Hertford GN, called at Webb's siding and Hertingfordbury on Wednesdays only and served Birchall, Smart's and Manure & Brick sidings only if required, with arrival at the junction at 12.26am. On weekdays a short trip working to the Manure & Brick siding departed Hatfield at 4.40am, the locomotive returning with empty wagons at 5.30am. On Sundays the first Down goods train departed Hatfield at 6.45am working through to Hertford GE with a 15 minutes allowance for shunting at Cowbridge. The train then departed Hertford GE to Hertford GN at 7.50am, when the locomotive worked the 8.25am Up passenger train to Hatfield calling at Cole Green only and arriving at 8.45am. The engine and stock then worked back to Hertford, departing the

GNR working timetable 1897, Up direction.

junction at 9.53am calling at Cole Green and Hertingfordbury and arriving at Cowbridge at 10.14am. The engine then stabled the coaching stock and worked the 10.35am ex Hertford Up goods calling at Birchall siding, Smart's siding and Manure & Brick siding only if required, arriving Hatfield at 12.00 noon. The afternoon workings commenced with a light engine departing Hatfield at 5.00pm to work the 6.25pm Up passenger service from Hertford calling at Cole Green only and arriving at Hatfield at 6.46pm. The last Down passenger service departed Hatfield at 7.30pm arriving at Hertford 21 minutes later, before the engine and stock returned Up road as a mixed train departing the county town at 8.20pm with calls at Hertingfordbury and Cole Green before arriving back at the junction at 8.48pm.

The working timetable for **1900** was virtually identical to that of 1897 save for some minor timing changes. In the Down direction the 6.20am goods ex Hatfield only ran when necessary between Hertford GN and Hertford GE, and was not to stop at Hertingfordbury and Webb's siding if it was liable to delay the 7.45am Up passenger train from Hertford. If this occurred the engine worked a 'Q' 'as and when required' goods train departing Hertford at 7.55am to Cole Green specifically to work Webb's siding and Hertingfordbury, before returning as engine and brake van from Cole Green at 8.20am. The 12.25pm goods train ex Hatfield to Cole Green was extended to Hertford GN and Hertford GE when necessary, arriving at 2.05pm and returning at 2.20pm as a through goods working to Hatfield arriving at 3.47pm. If it was not necessary for the 12.25pm Down goods to travel beyond Cole Green the train returned to Hatfield departing Cole Green at 1.38pm, calling at Smart's siding and arriving at Hatfield at 2.07pm. The 5.04pm and 5.41pm Down passenger trains ex Hatfield departed from the Down main-line platform as they were through workings from King's Cross. The 2.45amMX Up goods from Hertford GE was, when necessary, to take loaded wagons from Brazier's siding and place empty wagons in position, and on such occasions departed Hertford GN at 3.30am instead of 3.05am, running correspondingly later to Hatfield. The 7.45am passenger train ex Hertford was permitted to take cattle traffic from Cole Green on Mondays for Luton market and Tuesdays for Hitchin market provided the wagons were fitted with brake pipes. The 1.20pm ex Hertford passenger train was permitted to take vehicles containing vegetable traffic for Manchester provided the wagons were fitted with brake pipes, the vehicles being transferred to Down main-line goods No. 328 at Hatfield.

The working timetable for **1905** showed a service of thirteen passenger trains in the Down direction on weekdays with an addition

GNR working timetable 1905, Down direction.

12.39amFO train calling at Cole Green and Hertford GN only. All trains called at both intermediate stations whilst the 8.23am ex Hatfield was permitted to take cattle wagons if the vehicles were fitted with brake pipes. The 5.04pm and 5.41pm from Hatfield were through trains from King's Cross and departed from the Down main platform at the junction. Trains were allowed between 21 and 24 minutes for the 9 miles 47 chains journey between Hatfield and Hertford. On the Up road the weekday timetable showed twelve passenger services allowed 20 to 23 minutes for the journey augmented by the 4.20pmSO mixed train which was allowed 27 minutes. The initial train of the day, 7.45am ex Hertford, was permitted to take cattle traffic from Cole Green on Mondays for Luton market and on Tuesdays for Hitchin market provided the wagons were fitted with brake pipes. The 1.20pm ex Hertford could convey vegetable traffic destined for Manchester, again provided the vehicles were fitted with brake pipes, the wagon or wagons being transferred at Hatfield to a Down main-line freight service. Of the freight services, the 1.35amMX ex Hatfield was a through service to Hertford GE arriving at 2.15am after a 15-minute sojourn at Hertford GN. The locomotive returned with the 2.45amMX ex Hertford GE calling at Hertford GN and Webb's siding, Birchall siding and Smart's siding only if required, with arrival back at Hatfield at 4.00am. This train when necessary took loaded wagons from Brazier's siding and placed empties in position and on such occasions departed Hertford at 3.30am and ran correspondingly later throughout to Hatfield. If required this train also attached wagons of gravel at Smart's siding east of Hertford and worked the vehicles to Hatfield. At 4.40am a short 5-minute trip working was made to Manure & Brick siding returning from there at 5.40am. The next Down working from Hatfield departed at 5.57am, conveying newspapers and mail for Cole Green and Hertford, and conveying wagons destined for Hertford GN and Hertford GE only. On arrival at 6.55am the engine returned with the 7.10am Up goods, which served the Gas Works siding and Manser and Gray & Miles sidings if required, and terminated at Hertford GN at 7.30am. After this the engine worked the 7.45am Up passenger train to Hatfield. The convoy of freight did not falter, for the next Down goods departed Hatfield at 6.20am making mandatory calls

GNR working timetable 1905, Up direction.

at Smart's siding and Cole Green, and served Sinclair's and Smart's sidings, Hertingfordbury and Webb's sidings if required before arrival at Hertford GN at 7.35am. The train was only extended to Hertford GE when necessary and was not to serve Hertingfordbury and Webb's siding if it was to delay the 7.45am Up passenger train from Hertford. It the train was extended to Hertford GE the engine and brake van returned at 8.30am arriving at Hertford GN 5 minutes later, when the engine worked the 8.50am Up passenger train. The afternoon goods service departed Hatfield at 12.25pm calling at Digswell, Lord Cowper's, Attimore Hall and Birchall sidings only if required and ran through to Hertford GE arriving at 2.05pm. The train returned at 2.20pm serving Hertford GN for 15 minutes and Cole Green for 32 minutes before arriving back at Hatfield at 3.47pm. The penultimate goods train of the day was the 4.10pm SX ex Hertford, making mandatory calls at Hertingfordbury and Cole Green with conditional calls at Webb's and Smart's sidings, with arrival at Hatfield at 5.37pm. At 7.09pm a path was provided for a light engine to return from Hertford to Hatfield arriving at 7.29pm. The final working, the 11.12pm ex Hertford, called at Webb's siding and Hertingfordbury only on Saturdays and Birchall, Smart's and Manure & Brick sidings only if required, reaching Hatfield at 12.26am. On Sundays the 6.45am goods train ex Hatfield worked through to Hertford GE arriving at 7.40am, with a 15-minute allowance for shunting at Hertford GN. The engine returned with the 7.50am Up goods to Hertford GN before working the 8.25am Up passenger train to Hatfield calling at Cole Green only. The engine and stock then returned with the 9.53am passenger train from Hatfield, which served Cole Green and Hertingfordbury before arriving at Hertford at 10.14am. The locomotive then hauled the 10.35am Up goods train, which made conditional stops at Birchall, Smart's and Manure & Brick sidings only if required, with arrival at Hatfield at 12.00 noon. At 5.00pm the Sunday service resumed with a light engine running to Hertford to work the 6.25pm Up passenger train calling at Cole Green only. After arrival at Hatfield the engine and stock formed the 7.30pm Down passenger service to Hertford calling at Cole Green only, arriving Hertford at 7.51pm before forming the 8.20pm Up mixed train to Hatfield calling at Hertingfordbury and Cole Green with a 28-minute run to the junction.

The **1910** working timetable showed thirteen FX and fourteen FO weekday passenger services in the Down direction, and eleven passenger trains and one mixed train on the Up road. In the Down direction the 8.23am and 11.38am ex Hatfield were permitted to take cattle wagons if the vehicles were fitted with brake pipes whilst the 5.04pm and 5.41pm trains ex Hatfield through trains from King's Cross started from the Down main-line platform instead of

GNR working timetable 1910, Down direction.

the Hertford bay. All trains called at Cole Green and Hertingfordbury and were permitted 21 minutes running time for the 9 miles 47 chains journey. The additional FO Down working departed Hatfield at 1.07am calling at Cole Green but also served Hertingfordbury when required to set down passengers from King's Cross. In the Up direction the SO mixed train departing Hertford at 4.20pm served both intermediate stations and was allowed 27 minutes for the journey. Goods traffic was handled by three MO and four MX trains in the Down direction and 5SX and 3SO services on the Up road. The 1.30amMX ex Hatfield conveyed traffic for Hertford GN and Hertford GE only, as did the 6.00amMO ex Hatfield, whilst the 5.57amMX departure also took wagons containing general goods for delivery to the GER yard, detaching the vehicles in the shed road. This train also conveyed newspapers and mail bags from Hatfield to Cole Green and Hertford. The 6.30am goods ex Hatfield called at Sinclair's and Smart's sidings if necessary and only ran if required between Hertford GN and Hertford GE; this train omitted serving Hertingfordbury and Webb's siding if it would delay the 7.45am Up passenger train from Hertford. The 12.25pm ex Hatfield served Digswell, Lord Cowper's, Attimore Hall and Birchall sidings if required. In the Up direction the 2.45amMX ex Hertford GE when necessary conveyed wagons for Brazier's siding and placed empties in position, and on such occasions departed Hertford GN at 3.30am running correspondingly later to Hatfield. The train also attached gravel wagons at Smart's gravel siding east of Hertford GN and worked the traffic through to Hatfield. The 7.10am ex Hertford GE called at Gas Works and Manser's sidings if required and transferred cattle wagons to Hertford GN, which were then worked forward by the 7.45am passenger train ex Hertford. The 8.20am engine and brake van from Hertford GE to Hertford GN only ran if necessary. The afternoon Up goods 4.15pm ex Hertford called at Webb's and Smart's sidings only if required, whilst the 11.12pm ex Hertford served Birchall, Smart's, and Manure & Brick Company sidings if required and called at Webb's siding and Hertingfordbury on Saturdays only. Two light engine workings operated in the Up direction: 1.38amFO ex Hertford after working the 1.07am Down service from Hatfield, and at 7.09pm after working the 6.25pm Down passenger train ex Hatfield. The Sunday

GNR working timetable 1910, Up direction.

working timetable in 1910 showed the first Down working as a goods train departing Hatfield at 6.45am, which after a 15-minute allowance at Hertford GN worked through to Hertford GE arriving at 7.40am. The engine returned with a goods trip from Hertford GE departing at 7.50am to Hertford GN prior to working the 8.25am Up passenger service to Hatfield calling only at Cole Green. After arrival at 8.46am the engine and stock worked a return passenger service to Hertford departing at 9.33am, calling at Cole Green and Hertingfordbury with arrival at Hertford at 9.54am. The engine after shunting stock formed a goods train which departed Hertford at 10.35am to Hatfield calling at Birchall, Smart's and Manure & Brick Company sidings only if required, with arrival at the junction at 12.00 noon. In the afternoon an engine worked light to Hertford, departing Hatfield at 5.30pm and arriving at 5.52pm to work the 6.25pm Up passenger service calling at Cole Green only with arrival at Hatfield at 6.46pm. The last Down passenger service departed the junction at 7.37pm calling at Cole Green with arrival at Hertford at 7.58pm. The return working ran as a mixed train departing Hertford at 8.20pm and after calling at Hertingfordbury and Cole Green arrived at Hatfield at 8.48pm.

By **1911** the timings between Hertford and King's Cross by the GNR route with a change of trains at Hatfield varied between 55 and 61 minutes for the 27¼ miles journey. In comparison, the fastest time offered on the rival 24¼ miles GER route from Liverpool Street to Hertford was 49 minutes. A typical example of the service offered by the GN during the morning and evening on weekdays was as shown left.

The GNR public timetable for **1915** showed the service below on the branch.

Despite the outbreak of World War One the **1916** weekday train services on the Hertford branch showed few changes. In the Down direction a service of twelve passenger trains were provided with eleven services on the Up road. The conveyance of freight was maintained by three MO and four MX goods trains on the Down road and four MO and five MX services in the Up direction. There was also a 'Q' 'as and when required' engine and brake van short working from Hertford GE to Hertford GN, and a light engine working from Hertford departing 7.09pm after working the 6.25pm Down passenger train from Hatfield. All Down weekday passenger services called at Cole Green and Hertingfordbury, and in addition the 8.23am, 11.36am, 3.16pm, 6.25pm and 9.46pm ex Hatfield could work not exceeding three wagons of cattle if the vehicles were fitted with brake pipes. Not more than one wagon was to be attached behind the rear brake van. If it was necessary to attach more than one wagon behind the rear brake van an additional brake van was to be attached at the rear. The 5.04pm and 5.41pm ex

MORNING AND EVENING PASSENGER TIMETABLE 1911						
Up		am	am	am	am	am/pm
Hertford	dep	7.45	8.50	9.25	10.45	11.40
Hertingfordbury	dep	7.49	8.54	9.29	10.49	11.44
Cole Green	dep	7.54	8.59	9.34	10.54	11.51
Hatfield	arr	8.06	9.11	9.45	11.06	12.03
King's Cross	arr	8.40	9.44	10.20	11.40	12.47
Down		pm	pm	pm	pm	pm	pm
King's Cross	dep	4.39	5.10	5.49	7.00	8.50	10.00
Hatfield	dep	5.04	5.41	6.25	7.33	9.36	10.40
Cole Green	dep	5.18	5.56	6.39	7.45	9.48	10.52
Hertingfordbury	dep	5.22	6.00	6.43	7.49	9.52	10.56
Hertford	arr	5.27	6.05	6.48	7.54	9.57	11.01

PASSENGER TIMETABLE FOR 1915														
Weekdays									SX	SO				
Up		am	am	am	am	am	pm	pm	pm	pm	pm	pm	pm	pm
Hertford	dep	7.45	8.50	9.25	10.45	11.40	1.20	2.35	4.05	4.10	5.45	7.00	8.20	10.10
Hertingfordbury	dep	7.49	8.54	9.29	10.49	11.44	1.24	2.39	4.09	4.14	5.49	7.04	8.24	10.14
Cole Green	dep	7.54	8.59	9.34	10.54	11.51	1.29	2.44	4.14	4.19	5.57	7.09	8.29	10.19
Hatfield	arr	8.06	9.11	9.45	11.06	12.03	1.40	2.56	4.26	4.31	6.08	7.20	8.40	10.30
King's Cross	arr	8.40	9.44	10.20	11.40	12.47	2.27	3.40	5.09	5.09	6.47	7.59	9.16	11.09
Weekdays									H	H				FO
Down		am	am	am	am	am	pm	pm	pm	pm	pm	pm	pm	am
King's Cross	dep	7.45	8.45	9.20	11.10	11.45	1.15	2.30	4.30	5.10	5.49	7.00	9.00	10.00	12.19
Hatfield	dep	8.23	9.20	9.55	11.38	12.21	1.55	3.16	5.04	5.41	6.25	7.33	9.41	10.40	1.07
Cole Green	dep	8.34	9.35	10.07	11.50	12.33	2.07	3.28	5.18	5.56	6.39	7.45	9.53	10.52	1.20
Hertingfordbury	dep	8.38	9.39	10.11	11.54	12.37	2.00	3.32	5.22	6.00	6.43	7.49	9.57	10.58	B
Hertford	arr	8.43	9.44	10.16	11.59	12.42	2.16	3.37	5.27	6.05	6.48	7.54	10.02	11.01	1.28

Sundays Up		am	pm	pm				**Sundays Down**		am	am
Hertford	dep	8.25	6.25	8.20				King's Cross	dep	8.50	7.00
Hertingfordbury	dep	8.29	6.29	8.25				Hatfield	dep	9.39	7.37
Cole Green	dep	8.34	6.34	8.37				Cole Green	dep	9.51	7.49
Hatfield	arr	8.46	6.46	8.48				Hertingfordbury	dep	9.55	7.53
King's Cross	arr	9.53	7.43	9.42				Hertford	arr	10.00	7.58

B Stops when required to set down passengers from King's Cross only, please advise guard at Hatfield.
H Through train London to Hertford.
FO Fridays only between Hatfield and Hertford.

HATFIELD AND HERTFORD BRANCH.

SINGLE LINE TRAIN STAFF STATIONS:—HATFIELD, COLE GREEN, HERTFORD (G.N.) AND HERTFORD JUNCTION (G.E.).

WEEK DAYS.

Distance from Hatfield M.	C.	DOWN.		2 Gds. R a.m.	5 Goods. ER a.m.	5	6 Gds. CG a.m.	8 Pass. A a.m.	9 Pass a.m.	10 Pass. F a.m.		12 Pass. A a.m.	13 Pass. p.m.	14 Gds. p.m.	15 Pass. p.m.	16 Pass. A p.m.	17 Pass. M p.m.	18 Pass. M p.m.
					2 up			5 up	8 up	9 up		10 up	11 up	11 up	12 up	14 up	16 and 17 up	18 up
...	...	HATFIELD	dep.	1 30	6 0	5 57	6 20	8 23	9 20	9 55	...	11 38	12 21	12 25	1 55	3 16	5 4	5 41
...	35	Manure & brick siding	„		...	Conveys Newspapers and Mail Bags from Hatfield to Cole Green and Hertford.	...	...	...	...	...	...	...	...	...	...	...	...
1	64½	Smart's siding	„		...		6 45	...	...	...	...	...	...	...	...	...	...	...
2	76½	Digswell siding	„	Mondays excepted.	...		...	...	...	...	...	...	...	X	...	...	...	...
3	13½	Lord Cowper's siding	„		...		...	...	...	...	...	...	...	X	...	...	...	...
4	19¾	Attimore hall siding	„		...		...	...	...	...	...	...	...	X	...	...	...	...
5	...	Birchall siding	„		...		...	...	...	...	...	...	...	X	...	...	...	...
...	...	Sinclair's siding	„		...		X	...	...	...	...	...	...	...	...	...	...	...
6	30¾	COLE GREEN	arr.	1 48	6 16	6 13	7 0	8 33	9 31	10 6	...	11 49	12 32	1 25	2 6	3 27	5 17	5 55
				1 up					9 up			11 up		12 up		15 up	18 up	19 up
			dep.	1 50	6 18	6 15	7 15	8 34	9 35	10 7	...	11 50	12 33	1 35	2 7	3 28	5 18	5 56
7	75½	Smart's siding	„	...	...	...	X	...	...	...	...	...	...	...	...	...	...	...
8	1¾	Hertingfordbury	arr.	...	Mondays only.	Mondays excepted.	...	8 37	9 38	10 10	...	11 53	12 36	...	2 10	3 31	5 21	5 59
			dep.	...	...	...	X	8 38	9 39	10 11	...	11 54	12 37	...	2 11	3 32	5 22	6 0
8	32¾	Webb's siding	„	...	...	...	X	...	...	...	...	...	...	...	...	...	...	...
9	47	HERTFORD (G.N.)	arr.	2 0	6 28	6 25	7 35	8 43	9 44	10 16	...	11 59	12 42	1 45	2 16	3 37	5 27	6 5
							5 up											
			dep.	2 15	6 48	6 45	7 45	...	...	...	...	...	...	1 55	...	...	...	...
10	50¼	HERTFORD (G.E.)	arr.	2 25	6 58	6 55	8 0	...	...	...	...	...	...	2 5	...	...	...	...

DOWN—continued.		WEEK DAYS—continued. 19 Pass. A p.m.	20 Pass. F p.m.	22 Pass. A p.m.	SUNDAYS. 1 Gds. a.m.	2 Pass. a.m.	3 Lgt. Eng. p.m.	4 Pass. p.m.
		19 up	20 and 21 up	22 up		2 up		3 up
HATFIELD	dep.	6 25	7 33	9 46	6 45	9 39	5 30	7 37
Manure & brick siding	„	...	...	...	...	...	...	...
Smart's siding	„	...	...	...	...	...	...	...
Digswell siding	„	...	...	...	...	...	...	...
Lord Cowper's siding	„	...	...	...	...	...	...	...
Attimore hall siding	„	...	...	...	...	...	...	...
COLE GREEN	arr.	6 38	7 44	9 57	7 3	9 50	5 41	7 48
	dep.	6 39	7 45	9 58	7 5	9 51	5 42	7 49
Smart's siding	„	...	...	...	...	...	...	...
Hertingfordbury	arr.	6 42	7 48	10 1	...	9 54	...	...
	dep.	6 43	7 49	10 2	...	9 55	...	7 53
Webb's siding	„	...	...	...	...	...	...	...
HERTFORD (G.N.)	arr.	6 48	7 54	10 7	7 15	10 0	5 52	7 58
	dep.	...	...	...	7 30	...	...	...
HERTFORD (G.E.)	arr.	...	...	...	7 40	...	...	...

WEEK DAYS.

Distance from Hertford, G.E. M.	C.	UP.		2 Gds. I a.m.	4 Gds. P a.m.	5 Pass. BP a.m.	7 Eng. & Bk a.m.	8 Pass. a.m.	9 Pass. a.m.	10 Pass. a.m.	11 Pass. a.m.	12 Pass. p.m.		14 Pass. p.m.	15 Gds. p.m.	16 Pass. p.m.	17 Pass. p.m.	18 Goods. p.m.	18 Goods. p.m.
...	...	HERTFORD (G.E.)	dep.	2 45	7 10	...	8 30	...	...	...	...	...	...	...	2 20				
...	27¾	Gas works siding	„		X	...	...	...	...	...	...	...	...	...	...				
...	...	Manser's & Gray & Miles' sdgs	„	Mons. expt.	X	...	...	...	...	...	...	...	...	...	...	Sats. exceptd.	Sats. only.	Sats. excepted.	Sats. only.
...	...	McMullen's siding	„		...	...	...	...	...	...	...	...	...	...	...				
1	3¼	HERTFORD (G.N.)	arr.	2 55	7 30	...	8 35	...	...	...	...	...	...	...	2 30				
						6 dn		8 dn						15 dn		16 dn	16 dn		
			dep.	3 5	...	7 45	...	8 50	9 25	10 45	11 40	1 20	...	2 35	2 45	4 5	4 10	4 15	4 20
2	17¾	Webb's siding	„	X	...	...	...	...	...	...	...	...	...	...	S	...	...	X	X
2	48¾	Hertingfordbury	arr.	...	...	7 48		8 53	9 28	10 48	11 43	1 23	...	2 38	...	4 8	4 13	4 23	4 28
			dep.	...	...	7 49		8 54	9 29	10 49	11 44	1 24	...	2 39	T	4 9	4 14	4 45	4 50
2	55	Smart's siding	„	...	...	...		...	...	...	...	...	...	...	...	...	...	X	X
4	19⅞	COLE GREEN	arr.	3 20	...	7 53	When necessary.	8 58	9 33	10 53	11 48	1 28	...	2 43	2 55	4 13	4 18	4 53	4 58
									9 dn		12 dn	14 dn			16 dn			17 dn	17 dn
			dep.	3 22	...	7 54		8 59	9 34	10 54	11 51	1 29	...	2 44	3 27	4 14	4 19	5 10	5 19
		Sinclair's siding	„	...	...	...		...	...	...	...	...	...	...	...	...	...	...	...
5	50½	Birchall siding	„	X	...	...		...	...	...	...	...	...	...	...	...	...	...	...
6	30¾	Attimore hall siding	„	...	...	...		...	...	...	...	...	...	...	...	...	...	...	...
7	37	Lord Cowper's siding	„	...	...	...		...	...	...	...	...	...	...	...	...	...	...	...
7	54	Digswell siding	„	...	...	...		...	...	...	...	...	...	...	...	...	...	...	...
8	66	Smart's siding	„	X	...	...		...	...	...	...	...	...	...	...	...	...	...	...
10	15½	Manure & brick siding	„	...	...	...	...	...	...	...	...	...	...	...	...	...	...	...	...
10	50¼	HATFIELD	arr.	4 0	...	8 6	...	9 11	9 45	11 6	12 3	1 40	...	2 56	3 47	4 26	4 31	5 37	5 37

UP—continued.		WEEK DAYS—continued 19 Pass. p.m.	20 Pass. p.m.	21 Lt. Eg p.m.	22 Pass. p.m.	26 Gds. p.m.	SUNDAYS. 1 Gds. a.m.	2 Pass. a.m.	3 Pass. p.m.	4 Mixd. p.m.
HERTFORD (G.E.)	dep.	...	...	...	...	...	7 50	...	...	...
Gas works siding	„	...	...	...	...	...	...	...	...	...
Manser's & Gray & Miles' siding	„	...	...	...	...	...	...	...	...	...
McMullen's siding	„	...	...	...	...	...	...	...	...	...
HERTFORD (G.N.)	arr.	...	...	...	...	...	8 0	...	...	...
		17 dn	19 dn		20 dn	22 dn	2 dn	1 dn	3 dn	4 dn
	dep.	5 45	7 0	7 9	8 20	10 30	10 35	8 25	6 25	8 20
Webb's siding	„	...	...	...	...	D	...	...	...	...
Hertingfordbury	arr.	5 48	7 3	...	8 23	D	...	...	...	8 24
	dep.	5 49	7 4	...	8 24	...	...	8 29	6 29	8 25
Smart's siding	„	...	...	...	...	...	...	...	...	...
COLE GREEN	arr.	5 53	7 8	7 17	8 28	10 43	10 50	8 33	6 33	8 31
		18 dn								
	dep	5 57	7 9	7 18	8 29	10 44	10 52	8 34	6 34	8 37
Sinclair's siding	„	...	...	...	...	...	...	...	...	...
Birchall siding	„	...	...	...	...	X	X	...	...	...
Digswell siding	„	...	...	...	...	...	...	...	...	...
Smart's siding	„	...	...	...	...	X	X	...	...	...
Manure & brick siding	„	...	...	...	...	X	X	...	...	...
HATFIELD	arr.	6 8	7 20	7 29	8 40	11 39	12 0	8 46	6 46	8 48

A May take not exceeding 3 wagons cattle if wagons are fitted with brake pipes. Not more than 1 wagon may be attached behind rear brake. If it be necessary to attach more than one wagon behind rear brake an additional brake van must be attached at extreme rear. B May take not exceeding 3 wagons cattle from Cole Green on Mondays for Luton and on Tuesdays for Hitchin if wagons are fitted with brake pipes. C When necessary Hertford G.N. to G.E. D Will stop on Saturdays only. E Takes wagons for Hertford G.N. and for G.E. line only. F May take not exceeding three wagons cattle if wagons are fitted with brake pipes, and these may be attached, if necessary, next engine. G No. 6 down goods must not stop at Hertingfordbury and Webb's Siding if likely to delay 5 up passenger train. I No. 2 up will, when necessary, take loaded wagons for Brazier's Siding and place empties in position, and on such occasions will leave Hertford at 3.30 a.m. and run correspondingly later to Hatfield; also attaches gravel at Smart's gravel pit, east of Hertford, and works same to Hatfield when necessary. M 17 and 18 down start from Hatfield down main line platform. P Cattle traffic from G.E. line transferred at Hertford by 4 up goods may be conveyed to Hatfield by 5 up passenger train. The wagons must be attached to the rear of the passenger train, and a brake van attached behind the cattle. R 2 and 5 down must take wagons containing general goods for delivery to the G.E. yard and detach in Shed road. Refrigerator vans containing meat must be left in Shed road at G.N. station. 2 down to stop at Hertford New siding, when necessary, to attach empties. Hertford to instruct guard of 26 up when it is necessary for 2 down to stop. S Will call at Webb's Siding to attach wagons from Contractor and to transfer gravel from Hertingfordbury Pit to Webb's Siding when necessary. Stationmaster, Hertingfordbury, to advise Hertford when the train is required to call at the Siding. T May convey gravel from Hertingfordbury on Saturdays when necessary.

Traffic for Messrs. McAlpine and Sons must be placed in the new siding near Hertford Down distant signal, instead of being put into Messrs. Webb's Siding, Hertingfordbury. If there is not time for down trains to detach traffic at the new siding and reach Hertford without causing delay to up passenger trains the wagons must be taken through to Hertford and then propelled to the siding.

GNR working timetable 1916.

Hatfield being through services from King Cross started from the Down main platform. The 9.55am and 7.33pm ex Hatfield could take not exceeding three wagons of cattle if the wagons were fitted with brake pipes and these could be attached if necessary behind the engine. In the Up direction all passenger services called at Hertingfordbury and Cole Green. Of the Down goods trains the 1.30amMX, 6.00amMO and 5.57amMX ex Hatfield were required to take wagons containing general goods for delivery to Hertford GE yard for detaching in the shed road. Refrigerated vans containing meat had to be left in the shed road at Hertford GN. All three trains conveyed wagons for Hertford GN and Hertford GE only, and in addition the 5.57amMX conveyed newspapers and mailbags for Cole Green and Hertford. The 6.20am Down goods ex Hatfield when necessary was extended beyond Hertford GN to Hertford GE and was not to call at Hertingfordbury or Webb's siding if it would delay the 7.45am Up passenger service from Hertford. This train also served Sinclair's and Smart's sidings. Digswell, Lord Cowper's, Attimore Hall and Birchall sidings were served by the 12.25pm ex Hatfield. In the Up direction the 2.45amMX ex Hertford GE when necessary conveyed loaded wagons for Brazier's siding and placed empties in position and departed Hertford GN at 3.30am instead of 3.05am. The 7.05am ex Hertford GE served Gas Works and Manser's sidings if required, whilst the 8.30am engine and brake van ex Hertford GE only ran if required. In the afternoon the

Working Timetable for 1919

Down Weekdays		5 Gds MO am	5 Gds MX am	6 Gds CG am	8 Pass am	9 Pass am	10 Pass am	13 Pass pm	14 Gds pm	15 Pass pm	17 Pass pm	18 Pass pm	19 Pass pm	20 Pass pm		
Hatfield	dep	6.00	5.57	6.20	8.23	9.20	9.55	12.21	12.25	1.55	5.04	5.41	6.25	7.57		
Manure & Brick siding																
Smart's siding				6.45												
Digswell siding									X							
Lord Cowper's siding									X							
Attimore Hall siding									X							
Birchall siding									X							
Sinclair's siding																
Cole Green	arr	6.16	6.13	7.00	8.33	9.31	10.06	12.32	1.20	2.06	5.17	5.55	6.38	8.08		
	dep	6.18	6.15	7.15	8.34	9.35	10.07	12.33	1.35	2.07	5.18	5.56	6.39	8.09		
Smart's siding				X												
Hertingfordbury	arr				8.37	9.38	10.10	12.36		2.10	5.21	5.59	6.42	8.12		
	dep			X	8.38	9.39	10.11	12.37		2.11	5.22	6.00	6.43	8.13		
Webb's siding				X												
Hertford GN	arr	6.28	6.25	7.35	8.43	9.44	10.16	12.42	1.45	2.16	5.27	6.05	6.48	8.19		
	dep	6.48	6.45	7.45					1.55							
Hertford GE	arr	6.58	6.55	8.00					2.05							

Up Weekdays		4 Gds P am	5 Pass P am	7 E&B Q am	8 Pass am	9 Pass am	10 Pass am	11 Pass am	12 Pass pm	15 Gds pm	17 Pass pm	18 Gds pm	19 Pass pm	20 Pass pm	22 Pass pm	25 Gds pm
Hertford GE	dep	7.10		8.30						2.20						
Gas Works siding		X														
Manser's & Gray & Miles' sdg		X														
McMullens siding																
Hertford GN	arr	7.30		8.35						2.30						
	dep		7.45		8.50	9.25	10.40	11.33	1.15	A	4.10	4.20	5.45	7.10	8.28	8.45
Webb's siding												X				D
Hertingfordbury	arr		7.48		8.53	9.28	10.43	11.38	1.18		4.13	4.28	5.48	7.13	8.31	
	dep		7.49		8.54	9.29	10.44	11.39	1.19		4.14	4.50	5.49	7.14	8.32	D
Smart's siding												X				
Cole Green	arr		7.53		8.58	9.33	10.48	11.43	1.23		4.18	4.48	5.53	7.18	8.36	8.58
	dep		7.54		8.59	9.34	10.49	11.44	1.24		4.19	5.19	5.57	7.19	8.37	9.15
Sinclair's siding																
Birchall siding																X
Digswell siding																
Smart's siding																X
Manure & Brick siding																X
Hatfield	arr		8.16		9.11	9.45	11.00	11.55	1.35		4.31	5.37	6.08	7.30	8.48	9.53

2.20pm ex Hertford GE, 2.45pm ex Hertford GN service, called at Webb's siding to attach wagons from contractors and transfer gravel from Hertingfordbury to Webb's siding when necessary, the station master at Hertingfordbury advising Hertford when the train required to call at the siding. This train also conveyed gravel from Hertingfordbury SO. The 4.15pmSX, 4.20pmSO Up service called at Webb's siding and Smart's sidings if required, whilst the final train of the day, 10.30pm ex Hertford, called at Webb's siding and Hertingfordbury on SO as well as serving Birchall, Smart's and Manure & Brick Company sidings if required, terminating at Hatfield at 11.39pm. At this period the construction of the Wood Green to Stevenage extension was well under way and the branch played a key role in the works. A footnote advised that traffic for Messrs McAlpine & Sons must be placed in the new siding near Hertford Down distant signal, instead of being put into Messrs Webb's siding, Hertingfordbury. If there was not time for Down trains to detach traffic at the new siding and reach Hertford without causing delay to Up passenger trains the wagons had to be taken through to Hertford and then propelled to the siding. The working timetable for Sunday 1916 showed the first Down working as the 6.45am goods train ex Hatfield to Hertford GN and arriving at Hertford GE at 7.40am. The engine returned with the Up goods at 7.50am to Hertford GN from whence it worked the 8.25am passenger train to Hatfield calling at Cole Green only and with arrival at 8.46am. The engine then returned with the 9.39am Down passenger train calling at both Cole Green and Hertingfordbury, arriving at Hertford at 10.00am, from where it departed at 10.35am with the Up goods train which had conditional stops at Birchall, Smart's and Manure & Brick Company sidings before reaching Hatfield at 12.00 noon. The Sunday service resumed with a light engine departing Hatfield at 5.30pm to work the 6.25pm Up passenger service from Hertford calling only at Cole Green with arrival at the junction at 6.46pm. The first afternoon Down passenger service departed Hatfield at 7.37pm calling at Cole Green only with arrival at Hertford at 7.58pm before the engine and stock formed the final Up passenger service departing at 8.20pm serving both intermediate stations, and because of a 6-minute stand at Cole Green, reached Hatfield at 8.48pm.

The post-war working timetable for **1919** showed a slight increase in the branch services.

Down Sundays		1 Gds am	2 Pass am	3 LE pm			Up Sundays		1 Gds S am	2 Pass am	3 Pass pm
Hatfield	dep	6.45	9.39	5.30			Hertford GE	dep	7.50		
Manure & Brick siding							Gas Works siding				
Smart's siding							Manser's & Grays & Miles' sdg				
Digswell siding							McMullens siding				
Lord Cowper's siding							Hertford GN	arr	8.00		
Attimore Hall siding								dep	10.35	8.25	6.25
Birchall siding							Webbs siding				
Sinclair's siding							Hertingfordbury	arr			6.28
Cole Green	arr	7.03	9.50	5.41				dep		8.29	6.29
	dep	7.04	9.51	5.42			Smart's siding				
Smart's siding							Cole Green	arr	10.50	8.33	6.33
Hertingfordbury	arr		9.54					dep	10.52	8.34	6.34
	dep		9.55				Sinclair's siding				
Webb's siding							Birchall siding		X		
Hertford GN	arr	7.15	10.00	5.52			Digswell siding				
	dep	7.30					Smart's siding		X		
Hertford GE	arr	7.40					Manure & Brick siding		X		
							Hatfield	arr	12.00	8.46	6.46

A Engine to work No. 18 Up train.
C Will run when necessary Hertford GN to Hertford GE.
D Will stop on Saturdays only.
E Takes wagons for Hertford GN and for GE line only.
G No. 6 Down goods must not stop at Hertingfordbury and Webb's siding if likely to delay No. 5 Up passenger train.
H Will not convey cattle traffic. Horse boxes and carriage trucks will not be conveyed from Cole Green.
P Cattle traffic from GE line transferred by No. 4 Up goods may be conveyed to Hatfield by No. 5 Up passenger train. The wagons must be attached to the rear of the passenger train and a brake van attached behind the cattle wagons.
Q Runs when required.
R No. 5 Down must take wagons containing general goods for delivery to the GE yard and detach in shed road. Refrigerator vans containing meat must be left in the shed road at the GN station.
S Engine to work No. 2 Up and No. 2 Down passenger trains.
   Horse boxes and other 4-wheeled vehicles containing passenger rated traffic may be conveyed on any ordinary passenger train except that No's 8 and 9 Up will convey such traffic from Cole Green.
   In the event of a goods service not being available 1 to 3 wagons of cattle if fitted with brake pipes may be attached to any ordinary passenger train except No's 8 and 9 Up.
X Calls if required.

In **1922**, the final year of GNR ownership, the working timetable showed a weekday service of nine passenger and four goods trains in the Down direction balanced by ten passenger, four goods trains and one light engine working on the Up road. All Down passenger services were allowed 21 minutes for the 9 miles 47 chains journey, except the 12.10pmSO, 4.58pmSX and 6.25pmSX which called at Welwyn Garden City to take up or leave contractors' workmen only, and were allowed 2 minutes extra running time. In the Up direction all passenger services called at both intermediate stations and were also allowed 21 minutes for the journey save the 7.42am ex Hertford which called at Welwyn Garden City to take up or leave contractors' workmen and was allowed 24 minutes. Of the goods services, the 6.00amMO and 5.57amMX ex Hatfield conveyed wagons for Hertford GN and GE only, whilst the latter service conveyed newspapers and mail bags from Hatfield to Cole Green and Hertford; this service also conveyed wagons containing general goods for delivery to the GE yard and detached them in the shed road. Refrigerated vans containing meat were to be left in the shed road at the GN station. The 6.20am ex Hatfield made a mandatory call at Smart's siding and conditional calls at Sinclair's and Smart's sidings, Hertingfordbury and Webb's siding, and was extended beyond Hertford GN to Hertford GE if required. This train was not to call at Hertingfordbury or Webb's siding if it was likely to delay the 7.42am Up passenger service from Hertford. The 12.25pm goods from Hatfield called at Digswell, Lord Cowper's, Attimore Hall and Birchall sidings if necessary and ran through to Hertford GE, whilst a short trip working departed Herford GN to Hertford GE at 7.55pm. In the Up direction, the 7.10am ex Hertford GE to Hertford GN made conditional calls at Gas Works and Manser's sidings as well as conveying cattle traffic from the GER which was worked forward to Hatfield by the 7.42am Up passenger train ex Hertford. The engine working the 2.20pm from Hertford GE, after standing and shunting at Hertford GN, worked the 4.20pm Up goods calling at Webb's siding and Smart's sidings if required, arriving at Hatfield at 5.31pm. The final Up working, departing Hertford GE at 7.15pm, served intermediate sidings if required before arrival at Hertford GN at 7.25pm. The engine then worked the 8.40pm Up goods calling at Webb's siding and Hertingfordbury SO and Smart's and Welwyn Garden City sidings if required with arrival at Hatfield at 9.53pm. The 8.20pm ex Hertford GE engine and brake van to Hertford GN only ran when necessary. On Sundays in 1922 one passenger, one goods train and a light engine worked in the Down direction balanced by two passenger and one goods train on the Up road. In the Down direction the engine working the 6.45am goods train ex Hatfield worked through to Hertford GE with 15-minute layover at Hertford GN. The goods train returned from Hertford GE at 7.50am when the engine then worked a round trip to Hatfield departing Hertford at 8.25am with a passenger train calling at Cole Green only, arriving at the junction at 8.46am before returning with the 9.39am ex Hatfield Down passenger working calling at Cole Green and Hertingfordbury with arrival at Hertford at 10.00am. The engine then worked the 10.35am Up goods serving Birchall, Smart's and Manure & Brick Company sidings if required with arrival at Hatfield at 12.00 noon. For the afternoon service a light engine departed Hatfield at 5.30pm arriving at Hertford at 5.52pm in good time to work the 6.25pm Up passenger calling at Cole Green only with arrival at Hatfield at 6.46pm.

The miners' strike in **1926** brought a reduction in services as the L&NER, bereft of essential coal supplies, reduced train mileage to conserve fuel. On the Hatfield to Hertford North branch the passenger service was reduced to seven SX and eight SO trains in the Down directions and seven trains in the Up direction. No Sunday services were operated. Departures from Hatfield were 8.23am, 9.20am, 12.10pm, 3.06pmSO, 5.07pm, 5.42pm, 6.32pm and 7.40pm, whilst Up services left Hertford North at 7.42am, 8.50am, 9.25am, 11.35am, 4.20pm, 5.43pm and 7.04pm.

The opening of the new Hertford North station on and from **2nd June 1924** and the diversion of the main services from King's Cross to Hertford to the new line via Wood Green and Enfield Chase resulted in a drastic alteration to services on the Hatfield to Hertford branch, which was relegated to a secondary route. The **1928** working timetable showed a weekday service of seven SX and nine SO passenger services in the Down direction, with all trains calling at the new station at Welwyn Garden City as well as Cole Green and Hertingfordbury, and terminating at Hertford North with timings varying from 22 to 24 minutes for the 9 miles 04 chains journey. A feature of the SX timetable was the absence of a train between 12.08pm and the 5.07pm ex Hatfield, which was rectified SO by the running of the 1.52pm and 3.06pm ex Hatfield. In the Up direction, eight passenger services operated on weekdays between Hertford North and Hatfield with timings between 21 and 24 minutes and all trains calling at all stations. Horseboxes and other 4-wheel vehicles containing passenger-rated traffic could be conveyed on any passenger train except the 8.50am and 9.25am ex Hertford North which could not convey such traffic from Cole Green. In the event of goods services not being available up to three wagons of cattle, if the vehicles were fitted with brake pipes, could be attached to any passenger train except the 8.50am and 9.25am Up services from Hertford North. Freight traffic on weekdays was handled by five MO and six MX goods trains in the Down direction and eight services in the Up direction, although some were only short trip workings. On the Down road the day began with the 1.00amMX Class 'B' ex-Hatfield which ran through to Hertford East and conveyed wagons for Stratford Market. After arrival at Hertford East at 1.40am the train returned direct to Hatfield as a Class 'B' departing at 2.15am with a 42-minute timing to the junction. The next Down working departed Hatfield at 5.45am as a Class 'B' train conveying newspapers and mailbags to Cole Green and Hertford Old Yard. With 20 minutes allowed at the former GNR station the train terminated at Hertford East at 6.43am. This train returned at 6.52am serving Gas Works and Manser's sidings if required with arrival at Hertford Old at 7.18pm. A third Down goods, running as Class 'D', departed Hatfield at 6.20am calling at Welwyn Garden City, Digswell siding to drop off newspapers, Holwell siding, Hertingfordbury and Webb's siding if required, then a 10-minute stop at Hertford Old before terminating at Hertford East at 8.10am. This working returned from Hertford East at 8.20am to terminate at Hertford Old 5 minutes later. A Class 'D' goods departed Hatfield at 10.00am calling at Digswell siding to detach only and Lord Cowper's siding before terminating at Cole Green at 11.06am, from whence it returned at 11.20am calling at Holwell siding if required and terminating at Hatfield at 11.40am. The next Class 'D' goods departed Hatfield at 12.25pm and served Digswell, Lord Cowper's, Attimore Hall and Birchall sidings if required with 15 minutes at Cole Green, then 10 minutes at Hertford Old to terminate at Hertford East at 2.17pm. Returning at 2.27pm to Hertford Old, the engine then worked the 4.20pm passenger train from Hertford North to Hatfield. The 1.45pmSX Class 'D' goods ex Hatfield was another short working to Cole Green calling at Digswell siding; this train also served Twentieth

Mile siding departing 2.05pm and the Shredded Wheat Company siding departing 2.30pm. After terminating at Cole Green at 3.03pm the train returned at 3.15pm, calling at Holwell siding with arrival at Hatfield at 3.50pm. A light engine working from Hertford North departing 8.12pmSX to Hertford East provided the motive power for the 8.50pm Up goods to Hatfield calling at Hertford Old, Webb's, Hertingfordbury, Cole Green, Holwell, Birchall, Twentieth Mile and Mount Pleasant sidings, all if required, with arrival at Hatfield at 11.50pm. On SO the train departed Hertford East at 9.00pm with a mandatory call at Hertford Old and conditional calls at Hertingfordbury, Cole Green, Holwell, Birchall sidings then Welwyn Garden City with arrival at Hatfield at 10.50pm. Only one goods service worked across the branch on a Sunday, departing Hertford East at 1.15am with arrival at Hatfield at 1.54am, worked by the engine of the 12.00 midnightSO Down goods from Hatfield; this Up train conveyed traffic from Mint Street, Victoria Docks and Thames Wharf destined for stations south of Peterborough.

The **July 1930** working timetable for the branch showed seven SX and nine SO passenger trains in the Down direction on weekdays together with five MO and six MX goods trains, although not all of the latter ran the full distance and were short workings. The service was augmented by paths for two light engine movements SX: at 4.05pm from Hatfield to Hertford Old station and 8.12pm from Hertford North to Hertford East. Of the Down passenger services, all trains called at all stations with timings varying from 20 to 25 minutes for the journey between Hatfield and Hertford North. The additional SO services departed Hatfield at 1.52pm and 3.06pm, thus on SX there was no service from Hatfield for almost five hours, reflecting the change in travel patterns with passengers from London using the direct line via Enfield Chase and the greater use by the populace of the local bus services. Horseboxes and other 4-wheel vehicles containing passenger-rated traffic could be conveyed by any Down passenger train. In the event of a goods service not being available up to three wagons of cattle could be attached to any passenger service provided the wagons were fitted with brake pipes. The initial Down goods working on weekdays was the 1.00am MX Class 'B' ex Hatfield through to Hertford East, which conveyed traffic from stations south of Peterborough for Mint Street and Victoria Docks and also vegetable traffic for Stratford Market. The 5.45am Class 'B' ex Hatfield conveyed newspapers and mail bags from Hatfield to Cole Green and Hertford Goods and also conveyed wagons containing general goods for delivery to Hertford East yard. This was followed by the 6.20am Class 'D' ex Hatfield which served Smart's siding, unloaded newspapers at Digswell siding and called at Holwell siding only of required. After 15 minutes at Cole Green the train called at Hertingfordbury and Webb's siding only if required before continuing to Hertford Old and Hertford East. This train was not to stop at Hertingfordbury and Webb's siding if it was likely to delay the 7.40am passenger train ex Hertford North. A 'Q' 'as and when required' Class 'D' train departed Hatfield at 10.00am for Cole Green, detaching wagons at Welwyn Garden City and with a mandatory call at Digswell siding called at Lord Cowper's, Attimore Hall and Birchall sidings only if required. Another Class 'D' freight departed Hatfield at 12.25pm serving Digswell and Holwell sidings if required before continuing to Hertford Old and Hertford East. This was followed by a the 1.45pm Class 'D' from Hatfield to Welwyn Garden City serving Twentieth Mile siding and the Shredded Wheat siding en route. The last train of the day was the 12.00 midnightSO Class 'B' through to Hertford East conveying wagons for Stratford Market next the engine, this train also conveyed traffic from south of Peterborough for Mint Street and Victoria Dock and vegetable traffic for Stratford Market. Two light engine paths were also provided at 4.05pmSX ex Hatfield to Hertford Old Goods and 8.17pmSX working from Hertford North to Hertford East. In the Up direction the timetable showed eight passenger trains on weekdays augmented by seven MSO and eight MSX goods trains together with one light engine working. All Up passenger services called at all stations between Hertford North and Hatfield, with the last train departing Hertford North in the evening as early as 7.04pm. As with Down services, horseboxes and other 4-wheel vehicles containing passenger-rated traffic could be conveyed by any passenger service except the 8.50am and 9.25am ex Hertford North which could not convey such traffic from Cole Green. Up to three wagons of cattle could be attached to any passenger train except the above two services from Hertford North provided the vehicles were fitted with brake pipes. The Up goods train service commenced with the 2.35amMX Class 'B' ex Hertford East which conveyed traffic from Mint Street, Victoria Docks and Thames Wharf for stations south of Peterborough, working through to Hatfield arriving at 3.13am, followed by the 6.58am Class 'D' trip working from Hertford East to Hertford Old calling on the way at Gas Works and Manser and Gray & Miles sidings if required. Another trip working departed Hertford East at 8.20am with a 5-minute timing to Hertford Old. At 11.20am the return 'Q' 'as and when required' goods departed Cole Green for Hatfield calling at Holwell siding if required, whilst the 3.40pmSX Class 'D' ex Welwyn Garden City returned to Hatfield arriving at 3.50pm. At 2.27pm a short trip working ran from Hertford East to Hertford Old ready to shunt the yard and form the 7.20pm Up goods to Hatfield calling at Webb's siding and Hertingfordbury if required and Welwyn Garden City to pick up transshipments before arriving at the junction at 8.25pm. The last working of the day departed Hertford East at 9.00pm, the SX train calling at Webb's siding if required, Hertingfordbury, Cole Green, Holwell and Birchall sidings, Welwyn Garden City and Mount Pleasant siding, with arrival at Hatfield at 11.50pm. On SO the train called at Hertingfordbury, Cole Green and then Holwell and Birchall sidings and Welwyn Garden City only if required, with the earlier arrival at Hatfield at 10.50pm. Both the SX and SO services were worked by two guards. The one Sunday working was a Class 'B' goods train which departed Hertford East 1.15am working through to Hatfield arriving 1.55am, conveying traffic from Mint Street, Victoria Docks and Thames Wharf for stations south of Peterborough.

The working timetable for **1936** showed eight passenger services WSX, nine WO and ten SO trains in the Down direction together with nine SX and ten SO passenger services on the Up road. In the Down direction the 5.55am ex Hatfield ran non-stop between Welwyn Garden City and Hertford North with all other services calling at Cole Green and Hertingfordbury. The 1.52pm ex Hatfield operated WSO with arrival at Hertford North at 2.16pmSO and 2.17pmWO. As in previous years, horseboxes and other 4-wheel vehicles containing passenger rated traffic could be conveyed on any Down passenger train. In the event of a goods service not being available up to three wagons of cattle could be attached to any passenger train provided the vehicles were fitted with brake pipes. On the Up road all passenger trains served Hertingfordbury, Cole Green and Welwyn Garden City. The additional Saturday services departed Hertford North at 2.34pm and 9.30pm. As with the Down services, horseboxes and other 4-wheel vehicles containing passenger rated traffic could be conveyed on any passenger train except the

HATFIELD AND HERTFORD BRANCH.

SINGLE LINE (Staff and Ticket). TRAIN STAFF STATIONS:—HATFIELD, COLE GREEN AND HERTFORD NORTH (Long Section Staff Hatfield to Hertford North when Cole Green closed).
*** HERTFORD NORTH AND HERTFORD EAST JUNCTION.**

A metal ticket with Annett's key attached is provided for Cole Green and Hatfield Section for purpose of unlocking the points of intermediate sidings.
* See instruction under heading "Hertford North" on page 137 of appendix to W.T.T.

WEEK DAYS.

Distance from Hatfield M.	C.	DOWN.	1	3	4		6	7	9	10		11	12	13		14	15	16	17	18	19		20	21	23	24
			Gds.	Gds.	Pass		Gds.	Pass	Pass	Gds.		Pass	Gds.	Gds.		Pass	Pass	Lgt Eng	Pass	Pass	Pass		Pass	Lgt. Eng	Lgt. Eng	Gds.
		Class of Train	B	B			D			D			D	D	D											B
			MX											WSX	WO	WSO	SO	WSX			SX	SO			SO	SO
M.	C.		a.m	a.m.	a.m.		a.m.	a.m.	a.m.	a.m.		p.m.	p.m.	p.m.	p.m.	p.m.	p.m	p.m	p.m	p.m	p.m	p.m.	p.m	p.m	p.m.	mdt.
			J	e			H	5 up	7 up	F			12up						17up				21up			J
...	...	HATFIELD .... dep.	1 0	5 35	5 55	...	6 2	8 21	9 20	10 0	...	1214	1225	1 45	1 58	1 52	3 6	4 15	5 7	5 40	6 26	6 32	7 40		10 0	12 5
...	35	Manure & brick sdg. ,,	...	...	...	...	...	...	...	...	...	...	...	...	...	...	...	...	...	...	...	...	...		...	...
1	64½	Smart's siding ...... ,,	...	...	...	...	...	...	...	...	...	...	...	...	...	...	...	...	...	...	...	...	...		...	...
2	50½	Welwyn Gdn. City. ,,	...	...	6 1	...	6A25	8 27	9 26	10 57	...	1220	...	2 10	3 40	1 58	3 12	...	5 12	5 48	6 34	6 :8	7 46		...	...
2	76½	Digswell siding...... ,,	...	...	...	...	...	...	...	...	...	...	...	...	...	...	...	...	...	...	...	...	...		...	...
3	13½	Lord Cowper's sdg. ,,	...	...	...	...	...	...	...	...	...	...	...	...	...	...	...	...	...	...	...	...	...		...	...
4	19¾	Attimore hall siding ,,	...	...	...	...	...	...	...	*	...	...	...	...	...	...	...	...	...	...	...	...	...		...	...
5	...	Birchall siding ...... ,,	...	...	...	...	...	...	...	*	...	...	...	...	...	...	...	...	...	...	...	...	...		...	...
...	...	Holwell siding ...... ,,	...	...	...	...	*	...	...	*	...	...	*	...	...	...	...	...	...	...	...	...	...		...	...
6	30¾	COLE GREEN arr.	...	...	...	...	6 37	8 33	9 32	11F35	...	1226	1 20	...	3 55	2 6	3 18	4 27	5 19	5 55	6 43	6 46	7 53	8.12 p.m. Light Engine from Hertford North.	...	1221
									9 up				13up					17up					22up			
		COLE GREEN dep.	...	...	...	...	6 45	8 34	9 35	...	...	1227	1 35	Twentieth Mile Sidg. dep. 2.5 p.m.—Shredded Wheat Co.'s Sidg. arr. 2.10 p.m.	...	2 7	3 19	4 30	5 20	5 57	6 44	6 47	7 54	...	...	1223
8	1¾	Hertingfordbury arr.	...	...	...	...	..	8 37	9 38	...	...	1230	...		...	2 10	3 22	.	5 23	6 1	6 47	6 50	7 57	...	...	...
		Hertingfordbury dep.	...	...	...	...	*	8 38	9 39	...	...	1231	...		...	2 11	3 23	...	5 24	6 2	6 48	6 51	7 58	...	...	...
8	32¾	Webb's siding .. ,,	...	...	...	...	*	..	..	...	...	...	...		...	..	...	...	..	...	...	...	..	...	...	...
...	...	Hertford North Station Box arr.	1 24	6 0	...	...	7 3	...	...	...	...	...	1 46		...	...	...	4 38	...	...	...	...	...	8 13	...	1230
		Hertford North Station Box dep.	1 25	6 1	..	...	7 4	...	...	...	...	...	1 48		...	...	...	4 39	...	...	...	...	...	8 14	...	1231
9	4	HERTFORD N. arr.	...	...	6 15	...	..	8 43	9 44	...	...	1236			...	2P16	3 28		5 28	6 6	6 52	6 55	8 3	...	1019	...
9	47	HERTFORD GOODS (OLD STN.) arr.	...	6 5	...	...	7 6	..	..	..	..	..	1 52		...	...	...	4 43	...	...	...	...	...	8 18	...	...
		HERTFORD GOODS (OLD STN.) dep.	...	6 20	...	...	7 40	...	..	...	...	..	2 12		...	...	...	5 45	...	...	...	...	...	...	...	...
10	50½	HERTFORD E. arr.	1 40	6 30	...	...	7 55	..		...	.	...	2 22		...	..	..	5 55	..	...	...	...	...	...	...	1245

Nos. 1 and 24 will convey traffic from stations south of Peterboro' for Mint Street and Victoria Docks and also vegetable traffic for Stratford Market detached at Hatfield from 497 up main line.

A Stop to leave newspapers.

e **Takes wagons containing general goods for delivery to Hertford East yard.** Conveys newspapers and mail bags from Hatfield to Cole Green and Hertford Goods Yard.

F Welwyn Garden City Siding arrive 10,10 a.m. On Saturdays to arrive Cole Green at 11.6 a.m.

H **No. 6 down goods must not stop at Hertingfordbury and Webb's Siding if likely to delay 4 up passenger train**

J Wagons for Stratford Market to be formed together next engine.

P Due 2.17 p.m. on Wednesdays.

Horse boxes and other four-wheeled vehicles containing passenger rated traffic may be conveyed on any down passenger train. In the event of a goods service being available, 1 to 3 wagons of cattle, if fitted with brake pipes, may be attached to any down passenger train.

WEEK DAYS. — SUNS

UP.	1		3	4	5	6	7	9		11	12	13	14	15		16	17	18	21	23		24	26	27	28	SUNS 1
	Gds.		Gds.	Pass	Pass.	Gds.	Pass	Pass		Gds. Z	Pass	Pass	Pass	Gds.		Gds.	Pass	Pass	Pass	Gds. Z		Lgt. Eng	Gds.	Gds.	Pass	Gds.
Class of Train.	B		D							D				D	D	D							D	D		B
	MX												SO	WSX	WO					SX			SX	SO	SO	
	a.m		a.m.	a.m.	a.m.	a.m.	a.m.	a.m.		a.m.	a.m.	p.m.	p.m.	p.m.	p.m.	p m.	p.m.	p.m.	p.m	p.m		p.m	p.m.	p.m	p.m.	a.m.
HERTFORD EAST dep	2 40	...	6 43	...	...	8 20	...	...	...	...	...	...	...	...	...	2 27	...	...	...	7 35	For notes see page 89. Worked by engines of 16 and 19 Down.	..	...	...	...	1 15
Gas works siding... ,,	...	...	*	...	...	...	...	...	...	...	...	...	...	...	...	...	...	...	...	...		..	...	...	...	...
Manser's and Gray and Miles' sidings ...... ,,	...	...	*	...	...	...	...	...	...	...	...	...	...	...	...	...	...	...	...	...		..	...	...	...	...
McMullen's siding ..	...	...	..	...	...	...	...	...	...	...	...	...	...	...	...	...	...	...	...	...		..	...	...	...	...
HERTFORD GOODS (OLD STATION) arr.	...	...	7 3	...	...	8 25	...	..	...	...	...	..	...	...	...	2 37	...	...	...	7 45		..	...	...	...	1 25
HERTFORD GOODS (OLD STATION) dep.			.	...		...	...	...	...	...	...	...	...	...	...	...	...	...	...	8 3		..	9 30	9 14		1 27
HERTFORD NORTH arr.	Y																							9 22		
HERTFORD NORTH dep.	..	...	.	7 7	7 40	...	8 50	9 25	...	...	1135	1 17	2 34	...	...	...	4 20	5 45	7 7	8 7		8 12		1030	9 30	...
Hertford North Station Box arr.	2 54	...	...	...	...	...	...	...	...	...	...	...	...	...	...	...	...	...	...	...		8 13	...	..	...	1 28
Hertford North Station Box dep.	2 55	...	...	...		...	...	...	...	...	...	...	...	...	...	...	...	...	...	...		8 14	...		...	1 29
Webb's siding ... ,,	...	...	...	...	...	...	...	...	...	...	...	...	...	...	...	...	...	...	...	...		To Hertford Goods.	*	...	...	...
Hertingfordbury arr.	...	...	...	7 10	7 43	...	8 52	9 28	...	...	1138	1 20	2 37	...	...	...	4 23	5 48	7 10	Welwyn G.C. arr. 8.24 p.m.			9 39	1038	9 33	...
Hertingfordbury dep	...	...	...	7 11	744	...	8 53	9 29	...	...	1139	1 21	2 38	...	...	...	4 24	5 49	7 11				9 48	1048	9 34	...
COLE GREEN arr	...	..	...	7 15	7 88	...	8 57	9 33	...	..	1143	1 25	2 42		...	...	4 28	5 53	7 15	8 15			9 55	1055	9 38	
	...		...	...		...	...	9 dn	...			12dn	...	...	...	...		18dn	...				...	...	...	
COLE GREEN dep.	...	...	...	7 16	7 49	...	8 58	9 34	...	1151	1144	1 26	2 43	...	4 10	...	4 29	5 56	7 16	8 16		...	10 5	11 5	9 39	..
Holwell siding ... ,,	...	...	...	...	...	...	...	...	...	...	...	...	...	...	...	...	...	...	...	...		...	10 30	*	...	...
Birchall siding ... ,,	...	...	...	...	...	...	...	...	...	...	...	...	...	...	...	...	...	...	...	...		...	11 2	*	...	...
Digswell siding ... ,,	...	...	...	...	...	...	...	...	...	...	...	...	...	...	...	...	...	...	...	...		...	...	...	...	...
WelwynG'denCity ,,	...	...	...	7 23	7 56	...	9 5	9 41	...	...	1151	1 33	2 50	3 55	...	Engine to work 17 up	4 36	6 3	7 23	8 45		...	...	*	9 46	...
Twentieth Mile .. ,,	...	...	...	...	...	...	...	...	...	...	...	...	...	...	...		...	...	...	...		...	11 32	...	...	...
Smart's siding ..	...	...	...	...	...	...	...	...	...	...	...	...	...	...	...		...	...	...	...		...	...	...	...	...
Manure &brick s'd'g	...	...	...	...	...	...	...	...	...	...	...	...	...	...	...		...	...	...	...		...	...	...	...	...
Mount Pleasant .. ,,	...	...	...	...	...	...	...	...	...	...	...	...	...	...	...		...	...	...	...		...	11 52	..	...	..
HATFIELD arr	3 18	...	...	7 29	8 2	...	9 11	9 47	...	12 7	1157	1 39	2 55	4 5	4 25		4 42	6 9	7 29	8 53		...	11 55	1220	9 52	1 55

No. 1 weekdays and 1 up Sundays will convey traffic from Mint Street, Victoria Docks and Thames Wharf for stations south of Peterboro'.

Z Drivers of No. 11 Up and No. 23 Up Goods when required to work at the sidings between Cole Green and Hatfield will convey metal ticket from Cole Green as authority to proceed, and on arrival at Hatfield the metal ticket must be handed to person in charge of the Train Staff working, who must place it in the ticket box. The metal ticket must be returned to Cole Green, properly secured as a "Value" by the next train. On arrival at Cole Green it must be placed in the ticket box.

Y When there are 10 or more wagons detached at Hertford Goods from No. 1 up goods the engine brake and guard must return from Hatfield and work these wagons specially from Hertford Goods to Hatfield.

Horse boxes and other four-wheeled vehicles containing passenger rated traffic may be conveyed on any up passenger train except that Nos. 7 and 9 will not convey such traffic from Cole Green.
In the event of a goods service not being available, 1 to 3 wagons of cattle, if fitted with brake pipes may be attached to any up passenger train except Nos. 7 and 9.

L&NER working timetable 1936.

8.50am and 9.25am ex Hertford North which could not convey such traffic from Cole Green. In the event of a goods service not being available, up to three wagons of cattle could be attached to any passenger service provided the vehicles were fitted with brake pipes, with the exception of the above two trains from Hertford North. The initial Down goods train departed Hatfield at 1.00amMX as a Class 'B' working through to Hertford East conveying wagons for Stratford Market attached next the engine. This train also conveyed traffic from stations south of Peterborough destined for Mint Street and Victoria Docks, also vegetable traffic for Stratford Market. At 5.35am another Class 'B' train departed Hatfield to Hertford Goods, arriving 6.05am and departing 15 minutes later for Hertford East arriving at 6.30am. This train took wagons of general goods to Hertford East yard and conveyed newspapers and mail bags from Hatfield to Cole Green and Hertford Old. A Class 'D' train departed Hatfield at 6.02am making mandatory calls at Welwyn Garden City and Cole Green and serving Hertingfordbury and Webb's siding only if required; after a 34-minute allowance at Hertford Old the train continued to Hertford East. This train was not to call at Hertingfordbury and Webb's siding if it was likely to delay the 7.07am Up passenger train from Hertford North. By this date the 10.00am Class 'D' train ex Hatfield to Cole Green ran each weekday serving Welwyn Garden City and then Lord Cowper's siding, Attimore Hall siding and Birchall siding only if required, with arrival at Cole Green at 11.06amSO and 11.35amSX. The first afternoon goods service ran as a Class 'D' departing Hatfield at 2.25pm as a through working to Hertford East, with a conditional call at Holwell siding, 15 minutes at Cole Green and 20 minutes at Hertford Old arriving at Hertford East at 3.22pm. On WSX a short Class 'D' working departed Hatfield at 1.45pm for Welwyn Garden City but on WO the train departed at the later time of 1.58pm and terminated at Cole Green. The final Down goods train of the day was the 12.05amSO ex Hatfield working through to Hertford East arriving at 12.45am, conveying wagons for Stratford Market formed next the engine and conveying similar traffic as the 1.00amMX train. In the Up direction the 2.40amMX Class 'B' goods ex Hertford East ran as a through working to Hatfield arriving 3.18am. If, however, ten or more wagons were detached at Hertford Goods the engine and brake van with a guard was required to return to Hatfield and work these wagons specially from Hertford Old Goods to Hatfield. A short Class 'D' trip working departed Hertford East at 6.43am with a 20-minute timing to Hertford Old to allow for shunting Gas Works and Manser and Gray & Miles sidings en route. This was followed by another trip working from Hertford East to Hertford Old departing 8.20am. The return Class 'D' working from Cole Green, departing at 11.51am, arrived at Hatfield at 12.07pm The driver of this train when required to work at intermediate sidings between Cole Green and Hatfield was required to convey a metal ticket from Cole Green as authority to proceed and on arrival at Hatfield the metal ticket was to be handed to the person-in-charge of the Train Staff working who was responsible for placing it in the Ticket Box. The metal ticket was to be returned to Cole Green as a 'value' item by the next available train and on arrival at Cole Green was to be placed in the Ticket Box at that station; the same conditions applied to the 7.55pmSX goods ex Hertford East to Hatfield. On WSX the return goods working from Welwyn Garden City departed at 3.55pm but on WO the trip returned from Cole Green departing at 4.10pm with a 15-minute run to Hatfield. Another short Class 'D' trip working departed Hertford East at 2.27pm for Hertford Old, the engine then working the 4.20pm Hertford North to Hatfield passenger train. The 7.55pmSX goods ex Hertford East shunted 18 minutes at Hertford Old before continuing to Welwyn Garden City arriving 8.24pm, and departed 21 minutes later for Hatfield. This train was double headed from Hertford North to get the second locomotive back to Hatfield shed. The final Class 'D' working departed Hertford Old at 9.30pmSX and 9.14pmSO. The SX train made a conditional call at Cole Green, Holwell siding, Birchall siding, Welwyn Garden City and Mount Pleasant siding, arriving at Hatfield at 11.55pm. The SO train called at Hertford North from 9.22pm to 10.30pm before serving Hertingfordbury, Cole Green, Holwell siding, Birchall siding and Welwyn Garden City, with arrival at Hatfield at 12.20am on Sunday. Last, but not least, the sole Sunday working was the 1.15am Class 'B' goods ex Hertford East to Hatfield; this train conveying traffic from Mint Street, Victoria Docks and Thames Wharf for stations south of Peterborough. In the Down direction a light engine departed Hatfield 4.15pmWSX for Hertford Old where it shunted for an hour before continuing to Hertford East to work the 7.35pm Up train with the engine of the 6.26pmSX, 6.32pmSO ex Hatfield Down train. Another short engine working was the 6.12pm Hertford North to Hertford Old.

On the outbreak of World War Two and after the initial alarm of imminent invasion, train services were restored on most lines but between Hatfield and Hertford North the weekdays service provided for only four SX and five SO passenger trains in the Down direction and five SX and six SO in the Up direction.

The **1940** timetable was as shown below.

The freight train working timetable for **1942** showed a uniform weekday service of six MX, five MO and five SO trains in each direction. On the Down road the 12.50amMX Class 'B' ex Hatfield was a through working to Hertford East conveying wagons for Stratford Market. This train also picked up wagons left at Hertford North for transfer to the GE section. The 6.08am Class 'B' ex Hatfield called at Hertford Old station before continuing to Hertford East arriving at 7.15am. At 6.30am a short working departed Hatfield for Welwyn Garden City, after which there was a lull in freight working until the 12.45pm Class 'D' ex Hatfield

Passenger Timetable for 1940						
Down				SO		
		am	am	am/pm	pm	pm
London King's Cross	dep		7.20	10.10	3.25	5.45
Hatfield	dep	5.50	8.20	12.00	4.30	6.21
Welwyn Garden City	dep	5.57	8.27	12.07	4.37	6.28
Cole Green	dep	6.06	8.36	12.16	4.46	6.37
Hertingfordbury	dep	6.10	8.40	12.20	4.50	6.41
Hartford North	arr	6.15	8.45	12.25	4.55	6.48
Up				SO			
		am	am	pm	pm	pm	pm
Hertford North	dep	7.18	9.15	12.45	3.55	5.25	6.58
Hertingfordbury	dep	7.22	9.19	12.49	3.59	5.29	7.02
Cole Green	dep	7.28	9.25	12.55	4.05	5.35	7.08
Welwyn Garden City	dep	7.35	9.32	1.02	4.12	5.42	7.15
Hatfield	arr	7.43	9.40	1.10	4.20	5.50	7.23
London King's Cross	arr	8F18	10F02	2.09	5F12	6.38	8.25
F Change at Welwyn Garden City.							

HATFIELD AND HERTFORD BRANCH.

SINGLE LINE. Short Section Key Token, Hatfield—Cole Green. Train Staff and Ticket, Cole Green—Hertford North. (Long Section Key Token, Hatfield—Hertford North when Cole Green closed).

Trains may be shut in at Welwyn Garden City Goods Yard, I.C.I. Siding, Norton's Siding and Holwell Siding when Short Section Key Token Working is in operation.

*** HERTFORD NORTH AND HERTFORD EAST JUNCTION.**

* See instruction under heading "Hertford North" on page 352 of appendix to W.T.T.

Distance from Hatfield. M.	C.	DOWN.		WEEK DAYS. 21	22		24	25		26	27		28		SUNDAYS. 1	2				
				Gds.	Gds.		Gds	Gds.		Gds	Gds.		Gds.		Gds.	Gds.				
		Class of train		B	B		D	D	D	D	D	D	D		B	D				
				MX				SX	SO	SX	SX	SO	Q							
				a.m.	a.m		a.m.	p.m.	p.m.	p.m.	p.m.	p.m.	p.m.		a.m.	a.m				
				J											J					
...	...	**HATFIELD**	dep.	12 50	6 8	...	6 30	12 45	2 20	...	1 12	1 20	10 15	...	12 50	6 0	...	...	...	...
...	35	Manure & Brick Siding	„	...	...	...	...	...	...	...	...	...	...	...	...	...	...	...	...	...
1	61½	Smart's Siding	„	...	pass	...	arr.	...	...	...	...	...	...	...	...	...	...	...	...	...
2	50½	Welwyn Garden City	„	...	6 13	...	6 37	1 F2	...	...	7P30	7P30	...	...	...	6 8	...	...	...	...
2	76½	Digswell Siding	„	...	...	...	...	...	...	...	...	...	...	...	...	...	...	...	...	...
4	19¾	Attimore Hall Siding	„	...	...	...	...	...	...	...	...	...	...	...	...	...	...	...	...	...
5	...	Birchall Siding	„	...	...	...	...	...	...	...	...	...	...	...	...	...	...	...	...	...
5	39¼	Holwell Siding	„	...	...	...	...	...	...	...	...	...	11K10	...	...	...	...	...	...	...
6	30¾	**COLE GREEN**	arr.	...	...	...	...	1 10	2 35	...	7 40	7 40	...	...	...	...	...	...	...	...
			dep.	...	...	...	...	1 11	2 45	2 50	7 41	7 41	...	...	...	...	...	...	...	...
8	1¾	Hertingfordbury	arr.	...	...	...	...	...	...	...	...	...	...	...	...	...	...	...	...	...
			dep.	...	...	...	...	...	...	...	...	...	...	...	...	...	...	...	...	...
		Webb's Siding	„	...	...	...	...	...	...	...	...	...	...	...	...	...	...	...	...	...
8	32½	Hertford North Station Box	arr.	1 14	6 31	...	...		2 55	3 0	...	...	...	...	1 14	...	...	...	...	
...	...		dep.	1 25	6 32	...	...	...	3 20	3 20	...	...	...	...	1 25	...	...	...	...	
9	4	**HERTFORD NORTH**	arr.	...	...	...	...	1 20	...	...	7 50	7 50	11 26	...	...	...	...	...	...	...
9	47	HERTFORD GOODS (OLD STATION)	arr.	...	6 36	...	...	...	3 25	3 25	...	...	...	...	...	...	...	...	...	...
			dep.	...	7 5	...	...	...	3 55	3 55	...	...	...	...	...	...	...	...	...	...
10	53½	**HERTFORD EAST**	arr.	1 40	7 15	...	...	...	4 5	4 5	...	...	...	...	1 40	...	...	...	...	...
				...	...	...	...	...	...	...	...	...	...	...	...	...	...	...	...	...

Nos. 21 M.X. & 1 Su.O. will convey traffic from stations south of Peterboro' for Mint Street and Victoria Docks and also vegetable traffic for Stratford Market detached at Hatfield from 452 up main line.

F Arr 12.52 p.m.
J Wagons for Stratford Market to be formed together next engine. Attach at Hertford North wagons off 519 or 542 Down.
K Arr. 10.33 p.m.
P Due 1.19 p.m. **SX**, 1.27 p.m. **SO.**

Distance from Hertford East. M.	C.	UP.		WEEK DAYS. 21	22	24		25		26		27	28	SUNDAYS. 1	2					
				Gds.	Gds.	Gds.	E&B	Gds.		Gds.		Gds.	E &B	Gds.	Gds.					
		Class of Train		B	D	D	D	D		D		D		B	D					
				MX				SX					Q							
						SX	SO													
				a.m.	a.m.	p.m.	p.m.	p.m.	p.m.	p.m.		p.m.	p.m.	a.m.	p.m.					
		HERTFORD EAST	dep.	2 40	7 30	...	...	...	...	4 20	...	...	...	2 40	...	...	...	...	...	...
...	...	Gas Works Siding	„	...	...	...	...	...	...	...	...	...	...	...	...	...	...	...	...	...
...	...	Manser's and Gray and Miles' Sidings	„	...	...	...	...	...	...	...	...	...	...	...	...	...	...	...	...	...
...	...	McMullen's Siding	„	...	...	...	...	...	...	...	...	...	...	...	...	...	...	...	...	...
1	6½	HERTFORD GOODS (OLD STATION)	arr.	...	7 35	...	...	...	...	4 30	...	...	...	...	...	...	...	...	...	...
			dep.	...	...	...	...	...	...	7 4	...	...	...	...	...	...	...	...	...	...
	49½	**HERTFORD NORTH**	arr.	...	...	...	...	...	...	...	...	...	...	...	...	...	...	...	...	...
			dep.	...	...	...	...	2 0	...	...	...	8 30	11 40	...	...	...	...	...	...	...
2	21	Hertford North Station Box	arr.	2 54	...	...	...	...		7 9	...	...	...	2 54	...	...	...	...	...	...
			dep.	2 55	...	...	...	...		7 15	...	...	...	2 55	...	...	...	...	...	...
...	...	Webb's Siding	„	...	...	...	...	...	...	...	...	*	...	...	...	...	...	...	...	...
2	51¾	Hertingfordbury	arr.	...	...	...	...	...	...	...	...	...	...	...	...	...	...	...	...	...
			dep.	...	...	...	...	...	...	...	...	*	...	...	...	...	...	...	...	...
4	22¾	**COLE GREEN**	arr.	...	...	...	...	2 8		7 25	...	8 40	...	...	...	...	...	...	...	...
			dep.	...	...	...	...	...		7 42	...	8 50	...	...	...	...	...	...	...	...
5	14¼	Holwell Siding	„	...	...	...	...	...	...	...	...	*	...	...	...	...	...	...	...	...
5	53½	Birchall Siding	„	...	...	...	...	...	...	...	...	*	...	...	...	...	...	...	...	...
7	57	Digswell Siding	„	...	...	...	...	...	...	...	...	...	...	...	...	...	...	...	...	...
8	3	Welwyn Garden City	„	...	...	12 20	12 30	...	...	...	...	9F 30	...	...	2 20	...	...	...	...	...
...	...	Twentieth Mile	„	...	...	...	...	...	...	...	...	...	...	...	...	...	...	...	...	...
8	69	Smart's Siding	„	...	...	...	...	...	...	...	...	...	...	...	...	...	...	...	...	...
10	18½	Manure & Brick Siding	„	...	...	...	...	...	...	...	...	...	...	...	...	...	...	...	...	...
...	...	Mount Pleasant	„	...	...	...	...	...	...	...	...	...	...	...	...	...	...	...	...	...
10	53½	**HATFIELD**	arr.	3 18	...	12 30	12 37	...		8 0	...	9 40	12 0	3 18	2 30	...	...	...	...	...

No. 21 weekdays and 1 up Sundays will convey traffic from Mint Street, Victoria Dock and Thames Wharf for Stations south of Peterboro'.

F. Welwyn Garden City arr. 9.0 p.m.

L&NER working timetable 1942, freight.

called at Welwyn Garden City for 10 minutes before continuing to Hertford North where it terminated at 1.20pm. On SO the 2.20pm ex Hatfield called at Cole Green for 10 minutes before shunting at Hertford North for 25 minutes, continuing to Hertford Old and ultimately Hertford East arriving 4.05pm. On SX the 2.50pm ex Cole Green ran in the same timings to Hertford East. The final trains of the day departed Hatfield at 1.12pmSX and 1.20pmSO, and after a lengthy call at Welwyn Garden City ran through to Hertford North arriving at the uniform time of 7.50pm. In the Up direction the 2.40amMX Class 'B' ex Hertford East ran as a through train to Hatfield arriving at 3.18am. The 7.15am arrival at Hertford East returned at 7.30am to Hertford Old, whilst the short Down working arriving at Welwyn Garden City at 6.37am, after shunting the yard returned to Hatfield departing Welwyn Garden City at 12.20pmSX and 12.30pmSO, with a 10 and 7 minutes running time between stations. The 1.30pm arrival at Hertford North returned at 2.00pmSX to Cole Green, arriving at 2.08pm before returning to Hertford East calling at Hertford Old. The 4.20pm Class 'D' ex Hertford East shunted Hertford Old from 4.30pm until 7.00pm before calling at Cole Green 7.25pm until 7.42pm, with arrival at Hatfield at 8.00pm. The final train of the day, 8.30pm ex Hertford North, made mandatory calls at Cole Green and Welwyn Garden City before arrival back at Hatfield at 9.40pm. This train also served Webb's siding, Hertingfordbury, Holwell siding and Birchall siding if there was any traffic to collect. A 'Q' 'as and when required' path was available for a 10.15pm Class 'D' ex Hatfield serving Holwell siding 10.33pm until 11.10pm, continuing to Hertford North before the engine and brake van returned at 11.40pm to Hatfield, arriving at 12.00midnight. On Sundays two trains ran in each direction: the 12.50am Class 'B' ran through to Hertford East arriving at 1.45am conveying wagons for Stratford Market, returning from Hertford East at 2.40am arriving at Hatfield at 3.18am. The second train was a short trip working to Welwyn Garden City departing Hatfield at 6.00am; after shunting the yard the train returned as the 2.20pm Class 'D' with a 10-minute run to Hatfield.

The public timetable for **1943** showed an almost identical service to previous years since the outbreak of war, but with an additional train each way on Saturdays, although by now the branch trains conveyed only Third Class accommodation. All trains called at Welwyn Garden City, Cole Green and Hertingfordbury, and Down trains departed Hatfield at 5.50am, 8.22am, 11.27amSO, 12.50pmSO, 5.00pm and 6.33pm, whilst Up services departed Hertford North at 7.10am, 9.20am, 12.02pmSO, 1.35pmSO, 3.55pm, 5.38pm and 7.08pm.

The passenger train working timetable for **1944** showed a sparse service of four SX and six SO services in the Down direction, calling all stations from Hatfield to Hertford North with timings of 25 and 26 minutes for the 9 miles 04 chains journey, except for the 4.56pm ex Hatfield which was detained at Welwyn Garden City from 5.03pm to 5.10pm for connections, with arrival at Hertford North at 5.28pm. In the Up direction five SX and seven SO trains operated, again with 25 minute timings except for the 5.28pm ex Hertford North which stood at Welwyn Gardens City from 5.55pm until 6.12pm with arrival at Hatfield at 6.19pm.

From **September 1944** branch passenger services to and from Hertford North departed and terminated at Welwyn Garden City. An interesting innovation from 1945 was the through train from Hertford North to Broad Street via Cole Green which commenced its working as the 6.20am Finsbury Park to Hertford North via Cuffley. The train then formed the 7.28am departure to Broad Street via Hertingfordbury, Cole Green, Welwyn Garden City and Hatfield thence calling all stations to New Barnet, Finsbury Park and with arrival at Broad Street at 8.48am. There was no reciprocal Down working.

The **1947** timetable (overleaf) hardly encouraged rail travel across the branch, with a 7-hour gap in the SX service in the middle of the day on the Up road and an even greater gap of almost eight hours in the Down direction. Some of the publications even advised the existence of the alternative bus service! One crumb of comfort was the running of one train in each direction on Sundays, although these omitted calling at Cole Green and Hertingfordbury.

The first working timetable under **nationalisation** showed five SX and six SO passenger trains working between Welwyn Garden City and Hertford North, with six SX and eight SO trains in the Up direction. All trains called at Cole Green and Hertingfordbury

HATFIELD AND HERTFORD NORTH BRANCH — 35

DOWN WEEKDAYS—(No Sunday Trains)

Distance from Hatfield M. C.		1 Pass. a.m.	3 Pass. a.m.	5 Pass. SO a.m.	7 Pass. S.O. p.m.	9 Pass. p.m.	11 Pass. p.m.
.. ..	Hatfield dep.	5 50	8 22	11 27	12 50	4 56	6 33
2 50½	Welwyn Garden City ,,	5 57	8 29	11 34	12 58	5A10	6 40
6 30¾	Cole Green ,,	6 6	8 38	11 43	1 7	5 19	6 49
8 1¾	Hertingfordbury ,,	6 11	8 43	11 48	1 12	5 24	6 54
9 4	Hertford North arr.	6 15	8 48	11 54	1 16	5 28	6 58
	Carriage Working No.	61	61	61	61	61	61

UP WEEKDAYS—(No Sunday Trains) A—Arr. 5.3 p.m.

Distance from Hertford North M. C.		2 Pass. a.m.	4 Pass. a.m.	6 Pass. SO p.m.	8 Pass. S.O. p.m.	10 Pass. p.m.	12 Pass. p.m.	14 Pass. p.m.	16 Pass. p.m.
.. ..	Hertford North dep.	7 10	9 20	12 2	1 35	4 15	5 38		7 8
1 24¼	Hertingfordbury ,,	7 14	9 24	12 6	1 39	4 19	5 42		7 12
2 53¼	Cole Green ,,	7 20	9 30	12 12	1 45	4 25	5 48		7 18
6 33½	Welwyn Garden City ,,	7 27	9 37	12 19	1 52	4 32	5 55	6 12	7 25
9 4	Hatfield arr.	7 35	9 45	12 27	2 0	4 40		6 19	7 33
	Carriage Working No.	61	61	61	61	61	61	61	

L&NER working timetable 1944, passenger.

Passenger Timetable for 1947

Down		Weekdays							Sundays	
		am	am	SO am	SO pm	pm	SX pm	SO pm	SX pm	pm
King's Cross	dep		7.18	10.45	12.15	4.22	5.34	5.27		12.05
Welwyn Garden City	dep	5.57	8.29	11.27	12.58	5.15	6.12	6.40	6.40	1.15
Cole Green	dep	6.06	8.38	11.36	1.07	5.24	6.21	6.49	6.49	
Hertingfordbury	dep	6.11	8.43	11.41	1.12	5.29	6.27	6.54	6.54	
Hertford North	arr	6.17	8.48	11.47	1.16	5.33	6.34	6.58	6.58	1.30

Up		Weekdays							Sundays	
		am	H am	am	SO pm	SO pm	pm	pm	pm	pm
Hertford North	dep	7.10	7.32	9.15	12.02	1.35	4.10	5.45	7.18	4.38
Hertingfordbury	dep	7.14	7.36	9.19	12.06	1.39	4.14	5.49	7.22	
Cole Green	dep	7.20	7.42	9.25	12.12	1.45	4.20	5.55	7.28	
Welwyn Garden City	arr	7.27	7.49	9.32	12.19	1.52	4.27	6.02	7.35	4.53
King's Cross	arr	8.13	8.46c	10.12	1.11	3.00	5.45a	7.10	8.35b	6.14

H Through train to Finsbury Park and Broad Street arrive 8.48am.
a Arrives King's Cross 6.06pmSO.
b Arrives King's Cross 9.19pmSO.
c For King's Cross change at Finsbury Park.

and were allowed between 18 and 22 minutes for the journey in the Down direction and 17 minutes on the Up road. All services were self contained to the branch, with the exception of the 7.28am from Hertford North which was a through train to Broad Street, calling all stations to Oakleigh Park, then Finsbury Park, Dalston and arriving in London at 8.48am. A feature of the branch timetable was the huge gap between services SX, with no train after the 8.29am ex Welwyn Garden City until 5.15pm, and from 9.15am until 4.10pm ex Hertford North. The additional SO trains only partly filled the vacuum, departing Welwyn Garden City at 11.27am and 12.58pm, returning from Hertford North at 12.02pm and 1.35pm. On Sundays one passenger service was provided in each direction, departing Welwyn Garden City at 1.15pm and returning from Hertford North at 4.38pm, both with 15-minute timings as the trains ran non-stop omitting the calls at the intermediate stations. Compared with earlier years the freight traffic was on the wane, resulting in a reduced goods train service on weekdays. The 12.10amMX ex Hatfield called at Welwyn Garden City for 30 minutes and after calling at Hertford North arrived at Hertford East at 1.40am, conveying traffic from stations south of Peterborough for Mint Street and Victoria Docks as well as vegetable traffic for Stratford Market. The train returned from Hertford East departing 2.40amMX and after calling at Welwyn Garden City for 15 minutes arrived at Hatfield at 3.40am. This train conveyed traffic from Mint Street, Victoria Docks and Thames Wharf for stations south of Peterborough. The next Down goods working, 5.30am Class 'B' from Hatfield, shunted at Welwyn Garden City from 5.38am to 6.10am before continuing to Hertford Old station when another 30 minutes was allowed for shunting before arrival at Hertford East at 7.15am. The engine then returned with the 7.30am Class 'D' train to Hertford Old. A Down working departed Hatfield at 11.00amSX for Welwyn Garden City and Cole Green arriving at 11.35am, returning from the intermediate station at 12.15pm as a Class 'B' train to Welwyn Garden City and Hatfield. The next goods working, 12.45pmSO or 1.45pmSX ex Hatfield, arrived 10 minutes later at Welwyn Garden City. Here after yard shunting the train ran in a common time forward at 2.35pm calling at Holwell sidings if required and Cole Green before continuing to Hertford Old where a 30-minute sojourn allowed for yard shunting before the train terminated at Hertford East at 4.05pm. The engine and brake van then returned with the 4.20pm Up goods to Hertford Old where much yard shunting took place before the train worked forward at 7.04pm to pick up traffic at Hertford North and Welwyn Garden City. The final Down service departed Welwyn Garden City at 8.00pm as a Class 'B' train through to Hertford North, arriving at 8.20pm and returning at 8.50pm with mandatory calls at Cole Green and Welwyn Garden City and conditional calls at Webb's siding, Hertingfordbury, Holwell siding and Birchall siding with arrival at Hatfield at 9.55pm. On Sundays the 12.10am Class 'B' train from Hatfield served Welwyn Garden City and Hertford North before continuing to Hertford East arriving at 1.40am; the train returned at 2.40am with the same stopping pattern as the outward journey conveying traffic from Mint Street, Victoria Docks and Thames Wharf for stations south of Peterborough.

The point-to-point timing allowances for freight trains between Welwyn Garden City and Hertford East in **1950** were as shown opposite.

The **1951** passenger working timetable showed five SX and six SO trains in the Down direction with all trains calling at all stations except the 5.07pmSO and 6.40pmSO ex Welwyn Garden City which ran non-stop to Hertford North. Timings varied between 16 and 20 minutes for the 6 miles 34 chains journey. In the Up direction six passenger and one ECS working ran SX with seven passenger services SO. The 7.28am ex Hertford North was a through service to Broad Street whist the 5.27pm ex Hertford North ran ECS to Welwyn Garden City. All passenger trains called at Hertingfordbury and Cole Green with the exception of the 5.47pmSO and 7.18pmSO ex Hertford North, which ran non-stop to Welwyn Garden City. An additional Class 'G' train departing Hertford North at 7.02pmSX worked through to Hatfield arriving at 7.30pm.

By **September 1952** the branch freight services ran on weekdays only. The first Class 'H' Down train departed Hatfield at 7.20am and called at Welwyn Garden City 7.30am to 7.50am before continuing to Hertford Old arriving at 8.10am, where the engine shunted as required before retuning light to Welwyn Garden City, departing Hertford at 9.05am with a 20-minute run to the junction. The engine then returned Down the branch with the 10.20am London refuse traffic Class 'H' train to Holwell siding, arriving 10 minutes later. More shunting ensued before the engine and brake van returned at 11.20am to Welwyn Garden City, arriving at 11.30am. On SO the engine and brake van continued through to Hatfield, arriving at 11.41am. On SX the engine returned light to Hertford Old, departing Welwyn Garden City at 11.40am and arriving at 12.00 noon, where it shunted the yard until 1.40pm, from whence it worked the Class 'K' goods train to Welwyn

Point-to-Point Timing Allowances 1950

Down		Class 7 and 8 Trains			Up		Class 7 and 8 Trains		
From	To	Starting Allowance Minutes	Stopping Allowance Minutes	Passing Allowance Minutes	From	To	Starting Allowance Minutes	Stopping Allowance Minutes	Passing Allowance Minutes
Welwyn G City	Hertford North	1	1	16	Hertford East	Hertford North	2	1	5
Welwyn G City	Norton sidings	1	1	2	Hertford North	Welwyn G City	2	1	17
Norton sidings	Attimore Hall	1	2	2	Hertford Old	Hertford North	2	1	2
Attimore Hall	Holwell sidings	1	2	3	Hertford North	Hertingfordbury	2	1	2
Howell sidings	Cole Green	1	2	3	Hertingfordbury	Cole Green	2	1	4
Cole Green	Hertingfordbury	1	1	4	Cole Green	Holwell sidings	1	1	3
Hertingfordbury	Hertford North	1	1	2	Holwell sidings	Attimore Hall	2	1	4
Hertford North	Hertford Old	1	1	2	Attimore Hall	Norton sidings	1	1	2
Hertford North	Hertford East	1	1	4	Norton sidings	Welwyn G City	1	1	2

WELWYN GARDEN CITY AND HERTFORD

SINGLE LINE—Short Section Key Token, Welwyn Garden City—Cole Green. Train Staff and Ticket, Cole Green—Hertford North. Long Section Key Token, Welwyn Garden City—Hertford North when Cole Green closed.

DOWN — WEEKDAYS

Distance from Welwyn Gdn. City			No.	2300	2302	2304	2306	2310	2310	2312	2314	2314
			Class	B	B	B	B	B	B	B	B	B
			Description									
M.	C.			am	am	am	SO PM	SO PM	SX PM	SX PM	SO PM	SX PM
..	..	Welwyn Garden City (T)		5 57	8 38	11 30	1 6	5 7	..	6 15	6 40	6 40
3	60	Cole Green (T) (S)		6 6	8 47	11 39	1 15	..	5 16	6 24	..	6 49
5	32	Hertingfordbury		6 11	8 52	11 44	1 20	..	5 21	6 29	..	6 54
6	34	Hertford North (T) (S)		6B17	8B58	11 48	1 24	5 23	5 25	6B35	6 56	6 58

HERTFORD AND WELWYN GARDEN CITY

SINGLE LINE—Short Section Key Token, Cole Green—Welwyn Garden City. Train Staff and Ticket, Hertford North—Cole Green. Long Section Key Token, Hertford North—Welwyn Garden City when Cole Green closed.

UP — WEEKDAYS

Distance from Hertford North			No.	2237	1617	2241	2243	2245	2247	2249	2251	2251	2255	2257	2257
			Class	B	B	B	B	B	B	C	B	B	G	B	B
			Description							ECS					
M.	C.			am	am	am	SO PM	SO PM	PM	SX PM	SO PM	SX PM	SX PM	SO PM	SX PM
..	..	Hertford North (T) (S)		7 10	7 28	9 13	12 2	1 35	3 45	5 27	5 47	5 47	7 2	7 18	7 18
1	2	Hertingfordbury		..	..	..	..	..	..	..	..	..	..	..	..
..	..	Hertingfordbury		7 14	7 32	9 17	12 6	1 39	3 49	..	5 51	..	..	..	7 22
2	54	Cole Green (T) (S)		..	..	..	..	..	..	5 37	..	..	..	..	..
..	..	Cole Green (T) (S)		7 20	7 38	9 23	12 12	1 45	3 55	5 38	5 57	..	..	..	7 28
6	34	Welwyn Garden City (T)		7 27	7 45	9 30	12 19	1 52	4 2	5 45	6 2	6 4	..	7 33	7 35

1617.—Through train to Broad Street. Forward times on page 57.
2255.—To Hatfield arrive 7.30 pm.

BR ER working timetable 1951 passenger.

HATFIELD, WELWYN GARDEN CITY AND HERTFORD

SINGLE LINE.—Key Token, Welwyn Garden City—Hertford North.

Trains may be shut in at Welwyn Garden City Goods Yard, I.C.I. Siding, Norton's Siding and Holwell Siding.

* HERTFORD NORTH AND HERTFORD EAST JUNCTION

* See instruction on page 185 of sectional appendix to W.T.T.

DOWN — WEEKDAYS / SUNDAYS

Distance from Hatfield		Description	No.	2568	2570	2572	2562	2574	2586	2578	2576	Sundays				
M.	C.	Class		H	H	H	G	K	K	G	H					
				am	am	am	SX am	SX PM	SO PM	PM	PM					
..	..	Hatfield		7 20	..	..	..	12 5	..	..	11 30	..	..	..	..	..
2	50	Welwyn Garden City (T)		7 30	..	..	..	12 15	3 15	..	11 40					
..	..	Welwyn Garden City (T)		7 50	8 15	10 20	11 40	12 40	3 40	7 5	12 0					
2	76	Digswell Siding														
4	19	Attimore Hall Siding														
5	0	Birchall Siding														
5	39	Holwell Siding		..	9 30	10 30	..	1 20	4 20	..	..					
6	30	Cole Green (T)														
..	..	Cole Green (T)														
8	1	Hertingfordbury														
..	..	Webb's Siding														
8	32	Hertford North Station Box														
..	..	Hertford North Station Box														
9	4	Hertford North (T)		..	..	9 46	..	1 40	4 40	..	12 20					
..	..	Hertford North (T)		..	..	..	11 58	..	..	7 23	12 45					
9	47	Hertford Goods (Old Station)		8 10	..	..	12 0	..	..	..	..					
..	..	Hertford Goods (Old Station)														
10	53	Hertford East		..	..	..	..	..	..	7 30	12 55					

2568.—Shunts Hertford as required.
2570.—Holwell Siding arrive 8.25 am. Forward to **2471** page 28.
2574.—Holwell Siding arrive 12.50 pm. Shunts at Hertford as required.
2576.—On SO arrives Hertford East 1.0 am.
2586.—Holwell Siding arrive 3.50 pm. Shunts at Hertford as required.

UP — WEEKDAYS / SUNDAYS

Distance from Hertford East		Description	No.	2589	2581	2583	2583	2585	2585	2587	Sundays				
M.	C.	Class		H	G	G	G	K	K	K					
						E & V	E & V								
				am	am	am	SO am	SO PM	SX PM	PM					
..	..	Hertford East		2 40	..	..	..	..	..	..	..	..	..	..	..
..	..	Gas Works Siding													
..	..	Mansers and Gray and Miles' Sdgs.													
..	..	McMullen's Siding													
1	6	Hertford Goods (Old Station)		..	..	9 45	..	1 40	1 40	6 0					
..	49	Hertford North (T)		2 54	..	..	..	1 50	1 50	..					
..	..	Hertford North (T)		3 4	9 48	..	..	1 51	1 51	..					
..	21	Hertford North Station Box													
..	..	Hertford North Station Box									*				
..	..	Webb's Siding								*					
2	51	Hertingfordbury								*					
..	..	Hertingfordbury													
4	22	Cole Green (T)								*					
..	..	Cole Green (T)													
5	14	Holwell Siding		..	..	11 20	..	..	..	..					
5	53	Birchall Siding													
7	57	Digswell Siding													
8	3	Welwyn Garden City (T)		3 24	10 5	11 30	..	2 10	2 10	6 40					
..	..	Welwyn Garden City (T)		3 50	..	..	11 31	..	2 20	7 0					
8	69	Smart's Siding													
10	18	Manure and Brick Siding													
..	..	Mount Pleasant													
10	53	Hatfield		..	4 0	..	..	11 41	2 30	7 10	..				

2589.—Attaches traffic at Welwyn Garden City for Hatfield Down Side.

BR ER working timetable 1952 freight.

Garden City arriving at 2.10pm. On SX the engine then ran light to Hatfield shed. The engine hauling the 8.15am Class 'H' goods train ex Welwyn Garden City shunted Holwell siding from 8.25am until 9.30am before continuing with the train to Hertford North, arriving 9.46am to work traffic thence on the Cuffley loop line. The next Down working, 12.05pm ex Hatfield, was allowed 25 minutes to shunt Welwyn Garden City yard before continuing to Holwell siding, where the engine shunted from 12.50pm until 1.20pm, before continuing with the train to Hertford North; the engine then shunting as required. A light engine path was available SO from Welwyn Garden City, departing 7.05pm to Hertford East arriving at 7.30pm, essentially to allow the transfer of engines between the GN and the GE sections. In the meantime the 6.00pm Class 'K' train ex Hertford Old called at Webb's siding, Hertingfordbury and Cole Green if required before shunting for 20 minutes at Welwyn Garden City and arriving at Hatfield at 7.10pm. The final train of the day, 11.30pm Class 'H' ex Hatfield, called at Welwyn Garden City for 20 minutes and another 25 minutes at Hertford North before arriving at Hertford East at 12.55am. The train returned at 2.40am, calling at Hertford North for 10 minutes and Welwyn Garden City from 3.24am to 3.50am to attach traffic for Hatfield Down side before terminating at Hatfield at 4.00am.

The BR(ER) freight working timetable for **September 1953** showed the undermentioned services.

As traffic dwindled so the service became fragmented: Cole Green and Hertingfordbury lost their freight facilities on and from 1st August 1962 and 5th March 1962 respectively, although they had been unstaffed public sidings since the withdrawal of the passenger service on 18th June 1951. Thereafter the private sidings branching off the single line near Welwyn Garden City were served by trip workings with no specific timings and these ceased altogether on 12th November 1981.

Freight Working Timetable September 1953

Down

M	Ch		Class Reporting No.	8 2570	8 2568	8 2580	8 2471
				am	am	am	am
0	00	Hatfield	dep		7.00		
2	50	Welwyn G C	arr		7.12		
			dep	6.45	7.57	9.30	
5	37	Holwell sdgs	arr	7.10		9.50	
			dep	7.30			10.05
9	04	Hertford North	arr	7.55	8.37		10.25
			dep		8.38		10.37
9	47	Hertford Goods	arr		8.45		+
			dep				
10	53	Hertford East	arr				

+ To Ashburton Grove.

Up

M	Ch		Class Reporting No.	EBV 2581	LE 2579	8 2585 SO	LE 2585 SO	8 2585 SX	LE 2585 SX
				am	am	pm	pm	pm	pm
0	00	Hertford East	dep						
1	06	Hertford Goods	arr						
			dep			12.38		1.15	
1	49	Hertford North	arr			12.45		1.23	
			dep	8.40		12.55		1.23	
2	21	Webb's sdg	dep						
2	51	Hertingfordbury	dep						
4	22	Cole Green	dep						
5	14	Holwell sdg	arr	9.00					
			dep		10.55 A				
8	03	Welwyn G C	arr		11.30	1.15		2.01	
			dep				1.30		2.16
10	53	Hatfield	arr				1.40		2.21

A Shunts Lincoln Electric Company siding.

In the final years, on Sundays only one passenger train operated across the branch in each direction. 'N7/2' Class 0-6-2T No. 69695 is approaching Hertingfordbury with the 4.58pm Hertford North to Welwyn Garden City train on 11th July 1948. The goods loop siding is in the foreground. *J.F. Aylard*

Excursions

Over the years the GNR provided the Hatfield to Hertford branch with a generous offer of excursion traffic whether by special train or by the availability of through tickets to a wide variety of destinations. Rural in character, it took some time for traffic to materialise as the area served was agricultural and much of the terrain formed part of large private estates. Agricultural workers' wages were low in 1858 when the line opened and as they formed the nucleus of the inhabitants of villages served, usually only middle and upper classes could enjoy the first outings by rail. There were exceptions, however, for the new railway was a novelty and almost everyone in the district sampled at least one journey in the early years. Gradual alterations came with the introduction of paid holidays and additional leisure periods when the excursion programme from Hertford and the branch stations was extended. Only a brief summary can be made of the many facilities offered.

On Tuesday 14th August 1866 a cheap excursion train ran from Wheathampstead and St. Albans via Hatfield to Rye House on the GER Hertford branch, where the gardens were open free of charge for visitors – the GNR engine and men working the train to Hertford Junction where a GE engine took over for the short run to Rye House. On Tuesday 21st August cheap day tickets were issued to King's Cross in connection with the Foresters Fete at Crystal Palace, the train departing Hertford at 8.12am and arriving at London at 10.15am, for the return fare of 2s 6d with the privilege of riding in covered carriages; the train returned from King's Cross at 10.15pm. In September 1866 the GNR ran an excursion to Ramsgate and Margate departing Hertford at 5.15am; a connecting train also ran from St. Albans to Hatfield, where passengers from both branches joined a main-line train which departed the junction at 5.50am. Margate was reached at 9.20am and Ramsgate at 9.35am. Fares from Hertford were 9s 6d First Class and 6s 0d Third Class; similar First Class fares were quoted from Hatfield but Third Class was 1s 0d cheaper.

By 1869 a full excursion programme was being offered to the residents of Hertford and other stations on the branch. On Wednesday 2nd February cheap return facilities were offered to King's Cross by the 11.10am train for people wishing to attend the pantomime; similar facilities were offered from St. Albans by the 11.25am train. At Hatfield, passengers from the branch trains joined the 11.45am departure to continue their journey to London. Fares from Hertford and St. Albans were 5s 0d First Class and 2s 6d Third Class, and from Hatfield 4s 0d First Class and 2s 0d Third Class. Later the same year, on 21st May cheap return tickets were issued from Hertford and the branch stations for Harpenden Races. Passengers departing from Hertford on the 9.55am and 11.10am trains at a First Class fare of 3s 6d and Third Class at 2s 0d were required to travel to Hatfield before changing onto the Dunstable branch service for the journey to Harpenden. In the evening, returning racegoers were given the luxury of a through train from Harpenden, departing at 7.10pm for Hertford via Hatfield.

A further excursion fare was offered from Hertford to Epsom for the Derby on 26th May 1869 with passengers departing Cowbridge on the 8.00am train. The 5s 0d First Class and 2s 6d Third Class tickets were issued to King's Cross whilst patrons wishing to travel on via the London & South Western Railway to Epsom were offered a through fare from Hertford 9s 0d First Class and 6s 6d Third Class. A through fare was also offered via the London, Brighton & South Coast Railway but charges were 6d dearer than via the rival South Western route.

The excursion programme developed by the GNR continued to include seaside destinations and a typical example offered to Hertford branch passengers on 14th June 1870 included through fares to the Kent resorts of Margate, Broadstairs and Ramsgate. Compared with four years earlier, the fares had increased to 10s 0d First Class and 5s 6d Third Class. Departure from Hertford was by special train at 6.40am. Later in the same month the cheap return fares to King's Cross offered to passengers departing on the 8.00am train were 4s 4d First Class and 2s 2d Third Class.

Regular cheap return fares for passengers wishing to attend the pantomime at the various London theatres in 1871 ceased on Wednesday 22nd February, when passengers catching the 11.10am train ex Hertford could take advantage of the 4s 4d First Class and 2s 2d Third Class fares. A similar offer on the St. Albans branch by the 11.25am departure charged fares of 3s 2d First Class and 1s 7d Third Class.

As mentioned earlier, during the spring of 1872 the GNR and GER authorities agreed to standardise the excursion fare structure from Hertford to London. Later in September there came a change of venue for the seaside excursion offered by the GNR when cheap fares were issued to Eastbourne and Brighton via King's Cross and the LB&SCR. Passengers wishing to take advantage of a day by the sea were required to leave Hertford on the 6.40am departure.

Brighton was again the destination for an excursion from the Hertford branch stations on Wednesday 3rd September 1873, whilst the following day cheap return fares were offered to New Barnet for the annual Barnet Fair. A fortnight later new destinations were offered to Hertford and district excursionists when arrangements were made for through bookings to Canterbury and Dover.

The annual flower exhibition held in the rectory grounds at Hertingfordbury on Thursday 30th July 1874 prompted the GNR to issue return tickets at single fares from Hatfield, Cole Green and Hertford, whilst at the end of August a special excursion ran through to Skegness. The latter was marred by the injury of a little girl who boarded the train at St. Neots, when she fell out of the train at Firsby. On 8th September, ninety-six employees and friends of McMullen's brewery forsook the GNR for their annual outing by joining the GER excursion from Hertford to Brighton. Despite the common fares policy to London, by this time both companies were vying for excursion traffic offering cheap fares to different destinations on the same day. Typical examples ran on 3rd October when the GER destination was Hunstanton and the GNR Ramsgate.

During the next two decades the destinations of excursions varied considerably when both the GNR and rival GER routes from Hertford offered town and village folk opportunities to visit places

Great Northern Railway.
A DAY AT THE SEA SIDE.
NEW PIER, 1¼ MILES LONG.
GRAND NEW PAVILION.
Electric Tramcars run the whole length of the Pier.
WEDNESDAY, Sept. 2nd, 1891,
A CHEAP DAY EXCURSION TO
SOUTHEND

Part of poster for excursion to Southend, 1891.

of interest and important events. Examples in 1891 included a full excursion to Doncaster on 25th June for the Royal Agricultural Society Show, the branch train portion being combined with the main-line train at Hatfield. In July excursion fares were offered to London, Southampton, Hastings and Eastbourne, whilst the following month during the school holiday the emphasis was more towards day excursions to seaside resorts. These included Bournemouth and Portsmouth. Poor weather during the bank holiday reduced numbers. The trend for shorter runs by through trains reflected in rival numbers departing Hertford on Monday 24th August 1891: over 900 left on the through GER train to Southend, with only ninety excursion tickets sold at Cowbridge for the Portsmouth run. On Wednesday 2nd September 1891 a cheap day excursion was offered from the branch stations to Southend via the North London and London, Tilbury & Southend railways to view the new 1¼-mile pier and pavilion. Trains departed Hertford at 8.35am, returning the same day from Southend at 7.00pm, with return fares of 9s 0d First Class and 4s 6d Third Class from all the branch stations and Hatfield.

By the 1900s the excursion programme offered to GNR passengers from Hertford and the branch stations included, after a change at Hatfield, through runs to destinations on the South Eastern & Chatham Railway and the North Eastern Railway. In June 1902 passengers could leave Hertford at 5.30am for Margate and Ramsgate for 6s 0d day return, 8s 6d 3- or 4-day return and 12s 0d for 6- or 8-day return Third Class fare, and in 1904 resorts included Scarborough, Bridlington, Filey, Whitby and Saltburn. Local cheap return fares were not forgotten and for the Whit Monday gathering on Hartham common over 2,000 passengers travelled by the strengthened branch services to Hertford. Unfortunately for the GNR this was rather overshadowed by the GER, which conveyed over double that total. Typical of GNR offers was the cheap excursion to Margate and Ramsgate on Saturday 14th June 1902 departing Hertford at 5.30am, Hertingfordbury 5.35am, Cole Green 5.40am and Hatfield at 6.00am at uniform day fares of 6s 0d, three or four days 8s 6d and five to six days 12s 0d. Day excursionists returned from Ramsgate (Harbour) at 5.35pm and Margate at 5.50pm.

ABOVE: GNR notice of excursion to Margate and Ramsgate 1902.
LEFT: GNR handbill advertising a cheap day excursion to London, October 1893.

On 30th June 1906 the GNR commenced issuing cheap weekend return tickets valid for travel anytime on Saturdays to Mondays from Hitchin. The *Hertford Mercury* hoped the facility would soon be made available at Hertford; the comments were fruitful for within a week cheap weekend tickets were made available at Hertford for travel to London by both the GNR and GER routes.

Saturday 7th July 1906 was a special day for many employees of Hertford when the annual Amalgamated Trades excursion ran to Yarmouth. The train was formed of GER engine and coaching stock, but departed from and returned to Hertford GNR station, which was considered to be more convenient for the 522 passengers boarding the train. Departing at 4.00am, the train finally reached its destination at 9.00am. Twelve hours were spent at the seaside resort before the special returned at 9.00pm, finally reaching Hertford at 2.00am in the early hours of Sunday. For the Christmas holiday period of 1906 the GNR introduced the Saturday to Monday any station to any station cheap tickets from Hertford and the branch stations.

On Saturday 5th July 1913 the ninth annual outing of the Amalgamated Trades of Hertford took place when about 400 workers from the town travelled to Brighton on a special train, which departed Hertford Cowbridge station at 4.40am with Brighton being reached at 7.40am. Employees travelling on the excursion included those from Webb & Company, Ekins & Company, E.J. Wickham, Ewen & Tomlinson, G. Garratt & Sons, H. Shephard & Company, Hertford Steam Laundry, Hertford Gas Company, the Panshanger Estate employees and Ware church bellringers. All spent a lengthy day at the resort until the return journey commenced at 10.10pm with the train arriving at Hertford at 1.40am on the Sunday morning.

During World War One the excursion programme was stopped but when peace resumed the seaside excursions to Skegness, Yarmouth, Bridlington, Lincoln, York and Scarborough continued by the L&NER. Excursion fares were offered to London for the pantomime as well as the Smithfield Show, and in the latter years to the capital for home games of Arsenal football club. During World War Two excursions were again curtailed but resumption after hostilities was cut short when the branch passenger service was withdrawn in June 1951.

Fares

The full single fare structure on the opening of the railway was:

Hertford To	First Class s d	Second Class s d	Third Class s d
Welwyn Junction	1 11	1 3½	0 8
Hatfield	2 3	1 6	0 9½
Potters Bar	3 3	2 2	1 2½
Barnet	3 9	2 8	1 6
Southgate	4 3	3 2	1 9
Hornsey	4 9	3 4	1 11½
Holloway	4 9	3 4	2 4
King's Cross	4 9	3 4	2 4

In mid-April 1858 the H&WJR Secretary wrote to the ECR asking if season ticket rates via both routes to London could be brought into line. The directors, wishing to safeguard their cheaper fare, replied on 28th April they did not consider the proposal desirable. To coincide with the 1859 Christmas holiday the GNR and ECR made arrangements for day return tickets to be issued from stations on the Hertford to Welwyn Junction line from Friday 23rd December to Wednesday 28th December inclusive. The receipts for the sales of season tickets in the first six months of 1861 was encouraging with the ECR share amounting to £110 18s 10d.

From September 1862 the GER commenced issuing weekend return tickets for distances over 20 miles valid from Friday to the following Monday. Their introduction incensed the GNR authorities as the issue contravened the agreement regarding competitive passenger fares to Hertford, Huntingdon and Peterborough, and was made without prior consultation between the two companies. After raising the issue at a board meeting the GNR directors decided not to make similar offers until further traffic figures were available.

The fare structure for the branch in 1870 from Hertford GN station was:

Hertford To	First Single s d	Second Single s d	Third Single s d
Hertingfordbury	4	3	1½
Cole Green	8	6	3
Hatfield	2 0	1 6	9
St. Albans	3 0	2 2	1 3½
Luton	3 6	2 6	1 6½
Dunstable (Church St)	4 6	3 4	2 1½

Whilst fares to London from the intermediate stations were:

London From	First Single s d	Second Single s d	Third Single s d
Hertingfordbury	7 0	5 0	— —
Cole Green	6 0	5 0	— —

In comparison, fares from Hertford to King's Cross were equivalent to those from the GER station to London Bishopsgate, much to the displeasure of passengers using the intermediate stations.

London From	First Single s d	Second Single s d	Third Single s d
Hertford	4 9	3 4	2 2

On and from 1st April 1872 Third Class passengers were conveyed by all trains on the GNR and GER routes to London and by 1873 the fares from London King's Cross to Hatfield and the branch stations had been considerably reduced, partly to counteract loss of patronage to the GER route.

King's Cross To	Single			Return		
	First Class s d	Second Class s d	Third Class s d	First Class s d	Second Class s d	Third Class s d
Hatfield	3 0	2 8	1 5½	5 0	3 9	2 11
Cole Green	4 3	3 0	2 0	6 8	5 0	4 0
Hertingfordbury	4 9	3 4	2 1½	8 0	5 9	4 3
Hertford	4 9	3 4	2 2	8 0	5 9	4 4

By 1873 ordinary return tickets issued on Fridays and Saturdays between London and Hertford were available for the return journey until the following Monday inclusive. Through bookings were also in operation between Hatfield and Hertford, and Watford and Rickmansworth via St. Albans.

Some fares to the branch stations were again adjusted in 1875 and the full tariff from King's Cross was:

King's Cross To	Single						Return					
	First Class		Second Class		Third Class		First Class		Second Class		Third Class	
	s	d	s	d	s	d	s	d	s	d	s	d
Hatfield	2	6	1	10	1	5½	5	0	3	8	2	11
Cole Green	3	6	2	7	2	0	6	8	5	0	4	0
Hertingfordbury	4	0	2	10	2	1½	8	0	5	6	4	3
Hertford	4	6	3	4	2	3	8	0	5	9	4	6

The fare structure from Hertford Cowbridge in 1877 was:

Hertford Cowbridge To	First Single		Second Single		Third Single	
	s	d	s	d	s	d
Hertingfordbury		4		3		1½
Cole Green		8		6		3
Hatfield	2	0	1	6		9
St. Albans	3	0	2	2	1	3½
Luton	3	6	2	6	1	6½
Dunstable (Church St)	4	6	3	4	1	11
King's Cross	4	6	3	4	2	0

Second Class accommodation and fares were abolished on GNR services after 31st October 1891.

On 26th November 1928 Hertford branch stations were included in a scheme to reduce 9,000 return fares on the GNR section to counteract loss of traffic to road competition.

Fares from King's Cross to the branch stations in 1935 were:

King's Cross To	First Class						Third Class					
	S		MR		CDR		S		MR		CDR	
	s	d	s	d	s	d	s	d	s	d	s	d
Hatfield	3	8½	4	6	3	5	2	3	3	0	2	3
Welwyn G City	4	2	5	3	3	11	2	6	3	6	2	7
Cole Green	4	5	5	9	4	0	2	8	3	8	2	8
Hertingfordbury	4	4	5	3	3	11	2	7	3	6	2	7
Hertford North	4	2	5	3	3	9	2	6	3	6	2	6
S Single MR Monthly Return CDR Cheap Day Return												

The fares quoted to Hertford North and Hertingfordbury were via Enfield Chase whilst Cole Green was via either route.

The fare structure in 1947 from King's Cross was:

King's Cross To	First Class						Third Class					
	S		MR		CDR		S		MR		CDR	
	s	d	s	d	s	d	s	d	s	d	s	d
Hatfield	5	3	6	5	5	3	3	1	4	3	3	1
Welwyn G City	6	0	7	5	6	0	3	8	4	11	3	8
Cole Green	—	—	—	—	—	—	3	9	5	3	—	—
Hertingfordbury	—	—	—	—	—	—	3	8	4	11	—	—
Hertford North	—	—	—	—	—	—	3	7	4	11	—	—
S Single MR Monthly Return CDR Cheap Day Return												

The fares quoted to Cole Green and Hertingfordbury were via Hatfield whilst to Hertford North was via Enfield Chase.

Goods Traffic

From the outset it was the intention of the H&WJR to become a through freight route from and to the eastern counties, as the early negotiations proved. On 11th November 1857 the ECR board discussed the adoption of through goods rates from Ware to Digswell Junction (*sic*) with the GNR and H&WJR directors, but the matter was concluded without agreement. After discussion on 28th April 1858 the proposed revenue sharing on the London to Hertford goods traffic via the GNR was forwarded to the Railway Clearing House.

Early in 1859 the ECR authorities announced that 1,927 tons of coal from the Midland collieries had been routed via the H&WJR line but as yet no firm contract had been agreed between the three parties. After much deliberation, arrangements were proposed but on 13th March 1861 the ECR board considered the GNR Company proposals for the Hertford goods traffic.

1. All rail transfers between Hertford GN station and Hertford ECR station to be made by the GNR Company.
2. An allowance of 2 miles to be taken out of the ECR mileage for such transfers.
3. Cartage in the town to be free to the ECR.
4. Hertford station-to-station cartage: the ECR to pay the GNR 6d per ton.
5. A minimum charge of 1s 6d per wagon to be charged for all traffic using the line.

Needless to say, these rather one-sided proposal were rejected outright at Bishopsgate.

As a result of the Amalgamation Act of June 1861 the GNR announced in November the proposed minimum charge of 2s 6d per ton for traffic passing across the Welwyn Junction to Hertford branch en route to Ware. The ECR strongly objected to the suggested rate as the yield from such receipts would be considerably less than that already received. After much deliberation, in February 1862 the GNR Victoria Docks agency proposed the ECR handle GNR Victoria Docks traffic via Hertford and not via Hackney Wick, with charges 2s 6d per ton terminals, 8s 6d per ton cartage and terminals, and 2s 6d per ton lighterage if required. In return the ECR Manager asked for restoration of traffic emanating north of Peterborough to be routed via Peterborough and not via Hertford. Seymour Clarke, the GNR General Manager, however insisted on the shortest routing available for the GNR to ECR destinations south of Harlow and west of Witham. As a result of the agreements, GNR Company traffic from the north destined for Ipswich, Colchester and Bury St. Edmunds temporarily routed via Hertford was restored to run via Peterborough.

Before the advent of the railway, the local carriers' carts were a common sight on the roads, linking the villages and towns of the area, especially for Hertford market. The initial freight handled confirmed the optimistic views of the promoters as barley, hay straw and vegetable traffic were transferred from farm and carriers' carts to the railway for rapid transit to and from Hertford, Luton, St. Albans, Hitchin and London markets. In addition to the root vegetable crops conveyed, including potatoes, swedes, carrots, turnips, and mangold wurzels, from the early 1920s sugar beet was grown and considerable loads were transferred from farm carts and horse drawn waggons to railway wagons at Hertford, Cole Green and Hertingfordbury goods yards for conveyance to the British

Sugar Corporation factories at Peterborough and Felstead. By the early 1950s most of this traffic had transferred to road haulage for direct delivery from farm to factory.

Milk was regularly sent from the branch stations and conveyed to dairies at Hertford in the then familiar 17-gallon churns. Two loads were dispatched during the summer months, one by an early morning service and then again in the late afternoon. Milk was only forwarded on an early morning train in the winter months. The area of Hertfordshire was not noted for prolific dairy farming and the relatively small amounts of traffic were quickly lost to road transport in the late 1930s, although it was resurrected for a time in World War Two when petrol rationing reduced the number of lorries on the road.

Before the coming of the railway, drovers herded animals along the roads to and from markets and prices fluctuated according to the condition of the beasts. The advent of the railway meant animals could be conveyed relatively quickly to local and London markets, arriving in a much fresher condition and therefore gaining a higher price. From the outset livestock handled at the branch stations was two-way traffic. The potential of the railway for speedy transportation of animals was soon realised and horses were regularly conveyed in wagons or horseboxes attached to passenger trains. Until World War Two, hunting horses were conveyed to or from local hunt meetings on twenty-four hours' notice being given to the forwarding station. Cattle wagons were a common feature until the early 1950s and the branch was used to convey livestock to Hertford, St. Albans, Enfield, Luton, Barnet, Dunstable, Hitchin, Ware and Bishop's Stortford markets. Certain passenger trains were permitted to convey cattle wagons on market days.

Coal and coke traffic was handled at all stations with coal received from amongst others: Bestwood, Langwith, Newstead, Kirkley, Hucknall, Sheepbridge, Stanton, Shirebrook West Hallam, Denby Hall, Cossall and Clipstone colleries. The wagons travelled via Peterborough, the coal being loaded in colliery private owner wagons as well as some GNR and L&NER wagons. In the 1920s and 1930s coke was also conveyed for horticultural purposes. As early as 27th March 1858 John and Jasper Gripper had established a coal wharf beside the railway at Hertford, which soon became known as Gripper's Wharf. From 1st January 1859 the brothers were advertising the following prices per ton for coal:

	£	s	d	
Stewart's, Wallsend	1	3	0	
Silkstone Wharncliff Company	1	1	6	
Flockton	1	0	6	
Barnsley House		18	6	
Hard Steam		18	6	
Coke		15	6	chauldron

These prices for transit via the GNR and the H&WJR were 1s 0d cheaper than fuel routed via the ECR. In addition to the quoted prices a delivery charge of 1s 6d per ton was made to customers in the town of Hertford.

By 1863 the Gripper Brothers were advertising the distribution of coal from their wharf at Hertford as well as Hertingfordbury and Cole Green, also Hertford, Ware, St. Margaret's, Broxbourne and Roydon stations on the GER. They survived until the 1890s, adding from 1865 stations on the Buntingford branch, but did not enjoy the exclusive rights for W.H. Dorrington, the Hertford seedsman was advertising the distribution of coal from the coal depot at Cowbridge station and also Priory Wharf in Railway Street. A large user of coal was the Hertford Gas & Light Company, then later taken over by the Tottenham & District Gas Board, later Eastern Gas Board, Tottenham Division, which had daily deliveries to their siding near the junction with the GER.

Hertford was the centre of the seed industry serving the surrounding agricultural area. As well as Dorrington, Edmund Illiot & Sons (established in 1867, surviving until the late 1920s) produced dried animal foods from the Town Roller Mills which was served by a siding branching off the track leading to McMullen's brewery. Inskip & Manser, linseed, cotton seed and rape oil manufacturers operating from Dicker's oil mill, were operational when the railway opened but after 1874 became Edward Manser & Company, surviving until the later 1920s.

Samuel Andrews, a building surveyor, established a builders' merchants and supply business at Priory and Folly wharves, Hertford but by the early 1870 the business was taken over by Robert Thornton and William Frampton Andrews who received much material by rail including, timber, slates, bricks and other items. The business later only operated from Priory Wharf and associated saw mills, and was taken over by Ewen & Tomlinson Limited in the late 1890s, when the commodities received and exported by rail included galvanised iron, fire clay and sanitary pipes. The business passed to Jewsons in the late 1930s.

At one time the largest revenue earned on goods traffic on the branch came from the conveyance of ballast and sand removed from pits established at several locations alongside the line. The principal developer of the industry was Josiah Smart senior, born at Sneinton, a village near Nottingham, in 1847. By 1875 he was married and living with his wife and two daughters in Stevenage. Josiah junior was born in 1879 and by 1881 Josiah senior's occupation was established as 'Senior Ashphalter/Pavior to the GNR'. He thus was responsible for overseeing the tarpaving work on the company's station platforms. Soon after the 1881 census he went into business on his own account and, because of his connections with the GNR, entered into agreement on 23rd July 1886 with the Marquess of Salisbury for the lease of two acres of land forming part of Woodhall Lodge farm in the Hatfield Parish for the purpose of extracting sand and gravel. Four years later he purchased land at Holwell Hyde, Hatfield from Baron Braye and others for similar purposes. By now he was advertising in areas covering Hitchin, Stevenage, Barnet and Finsbury Park, offering estimates for surfacing of garden paths, footpaths, carriage drives and other hard surfaces with an address in Stevenage and the GNR goods yard at Finsbury Park. He had also patented a 3-ply asphalt used in GNR railway tunnels. He then entered into an agreement with Earl Cowper on 29th September 1892 for his tenant William Hill of Birchall or Birchold Farm to extract sand and gravel from land at Holwell for a period of fourteen years, and as a result a siding was established. Agreements were also made with Earl Cowper to extract sand and gravel from land belonging to Place Farm, Wheathampstead on the Dunstable branch.

Smart's company also had other sites at Roxford Lane, Hertingfordbury and Mead Lane, Hertford. In the latter years of the 19th century Josiah senior further expanded and rented two sites north of Hatfield: at Mount Pleasant on part of Great Heath Field, described in 1899 as brick works, and the second site north of the first close to Woodhall Farm Lodge (Twentieth Mile), both were served by sidings off the Hatfield to Hertford branch single line. Josiah junior was engaged in the activities of the firm, recorded in the 1901 census as manager of the family Asphalt & Tarpavement Contracting Company. Josiah senior died on 9th March 1915, when Josiah junior took sole charge of the firm and in 1916 he purchased the freehold of gravel pits and building land in Mead Lane, Hertford, which had previously been rented from William Gray. Consisting of 13 acres together with a cottage, the purchase price was £1,750. Several other sites were purchased for gravel extraction throughout the 1920s, when the establishment at Hertford was advertised as Gravel Merchants of Gashouse Lane, but on 14th January 1929 it was announced the business had been taken over by Constable, Hart & Company. In 1933 the local directory showed the establishment as Smarts, Tar Distillery Limited, The Distillers Works, Mead Lane, Hertford, but the business was sold to the Prince Regent Tar Company Limited before 1940. Josiah junior died in February 1940, at which time ballast was still being extracted from some of his pits.

Along the line at Hertingfordbury, Webb dealt with leather for their glove factory at Horn's Mill, William Paye loaded bricks and tiles from the small brickworks located near the station, whilst Welch was purely an agricultural siding. William Paye, the author's great grandfather, subsequently worked out the pit at Hertingfordbury and transferred his works to Hoddesdon, later moving to Enfield Highway.

Barley was conveyed to the maltings at Ware and Hertford in considerable quantities and the establishing of McMullen's brewery at Hertford in 1827, together with other smaller establishments which were later absorbed, meant there was a ready market. Alcoholic beverage was an early conveyance on the new railway from Welwyn Junction to Hertford, included 10,000 butts of beer en route from Burton to Blackwall. The ECR charges for this service from Hertford to Blackwall for a trial period of eighteen months were 1s 6d per ton for terminal handling and 4s 0d per ton for warehousing. Gripper & Wightman were also established as maltsters operating at Hertford from 1898 until after World War Two. McMullen's were early customers of the railway when sidings were installed to serve the brewery and, when local supplies were insufficient, malt was brought from other stations on the GNR and GER and even from Scotland. Bottled beer was another export from the brewery, as were the occasional barrels of ale, but with a local clientele most of the ale was transported by road on horse drawn drays, then steam lorries and later motor lorries. As a bonus for arranging the delivery, placing and collection of wagons, various shunting staff were provided with a free pint of ale for their labours. For the majority of the time the shunter was on the GNR or L&NER GN section staff complement, but in the latter years Shunter Lawrence from Hertford East was the recipient of a free pint.

After the opening of the Shredded Wheat Factory at Welwyn Garden City in 1924 much of the grain received from abroad was routed from Millwall Docks via the GER Lea Valley line and thence to Hertford East for conveyance across the branch; bulk grain wagons were regularly conveyed daily and empty wagons returned by the same route. Before conveyance across the branch it was usual for the train of loaded grain wagons to be taken into one or other of the terminal platform roads at Hertford East station to allow the locomotive to run round the train prior the propelling the wagons

'N7/3' Class 0-6-2T No. 69704 is approaching Hertford North from Hertford Old with a train of grain wagons en route to the Shredded Wheat factory at Welwyn Garden City, on 28th June 1958. Underbridge No. 13 spanning the River Beane is in the foreground. Note the locomotive, then allocated to Hertford East shed (30B), is still carrying the passenger destination board. *J.F. Aylard*

to Hertford Old for a Hatfield or relieving Hertford locomotive to take the train forward to Welwyn Garden City. The grain wagons were notorious for leakage, and many being unfitted and loose coupled added to the spillage. At other times the wagons were taken into the platform road before the engine hauled them out to the old Down yard before running round. With the daily movement into and out of the platform or yard and rough shunting it became noticeable that wheat started to grow between the rails!

In the 1920s and early 1930s many roads in Hertfordshire were unmetalled dust tracks in summer and quagmires in winter. Hertfordshire County Council undertook a rolling programme of road improvements, which included levelling the surface before covering with granite chippings and tarmacadam. Most of the material was delivered by rail to the branch stations from where it was offloaded and taken to site by horse and wagon. The granite and tarmacadam were then levelled by steamroller.

The branch will always retain a memorable place in the annals of the pigeon racing fraternity of North London, for Cole Green and Hertingfordbury stations were the liberation point for many young birds taking part in their first race or setting out on time trials.

The following goods facilities were available at the branch stations:

HATFIELD
Loading dock
Loading gauge
Fixed crane, 5 tons capacity
Cattle pens
Cattle dock
Truck weighbridge
Weighing machines
Goods shed
Wagon turntable
Lock up for small packages

WELWYN JUNCTION
Loading gauge

WELWYN GARDEN CITY (AFTER 1926)
Loading dock
Loading gauge
Fixed crane, 10 tons capacity
Cattle dock
Cattle pens
Truck weighbridge
Weighing machine
Goods shed
Wagon turntable
Lock up for small packages

COLE GREEN
Loading dock
Loading gauge
Fixed crane, 1 ton capacity – later removed
Cattle pens
Cattle dock
Lock up for small packages

HERTINGFORDBURY
Loading gauge
Lock up for small packages

HERTFORD NORTH (FROM 1924)
Nil

HERTFORD COWBRIDGE
Loading dock
Loading gauges
Fixed crane, 5 tons capacity
Fixed crane, 3 x 1-ton in goods shed
Fixed crane, 10-ton on River Lea wharf
Cattle pens
Cattle dock
Truck weighbridge

Sturrock '270' series, later 'F5' Class, 0-4-2WT No. 279A shunting at Hatfield on 12th April 1902. The locomotive was withdrawn from traffic in April 1905. *LCGB/Ken Nunn*

North elevation of the large 90 feet by 35 feet goods shed provided by the GNR at Hertford Cowbridge. In the early years it was equipped with 3 x 1-ton fixed cranes on the loading and unloading platform, but these were later removed.
P. Whitaker

The large 90 feet by 35 feet goods shed located on the Up side on the main single line east of the station at Hertford Cowbridge seen in July 1954. *P. Whitaker*

Combined GNR/GER loading gauge located east of Hertford Cowbridge station in July 1952. *P. Whitaker*

GNR 5 tons capacity fixed crane in the coal yard at Hertford Cowbridge in July 1954. At one time there were also three 1-ton capacity fixed cranes in the goods shed. *P. Whitaker*

Weighing machine
Goods shed
Wagon turntable
Lock up for small packages
Stables

There were no facilities for unloading horses and carriages at Hertingfordbury.

Permitted Loads

In 1877 the maximum permitted loading of goods trains between Hatfield and Hertford was 25 vehicles in either direction with the following restrictions:

Hawthorn 4-wheel coupled engine	15 coal wagons and one brake van
	20 goods and coal wagons and one brake van
Sharp 4-wheel coupled engine	10 coal wagons and one brake van
	13 goods and coal wagons and one brake van

One brake van was permitted on each train, with maximum load of 25 empty vehicles.

The 1881 GNR Appendix to the Working Timetable gave the following loads for goods and mineral locomotives working between Hatfield and Hertford. The figures did not include brake vans. One guard was to ride in the brake van.

1. Six-wheel coupled tender engines with 17½-inch and 18-inch cylinders.
2. Six-wheel coupled tender engines with small cylinders.
3. Six-wheel coupled tank engines – large class.
4. Six-wheel coupled tank engines – small classes.

General and pick up goods	35 wagons
Coal, coke, stone and other minerals and heavy goods, contents of wagons averaging 8 tons each	25 wagons
Empty wagons	40 wagons

By 1905 the permitted loadings were:

A Six-wheel coupled tender engine.
B Four-wheel coupled tender engine.
C Large 4-wheel coupled tank engine including '1520' Class.
D Smaller 4-wheel coupled tank engine including '249' and '513' classes.

	A	B	C	D
Down general and pick up goods	28	28	28	25
Minerals and heavy goods	23	20	19	18
Empty wagons	35	30	30	30
Up general and pick up goods between Cole Green and Hatfield	28	26	26	25
Up general and pick up goods between Hertford and Cole Green	26	25	24	23

Tender engines were permitted to take 35 loaded wagons and tank engines 30 loaded wagons between Hatfield and Digswell sidings. One guard to ride with each brake van.

Later the loading of freight trains was amended to:

	Minerals	Wagon/Goods	Empties
Tender Class 'B' and 'C'	45	45	45
Tank Class 'K'	33	45	45
Tank Class 'L'	32	45	45
Tank Class 'M'	37	45	45

The load classifications of locomotives, which worked across the branch were:

Load Class	GNR Class	Wheel Arrangement	L&NER Class
'B'	'J4'	0-6-0	'J3'
'B'	'J5'	0-6-0	'J4'
'B'	'J22'	0-6-0	'J6'
'C'	'J7'	0-6-0	—
'K'	'F7'	0-4-2T	—
'K'	'G5'	0-4-4T	—
'L'	'F4'	0-4-2T	—
'L'	'F6'	0-4-2T	—
'L'	'G2'	0-4-4T	—
'M'	'C2'	4-4-2T	'C12'
'M'	'G1'	0-4-4T	'G1'

Under the L&NER the freight train loads on the Hatfield to Hertford branch were not to exceed 45 wagons in either direction, with individual loadings as under:

Engine Class	Minerals	Goods	Empties
'1'	42	45	45
'2'	45	45	45
'3'	45	45	45

The 'C12' Class 4-4-2Ts were permitted to convey 37 minerals, 45 goods or 45 empties.

By 1944 the following loadings were permitted between Welwyn Garden City and Hertford:

	No. '1' Class			No. '2' Class			No. '3' Class		
	M	G	E	M	G	E	M	G	E
Welwyn G C to Hertford	24	35	35	25	35	35	26	35	35
Hertford to Cole Green	18	27	30	19	28	30	21	30	30
Cole Green to Welwyn G C	19	28	30	21	30	30	23	30	30
Hertford to Welwyn G C	12	27	36	19	28	38	21	32	42

M Minerals   G Goods   E Empties

Tank engines were to have a 15-ton brake van at the tail of the train. Down trains requiring to cross another train at Cole Green were to be limited to 24 wagons and brake van. Trains consisting of through loads of empties from Welwyn Garden City to Hertford were permitted to convey the following loads: No. '1' Class engine 48 empties, No. '2' Class engine 50 empties and No. '3' Class engines 52 empties. Up trains requiring to cross Down trains at Cole Green were to be limited to 29 wagons and brake van. The loads for through trains were subject to length limits if requiring to cross another train at Cole Green.

11

Locomotives and Rolling Stock

The relatively light construction of the Hatfield to Hertford branch precluded the use of locomotives with heavy axle loading. Fortunately the GNR possessed ample locomotives of low route availability to work both passenger and freight services. The L&NER and later BR classified Hatfield to Hertford and later Welwyn Garden City to Hertford North as Route Availability 5 (RA5) with additional classes 'N2' and 'J50' of RA6 permitted, the Class 'N2' permitted for through running only and not to exceed 30 mph. Hertford North to Hertford East retained the RA5 classification. 'N7' Class locomotives were only permitted to double head trains in an emergency whilst all mainline diesel locomotives were prohibited from the line except to the sidings at Welwyn Garden City, leaving Class '08' 0-6-0 diesel electric shunting locomotives to convey freight traffic in the final few months before closure.

The 'Little Sharpie' Tank Engines

The GNR initially had few tank locomotives but from the outset Hertford branch passenger services were worked by 'Little Sharpie' 2-2-2 tank locomotives. The engines had been converted in 1852 from tender locomotives built by Sharp Brothers of Manchester between 1847 and 1849, and numbered 1 to 50 inclusive. Fourteen engines were converted to tank locomotives between January and July 1852 – No's 1, 2, 6, 9, 10, 18, 19, 35, 39, 40, 42, 45, 46 and 50 – with a further seventeen – No's 4, 5, 7, 11, 12, 13, 15, 20, 21, 22, 28, 29, 31, 32, 33, 37 and 43 – converted by the end of the year. From the opening of the Welwyn Junction to Hertford line they were the only tank engines in use on the GNR until 1865, except for three engines absorbed from the Nottingham to Grantham line in 1855, and No's 1, 2, 15 and 31 were regularly outbased at Hertford from Hatfield to work the branch. The 'Little Sharpies' had limited coal and water capacity and the necessity to replenish supplies at frequent intervals rendered the class unpopular with the operating authorities. The principal dimensions of the class were:

Cylinders		15 ins x 20 ins	
Motion		Stephenson with slide valves	
Boiler	Max diameter	3 feet 6¾ ins	
	Barrel length	10 feet 0 ins	
	Firebox	3 feet 0 ins	
Heating surface			
	Tubes	147 x 1¾ ins	690.3 sq feet
	Firebox		57.9 sq feet
	Total		748.2 sq feet
Leading wheels		3 feet 6 ins	
Driving wheels		5 feet 6 ins	
Trailing wheels		3 feet 6 ins	
Wheelbase		15 feet 9 ins	
Axle loading			
	Leading wheels	8 tons 13 cwt	
	Driving wheels	7 tons 15 cwt	
	Trailing wheels	7 tons 0 cwt	
Water capacity		420 gallons	

In 1858, eight of the 2-2-2 tank locomotives were further altered and rebuilt into 0-4-2 wheel arrangement with an added well tank beneath the bunker. No's 7, 12, 20, 39, 40, 42, 43 and 46 received the modification and were initially allocated to work traffic in the Leeds and Wakefield, and Leeds, Bradford and Halifax areas. By August 1863 all were back in the London area and equipped with condensing gear for working Metropolitan line services before being displaced by new Sturrock designed '241' series 'Back Tanks' in 1865. In January 1866 the last 'Sharpie' 0-4-2 tank locomotive was displaced from the GNR Metropolitan services and after repairs four, No's 3, 25, 44 and 46, were sent to Hatfield shed for further service on the branches to Hertford, St. Albans and Dunstable where motive power *'was not sufficiently provided for before'.*

The GNR initially used 'Little Sharpie' 2-2-2 tank locomotives on Hertford branch services, the locomotives being built by Sharp Brothers of Manchester between 1847 and 1849. They had limited coke and water capacity, which necessitated replenishing at frequent intervals. *Author's collection*

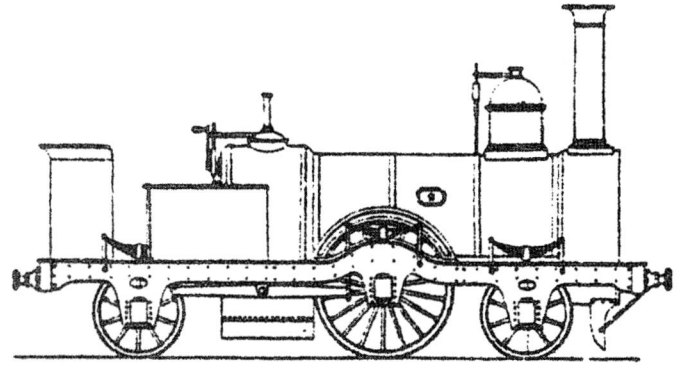

'Little Sharpie' 2-2-2Ts which worked the initial services on the Hatfield to Hertford branch.

The ECR Gooch 'B' Class 2-2-2 Well Tanks

For the short period the ECR was working the Hertford to Welwyn Junction services the company provided Gooch 'B' Class 2-2-2 well tank locomotives to haul both passenger and mixed trains and it was a member of the class which came to grief in the accident at Hertford on 9th April 1859. The well tanks were built at Stratford Works: No. 7 entering traffic in June 1853, No. 8 in August 1853 and No's 9 to 12 in April 1854. No's 7 and 12 were recorded working the Broxbourne to Hertford branch and it is possible the others were outbased at the shed sometime in their career also to work the branch thence to Welwyn Junction. No. 11 was the first to be withdrawn in March 1871, followed by No. 10 in November of the same year; No. 12 was scrapped in January in 1874, No. 7 in June and No. 9 in August of the same year. No. 8 was converted into an inspection engine in December 1874 and survived in much altered form for another nine years, being withdrawn in March 1883.

The leading dimensions of the 'B' Class were:

Cylinders	2 outside	12 ins x 22 ins	
Motion		Stephenson with slide valves	
Boiler	Max diameter	3 feet 3½ ins	
	Length	10 feet 0 ins	
Firebox	outside length	3 feet 6 ins	
Heating surface			
	Tubes	127 x 1⅞ ins	638.52 sq feet
	Firebox		69.17 sq feet
	Total		707.69 sq feet
Grate area		9.41 sq feet	
Boiler pressure		110 psi	
Leading wheels		3 feet 8 ins	
Driving wheels		6 feet 6 ins	
Trailing wheels		3 feet 8 ins	
Wheelbase		12 feet 0 ins	
Weight in working order		23 tons 19 cwt	
Max axle loading		9 tons 14 cwt	

By the end of 1865 the motive power position on the GNR was far from healthy and Archibald Sturrock, having been in office as Locomotive Engineer since 1850, deemed it necessary to purchase additional locomotives. Included in his submission was a request for a special class of engine to work the Hertford, Luton and Dunstable services. Early in 1866 the Board of Directors appointed a committee to investigate Sturrock's application and reporting back on 6th February they turned down the request and recommended the Locomotive Engineer *'to alter some of the existing engines to suit the curves of the line'*. In 1866 the following Sharp 2-2-2T locomotives were still allocated to Hatfield to work the branches: No's 1, 2, 15 and 31, with 0-4-2Ts No's 3, 25 and 44.

The '241' and '271' Engines

In 1865 Archibald Sturrock introduced into service ten 0-4-2 well tank locomotives, No's 241 to 250 inclusive, for use on the expanding London suburban service as well as working the Metropolitan line services. Their design was evolved from the 'Little Sharpie' 0-4-2 tank locomotive conversions and they were built by the Avonside Engine Company. A further fifteen were authorised in January 1866 as the initial ten were at work with no spare capacity. These were required for the traffic to Victoria, the Highgate and Edgware lines, and the Hitchin to Cambridge branch. Sturrock then requested special engines with *'Caillet's built up axles'* for working over the sharp curves of the Hatfield to Luton and Dunstable line, the St. Albans branch and Hertford branch. However, the directors refused this request and the London suburban tank engine order was reduced to ten. These very similar locomotives, No's 270 to 279 inclusive, entered service in 1867, the first five being built by Neilson & Company and the remainder by the Avonside Engine Company. Both classes were rebuilt with new boilers in 1878 and 1881. Most of the engines in their career were at one time used on the Hatfield branches where they could handle most of the lightweight passenger diagrams as well as proving their worth on the moderately heavy freight trains.

The '241' and '270' classes were as follows:

GNR No.	Built	Duplicate List	Withdrawn
241	October 1865	February 1879	December 1899
242	October 1865	June 1880	July 1899
243	October 1865	March 1879	July 1900
244	November 1865	November 1878	December 1899
245	November 1865	June 1879	June 1905
246	November 1865	December 1878	April 1902
247	November 1865	November 1879	January 1903
248	November 1865	August 1880	September 1902
249	December 1865	December 1879	May 1899
250	January 1866	May 1879	May 1898
270	February 1867	September 1901	February 1904
271	February 1867	—	April 1902
272	March 1867	—	June 1898
273	March 1867	—	October 1901
274	March 1867	—	December 1900
275	February 1867	April 1904	July 1905
276	February 1867	—	July 1901
277	March 1867	—	May 1900
278	March 1867	May 1904	November 1905
279	April 1867	May 1904	April 1905

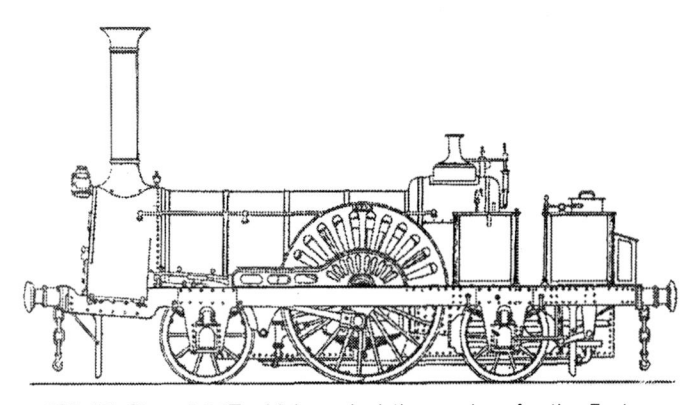

ECR 'B' Class 2-2-2T which worked the services for the Eastern Counties Company.

The principal dimensions of the '241' Class were:

Cylinders	2 inside	16 ins x 22 ins
Motion		Stephenson with slide valves
Boiler	Max diameter	4 feet 1 in.
	Barrel length	10 feet 0 ins
	Firebox	4 feet 6 ins
Heating surface		
	Tubes	146 x 2 ins 790.0 sq feet
	Firebox	64.0 sq feet
	Total	854.0 sq feet
Grate area		12.5 sq feet
Boiler pressure		150 psi
Coupled wheels		5 feet 6 ins
Trailing wheels		4 feet 0 ins
Tractive effort		10,863 lbs
Length over buffers		23 feet 10 ins
Wheelbase		19 feet 3 ins
Weight in working order		39 tons 12 cwt
Max axle loading		13 tons 14 cwt
Water capacity		1,000 gallons
Coal capacity		15 cwt (coke)

Amendments as a result of rebuilding:

Boiler	Max diameter	4 feet 0½ ins
	Barrel length	10 feet 0 ins
	Firebox	4 feet 6 ins
Heating surface		
	Tubes	162 x 1⅝ ins

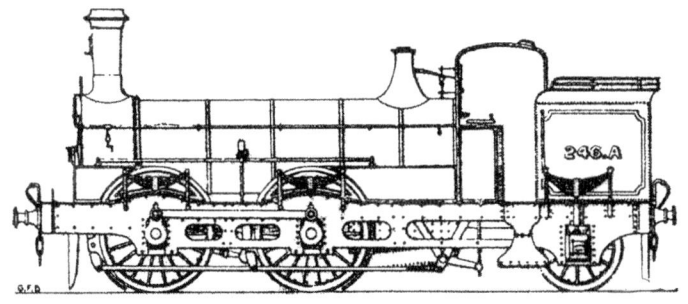

ABOVE: Sturrock '241' Class 0-4-2WT.

Sturrock '241' series 0-4-2WT No. 248A, built by the Avonside Engine Company in 1865, later became 'F5' Class in the Ivatt '1900' classification. It is seen at Hatfield in the last years of its life when fitted with a Stirling 4 feet 5 inches diameter boiler. The locomotive was withdrawn in 1902. *LCGB/Ken Nunn*

The leading dimensions of the '270' Class were:

Cylinders	2 inside	16½ ins x 22 ins
Motion		Stephenson's link
Boiler	Max diameter	4 feet 1 in.
	Barrel length	10 feet 0 ins
	Firebox	4 feet 9 ins
Heating surface		
	Tubes	146 x 2 ins 788.00 sq feet
	Firebox	86.75 sq feet
	Total	874.75 sq feet
Grate area		13.6 sq feet
Boiler pressure		160 psi
Coupled wheels		5 feet 6½ ins
Trailing wheels		4 feet 0½ ins
Tractive effort		12,250 lbs
Length over buffers		30 feet 3 ins
Wheelbase		20 feet 3 ins
Weight in working order		43 tons 10 cwt
Max axle loading		15 tons 0 cwt
Water capacity		1,080 gallons

Amendments as a result of rebuilding:

Boiler	Max diameter	4 feet 5 ins
	Barrel length	10 feet 0 ins
	Firebox	4 feet 6 ins
Heating surface		
	Tubes	162 x 1⅝ ins

STURROCK '126' CLASS, LATER 'F4' AND 'F6' CLASS

In 1868 there was an urgent requirement for additional passenger tank locomotives to work the steadily increasing suburban traffic in the London area. The GNR board was initially opposed to the provision of passenger tank classes but then relaxed their opposition, allowing Stirling to proceed with the construction of thirteen 0-4-2 well tank locomotives at Doncaster Works. The '126' Class as they were known appeared in small batches: No's 126 and 127 in 1868; four, No's 123, 125, 129 and 131 in 1869; three, No's 121, 122 and

132 in 1870, and the balancing four, No's 116, 117, 118 and 119 in 1871. The initial two were placed at work in the West Riding district whilst the remainder, equipped with condensing gear, worked turn and turn about with Sturrock classes on the London suburban routes. The class did not venture onto the Hertford branch on a regular basis until 1884 when with the later 0-4-4 back tanks they monopolised the King's Cross to Hatfield and Hertford services. Between 1884 and 1889 the whole class was rebuilt with a 4 feet 2½ inch diameter boiler and became Class 'F4', whilst No's 116, 117, 118, 122 and 132 received a 4 feet 5 inch diameter domed boiler between 1899 and 1907 to become Class 'F6'. The Hatfield and Hertford work continued after the influx of the Stirling side tank engines from the 1890s and continued through to the early 1900s. On the introduction of the Ivatt 'C2' Class 4-4-2 tank locomotives from 1899, all the '126' Class well tanks were transferred to Hatfield to work the branches and some later moved further out to country sheds. Between 1898 and 1903 Hatfield regularly used No's 121, 129 and 132 together with unrebuilt No. 116 on the sharply timed 4.30pm King's Cross to Hertford semi-fast train. No's 117, 121 and 132 were still at Hatfield in January 1904. No. 121, on a relatively high mileage and due for shops, was the official snow plough engine, having brackets affixed to the top of the smokebox for attaching the plough, and worked as required clearing the main line and the branches. Locomotives known to have worked from Hatfield included:

GNR No.	Duplicate List	Withdrawn
116A	July 1903	September 1918
117	December 1904	December 1916
121	December 1904	June 1905
129	December 1905	July 1906
132	December 1905	June 1908

The leading dimensions of the 'F4' Class were:

Cylinders	2 inside	17½ ins x 24 ins	
Motion		Stephenson with slide valves	
Boiler	Max diameter	4 feet 2½ ins	
	Barrel length	10 feet 0 ins	
	Firebox	4 feet 10 ins	
Heating surface			
	Tubes	186 x 1⅝ ins	764.0 sq feet
	Firebox		85.33 sq feet
	Total		849.33 sq feet
Grate area		14.06 sq feet	
Boiler pressure		160 psi	
Coupled wheels		5 feet 8 ins	
Trailing wheels		4 feet 2 ins	
Tractive effort		14,700 lbs	
Wheelbase		20 feet 3 ins	
Length over buffers		33 feet 0 ins	
Weight in working order		44 tons 4 cwt	
Water capacity		1,000 gallons	
Coal capacity		1 ton 10 cwt	

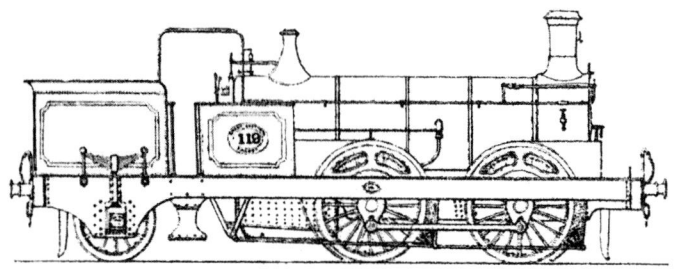

Sturrock '126' Class 0-4-2WT, later classes 'F4' and 'F6'.

Detail differences of the 'F6' Class with Ivatt domed boiler were:

Boiler	Max diameter	4 feet 5 ins	
	Barrel length	10 feet 1 in.	
Heating surface			
	Tubes	215 x 1¾ ins	1,016.0 sq feet
	Firebox		94.0 sq feet
	Total		1,110.0 sq feet
Grate area		16.0 sq feet	
Boiler pressure		140 psi	
Tractive effort		12,862 lbs	
Weight in working order		44 tons 18 cwt	
Max axle loading		17 tons 0 cwt	

The Stirling 'F7' Class

In January 1876 Patrick Stirling prepared drawings for a new class of tank locomotive to work the Essendine to Stamford and Stamford to Wansford branches. The plethora of curves and two weak underbridges required a short wheelbase and adoption of saddle tank and small coal bunker, with the smallest boiler ever adopted by Stirling on one of his own engines. The first engine to the new design, Doncaster Works reference N, No. 502 emerged on 3rd August 1876, to be followed by No. 501 on 6th September and later by No. 503 on 20th December. All three were put to work on the branches from Stamford enabling older locomotives with the same running number to be withdrawn. A fourth locomotive, No. 161, entered traffic on 12th February 1877 and acted as spare engine, deputising when any of the 0-4-2 saddle tank engines were undergoing maintenance or works repair. When not required to work on the branches No. 161 worked away for short periods at Leeds and Bradford. With the increase in traffic on the Stamford branches and the restriction on the use of other GNR tank engines, the decision was taken to introduce a further two 0-4-2 saddle tank locomotives of similar design and same dimensions as the original quartet.

Designated under Doncaster Works reference 2, the first of the pair, No. 631 (Works No. 241), with detailed differences to the cab from the original engines, was completed on 24th June 1878, whilst No. 632 (Works No. 244) was released to traffic on 6th August 1878. All six engines were equipped with the vacuum brake fittings during 1881 and 1882 but soon the choice of six engines specifically to work the Stamford branches was considered excessive and subsequently No's 631 and 632 were transferred away to work in the West Riding district on the Pudsey branch from Stanningley. By the late 1890s No's 501 and 631 were at Hatfield to work the St. Albans and Hertford branches, but by 1902 No. 631 was back in the West Riding.

In June 1900 the 0-4-2 saddle tank locomotives were allocated to GNR Class 'F7' with new load classification 'K'. No. 631 never

ABOVE: Six members of Stirling 'F7' Class 0-4-2T were built between 1876 and 1878 especially to work the Essendine to Stamford and Stamford to Wansford branches, but the number proved excessive and in the 1890s No's 501 and 631 were transferred to Hatfield to work the St. Albans and Hertford routes. Here No. 501 is shown at Essendine on 16th July 1904. *LCGB/Ken Nunn*

FACING PAGE: GNR 'F4' Class 0-4-2WT No. 129A at Hatfield on 12th April 1902. Locomotives of this class handled Hertford branch passenger trains for many years until the arrival of the larger 'Back Tanks'. Withdrawn from traffic in July 1906. *LCGB/Ken Nunn*

returned south and was the first of the class to be withdrawn from service on 11th February 1904. By the end of 1905 No's 501, 502 and 503 were back working the Stamford branches before No. 501 was withdrawn from service in September 1906. The decision was soon cancelled, probably because no suitable replacement could be found, and the engine was reinstated and returned to Peterborough. No. 161, which had been permanently allocated to Leeds, returned south and took turns on the Stamford diagrams until withdrawal on 6th September 1907. In 1911 the GNR civil engineer commenced a programme of work to relay the permanent way and strengthen the bridges on the Stamford branches to permit heavier engines to work the services. No's 501, 502 and 503 soldiered on until 1913 when No. 502 was withdrawn on 22nd January, No. 501 on 18th March and No. 503 on 4th June. No. 632, which received the boiler from No. 161 in October 1911, survived World War One having served at Boston, although before withdrawal on 6th November 1918 as the last member of the class it had been transferred to Peterborough to work the Stamford branches in its final days. The engine subsequently worked for a few months at Swanwick Colliery.

The leading dimensions of the GNR 'F7' Class were:

Cylinders	2 inside	16 ins x 22 ins	
Motion		Stephenson with slide valves	
Boiler	Max dia. outside	4 feet 0½ ins	
	Barrel length	9 feet 3 ins	
Firebox	Outside length	4 feet 6 ins	
Heating surface			
	Tubes	169 x 1⅝ ins	689.0 sq feet
	Firebox		74.0 sq feet
	Total		763.0 sq feet
Grate area		12.75 sq feet	
Boiler pressure		160 psi	
Coupled wheels		5 feet 1 ins	
Trailing wheels		3 feet 7 ins	
Tractive effort		12,557 lbs	
Length over buffers		23 feet 10 ins	
Wheelbase		15 feet 0 ins	
Weight in working order		39 tons 0 cwt	
Max axle loading		14 tons 16 cwt	
Coal capacity		2 tons 0 cwt	
Water capacity		800 gallons	

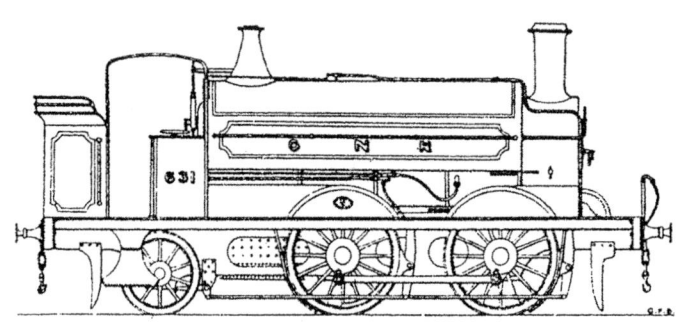

Stirling 'F7' Class 0-4-2T No. 631 which regularly worked the Hertford branch when allocated to Hatfield.

GNR '120' Class later 'G2' Class 0-4-4T 'Back Tank' No. 249 prepares to leave Hatfield with a branch goods train on 13th September 1902. The locomotive was withdrawn from traffic in 1911.
LCGB/Ken Nunn

The Class '120'/'G2' 'Back Tanks'

The next class to be associated with the branches from Hatfield was the '120' Class 0-4-4 tank locomotives. Forty-six of the 'Back Tanks' as they were nicknamed were built at Doncaster between 1872 and 1881 and although of the same basic design, successive batches had minor variations. They were essentially a bogie version of the '126' Class 0-4-2 well tanks but water was carried in a tank measuring 6 feet 11 inches wide by 4 feet 0 inches high positioned above the bogie. In the Ivatt June 1900 Engine Classification the '120' Class were redesignated to Class 'G2'. When new, the initial five of the class were allocated to duties in the West Riding but later engines equipped with condensing gear supplemented the Sturrock and Stirling 0-4-2 tank engines on suburban services from King's Cross. With the arrival of the larger 'G1' Class 0-4-4 tank locomotives from 1881 the 'Back Tanks' were transferred to Hatfield to work diagrams to Moorgate Street and the branches to Hertford, Dunstable and St. Albans. After the arrival of the Ivatt 'C2' Class 4-4-2 tank locomotives in 1899 further engines emigrated from King's Cross to Hatfield, while others transferred to Colwick, Leeds and Bradford. Those at Hatfield were often called upon to work the 4.30pm King's Cross to Hertford train, which with a tail load of four or five 6-wheel coaches was allowed six minutes running time from King's Cross to Finsbury Park and thirteen minutes thence from a standing start to stopping at Potters Bar, a distance of 10½ miles. By 1905 eighteen of the class, No's 243, 244, 245, 247, 249, 510, 511, 513, 515, 528, 530, 531, 622, 623, 624, 625, 628 and 655, had served at Hatfield, working the main line and branches, and as late as 1912 No's 245, 247, 515 and 531A were still at work at the Hertfordshire shed.

GNR No.	To Duplicate List	Withdrawn
243	—	October 1910
244	—	April 1913
245	—	December 1916
247	—	May 1914
249	—	November 1911
510	—	September 1907
511	—	July 1911
513	—	November 1908
515	—	March 1920
528	—	July 1908
530	November 1911	May 1919
531A	November 1911	June 1919
622	—	September 1908
623	—	July 1907
624	December 1919	January 1921
625	—	September 1903
628	—	December 1909
655	—	January 1921

'120' Class 'Back Tank' 0-4-4T, later Class 'G2'.

The principal dimensions of the 'G2' Class were:

Cylinders	2 inside	17½ ins x 24 ins	
Motion		Stephenson with slide valves	
Boiler	Max diameter	4 feet 5 ins	
	Barrel length	9 feet 10 ins	
	Firebox	4 feet 6 ins	
Heating surface			
	Tubes	201 x 1⅝ ins	869.03 sq feet
	Firebox		83.17 sq feet
	Total		952.20 sq feet
Grate area		12.75 sq feet	
Boiler pressure		160 psi	
Coupled wheels		5 feet 7 ins	
Trailing wheels		3 feet 1 in.	
Tractive effort		14,919 lbs	
Length over buffers		33 feet 5 ins	
Wheelbase		22 feet 6 ins	
Weight in working order		45 tons 10 cwt	
Max axle loading		14 tons 14 cwt	
Water capacity		1,000 gallons	
Coal capacity		2 tons 10 cwt	

The '766'/'G1' Class

In 1889 Stirling introduced into service his '766' Class 0-4-4 tank locomotives for Metropolitan and London traffic. Ten were built in 1889/90 followed by five in 1891, ten in 1892/3 and a further four in 1895. They were a substantial improvement on the '126' Class and the 'Back Tanks', and in the 1900 Engine classification all twenty-nine were designated to Class 'G1'. All engines were built with condensing gear but when the class was transferred from the London area in 1907 this was removed. In 1905 all but three were allocated to the London district with a few out-stationed at Hatfield, where they worked on the main-line suburban services as well as the branches. On 15th February 1907 No. 931 suffered a broken

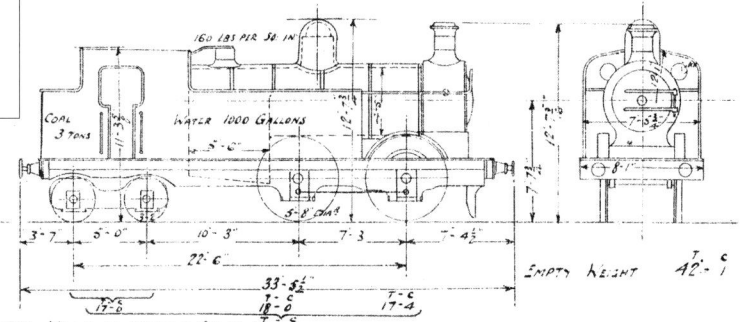

RIGHT: Stirling '766' Class. Later L&NER 'G1' Class 0-4-4T.

GNR, later L&NER 'G1' Class, No. 770 was based at Hatfield in the latter stages of its life and is here shown in lined GNR livery. The locomotive was withdrawn from traffic in June 1925. *Author's collection*

left-hand crank web whilst the locomotive was shunting Smart's gravel pit siding near Hertingfordbury. The fault went unnoticed but fortunately the strap held until the locomotive reached Cole Green, where the strap holding the crank together fractured whilst the locomotive was stationary thus obviating what might have been a serious mishap. The arrival of the Ivatt 0-8-2 and later 'N1' Class 0-6-2 tank locomotive classes allowed locomotives to be transferred away to Colwick and Leeds and by 1912 only No's 766 to 770 were working from Hatfield as well as on lighter inner suburban work. The arrival of additional 'N1' Class locomotives meant further transfers away and by 1919 0-4-4 tank locomotives No's 933 and 936 were at Hatfield, with No's 767, 770 and 931 added in August 1921. As L&NER 'G1' Class working from Hatfield in 1923, No's 767 and 770 were regularly diagrammed on the Hertford branch. In October of that year the latter received an N suffix becoming 770N when it was painted black with red lining.

GNR No.	L&NER 1924 No.	Withdrawn
766	3766	February 1927
767*	—	January 1924
768	—	August 1921
769	—	June 1924
770	—	June 1925
931	—	November 1922
933	—	July 1921
936	—	February 1921
937	—	June 1921

NOTE: * Fitted with 4 feet 2½ ins boiler.

The leading dimensions of the class were:

Cylinders	2 inside	18 ins x 26 ins
Motion		Stephenson with slide valves
Boiler	Max diameter	4 feet 5 ins
	Barrel length	10 feet 1 in.
	Firebox	5 feet 6 ins
Heating surface		
	Tubes	213 x 1¾ ins	1,016.0 sq feet
	Firebox		103.0 sq feet
	Total		1,119.0 sq feet
Grate area		16.25 sq feet
Boiler pressure		160 psi
Coupled wheels		5 feet 8 ins
Trailing wheels		3 feet 2 ins
Tractive effort		16,846 lbs
Length over buffers		33 feet 5½ ins
Wheelbase		22 feet 6 ins
Weight in working order		52 tons 4 cwt
Max axle loading		18 tons 0 cwt
Water capacity		1,000 gallons
Coal capacity		3 tons 0 cwt

The detailed differences of locomotives fitted with 4 feet 2½ ins boilers were:

Boiler	Max diameter	4 feet 2½ ins	
Heating surface			
	Tubes	174 x 1¾ ins	830.0 sq feet
	Firebox		94.0 sq feet
	Total		924.0 sq feet
Weight in working order		53 tons 9 cwt	
Max axle loading		17 tons 16 cwt	

The 'C2'/'C12' Class

A class associated with the Hatfield branches for some years was Ivatt's 'C2' Class 4-4-2 tank locomotives, later classified 'C12' by the L&NER. Originally introduced between 1898 and 1907 for use in the West Riding of Yorkshire and on the London suburban services, they were later superseded by Gresley's 'N1' Class and 'N2' Class 0-6-2 tank locomotives. Soon after World War One most of the London-based engines were sent to country districts for use on branch line services and the Nottingham district suburban trains. No. 1501 was built with a full length chimney and high dome which prevented it working to Moorgate Street so in December 1901 the condensing apparatus was removed and the engine transferred from King's Cross to Hatfield where it later received bogie brakes; it later moved on to Leeds to work West Riding services. Other members of the class were sent to Hatfield for use on the branches in 1914 and by 1921 No's 1514 and 1531 were working on the Hatfield to Hertford passenger turns and by 1922 No's 1534, 1537, 1541, 1548 and 1550 were the five allocated to the Hertfordshire shed for use on the branches. Later some were replaced by 'N1' Class from 1920 and transferred away.

GNR 'C2' Class, later L&NER 'C12' Class 4-4-2T.

The leading dimensions of the class were:

Cylinders	2 inside	18 ins x 26 ins
Motion		Stephenson with slide valves
Boiler	Max diameter	4 feet 5 ins
	Barrel length	10 feet 1 in.
Firebox		5 feet 6 ins
Heating surface		
	Tubes	213 x 1¾ ins 1,016.0 sq feet
	Firebox	103.0 sq feet
	Total	1,119.0 sq feet
Grate area		16.25 sq feet
Boiler pressure		170 psi
Leading wheels		3 feet 8 ins
Coupled wheels		5 feet 8 ins
Trailing wheels		3 feet 8 ins
Tractive effort		17,900 lbs
Length over buffers		36 feet 9¼ ins
Wheelbase		27 feet 3 ins
Weight in working order		62 tons 6 cwt
Max axle loading		18 tons 0 cwt
Water capacity		1,350 gallons
Coal capacity		2 tons 5 cwt

GNR No.	L&NER 1924 No.	L&NER 1946 No.	BR No.	Withdrawn
1501	4501	7359	—	August 1949
1502	4502	7360	67360	January 1955
1511	4511	7389	67369	July 1954
1512	4512	—	—	April 1937
1514	4514	7371	67371	April 1955
1531	4531	7384	67384	May 1956
1534	4534	7385	67385	April 1955
1537	4537	7387	67387	February 1955
1541	4541	7391	67391	January 1958
1548	4548	7398	67398	November 1958
1550	4550	—	—	December 1938

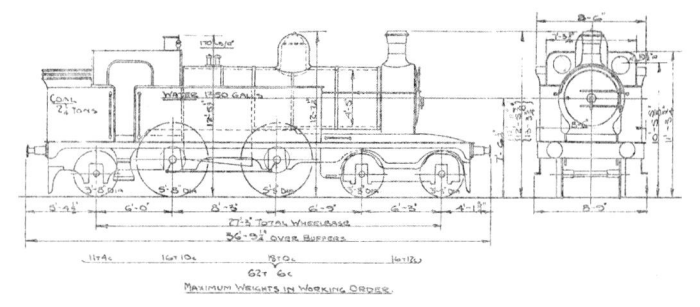

GNR 'C2' Class, later L&NER 'C12' Class, 4-4-2Ts were regularly based at Hatfield to work the three branches. L&NER No. 4511 waits its next turn of duty at Hatfield.
Author's collection

The 'S44'/'G4' Class

In 1929 two members of the GER 'S44' Class 0-4-4 tank locomotives, reclassified by the L&NER as 'G4' Class 0-4-4, were allocated to Hatfield when No's 8100, 8114 and 8124 shared duties on all three branches. Forty locomotives were built to the design of James Holden between 1898 and 1901 at Stratford especially for handling the heavy suburban trains on the Liverpool Street to Enfield and Chingford lines. Withdrawal of the class commenced in 1929 when many displaced from the suburban duties migrated to country depots and as No's 8100, 8114 and 8124 were equipped with vacuum ejectors they were suitable for working from the former GNR shed but their sojourn was relatively short.

GER No.	L&NER 1924 No.	Withdrawn
1100	8100	July 1931
1114	8114	September 1931
1124	8124	September 1934

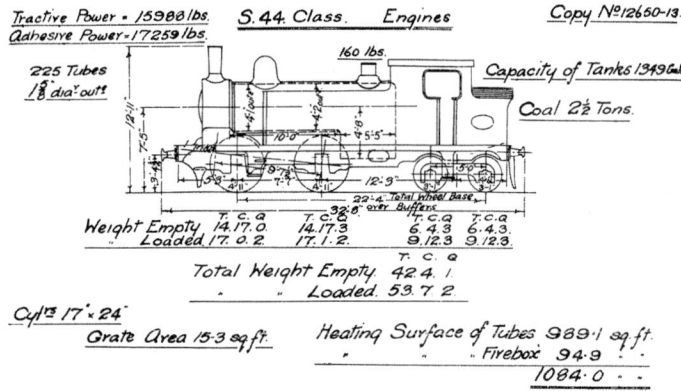

GER 'S44' Class, later L&NER 'G4' Class 0-4-4T.

The leading dimensions of the 'G4' Class were:

Cylinders	2 inside	17 ins x 24 ins	
Motion		Stephenson with slide valves	
Boiler	Max diameter	4 feet 2 ins	
	Barrel length	10 feet 0 ins	
	Firebox	5 feet 5 ins	
Heating surface			
	Tubes	225 x 1⅝ ins	989.1 sq feet
	Firebox		94.9 sq feet
	Total		1,084.0 sq feet
Grate area		15.3 sq feet	
Boiler pressure		160 psi	
Coupled wheels		4 feet 11 ins	
Trailing wheels		3 feet 1 in.	
Tractive effort		15,988 lbs	
Length over buffers		32 feet 8 ins	
Wheelbase		22 feet 4 ins	
Weight in working order		53 tons 8 cwt	
Max axle loading		17 tons 1 cwt	
Water capacity		1,349 gallons	
Coal capacity		2 tons 10 cwt	

The 'N1' Class

After the unsuccessful experiment of using 'R1' Class 0-8-2 tank locomotives on London area suburban services, Ivatt introduced his 'N1' Class 0-6-2 tank locomotives from 1907, initially to relieve the 'C2' Class later 'C12' Class 4-4-2Ts on the exacting task. The prototype No. 190 worked empty coaching stock trains into and out of King's Cross before appearing on GNR passenger services but the engine was too heavy for use on the Metropolitan widened lines and was initially sent to Hatfield to work the branches before being sent north to the West Riding. The subsequent fifty-five

In 1929 two members of the ex-GER 'S44' Class 0-4-4Ts, later designated to Class 'G4' by the L&NER, were allocated to Hatfield shed for evaluation on the branches. No. 8123 is typical of the class, which was not popular with Hatfield men, and the engines were soon handed back to the GE section. *Author's collection*

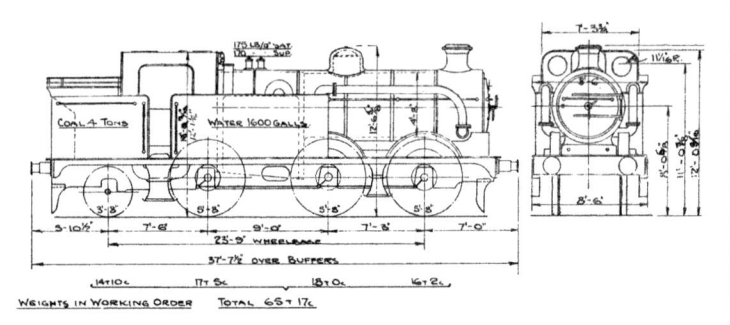

The pioneer Ivatt 'N1' Class 0-6-2T No. 190 differed from the remainder of the class by having larger side tanks and other features. Here in GNR livery it waits to work a train from Hatfield to Hertford on 31st May 1919. The locomotive was later transferred away to Yorkshire sheds. *LCGB/Ken Nunn*

GNR/L&NER 'N1' Class 0-6-2T.

GNR No.	L&NER 1924 No.	L&NER 1946 No.	BR No.	Withdrawn
190	3190	9430	69430	December 1956
1554	4554	9434	69434	March 1959
1559	4559	9439	69439	November 1955
1560	4560	9440	69440	March 1957
1561	4561	9441	69441	May 1955
1564	4564	9444	69444	October 1956
1567	4567	9447	69447	October 1956
1569	4569	9449	69449	April 1955
1575	4575	9455	69455	May 1955
1577	4577	9457	69457	April 1957
1578	4578	9458	69458	November 1955
1582	4582	9462	69462	April 1959
1584	4584	9464	69464	August 1955
1586	4586	9466	69466	July 1955
1587	4587	9467	69467	July 1956
1588	4588	9468	69468	March 1954
1589	4589	9469	69469	April 1957
1590	4590	9470	69470	August 1956
1595	4595	9475	69475	April 1955
1597	4597	9477	69477	April 1959
1600	4600	9480	—	June 1951
1601	4601	9481	69481	May 1956
1602	4602	9482	69482	August 1954
1603	4603	9483	69483	March 1955
1604	4604	9484	69484	September 1957
1605	4605	9485	69485	November 1954

members of the class – introduced in batches of ten between 1907 and 1911, with fifteen built in 1911-12 and the last ten in 1912 – were all built at Doncaster Works. Some initially followed No. 190 to the West Riding but others were employed on the King's Cross suburban trains and cross-London freight services. Before grouping No. 190 had returned to Hatfield as the sole member of the class at the shed but by 1924 No's 190 and 1569N were working the Hertford services together with No's 1560N and 1564N on loan from Ardsley shed. The 'N1's were not popular on the three Hatfield branches due to axle weight and wear and tear on tyres and axles because of the sharp curves encountered; they were soon replaced by ex-GER 'N7' Class tank locomotives No's 994 and 995, whilst on 28th June 1924 No. 993 arrived to release No. 1569N to go north. Despite the earlier problems, once the branch permanent way had been improve Hatfield retained at least three of the class, reducing to two just before the outbreak of World War Two, to work the branches and it was 1947 before the last of the class had left the shed. The following were known to have worked between Hatfield and Hertford during their time at the Hertfordshire depot.

The principal dimensions of the 'N1' Class were:

Cylinders	2 inside	18 ins x 26 ins	
Motion		Stephenson with slide valves	
Boiler	Max diameter	4 feet 8 ins	
	Barrel length	10 feet 1 in.	
Firebox		6 feet 4 ins	

		Saturated	Superheated
Heating surface			
	Tubes	1,130.0 sq feet	562.0 sq feet
	Firebox	120.0 sq feet	118.0 sq feet
	Flues	—	257.0 sq feet
	Total evaporative	1,250.0 sq feet	937.0 sq feet
	Superheater	—	192.0 sq feet
	Total	1,250.0 sq feet	1,129.0 sq feet
Tubes		238 x 1¾ ins	118 x 1¾ ins
Flues		—	18 x 5¼ ins
Elements		—	18 x 1¼ ins
Grate area		19.0 sq feet	19.0 sq feet
Boiler pressure		175 psi	170 psi
Coupled wheels		5 feet 8 ins	
Trailing wheels		3 feet 8 ins	
Tractive effort		18,427 lbs	17,900 lbs
Length over buffers		35 feet 7½ ins	36 feet 7½ ins
Wheelbase		23 feet 3 ins	23 feet 9 ins
Weight in working order		64 tons 14 cwt	65 tons 17 cwt
Max axle loading		18 tons 0 cwt	18 tons 0 cwt
Water capacity		1,600 gallons	
Coal capacity		4 tons 0 cwt	

The 'N2' and 'N2/4' Classes

Following the introduction of the 'N1' Class 0-6-2Ts it was considered the motive power position for suburban services was adequate, but after the end of World War One thoughts were put to providing a larger and more powerful locomotive with high-pitched boiler and shorter chimney to keep within the Metropolitan loading gauge. Nigel Gresley, having assumed control of the locomotive department, introduced sixty of his 'N2' Class 0-6-2 tank locomotives into service in 1920 and 1921, ten built by Doncaster and fifty by the North British Locomotive Company, with a further forty-seven added between 1925 and 1929. These came in four series: No's 2583 to 2594 built by Beyer, Peacock & Company in 1925; the '892' series No's 892 to 897 by Doncaster in 1925; the '2662' series No's 2662 to 2681 by Hawthorn, Leslie & Company in 1928/9 and 2682 to 2684 by the Yorkshire Engine Company in 1928, and lastly the '2685' series No's 2685 to 2690 by the Yorkshire Engine Company in 1928/9. Although designed for London suburban work, members of the class subsequently worked suburban service around Edinburgh, Glasgow and Dundee. In May 1921 new locomotives No's 1759, 1760, 1761, 1762 and 1763 were allocated to Hatfield to work the branches, joined in August by 1766. At grouping the first five remained but No. 1766 was transferred to King's Cross. In September 1930 new 'V1' Class 2-6-2 tank locomotives replaced 'N2' Class locomotives allocated to Scottish sheds and fourteen locomotives – No's 2588, 2589, 2685, 2686, 2687, 4725, 4727, 4730, 4733, 4734, 4735, 4736, 4737 and 4738 – were transferred south and allocated to Hatfield. The allocation was increased with the arrival of No. 2586 in March 1931. This locomotive had previously been sent to Cambridge and outbased at Bishop's Stortford before going to Stratford. All locomotives moved back north in January 1932, except for No's 2586 and 4730 which were transferred to Kipps in November 1932. Thereafter the Hatfield allocation of 'N2' Class engine fluctuated, with only two of the class at the shed in 1933 increasing to fourteen by 1947.

There was a reluctance to work the Hertford branch with these engines as the footplate staff considered them to be *'top heavy'* on the undulating road and preference was always given to working the services with 'N7' Class 0-6-2Ts. Nevertheless, they worked both passenger and freight services on occasions but were prohibited from working stopping services between Hertford North and Welwyn Garden City. On one occasion an 'N2' working light engine chimney first from Hatfield to Hertford with its side tanks

'N2/4' Class 0-6-2T No. 69572 waits to depart from the bay platform at Hertford North with the 1.31pm train to King's Cross on 20th September 1958. The parachute water tank was one of a pair provided at the station to replenish locomotives. *F. Hornby*

full of water began flailing from side to side on the undulating road and derailed near Cole Green. At the joint inquiry the driver stated that despite observing the road speed the engine was rolling alarmingly. The line was shut for the rest of the day and was not reopened until the following morning after the King's Cross breakdown train re-railed the engine. The 'N2's had already been banned from working passenger services over the Dunstable branch from November 1952 resulting in Hatfield shed receiving an influx of 'N7' Class 0-6-2Ts in place of the 'N2's, which were transferred away. At the same time it was reiterated that 'N2' Class locomotives were only to work through services across the Hertford branch from Welwyn Garden City, thus obviating stops at intermediate stations or sidings.

Locomotives known to have been allocated to Hatfield to work over the three branch lines included those listed below.

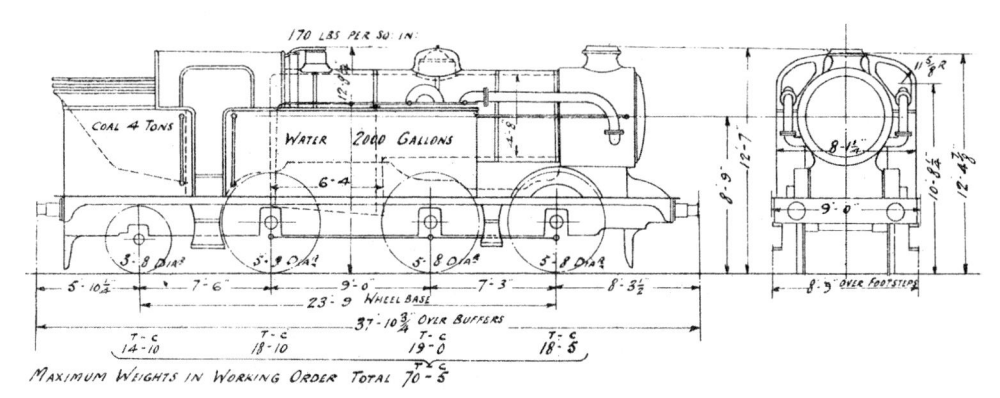

GNR/L&NER 'N2' Class 0-6-2T.

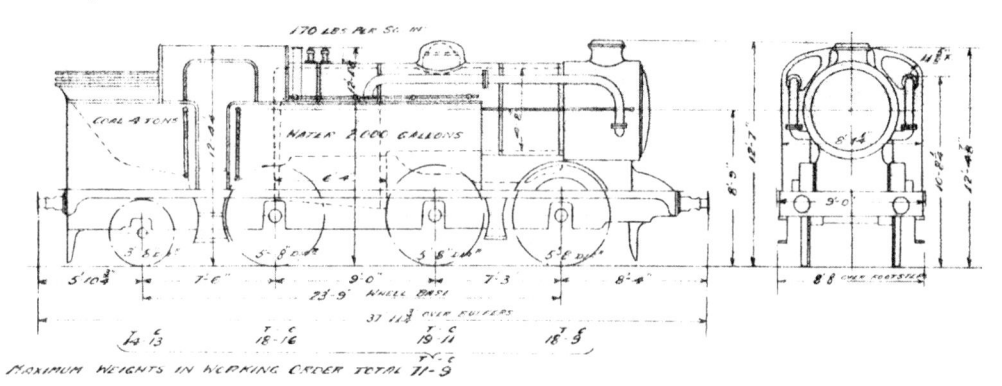

GNR/L&NER 'N2/4' Class 0-6-2T.

GNR No.	L&NER 1924 No.	L&NER 1946 No.	BR No.	Withdrawn		GNR No.	L&NER 1924 No.	L&NER 1946 No.	BR No.	Withdrawn	
1609	4609	9493	69493	December 1958	(1)		2583	9550	69550	September 1958	(2)
1610	4610	9494	69494	January 1958	(1)		2584	9551	69551	December 1958	(2)
1722	4722	9501	69501	November 1957	(1)		2585	9552	69552	May 1960	(2)
1723	4723	9502	69502	May 1958	(1)		2586	9553	69553	December 1959	(2)
1725	4725	9504	69504	September 1962	(1)		2587	9554	69554	June 1958	(2)
1727	4727	9506	69506	May 1961	(1)		2588	9555	69555	April 1959	(2)
1730	4730	9509	69509	October 1960	(1)		2589	9556	69556	December 1959	(2)
1733	4733	9512	69512	July 1962	(1)		2591	9558	69558	June 1957	(2)
1734	4734	9513	69513	May 1961	(1)		2592	9559	69559	July 1957	(2)
1735	4735	9514	69514	September 1955	(1)		2593	9560	69560	October 1960	(2)
1736	4736	9515	69515	July 1959	(1)		2665	9571	69571	June 1961	(4)
1737	4737	9516	69516	January 1961	(1)		2671	9577	69577	May 1959	(4)
1738	4738	9517	69517	August 1959	(1)		2674	9580	69580	September 1961	(4)
1752	4752	9531	69531	July 1961	(1)		2676	9582	69582	September 1960	(4)
1755	4755	9534	69534	February 1959	(1)		2678	9584	69584	July 1959	(4)
1758	4758	9537	69537	April 1959	(1)		2680	9586	69586	March 1961	(4)
1759	4759	9538	69538	September 1962	(1)		2681	9587	69587	July 1960	(4)
1760	4760	9539	69539	June 1946	(1)		2682	9588	69588	February 1960	(4)
1761	4761	9540	69540	July 1960	(1)		2683	9589	69589	March 1960	(4)
1762	4762	9541	69541	August 1959	(1)		2684	9590	69590	June 1957	(4)
1763	4763	9542	69542	April 1959	(1)		2685	9591	69591	August 1959	(3)
1764	4764	9543	69543	September 1961	(1)		2686	9592	69592	September 1961	(3)
1767	4767	9546	69546	September 1962	(1)		2687	9593	69593	September 1962	(3)
1768	4768	9547	69547	June 1959	(1)		2688	9594	69594	January 1960	(3)
1769	4769	9548	69548	July 1959	(1)						
Notes:	1. Class 'N2/1'.		2. Class 'N2/2'.		3. Class 'N2/3'.		4. Class 'N2/4'.				

The principal dimensions of the 'N2' Class were:

Cylinders	2 inside	19 ins x 26 ins	
Motion		Stephenson with 8-ins piston valves	
Boiler	Max diameter	4 feet 8 ins	
	Barrel length	10 feet 1 in.	
Firebox		6 feet 4 ins	
Heating surface		Twin tube superheater	
	Tubes	107 x 1¾ ins	510.0 sq feet
	Flues	34 x 4 ins	370.0 sq feet
	Firebox		118.0 sq feet
	Total evaporative		998.0 sq feet
	Superheater		207.0 sq feet
	Total		1,205.0 sq feet
Grate area		19.0 sq feet	
Boiler pressure		170 psi	
Coupled wheels		5 feet 8 ins	
Trailing wheels		3 feet 8 ins	
Tractive effort		19,945 lbs	
Wheelbase		23 feet 9 ins	
Water capacity		2,000 gallons	
Coal capacity		4 tons	

Differences of locomotives equipped with 18-element superheater:

Heating surface			
	Tubes	118 x 1¾ ins	562.0 sq feet
	Flues	18 x 5¼ ins	257.0 sq feet
	Firebox		118.0 sq feet
	Total evaporative		937.0 sq feet
	Superheater		192.0 sq feet
	Total		1,129.0 sq feet

Other detailed differences:

Class	N2/1 and N2/2	N2/3	N2/4
Length over buffers	37 feet 10¾ ins	37 feet 10¾ ins	37 feet 11¾ ins
Weight in working order	70 tons 5cwt	70 tons 8 cwt	71 tons 9 cwt
Max axle loading	19 tons 0 cwt	20 tons 0 cwt	19 tons 11 cwt

The 'N7' Class

The class generally associated with the Hatfield to Hertford branch passenger services and later from Welwyn Garden City was the Gresley L&NER 'N7' Class 0-6-2 tank locomotives, based on A.J. Hill's GER design which had a long association with Hatfield shed. As early as January 1924 No's 7992, 7993, 7994 and 7995, built at Stratford, were initially allocated to Hatfield but then gravitated to other depots, whilst No's 457, 913 and 919 were then allocated to the Hertfordshire shed and took up duties on the main line and branches. They were subsequently transferred to Stratford in December 1930, January 1931 and September 1930 respectively. Another three, No's 2659, 2660 and 2661, after running in at Eastfield shed, Glasgow, were allocated to Hatfield. The allocation was enhanced with the arrival of eleven Westinghouse brake fitted locomotives new from Gorton works: No's 2631 to 2641 inclusive. Their stay was fairly short for No's 2632 to 2636 were transferred to Stratford in January 1929 and out-based at Hertford East shed, whilst No's 2637 to 2639 followed in April 1929. At the same time, No's 2642 to 2661 were transferred to Hatfield as replacements. From 1931 to 1939 these locomotives remained at Hatfield working the three branches and covering work on the main lines. During this period, however, some engines were transferred away for short periods: No's 2653, 2657, 2660 and 2661 going to Cambridge in March 1933 and outbased at Bishop's Stortford as replacement for the 'D13' Class 4-4-0 tender locomotives when the turntable was out of use, before returning to the GN in May. They, however, were soon transferred to Stratford. No. 2659 was transferred to Stratford in September 1933 to be followed by 2645 in December 1937. No. 2644 went to Stratford for a short period in 1933 but then returned to Hatfield before going to the GE permanently in 1939. Others moved to Stratford were No's 2642 and 2647 in 1938, 2646 and 2648 in 1939 and finally No. 2643 in 1940. Early in 1942 No's 2649 to 2652 inclusive, 2654, 2655, 2656 and 2658 were transferred to Bradford but returned to Hatfield in 1943 and 1944 after 'A5' Class 4-6-2 tank locomotives displaced them on Yorkshire routes.

Hertford East based 'N7' Class locomotives also worked across the branch with grain trains en route from London Docks to Welwyn Garden City for the Shredded Wheat factory, returning with the empty grain wagons. In the latter years of steam traction, Hertford East locomotive and men were responsible for shunting Welwyn Garden City goods yards and sidings; No. 1 diagram, rostered for an 'N7' Class engine, working 5.00am to 10.00pmSX, and 5.00am to 12.00 noon then 2.15pm to 7.00pm and finally 7.30pm to 10.00pmSO. Crews changed over during the day. This obviated the use of a Hatfield engine, which would have required time-consuming shunting across the main line.

In the final months of steam operation Hatfield shedmaster was instructed to keep his run-down fleet of 'N7's in operation and *'run them into the ground'* until modern replacements could be delivered. No. 69632 was a firm favourite and always kept in good condition, No. 69618 was not popular with the train crews for being right-hand drive; No. 69648 was infamous for always having blocked tubes; whilst No. 69692 and 69698, being transferred from South Lynn, had low mileage. No. 69704 also proved popular with staff and was reliable until withdrawal. When No. 69629, which was in a *'rough condition'*, incurred hot boxes it was thought the locomotive would be scrapped; it was sent to New England shed for lifting as Hatfield could not carry out the necessary repair but the foreman at New England decided against any repairs and sent it to Doncaster for condemnation, but en route via the GN and GE Joint line the message was received that it was imperative to keep the Hatfield 'N7' operative for a few more months. Thus when it reached Lincoln the local staff carried out remedial repairs and the locomotive was sent back to Hatfield.

Locomotives known to have been based at Hatfield and worked across the Hertford branch included those listed opposite.

FACING PAGE: 'N7/5' Class 0-6-2T No. 69632 waits hopefully for passengers in the Up back platform at Welwyn Garden City before departing with the Hertford North branch train on 15th June 1951. In the left background is the large 80-feet-long goods shed provided in the Up yard at the station in 1932. *Author's collection*

L&NER 1924 No.	L&NER 1946 No.	BR No.	Withdrawn		L&NER 1924 No.	L&NER 1946 No.	BR No.	Withdrawn	
7991	9613	69613	November 1959	(4)	2636	9676	69676	February 1959	(3)
7992	9614	69614	December 1960	(4)	2637	9677	69677	November 1960	(3)
7993	9615	69615	September 1960	(4)	2638	9678	69678	September 1961	(3)
7994	9616	69616	January 1959	(4)	2639	9679	69679	January 1961	(3)
7995	9617	69617	July 1960	(4)	2640	9680	69680	December 1960	(3)
7996	9618	69618	September 1961	(4)	2641	9681	69681	December 1960	(3)
7998	9620	69620	November 1960	(4)	2642	9682	69682	December 1960	(3)
457	9626	69626	June 1959	(5)	2643	9683	69683	February 1960	(3)
460	9627	69627	March 1959	(5)	2644	9684	69684	August 1960	(3)
471	9629	69629	August 1960	(5)	2645	9685	69685	December 1960	(3)
475	9631	69631	January 1961	(5)	2646	9686	69686	September 1961	(3)
826	9632	69632	September 1962	(5)	2647	9687	69687	December 1960	(3)
829	9635	69635	March 1959	(5)	2648	9688	69688	November 1960	(3)
832	9637	69637	March 1959	(5)	2649	9689	69689	March 1957	(2)
833	9638	69638	May 1959	(5)	2650	9690	69690	January 1961	(3)
834	9639	69639	January 1959	(5)	2651	9691	69691	December 1960	(3)
837	9640	69640	September 1962	(5)	2652	9692	69692	September 1962	(3)
852	9644	69644	January 1959	(5)	2653	9693	69693	September 1961	(3)
867	9648	69648	August 1960	(5)	2654	9694	69694	November 1960	(3)
868	9649	69649	July 1959	(5)	2655	9695	69695	December 1958	(2)
870	9650	69650	May 1959	(5)	2656	9696	69696	April 1961	(3)
913	9654	69654	December 1960	(5)	2657	9697	69697	September 1962	(3)
919	9657	69657	June 1959	(5)	2658	9698	69698	September 1961	(3)
2631	9733	69733	October 1960	(3)	2659	9699	69699	November 1960	(3)
2632	9672	69672	October 1959	(3)	2660	9700	69700	December 1960	(3)
2633	9673	69673	September 1961	(3)	2661	9701	69701	December 1960	(3)
2634	9674	69674	June 1961	(3)	2602	9704	69704	October 1960	(3)
2635	9675	69675	June 1961	(3)	2607	9709	69709	November 1960	(3)

NOTES: 2. Class 'N7/2'. 3. Class 'N7/3'. 4. Class 'N7/4'. 5. Class 'N7/5'.

The leading dimensions of the 'N7/3', 'N7/4' and 'N7/5' classes were:

Cylinders	2 inside	18 ins x 24 ins	
Motion		Walschaerts with 9-ins piston valves	
Boiler	Max diameter	4 feet 9 ins	
	Barrel length	9 feet 7 ins	
Firebox		6 feet 0 ins	
Heating surface			
	Tubes	132 x 1¾ ins	599.6 sq feet
	Flues	8 x 5 ins	231.2 sq feet
	Firebox		107.3 sq feet
	Total evaporative		938.1 sq feet
	Superheater		134.2 sq feet
	Total		1,072.3 sq feet
Grate area		17.7 sq feet	
Boiler pressure		180 psi	
Coupled wheels		4 feet 10 ins	
Trailing wheels		3 feet 9 ins	
		3 feet 6 ins*	
Tractive effort		20,512 lbs	
Length over buffers		35 feet 0½ ins	
		34 feet 11 ins*	
		34 feet 10 ins+	
Wheelbase		23 feet 0 ins	
Max axle loading		7 tons 16 cwt	
		18 tons 19 cwt*	
		17 tons 8 cwt+	
Weight in working order		62 tons 19 cwt	
		64 tons 0 cwt*	
		61 tons 16 cwt+	
Water capacity		1,600 gallons	
Coal capacity		3 tons 5 cwt	

NOTES:
* 'N7/3' Class.
+ 'N7/4' Class.

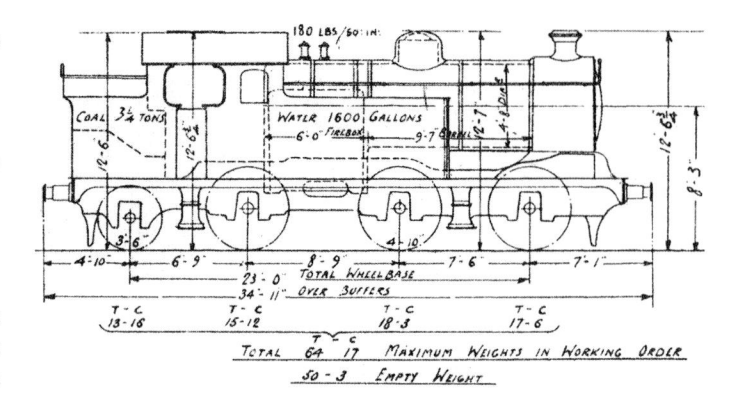

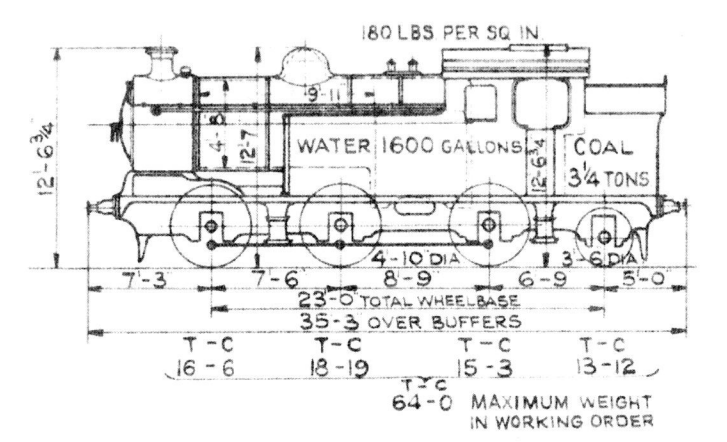

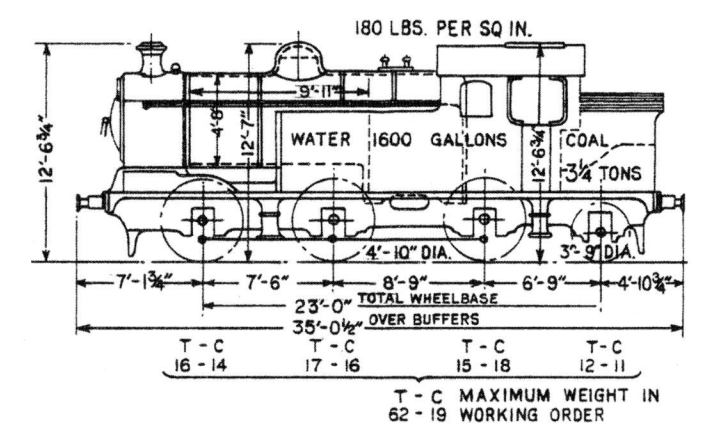

TOP RIGHT: L&NER 'N7/2' Class 0-6-2T.
CENTRE RIGHT: L&NER 'N7/3' Class 0-6-2T.
BOTTOM RIGHT: L&NER 'N7/5' Class 0-6-2T.

BELOW: 'N7/3' Class 0-6-2T No. 69683 departing from Hertford East with a train for Liverpool Street on 7th July 1958. The connecting line from Hertford Cowbridge can be seen on the far right behind the grounded coach body as it approaches the junction between the former GN and GE systems.
P. Whitaker

GCR '9C', '9F' AND '9O' Classes, L&NER 'N5' Class

In 1891 Thomas Parker, the Locomotive Superintendent of the Manchester, Sheffield & Lincolnshire Railway, introduced his second design of 0-6-2 tank locomotives into traffic. The prototype engine No. 7 was notable at the time for being the first locomotive constructed by a British company to be fitted with a Belpaire firebox. Once Parker was satisfied with the design, a total of 129 were built by the MS&LR at Gorton Works, or by the neighbouring contractor Beyer, Peacock & Company. They became the standard shunting and light goods engine of the Great Central Railway, successor to the MS&LR, as classes '9C', '9F' and '9O', and during their long and useful lives some were later in L&NER and BR days transferred to work on former GER and GNR lines. The L&NER reclassified the 0-6-2Ts to 'N5' and in March 1934 No. 5533 arrived at Hatfield to work on the branches whilst another, No. 5930, was allocated to Hornsey in June 1935 before moving on to Hatfield in September 1935. The locomotives were regularly used on the Hertford North services in preference to the other branches. No. 5930 moved back to the GC section in April 1937 and was immediately replaced by sister engine No. 5535 which was transferred in from Stratford. Their stay was relatively short for No's 5533 and 5535 was transferred away to Ardsley in April 1941. No. 5533 again served on the former GNR when as No. 69266 it worked the Essendine to Stamford branch and served as Peterbrough North station pilot in the late 1950s.

GCR No.	L&NER 1924 No.	L&NER 1946 No.	BR No.	Withdrawn
533	5533	9266	69266	November 1960
535	5535	9268	69268	January 1960
930	5930	9354	69354	February 1960

The principal dimensions of the 'N5' Class were:

Cylinders	2 inside	18 ins x 26 ins	
Motion		Stephenson with slide valves	
Boiler	Max diameter	4 feet 4 ins	
	Barrel length	10 feet 8⅛ ins	
Firebox		6 feet 0 ins	
Heating surface		Saturated	
	Tubes	190 x 1¾ ins	964.0 sq feet
	Firebox		99.0 sq feet
	Total		1,063.0 sq feet
Grate area		18.3 sq feet	
Boiler pressure		160 psi	
Coupled wheels		5 feet 1 in.	
Trailing wheels		3 feet 6 ins	
Tractive effort		18,781 lbs	
Length over buffers		36 feet 8⅛ ins	
Wheelbase		22 feet 6 ins	
Weight in working order		62 tons 7 cwt	
Max axle loading		17 tons 0 cwt	
Water capacity		1,360 gallons	
Coal capacity		3 tons 0 cwt	

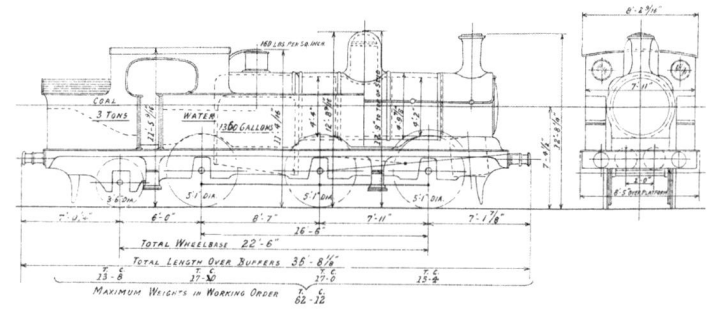

GCR '9C', '9F' and '9O' classes, later L&NER 'N5' Class 0-6-2T.

'N5' Class 0-6-2T No. 5535 was one of three former Great Central Railway '9C', '9F' and '9O' Class locomotives allocated for a short period to Hatfield. Here it is working a train from Hertford alongside the main line between Welwyn Garden City and Hatfield in 1937 with a two-coach Gresley articulated non-gangway set. *Author's collection*

The 'M15'/'F4' and M15R'/'F5' Classes

On 10th June 1922 GER 'M15R' Class 2-4-2 tank locomotive No. 94 worked through from Hertford to Hatfield with a special passenger train, whilst on 24th March 1925 'F4' Class No. 7221 was allocated on loan to Hatfield to cover for 'C12' Class No. 1569N which was under repair. The stay was fairly brief for the locomotive was returned to the GE section on 6th May 1925. The 'M15' Class was designed by T.W. Worsdell with the first locomotives entering service in 1884. Between 1903 and 1909 another 120 locomotives were built, and from 1911 to 1923 the GER rebuilt thirty locomotives with a higher boiler pressure and designated them 'M15R'. The earliest-built locomotives were all condemned by 1929, whilst the L&NER classified the 'M15's as Class 'F4' and the rebuilt locomotives Class 'F5'. The classes were nicknamed 'Gobblers' because the earlier locomotives with Joy's valve gear had a voracious appetite for coal.

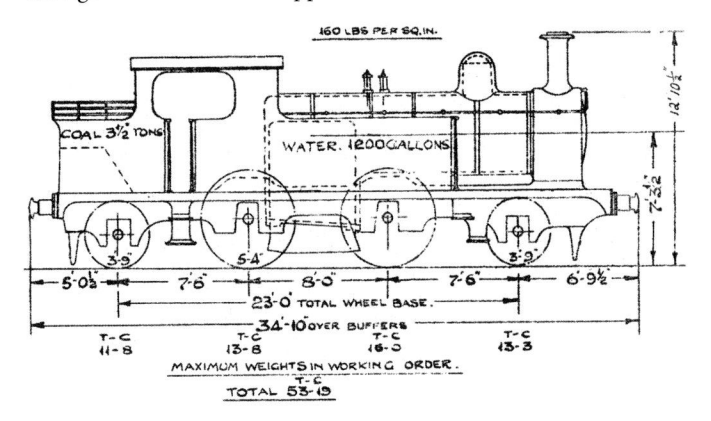

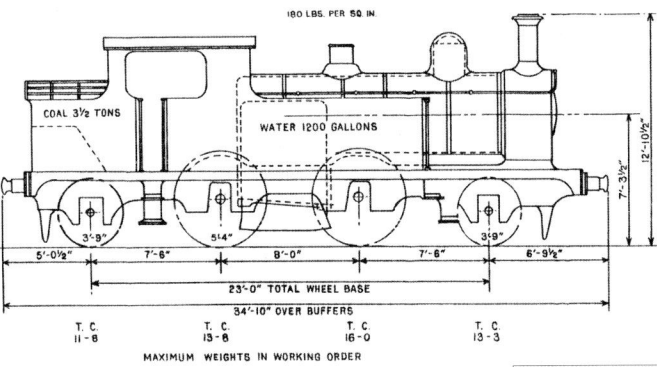

GER No.	L&NER 1924 No.	L&NER 1946 No.	BR No.	Withdrawn
94	7094 (F5)	7203	67203	December 1957
221	7221 (F4)	—	—	June 1934

The principal dimensions of the 'M15' Class were:

Cylinders	17½ ins x 24 ins	
Motion	Stephenson with slide valves	
Boiler Max diameter	4 feet 2 ins	
Barrel length	10 feet 2½ ins	
Firebox	5 feet 5 ins	
Heating surface		
Tubes	227 x 1⅝ ins	1,018.0 sq feet
Firebox		98.4 sq feet
Total		1,116.4 sq feet
Grate area	15.3 sq feet	
Boiler pressure	160 psi	
Leading wheels	3 feet 9 ins	
Driving wheels	5 feet 4 ins	
Trailing wheels	3 feet 9 ins	
Tractive effort	15,618 lbs	
Length over buffers	34 feet 10 ins	
Wheelbase	23 feet 0 ins	
Weight in working order	51 tons 11 cwt	
Max axle loading	14 tons 18 cwt	
Water capacity	1,200 gallons	
Coal capacity	3 tons 10 cwt	

The detailed differences of the 'M15R' Class were:

Heating surface		
Tubes		1,018.0 sq feet
Firebox		96.7 sq feet
Total		1,114.7 sq feet
Grate area	15.2 sq feet	
Boiler pressure	180 psi	
Tractive effort	17,571 lbs	
Weight in working order	53 tons 19 cwt	
Max axle loading	16 tons 0 cwt	

Top: GER 'M15' Class, later L&NER 'F4' Class 2-4-2T.

Above: GER 'M15R' Class, later L&NER 'F5' Class 2-4-2T.

Right: GER 'M15' and 'M15R', later L&NER 'F4' and 'F5', Class 2-4-2Ts were the mainstay of the GER Hertford branch services for many years, and they often trip worked wagons to the Hertford GN station. Here No. 180 passes Hertford station signal box circa 1920; the GNR connection can be seen to the left approaching the junction between the two lines of fence. No. 180 of the 'F4' Class was renumbered 7160 by the L&NER and was subsequently renumbered 7174 in 1946 before being withdrawn in December 1954. In 1925, 'F4' Class No. 7221 was allocated on loan to Hatfield shed for a short period to cover for 'C12' Class No. 1569N, which was under repair. *R. Leggett*

Oliver Bulleid, later Chief Mechanical Engineer of the Southern Railway, was the officer in charge of the experimental Dick, Kerr 4-wheel railcar purchased by the GNR during trials on the branch in 1904/5. It was hoped the car could be utilised on lightly used services and two halts were opened in association with its operation, one beside the level crossing at Attimore Hall and the other by the level crossing at Hatfield Hyde. The railcar was constantly failing in traffic, resulting in the vehicle spending many weeks out of traffic, and the trials were not a success. Subsequently the two halts were closed on and from 1st July 1905. *Author's collection*

Petrol and Steam Railcars

The costs of operating conventional steam trains over lightly used branch lines was by 1904 causing concern at GNR headquarters and like many railways the company was seeking ways of reducing expenditure. One alternative was the use of lightweight petrol engine railcars and Oliver Bury, the GNR General Manager, negotiated with Dick, Kerr & Company of Preston who offered to allow the company to conduct extended trials with one of their models during the autumn of that year. Dick, Kerr selected a special design of 4-wheel car based on tramway design and provided the vehicle with two petrol engines to minimise the risk of breakdown in service and provide better weight distribution. Two standard 4-cylinder Daimler engines capable of developing 36 hp were supplied by the Daimler Motor Company of Coventry who also made a large part of the transmission. Seating for thirty-two passengers was arranged in four blocks of transverse seats, 3 feet 2 inches long by 1 feet 8 inches deep set 2 feet 0 inches apart on either side of a 1-foot-wide gangway. The driving compartments provided at each end of the vehicle were approximately 4 feet 0 inches in depth. Only a hand brake was provided.

After delivery to Doncaster Works for inspection in September 1904, the car ran light to London and was then sent to Hatfield depot for evaluation trials over the three branch lines. On the last Sunday of the month the vehicle worked to St. Albans and from the following week ran a series of tests over the Hertford branch, which continued over several months, some in extremely snowy weather. So confident were the GNR operating officers of the success of the car that new inexpensive lineside halts were opened beside the level crossings at Hatfield Hyde and Attimore Hall in January 1905. At first four round trips were made each weekday from Hatfield to Hertford between timetabled trains but no passengers were conveyed. H.A. Ivatt detailed one of his apprentices O.V.S. Bulleid, later Chief Mechanical and Electrical Engineer of the Southern Railway, to observe and report on the tests. On 7th February 1905 the car made a trial run on the Dunstable branch, running as far as Luton from whence it returned to Hatfield at 2.40pm. The experiment was not successful and the car returned for further trials on the Hertford line before actually entering service for a short period. Bulleid, responsible for maintaining the vehicle, could only keep the car available by 'burning the midnight oil', as the gearboxes gave constant problems. Grindling, the Chief Traffic Manager, reported to his directors on the Traffic Committee on 5th April:

We have for some time been experimenting with a small Motor Car driven by petrol engines. This car has not proved sufficiently reliable for regular service, and Mr Bury agrees that, for the present, it will be wiser to follow the example of the other companies whose cars we have inspected and adhere to steam power.

Despite its faults and failures the car was actually purchased from Dick, Kerr & Company at a cost of £1,244 but the experimental running soon ceased. Public and working timetables of the period do not show any regular use of a one-class vehicle on the Hertford branch so its use was sporadic; on 1st July 1905 the two halts specially provided for use with the car were closed. The car was initially un-numbered during its trial period on the branches but was then numbered 4 and finished in varnished teak livery. It was finally withdrawn from stock in the latter months of 1908. The leading dimensions of the car were:

Length over body	33 feet 6 ins
Max width	9 feet 0 ins
Height above rail	11 feet 7 ins
Wheels	3 feet 0 ins
Wheelbase	15 feet 0 ins
Weight in working order	11 tons 0 cwt
Fuel capacity	Sufficient for 400 route miles
Seating Third Class	32

Whilst the trials were being conducted with the petrol car, Ivatt was turning his attention to the provision of steam railcars and after discussion with the Locomotive Committee in 1904 two GNR officers – J.R. Bazin of the Locomotive Department and T. Smith of the Traffic Department – were delegated to visit and evaluate steam railcar working on the Great Western Railway and Taff Vale Railway. The duo reported back on 21st January 1905, stating the GWR

GNR railmotor No. 2 was used on trials on both the St. Albans and Hertford branches from Hatfield but failed miserably when negotiating the sharp curves encountered on both lines, particularly the latter when on the first run it had great difficulty on the 8 chains radius curve as the branch left the main line at Digswell. Difficulty was also experience topping up with water supplies at Hertford and No. 2 joined the other railcar units working on Lincolnshire and North London branches. It was also used for a short period on shuttle services between Hitchin and Hertford North via Watton-at-Stone.
Author's collection

operated two types of steam car whilst the TVR used only one type. A survey of GNR branch lines considered suitable for steam railcar operation included Finchley to Edgware, Essendine to Stamford, Stamford to Wansford, Essendine to Bourne and Sleaford, Firsby to Skegness, Louth to Willoughby, Louth to Grimsby, as well as the Nottingham suburban line and several routes in Yorkshire. The report also concluded that the Hatfield to St. Albans branch could be worked by two Third Class-only railcars, one standing spare and no trailer cars, whilst the Hatfield to Hertford branch would benefit from two Composite steam railcars covering eight return trips on weekdays with the other journey being covered by conventional steam train. The report was considered by W.J. Grinling, the Chief Traffic Manager, who suggested the Composite cars should be 62 feet 6 inches in length with accommodation for eight First, twenty-eight Third Class smoking and twenty-eight Third Class non-smoking, making a total of sixty-four seats. On 28th February Ivatt wrote to R. Wigram, a director, that after discussion at the Locomotive Committee meeting Grinling had altered his requirement to a car containing about fifty-two seats of which eight were to be for First Class passengers. There was also to be a luggage compartment and to meet this specification the body was to be 49 feet in length, which with the engine section would make a total length of 62 feet. It was also to be powerful enough to haul a trailer bogie coach holding seventy passengers or an ordinary 6-wheel coach and attain a maximum speed of about 35 mph on a level road. The basic design was for the locomotive section to be detachable from the car in order to carry out repairs. The engines had locomotive-type boilers carried on four wheels and each carriage section ran on a 4-wheel bogie at the rear end.

On 5th April 1905 Ivatt advised the board that two cars had been ordered from Kitson & Co. of Leeds at £2,400 each, two from Avonside at £2,440 each and, because prices were considered exorbitant, two were to be built at Doncaster Works at a price of £2,153 each. The six were numbered in the range 1 to 6 inclusive and were classified 'M', although later No. 4 was reserved for the petrol car, and the allocated numbers were increased with the addition of No's 7 and 8. No. 2 was released from Doncaster Works on 3rd October 1905 followed by No. 1 on 27th of the same month. The two cars built by Kitson, No's 5 and 6, entered traffic in December 1905, whilst the Avonside pair, No's 7 and 8, were not delivered until February 1906. The scheme proposed by Bazin and Smith envisaged a total fleet of twenty-seven steam railcars, of which four were required to be stabled at Hatfield to work the St. Albans and Hertford branches. It was mooted that a shed to accommodate the four be built in the angle where the St. Albans branch diverged from the Dunstable branch north of Hatfield station, separating them from the smoky atmosphere of the engine shed. Because of the reduced number built the steam railcars never operated from Hatfield and the shed was never constructed.

On release to traffic the steam cars initially worked from Louth to Grimsby, Louth to Mablethorpe and Willoughby, Finchley to Edgware, and Ossett to Batley. By 1907 one of the cars was transferred to Hitchin to work a shuttle service to Letchworth and Baldock, to be followed by a second in 1909 and by 1914 they had diagrammed working on the main line to Hatfield. In 1918 all six units were placed in store at Doncaster Works. By 1922/3 they were refurbished and put into running order but the only regular work for two – No's 5 and 6 – was at Hitchin where from 6th June 1924 they worked the newly introduced weekdays only passenger service to Hertford North via Stevenage. Their reign was fairly short for by November 1924 the steam cars were replaced by conventional steam hauled trains. Thus the Hatfield to Hertford branch saw the steam railcars work at both ends of the system but never regularly across the branch. The only recorded visit was in the early days when No. 2 worked a trial trip from Hatfield to Hertford. The journey was unsuccessful for the car almost stalled negotiating the extremely sharp curve at Welwyn in both directions and then had difficulty in obtaining water at Hertford station. The curve to the St. Albans branch at Hatfield was of equal sharpness and it was possibly for these reasons the steam railcars were not used on the branches from Hatfield. To conclude the saga, No's 7 and 8 were withdrawn in December 1925, whilst No's 1, 2, 5 and 6 were withdrawn in December the following year. All engine units were condemned in May 1927.

THE HAWTHORN 0-4-2 ENGINES

In the early years on the branch R. & W. Hawthorn 0-4-2 outside frame 'luggage' tender engines were based at Hatfield to work the branch goods services. Fifteen locomotives, numbered 101 to

115, entered service with the GNR between April 1848 and May 1849. They appear to have been fairly successful but No. 111 was converted by Sturrock to a 0-6-0 saddle tank locomotive in April 1863. Stirling rebuilt the entire class except No. 111 from April 1866 and they were again re-boilered from the early 1880s. Many of the class were concentrated at Hatfield for some years and in 1866 No's 101, 102, 104, 107, 108, 112 and 115 were at the shed, whilst as late as 1881 No. 102A, by now on the duplicate list, was still providing active service. On the Hertford branch passenger services, as with those to St. Albans and Dunstable, Sharp 0-4-2T rebuild engines provided the main motive power but the 0-4-2 tender locomotives often deputised and, as there were no turntables provided at the destinations away from Hatfield, the return working was tender first. To protect the enginemen, weather boards with circular windows were provided on the tenders of selected locomotives. Locomotives working across the branch to Hatfield to Hertford included:

GNR No.	To Duplicate List	Withdrawn
101	December 1881	November 1897
102	December 1881	December 1890
104	October 1882	June 1891
107	June 1885	February 1892
108	June 1885	June 1893
112*	December 1883	August 1904
115	June 1884	October 1896

Note: * No. 112A on the duplicate list from December 1899 to August 1904.

The leading dimensions of the Hawthorn 0-4-2 locomotives as rebuilt by Stirling with a domeless raised firebox were:

Cylinders	2 inside	16 ins x 24 ins	
Motion		Stephenson with slide valves	
Boiler	Max diameter	3 feet 11 ins	
	Barrel length	10 feet 0 ins	
Firebox		4 feet 9 ins	
Heating surface			
	Tubes	148 x 1⅞ ins	744.5 sq feet
	Firebox		74.0 sq feet
	Total		818.5 sq feet
Grate area		10.0 sq feet	
Boiler pressure		120 psi	
Coupled wheels		5 feet 0 ins	
Trailing wheels		3 feet 6 ins	
Engine wheelbase		14 feet 0 ins	
Weight in working order			
	Engine	28 tons 0 cwt	
Max axle loading		11 tons 10 cwt	

Later Stirling rebuilds with a straightback boiler had the following detailed differences:

Boiler	Max diameter	4 feet 0½ in.
Firebox		4 feet 10 ins
Weight in working order		28 tons 4 cwt

The '116' Class

Another class of goods engine to be allocated to Hatfield in the 1860s was the '116' Class 0-6-0 tender locomotives. Fifteen were built by E.B. Wilson and the balancing fifteen by R. & W. Hawthorn, and they entered service between October 1850 and February 1851. Between 1864 and 1866 the class received new boilers designed by Sturrock with round topped domes and at the same time eight were converted into 0-6-0 saddle tank engines. The tender locomotives were employed chiefly on coal trains but with the introduction of more powerful locomotives were gradually relegated to main-line pick-up goods and branch line duties. No's 154 and 156 were employed in that capacity when allocated to Hatfield between 1864 and 1866. The thirty-one locomotives of the class were numbered 116 to 158 plus 167.

GNR No.	Built	Rebuilt	Duplicate List	Withdrawn
154	January 1851	1866	November 1879	March 1883
156	January 1851	1861	February 1888	1889

The leading dimensions of the '116' Class in later years were:

Cylinders		16 ins x 24 ins	
Motion		Stephenson with slide valves	
Boiler	Max diameter	3 feet 10 ins	
	Barrel length	10 feet 0 ins	
Firebox		3 feet 10½ ins	
Heating surface			
	Tubes	158 x 2 ins	815.0 sq feet
	Firebox		78.0 sq feet
	Total		893.0 sq feet
Boiler pressure		120 psi	
Coupled wheels		5 feet 0 ins	
Engine wheelbase		14 feet 0 ins	

The Stirling 'F2' and 'F3' Classes

Patrick Stirling designed a ubiquitous 0-4-2 mixed traffic tender locomotive for handling all types of traffic, from heavy excursion work to fast goods services. A total of 154 were built between 1868 and 1895 consisting of 117 engines classified in series '18', all built at Doncaster save thirty constructed by Sharp, Stewart and twenty by Kitson & Company. Four locomotives in series '218' were constructed at Doncaster and the balancing thirty-three in series '103' were also built at the Yorkshire works. Under the Ivatt June 1900 Engine Classification the '218' series were reclassified to 'F1'. Both the other series were designated Class 'F2', except for those rebuilt by Ivatt which became Class 'F3'. Under the power classification the 'F2' Class became load 'R' and the 'F3' were designated 'P'. As 'maids of all work' they were found across the entire GNR network, from working London suburban services to cross-country trains in Lincolnshire. Only towards the end of their long and illustrious career were they specifically allocated to Hatfield to work the branch traffic, when one could be found deputising for the usual tank engine on the Hertford branch. No. 43 was involved in the accident at Hatfield in 1891.

Locomotives specifically noted at the Hertfordshire shed are listed overleaf.

Class	GNR No.	Built	Duplicate list	Withdrawn
Series '18'				
'F2'	592	June 1876	November 1914	April 1921
'F3'	25A	September 1870	June 1910	April 1921
'F3'	565A	October 1876	August 1913	November 1919
'F2'	562	March 1876	—	August 1905
Series '103'				
'F2'	10A	April 1887	October 1908	April 1921
'F2'	12A	July 1887	November 1908	October 1912
'F2'	20	May 1888	—	November 1918
'F2'	104	October 1882	—	July 1921
'F2'	112	December 1883	—	November 1918
'F2'	43	November 1888	—	January 1907
Series '218'				
'F1'	11	May 1869	—	October 1904

The leading dimensions of the '18' series as rebuilt were:

Cylinders	2 inside	17½ ins x 24 ins	
Motion		Stephenson with slide valves	
Boiler	Max diameter	4 feet 2½ ins	
	Barrel length	10 feet 0 ins	
	Firebox	5 feet 6 ins	
Heating surface			
	Tubes	169 x 1⅝ ins	743.0 sq feet
	Firebox		94.5 sq feet
	Total		837.5 sq feet
Grate area		16.0 sq feet	
Boiler pressure		140 psi	
Coupled wheels		5 feet 7½ ins	
Trailing wheels		3 feet 7½ ins	
Tractive effort		12,957 lbs	
Length		23 feet 0 ins*	
Engine wheelbase		15 feet 2 ins*	
Weight in working order		32 tons 3 cwt*	
Water capacity		2,400 gallons	
		2,600 gallons	
Coal capacity		5 tons 0 cwt	

Stirling 'F2' Class 0-4-2 tender locomotive.

The leading dimensions of the '103' series as rebuilt with an Ivatt domed boiler were:

Cylinders	2 inside	17½ x 24 ins	
Motion		Stephenson with slide valves	
Boiler	Max diameter	4 feet 5 ins	
	Barrel length	10 feet 1 in.	
	Firebox	5 feet 6 ins	
Heating surface			
	Tubes	215 x 1¾ ins	1,020.7 sq feet
	Firebox		103.1 sq feet
	Total		1,123.8 sq feet
Grate area		17.8 sq feet	
Boiler pressure		160 psi	
Coupled wheels		5 feet 7½ ins	
Trailing wheels		4 feet 1½ ins	
Tractive effort		14,809 lbs	
Length		24 feet 0 ins*	
Wheelbase		15 feet 3 ins*	
Weight in working order		35 tons 2 cwt	
Water capacity		2,600 gallons	
Coal capacity		5 tons 0 cwt	

Series '218' had the following detail differences from the series '18' engines:

Boiler	Max diameter	4 feet 2½ ins	
	Barrel length	10 feet 0 ins	
	Firebox	4 feet 6 ins	
Heating surface			
	Tubes	174 x 1¾ ins	823.0 sq feet
	Firebox		not known
Grate area		12.75 sq feet	

NOTE: * Engine only.

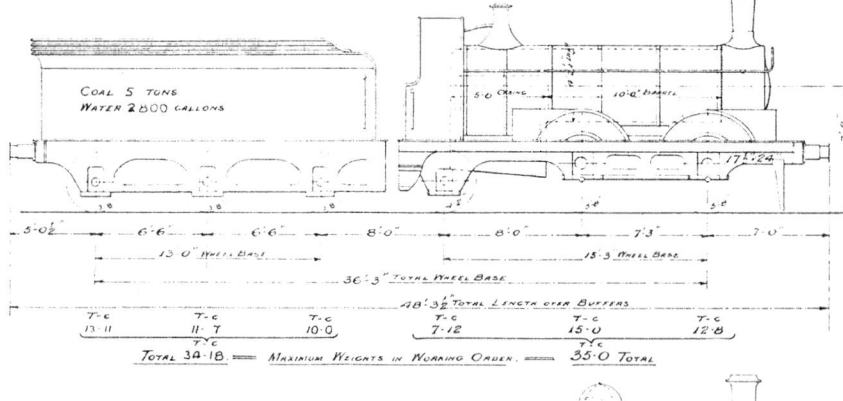

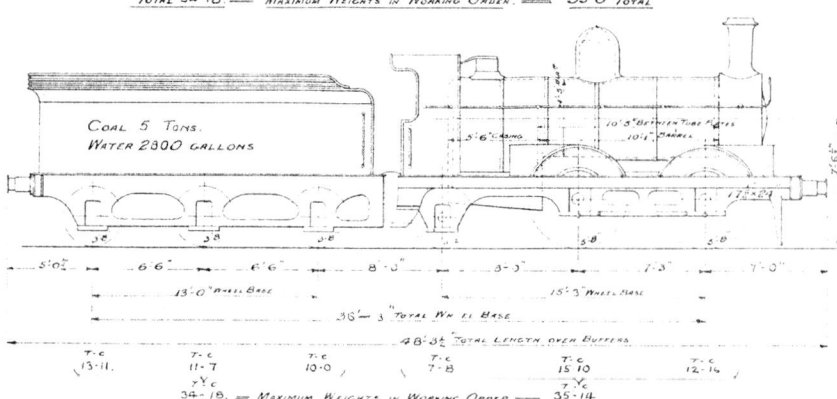

Stirling 'F3' Class 0-4-2 tender locomotive.

Stirling '18' Class, later GNR 'F2' Class 0-4-2 tender locomotives were occasionally employed on Hertford branch passenger services. Here No. 205 heads a typical suburban train formed of 6-wheel stock en route to Nottingham Victoria.
Author's collection

THE GNR 'J4' AND 'J5' CLASSES, LATER L&NER 'J3' AND 'J4'

Three classes associated with the Hatfield branches on an irregular basis over the years were Stirling and Ivatt's GNR classes 'J4', 'J5' and 'J6' 0-6-0 tender locomotives. Initially developed in 1873, the thirty-eight of the '171' series were built at Doncaster Works from that date until 1881. The following '716' series comprised of ten engines built by Vulcan Foundry between August and November 1882 and twenty built by Dübs & Company from June to November 1882. The balancing ten of this series was built at Doncaster Works in 1886. The sixty-two members of the '322' series were all built at Doncaster between 1887 and 1894, whilst the fifteen '1031' series were completed by Dübs & Company in 1896; these locomotives were later designated GNR Class 'J6'. When Ivatt took up his appointment as Locomotive Superintendent in March 1896, he adopted the ten '1081' series built in the same year at Doncaster for further development and between 1897 and 1901 arranged for another 133 engines to be constructed. Starting with ten locomotives in the '1091' series built by Dübs & Company in 1897/8, the '315' series followed with ten built at Doncaster in 1898 and fifteen by Dübs & Company. The '343' series completed the order with forty built at Doncaster in 1899 and 1900, twenty-five by Kitson & Company in 1900 and thirteen by Dübs in 1901. These 143 engines were designated 'J5' in 1900 and over the years 125 of the earlier 'J6' Class were rebuilt to conform to Class 'J5'.

In May 1912 Gresley commenced equipping some of the class with 4 feet 8 inch diameter boilers and seventy-one locomotives were converted by grouping, with the L&NER converting a further eighty-two engines. The rebuilds became GNR Class 'J4'. The 228 survivors of the 'Standard Goods' Class were reclassified by the L&NER: the GNR 'J4' Class becoming L&NER Class 'J3' and GNR Class 'J5' becoming L&NER Class 'J4'. The various locomotives allocated to Hatfield occasionally worked passenger trains between Hatfield and Hertford covering for a failed tank locomotive and also worked for many years the regular goods trains, engineer's specials and out of course or special freight traffic.

Stirling and Ivatt GNR 'J4' and 'J5' Class 0-6-0 tender locomotives were used on branch goods services when allocated to Hatfield but also covered passenger workings in the event of the failure of a tank locomotive. No. 1142 of Class 'J4' hauls a typical passenger train at Basford in February 1910 with a formation of 6-wheel coaches similarly found on the Hertford branch. No. 1142 became L&NER 'J3' Class and was renumbered 4142 before withdrawal from service in September 1940.
Author's collection

They were highly unpopular with footplate crews when tender first running was required.

Locomotives known to have worked between Hatfield and Hertford were:

L&NER Class	GNR No.	L&NER 1924 No.	L&NER 1946 No.	BR No.	Withdrawn
—	171	—	—	—	December 1913
—	322	—	—	—	April 1920
'J3'	384	3384	—	—	January 1936
'J3'	387	3387	4141	64141	September 1953
'J3'	1031	4031	—	—	October 1931
'J3'	1099	4099	—	—	November 1937
'J3'	1100	4100	4117	—	June 1952
'J3'	1136	4136	—	—	March 1948
'J3'	1169	4169	—	—	August 1936
'J3'	1170	4170	—	—	August 1933
'J4'	101	3101	—	—	June 1928
—	154	—	—	—	November 1913
—	650	—	—	—	August 1912
'J3'	716	3716	—	—	July 1931
'J3'	717	3717	—	—	November 1939
'J4'	745	3745	—	—	October 1928
'J4'	746	—	—	—	January 1926

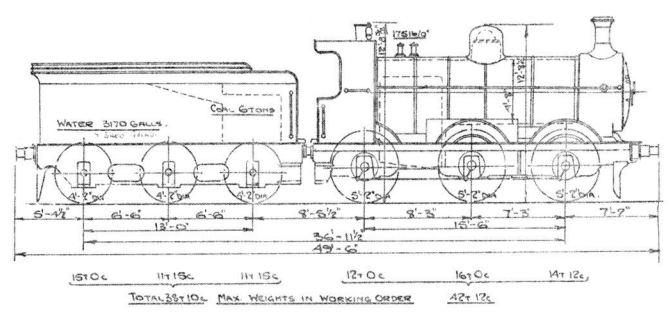

The leading dimension of the L&NER 'J3' Class were:

Cylinders		17½ ins x 26 ins
Motion		Stephenson with slide valves
Boiler	Max diameter	4 feet 8 ins
	Barrel length	10 feet 1 in.
Firebox		5 feet 6 ins
Heating surface		
	Tubes	238 x 1⅜ ins 1,130.0 sq feet
	Firebox	105.0 sq feet
	Total	1,235.0 sq feet
Firebox grate area		16.25 sq feet
Boiler pressure		175 psi
Coupled wheels		5 feet 2 ins
Tender wheels		4 feet 2 ins
Length over buffers		49 feet 6 ins*
Tractive effort		19,105 lbs
Wheelbase	Locomotive	15 feet 6 ins
	Tender	13 feet 0 ins
	Total	36 feet 11½ ins
Weight in working order		
	Locomotive	42 tons 12 cwt
	Tender	38 tons 10 cwt
	Total	81 tons 2 cwt
Max axle loading		16 tons 0 cwt
Water capacity		3,170 gallons
Coal capacity		6 tons

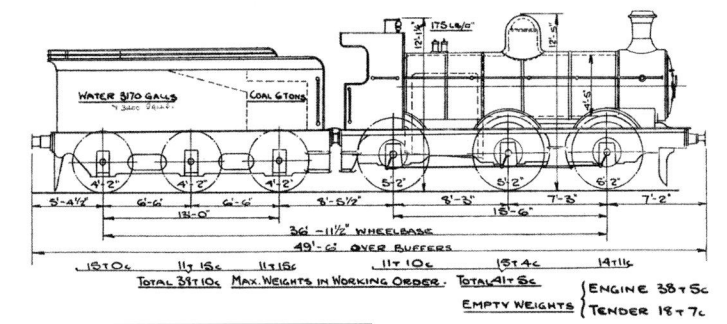

NOTE: *   Engine and tender.

ABOVE LEFT: GNR 'J4' Class, later L&NER 'J3' Class 0-6-0.

ABOVE RIGHT: GNR 'J5' Class, later L&NER 'J4' Class 0-6-0.

GNR 'J4' Class, later L&NER 'J3' Class, 0-6-0 tender locomotives were responsible for much of the goods work on the Hatfield branches. Here No. 4032 languishes at Hatfield shed circa 1936. In the background is former GCR, later L&NER 'N5' Class, 0-6-2T, one of a pair allocated to the Hertfordshire shed for a short period.   *Author's collection*

The principal dimensions of the L&NER 'J4' Class were:

Cylinders	17½ ins x 26 ins	
Motion	Stephenson with slide valves	
Boiler Max diameter	4 feet 5 ins	
Barrel length	10 feet 1 in.	
Firebox	5 feet 6 ins	
Heating surface		
Tubes	213 x 1¾ ins	1,016.0 sq feet
Firebox		103.0 sq feet
Total		1,119.0 sq feet
Firebox grate area	16.25 sq feet	
Boiler pressure	170 psi	
Coupled wheels	5 feet 2 ins	
Tender wheels	4 feet 2 ins	
Tractive effort	18,560 lbs	
Length over buffers	49 feet 2 ins*	
Wheelbase Locomotive	15 feet 6 ins	
Tender	13 feet 0 ins	
Total	36 feet 11½ ins	
Weight in working order		
Locomotive	41 tons 5 cwt	
Tender	34 tons 8 cwt	
Total	76 tons 3 cwt	
Max axle loading	15 tons 4 cwt	
Water capacity	2,800 gallons	
Coal capacity	5 tons 0 cwt	

NOTE: * Engine and tender.

THE GNR 'J21'/L&NER 'J1' CLASS

In 1908 H.A. Ivatt introduced into traffic fifteen 0-6-0 tender locomotives to GNR Class 'J21' numbered 1 to 15, all being built at Doncaster works. Although intended for use on fast main-line goods trains, members of the class often worked on passenger duties. With the advent of more powerful Gresley Class 'K1' 2-6-0 tender locomotives in 1912/13 the 0-6-0s were relegated to more menial tasks and it was during this period that some were allocated to Hatfield shed and were regularly employed on Dunstable to King's Cross through passenger services, with the occasional foray to Hertford and St. Albans covering for failed tank locomotives. The class was redesignated 'J1' by the L&NER and from the early 1930s the locomotives were transferred away to the West Riding and Peterborough and visits to the Hatfield branches became rare. During World War Two the class was divided between Gorton and Colwick, but just after nationalisation three engines, No's 5003, 5010 and 5013, returned south to Hitchin where as No. 65013 became last of the class before withdrawal in 1954. In the final year it worked an engineers train between Welwyn Garden City and Hertford North.

GNR No.	L&NER 1924 No.	L&NER 1946 No.	BR No.	WITHDRAWN
1	3001	5000	—	August 1947
2	3002	5001	—	August 1947
3	3003	5002	65002	August 1954
11	3011	5010	65010	January 1953
13	3013	5012	—	August 1947
14	3014	5013	65013	November 1954

The principal dimensions of the 'J21'/'J1' Class were:

Cylinders 2 inside	18 ins x 26 ins	
Motion	Stephenson with slide valves	
Boiler Max diameter	4 feet 8 ins	
Barrel length	10 feet 1 in.	
Firebox	6 feet 4 ins	
Heating surface		
Tubes	238 x 1¾ ins	1,130 sq feet
Firebox		120 sq feet
Total		1,250 sq feet
Grate area	19.0 sq feet	
Boiler pressure	175 psi	
Coupled wheels	5 feet 8 ins	
Tender wheels	4 feet 2 ins	
Tractive effort	18,427 lbs	
Length over buffers	50 feet 5½ ins*	
Wheelbase Locomotive	16 feet 3 ins	
Tender	13 feet 0 ins	
Total	37 feet 8 ins	
Weight in working order		
Locomotive	46 tons 14 cwt	
Tender	43 tons 2 cwt	
Total	89 tons 16 cwt	
Water capacity	3,500 gallons	
Coal capacity	6 tons 10 cwt	

NOTE: * Engine and tender.

The tenders originally fitted to the class were gradually removed and tenders with 3,170 gallon and 3,140 gallon capacity were later provided.

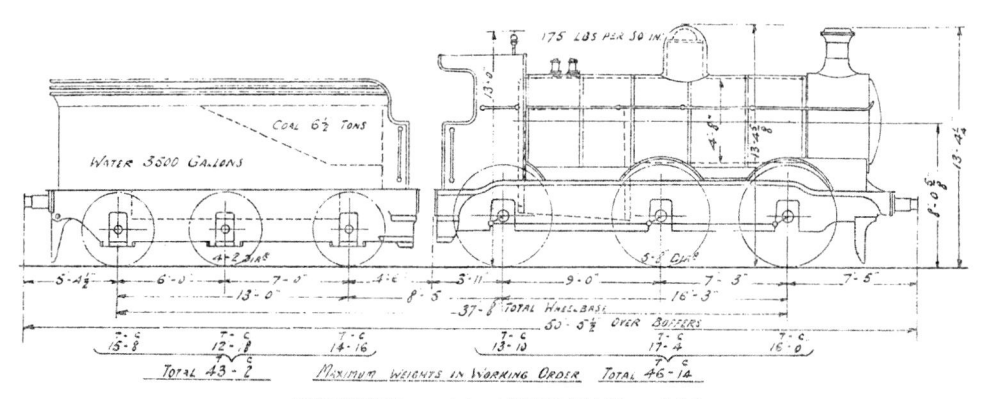

GNR 'J21' Class, later L&NER 'J1' Class 0-6-0.

The 'J22'/'J6' Class

Another class, which made occasional visits to the Hatfield to Hertford branch were the Ivatt GNR 'J22' Class 0-6-0 tender locomotives, later designated 'J6' by the L&NER. A total of 110 engines built between 1911 and 1922 were the final development of the Ivatt 0-6-0 tender locomotive designs with traditional Doncaster outline and were fitted with superheated boilers. Hatfield shed had no regular allocation of the class until shortly before World War Two, when four were allocated to the shed to work through passenger trains from Dunstable to King's Cross. However, the depot borrowed members of the class from Hornsey and Hitchin sheds to work out-of-course freight and engineers trains, and from their introduction until the final withdrawal from traffic the 'J6' Class were a firm favourite with footplate staff. The following locomotives are known to have worked across the Hertford branch.

GNR No.	L&NER 1924 No.	L&NER 1946 No.	BR No.	Withdrawn
539	3539	4188	64188	October 1959
585	3585	4234	64234	December 1959
590	3590	4239	64239	October 1959
591	3591	4240	64240	August 1960
602	3602	4251	64251	October 1960
607	3607	4256	64256	April 1960

The leading dimensions of the 'J6' Class were:

Cylinders		19 ins x 26 ins	
Motion		Stephenson with slide valves	
Boiler	Max diameter	4 feet 8 ins	
	Barrel length	10 feet 1 in.	
Firebox		6 feet 4 ins	
Heating surface			
	Tubes	118 x 1¾ ins	562.0 sq feet
	Flues	18 x 5¼ ins	257.0 sq feet
	Firebox		118.0 sq feet
	Total evaporative		937.0 sq feet
	Superheater	18 x 1¼ ins	192.0 sq feet
	Total		1,129.0 sq feet^
Firebox grate area		19.0 sq feet	
Boiler pressure		170 psi	
Coupled wheels		5 feet 2 ins	
Tender wheels		4 feet 2 ins	
Tractive effort		21,875 lbs	
Length over buffers		52 feet 6 ins	
Wheelbase	Locomotive	16 feet 3 ins	
	Tender	13 feet 0 ins	
	Total	38 feet 10 ins	
Weight in working order			
	Locomotive	50 tons 10 cwt	
	Tender	43 tons 2 cwt	
	Total	93 tons 12 cwt	
Max axle loading		18 tons	
Water capacity		3,500 gallons	
Coal capacity		6 tons 10 cwt	

Notes:
^ With superheater.
* Engine and tender.

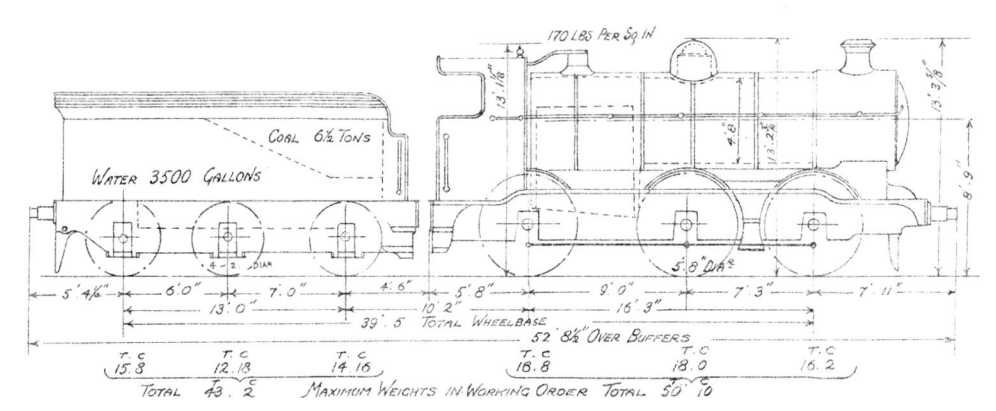

GNR 'J22' Class, later L&NER 'J6' Class, 0-6-0.

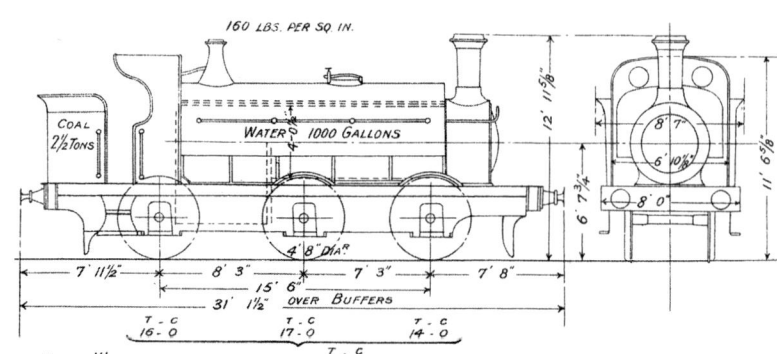

GNR 'J15' Class, later L&NER 'J54' Class, 0-6-0ST.

The GNR 'J15', Later L&NER 'J54'/'J55' Classes

For many years the GNR allocated a 'J15' Class 0-6-0 tank locomotive for shed pilot and general shunting duties at Hatfield. A total of fifty-six engines were built to the design of Patrick Stirling between 1874 and 1892 at Doncaster Works. The boilers, cylinders and wheel spacings were identical to the Class 'J6' 0-6-0 goods engines. The six original engines in the '494' series were built in 1874, to be followed by ten in the '500' series the following year. Then came the '634' series, which appeared between 1880 and 1891, to be followed by seven locomotives in 1891 and 1892. Robert Stephenson & Company provided ten in 1891 with Neilson providing a similar number to bring the total to ninety-five. They were distributed throughout the GNR system and twenty-seven of the original design were rebuilt with enclosed cabs in 1891 and 1892. At grouping the design with open cabs became L&NER Class 'J54/1' and the remainder 'J54/2'. Hatfield had one locomotive allocated in 1902 and at grouping No's 855, 901 and 909 of Class 'J54/2' were based at the Hertfordshire shed.

GNR No.	L&NER 1924 No.	L&NER 1946 No.	BR No.	Withdrawn
855	3855	—	—	February 1930 (1)
901	3901	—	—	September 1934 (1)
909	3909	—	—	June 1928

Note: 1. Later rebuilt to Class 'J55'.

The principal dimensions of the 'J54' Class were:

Cylinders	2 inside	17½ ins x 26 ins
Motion		Stephenson with slide valves
Boiler	Max diameter	4 feet 0½ ins
	Barrel length	10 feet 1 in.
Firebox		5 feet 6 ins
Heating surface		
	Tubes	163 x 1¾ ins 778.0 sq feet
	Firebox	85.0 sq feet
	Total	863.0 sq feet
Grate area		16.0 sq feet
Boiler pressure		160 psi
Coupled wheels		4 feet 8 ins
Tractive effort		19,334 lbs
Wheelbase		15 feet 6 ins
Length over buffets		31 feet 1½ ins part 1
		31 feet 9½ ins part 2
Weight in working order		47 tons 0 cwt part 1
		48 tons 10 cwt part 2
Max axle loading		17 tons 0 cwt part 1
		17 tons 10 cwt part 2
Water capacity		1,000 gallons
Coal capacity		2 tons 0 cwt

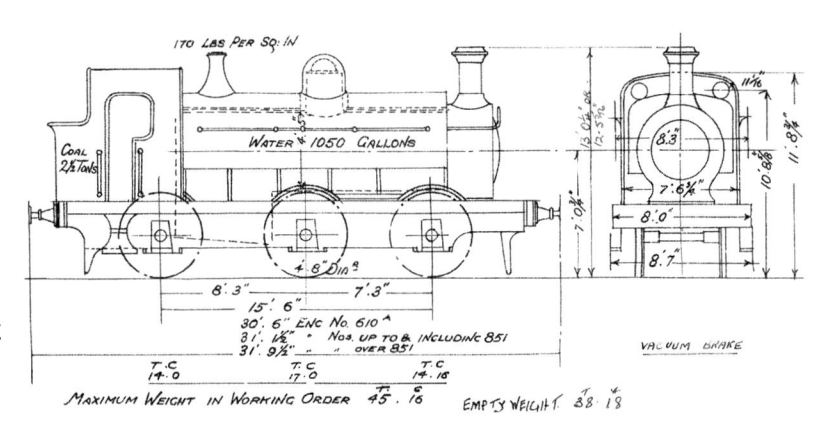

GNR 'J15' Class, later L&NER 'J55' Class 0-6-0ST.

The detail differences as rebuilt to Class 'J55' were:

Boiler	Max diameter	4 feet 5 ins	
Heating surface			
	Tubes	213 x 1¾ ins	1,016.0 sq feet
	Firebox		103.0 sq feet
	Total		1,119.0 sq feet
Grate area		16.25 sq feet	
Boiler pressure		170 psi	
Tractive effort		20,548 lbs	
Length over buffers		31 feet 9½ ins	
Weight in working order		50 tons 0 cwt	
Max axle loading		17 tons 0 cwt	
Water capacity		1,050 gallons	
Coal capacity		2 tons 10 cwt	

The 'J18'/'J57' Class

Another class of shunting locomotive allocated to Hatfield for shed pilot and trip working was the GNR 'J18' Class 0-6-0 saddle tank locomotives built by Stirling as his '684' series with eight engines being built in pairs between 1882 and 1892. They were primarily intended for working traffic to London's East End docks and had to pass under the GER main line at Stratford Low Level where the headroom at the time was only 11 feet 6 inches. Officially recorded *for the Blackwall traffic*, they were primarily used for working the freight trains to and from the GNR depots at Royal Mint Street, Poplar Dock and Thames Wharf reached by running powers over the GER and the North London Railway. Apart from two, all engines spent their life in the London area and after displacement from their original intended work No's 684 and 685 were allocated to Hatfield. After grouping the L&NER reclassified the locomotives to Class 'J57' and added 3000 to their original number. Their Hertfordshire days were, however, numbered for No. 3684 was transferred away to Ardsley and early scrapping, whilst No. 3685 was sent to Doncaster by which time the ex-GER 0-6-0Ts had taken their place at Hatfield. No. 3684 had a domeless boiler whilst No. 3685 was equipped with a 4 feet 5 inch diameter domed boiler.

GNR No.	L&NER 1924 No.	Withdrawn
684	3684	September 1930
685	3685	June 1938

The principal dimensions of the 'J57' Class with domeless boiler were:

Cylinders	2 inside	17½ ins x 24 ins	
Motion		Stephenson with slide valves	
Boiler	Max diameter	4 feet 0½ ins	
	Barrel length	10 feet 1 in.	
	Firebox	5 feet 6 ins	
Heating surface			
	Tubes	163 x 1¾ ins	778.0 sq feet
	Firebox		85.0 sq feet
	Total		863.0 sq feet
Grate area		16.0 sq feet	
Boiler pressure		160 psi	
Coupled wheels		4 feet 0½ ins	
Tractive effort		20,610 lbs	
Length over buffers		31 feet 1½ ins	
Wheelbase		15 feet 6 ins	
Weight in working order		43 tons 6 cwt	
Max axle loading		15 tons 12 cwt	
Coal capacity		2 tons	

Locomotives fitted with a domed boiler had the following detail differences.

Boiler	Max diameter	4 feet 5 ins	
Heating surface			
	Tubes	213 x 1¾ ins	1,016.0 sq feet
	Firebox		103.0 sq feet
	Total		1,119.0 sq feet
Grate area		16.25 sq feet	
Boiler pressure		170 psi	
Tractive effort		21,896 lbs	
Weight in working order		47 tons 4 cwt	
Max axle loading		16 tons 12 cwt	

The 'J13'/'J52' Class

A prolific class of 0-6-0 saddle tank shunting locomotive, the Ivatt 'J13' Class – introduced between 1894 and 1909 as a development of Stirling's 'J14' Class 0-6-0STs – strangely saw little use on the Hertford branch. Initially they were concentrated in large marshalling yards and also worked cross-London freights and only towards the end of their career did members of the class have any regular work from Hatfield. However, a few penetrated the rural charms of Hertfordshire on pick-up goods and two were given the opportunity to works special trains. No. 68878 worked the Railway Correspondence & Travel Society's Hertfordshire Railtour train over the St. Albans branch on 30th April 1955, taking over from 'B12/3' Class No. 61576 which had worked through from St. Pancras to Hatfield via the ex GE Hertford branch and on via Hertford Old and Cole Green to Hatfield. On withdrawal from traffic in May 1959 No. 68846 was purchased for preservation by Captain W.G. Smith and restored to GNR livery as No. 1247. It was initially stabled at Mowlem's yard at Marshmoor, south of Hatfield, and during its sojourn worked several railtours, including the South Bedfordshire Locomotive Society 'Lea Flyer' tour from Luton Bute Street to Hertford across the Welwyn Garden City to Hertford branch on 16th September 1961, and even worked on a train from London to the Bluebell Railway in Sussex. Locomotives known to have worked across the branch included:

GNR No.	L&NER 1924 No.	L&NER 1946 No.	BR No.	Withdrawn
1247	4247	8846	68846	May 1959
1268	4268	8867	68867	February 1958
1279	4279	8878	68878	May 1956
1286	4286	8885	68885	September 1956

The leading dimensions of the 'J52' Class 0-6-0STs were:

Cylinders	2 inside	18 ins x 26 ins	
Motion		Stephenson with slide valves	
Boiler	Max dia outside	4 feet 5 ins	
	Barrel length	10 feet 6 ins	
	Firebox	5 feet 6 ins	
Heating surface			
	Tubes	213 x 1¾ ins	1.061.0 sq feet
	Firebox		103.0 sq feet
	Total		1,164.0 sq feet
Grate area		16.25 sq feet	
Boiler pressure		160 psi	
Coupled wheels		4 feet 8 ins	
Tractive effort		20,456 lbs	
Wheelbase		15 feet 6 ins	
Weight in working order		51 tons 14 cwt	
Max axle loading		18 tons 0 cwt	
Water capacity		1,100 gallons	
Coal capacity		3 tons 0 cwt	

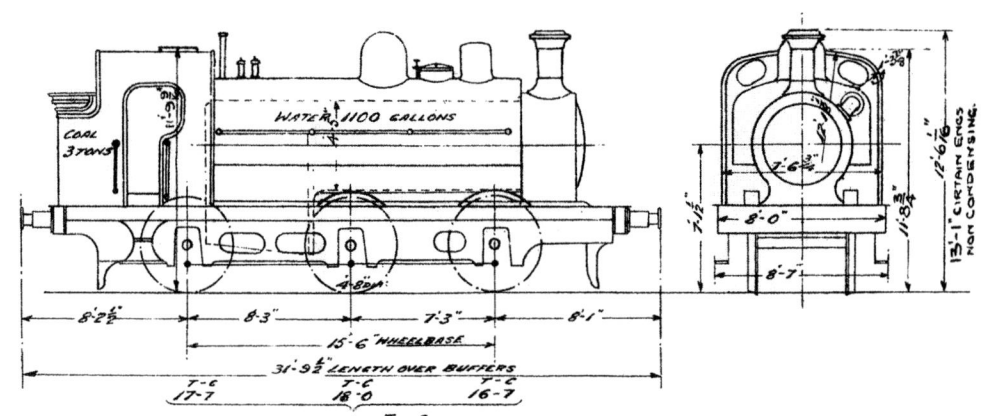

GNR 'J13' Class, later L&NER 'J52' Class, 0-6-0ST.

A fine study of 'J52' Class 0-6-0ST preserved as GNR No. 1247 standing at Hertingfordbury whilst hauling the South Bedfordshire Locomotive Society 'Lea Flyer' rail tour on 16th September 1961. *R.C. Riley*

The 'B12/3' Class

Possibly the largest tender locomotive to work across the branch, albeit on a railway enthusiasts special, was 'B12/3' Class 4-6-0 No. 61576 which hauled the Railway Correspondence & Travel Society Hertfordshire Rail Tour on 30th April 1955 between London St. Pancras and Hatfield via the ex-GER Hertford East branch and thence to Welwyn Garden City via Cole Green. The locomotive was a Gresley rebuild of Holden's 'S69' Class first introduced in 1911 when the GER authorities were finding the Claud Hamilton 4-4-0 tender locomotives struggling with ever-increasing heavy trains. Known as the '1500's from the running number of the initial locomotive, a total of seventy-one were built at Stratford and by William Beardmore & Company to 1921, although No. 1506 was totally written off after a fatal crash at Colchester and the number was never reused. After grouping the locomotives were allocated to Class 'B12' and a further ten were built by Beyer, Peacock & Company, later rebuilt to Class 'B12/3' including No. 8576, later 61576.

GER No.	L&NER 1924 No.	L&NER 1946 No.	BR No.	Withdrawn
—	8576	1576	61576	January 1959

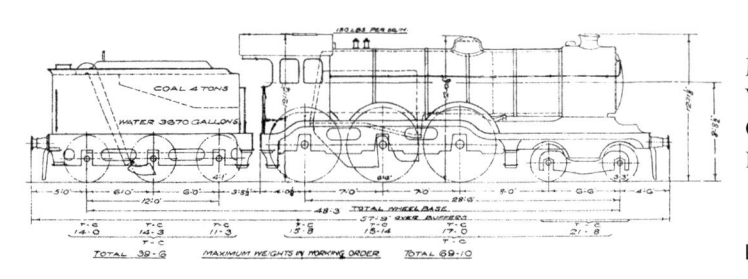

The leading dimensions of the 'B12/3' Class were:

Cylinders	2 inside	20 ins x 28 ins	
Motion		Stephenson with 10-ins piston valves	
Boiler	Max diameter	5 feet 6 ins	
	Barrel length	12 feet 7½ ins	
Firebox		10 feet 1½ ins	
Heating surface			
	Tubes	143 x 2 ins	979.0 sq feet
	Flues	24 x 5¼ ins	426.0 sq feet
	Firebox		154.0 sq feet
	Total evaporative		1,559.0 sq feet
	Elements	24 x 1⁷⁄₃₂ ins	315.0 sq feet
	Total		1,874.0 sq feet
Grate area		21.0 sq feet	
Boiler pressure		180 psi	
Leading wheels		3 feet 3 ins	
Coupled wheels		6 feet 6 ins	
Tender wheels		4 feet 1 ins	
Tractive effort		21,969 lbs	
Length over buffers		57 feet 9 ins*	
Weight in working order			
	Engine	69 tons 10 cwt	
	Tender	39 tons 6 cwt	
	Total	108 tons 16 cwt	
Max axle loading		17 tons 0 cwt	
Water capacity		3,670 gallons	
Coal capacity		4 tons 0 cwt	

Note: * Engine and tender.

Left: L&NER 'BI2/3' Class 4-6-0 tender locomotive.

The 'R24'/'J67' and 'R24R'/'J69' Classes

From 1930 until 1951 Hatfield shed was allocated at least one member of the ubiquitous GER 'R24' and 'R24R' Class 0-6-0 tank locomotives for shed shunting and local trip working. Nicknamed 'Buckjumpers' and designed by James Holden, the locomotives were built at Stratford Works between 1890 and 1904. Those fitted with the Westinghouse brake for passenger work gained fame on the 'Jazz' suburban services from Liverpool Street to Enfield and Chingford, whilst others were drafted to country depots. The L&NER after 1923 reclassified them to 'J67' and 'J69' with sub-sections and, finding there was an excess of the locomotives on the GE section, many were reallocated away from their native territory. Amongst the migrants were two sent to Hatfield in November 1930, initially for evaluation purposes as a possible replacement for the withdrawn of ex-GNR 'J54' Class 0-6-0Ts. Thereafter until the withdrawal of steam traction Hatfield was home to at least one or two of the class. As well as shed and yard shunting they made occasional forays to the St. Albans and Hertford branches and on the latter line were used on trip workings to intermediate sidings as far as Cole Green. Locomotives known to have worked across the branch were:

Class	GER	L&NER 1924 No.	L&NER 1946 No.	BR No.	Withdrawn
'J69/1'	195	7195	8602	68602	November 1959
'J67/1'	261	7261	8587	68587	November 1959
'J69/1'	370	7370	8546	68546	May 1958
'J69/1'	389	7389	8565	68565	August 1962
'J67/2'	396	7396	8572	68572	November 1954

Above: From 1930 until 1951 Hatfield shed was allocated one or two of the ubiquitous former GER 'R24' and 'R24R', later L&NER 'J67' and 'J69', Class 0-6-0Ts for general shunting duties and freight trip workings. Here 'J69/1' Class No. 7389 stands ahead of a GNR 0-6-0 tender locomotive in the shed yard in 1935. The locomotive became 8565 in the 1946 renumbering scheme and then BR No. 68565 before withdrawal from service in August 1962.
Author's collection

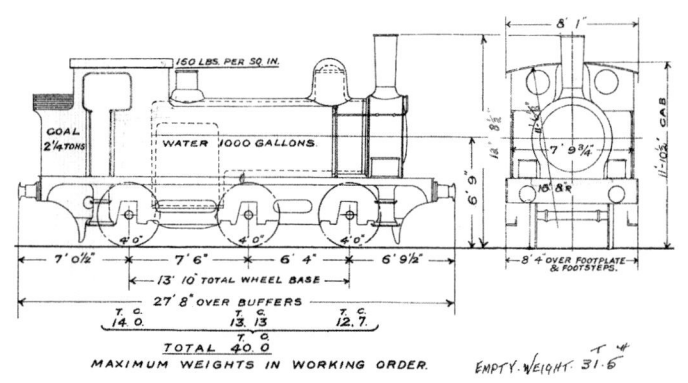

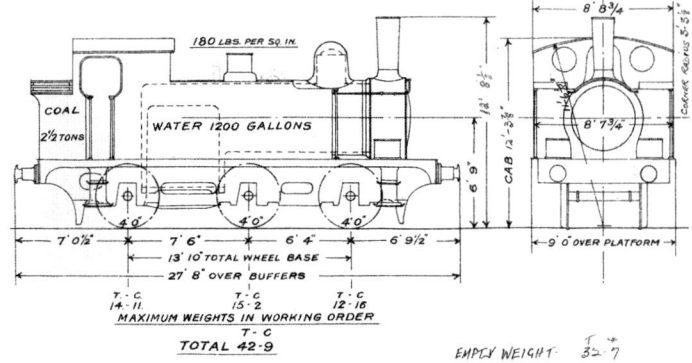

GER 'R24' Class, later L&NER 'J67' Class 0-6-0T.

GER 'R24R' Class, later L&NER 'J69' Class 0-6-0T.

The leading dimensions of the 'J67/1' Class were:

Cylinders 2 inside	16½ ins x 22 ins	
Motion	Stephenson with slide valves	
Boiler Max diameter	4 feet 2 ins	
Barrel length	9 feet 1 in.	
Firebox	4 feet 6 ins	
Heating surface		
Tubes	227 x 1⅝ ins	909.4 sq feet
Firebox		78.0 sq feet
Total		987.4 sq feet
Grate area	12.4 sq feet	
Boiler pressure	160 psi	
Coupled wheels	4 feet 0 ins	
Tractive effort	16,970 lbs	
Length over buffers	27 feet 8 ins	
Wheelbase	13 feet 10 ins	
Weight in working order	40 tons 0 cwt	
Max axle loading	14 tons 0 cwt	
Water capacity	1,000 gallons	
Coal capacity	2 tons 5 cwt	

The detail differences of the 'J69/1' Class were:

Firebox	6 feet 2¹⁄₁₆ ins	
Heating surface		
Firebox		86.77 sq feet
Total		996.17 sq feet
Grate area	14.5 sq feet	
Boiler pressure	180 psi	
Tractive effort	19,091 lbs	
Weight in working order	42 tons 9 cwt	
Max axle loading	15 tons 2 cwt	
Water capacity	1,200 gallons	
Coal capacity	2 tons 10 cwt	

THE BR CLASS '03' DIESEL SHUNTER

With the withdrawal of steam traction for shunting duties, Hatfield was allocated two BR Class '03' 204 hp diesel mechanical shunting locomotives, No's D2001 and D2002. The pair also worked local trips to adjacent sidings on the former Hertford and St. Albans branches before returning to Hatfield yard. When outbased at Luton they were occasionally called upon to work freight trips to Dunstable and back. D2002 worked such a trip on 17th February 1959.

A third locomotive was added to the allocation and their duties in October 1959 were as under:

Diagram 1   Down yard pilot.
Diagram 2   Welwyn Garden City yard pilot.
Diagram 3   Spare for maintenance.

It quickly became clear the locomotives were totally underpowered for such duties and they were subsequently transferred to Hitchin to join several already allocated to that shed.

The leading dimensions of the '03' Class were:

Weight in working order	30 tons 4 cwt
Tractive effort	15,300 lbs
Wheelbase	9 feet 0 ins
Wheel diameter	3 feet 7 ins
Width overall	8 feet 6 ins
Length overall	26 feet 0 ins
Height overall	12 feet 2⁷⁄₁₆ ins
Minimum curve negotiable	2 chains
Maximum speed	28½ mph
Fuel tanks	300 gallons
Brakes	Compressed air, vacuum and hand
Sanding	Compressed air operated
Power equipment	8-cylinder diesel engine – Gardner 8L3 type 204 hp at 1,200 rpm
Transmission	
Fluid coupling	Vulcan Sinclair type 23, capacity 8½ gallons
Gearbox	Wilson Drewry CA5 R7 compressed air operated
Reverse gear and final drive	type RF11

THE BR CLASS '08' DIESEL SHUNTER

The initial decline in steam operation on the lines came in February 1958 when three Class 'DEJ5' diesel electric shunting locomotives, No's D3476, D3477 and D3478, were allocated to Hatfield and normally outbased at Luton. They departed Hatfield early on a Monday morning and remained at Luton until later the following Saturday when a return journey was made to the parent shed for maintenance and fuelling. After the initial tranche they were joined by D3475 and D3490, but the latter was soon transferred away to Boston coded 40F and No's D3689 and D3690 came to Hatfield in 1960. In October 1959 the allocation of the shunting locomotives was altered as overleaf.

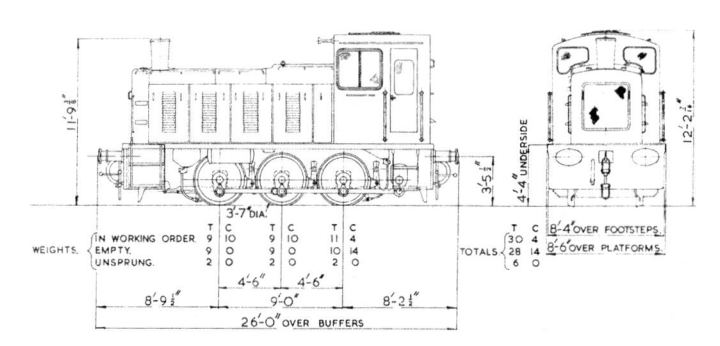

BR Class '03' 0-6-0 diesel mechanical shunting locomotive.

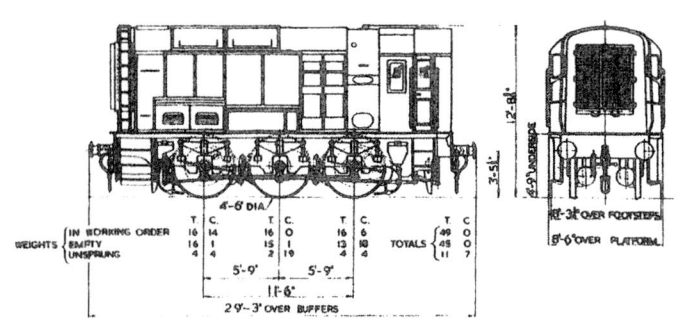

BR Class '08' diesel electric shunting locomotive.

Diagram 1 Monday to Luton where it worked all week returning to Hatfield on Saturday.
Diagram 2 Early morning freight train to Luton before working back to Hatfield the same evening.
Diagram 3 Early morning freight train to Hertford before working back the same evening.
Diagram 4 Spare at Hatfield for maintenance and yard duties.

The initial allocation was fitted with GEC equipment and had Blackstone engines, whilst D3689 and D3690 had English Electric equipment. The principal dimensions of the Blackstone 350 hp locomotives, which later became BR Class '08' were:

Type	0-6-0
Weight in working order	48 tons
Tractive effort	35,000 lbs
Wheelbase	11 feet 6 ins
Wheel diameter	4 feet 6 ins
Width overall	8 feet 10 ins
Length overall	29 feet 3 ins
Height overall	12 feet 8⅝ ins
Minimum curve negotiable	3 chains
Max speed	20 mph
Fuel tanks Main	585 gallons
Service	83 gallons
Total	668 gallons
Lubricating oil sump	45 gallons
Cooling water	
Radiator	90 gallons
Engine	50 gallons
Total	140 gallons
Brakes	Compressed air and hand brake on the locomotive
	Vacuum brake equipment provided to work fitted stock and give proportional air braking on the locomotive when so working
Engine	6-cylinder diesel – Blackstone ER 6T type 350 hp at 750 rpm
Main generator	DC self ventilated GEC WT 821 type, 1 hour rating 228 kw, 600 amps, 380 volts at 750 rpm
Auxiliary generator	DC self ventilated GEC type WT 700, 1 hour rating 9.2 kw, 92 volts, 100amps, 2,520 rpm
Traction motors	DC force-ventilated 4 pole GEC type WT 360, 1 hour rating, 2 x 152hp, 360 volts, 370 amps at 800 rpm
Air compressor	Westinghouse DH 16, motor driven
Exhausters	Westinghouse 3V72, motor driven

Facilities and Staff

When the Great Northern Railway opened between Peterborough and London on 7th August 1850 no engine shed was provided at Hatfield. Late in 1851 Archibald Sturrock, the Locomotive Superintendent, made application for a carriage turntable 16 feet in diameter and on 15th September 1852 he requested a carriage shed at an estimated cost of £130, which the board approved. It is almost certain that stabling for locomotives was provided at the same time for there is evidence both facilities were available in 1854. This dead-end building, measuring 215 feet by 35 feet, covered two roads and was fully justified with the opening of the three branches from Hatfield. The roof of the building was single gable with slate on wood supported on iron beams.

On 31st August 1886 new works authorised improvements to the station including an extension to the south siding and demolition of the carriage shed beside the engine shed and conversion of the latter to a through building. It had been the intention to relocate the depot to a site 60 chains north of the station but the cost was considered prohibitive as it entailed doubling the St. Albans branch approach to the station and increased costs by £13,000, so *'the engine shed will remain for the time being'*. The extension of the roads through the shed was also aborted following complaints made on 7th January 1892 from residents of neighbouring houses objecting to *'more or less continual nuisance of smoke'*. In the early months of 1892 the Locomotive Engineer submitted plans for new facilities for the maintenance of engines at Hatfield. Over the years the existing accommodation had been *'inadequate for the day-to-day servicing and repairs for the larger number of engines allocated to the depot for main line and branch work'*. Whilst improvements had been made to the goods yard and passenger station, together with associated signalling, the locomotive department had been almost

A shed foreman's nightmare! With few branch services and a reduction of outer suburban trains on Sundays, many locomotives were stabled at Hatfield shed, so that accommodation was very restricted. Here a selection of 'N2' and 'N7' Class 0-6-2Ts stand boiler to bunker waiting their next turn of duty. *Author's collection*

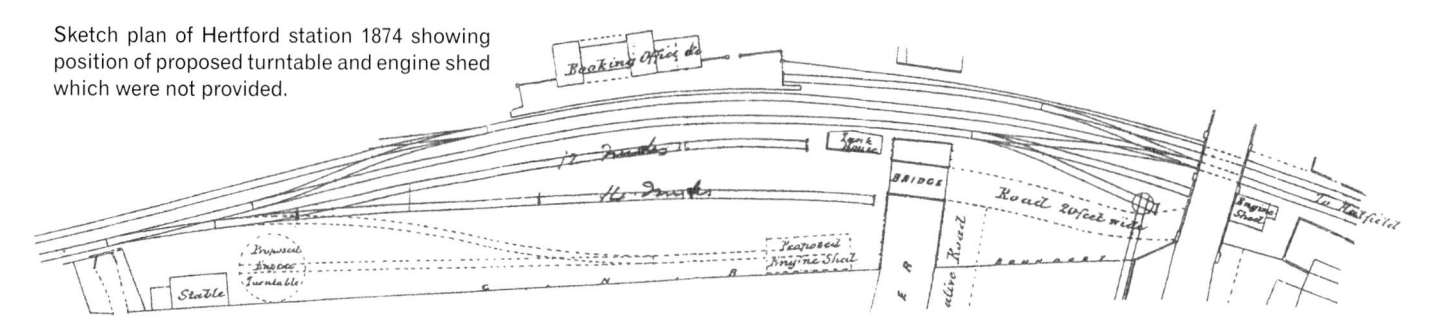

Sketch plan of Hertford station 1874 showing position of proposed turntable and engine shed which were not provided.

overlooked. This omission was to be rectified when a request was made for a small engine shed with undercover capacity for eight engines, together with a coaling stage, engine turntable and engine holding siding. The scheme was placed before the Board on 1st April 1892 when the General Manager was instructed to provide more details of the plans. Salvation almost came when sparks from a locomotive set fire to the roof timbers of the existing building causing considerable damage. As a result of the loss of most of the roof, the inspection pits within the shed flooded during wet weather and the routine maintenance and repairs of engines suffered as a consequence.

An urgent request for repairs was agreed on 26th July 1901 after Ivatt reported to the Locomotive Committee the building had suffered from corroded iron beams caused by many years of permanent dampness and sulphuric acid, and replacement of the roof was essential at a cost of £1,500. This was considered excessive and a sum of £310 was sanctioned for repairs. Ivatt was asked to re-investigate. In the end the existing type of roof was retained with the iron beams supported by wooden trusses at a total cost of £190. By this period the western shed road had been extended through the building resulting in an increase in stabling siding. The new opening had rolled steel joists in the wall bearing on new pad stones and new brickwork was formed above this lintel, although the roof retained its original profile and central raised ventilators. In early grouping years the roof was raised by some two feet and smoke ventilators were fitted over each of the shed roads. At the same time a new chimney was added to the foreman's office.

An increased allocation of locomotives to Hatfield after World War One necessitated additional inspection work to be preformed in the open. As no siding outside the engine shed was equipped with an inspection pit the locomotive superintendent requested the provision of additional facilities. Authority for a new 75-foot engine inspection pit at Hatfield was given on 16th April 1920 at the estimated cost of £165 but when the work was completed on 6th May 1921 the cost had increased to £273, £108 above budget because of unforeseen drainage difficulties. Little else appears to have

The southern aspect of Hatfield shed on 24th April 1960 with 'N2/1' Class 0-6-2T No. 69531 standing on No. 1 road. The modernised frontage to the older building is evident.
K. Fairey

Above: The cramped stabling facilities at Hatfield shed are well demonstrated by the close positioning of an 'N7' Class 0-6-2T and the following 'N2' Class 0-6-2T. Close behind another 'N7' Class locomotive waits to move forward. *Author's collection*

The south aspect of Hatfield engine shed on 23rd May 1959 showing the cramped position of the depot coded 34C by British Railways. A Class 'N2' 0-6-2T bearing the destination board MOORGATE on the bunker is receiving attention. *F. Hornby*

been carried out to improve facilities at the shed other than in 1929 a 10 cwt skip-type mechanical coaling plant was provided to ease fuelling of locomotives at Hatfield. A coking platform constructed of timber was initially supplied and this was later replaced by an open air coaling stage.

In the heyday of the branch in 1925, of the fifteen weekday engine diagrams operated by Hatfield shed only six involved work to and from Hertford. Diagram 1 on both MO and MX and diagram 2 MX required the locomotive to haul a return goods trip to Cole Green, whilst diagram 5 spent most of the early part of the day on the Hertford line before working the Dunstable branch. Diagram 7 engine and men spent the whole day working to Hertford and back between shunting duties at Hatfield. In complete contrast, the locomotive working diagram 11 was only involved in an SO return working from Hatfield to Hertford. The engine on diagram 12 was employed for the greater part of the day on the branch interspersed with one round trip from Hatfield to King's Cross. No Sunday trains were operated.

In 1929 twenty-nine locomotives were allocated to Hatfield depot worked by fifty-five sets of men, four sets working the 'Suburban link', increasing two years later to thirty engines but this was reduced in the mid 1930s to totals varying from twenty-six to

RIGHT: The south end of Hatfield shed in the early 1900s with two '126' Class 0-4-2WTs led by No. 116A and '120' Class 0-4-4 'Back Tank' No. 249 nearest the single opening. In later years the opening was doubled to two tracks. Note the close proximity of the housing to the depot.
Author's collection

FACING PAGE BOTTOM: The north end of Hatfield shed with 'N7/5' Class 0-6-2T No. 69631 waiting its next diagrammed working on 6th June 1959. Note the close proximity of the company houses where it was almost impossible to hang out the 'white' washing on a Monday morning! *N. Browne*

HATFIELD DEPOT

WEEK DAYS.

No. 1.

arr. a.m.	MX	dep. a.m.
......	On Duty	2 0
......	Loco'	2 45 L
......	Hatfield	3 0 G
3 39	Luton	6 20
6 34	Dunstable	7 11
8 2	Hatfield	9 15 E
9 25	St. Albans	9 32
9 44	Hatfield	10 0 G SO
10 56	Cole Green	11 20 G SO
11 40	Hatfield	12 15
p.m.		p.m.
1 16	Dunstable	1 50
2 3	Luton	4 0
4 14	Dunstable	5 17
5 30	Luton	6 30
6 44	Dunstable	9 0 G
10 57 ...	⎧ Hatfield	L
p.m.	⎨	
12 55u	⎩	
......	Loco'	......

Second set from 11.45 a.m.

Third set travel passenger to Luton.

No. 1.

arr. a.m.	MO	dep. a.m.
......	On Duty	3 50
......	Loco'	4 35 L
......	Hatfield	4 40 AG
5 20	Luton	5 25 E
5 40	Dunstable	6 0
6 15	Luton	7 34
7 48	Dunstable	8 15
9 10	Hatfield	10 0 G
10 56	Cole Green	11 20 G
11 40	Hatfield	12 15
p.m.		p.m.
1 16	Dunstable	1 50
2 3	Luton	4 0
4 14	Dunstable	5 17
5 30	Luton	6 30
6 44	Dunstable	9 0 G
10 57	Hatfield	L
......	Loco'	......

Second set from 11.45 a.m.

Third set passenger to Luton.

(A) Coupled to engine of No. 2 diagram.

No. 2 MX.

a.m. arr.		a.m. dep.
......	On Duty	3 5
......	Loco'	3 50 L
......	Hatfield	4 5 G
5 35	Dunstable	6 0
6 15	Luton	7 34
7 48	Dunstable	8 15
9 10	Hatfield	10 0 SX G
10 56	Cole Green	11 20 SX G
11 40	Hatfield	9 55 SO
10 21	Hitchin	L
......	Hatfield Loco'	......
p.m.		p.m.
......	Hatfield	⎧ 2 10 G SX
		⎨ 2 7 G SO
4 57	Dunstable	5 57 G
8 10	Hatfield	L
......	Loco'	......

Second set from 1.20 p.m.

No. 5.

arr. a.m.		dep. a.m.
......	On Duty	5 15
......	Loco'	6 0 L
......	Hatfield	6 20 G
8 0	Hertford E.	8 20 E & B
8 25	Hertford Old	L
......	Hertford N.	8 50
9 11	Hatfield	9 20
9 44	Hertford	11 35
11 55	Hatfield	p.m. 12 10
SX 12 31 ⎱	Hertford	1 15
SO 12 33 ⎰		
1 35	Hatfield	2 0
2 56	Dunstable	3 50
4 42	Hatfield	5 40
5 50	Ayot	6 5
6 15	Hatfield	6 33
7 30	Dunstable	7 47
8 54	Hatfield	......
......	Hatfield	9 53 SO
10 27	Luton	11 0 SO
11 13	Dunstable	11 20 SO
11 33	Luton	11 57 SO G
a.m.		
12 50	Hatfield	L
......	Loco'	......

Second set 12.0 noon.

Third set 9.53 p.m. SO

No. 7.

arr. a.m.		dep. a.m.
......	On Duty	4 30
......	Loco'	5 50 L

Shunt Hatfield 6.0 a.m. to 8.0 a.m.

......	Hatfield	8 23
8 43	Hertford N.	9 25
9 45	Hatfield	9 55
10 16	Hertford N.	11 0
11 20	Hatfield	......

Shunt Up Yard.

p.m.		p.m.
......	Hatfield	12 25 G
2 5	Hertford E.	2 20 G
2 30	Hertford Old	L
......	Hertford N.	4 10 SX 4 20 SO
4 41 SO 4 31 SX	Hatfield	5 7
5 30	Hertford N.	5 43
6 7	Hatfield	6 32
6 55	Hertford N.	L
......	Hertford Old	7 20 G
8 12	Hatfield	L
......	Loco'	......

Second set from 12.10 p.m.

No. 11.

arr. a.m.		dep. a.m.
......	On Duty	8 10
......	Loco'	8 55 L
......	Hatfield	9 15
9 44	King's Cross	11 0 MTX
11 41	Ayot	12 45 MTX
p.m.		p.m.
12 55	Hatfield	5 8 MTSX
5 18	Ayot	5 27 MTSX
6 5	King's Cross	11 45 WSX
a.m.		
12 24	Hatfield	......
......	King's Cross	11 45 WO
		a.m.
12 58	Letchworth	1 10 E ThO
1 36	Hatfield	......
12 55	Hatfield	3 6 SO
3 27	Hertford	3 40 L SO
4 0	Hatfield Loco	......

Second set from 5.8 p.m. MTSX

Passengers to King's Cross by 795 up MTO

No. 12.

arr. a.m.		dep. a.m.
......	On Duty	4 30
......	Loco'	5 15 L
......	Hatfield	5 45 G
6 43	Hertford E.	6 58 G
7 18	Hertford Old	L
......	Hertford N.	7 42
8 6	Hatfield	9 31
10 8	King's Cross	11 5
11 55	Hatfield	L
p.m.		p.m.
......	Loco'	5 30 L
......	Hatfield	5 42
6 5	Hertford N.	6 10 L
6 15	Hertford Old	L
......	Hertford N.	7 4
7 24	Hatfield	7 40
8 1	Hertford N.	8 12 L SX
8 22	Hertford E.	8 32 G SX
8 42	Hertford Old	8 45 G SX
10 20	Hatfield	L SX
......	Loco'	......
......	Hertford N.	8 30 G SO
8 40	Hertford E.	9 0 SO
9 10	Hertford Old	9 20 SO
10 50	Hatfield	L SO
......	Loco'	......

Second set on duty 4.45 p.m.

Hatfield depot locomotive and enginemen's diagram 1925; only diagrams involving work on the Hertford branch are shown.

twenty-eight engines as a result of a slight loss of local passenger and goods traffic. By 1957, after the loss of the St. Albans and Hertford passenger traffic, Hatfield motive power depot still had a staff of 123, of which about fifty sets of men were footplate staff working to such diverse places as London, Hertford, St. Albans, Dunstable and Peterborough. The footplate staff had strong union representation, with Driver Joe Deeley as chairman of the Local Departmental Committee. Hatfield depot, which was allocated shed code 34C in the King's Cross district in 1951 by BR, closed on 2nd January 1961. At the same time, engines allocated to Hertford East carried shedplates denoting 30B in the Stratford District.

In the early years after joint working with the ECR, two engines from Hatfield were outbased at Hertford, where primitive facilities were provided. Because of restricted space the small engine shed at Hertford was in fact located under No. 2 arch of Port Hill overbridge, with an extension 25 feet westwards beyond the structure which was enclosed by a 32-foot timber building forming an extension of the overbridge arch. The total building was 62 feet in length by 17 feet in width and had a 12-foot inspection pit immediately to the east of the bridge arch. A coal/coke loading stage was also provided but, although mooted, no turntable was installed as most passenger services were worked by tank engine and freight trains hauled by tender locomotives invariably worked through to the GER yard where GNR locomotives used the GER 36 feet diameter turntable. On occasions passenger engines also ventured to the GER turntable if revised running was required.

After complaints from residents living near the station, led by William Rolfe on 4th July 1868, regarding smoke emanating from the shed, an instruction was issued that coke was to be used instead of coal and then proposals for a new shed to be located at the east end of the goods yard together with new sidings. Ultimately the stabling of two locomotives proved inconvenient and a second shed was constructed measuring 60 feet by 20 feet close to the bridge spanning the River Lea, with an associated coaling stage. It appears then that one locomotive was stabled in each shed. By 1876 only one engine was allocated and from 1883 all workings started and finished at Hatfield, and soon after both Hertford sheds became derelict and were demolished.

With the conversion of the Hertford branch between Hatfield and Welwyn Garden City with effect from 17th September 1944, it was deemed that Hertford East shed would work some of the diagrams between Hertford and Welwyn Garden City and two sets of men were duly transferred from Hatfield to Hertford East depot to take up the new work. There was always a promotional movement between the two sheds after grouping and it was volunteers who agreed to accept the transfer between depots. In October 1952 rumours were rife about the closure of Hatfield shed when Hornsey footplate staff started learning the road to St. Albans and Dunstable. At this stage Hertford East engines and men increased their work on the Hertford to Welwyn Garden City section as well as carrying out shunting at the latter. The fears that Hornsey men would take over the St. Albans and Dunstable

Looking east from Hertford Station signal box in 1911 showing the two-road engine shed to the left with access at the far end of the building. Hard by the shed and adjacent to the Up main line is the 44 feet 9 inches diameter turntable, which was occasionally used by GNR engines. The goods shed part of the original 1843 passenger station, to the right, casts a shadow over the Down main line and the scissors crossover in the foreground. The GNR single line branch is to the extreme left running at a lower level. *GERS/Windwood 609*

branches proved unfounded, but Hertford East men continued to share the workings between Hertford Old and Welwyn Garden City with Hatfield men. A problem which occasionally arose was when a locomotive was required to carry out a vacuum brake test on trains in Welwyn Garden City yard for the GN section, when a Westinghouse fitted 'N7' Class engine was working the diagram and had trouble raising the vacuum. It was therefore an unwritten law that no Westinghouse fitted Class 'N7' engine was to work to Welwyn Garden City or Hatfield.

Whistle Codes

The engine whistle codes for the Hatfield branches stipulated in 1877 were:

Hatfield South signal box:

To or from spur	2 short, 1 long
Crossover between Down sidings and Down main line and spur	5

Hatfield North signal box:

Main lines	1
To and from Hertford	2
From Luton	3
From sidings to St. Albans	2 long
From sidings to Luton	3
From sidings to Down main line	1 long
From back platform to St. Albans	2 long
From back platform to Down main line	2
From sidings to spur	4 with pause between 2nd and 3rd
From west sidings to St. Albans	1 long and 1 short
From west sidings to Luton	2 long and 1 short
From sidings to Down main line	1 long
From St. Albans	3 long
Through road Up sidings to Up slow line	1 long
Down main line to Down sidings	1 long
South end of slip in Up main line	4
North end of slip in Down main line	4
Crossover between Up main and Up slow line	4 with pause between 2nd and 3rd

Twentieth Mile:

Up siding	3

The engine whistle codes stipulated by the GNR in 1881 were:

Hatfield North signal box:

Hertford line	2
From Luton	3
Sidings to St. Albans	2 long
Sidings to Down main line	1 long
Back of platform to St. Albans	2 long
Back of platform to Down main line	2
Sidings to spur	4 with pause between 2nd and 3rd
West sidings to St. Albans	1 long and 1 short
West sidings to Luton	2 long and 1 short
Sidings to Down main line	1 long
Luton to Up main line	3
Luton to Up slow line	1 crow
Luton to west face of Down platform	2 crow
St. Albans to Up main line	5
St. Albans to Up slow line	2 long
St. Albans to west face of Down platform	2 long, 2 short
West face of Down platform to St. Albans	2 long, 2 short
West face of Down platform to Luton	2 crow
Crossover between Up main and Up slow line	4 with pause between 2nd and 3rd
Up shunting siding to Up fast line	1 crow
Up shunting siding to slow line	2 crow

Hertford:

To or from the GER	3
Cattle dock	1 long
Long Bank siding	2 long
Goods warehouse and coal sidings	1 long, 1 short
McMullen's siding	1 long, 2 short
Engine shed	1 long, 3 short
Dicker's mill and wharf siding	6
Andrew's siding	1 crow
Gas works	2 crow

The GER whistle code applicable to GNR enginemen at Hertford in 1891 was:

Hertford Junction:

Main line – to or from Hertford passenger station	1 distinct sound

In 1929 a 10 cwt lightweight skip-type mechanical coaling plant was provided at Hatfield shed to assist with the fuelling of locomotives and eliminate much of the hand-coaling. The structure was provided by Stothert & Pitt of Bath and was of minimum width enabling the coal and locomotives to be as close together as possible. A wide base provided ample stability and the equipment was entirely clear of loading gauge.

To or from the goods yard	2 distinct sounds
To or from the Great Northern branch	3 distinct sounds
To or from engine turntable and shed	4 distinct sounds
To or from the back road	5 distinct sounds
To or from engine turntable	1 long and 1 crow

Hertford Station:

To or from the south platform line	1 distinct sound
To or from the north platform line	2 distinct sounds
To or from siding at the back of south platform	3 distinct sounds
To or from siding between the platform lines	4 distinct sounds
To or from siding at the back of north platform	5 distinct sounds

The engine whistle codes in 1905 for the Hertford Branch were:

Hatfield No. 2 signal box:

Hertford line	2, 1 crow
Hertford line and Down main	1 crow, 1 short
Hertford line and Down goods	1 crow, 4 short
Hertford line and Luton line	1 short, 1 long
Hertford line and St. Albans line	2 short, 1 crow
Hertford line and carriage siding	1 long, 1 crow
Up main to Up goods, set back	1, pause, 2
Up main to Down goods	1 crow, 2 short
Up main and Luton line	3
Up main and St. Albans line	5
Up main and carriage siding	3, pause, 1
Up slow and Up siding	1 long
Up slow and Hertford line	2
Up slow and Down main	3 long
Up slow and Down goods	1 crow, 3 short
Up slow and Luton line	1 crow
Up slow and St. Albans line	2 long
Up slow and carriage siding	3, pause, 2
Up siding and Hertford line, southern	4, pause, 1
Up siding and Hertford line, northern	1 long, 2 short
Up siding No. 1 and Down main	2
Up siding No. 1 and Down goods	1 crow, 5 short
Up siding No. 1 to Luton line	4
Up siding No. 1 to St. Albans line	6
Up siding No. 1 and carriage siding	1, pause, 3
Up goods line to Up slow, disc	2, pause, 2
Up sidings to Hertford line	4
Up sidings to Down main	1 long
Up sidings to Down goods	2 crows
Up sidings to Luton line	3
Up sidings to St. Albans line	2 long
Up sidings to carriage siding	3, pause, 3
Luton line to Up sidings	2 long, 2 short
St. Albans line to Up sidings	1 long, 1 short

Hatfield No. 3 signal box:

Western platform to St. Albans	2 long, 2 short
Western platform to Luton	3
Western platform and Down main	2
Western platform and Down goods	2 long, 1 crow
Down goods to St. Albans	5, 2 short
Down goods to Luton	5, 3 short
Down goods line	5
Down goods and spur	1 crow
Down goods and Up main line	1 crow, 2 short
Down goods and Up slow line	1 crow, 3 short
Down goods and Hertford line	1 crow, 4 short
Down goods and Up sidings	1 crow, 5 short
Down goods line set back	5
Goods yard and spur	2, pause, 2
Goods yard and St. Albans	1 long, 1 short
Goods yard to Luton	2 long, 1 short
Goods yard and Down main	1 long
Goods yard and Down goods	1 long, 3 short
Luton line advance signal	3
Luton line outer stop signal	3
Luton line to Up slow	1 crow
Luton line to Up main	3
Luton line to western platform	2 crow
Luton line to Hertford line	1 long, 1 short
St. Albans line to Up slow	2 long
St. Albans line to Up main	5
St. Albans line to Hertford line	2 long, 1 crow
St. Albans line to western platform	2 long, 2 short
St. Albans line and carriage siding	2 short, 1 crow

Twentieth Mile:

Up Hertford line	2

Cole Green:

Siding and Down main	3
Siding and Up main	1 long
Single line to Down main	1 crow
Up main to single line	4

Hertford:

Great Eastern Railway	3
Cattle dock	1 long
Long bank siding	2 long
Goods warehouse and coal sidings	1 long, 1 short
McMullen's siding	1 long, 2 short
Engine shed	1 long, 3 short
Dicker's Mill and wharf siding	6
Andrew's siding	1 crow
Gas Works	2 crows
Running line and No. 1 siding eastern crossover	5
Running line and No. 2 siding western crossover	1 crow
Running line and No. 2 siding	1 long
Running line and No. 3 siding	4

Drivers of Up goods, coal and brick trains not booked to stop at Hatfield but which required to stop there for water were required to sound one crow on the whistle when passing Woolmer Green signal box and the signalman there then advised the signalmen at Digswell, Welwyn Garden City and Hatfield No. 2 signal boxes of the circumstances. The engine requiring water was required to stop at the water crane at the north end of Hatfield station unless the driver was specifically instructed to proceed to the south end crane for water. Drivers of trains on the Up goods line were required

'N7/5' Class 0-6-2T No. 69632, complete with express train headcode, approaching Hertingfordbury with the Railway Correspondence & Travel Society's Hertfordshire No. 2 railtour on 27th April 1958. The train is formed of Gresley L&NER corridor coaches in carmine and cream livery whilst the locomotive has the smokebox ring embellished. *Author's collection*

to sound the engine whistle on approaching Smart's siding near Welwyn Garden City whenever a train was working the siding.

Strangely, after the excessive number of whistles codes stipulated by the pre-grouping companies, the L&NER advised no specific whistles for the main line or the branch at Hatfield or Hertford North, whilst the requirements at Hertford East were the same as for Hertford Station in 1891 save that the whistles were short and with the addition of *'to or from the engine turntable 3 short, pause 3 short'*. By 1942 the whistle code at **Hertford East** was:

To or from the south platform	1 short
To or from the north platform	2 short
To or from the siding at the back of the south platform	3 short
To or from the siding between the platforms	4 short
To or from the siding at the back of the north platform	5 short
To or from the engine turntable	3 short, pause, 3 short

HEADCODES

The engine headcode used by the GNR on the Hertford branch services was one white light under the chimney and one white light over the right-hand buffer looking from the locomotive cab, for ordinary passenger and excursion trains as well as empty coaching stock workings. Goods, mineral or ballast trains carried one white light over the left-hand buffer, whilst light engines carried one white light over the right-hand buffer. If a special train was run at short notice with no printed or written notice, the engine carried the normal headcode and an additional lamp on the chimney. Once the Railway Clearing House had established the standard engine headcode, locomotives carried the normal white light at the base of the chimney for stopping passenger services and the specific freight train class headcode for branch goods trains.

WATER SUPPLIES AND TURNTABLES

Locomotive water supplies at Hatfield initially came from a local stream, which fed a 10,000 gallons capacity storage tank. By March 1862 Sturrock considered this as inadequate and requested approval for a sum of £150 to deepen it by 4 feet, thereby doubling the capacity to 20,000 gallons – the shortfall of water being particularly noticeable during period of heavy demand or on stormy days. The Locomotive Engineer, however, reported on 7th March 1864 that the water supply was *'good at present due to heavy rains'*. On 4th February 1864 a request had been made to further develop the spring and he subsequently received approval for a sum of £1,085 to excavate a well yielding 40,000 gallons a day and install the necessary engine pumps and pump house. Ultimately two wells were sunk producing 30 million gallons of water annually. In the 1886 improvements the water tank was enlarged to hold 29,000 gallons. This sufficed until 1927 when authority given to sink a new bore hole and this was completed the following year.

By 1905 water for locomotives was available at **Hatfield** as under:

Standpipe	South of No. 1 signal box Down home signal	Down goods line
Crane	North end of Down main platform	Down main line
Standpipe	North end of Luton and St. Albans platform	Platform line
Crane	Just south of coal stage (Down side)	Coal stage line
Standpipe	North end of Hertford platform	Hertford line
Standpipe	South end of Up platform	Up slow and Up platform

And at **Hertford**:

Standpipe	West end of platform	Platform line

Water was also available at Hertford GER station.

ENGINE HEAD LAMPS.

It has been decided to adopt the following description and arrangement of Head Lamps for all Engines running on the Great Northern Railway.

The existing Lamps and Lamp Brackets on the Engines and Tenders are being altered, so that the new rule may be absolute from 1st August, 1881, from which time the Station Staff and Signalmen at intermediate Signal Boxes must report every case in which the proper distinguishing Disc, Board or Head Lamp or Lamps, are not carried.

1. Express and fast passenger trains,—and through express fish and meat trains having to be run at the same rate of speed as passenger trains,—booked to stop at principal stations only; also break down trains when proceeding to clear the line.

2. Express and fast passenger trains, excursion and other special passenger trains—and through express fish and meat trains having to be run at the same rate of speed as passenger trains—booked to stop at principal stations only; *which are not in the general working time books, but which are entered in the weekly working tables, or of which other special printed or written notice has been issued.*

3. Ordinary passenger and excursion trains booked to stop at other than principal stations,—and trains of empty coaching stock.

4. Express and fast goods trains,—and meat, fish, and cattle trains which have to be run at the same rate of speed as express goods trains, also trains of empty meat, fish, or cattle wagons.

5. Through goods, mineral and ballast trains, which have not to stop on the journey for the purpose of loading or unloading, and trains of empty wagons.

6. Goods, mineral and ballast trains which have to stop on the journey for the purpose of loading or unloading,—and break down trains returning from obstruction of line.

7. Light Engines,—and shunting engines when on a running line or proceeding from one yard to another.

8. Shunting engines when employed after dusk in station yards and sidings a head and tail lamp, each showing a *red* light.

9. When an additional or special train, of the description shown by Nos. 1, 2, 3, 4, 5 or 6, is run, of which no printed or written notice has been given to the signalmen, the head lamp or lamps prescribed above must be used, and in addition, *a special lamp must be carried near the top of the chimney*, thus:—

10. When single line working is temporarily adopted on any portion of the Great Northern Railway usually worked as a double line, all engines running in the wrong direction must carry a *red* head light or head lights, instead of the head lights ordinarily used.

11. Where not otherwise specially ordered the head lights must be *white*.

12. The head lamps must always be carried in their ordinary position whether lighted or not.

13. The *special* regulations for exceptional head lamps, discs and boards as given below, must be carefully observed.

Great Northern Engines when on Foreign Lines.

14. Great Northern passenger train engines when on the Swinton and Knottingley (Midland and North Eastern) joint line, must have one lamp with blue glass.

15. Great Northern engines when between Eggington Junction and Tutbury, must have one lamp with green glass on left buffer, and one with white glass on right buffer.

16. Great Northern engines when passing over the Metropolitan Company's widened lines must carry a lighted head lamp (white) by day as well as by night.

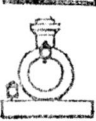

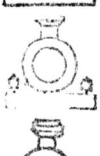

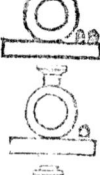

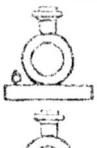

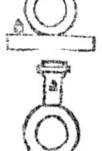

GNR engine headcodes 1881.

Above: Hertford North station from the south with an 'N2' Class 0-6-2T waiting in the Down Back platform with a train for King's Cross. The Down and Up lines serve their respective platforms and in the centre parachute water tanks are provided to replenish locomotive supplies. The Up starting signal upper arm denotes the route to the main line and the lower arm the connection to the Welwyn Garden City branch.
Author's collection

Later, water was available at Hatfield from a column at the south end of the Up platform for Up passenger independent and Up platform lines; at the north end of Luton and St. Albans platform foe western platform lines; at the north end of Down main platform for Down main line; at the Down side south of coal stage for coal stage and siding in Down yard; north end of transship platform for Up passenger independent and yard lines. At Welwyn Garden City water was available from 1944 from a crane next to the Up reception line. Along the branch at Hertford North, water supplies were available from a water column at the south end of the Up main platform for locomotives standing on the Up main line and also between the western platform line and the run round road serving both roads. At Hertford Cowbridge, later Hertford Old, water was available from a parachute tank located opposite the west end of the station platform and from a crane located at the west end of the station platform. To footplate staff the water was considered satisfactory for locomotive boilers and no molasses were added to the supply.

Hatfield was originally provided with an engine turntable 40 feet diameter installed, as a requirement of the Board of Trade, at the north end of the yard in August 1860. It was enlarged to 44 feet 7 inches in 1886 and subsequently to 46 feet 0 inches in diameter. A 36 feet diameter turntable was also available for use at Hertford GER engine shed, later extended to 44 feet 9 inches.

BREAKDOWN VEHICLES

The importance of Hatfield as a motive power stabling point, handling traffic on the main line as well as the three branches, rendered it necessary to cover all emergencies and breakdowns. After a few relatively minor failures on the Hertford and Luton lines and the accident at Welwyn Junction on 3rd May 1864, Archbald Sturrock, the GNR Locomotive Engineer requested the provision of a complete breakdown train for stabling at Hatfield. The request was readily agreed and on 7th February 1865 the board sanctioned the purchase of a crane and all the necessary tools. The train was eventually provided in 1866, when the leading vehicle was a Doncaster-built 8 tons capacity hand crane. In the event of a derailment or accident, the Hatfield to Hertford branch including as far as Hertford East Junction was covered by Hatfield Breakdown Vans, which were equipped with the requisite re-railing jacks and equipment. The timber wagon re-railing ramps available at Hatfield and Hertford were not on any account to be used for re-railing locomotives, although on some occasions when engines became derailed by one pair of wheels, these ramps were found most useful. Ropes were also used to assist in the re-railing of locomotives. In dire emergencies King's Cross 35 tons capacity breakdown crane No. 941593 was permitted to attend; this crane, formerly GER No. 6A, was built by Ransomes & Rapier in 1915 and received its L&NER number in 1938. It was replaced in 1940 by 45-ton crane No. 941600 built by Cowans, and then from 1943 by Ransomes & Rapier No. 941601, later 330102, 45-ton steam crane allocated to cover accidents and mishaps between Welwyn Garden City and Hertford East Junction exclusive in addition to the Hatfield Tool Vans.

COACHING STOCK

Unlike locomotives, the GNR placed no weight or loading gauge restrictions on rolling stock used on the branch and conventional coaching stock was utilised, initially graduating from ancient 4-wheel vehicles of various vintage, and by 1877 the load limit for passenger trains between Hatfield and Hertford was eighteen 4-wheel vehicles. Where the load was six or fewer coaches including the brake van, one guard was to ride in each brake van; from seven to twelve coaches two brake vans were required, each with a guard, whilst thirteen to eighteen vehicles necessitated three brake vans each attended by a guard, although it is almost certain these loads were never operated because of platform length limitations. At this time vehicles were close-coupled, oil lit, and the guard's brake van had a raised lookout.

By 1905 the load limit was forty-five pairs of wheels, equal to fifteen 6-wheel coaches. When working without continuous brake the number of carriages including brake van was five with one guard riding in the brake van. When at least one half of the vehicles were fitted with continuous brakes worked from the locomotive, for up to six vehicles one brake van attended by a guard was required; from seven to twelve vehicles two brake vans, each attended by a guard, and for thirteen to fifteen vehicles three brake vans were stipulated, each attended by a guard. When the train was fitted throughout with continuous brake worked from the engine up to eight vehicles required a brake van attended by a guard, and nine to fifteen vehicles required two brake vans each attended by a guard. For the comfort of passengers, before continuous steam heating was provided on trains, foot warmers were available to all classes of travel between 1st November and 30th April.

The situation continued until cast-offs from the London suburban service infiltrated on the Hatfield branches; from the early 1890s the branch trains were formed of 6-wheel Composites, Thirds and Brake Thirds designed by E.F. Howlden and examples are shown below. Second Class accommodation was withdrawn from the GNR on 1st November 1891. The continuing use of 6-wheel stock on passenger services catered for all requirements.

The leading dimensions of the 6-wheel vehicles were:

Diagram	156	245	301
Type	6-wheel Composite	6-wheel Third	6-wheel Brake Van
Length over buffers	36 ft 3 ins	35 ft 6 ins	35 ft 4½ ins
Length over body	32 ft 10½ ins	32 ft 1½ ins	32 ft 0 ins
Height overall	12 ft 4⅛ ins	12 ft 4⅛ ins	12 ft 4⅛ ins
Width over body	8 ft 2 ins	8 ft 2 ins	8 ft 2 ins
Width over guard's ducket	—	—	8 ft 10¾ ins
Wheelbase	23 ft 2 ins	22 ft 3 ins	22 ft 4 ins
Seating			
First Class	12	—	—
Third Class	30	50	—
Luggage	—	—	5 tons
Weight empty	14 tons 10 cwt	13 tons 9 cwt	12 tons 18 cwt

A breakdown crane lifting the former Liverpool & Manchester Railway 0-4-2 locomotive *Lion* from a low loader at Cole Green on 3rd June 1951 prior to appearing in the filming of *The Lady with a Lamp* starring Anna Neagle as Florence Nightingale.

LCGB/Ken Nunn

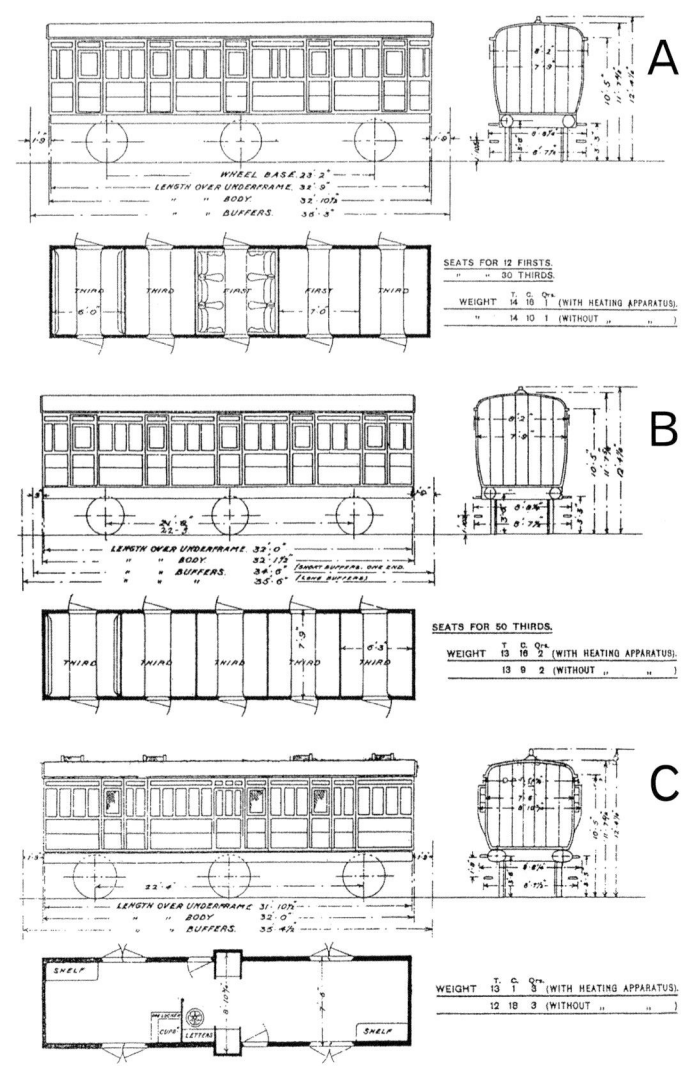

(A) GNR 6-wheel Composite to diagram 156.
(B) GNR 6-wheel Third to diagram 245.
(C) GNR 6-wheel brake van to diagram 301.

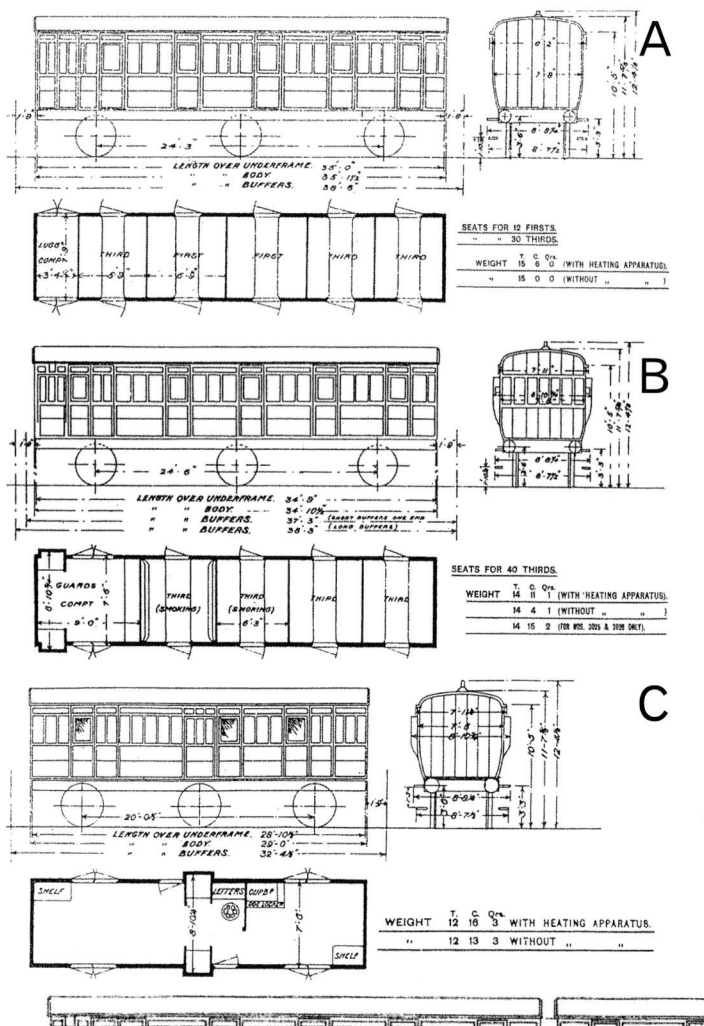

Diagram	154	281	303
Type	6-wheel Composite	6-wheel Brake Third	6-wheel Luggage Brake
Length over buffers	38 ft 6 ins	38 ft 3 ins	32 ft 4½ ins
Length over body	35 ft 1½ ins	34 ft 10½ ins	29 ft 0 ins
Height overall	12 ft 4⅛ ins	12 ft 4⅛ ins	12 ft 4⅛ ins
Width over body	8 ft 2 ins	7 ft 11 ins	7 ft 11¼ ins
Width over guard's ducket	—	8 ft 10¾ ins	8 ft 10¾ ins
Wheelbase	24 ft 3 ins	24 ft 6 ins	20 ft 0½ ins
Seating			
First Class	12	—	—
Third Class	30	40	—
Luggage	1 ton	1 ton	5 tons
Weight empty	15 tons 6 cwt	14 tons 11 cwt	12 tons 16 cwt

During the latter part of the first decade of the twentieth century, many of the former 6-wheel stock were converted to 2-car and 3-car articulated sets, which gave the vehicles a further lease of life. As well as working on the main line many were allocated to former GNR branch lines. During this period the Hatfield branches were allocated sets and it is known that diagram 197 and 198 twin sets worked the services augmented by diagram 218K and 218N triple articulated sets. Other diagram vehicles were probably utilised but the leading dimensions of diagram 197, 198 and 218K and 218N sets are given here.

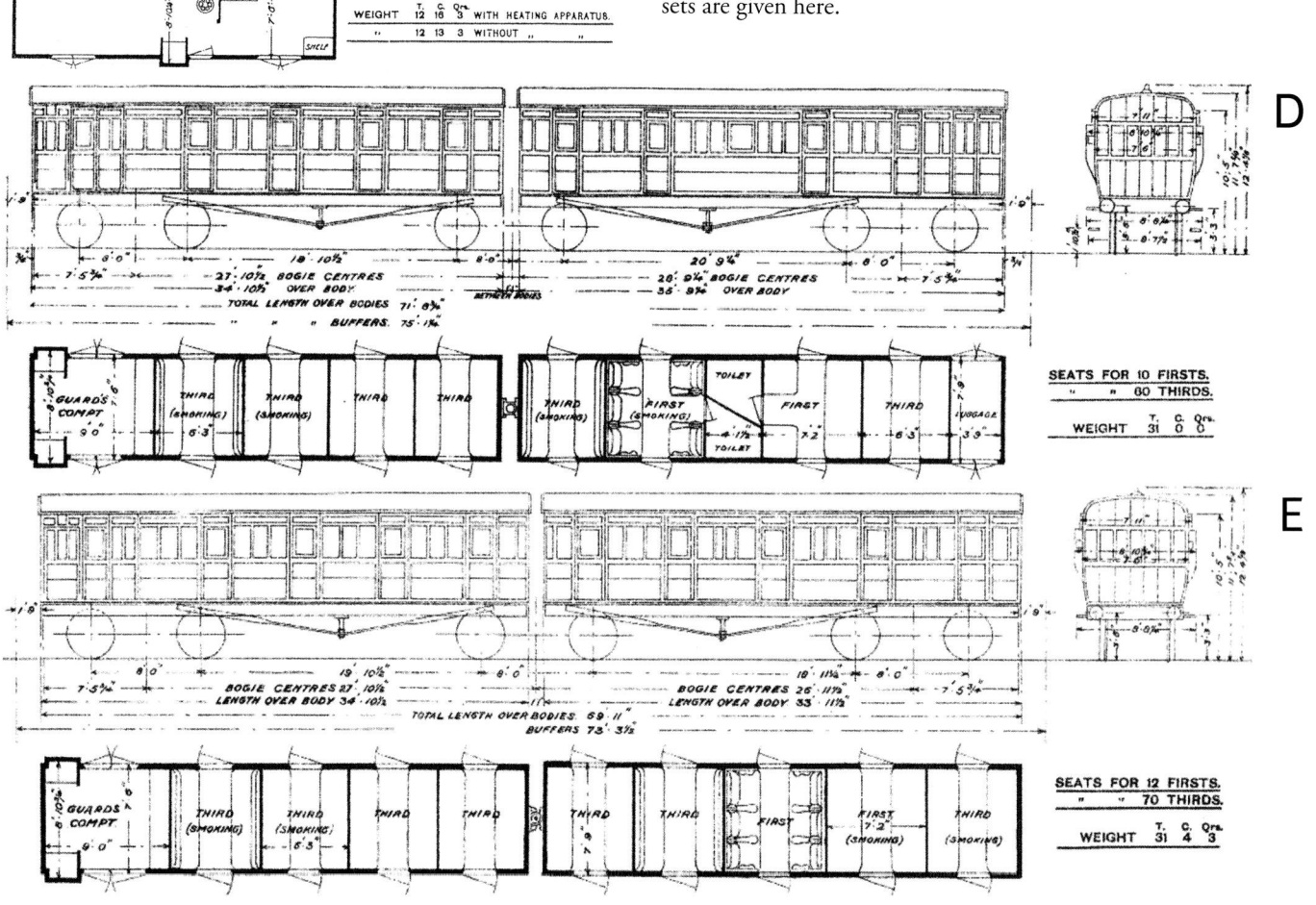

DIAGRAM 197 HOWLDEN TWIN ARTICULATED SET		
	Brake Third	Composite
Length over buffers	75 feet 1¾ ins*	
Length over body	34 ft 10½ ins	35 ft 9¼ ins
Max width	8 ft 8¼ ins	8 ft 8¼ ins
Max width over guard's duckets	8 ft 10¾ ins	—
Max height	12 ft 4⅛ ins	12 ft 4⅛ ins
Wheelbase	64 ft 7¾ ins*	
Seating		
First Class	—	10
Third Class	40	20
Weight in working order	31 tons 0 cwt*	

NOTE: * Total set.

DIAGRAM 198 HOWLDEN TWIN ARTICULATED SET		
	Brake Third	Composite
Length over buffers	73 feet 3½ ins*	
Length over body	34 ft 10½ ins	33 ft 11½ in
Max width	8 ft 7½ ins	8 ft 7½ ins
Max width over guard's duckets	8 ft 10¾ ins	—
Max height	12 ft 4⅛ ins	12 ft 4⅛ ins
Wheelbase	62 ft 10¼ ins*	
Seating		
First Class	—	12
Third Class	40	30
Weight in working order	31 tons 4 cwt 3 qtrs*	

NOTE: * Total set.

DIAGRAM 218K HOWLDEN TRIPLE ARTICULATED SET			
	Brake Third	Third	Composite
Length over buffers	107 ft 10 ins*		
Length over body	34 ft 10 ins	32 ft 1½ ins	35 ft 3½ ins
Max width	8 ft 8¼ ins	8 ft 8¼ ins	8 ft 8¼ ins
Max width over guard's duckets	8 ft 10¾ ins	—	—
Max height	12 ft 4⅛ ins	12 ft 4⅛ ins	12 ft 4⅛ ins
Wheelbase	97 ft 9¾ ins*		
Seating			
First Class	—	—	10
Third Class	30	50	20
Weight in working order	43 tons 14 cwt 2 qtrs*		

NOTE: * Total set.

DIAGRAM 218N HOWLDEN TRIPLE ARTICULATED SET			
	Brake Third	Brake Third	Composite
Length over buffers	110 feet 2 ins*		
Length over body	34 ft 10½ ins	34 ft 10½ ins	34 ft 10½ ins
Max width	8 ft 8¼ ins	8 ft 8¼ ins	8 ft 8¼ ins
Max width over guard's duckets	8 ft 10¾ ins	8 ft 10¾ ins	—
Max height	12 ft 4⅛ ins	12 ft 4⅛ ins	12 ft 4⅛ ins
Wheelbase	99 ft 8½ ins*		
Seating			
First Class	—	—	18
Third Class	40	40	20
Weight in working order	44 tons 9 cwt 0 qtrs*		

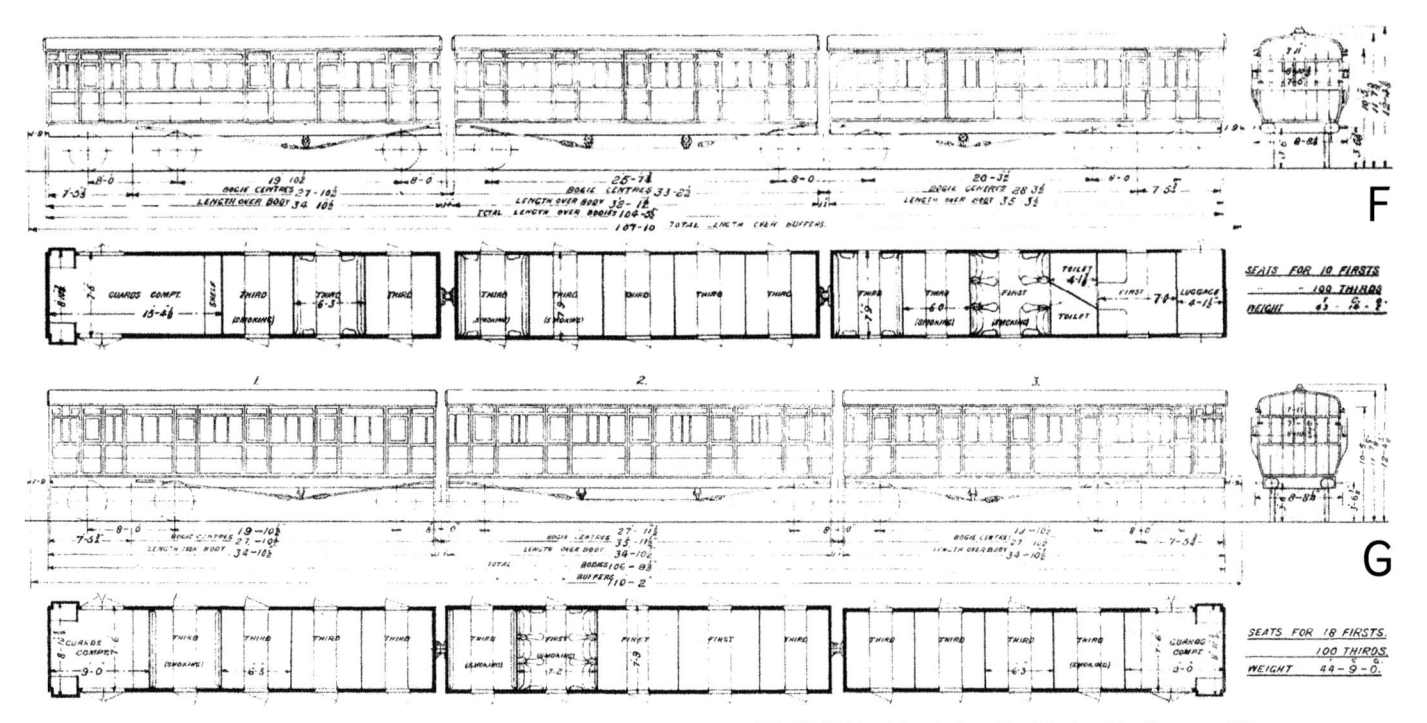

NOTE: * Total set.

(A) GNR 6-wheel Composite to diagram 154.
(B) GNR 6-wheel Brake Third to diagram 281.
(C) GNR 6-wheel Luggage Brake to diagram 303.
(D) GNR Howlden twin articulated set to diagram 197.
(E) GNR Howlden twin articulated set to diagram 198.
(F) GNR Howlden triple articulated set to diagram 218K.
(G) GNR Howlden triple articulated set to diagram 218N.

The variety of L&NER coaching stock used on the branch services in the latter years included Gresley non-gangway twin Brake Composite sets to diagram 107 and 108 and twin Brake Third sets to diagram 105 and 125 with the following dimensions:

Diagram	107	108
Type	Brake Third	Composite
Length over body	51 ft 1½ ins	51 ft 1½ ins
Width over body	9 ft 3 ins	9 ft 3 ins
Seating		
First Class	—	23
Third Class	40	39

Diagram	105	125
Type	Third	Brake Third
Length over body	51 ft 1½ ins	51 ft 1½ ins
Width over body	9 ft 3 ins	9 ft 3 ins
Seating		
First Class	—	—
Third Class	80	50

Facilities for the gas replenishment of coaches at Hatfield were first mooted early in 1864 when the station became the terminal and starting point for outer suburban trains from King's Cross as well as the Dunstable and Hertford branches. At that point in time, all branch traffic was worked by coaches equipped with oil lighting, and therefore gas filling was only pertinent to vehicles on the main line. The General Manager and Locomotive Engineer on 22nd November 1864 advised against the establishment of a gas making plant but their objections were overruled by the directors who requested details of the consumption of gas together with the estimated quantity required for refilling trains and costs of additional equipment required to produce the gas for rolling stock. On 20th December the engineer reported the local gas company would not reduce their charge for gas quoted at 5s 3d per 1,000 cubic feet as it was their rule to appropriate any surplus after paying 5 per cent to their shareholders and with the surplus reduce the price of gas to their customers. The engineer thought the GNR Company would benefit on these terms and subsequently requested the Hatfield Gas Company as to what charges they would make over a three year period.

In order to maximise the utilisation of passenger and freight rolling stock in GNR days, Hatfield station master was required to advise Grantham rolling stock department of spare vehicles on hand by 7.00am each day. Day-to-day maintenance of coaching stock was the responsibility of the carriage examiner based at Hatfield.

Wagons

A brief description of freight rolling stock provided by the GNR for the conveyance of goods traffic on all three branches from Hatfield is appropriate. The details are not exhaustive but give guidance to the general user vehicles. The wagons operated by the GNR in the early years were wooden open vehicles with side doors and were fitted with dumb buffers. Where grain, straw or other merchandise was susceptible to wet weather a tarpaulin sheet was utilised to protect the contents of the wagon. The brake van at the tail of the train would have been a 10-ton vehicle. From the 1870s,

Class 'N7/2' 0-6-2T No. 69695 waits patiently in the Up back platform at Welwyn Garden City with the branch train to Hertford North on 16th June 1951, the last day of regular passenger train operation. The train was formed of two 2-coach articulated non-gangway suburban stock. *Author's collection*

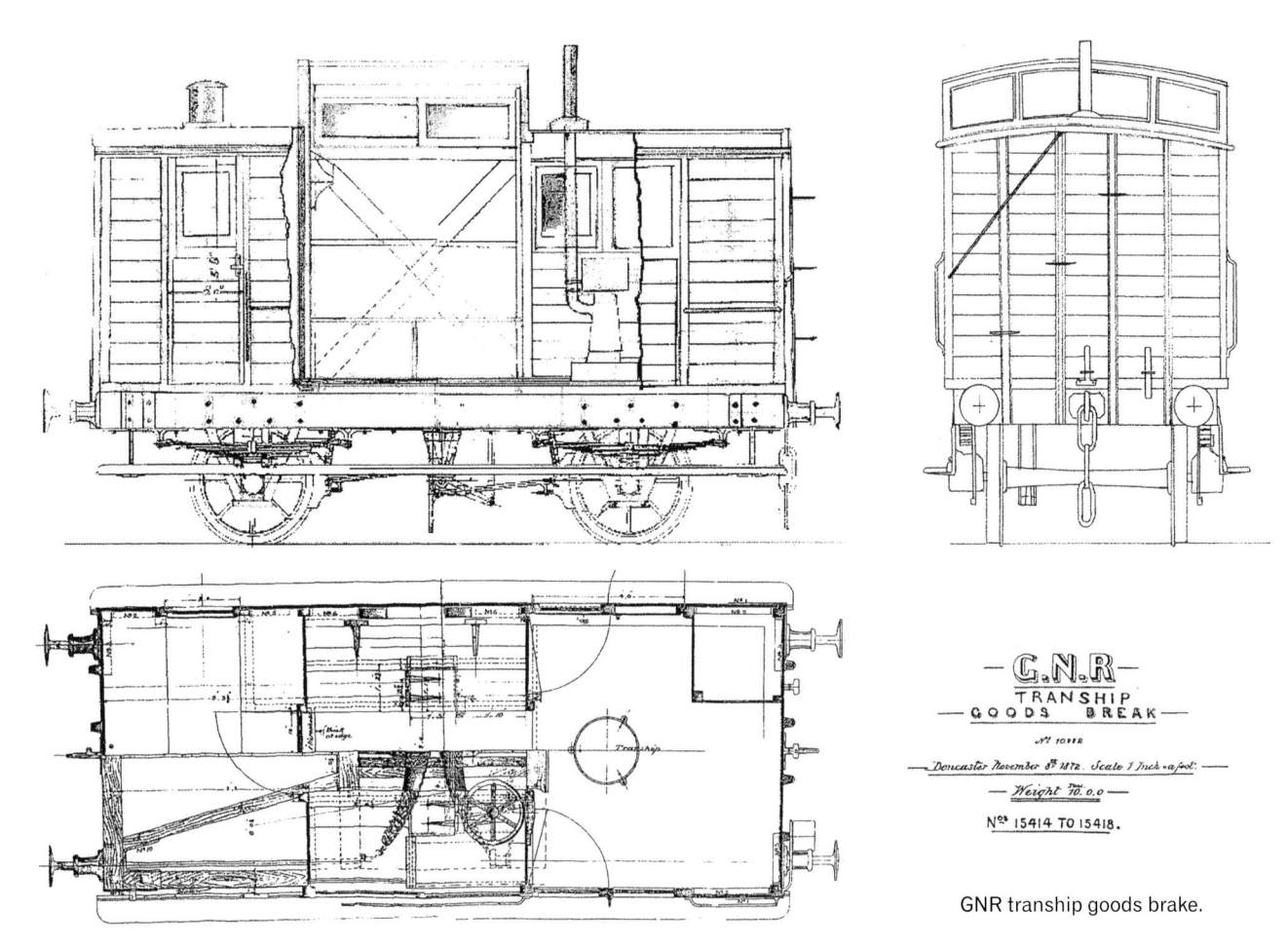

G.N.R
TRANSHIP
GOODS BREAK
Nº 10112
Doncaster November 8th 1872. Scale 1 Inch a foot.
Weight 70.0.0
Nºs 15414 TO 15418.

GNR tranship goods brake.

Freight played a large part in the revenue earnings on the Hatfield to Hertford branch as the GNR encouraged the opening of many sidings. Here a typical branch goods train hauled by '120' Class, later 'G2' Class, 0-4-4T No. 531 trundles up the branch alongside the main line en route to Hatfield. *Author's collection*

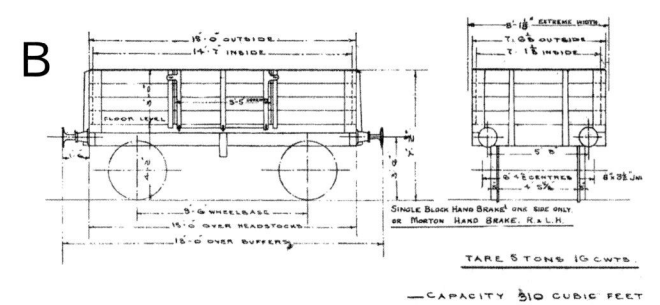

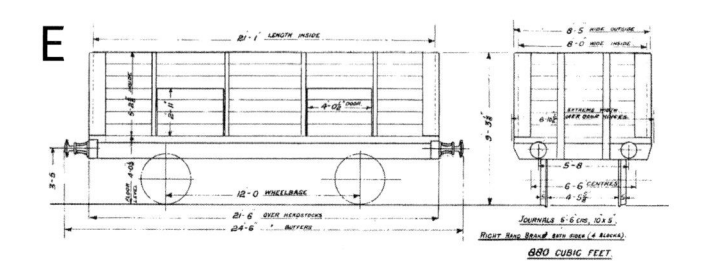

(A) GNR 9-ton 4-plank open goods or coal wagon of 1870.
(B) GNR 9-ton 4-plank open wagon.
(C) GNR 9-ton low sided wagon.
(D) GNR ordinary goods brake van, 10, 15 or 20-tons.
(E) GNR 20-ton coal wagon.

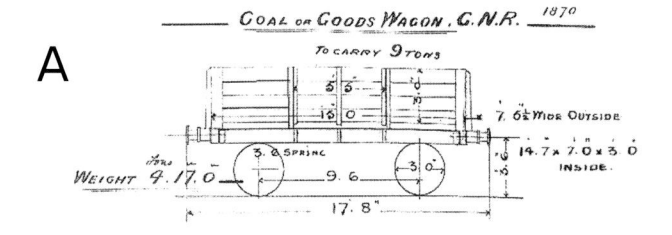

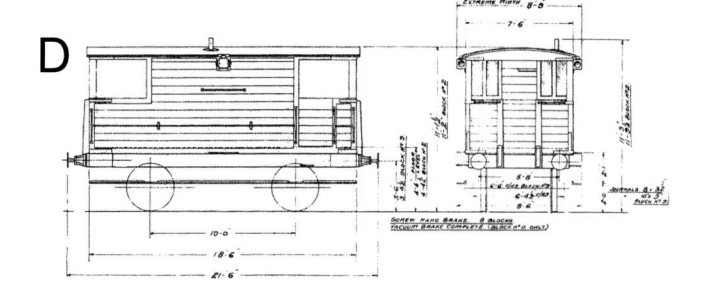

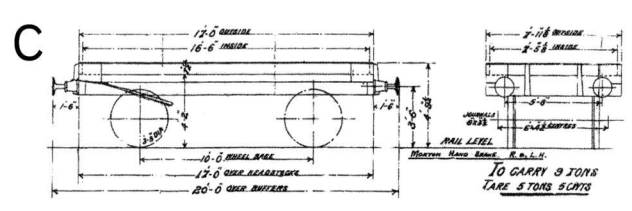

An early morning view of the goods yard at Hatfield showing the vast amount of traffic exchanged to and from the three branch lines in a relatively cramped area. This view looking south shows the passenger station to the right. *Author's collection*

for the conveyance of general merchandise and minerals the GNR Company utilised 9 tons capacity 4-plank-bodied open wagons with wooden frames, 9 feet 6 inches wheelbase and 17 feet 8 inches length over buffers. These wagons were gradually superseded by 9-ton 4-plank opens measuring 15 feet 0 inches over headstocks and wheelbase of 9 feet 6 inches, 9 tons capacity 6-plank opens with 9 feet 6 inches wheelbase and measuring 15 feet 0 inches over headstocks, and 10 tons capacity opens with 10 feet 0 inches wheelbase and measuring 19 feet 0 inches over headstocks.

Two varieties of low machine wagons would have been used, both of 9 tons capacity, one with 9 feet 6 inches wheelbase and 18 feet 0 inches over headstocks, and the other 10 feet 0 inches wheelbase and 19 feet 0 inches over headstocks. For fruit and vegetable traffic, ventilated covered vans of 6 and 8 tons capacity were provided, measuring 16 feet 10 inches over buffers. Later 8 tons capacity covered goods vans with 9 feet 10 inches wheelbase and overall height of 11 feet 4 inches were also utilised. Another variation of the same dimension had 10 feet 0 inches wheelbase.

Cattle traffic on the branches would have brought several types of cattle truck to cater for the trade, including 6 tons capacity vehicles measuring 18 feet 2½ inches, and later 6 tons capacity measuring 19 feet 0 inches. Both were equipped with through vacuum brake pipes, screw couplings and oil-lubricated axleboxes. At the tail of the train could be found a 4-wheel brake van of 10, 13, 15 or 20 tons capacity, all measuring 21 feet 6 inches over headstocks and having 10 feet 0 inches wheelbase. In addition, many wagons owned by other railway companies were used to deliver and collect agricultural and malt traffic, whilst coal and coke supplies usually came in private owner coal wagons. These fell into two categories: those belonging to the collieries, and merchant and coal factor wagons. The GNR also operated a fleet of coal wagons and the following were noted on the lines to Hertford, St. Albans and Dunstable: 9 tons and 10 tons capacity 7-plank, 9 tons capacity 5-plank and 6-plank, 10-ton capacity 5-plank and 15-ton capacity 8-plank, all with 9 feet 6 inches wheelbase and measuring 15 feet 0 inches over headstocks. Locomotive coal for Hatfield depot was delivered in 10-ton 7-plank open wagons, 15 tons capacity 8-plank, 12 tons capacity 7-plank and 20 tons capacity 9-plank opens, the latter with 12 feet wheelbase and body length of 21 feet 6 inches.

After grouping the GNR wagons continued in use but gradually L&NER standard designed wagons made an appearance. The most numerous were probably the 12-ton 5-plank opens with 8 feet 0 inches wheelbase to code 2 and 12-ton 6-plank opens with 10 feet 0 inches wheelbase to code 91 built after 1932. Later types included 13-ton 7-plank opens wagons to code 162 measuring 16 feet 6 inches over headstocks and with 9 feet 0 inches wheelbase. All were used on vegetable and sugar beet traffic as well as general merchandise. Fitted and unfitted 12 tons capacity 9 feet 0 inches wheelbase covered vans to code 16 conveyed perishable goods, fruit and malt, and later some were designated for fruit traffic only. Vans of 12 tons capacity to code 171 with steel underframes and pressed corrugated steel ends were introduced whilst at the same

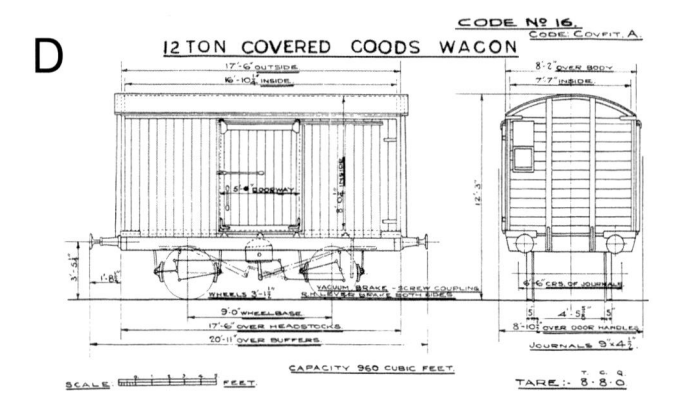

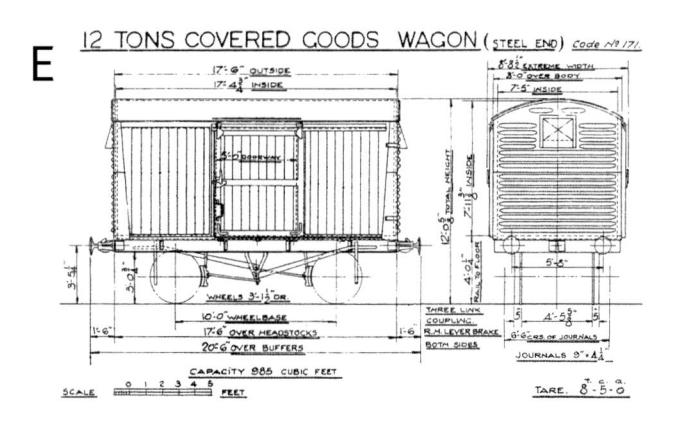

(A) L&NER 12-ton 5-plank open wagon to code 2.
(B) L&NER 12-ton 6-plank open wagon to code 91.
(C) L&NER 13-ton 7-plank open wagon to code 162.
(D) L&NER 12-ton covered van to code 16.
(E) L&NER 12-ton covered van with steel ends to code 171.

time the wheelbase was extended to a length of 10 feet 0 inches. Specific fruit vans with both 9 feet 0 inches and 10 feet 0 inches wheelbase saw service on the Hatfield branches for malt traffic. Agricultural machinery was conveyed on 'lowfit' wagons. L&NER brake vans provided for the branch freight traffic included 20-ton 'Toad B' to code 34 and 'Toad E' to code 64 vehicles with 10 feet 6 inches wheelbase and measuring 22 feet 5 inches over buffers. Later 'Toad D' brake vans to code 61 and measuring 27 feet 5 inches over buffers were also employed. After nationalisation many of the older wooden-bodied open wagons were scrapped and much of the traffic was conveyed in 16-ton all-steel mineral wagons. 20-ton bulk grain wagons were a regularly used on the trains destined for the Shredded Wheat factory at Welwyn Garden City in the latter years of operation.

In the GNR days the body, solebar and headstocks of ordinary goods wagons were painted oxide brown, sometimes called 'milk chocolate', whilst ironwork below the solebar level, buffer guides, buffers, drawbar plates and couplings were black. Lettering was white. The L&NER wagon livery was grey for non-fitted wagons and covered vans, whilst all vehicles fitted with automatic brakes, including brake vans, were painted brown red oxide, which changed to bauxite around 1940. Similar liveries were carried in BR days.

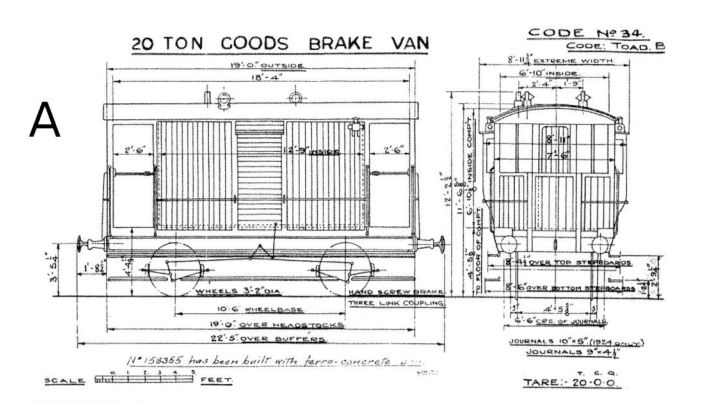

In the event of a derailment, wagon re-railing ramps were available at Hatfield, Hertford, St. Albans, Luton and Dunstable stations. These ramps, used by station and shunting staff, were provided to obviate the necessity to call out the breakdown train. The ramps were not to be used for re-railing locomotives or tenders but in practice were useful for re-railing when only one pair of locomotive wheels became derailed. Ropes were also used to re-rail itinerant wagons. A wagon examiner was based at Hatfield in GNR and L&NER days for general examination of rolling stock.

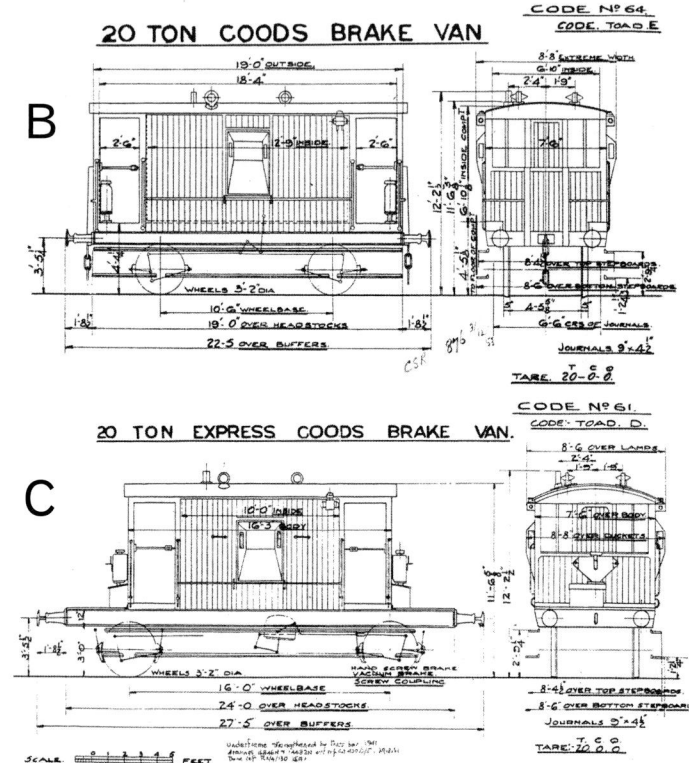

(A) L&NER 20-ton 'Toad B' goods brake van to code 34.

(B) L&NER 20-ton 'Toad E' goods brake van to code 64.

(C) L&NER 20-ton 'Toad D' goods brake van to code 61.

Left: 'N7/3' Class 0-6-2T No. 69692 hauling a brake van over Attimore Hall level crossing on Saturday 27th February 1960 en route to Holwell sidings to pick up empty wagons. The gates at this period were opened and closed by members of the train crew.
T. Middlemass

Appendix 1

Level Crossings

No.	Location	Mileage from King's Cross M Ch	Local Name	Status
Main Line				
	Hatfield Station	17 54½		
4	Hatfield & Welwyn G C	19 09¾		Footpath
	Welwyn Garden City Station	20 25		
5	Welwyn GC & Welwyn North	20 36	Digswell Lodge	Public^
Branch				
1	Welwyn G C & Cole Green	20 78½	Lord Cowper's	Footpath
2	Welwyn G C & Cole Green	21 34	Bramley Hill	Public¹
3	Welwyn G C & Cole Green	21 55		Footpath
4	Welwyn G C & Cole Green	21 66¾	Attimore	Public
	Attimore Halt	21 67		
5	Welwyn G C & Cole Green	22 07		Occupation
6	Welwyn G C & Cole Green	22 38	Birchall/Hatfield Hyde	Public
	Hatfield Hyde Halt	22 39		
7	Welwyn G C & Cole Green	22 58½	Holwell No. 1	Occupation+
8	Welwyn G C & Cole Green	22 59	Holwell No. 2	Occupation+
9	Welwyn G C & Cole Green	22 76¼	Holwell No. 3	Occupation+
10	Welwyn G C & Cole Green	23 00¾		Footpath*
11	Welwyn G C & Cole Green	23 09		Footpath*
12	Welwyn G C & Cole Green	23 16		Footpath*
13	Welwyn G C & Cole Green	23 26	Holwell Hyde Farm	Footpath
14	Welwyn G C & Cole Green	23 63½		Occupation
	Cole Green Station	24 05		
15	Cole Green & Hertingfordbury	24 12		Footpath
16	Cole Green & Hertingfordbury	24 27	Letty Green	Footpath
17	Cole Green & Hertingfordbury	24 52		Occupation
18	Cole Green & Hertingfordbury	24 58½		Footpath
19	Cole Green & Hertingfordbury	25 00½		Occupation
20	Cole Green & Hertingfordbury	25 21		Occupation
	Hertingfordbury Station	25 56		
21	Hertingfordbury & Hertford	25 62	Hertingfordbury	Footpath
22	Hertingfordbury & Hertford	26 13½		Occupation
	Hertford North Station	26 37		
23	Hertingfordbury & Hertford	27 20	Port Hill	Occupation
	Hertford Station	27 21½		
24	Hertford & Hertford GER	27 27		Occupation
25	Hertford & Hertford GER	27 46	Dicker Mill	Public
	Junction with GER	27 77		

Notes:
    ^ Closed and replaced by Digswell Lodge Farm overbridge No. 67A; 1896.
    * Closed 10th December 1919.
    + Closed November 1940.
    ¹ also known as Crossley Hill.

Appendix 2
Bridges and Culverts

Bridge No.	Location	Mileage M	Mileage Ch	Local Name	Under or Over	Type	Spans	Square Span Ft	Square Span In	Skew Span Ft	Skew Span In	Construction
Main Line												
59	Potters Bar & Hatfield	17	50	Town footbridge	Over	Public	4	49	9			Brick abutments, wrought iron lattice girders, cast iron columns and brick piers, plank floor, two stone staircases to street, iron treads.
								49	3			Over goods yard and Down goods line.
								60	9			Over goods yard and Down goods line.
								29	9			Over Down siding, Down and Up main lines and Up slow line. Over Up local line and carriage siding. Constructed 1887. Smoke plates fixed over main and slow lines and strengthened in 1906.
60	Hatfield Station	17	55¾	Station footbridge	Over	Railway	2					Wrought iron lattice girders, cast iron columns, plank floor, wood screens, corrugated iron covering, two cast iron staircases to Up platform, oak treads, one wrought iron staircase to Down platform, oak treads.
								35	9			Over Down and Up main lines.
								17	7			Over Up slow. Constructed 1865. Girder repaired and strengthened 1912. Smokeboards over Down and Up main, and Up slow lines.
61	Hatfield & Welwyn	17	74	St. Albans Road	Over	Public		103	0			Brick abutments. Constructed in 1865. East abutment set back and bridge reconstructed 1908 with steel girders, steel joists and jack arches. Smoke plates fixed over all lines. Roadway maintained by Hertfordshire County Council from 1909.
62	Hatfield & Welwyn	18	02	Wrestler's	Over	Public	3	26 0 each		32 0 each		Brick abutments and piers, corrugated iron screens. Roadway for length of 285 yards maintained by Hertfordshire County Council from 1913.
—	Hatfield & Welwyn	18	15	Wrestler's Culvert	Under			2	0	diameter		Brick, barrel, skew across line. Lengthened Down side 1895.
—	Hatfield & Welwyn	18	30	Mount Pleasant Culvert	Under			2	0	diameter		Brick, barrel. Lengthened Down side 1895.
63	Hatfield & Welwyn	18	39¼	Blue Bridge	Over	Public	3	26 0 each		each		Brick abutments and piers, western span reconstructed and lengthened 1895. Roadway for length of 180 yards maintained by Hertfordshire County Council from 1913.
—	Hatfield & Welwyn	18	55	River Lea Culvert	Under			3	0	diameter		Brick, barrel, skew across line. Lengthened Down side 1895.

APPENDICES

Bridge No.	Location	Mileage M	Mileage Ch	Local Name	Under or Over	Type	Spans	Square Span Ft	Square Span In	Skew Span Ft	Skew Span In	Construction
64	Hatfield & Welwyn	18	58	River Lea	Under	Occupation		30	0	—	—	Brick abutments and piers.
							5	30	0	—	—	Under Luton line, constructed 1895.
							5	29	9	—	—	Under Down slow, Down main, Up main and Up goods lines, constructed 1850.
								29	9	—	—	
							3	30	8	—	—	Under Hertford line, constructed 1876.
—	Hatfield & Welwyn	18	59	River Lea Culvert	Under			3	0	diameter		Brick, barrel. Lengthened Down side 1895.
65	Hatfield & Welwyn	18	74	Pearts	Under	Occupation						Brick abutments and piers.
							5	13	0	each		Under Luton line, constructed 1895.
							5	13	0	each		Under Down slow and Down and Up main, constructed 1850.
							1	13	0	—	—	Under Up goods and Hertford line, constructed 1868.
—	Hatfield & Welwyn	18	79½	Pearts Culvert	Under			2	0	diameter		Brick, barrel. Lengthened Down side 1895.
—	Hatfield & Welwyn	19	03	Pearts Culvert	Under			2	0	diameter		Brick, barrel, skew across line. Lengthened Down side 1895.
66	Hatfield & Welwyn	19	36½	Titmus	Over	Occupation	3	26	0	each		Brick abutments and piers. Western span reconstructed 1895.
67	Hatfield & Welwyn	19	64½	Hatfield Hyde	Over	Public	3	26	0	27	0	Brick abutments and piers.
								each		each		Roadway for length of 180 yards maintained by Hertfordshire County Council from 1913.
—	Hatfield & Welwyn	20	31	Pear Tree Crossing Culvert	Under			2	0	diameter		Brick, barrel, skew across line. Lengthened Down side 1895.
—	Hatfield & Welwyn	20	35	Pear Tree Crossing Culvert	Under			1	6	diameter		Brick, barrel. Lengthened Down side 1895.
67A	Hatfield & Welwyn	20	37½	Digswell Lodge Farm	Over	Public	1	104	0	—	—	Concrete abutments, faced with blue brick, steel girders and trough flooring. Smoke plates fitted over all lines. Constructed 1896.
67C	Welwyn GC	20	28	footbridge	see text							
BRANCH												
1B	Hatfield & Cole Green	20	75	Bessemer Road	Under	Public	1	55	3	56	2	Concrete abutments, wing walls, brick faced. Built 1959. Width between parapets 18ft 9ins.
1A	Hatfield & Cole Green	21	01	Tewin Road	Under	Public	3	8	0	8	3	Welded steel girders, RSJ in concrete floor. Built 1925.
								24	0	24	6	Maintained by Hertfordshire County Council agreement dated 6th June 1925 and 20th April 1957.
								24	0	24	6	
1	Hatfield & Cole Green	23	40	Sandy Road	Over	Public		28	0	31	10	Brick abutments, arch and parapets. Roadway for length of 200 yards maintained by Hertfordshire County Council agreement of 27th June 1913. Sold to Hertfordshire County Council 12th March 1974.
2	Hatfield & Cole Green	24	01¾	Cole Green	Under	Public		25	0	30	7	Brick abutments and arch, timber screens on parapets. No. 4 wrought iron ties and cast iron star plates. L.R. Sold to Hertfordshire County Council 12th March 1974.
—	Cole Green & Hertingfordbury	24	36½	Culvert	Under			3	6	diameter		Brick, barrel, skew across line.
3	Cole Green & Hertingfordbury	24	37¼	Letty Green	Under	Public		25	1	26	2	Brick abutments and arch. L.R. Sold to Hertfordshire County Council 12th March 1974.

Bridge No.	Location	Mileage M	Mileage Ch	Local Name	Under or Over	Type	Spans	Square Span Ft	Square Span In	Skew Span Ft	Skew Span In	Construction
—	Cole Green & Hertingfordbury	24	60	Culvert	Under			3	6	diameter		Brick, barrel, skew across line.
4	Cole Green & Hertingfordbury	24	68½	Birch Green, also known as Staines Green	Over	Public	1	24	11	26	5	Brick abutments, cast iron girders, jack arches, brick parapets. Sold to Hertfordshire County Council 12th March 1974.
—	Cole Green & Hertingfordbury	25	05	Culvert	Under			3	6	diameter		Brick, barrel, skew across line.
5	Cole Green & Hertingfordbury	25	50½	Hertingfordbury	Under	Public	1	25	0	—	—	Brick abutments and arch, wood handrail on parapets. Sold to Hertfordshire County Council 12th March 1974.
—	Cole Green & Hertingfordbury	25	51	Culvert	Under			3	6	diameter		Brick, barrel, skew across line.
6	Hertingfordbury & Hertford	25	78½	Wells	Over	Occupation	1	28	0	—	—	Brick abutments and arch. Sold to Hertfordshire County Council 12th March 1974.
7	Hertingfordbury & Hertford	26	06	Footbridge	Over	Occupation	3	20 1, 24 10, 21 3		21 2, 26 9, 21 8		Over Down side cutting. Over line. Over Up side cutting. Brick abutments and piers. Timber span. Sold to Hertfordshire County Council 12th March 1974.
8	Hertingfordbury & Hertford	26	15½	Cattle Arch	Under	Occupation	1	12	0	12	9	Brick abutments and arch. Sold to Hertfordshire County Council 12th March 1974.
9	Hertingfordbury & Hertford	26	24	River Mimram	Under		3	12 0, 51 6, 12 0		21 North, 26 Centre, 21 South		Four cast iron cylinders on concrete piers. Reconstructed 1891 with steel main and cross girders and trough flooring, cast iron standards and wrought iron pipe handrail.
10	Hertingfordbury & Hertford	26	36¾	Hertingfordbury Road	Under	Public	1	25	1	26	0	Brick abutments and arch, strengthened 1913 with 3 tie bolts, 18 inches of concrete on top and 7 feet of concrete behind retaining walls and asphalted wood screens. Demolished by explosives, Sunday 6th August 1967 for road widening by Hertfordshire County Council.
11	Hertingfordbury & Hertford	26	51	Footbridge	Over	Public						Removed 1914. Replaced by Enfield branch footbridge No. 41.
12	Hertingfordbury & Hertford	26	59¾	North Road	Under	Public	1	34	11	42	2	Brick abutments. Reconstructed 1904 with steel main girders, trough flooring and screens. Removed 1967, superstructure only. Abutments and wing walls remained.
—	Hertingfordbury & Hertford	26	64¾	Culvert	Under			2	6	diameter		Brick, barrel.
13	Hertingfordbury & Hertford	26	66¾	River Beane	Under		3	19 11, 51 6, 19 11		19 North, 51 Centre, 19 South		Four cast iron cylinders on concrete piers. Reconstructed 1891 with steel main and cross girders and trough flooring, cast iron standards, wrought iron pipe handrails. Removed 1971.

Bridge No.	Location	Mileage M CH	Local Name	Under or Over	Type	Spans	Square Span FT IN	Skew Span FT IN	Construction
14	Hertingfordbury & Hertford	26 76	Molewood	Under	Public	1	14 9	17 1	Brick abutments, cast iron girders, timber longitudinals, planked floor. Strengthened 1901 with additional cast iron girders. Removed April 1966, abutments and wing remained.
15	Hertingfordbury & Hertford	27 04½	Port Vale	Over	Public	1	23 10	— —	Brick abutments, cast iron girders, jack arches, wood screen on parapet.
16	Hertingfordbury & Hertford	27 06½	Thompson	Over	Occupation	1	23 11	24 5	Brick abutments, cast iron girders, jack arches, brick parapet.
17	Hertingfordbury & Hertford	27 16	Port Hill	Over	Public	5	15 1 21 11 15 1	— — — — — —	Two over Down side cutting and siding, brick arch. Over line, cast iron girders and brick jack arches. Two over Up side cutting, brick arch and timber screen to No. 2 arch. Brick abutments and piers.
18	Hertingfordbury & Hertford	27 18¾	River Beane	Under		1	33 0	— —	Brick abutments. Under Down side shunting siding, two cast iron girders under each rail, timber longitudinals and plank floor. Under running lines, reconstructed with steel trough girders and floor plates, timber longitudinals. Under Up side shunting siding, cast iron girders and floor plates. Rebuilt 1904.
19	Hertford GN & GE	27 26¾	Cattle Arch	Under	Occupation	1	10 0	— —	Brick abutments. Reconstructed 1906 with steel trough girders and planked flooring.
20	Hertford GN & GE	27 32¾	Mill Tail	Under		8	— —	137 3	Brick abutments and piers, and timber piles, longitudinal timbers and timber handrail.
21	Hertford GN & GE	27 41	River Lea	Under		1	35 0	39 3	Brick abutments. Bridge widened in 1915. Wrought iron main girders strengthened. New cross steel girders and timber. Longitudinals fixed, planked flooring.
Wood Green to Langley Junction									
			Bridges Crossing the Hertford Branch						
39	Bayford & Hertford North	19 01¼ to 19 15	Hertford Viaduct	Over	Railway & River Mimram	20	30 9 32 6 30 6 32 6	— — — — 64 10 — —	7 spans of brick segmental arches. 6 spans of brick segmental arches. 1 span of steel girders. 6 spans of brick segmental arches. North abutments concrete. South abutments concrete. Total length 291½ yards. Built 1915.
41	Bayford & Hertford North	19 41½	Footbridge	Over	Public	3	26 6 110 0 12 6	— — 116 11½ — —	Concrete abutments and piers faced with brickwork, side span brick segmental arches, main span two steel pale girders with timber frame. Clear width 6 feet 10 inches. Built 1915.

Bibliography

General Works
Groves, N., *Great Northern Railway Locomotive History*, RCTS
Joby, R.S., *Forgotten Railways of East Anglia*, David and Charles
Nock, O.S. *The Great Northern Railway*, Ian Allan
RCTS, *Locomotives of the LNER*
Waywell, R., *Industrial Railways and Locomotives: Hertfordshire and Middlesex*, Industrial Railway Society
Wrottesley, John, *The Great Northern Railway*, Vols 1, 2 and 3, Batsford

Periodicals
Bradshaw's Railway Guide
Bradshaw's Railway Manual
British Railways Eastern Region Magazine
Buses Illustrated
Herepath's Journal
Locomotive Carriage and Wagon Review
LNER Magazine
Railway Magazine
Railway World
Railway Year Book
Trains Illustrated

Newspapers
Hertfordshire Mercury
Hertford Mercury & Reformer
Herts Guardian
Luton Reporter

Minute Books
Great Northern Railway
Eastern Counties Railway
Great Eastern Railway
London and North Eastern Railway

Working Timetables
Great Northern Railway
Eastern Counties Railway
Great Eastern Railway
London and North Eastern Railway
British Railways (Eastern Region)

Appendices to Working Timetables
Great Northern Railway
Great Eastern Railway
London & North Eastern Railway
British Railways (Eastern Region)

Miscellaneous Working Instructions
Great Northern Railway
Great Eastern Railway
London & North Eastern Railway
British Railways (Eastern Region)

Acknowledgements

The publication of this history would not have been possible without the assistance of many people. In particular I should like to thank:

The late A.R. Cox
The late W. Fenton
The late G. Woodcock
The late Dr I.C. Allen
The late Canon C. Bayes
The late Peter Proud
The late R.C. (Dick) Riley

Peter Webber
The late John Aylard
The late Eric Neve
The late Malcolm (Tom) Heugh
The late T. Hatton
The late J.E. Kite
The late Michael Back

Chris Cock
John Petrie
Doug Stephenson
The late R.A.H. Weight
Stephen Ruff
Ed Graves
P. Theobald

I am extremely grateful for the assistance rendered by David Dent with his encyclopedic knowledge of the Hertford area and for information given by Barry Gray who has conducted walking tours over the remnants of the branch.

Also to staff at King's Cross Divisional Manager's Office, King's Cross Chief Civil Engineer's Office, Hatfield Motive Power Depot, Hertford East Motive Power Depot, King's Cross Chief Signal and Telegraph Department.

Thanks also to the House of Lords Record Office, National Archives, British Library Newspaper Library, British Railways (Eastern Region), Members of the Great Northern Railway Society, Members of the Great Eastern Railway Society, Hertford County Record Office, Hertford Museum, Hertfordshire Archives and Local Studies and Hatfield Local History Society.

APPENDICES

Bridge No.	Location	Mileage M Ch	Local Name	Under or Over	Type	Spans	Square Span FT IN.	Skew Span FT IN.	Construction
14	Hertingfordbury & Hertford	26 76	Molewood	Under	Public	1	14 9	17 1	Brick abutments, cast iron girders, timber longitudinals, planked floor. Strengthened 1901 with additional cast iron girders. Removed April 1966, abutments and wing remained.
15	Hertingfordbury & Hertford	27 04½	Port Vale	Over	Public	1	23 10	— —	Brick abutments, cast iron girders, jack arches, wood screen on parapet.
16	Hertingfordbury & Hertford	27 06½	Thompson	Over	Occupation	1	23 11	24 5	Brick abutments, cast iron girders, jack arches, brick parapet.
17	Hertingfordbury & Hertford	27 16	Port Hill	Over	Public	5	15 1 21 11 15 1	— — — — — —	Two over Down side cutting and siding, brick arch. Over line, cast iron girders and brick jack arches. Two over Up side cutting, brick arch and timber screen to No. 2 arch. Brick abutments and piers.
18	Hertingfordbury & Hertford	27 18¾	River Beane	Under		1	33 0	— —	Brick abutments. Under Down side shunting siding, two cast iron girders under each rail, timber longitudinals and plank floor. Under running lines, reconstructed with steel trough girders and floor plates, timber longitudinals. Under Up side shunting siding, cast iron girders and floor plates. Rebuilt 1904.
19	Hertford GN & GE	27 26¾	Cattle Arch	Under	Occupation	1	10 0	— —	Brick abutments. Reconstructed 1906 with steel trough girders and planked flooring.
20	Hertford GN & GE	27 32¾	Mill Tail	Under		8	— —	137 3	Brick abutments and piers, and timber piles, longitudinal timbers and timber handrail.
21	Hertford GN & GE	27 41	River Lea	Under		1	35 0	39 3	Brick abutments. Bridge widened in 1915. Wrought iron main girders strengthened. New cross steel girders and timber. Longitudinals fixed, planked flooring.
Wood Green to Langley Junction									
39	Bayford & Hertford North	19 01¼ to 19 15	Hertford Viaduct	Over	Railway & River Mimram	20	30 9 32 6 30 6 32 6	— — — — 64 10 — —	7 spans of brick segmental arches. 6 spans of brick segmental arches. 1 span of steel girders. 6 spans of brick segmental arches. North abutments concrete. South abutments concrete. Total length 291½ yards. Built 1915.
Bridges Crossing the Hertford Branch									
41	Bayford & Hertford North	19 41½	Footbridge	Over	Public	3	26 6 110 0 12 6	— — 116 11½ — —	Concrete abutments and piers faced with brickwork, side span brick segmental arches, main span two steel pale girders with timber frame. Clear width 6 feet 10 inches. Built 1915.

Bibliography

GENERAL WORKS
Groves, N., *Great Northern Railway Locomotive History*, RCTS
Joby, R.S., *Forgotten Railways of East Anglia*, David and Charles
Nock, O.S. *The Great Northern Railway*, Ian Allan
RCTS, *Locomotives of the LNER*
Waywell, R., *Industrial Railways and Locomotives: Hertfordshire and Middlesex*, Industrial Railway Society
Wrottesley, John, *The Great Northern Railway*, Vols 1, 2 and 3, Batsford

PERIODICALS
Bradshaw's Railway Guide
Bradshaw's Railway Manual
British Railways Eastern Region Magazine
Buses Illustrated
Herepath's Journal
Locomotive Carriage and Wagon Review
LNER Magazine
Railway Magazine
Railway World
Railway Year Book
Trains Illustrated

NEWSPAPERS
Hertfordshire Mercury
Hertford Mercury & Reformer
Herts Guardian
Luton Reporter

MINUTE BOOKS
Great Northern Railway
Eastern Counties Railway
Great Eastern Railway
London and North Eastern Railway

WORKING TIMETABLES
Great Northern Railway
Eastern Counties Railway
Great Eastern Railway
London and North Eastern Railway
British Railways (Eastern Region)

APPENDICES TO WORKING TIMETABLES
Great Northern Railway
Great Eastern Railway
London & North Eastern Railway
British Railways (Eastern Region)

MISCELLANEOUS WORKING INSTRUCTIONS
Great Northern Railway
Great Eastern Railway
London & North Eastern Railway
British Railways (Eastern Region)

Acknowledgements

The publication of this history would not have been possible without the assistance of many people. In particular I should like to thank:

- The late A.R. Cox
- The late W. Fenton
- The late G. Woodcock
- The late Dr I.C. Allen
- The late Canon C. Bayes
- The late Peter Proud
- The late R.C. (Dick) Riley
- Peter Webber
- The late John Aylard
- The late Eric Neve
- The late Malcolm (Tom) Heugh
- The late T. Hatton
- The late J.E. Kite
- The late Michael Back
- Chris Cock
- John Petrie
- Doug Stephenson
- The late R.A.H. Weight
- Stephen Ruff
- Ed Graves
- P. Theobald

I am extremely grateful for the assistance rendered by David Dent with his encyclopedic knowledge of the Hertford area and for information given by Barry Gray who has conducted walking tours over the remnants of the branch.

Also to staff at King's Cross Divisional Manager's Office, King's Cross Chief Civil Engineer's Office, Hatfield Motive Power Depot, Hertford East Motive Power Depot, King's Cross Chief Signal and Telegraph Department.

Thanks also to the House of Lords Record Office, National Archives, British Library Newspaper Library, British Railways (Eastern Region), Members of the Great Northern Railway Society, Members of the Great Eastern Railway Society, Hertford County Record Office, Hertford Museum, Hertfordshire Archives and Local Studies and Hatfield Local History Society.

Index

absorption of HL&DR by GNR 35, 36
accidents and incidents 19, 24, 26, 28, 29, 34, 36, 37, 38, 39, 41, 43, 47, 48 *et seq*, 55, 61, 62, 63, 90
Acts of Parliament 9, 10, 11, 14, 18, 25, 29, 35, 37, 38, 53, 56, 62, 72, 74
agreements between HL&DR and GNR, also GNR with ECR 20 *et seq*, 30 *et seq*
amalgamation H&WJR and LD&WJR 21 *et seq*, 33

Bedfordshire, Hertfordshire & Essex Railway 10
Birkinshaw, John Cass, Engineer 14 *et seq*
block signalling introduction 48, 68
Board of Trade inspections 10, 23, 24, 32, 42, 44, 61, 63, 74, 76, 77
breakdown arrangements 264
bridges and culverts 274-7
bus competition 64 *et seq*

closure
  of branch to freight traffic 75
  of branch to passenger traffic 95 *et seq*
  of Hertford Old to passenger traffic 87 *et seq*
  of signal boxes 72-3
coaching stock 264 *et seq*
Cole Green
  extension to platform 47
  general 118 *et seq*
  improvements 53 *et seq*
  opening 27, 36
combination of Hertford GN and GE stations, proposals 46-7
complaint re putrid matter 48
Cuffley to Langley Junction 72 *et seq*
cutting of first sod 15

Dicker Mill Crossing 151, 153
Digswell 14 *et seq*

East Hertfordshire Railway 48
Eastern Counties Railway 10, 12 *et seq*
  branch to Hertford 9
engine and men's diagrams 222, 258
engine headcodes 262-3
engine loads summary 222
engine route availability 223
engine shed
  Hatfield 254-7
  Hertford 255
engine whistle codes 260-61
excursion traffic 214 *et seq*
extension of service, Welwyn Junction to Hatfield 33

fares 216-17

filming at stations 80, 85, 87
freight facilities at stations 220
freight traffic 217 *et seq*

goods facilities summary 220 *et seq*
goods traffic 217 *et seq*
gradient diagram 97
Great Eastern Railway 37 *et seq*
Great Northern Railway 11 *et seq*
  Hornsey–Hertford Act 39
  HL&DR takeover 35, 36
  Sr Albans–Hertford Act 10

Hatfield 11, 97 *et seq*
  Hertford bay improvements 56
headcodes 262-3
Hertford GER station 154-6
Hertford GNR station 6 *et seq*
Hertingfordbury station 27, 47, 124 *et seq*

junction, Welwyn 21 *et seq*

Kirk and Parry, contractors 37

level crossings 273
loading of freight trains 222
local superintendence 185
long section and short section single line working 170

*A BR/Sulzer Type 2 diesel electric locomotive approaching Hertford North with a train from King's Cross formed of two quad-art non-gangway coaches. The train is passing Hertford North signal box and the connection to the line from Hertford East and the branch to Welwyn Garden City.
Author's collection*

locomotives
  British Railways
    '03' Class DM shunting 0-6-0   253
    '08' Class DE shunting 0-6-0   253-4
  Eastern Counties Railway
    Gooch 'B' Class 2-2-2WT   224-5
  Great Central Railway
    '9C', '9F', '9O' L&NER 'N5' Class 0-6-2T 239
  Great Eastern Railway
    'Ml5'/'Ml5R' L&NER 'F4'/'F5' 2-4-2T 240
    'R24'/'R24R' L&NER 'J67'/'J69' 0-6-0T 252
    'S44' L&NER 'G4' Class 0-4-4T   232
  Great Northern Railway
    '116' Class 0-6-0   243
    '120'/'G2' Class 0-4-4 'Back Tanks'   229
    '241' and '271' Class 0-4-2WT   224
    'C2'/'C12' Class 4-4-2T   231
    'F2'/'F3' Class 0-4-2   243-5
    'G1' Class 0-4-4T   229-30
    Hawthorn 0-4-2   242-3
    'J4'/'J5' Class 0-6-0   245-6
    'J13' L&NER 'J52' 0-6-0ST   250
    'J15' L&NER 'J54'/'J55' Class 0-6-0 248-9
    'J18' L&NER 'J57' Class 0-6-0ST   249
    'J21' L&NER 'J1' Class 0-6-0   247
    'J22' L&NER 'J6' Class 0-6-0   248
    'Little Sharpie' 2-2-2WT   223
    'N1' Class 0-6-2T   232-4
    'N2' Class 0-6-2T   234-6
  London & North Eastern Railway
    'N7' Class 0-6-2T   236-8
    'B12/3' Class 4-6-0   251

locomotive water supplies   262
locomotive turntables   262
London & North Western Railway   15 *et seq*

Metropolitan Junction Railway   10
Mount Pleasant brick siding   102

nationalisation   85 *et seq*
Northern & Eastern Railway   9

opening and closing times of signal boxes   183
opening of railway
  Cuffley to Langley Junction   73
  N&ER Broxbourne to Hertford   9
  Hertford to Welwyn Junction   23-4
  Welwyn Junction to Hatfield single line   44, 46

passenger traffic receipts   74-5
permanent way   165 *et seq*
  staff   166
point-to-point timing of freight trains   211
population figures   187
prospectus H&WJR   11

railcars
  Dick, Kerr petrol   241
  steam   241-2
railway enthusiasts' special trains   91 *et seq*
Rambles in Hertfordshire booklet   80
Regulation of Railways Act 1889   49 *et seq*
resignalling   48
route availability of locomotives   223
royal travellers   45, 62

sale of surplus railway equipment   27

semaphore signals   168 *et seq*
sidings, intermediate   102, 103, 111, 112, 115, 117, 124, 128, 130, 157, 158, 160, 161, 162
signalboxes   172 *et seq*
  opening and closing times   183
signalling   167 *et seq*
snowstorms   38, 84
speed limits   150, 153
staff outings, GNR   43, 47
station masters   185 *et seq*
strikes   69, 72

timetables   187-213
traffic staff   186
Train Staff and Ticket working   48, 167 *et seq*
Transport Act 1947   84

wagons including brake vans   268 *et seq*
Welwyn Garden City
  development   67 *et seq*
  halts   110, 111
  industrial development   72 *et seq*
  station   104 et seq
whistle codes, engine   260-61
widening of track formation   56 *et seq*
withdrawal of passenger service
  Hertford North to Hertford Old   72-3
  Welwyn Garden City to Hertford   87
working and public timetables   187-213
World War One   63 *et seq*
World War Two
  precautions and arrangements   83
  Railway Executive Committee   83
  war damage   84

Looking east from the end of Hertingfordbury station platform with the west-end headshunt and loop siding spanned by a loading gauge on the Up side of the line in the foreground.
Author's collection

*Cole Green
to
Hertford East*

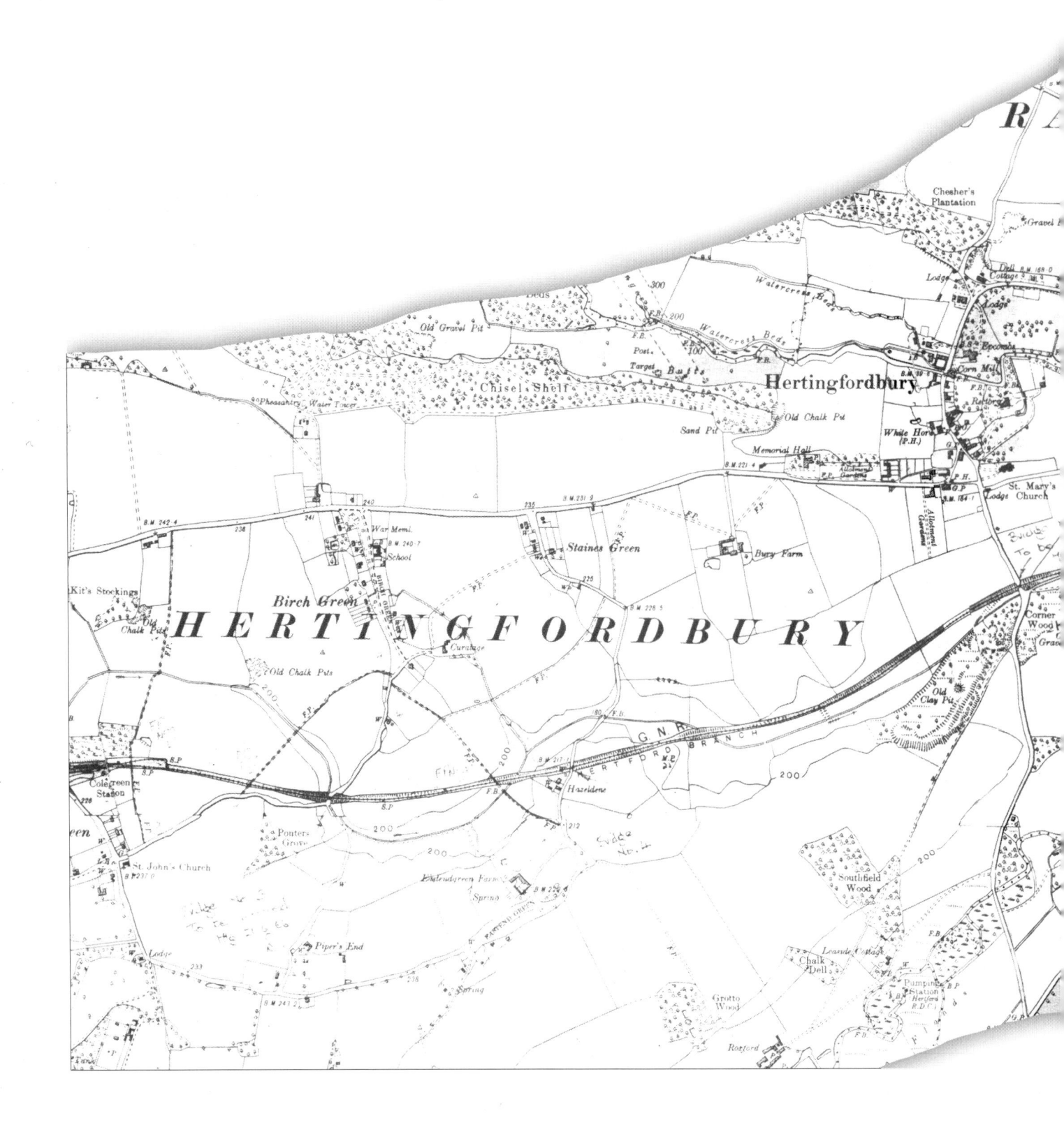